FROM RECOGNITIO

MW01274095

Essays on the Constitutional Entrenchment
of Aboriginal and Treaty Rights

More than thirty years ago, section 35 of the *Constitution Act, 1982,*
recognized and affirmed "the existing aboriginal and treaty rights of the
aboriginal peoples of Canada." Hailed at the time as a watershed moment
in the legal and political relationship between Indigenous peoples and
settler societies in Canada, the constitutional entrenchment of Aboriginal
and treaty rights has proven to be only the beginning of the long and
complicated process of giving meaning to that constitutional recognition.

In *From Recognition to Reconciliation,* twenty-three leading scholars
reflect on the continuing transformation of the constitutional relationship
between Indigenous peoples and the Canadian state. The book features
essays on themes such as the role of sovereignty in constitutional
jurisprudence, the diversity of methodologies at play in these legal and
political questions, and connections between the Canadian constitutional
experience and developments elsewhere in the world.

PATRICK MACKLEM is the William C. Graham Professor of Law in the
Faculty of Law at the University of Toronto.

DOUGLAS SANDERSON is an associate professor in the Faculty of Law at
the University of Toronto.

Contents

Part Five: Comparative Reflections

Acknowledgments

Contributors to this collection of essays presented earlier versions of their contributions at a conference occasioned by the thirtieth anniversary of the enactment of section 35 of the *Constitution Act, 1982*. We wish to thank the many participants for their constructive comments; Jennifer Brown and Aboriginal Affairs and Northern Development Canada, whose generous financial support made this event possible; our funding partner, the National Centre for First Nations Governance, and its president, hereditary chief Satsan (Herb George); Mayo Moran for her encouragement and support; and Jennifer Tam for her organizational assistance. We were fortunate to have Elijah Harper as our elder for the event, and we mourn his passing. We are also grateful to our colleague David Schneiderman, who offered valuable comments on the manuscript as a whole, and Daniel Quinlan of the University of Toronto Press for skilfully shepherding it to publication.

FROM RECOGNITION TO RECONCILIATION

Essays on the Constitutional Entrenchment
of Aboriginal and Treaty Rights

Introduction: Recognition and Reconciliation in Indigenous-Settler Societies

PATRICK MACKLEM AND DOUGLAS SANDERSON

On a clear day in early May 1990, two dozen black-gowned lawyers expectantly rose as one as the justices of the Supreme Court of Canada filed into the courtroom to render judgment in *R v Sparrow*.[1] The lawyers had reason to be attentive. *Sparrow* was the first decision of the Court to interpret section 35(1) of the *Constitution Act, 1982*, which provides that "the existing aboriginal and treaty rights of the aboriginal peoples of Canada are hereby recognized and affirmed." Section 35 was included in the constitutional reforms that ushered in formulas to amend the Constitution of Canada without the approval of the Parliament of the United Kingdom of Great Britain and the *Canadian Charter of Rights and Freedoms*. Lower courts across the country had offered a range of conflicting views on its nature and scope. Whatever the outcome, the Supreme Court of Canada's decision would have significant consequences for the constitutional relationship between Aboriginal peoples and the Canadian state.

At issue in *Sparrow* was the constitutionality of federal fishing regulations imposing a permit requirement and prohibiting certain methods of fishing. The Musqueam First Nation, located in British Columbia, had fished since ancient times in an area of the Fraser River estuary known as Canoe Passage. According to anthropological evidence at trial, salmon is not only an important source of food for the Musqueam but also plays a central role in Musqueam cultural identity. The Musqueam regard salmon as a race of beings that had, in "myth times," established a bond with humans, which required the salmon to come each year to

---

1 *R v Sparrow*, [1990] 1 SCR 1075.

give themselves to humans, who in turn treated them with respect by performing certain rituals. The Musqueam argued that the federal fishing requirements interfered with their Aboriginal fishing rights and, as a result of section 35(1), were invalid.

In jointly authored reasons by Chief Justice Dickson and Justice La Forest, a unanimous Court held that the constitutional recognition of Aboriginal and treaty rights "renounces the old rules of the game" and "calls for a just settlement for aboriginal peoples."[2] The Court found for the Musqueam nation and held that Aboriginal rights recognized and affirmed by section 35(1) include practices that form an integral part of an Aboriginal community's distinctive culture. If such rights existed as of 1982 – that is, if such rights had not been extinguished by state action before 1982 – then any law that unduly interferes with their exercise must meet relatively strict standards of justification. Specifically, such a law must possess a valid legislative objective, and any allocation of priorities after implementing measures that secure the law's objective must give top priority to Aboriginal interests. The Court also indicated that in future cases it might require that such laws infringe the right in question as little as possible, and that infringements be accompanied by fair compensation.

Understanding Aboriginal and treaty rights as constitutional checks on the exercise of the sovereign authority of the Canadian state, as the Court proposed in *Sparrow*, no doubt changed "the rules of the game." Yet what these changes mean in terms of the constitutional relationship between Aboriginal peoples and the Canadian state remain matters of deep contestation. In *Sparrow*, the Court was quick to declare that "while British policy towards the native population was based on respect for their right to occupy their traditional lands, ... there was from the outset never any doubt that sovereignty and legislative power, and indeed the underlying title, to such lands vested in the Crown."[3] Although Aboriginal and treaty rights check the exercise of sovereign power, they do not, according to the Court in *Sparrow*, challenge the constitutional validity of sovereignty itself.

Constitutional recognition of Aboriginal peoples and the fact of Canadian sovereignty was subsequently described by the Court as a

2 *Ibid* at 1105–06, quoting Noel Lyon, "An Essay on Constitutional Interpretation" (1988), 26 Osgoode Hall LJ 95, at 100.
3 *Ibid* at 1103.

relationship in need of "reconciliation." In *R v Van der Peet*, the Court was faced with a claim by the Sto:lo First Nation that it possessed an Aboriginal right to engage in commercial fishing. In developing a general approach to the interpretation of Aboriginal rights, Chief Justice Lamer, for a majority of the Court, stated, "With regards to s. 35(1), ... what the court must do is explain the rationale and foundation of the recognition and affirmation of the special rights of aboriginal peoples; it must identify the basis for the special status that aboriginal peoples have within Canadian society as a whole."[4] In Chief Justice Lamer's view, constitutional recognition of existing Aboriginal and treaty rights is based on the "simple fact" that "when Europeans arrived in North America, aboriginal peoples were already here, living in distinctive communities on the land, and participating in distinctive cultures, as they had done for centuries."[5] The purpose of section 35(1), in his opinion, is twofold: to constitutionally recognize the fact of prior Indigenous presence in North America and to reconcile this fact with the assertion of Crown sovereignty over Canadian territory.

One way the Court has sought to reconcile constitutional recognition of a prior Indigenous presence with Canadian sovereignty is to extend constitutional protection to Indigenous territories in the form of Aboriginal title. In *Delgamuukw v British Columbia*, hereditary chiefs of the Gitksan and We'suwet'en nations claimed Aboriginal title to 58,000 square kilometres of the interior of British Columbia. The Gitksan sought to prove historical use and occupation of part of the territory in question by entering as evidence their *adaawk*, a collection of sacred oral traditions about their ancestors, histories, and territories. The Wet'suwet'en entered as evidence their *kungax*, a spiritual song or dance or performance that ties them to their territory. Both the Gitksan and Wet'suwet'en also introduced evidence of their feast hall, in which they tell and retell their stories and identify their territories to maintain their connection with their lands over time. The trial judge admitted the above evidence but accorded it little independent weight, stating that, because of its oral nature, it could not serve as evidence of a detailed history of extensive land ownership.[6] He concluded that ancestors of the Gitksan and Wet'suwet'en peoples lived within the

---

4 *R v Van der Peet*, [1996] 2 SCR 507, at 537.
5 *Ibid* at 538 [emphasis deleted].
6 *Uukw v R*, [1987] 6 WWR 155, at 181 (BCSC).

territory in question prior to the assertion of British sovereignty, but predominantly at village sites already identified as reserve lands. As a result, he declared, the Gitksan and Wet'suwet'en did not own or possess Aboriginal title to the broader territory.[7]

On appeal, the Supreme Court of Canada ordered a new trial. Although its reasons for doing so were predominantly procedural, it took the opportunity to provide a definition of Aboriginal title that swept away many of the procedural and substantive hurdles Aboriginal people faced in their attempts to obtain legal recognition of their rights to ancestral territories. Specifically, the Court held that Aboriginal title is a communally held right in land and, as such, comprehends more than the right to engage in specific activities that may themselves constitute Aboriginal rights. Based on the fact of prior occupancy, Aboriginal title confers the right to exclusive use and occupation of land for a variety of activities, not all of which need be aspects of practices, customs, or traditions integral to the distinctive cultures of Aboriginal societies. The Court held further that the trial judge erred by placing insufficient weight on the oral evidence of the Gitksan and Wet'suwet'en: "[T]he laws of evidence must be adapted in order that this type of evidence can be accommodated and placed on an equal footing with the types of historical evidence that courts are familiar with, which largely consists of historical documents."[8]

Another way the Court has sought to reconcile the fact of a prior Indigenous presence with Canadian sovereignty is to conceive of treaties between Indigenous peoples and Canada as instruments of reconciliation, in *R v Sioui*.[9] The respondents in *Sioui* were members of the Huron band on the Lorette Indian reserve in Quebec. They were convicted of cutting down trees, camping, and making fires in a provincial park, contrary to provincial legislation. They alleged that they were engaged in ancestral customs and religious rites protected by a treaty entered into by the Huron and the Crown in 1760. Justice Lamer held for the Huron and offered a broad interpretation of the treaty's provision for "the free Exercise of [the Huron] religion, [and] their Customs."[10] Because the text of the treaty makes no mention of the territory over which treaty rights may be exercised, Quebec argued that the treaty right did not extend to activities performed in park territory.

---

7 [1991] 3 WWR 97, at 383 (BCSC).
8 *Delgamuukw v British Columbia, supra* at 1069.
9 [1990] 1 SCR 1025.
10 [1990] 1 SCR 1025, at 1074.

Justice Lamer held that this issue had to be resolved "by determining the intention of the parties ... at the time it was concluded."[11] He acknowledged the possibility of different interpretations of the parties' common intention and stated that the court must choose "from among the various possible interpretations of the common intention the one which best reconciles the Hurons' interests" and those of the Crown.[12] Justice Lamer was of the opinion that "the rights guaranteed by the treaty could be exercised over the entire territory frequented by the Hurons at the time, so long as the carrying on of the customs and rites is not incompatible with the particular use made by the Crown of this territory."[13]

These early efforts by the judiciary to comprehend Aboriginal and treaty rights as instruments of reconciliation have been refined in subsequent jurisprudence by the Court. But the Court's contributions, however refined, do not exhaust the meaning of recognition and reconciliation in Indigenous-settler societies. "Recognition" can and often does connote many different meanings in the context of Indigenous-settler relations. It can refer simply to the moment of constitutional entrenchment, a meaning underscored in the Canadian context by the text of section 35(1) itself. But recognition is a variable concept. Recognition can occur in a wide range of contexts outside of the constitutional sphere – most notably, as a political act – and constitutional recognition itself can assume different forms. One of these forms is recognition of a constitutional pluralism, an acknowledgment of a plurality of constitutional orders within the boundaries of Canada. Indigenous peoples, from before contact and to this day, constitute political and legal orders, exercising lawmaking authority over territory and people. The extent to which section 35(1) recognizes this complex fact of constitutional pluralism is critical to the evolving relationship between Indigenous peoples and the Canadian state.

"Reconciliation" also admits of many different interpretations. For our purposes, it plays the primary role of a constitutional objective ascribed primarily by the judiciary to the entrenchment of Aboriginal and treaty rights. "The reconciliation of the pre-existence of aboriginal societies with the sovereignty of the Crown," according to the Court,

---

11 *Ibid* at 1068.
12 *Ibid* at 1069.
13 *Ibid* at 1070.

is the underlying "purpose" of constitutional recognition of Aboriginal and treaty rights.[14] Reconciliation thus is a juridical concept developed by the judiciary to ascribe meaning and purpose to recognition. But it too carries a richer meaning. Reconciliation implicates acts and processes that seek to bring justice to Indigenous-settler relations in a host of legal, political, social, and methodological settings beyond the constitutional context of these relations. And what constitutes reconciliation, of course, is a matter of deep political contestation.

Each chapter in this collection, in its own way, explores recognition and reconciliation. Yet, while each is unique in its contribution, five central themes animate the collection as a whole. The first is the role that the concept of sovereignty occupies in constitutional jurisprudence relating to Indigenous peoples and Canada. Constitutional norms possess the capacity to unsettle the concept of Canadian sovereignty and to engage with concepts of Indigenous sovereignty. To the extent that Indigenous societies were sovereign nations prior to contact, and at least remnants of their sovereignty remain in the wake of Canada's emergence as a sovereign state, how are we to understand the nature of Canadian – and Indigenous – sovereignty today?

Patrick Macklem's chapter describes an ethos of constitutional pluralism in early encounters between Indigenous peoples and colonists in New France and British North America that failed to take root as an organizing principle for the relationship between Indigenous legal orders and the Canadian state. He identifies legal and political developments that replaced this ethos of legal pluralism with its antithesis: a monistic account of sovereignty, with decidedly non-Indigenous sources of legal authority initially grounded in British law and subsequently in the Constitution of Canada. Macklem then identifies three developments that could form a foundation for a resurgence of an ethos of legal pluralism. Two are occurring inside Canadian law, looking out to Indigenous legal norms for validation. The third is occurring beyond Canadian law and is not necessarily looking in to Canadian legal norms for validation.

Mark Walters highlights judicial resistance to questioning traditional conceptions of sovereignty and considers theoretical and practical reasons for doing so. He acknowledges that there are good reasons in legal principle for why judges might resist hearing challenges to the legal existence

---

14 *R v Van der Peet*, [1996] 2 SCR 507, at para 31.

of the Canadian state by Indigenous peoples. However, he also argues that, in certain circumstances, inquiry into the legality of Crown sovereignty may be an essential part of completing the task of building the Canadian state. According to Walters, most claims for Aboriginal rights do not represent existential challenges to Canada at all, and "Crown sovereignty" is invoked to obscure what is really just a balancing of Indigenous and non-Indigenous interests. If Aboriginal rights are sui generis, as courts have ruled, then it would appear that the judicial conception of Crown sovereignty in Aboriginal rights cases is equally sui generis. It is time, therefore, to dismantle the idea of Crown sovereignty with a view not to challenging but defending the ideal of legality in Canada.

In contrast, Jeremy Webber argues that judicial reluctance to engage with questions about Indigenous and Canadian sovereignty may have salutary consequences by permitting the accommodation of divergent interpretations of the location of sovereignty. He calls for an "agnostic constitutionalism," which brackets fundamental disagreements about Canadian and Indigenous sovereignty, "so that divergent positions on these fundamental issues might be permitted to persist in the medium or even long term, without those questions having to be decided once and for all." He develops these claims by engaging with four different conceptions of sovereignty vying for constitutional attention and exploring the role that conceptions of sovereignty have played in practical decision-making, both within and outside the courts.

Brian Slattery's contribution focuses on what the judiciary, notwithstanding its relative silence on questions relating to sovereignty, has said about the purpose of section 35. Slattery argues that by assuming that the two goals of recognition and reconciliation can be advanced by a single set of legal principles, the Court has gone astray. He recommends the formulation of two sets of principles: principles of recognition and principles of reconciliation. The former would enable courts to identify the full range of rights held by Indigenous peoples at the time they entered into settled relations with the Crown, that is, historical Aboriginal rights. The latter would govern the process of translating historical rights into contemporary rights. Although courts play the leading role in applying principles of recognition, they play a lesser, though still crucial, role in principles of reconciliation. Reconciliation cannot be imposed by judicial fiat – no matter how well-intentioned. As such, principles of reconciliation provide the legal framework within which a modern settlement of Indigenous claims may be achieved by treaty between Indigenous peoples and the Crown.

The second theme of this collection of essays is the methodologies at play in legal and political questions involving Indigenous peoples. Legal and political questions involving Indigenous peoples and the Canadian state raise complex methodological and epistemological questions about how particular categories and ways of understanding shape the development of constitutional norms and the boundaries of political possibility. Constitutional law offers several different potential paradigms for understanding Indigenous-state relations. Beyond the constitutional realm, epistemological assumptions about the nature of individual and collective identities shape and arguably constrain our capacity to make sense of Indigenous difference. Indigenous knowledge offers dramatically different categories and ways of understanding. What does "reconciliation" mean in the context of methodological and epistemological contestation?

Paul McHugh's contribution identifies the emergence of a loose intellectual consensus regarding "common law Aboriginal title" in the decade before the enactment of section 35. He argues that consensus replaced an older method of comprehending Indigenous-settler relations in terms of a "political trust" with what purported to be a form of property that appealed to a most intensively common law principle based upon longevity of possession. By the mid-1990s, as courts – not only in Canada but in Australia and New Zealand as well – amplified the proprietary dimensions of Aboriginal title and rights that section 35 recognizes, the doctrine's limitations as a constitutional mechanism for the structuring of Indigenous-settler relations became evident just as its retrospective gaze – and revisionist character – became even more pronounced. According to McHugh, more recent developments in all three jurisdictions do not discard the proprietary paradigm but add to it a reconceptualized notion of the "honour of the Crown." This has given section 35 a constitutional function beyond that of a reaffirmation of the proprietary paradigm that was already a hallmark in 1982.

Like McHugh, Dale Turner examines the common law character of the constitutional dialogue on the meaning and content of section 35(1). He notes that, when in Canadian courts, Indigenous peoples must articulate their arguments in the language of the common law when seeking constitutional justice in Canadian courts. Turner contends that, since 1982, Indigenous knowledge and ways of thinking have been "re-configured" in profound ways. Indigenous knowledge has come to be understood and valorized in two different, but related, contexts. First, there are the forms of Indigenous knowledge that are rooted in Indigenous homelands; second, there are the explanations of Indigenous knowledge that are used in Canadian courts of law. Turner links the tension between these two manifestations to the challenge of reconciliation.

Jean Leclair's contribution argues that the epistemological lens through which one examines legal and political realities entails normative consequences that are seldom fully appreciated by scholars interested in exploring the constitutional relationship between Indigenous peoples and Canada. Leclair interrogates some of the epistemological assumptions embedded in constitutional, political, and scholarly discourse about the nature of individual and collective identities, and their effect on dominant understandings of Indigenous-settler relations. He attempts to demonstrate that many of the accounts devoted to the recognition and reconciliation of Aboriginal peoples with Canadian sovereignty share unstated – and misguided – assumptions that each of the various communities implicated by these accounts – Aboriginal and non-Aboriginal – possesses a unitary "identity" and speaks in one voice. These accounts generate concepts that feed on incommensurability. Grounding constitutional norms instead on the dramatic complexities of individual and collective identities generates concepts that promote reconciliation.

The third theme engages with the evolution of an important, post-1982 jurisprudential innovation, the emergent constitutional obligation of government to consult with First Nations when exercising authority in ways that might interfere with an Aboriginal or treaty right. One of the most significant constitutional dimensions of the movement from recognition to reconciliation has been the emergence of a constitutional duty of federal and provincial governments, and arguably third parties, to consult with an affected Aboriginal community before engaging in action that likely will interfere with its Aboriginal or treaty rights. This duty has thrust governments, Aboriginal peoples, and third parties into complex political and legal relations, especially in the context of resource development and extraction on ancestral territories. On the one hand, the duty opens the door to comprehending reconciliation in economic terms by creating the possibility of a wide array of negotiated rights relating to risk and environmental impact assessment processes and royalty sharing. On the other hand, the duty creates onerous, ongoing procedural and substantive burdens on all parties concerned.

In recent years, the duty-to-consult doctrine also has become a springboard for discussions about Aboriginal economic participation, economic accommodation of potential Aboriginal and treaty rights claims, and what could more generally be thought of as an economic dimension of reconciliation. In his chapter, Dwight Newman asks whether the duty to consult doctrine has the potential for more successful furtherance of economic opportunities for Indigenous communities than other legal doctrines, particularly Aboriginal title. He argues that the doctrine has the potential, realized in some instances, of contributing to economic accommodation, but that there are also risks that it may contribute to certain unstable policy outcomes, accentuate some policy challenges, and pose an obstacle to certain highly desirable policy outcomes. He suggests some paths forward on the policy front for making consultation and economic reconciliation interact as harmoniously as possible.

In contrast, Michael Bryant argues that the costs of the duty to consult outweigh its benefits and it therefore should be abandoned as a legal doctrine. From a practical perspective, consultation is easy to identify as a duty, but, in Bryant's view, impossible on its own to fulfil as a standard of care. A major challenge with the duty to consult and accommodate is that it has produced unintended consequences, growing *ad absurdum* to require consultation on how to consult. But consulting in itself is not the objective. Unintentionally, the Court has established process as the ultimate goal. As such, the duty to consult has done more harm than good by multiplying processes and creating delays and uncertainty. Bryant argues that the better approach is to require the Crown to obtain the consent of Indigenous communities before embarking on major projects on traditional lands.

Sari Graben and Abbey Sinclair explore the role that the duty to consult plays in relation to the authority and responsibilities of administrative agencies and tribunals. The Supreme Court of Canada's reliance on tribunals to administer Aboriginal rights assumes that tribunals provide parties with early and accessible relief consistent with principles of justice espoused in the common law. In an attempt to evaluate this assumption, Graben and Sinclair use an empirical approach to determine whether the duty to consult has had an effect on tribunal decision-making in one particular tribunal, the National Energy Board (NEB). A quantitative and qualitative analysis of recent NEB decisions indicates that while it assesses the Aboriginal engagement activities of proponents, the NEB typically does not evaluate the adequacy of Crown consultation. The insights gained from this quantitative and qualitative assessment of tribunal authority suggests that empirical methods offer an important tool to evaluate whether agencies and tribunals take the duty to consult seriously.

The fourth theme animating this book is law and politics in action beyond the constitutional domain. This section explores how constitutional norms governing the relationship between Indigenous peoples and Canada that had been developed since 1982 affect tactical and strategic choices inside the courtroom and in broader legislative, regulatory, and political arenas. The chapter by Sébastien Grammond, Isabelle Lantagne, and Natacha Gagné explores the impact that constitutional norms have on efforts by Indigenous communities lacking official status as Indians to access the courts to secure the recognition of their Indigenous identities and their Aboriginal and treaty rights. In most cases, these attempts have failed. This chapter shows that these groups' lack of resources and their inability to conform to a popular, stereotyped image of an Indigenous community embedded in constitutional norms explain why courts have denied their claims. Grammond, Lantagne, and Gagné suggest that a marginalized group's visibility or invisibility is a material factor in determining whether courts will address its needs.

Kirsty Gover also explores questions of membership that section 35(1) fails to address, engaging with democratic theory to resolve tensions embedded in the *Indian Act* between descent-based membership rules and liberal theory. She draws on debates about the "boundary problem" in democratic theory to consider the normative challenges raised by descent-based membership in Indigenous communities. If a *demos* is necessarily bounded, so that some people are excluded, what normative principle could justify these exclusions? Liberal approaches to this question prioritize non-discrimination, potentially denying to kinship-based polities like First Nations the capacity to distribute membership by reference to characteristics listed as "prohibited grounds" in human rights law, including race and its cognates: descent, nationality, and ethnic origin. Gover draws parallels between Canadian citizenship law, the *Indian Act* regime, and First Nations' membership codes, all of which allocate membership by descent, and all of which exclude some descendants. Canadian human rights laws and methodologies, including those engaging section 35, could assist in the reconciliation of Indigenous and liberal forms of political organization.

Douglas Sanderson examines the gaps that constitutional norms produce, which must be filled in by legislative action to secure their effective realization, and proposes amendments to the federal *Indian*

Act to secure their effective realization. Constitutional recognition of Aboriginal and treaty rights does not provide positive direction to the Crown, and accordingly it needs to be supplemented by legislation, such as the *Indian Act*. The *Indian Act*, though, is plagued by problems. Sanderson argues that the *Indian Act* must be amended to do the work that is required by section 35 by setting out an appropriate relationship between Indigenous people and the Crown. Sanderson proposes a series of small legislative amendments, the first of which is aimed at demonstrating that Parliament and Indigenous peoples can work together by identifying those sections of the existing *Indian Act* that serve no legitimate purpose and whose elimination from the *Act* undermines no one's autonomy, property rights, or freedoms. The second set is designed to bring economic stability to First Nation communities, while remaining uncontroversial in the wider settler society.

Courtney Jung explores the migration of the concept of reconciliation from its constitutional roots to the political sphere. Specifically, she examines the politics surrounding the establishment and operation of Canada's Truth and Reconciliation Commission to address the legacy of the residential schools system and the limits and possibilities of transitional justice measures to promote Indigenous-settler reconciliation. The framework of transitional justice, originally devised to facilitate reconciliation in countries undergoing transitions from authoritarianism to democracy, has recently been employed in response to human rights violations against Indigenous peoples in societies not undergoing regime transition. Jung outlines some of the potential complexities involved in processing Indigenous demands for justice through a transitional justice framework. Treating Indigenous demands for justice as a matter of "human rights" is an ethically loaded project that may reinforce liberal and neoliberal paradigms that Indigenous peoples often reject. Whether transitional justice measures, such as apologies, truth commissions, and reparations, will serve primarily to legitimate the status quo between postcolonial states, settler societies, and Indigenous peoples, or whether they will promote reconciliation, will depend in part on the political context in which they take place.

Natalia Loukacheva examines post-1982 constitutional developments in the context of the establishment of Nunavut. Loukacheva argues that the political and economic viability of Nunavut is dependent on not only on its constitutional location in the structure of the Canadian state, but also the ability of local actors to respond to challenges. This chapter thus looks at the legal and socio-economic capacities of the

Nunavummiut to regain control over their territory and their ability to shape a sustainable future. In some ways, this future is predetermined by the devolution process currently in place for the region. However, the existing legal and political environment, including a possible devolution deal, will not in itself lead to political and economic viability. Sustainability, greater political autonomy, and, ultimately, reconciliation also depend upon people and their ability to make a difference.

The final part of this book contains chapters that relate the movement from recognition to reconciliation in Canada with legal and political developments in other jurisdictions. Jacinta Ruru's contribution compares the rights protected by section 35 of the *Constitution Act, 1982* in Canada to those protected by the Treaty of Waitangi in New Zealand to argue that the treaty ought to become a formal part of New Zealand's constitution. The Maori version of the Treaty of Waitangi states that the Maori would retain sovereignty over their lands and treasures, while the British version states that the Maori ceded sovereignty to the British Crown. Although the treaty is not part of New Zealand's domestic law, it is commonly said to form part of the country's informal constitution. Under New Zealand's constitutional system, however, Parliament is supreme and has no formal limits to its law-making power. She explores the extent to which the judiciary nonetheless has attributed a constitutional role to the Treaty of Waitangi.

Marcia Langton and Megan Davis's chapter invites an exploration of the extent to which Canadian constitutional developments have shaped constitutional reform in Australia. Australia's federal government recently established an expert panel – on which Langton and Davis served as members – to report on possible options for recognition of Aboriginal and Torres Strait Islander peoples in Australia's Constitution. Davis and Langton provide an overview of the expert panel's recommendations, set in the context of a discussion of the history of provisions of Australia's Constitution dealing with Aboriginal voting rights. The panel made recommendations that were likely to gain wide public support, as amendments to Australia's Constitution require approval by a double majority in a national referendum. Davis and Langton refer to the need for wide public support in explaining why the expert panel did not make recommendations similar to those contained in the Canadian Constitution or recommendations that contemplate the negotiation of treaties or an acknowledgment of Indigenous sovereignty.

John Borrows's contribution argues that reconciliation requires that Indigenous self-determination lie at the heart of a country's dealings with Indigenous peoples, and that Canada has not been successful in this respect. This is evident when one compares the inclusion of Aboriginal and treaty rights in Canada's Constitution with legislative provisions dealing with Native American issues in the United States. In contrast with Canada, the United States has placed self-determination at the centre of its relations with Indigenous peoples. Canada's failure has resulted in negative consequences for Indigenous peoples in three areas: the administration of government programs, the protection of Indigenous cultures, and the control over natural resources and economic development opportunities.

Michael Ignatieff's "Afterword," echoes many of the themes informing many of the contributions to this collection. He characterizes section 35 as the constitutional recognition of the constitutive place of Aboriginal peoples in the political identity and legal order of Canada. It recognizes their place in the founding narrative of Canada and acknowledges the state's obligations to fulfil specific treaty rights and Crown duties inherited from the past. Section 35 also has a generative, future-directed aspect, one that aims to create a practice of inter-societal law. It is designed to facilitate dialogue between two legal systems, on the basis of a primary recognition of existing rights and obligations. Section 35 also tacitly distinguishes between a jurisprudence focused on sovereignty and one focused on jurisdiction. For Ignatieff, section 35, being a part of the Constitution of Canada, tacitly restates the ultimate supremacy of Canadian law. It then goes on to frame the possibility of a jurisprudence of jurisdictions. Ignatieff identifies several features of such a jurisprudence for it to promote reconciliation.

By interrogating concepts of pluralism, sovereignty, and consultation, challenging dominant methodologies and epistemologies, exploring processes of recognition and reconciliation outside of the juridical environment, and engaging in comparative reflection, the essays in this book shed light on different features of the evolving relations between Indigenous peoples and the Canadian state. They invite the reader to look at the law and politics of Indigenous-settler societies in new ways. And they demonstrate how recognition and reconciliation are both means and ends of a just constitutional and political order.

PART ONE

Reconciling Sovereignties

1 Indigenous Peoples and the Ethos of Legal Pluralism in Canada

PATRICK MACKLEM

In a luminous book entitled *Shadow Nations*, Bruce Duthu reconstructs relations between Indian nations and the United States according to a founding "ethos of legal pluralism."[1] In its afterglow, many scholars will be inspired to approach their jurisdictions with a similar objective in mind. Writing from Canada, with its strong ties to legal pluralism in theory,[2] if not in practice, *Shadow Nations* led me to ask several questions. How receptive is the Canadian constitutional environment to conceiving of Indigenous-Canadian relations in accordance with a similar ethos of legal pluralism? Are there institutional and doctrinal openings for such a reconstruction to take root? What forms of structural and political resistance might act as impediments?

This chapter offers some preliminary reflections on these questions. It first outlines legal pluralism's promise in early encounters between Indigenous peoples and colonists in New France and British North America and offer reasons why legal pluralism thus far fails to characterize Indigenous-Canadian relations. It then identifies three developments that could form a foundation for its resurgence. Two are occurring inside Canadian law, looking out to Indigenous legal norms. The third is occurring beyond Canadian law and is not necessarily looking in to Canadian legal norms. My reflections on these developments provide little more

---

1 Bruce Duthu, *Shadow Nations: Tribal Sovereignty and the Limits of Legal Pluralism* (New York: Oxford University Press, 2013) at 1.
2 A fact duly noted in *ibid*, which engages the work on legal pluralism by several Canadian theorists, including Roderick MacDonald and Tim Schouls. See Roderick A MacDonald, "Metaphors of Multiplicity: Civil Society, Regimes and Legal Pluralism" (1998) 15 Ariz J Int'l & Comp L 69; Tim Schouls, *Shifting Boundaries: Aboriginal Identity, Pluralist Theory, and the Politics of Self-Government* (Vancouver: University of Vancouver Press, 2003).

than a foundation from which answers to these questions might flow. But I hope they shed some light on the receptivity of relations between Indigenous peoples and the Canadian state to an ethos of legal pluralism.

I

By "legal pluralism" I take Bruce Duthu's lead to refer to the existence of a plurality of legal orders existing within or across the territorial boundaries of a sovereign state.[3] Many institutional mechanisms give formal expression to the presence of a plurality of legal orders. A federal system constitutionally vests law-making authority in two levels of government, each relatively autonomous from the other in the production of legal norms. A state can also devolve power to regional and local levels of government, enabling the exercise of delegated law-making authority to a subsection of its population. Forms of minority protection may also promote legal pluralism, to the extent that they contemplate a minority community having a measure of law-making authority relatively shielded from the legislative power of the broader political community in which it is located.

But the legal pluralism relevant to *Shadow Nations* – and indeed to all rich accounts of Indigenous-settler relations – is one where the sources of legal validity themselves are plural. In the above examples, norms produced by legal actors other than a central government appear to possess legal validity by a plurality of sources. A provincial law is legally valid because it was enacted by a legislature possessing jurisdiction to enact it. A municipal bylaw is legally valid because it was enacted in accordance with relevant enabling legislation. A law promulgated by a minority community possesses legal validity because the community has a legal right to promulgate it. But ultimately the legal validity of

---

3 *Supra* note 1 at 11–12 ("the legal pluralist is intensely interested in identifying the forms of normative ordering, including legal systems, that have meaning to the socially plural societies occupying the same social field and examining the operation of those normative ordering systems in relation to the power of the state"). For more discussion of legal pluralism, see Paul Schiff Berman, *Global Legal Pluralism: A Jurisprudence of Law beyond Borders* (Cambridge: Cambridge University Press, 2012); Boaventura de Sousa Santos, *Toward a New Legal Common Sense: Law, Globalization, and Emancipation* (Cambridge: Cambridge University Press, 2002); Carol Weisbrod, *Emblems of Pluralism: Cultural Differences and the Law* (Princeton: Princeton University Press, 2002); William Connolly, *The Ethos of Pluralization* (Minneapolis: University of Minnesota Press, 1995).

each of these norms is derived from a singular source, the constitution of the state itself. In contrast, the legal pluralism that captures salient properties of Indigenous-settler relations is one of constitutional pluralism, where there exists a plurality of constitutional orders within and, conceivably, across state boundaries. In such an environment, there are multiple legal norms of different content, multiple sites of legal norm production, multiple legal sources for these sites, and multiple forms of norm enforcement. As a result, "legal reality," according to John Griffiths, is "an unsystematic collage of inconsistent and overlapping parts, lending itself to no easy legal interpretation."[4]

At the time of initial contact between Indigenous peoples and imperial powers and their colonial representatives, "legal reality" appeared receptive to an ethos of legal pluralism. Manifold Indigenous legal orders exercised law-making authority over territories and peoples in the Americas. The legal norms that constituted these legal orders specified and regulated the economic, social, and political practices of individuals and groups belonging to distinct Indigenous nations as well as relations between and among Indigenous nations. The legal validity of these norms lay in the nature of the legal orders from which they emanated. European settlement imported colonial legal norms whose validity depended ultimately on the legal systems of France and the United Kingdom. Colonial settlement also marked the genesis of a series of inter-societal encounters, some friendly, others hostile, with mistrust, trust, suspicion, and expectation alike participating in the formation of a pluralist ethos characteristic of such relations. In the words of Jeremy Webber, "[T]he distinctive norms of each society furnished the point of departure, determining the spirit of interaction, colouring the first interpretations of the other's customs, and shaping the beginning of a common normative language."[5]

---

4 John Griffiths, "What Is Legal Pluralism?" (1986) 24 J Leg Pluralism 1 at 4. Legal scholars, myself included, often cite this article as a classic articulation of legal pluralism. David Schneiderman's work on the British legal and political pluralists, including FW Maitland, Harold Laski, & John Neville Figgis, of the early twentieth century reveals Griffiths to have been a relative latecomer to the field. See David Schneiderman, "Harold Laski, Viscount Haldane, and the Law of the Canadian Constitution in the Early Twentieth Century" (1998) 48 UTLJ 521; Schneiderman, "Haldane Unrevealed" (2012) 57 McGill LJ 593.

5 Jeremy Webber, "Relations of Force and Relations of Justice: The Emergence of Normative Community between Colonists and Aboriginal Peoples" (1995) 33 Osgoode Hall LJ 623 at 627.

Contact thus set the stage for legally plural relationships between Indigenous peoples and colonial powers. Treaties negotiated early in the history of European expansion formalized efforts to achieve peaceful coexistence between Indigenous nations and newcomers to the continent. A 1665 peace treaty between the French Crown and four Indigenous nations belonging to the Iroquois Confederacy, for example, confirmed a cessation of conflict and a state of peace between the parties. The text of the treaty indirectly acknowledged the First Nations' continuing title to their territories and certain territorial rights of the French Crown in the settlements of Montreal, Trois-Rivières, and Quebec City.[6]

It would be a stretch, I think, to construe the 1665 treaty and others like it as formal evidence of a strong ethos of legal pluralism animating relations between Indigenous and colonial legal orders. "Legal reality" likely becomes legally plural gradually, as repeated interactions deepen inter-societal commitments to plural legal orders. But the early treaties do suggest a nascent legal pluralism at play among the parties. Premised on mutual recognition, they stand as formal markers of early encounters and interactions that had the potential – if deepened and multiplied – to evolve into a durable form of legal pluralism structuring Indigenous-settler relations on the continent.

Fast forward to today. There exist more than five hundred treaties between Indigenous peoples and the Crown in Canada from the shores of the Atlantic Ocean to the Yukon in the western Canadian Arctic. Where territories have not yet been subject to treaty, in most of British Columbia, First Nations are negotiating new treaties to structure their relationships with federal and provincial authorities. The enactment of section 35(1) of the *Constitution Act, 1982*, which recognizes and affirms "the existing aboriginal and treaty rights of the aboriginal peoples of Canada," has ushered in significant changes to the constitutional relationship between Indigenous peoples and the Canadian state.

---

6 *Treaty of Peace between the Iroquois and Governor de Tracy*, New York Papers 111 A28. The text of the treaty can be found in Clive Parry, ed, *The Consolidated Treaty Series*, vol IX (Dobbs Ferry, NY: Oceana, 1969–86) at 363; and EB O'Callaghan, ed, *Documents Relative to the Colonial History of the State of New York*, vol 3 (Albany: Weed, Parsons, 1856–61) at 21. For more discussion of the treaty, see Royal Commission on Aboriginal Peoples, *Treaty Making in the Spirit of Co-Existence: An Alternative to Extinguishment* (Ottawa: Minister of Supply and Services Canada, 1995) at 18–20.

The promise of a "common normative language" informing this relationship, however, remains unfulfilled. There are many complex reasons for its absence – reasons that span many domains, including epistemology, economics, politics, and law. But one account merits attention, even though it glosses over the complexity of what it seeks to explain. The ethos of legal pluralism immanent in early encounters between Indigenous and colonial peoples failed to take root and was replaced by its antithesis: a monistic account of constitutional order, with decidedly non-Indigenous sources of legal authority initially grounded in British law and subsequently grounded in the Constitution of Canada.

The question, of course, is why legal pluralism did not come to pass. Although the Crown entered into treaties with Indigenous peoples initially to secure its precarious legal and factual footing on Indigenous territories by acts of mutual recognition, the Crown began to negotiate treaties for different reasons. International law had come to stabilize claims of sovereignty by imperial powers over Indigenous territory. Constitutional law assumed a singular, hierarchical conception of sovereignty incapable of comprehending multiple sovereign actors on a given territory. As a result, the Crown no longer regarded a treaty as necessarily linked to its sovereignty over Indigenous territory.[7]

During the nineteenth century, perhaps as a result of the dramatic shift in demography and in the balance of military and economic power between Indigenous nations and the Crown, the treaty process from the Crown's perspective instead became a means of facilitating the relocation and assimilation of Indigenous peoples. The Crown increasingly saw the treaty process as a means of formally dispossessing Indigenous peoples of ancestral territory in return for reserve land and certain benefits to be provided by state authorities, rendering remote the possibility of legal pluralism becoming "legal reality."

Moreover, although the early treaties signalled a nation-to-nation relationship of mutual respect, the parties did not initially regard them as creating legal rights enforceable in a court of law. Instead, the treaty served as evidence of an ongoing relationship; rights and obligations

---

7 Compare PG McHugh, *Aboriginal Societies and the Common Law: A History of Sovereignty, Status, and Self-Determination* (New York: Oxford University Press, 2004) at 65 ("constitutional lawyers and courts cleaving intellectually to the unitary common law model of sovereignty – itself … largely a nineteenth-century model – were unable to recognize a shared or multiple version").

flowed not from the document itself but from the relationship formalized by the treaty.[8] This early process of generating norms of conduct and recognition operated against the backdrop of a colonial legal imagination that had yet to experience a radical separation of law and politics, in which certain issues are regarded as legal and others as political.

When law gradually emerged as a relatively autonomous sphere of social life, the judiciary began to address the legal consequences of the treaty process. Judicial interpretation of treaties started to occur in Canada only in the late 1800s, when courts held treaties to be political agreements unenforceable in a court of law. International law provides that an agreement between two "independent powers" constitutes a treaty binding on the parties to the agreement.[9] But because courts regarded Indigenous nations as uncivilized and thus not independent, they refused to view Crown promises as legally enforceable obligations under international or domestic law. This view was replaced gradually by a more accommodating approach that regarded a treaty as a form of contract.[10] Indigenous people were imagined as possessing legal personality similar to that possessed by non-Indigenous people in Canada and were therefore capable of entering into domestically binding agreements with the Crown.

But because treaties assumed the legal form of contract, their terms were subject to the exercise of unilateral legislative authority. Prior to 1982, this had the effect of permitting Parliament to unilaterally

---

8 Compare William Blackstone, *Commentaries on the Laws of England*, vol 1 (Oxford, 1765–9) at 428 (vision of a contract as dependent on the existence of a social relation and pre-existing rights and obligations). See also Patrick Atiyah, *The Rise and Fall of Freedom of Contract* (Oxford: Clarendon, 1979) at notes 40, 143 (eighteenth-century legal consciousness invoked the notion of promise "to support an independently existing duty"); Owen Kahn-Freund, *Blackstone's Neglected Child: The Contract of Employment*, 93 LQR 508 at 512 ("the contract is only an *accidentale*, not an *essentiale* of the relation").

9 See, e.g., James Crawford, ed, *Brownlie's Principles of Public International Law*, 8th ed (Oxford: Clarendon, 2012) at 58–70. It should be noted that, even if treaties between the Crown and First Nations were accorded "international treaty" status, this fact alone would not render them enforceable in domestic courts; implementing legislation would be required: see *AG Canada v AG Ontario (Labour Conventions)*, [1937] AC 326 (PC).

10 See, e.g., *Pawis v R* (1979), 102 DLR (3d) 602 (FCTD) at 610 ("[t]he right acquired by the Indians in those treaties was … necessarily subject to restriction through acts of the legislature, just as the person who acquires from the Crown a grant of land is subject in its enjoyment to … legislative restrictions").

regulate or extinguish existing treaty rights. Moreover, when courts viewed treaties as contractual agreements, they initially interpreted their substance in a manner that was blind to Indigenous expectations of the treaty process. Treaty rights were interpreted solely by reference to non-Indigenous legal norms and values. In the words of Dale Turner, treaties were "textualized in the language of the dominant European culture."[11]

Despite its nascent presence in early treaties, legal pluralism thus did not take root in Canada in part because the Crown began to negotiate treaties for reasons antithetical to pluralism's promise. And when treaties assumed legal form in Canadian law, Canadian legal institutions did not comprehend them as instruments of mutual recognition, where each party acknowledged a measure of legitimacy of the legal order of the other, and accordingly made arrangements for the coexistence and interaction of legal norms emanating from the two or more legal communities they represented. Their legal form as contracts rendered them unintelligible as instruments of mutual recognition. As contracts, they assumed a hierarchical legal relation between the Crown and Indigenous parties, given that the Crown in its legislative capacity had the authority to unilaterally override their terms. Their substance, too, rendered them unintelligible to legal pluralism, as Indigenous legal norms played no role in clarifying their terms.

Another set of factors contributing to the failure of legal pluralism relates to how Canadian law comprehended the legality of Indigenous interests in their territories. With British sovereignty came underlying Crown title, with a particularly brutal twist. The fiction of underlying Crown title was developed in feudal times to legitimate the then-existing kaleidoscopic pattern of landholdings in England by treating the Crown as the original occupant and actual landholders as holding title by way of (mostly fictional) grants from the Crown. Its transplantation to the colonial context was not accompanied by the complementary fiction that the actual Indigenous landholders held title by way of

---

11 Dale Turner, "From Valladolid to Ottawa: The Illusion of Listening to Aboriginal People," in Jill Oakes, Kathi Kinew, & Rick Riewe, eds, *Sacred Lands: Aboriginal World Views, Claims, and Conflicts* (Edmonton: Canadian Circumpolar Institute, 1998), 53–68 at 64. For a good example of this phenomenon, see *Pawis v R, supra* note 10 at 609–10 (interpreting a treaty provision establishing a "full and free privilege to hunt and fish" to mean that "no consideration is to be extracted from those entitled to hunt and fish").

a grant from the Crown. The fiction of underlying Crown title became a legal technology of Indigenous dispossession, radically disrupting the actual pattern of Indigenous landholding in British North America.

In the late 1800s, Canadian law, with its belated acceptance of a tepid form of common law Aboriginal title, did acknowledge that Indigenous peoples lived on and occupied the continent prior to European contact and, as a result, possess certain interests worthy of legal protection. This body of law prescribed ways of handling disputes between Indigenous and non-Indigenous peoples, especially disputes over land. It recognized, in common law terms, Indigenous occupation and use of ancestral lands,[12] described rights associated with Aboriginal title in collective terms vesting in Indigenous communities,[13] and purported to restrict settlement on Indigenous territories until these territories had been surrendered to the Crown.[14] It prohibited sales of Indigenous land to non-Indigenous people without the approval of and participation by Crown authorities.[15] And it prescribed safeguards for the manner in which such surrenders can occur and imposed fiduciary obligations on government in its dealings with Indigenous lands and resources.[16]

The common law of Aboriginal title, however, historically failed to protect Indigenous territories from settlement and exploitation. Law's inability to protect Indigenous territories was in part a function of broader social and historical realities associated with colonial expansion. Governments and settlers either misunderstood or ignored the law of Aboriginal title. Crown respect for the law of Aboriginal title was eroded by the decline of the fur trade and the waning of Indigenous

---

12 See, for example, *Hamlet of Baker Lake v Minister of Indian Affairs and Northern Development*, [1980] 1 FC 518 (FCTD).

13 See, for example, *Amodu Tijani v Secretary, Southern Nigeria*, [1921] 2 AC 399 (PC).

14 See, for example, *Guerin v R*, [1984] 2 SCR 335 at 383 ("[t]he purpose of this surrender requirement is clearly to interpose the Crown between the Indians and prospective purchasers or lessees of their land, so as to prevent the Indians from being exploited").

15 See, for example, *Canadian Pacific Ltd v Paul*, [1988] 2 SCR 654 at 677 (Aboriginal title cannot be transferred, sold, or surrendered to anyone other than the Crown).

16 See, for example, *R v Guerin, supra* note 14 at 382 (Aboriginal title "gives rise upon surrender to a distinctive fiduciary obligation on the part of the Crown to deal with the land for the benefit of the surrendering Indians"); see also *R v Sparrow*, [1990] 1 SCR 1075 at 1108 ("the Government has the responsibility to act in a fiduciary capacity with respect to Aboriginal peoples").

and non-Indigenous economic interdependence. Increased demands on Indigenous territories occasioned by population growth and westward expansion, followed by a period of paternalistic administration marked by involuntary relocations, only exacerbated the erosion of respect.

In addition to these external factors, law's failure to protect Indigenous territories can also be internally traced to legal choices of the judiciary. On more than one occasion, the judiciary suggested that Indigenous territorial claims might not possess any independent legal significance at all.[17] The possibility that Indigenous territories might not generate legal recognition by the Canadian legal order served as a legal backdrop for almost a century of relations between the Crown and Indigenous peoples, shaping legal expectations of governments, corporations, citizens, and other legal actors. It contributed to a perception that governments and third parties were relatively free to engage in a range of activity on ancestral lands – a perception that, in turn, legitimated unparalleled levels of government and third-party development and exploitation of Indigenous territories, which continue relatively unabated today.

Moreover, until recently, the legal significance that the judiciary attached to Indigenous territorial interests was minimal. Courts resisted characterizing Aboriginal title in proprietary terms, preferring instead to characterize it as a right of occupancy or a personal or usufructuary right,[18] or, more recently, as a sui generis interest.[19] Constructing Aboriginal title as a non-proprietary interest enabled its regulation and indeed its extinguishment by appropriate executive action,[20] disabled

---

17 See, for example, *St Catherines Milling & Lumber Co v R* (1888), 14 AC 46 (PC) (Aboriginal rights with respect to land and resources did not predate but were created by the royal proclamation and, as such, are "dependent on the good will of the Sovereign").

18 *Ibid* at 54; see also *Smith v R*, [1983] 1 SCR 554.

19 *Canadian Pacific Ltd v Paul*, [1988] 2 SCR 654 at 658 (Aboriginal title refers to an "Indian interest in land [that] is truly *sui generis*"); see also *R v Sparrow*, [1990] 1 SCR 1075 at 1112 ("[c]ourts must be careful ... to avoid the application of traditional common law concepts of property as they develop their understanding of ... the *sui generis* nature of Aboriginal rights").

20 See, for example, *Ontario (AG) v Bear Island Foundation*, [1991] 2 SCR 570 at 575 ("whatever may have been the situation upon signing of the Robinson-Huron Treaty, that right was in any event surrendered by arrangements subsequent to that treaty by which the Indians adhered to the treaty in exchange for treaty annuities and a reserve").

Indigenous titleholders from obtaining interim relief,[21] and frustrated access to the common law presumption of compensation in the event of expropriation.[22] Courts also indicated a willingness to view Aboriginal title as a set of rights to engage only in traditional practices on Aboriginal territory, that is, those practices that Indigenous people engaged in at the time the Crown acquired territorial sovereignty.[23] Each of these legal choices had a profound effect on the ability of Indigenous peoples to rely on Canadian law to protect ancestral territories from non-Indigenous incursion. Each also represented another nail in legal pluralism's coffin.

II

Notwithstanding this history, and to return to the questions posed at the outset, how receptive is the Canadian constitutional environment to conceiving of Indigenous-Canadian relations in accordance with the ethos of legal pluralism that animated their origins? Are there institutional and doctrinal openings for such a reconstruction to take root? What forms of structural and political resistance might act as impediments? There are three developments that could form a foundation for the recovery of legal pluralism. Two are occurring inside Canadian law, looking out to Indigenous legal norms. The third is occurring beyond Canadian law and is not necessarily looking in to Canadian legal norms.

The first development relates to the form and substance of treaty rights as understood by the Canadian judiciary. With the enactment of section 35(1) of the *Constitution Act, 1982*, treaty rights now assume the

---

21 A number of cases held that Aboriginal title does not constitute an interest in land sufficient to support the registration of a caveat or certificate of *lis pendens*, which would temporarily prevent activity on ancestral territory, pending final resolution of a dispute. See, for example, *Uukw v AGBC* (1987), 16 BCLR (2d) 145 (BCCA); *Lac La Ronge Indian Band v Beckman*, [1990] 4 WWR 211 (Sask CA); *James Smith Indian Band v Saskatchewan (Master of Titles)*, [1994] 2 CNLR 72 (Sask QB); but see *Ontario (AG) v Bear Island Foundation*, [1991] 2 SCR 570.

22 See, for example, *British Columbia v Tener*, [1985] 1 SCR 533 at 559, quoting *AG v De Keyser's Royal Hotel Ltd*, [1920] AC 508 at 542, per Lord Atkinson ("a statute is not to be construed so as to take away the property of a subject without compensation").

23 See, for example, *Baker Lake v Minister of Indian Affairs*, [1980] 1 FC 518 at 559 ("the common law ... can give effect only to those incidents of that enjoyment that were ... given effect by the [Aboriginal] regime that prevailed before"); *AG Ont v Bear Island Foundation*, [1985] 1 CNLR 1 at 3 (Ont SC) ("essence of Aboriginal rights is the right of Indians to live on the lands as their forefathers lived").

form of constitutional rights. No longer enforceable merely in the face of Crown inaction, treaties now constrain the exercise of legislative authority. To illustrate, in *R v Badger*,[24] at issue was whether the right to hunt contained in Treaty 8 provided a defence to a charge under Alberta's *Wildlife Act*, which prohibited hunting out of season and hunting without a licence. The Supreme Court of Canada held that Treaty 8 protected hunting for food on private property that was not put to a "visible, incompatible use," and that the right to hunt was a treaty right within the meaning of section 35(1) of the *Constitution Act*. The Court stated that "a treaty represents an exchange of solemn promises ... [and] an agreement whose nature is sacred." It reiterated that treaties should be interpreted in "a manner which maintains the integrity of the Crown" and that ambiguities or doubtful expressions in the wording of the treaty should be resolved in favour of Indigenous people.

Badger marks a significant transformation in the judicial understanding of a treaty's form and substance. No longer mere political agreements or contractual agreements, treaties now possess formal constitutional status. Their substance ought to be determined in a manner consistent with Indigenous understandings, flexible to evolving practices, inclusive of reasonably incidental practices, and in a way that best reconciles the competing interests of the parties.

Badger's requirement that treaties be interpreted in a manner consistent with Indigenous understandings implicitly rests on an ethos of legal pluralism. Though each treaty is unique in its terms and scope of application, Indigenous understandings of treaties are relatively uniform. Indigenous peoples entered into treaties with the Crown to formalize a relationship of continental coexistence. They initially sought military alliances before and during the war between Britain and France and also sought to maximize benefits associated with economic interdependence. As the nineteenth century progressed, Indigenous peoples sought to maintain their autonomous legal orders and traditional ways of life in the face of railway construction, surveying activity, non-Indigenous settlement of Indigenous territory, and an unprecedented rise in hunting, fishing, and trapping by non-Indigenous people. They sought to retain traditional authority over their territories and to govern their communities in the face of colonial expansion. In James Youngblood Henderson's words, "Aboriginal nations entered into the treaties

---

24 *R v Badger* [1996] 1 SCR 771.

as the keepers of a certain place."[25] Indigenous peoples regarded the treaty process as enabling the sharing of land and authority with non-Indigenous people while at the same time protecting their territories, economies, and forms of government from non-Indigenous incursion.

The new constitutional status of treaties also recovers the promise of legal pluralism. Understanding treaties as constitutional instruments opens the pluralist legal door to comprehending treaties as constitutional accords. As constitutional accords, they articulate basic terms and conditions of social coexistence and make possible the exercise of constitutional authority. Unlike legal contracts between the Crown and private citizens, which distribute power delegated by the state to private parties in the form of legally enforceable rights and obligations, treaties establish the constitutional parameters of state power itself.[26] Accordingly, treaties do not distribute delegated state power, they distribute constitutional authority. Treaties are therefore as much a part of the constitutional history of Canada as the *Constitution Act, 1867*, which distributes legislative power between the federal and provincial governments. Treaty rights are constitutional rights that flow to Indigenous peoples in exchange for allowing European nations to exercise a measure of sovereign authority in North America.

As constitutional accords, treaties operate as instruments of mutual recognition. Negotiations occur against a backdrop of competing claims of constitutional authority. The Crown enters negotiations under the assumption that it possesses jurisdiction and rights with respect to the territory in question; a First Nation enters negotiations on the assumption that it possesses jurisdiction and rights with respect to the same territory. The treaty process is a means by which competing claims of authority and right can be reconciled with each other by each party agreeing to recognize a measure of the authority of the other.[27] Recognition can occur geographically, as with a number of contemporary land

25 James [Sákéj] Henderson, "Interpreting Sui Generis Treaties" (1997) 36 Alta L Rev 46 at 64.
26 Compare Robert A Williams, Jr, *Linking Arms Together: American Indian Treaty Visions of Law & Peace, 1600–1800* (New York: Oxford University Press, 1997) at 105 ("[I]n American Indian visions of law and peace, a treaty connected different peoples through constitutional bonds of multicultural unity").
27 See generally Royal Commission on Aboriginal Peoples, *Treaty Making in the Spirit of Co-existence: An Alternative to Extinguishment* (Ottawa: Minister of Supply and Services Canada, 1995).

claims agreements that distribute jurisdiction between the parties on the basis of different geographical categories of land within the territory in question. Recognition can also occur by subject, whereby the parties distribute jurisdiction between themselves on the basis of various subject matters suitable for legislation. As an instrument of mutual recognition, a treaty is an ongoing process, structured but not determined by the text of the original agreement, by which parties commit to resolving disputes that might arise in the future through a process of dialogue and mutual respect.

Viewing treaties as constitutional accords is consonant with recent scholarly attempts to construct alternative legal histories of Indigenous-Crown relations. Legal histories typically trace the legal position of Indigenous peoples under Canadian law over time to demonstrate the redemptive potential, or lack thereof, of Canadian law for protecting Indigenous peoples from assimilation. What such histories lack, and what recent scholarship attempts to provide, is an appreciation of how Indigenous peoples actively participated in the production and reproduction of legal norms that structured their relations with non-Indigenous people on the continent. This scholarship, I believe, is consistent with what *Shadow Nations* identifies as "critical legal pluralism," an approach introduced by Kleinhaus and MacDonald that "focuses the spotlight on the citizen-subject and views them as sources of normativity in the sense that they are *law inventing*, not merely *law-abiding*, forces within a society."[28]

James Tully, for example, has interpreted the treaty process as a form of "treaty constitutionalism," whereby Indigenous peoples participate in the creation of constitutional norms governing Aboriginal-Crown relations.[29] Robert Williams has written of the "long-neglected fact that ... Indians tried to create a new type of society with Europeans on the multicultural frontiers of colonial North America."[30] Henderson has interpreted the treaty process as producing "treaty federalism" – a constitutional order grounded in the consent of Indigenous and non-Indigenous peoples on the continent.[31] What such scholarship shares

---

28 *Shadow Nations, supra* note 1 at 77, drawing from Martha-Marie Kleinhaus and Roderick A MacDonald, "What Is a Critical Legal Pluralism?" (1997) 12 Can JL & Soc 25.
29 James Tully, *Strange Multiplicity: Constitutionalism in an Age of Diversity* (Cambridge: Cambridge University Press, 1995) at 117.
30 Williams, Jr, *supra* note 26 at 9.
31 James Youngblood Henderson, "Empowering Treaty Federalism" (1994) 58 Sask L Rev 241.

is an appreciation of the active participation by Indigenous peoples in the production of basic legal norms governing the distribution of constitutional authority in North America.[32] Viewed through the prism of legal pluralism, the treaty process is a formal manifestation of such participation through its active production of constitutional accords that distribute constitutional authority on the continent.

The second development relates to the form and substance of Aboriginal title and rights. With the enactment of section 35(1) of the *Constitution Act, 1982*, and confirmed by the Supreme Court of Canada in *Delgamuukw v British Columbia*,[33] Aboriginal title shed its common law status and assumed the form of a constitutional right. Although the Court extensively described the nature and scope of Aboriginal title and the circumstances under which it can be justifiably interfered with by the Crown, it offered little insight into why Aboriginal title merits constitutional protection, holding simply that a "plain meaning" of the Constitution and precedent were conclusive of the issue.[34]

But a deeper account of the constitutional status of Aboriginal title rests on an ethos of legal pluralism. On this account, Aboriginal title is a constitutional – as opposed to a common law or statutory – norm, because it is an entitlement that is not conditional on the exercise of judicial and legislative authority. Instead, it is logically and historically antecedent to the exercise of judicial and legislative authority and owes its origins to facts and norms that predate the establishment of the Canadian state. Indigenous peoples possessed title to their territories according to their own laws prior to the establishment of a sovereign entity that assumed the legislative power to redistribute title to its citizens. In the words of Swepson and Plant, "[R[ights of ownership already accrue to indigenous populations, and are not ceded to them through the actions of nation-states."[35] Canada became a nation

---

32 See generally Webber, *supra* note 5; see also Sidney L Harring, *White Man's Law: Native People in Nineteenth-Century Canadian Jurisprudence* (Toronto: Osgoode Society for Canadian Legal History, 1998).

33 [1997] 3 SCR 1010.

34 The Court held that the text of s 35(1) and *R v Van der Peet*, [1996] 2 SCR 507 both suggest that s 35(1) provides constitutional status to those rights that were "existing" prior to 1982 and, given that Aboriginal title was a common law right existing in 1982, s 35(1) accords it constitutional status.

35 L Swepson & R Plant, "International Standards and the Protection of the Land Rights of Indigenous and Tribal Populations" (1985) 124 International Lab Rev 91 at 97.

state against the backdrop of a pre-existing distribution of territory among Indigenous nations. By recognizing and affirming Aboriginal title, section 35(1) extends constitutional validity to Indigenous legal norms that inform and make sense of this pre-existing distribution of Indigenous territory. It ensures that state power will be exercised in a manner that respects these Indigenous legal norms and the Indigenous legal orders to which they owe their existence.

Also relevant to a recovery of legal pluralism's promise is a shift in how the judiciary assesses the validity of a claim of Aboriginal title. Indigenous legal norms can participate in establishing the requisite exclusive occupation on which Aboriginal title rests. In the words of Lamer CJ in *Delgamuukw*,

> [I]f, at the time of sovereignty, an aboriginal society had laws in relation to land, those laws would be relevant to establishing the occupation of laws which are the subject of a claim of Aboriginal title. Relevant laws might include, but are not limited to, a land tenure system or laws governing land use.[36]

Elsewhere in his reasons, Lamer CJ stated that Indigenous laws governing trespass and conditional land use by other Indigenous nations, as well as treaties between and among Indigenous nations, also might assist in establishing the occupation necessary to prove Aboriginal title.[37]

Constitutional recognition of Indigenous legal norms is not restricted to the proof of Aboriginal title. Elsewhere the Court has suggested that Indigenous laws that were compatible with the assertion of Crown sovereignty and survived its assertion were "absorbed into the common law as rights," and, if not surrendered or extinguished, received constitutional recognition as Aboriginal rights by section 35(1).[38] This suggests that at least part of the reason something is an Aboriginal right in Canadian law is that it was an Indigenous legal norm at the time of the assertion of Crown sovereignty. Understanding Aboriginal rights as Indigenous legal norms renders section 35(1) a provision performative

---

36 *Delgamuukw v British Columbia*, [1997] 3 SCR 1010 at para 148.
37 *Ibid* at para 157.
38 *Mitchell v MNR*, 1 SCR 911 at para 10 per McLachlin CJ.

of legal pluralism by formally acknowledging the constitutional significance of Indigenous legal orders.

A third development relevant to a resurgence of an ethos of legal pluralism lies outside the confines of constitutional recognition and affirmation of Aboriginal and treaty rights. Indigenous legal scholars have
begun ambitious tasks of recovering and modernizing Indigenous legal
norms or traditions that historically contributed to the social ordering
of different Indigenous societies. This is no easy task, given the relative
inaccessibility of oral traditions and Indigenous languages as well as
the need to recover Indigenous patterns of being and ways of life dam-
aged by the history of colonialism.[39] One must then seek to identify the
ideas and beliefs that underpin such legal norms – in order to make
sense of them and understand their normative significance. And then
they need to be placed alongside non-Indigenous norms for comparison and contrast to determine ways in which they might assist in structuring Indigenous and non-Indigenous legal and political relations.

John Borrows, for example, in *Canada's Indigenous Constitution*,
details legal norms from the Mi'kmaq, Haudenosaunee, Anishnabek,
Cree, Metis, Canarrier, Nisga'a, and Inuit legal traditions.[40] Val Napoleon and Hadley Friedland focus on the *wetiko* in particular, a concept
in Cree and Anishnabek societies that describes a person who is harmful to others in prohibited ways and the traditions, processes, and principles developed to address people who fell within this legal category.[41]
A number of law schools in Canada have institutionalized this development by offering courses on Indigenous legal traditions. The University of Victoria on Vancouver Island has taken this one step further, by
working to offer a joint common law and Indigenous law degree.

Judicial decisions occasionally hint at an ethos of legal pluralism
informing their characterizations of relations between Indigenous peoples and the Canadian state. Chief Justice McLachlin, in *Haida Nation* and
Taku River, wrote of treaties as instruments that "reconcile pre-existing

---

39 For thoughtful reflections on the challenges this work faces, given the ongoing effects of colonialism on Indigenous identity formation, see Gordon Christie, "Culture,
   Self-Determination and Colonialism: Issues around the Revitalization of Indigenous
   Legal Traditions" (2007) 6 Osgoode Hall LJ 13.
40 John Borrows, *Canada's Indigenous Constitution* (Toronto: University of Toronto Press,
   2010) at 59–106.
41 Val Napoleon & Hadley Friedland, "Indigenous Legal Traditions: Roots to
   Renaissance" (2013) (on file with author).

Aboriginal sovereignty with assumed Crown sovereignty or *"de facto Crown sovereignty."*[42] The Court regularly refers to "the pre-existing societies of aboriginal peoples,"[43] Indigenous "legal systems,"[44] "pre-existing systems of aboriginal law,"[45] and "aboriginal peoples occupying and using most of this vast expanse of land in organized, distinctive societies with their own social and political structures."[46] And, in the following passage, Chief Justice McLachlin, in her dissent in *Van der Peet*, clearly summoned the spirit of legal pluralism:

> The history of the interface of Europeans and the common law with aboriginal peoples is a long one. As might be expected of such a long history, the principles by which the interface has been governed have not always been consistently applied. Yet running through this history, from its earliest beginnings to the present time is a golden thread – the recognition by the common law of the ancestral laws and customs of the aboriginal peoples who occupied the land prior to European settlement.[47]

Indeed, this passage seems to suggest that legal pluralism has always characterized the "the interface of Europeans and the common law with aboriginal peoples." But history tells us otherwise. Canadian courts describing relations between Indigenous peoples and Canada as legally plural, as important as this development is, does not make them so. For the ethos of legal pluralism to restart animating relations between Indigenous peoples and Canada, constitutional recognition of Indigenous governments sovereign within their spheres of authority, capable of exercising exclusive and concurrent law-making powers formally equivalent to their federal and provincial counterparts, would need to occur, coupled with a deepening of the recent developments traced in this chapter.

---

42 *Haida Nation v British Columbia (Minister of Forests)*, [2004] 3 SCR 511 at para 20; *Taku River Tlingit First Nation v British Columbia Project Assessment Director)*, [2004] 3 SCR 550. For an extended reflection on this approach, see Felix Hoehn, *Reconciling Sovereignties: Aboriginal Nations and Canada* (Saskatoon: Native Law Centre, University of Saskatchewan, 2012).

43 *R v Van der Peet*, *supra* note 34 at para 39, per Lamer CJ.

44 *R v Sappier; R . Gray*, [2006] 2 SCR 686 at para 45, per Bastarache J.

45 *Delgamuukw*, *supra* note 36 at para 145, per Lamer CJ.

46 *Mitchell v MNR*, [2001] 1 SCR 911 at para 9, per McLachlin CJ.

47 *Van der Peet*, *supra* note 34 at para 263.

Nor is legal pluralism a one-way street. When Indigenous legal orders themselves pay homage to the premises of legal pluralism, then it will truly begin to become "legal reality." The capacity of Indigenous legal orders to do so turns on, first, their capacity to resurrect Indigenous legal norms that can carry this message, and second, the willingness of the Canadian constitutional order to recognize, and affirm, its constitutional significance. Until then, Indigenous nations remain, to borrow Bruce Duthu's haunting phrase, shadow nations, waiting and working for a new dawn.

2 "Looking for a knot in the bulrush": Reflections on Law, Sovereignty, and Aboriginal Rights

MARK D. WALTERS*

I

It has been thirty years since "existing aboriginal and treaty rights" were constitutionally entrenched by section 35 of the *Constitution Act, 1982*, and it has been almost twenty-five years since I began thinking about what these words mean. In 1989, in my last term of law school, I wrote a paper for a seminar course taught by Noel Lyon in which I pretended to be the Supreme Court of Canada writing its first decision on section 35. I wanted to write a bold decision, and so I had my "judges" recognize Aboriginal sovereignty as part Canadian constitutional law. But rereading my paper recently, I was struck by just how cautious I was. The paper betrays the hallmarks of a keen, slightly obsequious law student wishing to ground each proposition in precedent – and in my case that meant drawing upon the old Marshall Court opinions from the United States that acknowledged that a kind of residual or diminished Aboriginal sovereignty survived the assertion of Crown sovereignty over North America.[1]

My teacher, Professor Lyon, was intellectually braver than I was. He wrote, at about the same time, that the dramatic constitutional reforms

* I am grateful for the research assistance of Stephanie Lalonde and for the funding assistance provided to me by the Social Sciences and Humanities Research Council of Canada.

1 See, e.g., *Worcester v Georgia*, 31 US (6 Pet) 515 (1832); *Cherokee Nation v Georgia*, 30 US (5 Pet) 1 (1831); Mark Walters, *"Lake Kamaniskeg Band Council v Minister for Indian and Northern Development"* (28 April 1989) [unpublished, on file with the author] (a paper submitted to Professor Noel Lyon, Faculty of Law, Queen's University).

of 1982 affirmed that section 35 was not just a "codification of the case law on aboriginal rights," but rather that it was a call for "a just settlement for aboriginal peoples" that involved "renounc[ing] the old rules of the game under which the Crown established courts of law and denied those courts the authority to question sovereign claims made by the Crown."[2] These were the bold words about law and sovereignty that I had been too afraid to express when writing my pretend Supreme Court of Canada judgment on section 35 – and yet these were the words that, within a year, were quoted with approval by Chief Justice Brian Dickson and Justice Gérard La Forest writing for the real Supreme Court of Canada in its first real section 35 case.[3] I remember reading this case, R v Sparrow, and thinking that the law in this area was moving fast, much faster than my pretend judges had been moving. Perhaps law professors and judges, at least judges in the country's highest court, can say things that law students cannot.

As I reflect upon the different approaches that my teacher and I took to Aboriginal rights, I can now see that we were both struggling with a basic tension between law's promise for justice and sovereignty's boundaries for justice. The very idea of Indigenous rights in modern law is a kind of paradox in which the law of the state is used to attack the sovereign foundations of the state in order to find justice.[4] In effect, section 35 asks judges to walk a fine line between undoing the legal order and redeeming the rule of law – it asks them to question the legality of the state in order to affirm the legality of the state. Naturally, questions arise as to whether ordinary legal methods and techniques are suited for this task. Does it even make sense, from the ordinary legal perspective, to suggest that the law of the state can question the legality of the state?

This is hardly a new question. It was one that the Spanish theologian Francisco de Vitoria paused to consider before he set out to examine the legality of Spain's invasion of the Americas. He acknowledged the argument that might be made against this examination, that "our sovereigns" were most "just and scrupulous" and so it would be "useless

---

2 Noel Lyon, "An Essay on Constitutional Interpretation" (1988) 26:1 Osgoode Hall LJ 95 at 100.
3 R v Sparrow, [1990] 1 SCR 1075 at 1105–06, 70 DLR (4th) 385 [Sparrow].
4 For a historical overview of the structure of Indigenous rights claims in the common law, see, e.g., PG McHugh, Aboriginal Societies and the Common Law: A History of Sovereignty, Status, and Self-Determination (Oxford: Oxford University Press, 2004).

but also presumptuous" to question the matter – that it would be "like looking for a knot in a bulrush and for wickedness in the abode of the righteous."[5] Vitoria rejected this argument. It was, he thought, entirely appropriate for jurists and theologians alike to inquire into the legality of sovereign claims over the Indians in the Americas. Looking for a knot in a bulrush or for wickedness in the abode of the righteous was, in his view, just the sort of thing that a *legal* perspective on sovereign action demanded.

Of course, it will be said that Vitoria wrote within a natural law tradition in which legality and morality were inseparable, and that questioning the legality of sovereignty is no longer possible under modern conceptions of law. Indeed, for most of the short history of section 35, judges seem to have adopted this (so-called) modern view of jurisprudence. The part of the *Sparrow* decision concerning sovereignty that courts have relied upon when interpreting section 35 has not been the quotation of Professor Lyon's bold assertion about renouncing the old rules of the game. Instead, attention has focused upon another passage in which Dickson CJ and La Forest J stated that, while the Crown respected the right of Aboriginal peoples to occupy their traditional lands, "there was from the outset never any doubt that sovereignty and legislative power, and indeed the underlying title, to such lands vested in the Crown."[6]

This sovereignty-without-a-doubt passage reflects deeply held judicial convictions and anxieties. Judges in British Columbia in the 1980s were perplexed by the claim made by the Gitksan and Wetsueten nations to "ownership and jurisdiction" over their ancestral territories. In refusing an injunction pending trial, they said that the claim was "a direct challenge to the sovereignty of the Crown," and when counsel for the Gitksan resisted this characterization, stating that they did *not* challenge Crown sovereignty but only insisted that decisions affecting Gitksan territories required their consent, one judge simply stated, "I see no difference."[7] After a long trial in this case, now known as *Delgamuukw v British Columbia*, Chief Justice Allan McEachern also characterized the claim for ownership and jurisdiction as a claim for

---

5 Franciscus de Victoria, *De Indis et de Ivre Belli Relectiones* [1532], ed by Ernest Nys, translated by John Pawley Bate (Washington, DC: Carnegie Institution, 1917) at 116.
6 *R v Sparrow, supra* note 3 at 1103.
7 *Westar Timber Ltd v Gitksan Wet'suwet'en Tribal Council* (1989), 60 DLR (4th) 453, 37 BCLR (2d) 352 (CA) Carrothers & Locke JJA.

Aboriginal sovereignty – a claim that he said was impossible in light of the sovereignty-without-a-doubt passage from *Sparrow*. That Aboriginal peoples found themselves under Crown sovereignty despite having never been conquered and having never surrendered to the Crown by treaty might seem unfair to them "on philosophical grounds," he wrote, but it made no difference to the "reality" of Crown sovereignty. "I am driven," the chief justice concluded, "to find that jurisdiction and sovereignty are such absolute concepts that there is no half-way house," and no court of law has "the jurisdiction to undo the establishment of the Colony, Confederation, or the constitutional arrangements which are now in place."[8]

The dispute in *Delgamuukw* about whether a claim under section 35 to ownership and jurisdiction over territory is really an attack on Crown sovereignty illustrates the contested dimensions within which the concept of sovereignty exists. But it also reflects the judicial fear that there is something about the very nature of Indigenous rights that threatens the basic fabric, or sovereign structure, of the legal order – that Indigenous claims represent for the state an *existential* challenge. It is in response to this existential challenge that judges have constructed a conception of "Crown sovereignty" that has a profound but distinctive – one is tempted to say sui generis – meaning in the Aboriginal rights context.

Something called "Aboriginal sovereignty" has been acknowledged too, though mostly by lower court judges in order to deny it. However, a more positive conception of Aboriginal sovereignty has long been a shadowy presence within Canadian legal discourse.[9] Finally, in 2004, that conception was brought into the direct light and the Supreme Court of Canada acknowledged "Aboriginal sovereignty" explicitly for

---

8 *Delgamuukw v British Columbia*, 79 DLR (4th) 185, at 285, 454 [1991] 5 CNLR 1 (BC Sup Ct).
9 Several lower court judges had acknowledged the idea of Aboriginal sovereignty: *Eastmain Band v Gilpin*, [1987] 3 CNLR 54, [1987] RJQ 1637 (Prov Ct) (a by-law made under the *Cree-Naskapi Act* was held to be the exercise of "a residual sovereignty as regards their local government" at 67); *Canadian Pacific Ltd v Matsqui Indian Band*, [2000] 1 FC 325, 176 DLR (4th) 35 (CA), Robertson JA, dissenting (a property tax by-law made by an Indian Band was an aspect of the "Aboriginal sovereignty over reserve lands" at para 193). At the Supreme Court of Canada, references to Aboriginal sovereignty have been more oblique: see *R v Sioui*, [1990] 1 SCR 1025, 70 DLR (4th) 427, Lamer CJ for the Court (noting that during the late eighteenth century "Indian nations had sufficient independence and played a large enough role in North America for it to be good policy to maintain relations with them very close to those maintained between sovereign nations" at 1052–53); *Mitchell v Canada (MNR)*, 2001 SCC 33, [2001] 1 SCR 911, Binnie J

the first time. In the cases of *Haida Nation* and *Taku River*, Chief Justice Beverley McLachlin stated that treaties were required "to reconcile pre-existing Aboriginal sovereignty with assumed Crown sovereignty," or "*de facto* Crown sovereignty," the respective "sovereignty claims" being "reconciled through the process of honourable negotiation."[10] These remarkable statements concerning the reconciling of sovereignties may, as Felix Hoehn has written, indicate a paradigm shift in Aboriginal rights law in Canada – a shift to a new "sovereignty paradigm."[11]

As important as the judicial recognition of Aboriginal sovereignty in 2004 was, the stunning thing about the *Haida Nation* and *Taku River* cases was the characterization of Crown sovereignty as de facto. The expression de facto in law is the converse of de jure – it is a state of affairs that exists in fact but not in law.[12] If, as the Court states, Aboriginal sovereignty is pre-existing and Crown sovereignty is only de facto, then it seems to follow that Aboriginal sovereignty is de jure. In other words, there are places in Canada today where legal sovereignty remains with Aboriginal nations, even though factual or practical sovereignty rests with the Crown. Whether the Court really meant to say this is perhaps open to debate. But one thing is clear: the two cases show that, in Canada, legality can question sovereignty in certain respects at

---

(Major J concurring) [*Mitchell*] (Binnie J advanced the complex and controversial idea of "merged" or "shared" sovereignty, according to which Aboriginal peoples "were not wholly subordinated to non-aboriginal sovereignty but over time became merger partners" at para 129). And, of course, the Supreme Court of Canada has on a number of occasions quoted passages from the classic nineteenth-century decisions of Chief Justice John Marshall of the United States Supreme Court on Indigenous peoples, including the statement from *Johnson v M'Intosh* that the rights of Indian nations in North America "to complete sovereignty, as independent nations, were necessarily diminished," but not, by implication, eliminated, by European claims to the new world: *Johnson v M'Intosh*, 21 US (8 Wheat) 543 (1823) at 572–74 [*Johnson v M'Intosh*], quoted in *Calder v British Columbia (AG)*, [1973] SCR 313, 33 DLR (3d) 618 Hall J, (Laskin CJ & Spence J concurring) at 381–83 [*Calder*]; *Guerin v R*, [1984] 2 SCR 335, 13 DLR (4th) 321, Dickson J for the majority at 378–79; *R v Van der Peet*, [1996] 2 SCR 507, 137 DLR (4th) 289, Lamer CJ for the majority at para 36 [*Van der Peet*].

10 *Haida Nation v British Columbia (Minister of Forests)*, 2004 SCC 73, [2004] 3 SCR 511 at para 20; *Taku River Tlingit First Nation v British Columbia (Project Assessment Director)*, 2004 SCC 74, [2004] 3 SCR 550 at para 42.

11 Felix Hoehn, *Reconciling Sovereignties: Aboriginal Nations and Canada* (Saskatoon: Native Law Centre, University of Saskatchewan, 2012) [Hoehn, *Reconciling Sovereignties*].

12 Brian Slattery, "Aboriginal Rights and the Honour of the Crown" (2005) 29 Sup Ct L Rev (2d) 433 at 437–38; Hoehn, *Reconciling Sovereignties, ibid* 34–35.

least – that the Supreme Court of Canada has begun to look for knots in the bulrush.

In this chapter, I cannot hope to address all of the unresolved points raised by *Haida Nation* and *Taku River* with regard to the question of sovereignty. My objective is far more modest. I intend, first, to offer some reflections about legal method and interpretation and how arguments about Aboriginal rights have been constructed over the course of the last thirty years. I shall then inquire more closely into what I shall describe as the sui generis conception of "Crown sovereignty" that permeates the case law on section 35 of the *Constitution Act, 1982*, with a view to contributing to the unfolding legal discourse on what it means for judges to recognize the necessity for reconciling sovereignties. In the end, I shall suggest that even if judges cannot undo the Canadian state, as McEachern CJ said, injustice cannot hide behind the concept of Crown sovereignty. As a construct of ordinary legal discourse, sovereignty is, like all ordinary legal constructs, something that must be constantly interpreted and reinterpreted over time to ensure that it contributes to the general understanding of law as an enterprise that integrates legality and legitimacy.

II

Back in the early 1990s, there appeared to be at least two ways to respond to the kind of reasoning found in Chief Justice McEachern's trial decision in *Delgamuukw*. One could attack the assumption that Crown sovereignty could have been established over what is now Canada without regard for Indigenous nations as if the land were legally empty and then challenge the notion that sovereignty is an absolute legal concept that is inconsistent with coexisting Aboriginal and Crown sovereignties.[13] Or one could bracket the question of sovereignty and pursue the challenge of building a robust theory of common law Aboriginal rights based either upon the basic insights of the old colonial cases on the continuity of local laws and rights within territories subjected to Crown sovereignty, or upon the ancient principles of English

13 See, e.g., Michael Asch & Patrick Macklem, "Aboriginal Rights and Canadian Sovereignty: An Essay on *R. v. Sparrow*" (1991) 29:2 Alta L Rev 498; Brian Slattery, "Aboriginal Sovereignty and Imperial Claims" (1991) 29:4 Osgoode Hall LJ 681; John Borrows, "Sovereignty's Alchemy: An Analysis of *Delgamuukw v. British Columbia*" (1999) 37:2 Osgoode Hall LJ 537.

property law, or both.[14] When I began graduate studies in 1990, after a dramatic summer that saw Elijah Harper's stand against the Meech Lake Accord and the tragic events at Oka, pursuing the sovereignty argument may have made sense. But I responded to the trial decision in *Delgamuukw* by following the common law argument.[15] My approach was no doubt influenced by the fact that I studied in England under a supervisor who wrote the modern book on colonial law.[16] But I was also inspired, I now think, by another of my teachers from my last year of law school, David Dyzenhaus, who had invoked the work of Fuller and Dworkin in arguing for the value of the common law interpretive perspective in response to state wickedness.[17] Something about the notion that the common law, even in the face of imperial aggression and colonial oppression, might find ways to reconcile diverse legal cultures intrigued me. Finally, there was a pragmatic reason for this approach, illustrated by the case law then emerging from Australia. In the late 1970s, judges in that country had rejected the claim that there was "an aboriginal nation which has sovereignty over its own people, notwithstanding that they remain citizens of the [Australian] Commonwealth" as "imprecise, emotional or intemperate."[18] But by 1992 they were prepared to recognize Aboriginal title at common law as a burden upon the radical title of the sovereign Crown because, although it required a reinterpretation of the common law in light of contemporary notions of justice and human rights, it did not "fracture the skeleton of principle which gives the body of our law its shape and internal consistency."[19]

14 Brian Slattery, *The Land Rights of Canadian Indigenous Peoples, as Affected by the Crown's Acquisition of Their Territory* (DPhil Dissertation, Oxford University, 1979) [unpublished]; Slattery, "Understanding Aboriginal Rights" (1987) 66 Can Bar Rev 727; Paul McHugh, *The Aboriginal Rights of the New Zealand Maori at Common Law* (PhD Dissertation, Cambridge University, 1987) [unpublished]; Kent McNeil, *Common Law Aboriginal Title* (Oxford: Clarendon, 1989); McNeil, "A Question of Title: Has the Common Law Been Misapplied to Dispossess the Aboriginals?" (1990) 16:1 Monash UL Rev 91.

15 Mark D Walters, "British Imperial Constitutional Law and Aboriginal Rights: A Comment on *Delgamuukw v. British Columbia*" (1992) 17:2 Queen's LJ 350.

16 JM Finnis, *Commonwealth and Dependencies*, in *Halsbury's Laws of England*, 4th ed, vol 6 (London: Butterworth, 1974) 315; revised in *Halsbury's Laws of England*, 4th ed, vol 6 (London: Butterworth, 1991) 345.

17 David Dyzenhaus, *Hard Cases in Wicked Legal Systems: South African Law in the Perspective of Legal Philosophy* (New York: Oxford University Press, 1991).

18 *Coe v Commonwealth*, [1979] HCA 68, 24 ALR 118, Gibbs J at paras 12, 21.

19 *Mabo v Queensland* (No 2), [1992] HCA 23; 175 CLR 1, Brennan J at para 29.

If the skeleton of law – the sovereignty of the Crown – was too scary for judges to confront, perhaps common law advancements in the area of Indigenous rights were possible by keeping the skeleton in the closet.

I now know that I was wrong to think that the common law argument can be separated from the sovereignty argument. I can now see that pursuing Aboriginal rights through a common law interpretive perspective leads, in the end, to the questions about the legality of sovereignty. But to see this point, it may be helpful to begin by trying to understand the judicial anxieties about the existential challenge presented by Indigenous claims.

To begin with, it is appropriate to acknowledge that, in one sense, this existential fear is warranted. If the sovereignty-without-a-doubt statement from *Sparrow* – "there was from the outset never any doubt that sovereignty ... vested in the Crown" – is read, as it can be, as a statement of historical fact, then its truth is easily denied. All one needs to do is to look at the three authorities that were cited by Dickson CJ and La Forest J in its support. They cited, first, *Johnson v M'Intosh*, the 1823 case in which Chief Justice John Marshall explained that Crown claims to America left Indigenous "sovereignty" "diminished," not gone.[20] Next they cited the *Royal Proclamation of 1763*, which protected the lands of the "Nations or Tribes of Indians" living under "our Sovereignty, Protection, and Dominion." However, neither the Crown's representative for Indian affairs in America at the time nor the imperial government in London that drafted the *Proclamation* thought that these words meant that Indigenous nations were under Crown sovereignty in the full sense.[21] Finally, they cited several pages from the decision in the seminal 1973 case of *Calder v British Columbia*, where, in turn,

---

20 *Johnson v M'Intosh, supra* note 9.
21 In 1764, the superintendent general of Indian affairs for the Northern Department denied that the nations of the Great Lakes region were under Crown "sovereignty" or "laws" (letter of Sir William Johnson to the Lords of Trade, 30 October 1764 in EB O'Callaghan, ed, *Documents Relative to the Colonial History of the State of New York*, vol 7 [Albany, NY: Weed, Parsons, 1856–61] 670 at 670–74). Royal instructions issued at the same time as the *Royal Proclamation of 1763* to the first governor of the new British province of Quebec not only instructed him to enforce the *Proclamation* but also observed that the province was "in part inhabited and possessed by several Nations and Tribes of Indians" with whom it was necessary "to cultivate and maintain a strict Friendship and good Correspondence, so that they may be *induced by Degrees*, not only to be good Neighbours to Our Subjects, but likewise themselves *to become good Subjects to Us*," and so the governor was "to assemble, and treat with the said

we find references to ambiguous readings of the *Proclamation*,[22] another reference to the passage in *Johnson v M'Intosh* recognizing the diminished sovereignty of Indigenous nations,[23] and, finally, a reference to the fact that the plaintiffs in the case, the Nisga'a Nation, themselves relied upon the "presumption" acknowledged in the old American and British cases that Native rights continued after the assertion of Crown sovereignty.[24] On the basis of the authorities they cited, then, Dickson CJ and La Forest J should have said, at very least, "There was from the outset *considerable doubt* about whether sovereignty vested in the Crown so as to displace fully the sovereignty and territorial rights of Aboriginal nations." In truth, however, it is more accurate to say that there was, from the outset, no doubt at all that some kind of Indigenous sovereignty persisted and was acknowledged by the Crown.

The Court has never returned to consider, directly at least, the sovereignty-without-a-doubt passage from *Sparrow*. This failure to engage critically with our colonial legal past is due, in part, to the Court's decisions in 1996 – section 35's *annus horribilis*. In that year, the Supreme Court of Canada ruled, in effect, the following: that Aboriginal rights were to be defined by a new rule, unheard of before in the common law, that would protect only those bits of Indigenous culture that might be traced to a time before the very first meetings between Aboriginal peoples and Europeans (meetings that, in some parts of the country,

---

Indians, promising and assuring them of Protection and Friendship" and also to inform himself as to the number, nature, and disposition of the Indians as well as "the Rules and Constitutions, by which they are governed or regulated" – which suggests, if anything, that Indigenous nations retained a certain sovereign distance from the Crown and were assumed to retain that distance even after treaties were made. See "Instructions to Governor Murray" in Adam Shortt & Arthur G Doughty, eds, *Documents Relating to the Constitutional History of Canada, 1759–1791*, vol 1 (Ottawa: SE Dawson, 1907) 181 at arts 61–63 [emphasis added].

22 *Calder, supra* note 9 at 328 (here Judson J observes that Aboriginal title is "dependent upon the goodwill of the Sovereign," a conclusion made by Lord Watson in *St Catherine's Milling & Lumber Co v R*, [1888] UKPC 70, 14 App Cas 46 at 54, based upon the *Royal Proclamation of 1763*; however, Lord Watson based this conclusion on passages in the *Proclamation* setting up a temporary ban on treaties to purchase Indian lands in the interior, and the fact that this ban was temporary, or subject to the goodwill of the Crown, is hardly inconsistent with some ongoing Indigenous sovereignty, since once the ban was lifted the requirement found in the proclamation to purchase land by treaty remained.

23 *Calder, ibid* at 383, Hall J dissenting.

24 *Ibid* at 402, Hall J dissenting.

occurred as early as the sixteenth century);[25] that if self-government was an Aboriginal right at all, it existed only in relation to fragments of governmental practice that can be traced to such culturally integral pre-contact practices;[26] and that there was no need to wade into "murky historical waters" to reconsider colonial legal history in order to determine if this new rule applied or not.[27] Critical re-evaluation of assumptions about our legal past, including assumptions about sovereignty, has been, in short, discouraged. Judges supposed that our legal history was unjust and unpromising, and they ignored the possibility that it might yield, through careful legal analysis, a richer, more complex understanding of Aboriginal rights than they assumed. Among the things we lost as a result of the decision to draw a line under our legal history was the possibility of giving real normative life to the *Royal Proclamation of 1763* through case-by-case constitutional exegesis of that document informed by the rich inter-cultural context of the covenant chain relationship between the Crown and the Great Lakes nations within which the *Proclamation* was created; instead the *Proclamation* seems to have become a dead branch on the living tree that is our Constitution.[28] In 1990, Professor Lyon's call for new rules in a new game sounded attractive, but by 1996 I began to think that the old rules of the game – the common law that recognized the continuity of working legal systems upon the assertion of Crown sovereignty rather than a rule about fragments of ancient cultures from a time before the arrival of the first Europeans – did not look too bad after all.[29]

---

25 *Van der Peet, supra* note 9. For a case dating contact in the sixteenth century, see *Newfoundland (Minister of Government Services and Lands) v Drew*, 2006 NLCA 53, [2006] NJ No 270.

26 *R v Pamajewon*, [1996] 2 SCR 821.

27 *R v Côté*, [1996] 3 SCR 139 at paras 41, 52, 138 DLR (4th) 385.

28 Indeed, the relevant provisions on Aboriginal rights found in the *Royal Proclamation of 1763* are thought by judges to have been repealed in 1774: *Chippewas of Sarnia Band v Canada (AG)* (2001) 51 OR (3d) 641 (CA); leave to appeal refused [2001] SCCA No 63. On the relations of intercultural normativity that informed the proclamation, see John Borrows, "Wampum at Niagara: The Royal Proclamation, Canadian Legal History and Self-Government" in Michael Asch, ed, *Aboriginal and Treaty Rights in Canada: Essays on Law, Equality, and Respect for Difference* (Vancouver: University of British Columbia Press, 1997) 155; Jeremy Webber, "Relations of Force and Relations of Justice: The Emergence of Normative Community between Colonists and Aboriginal Peoples" (1995) 33:4 Osgoode Hall LJ 623.

29 Mark D Walters, "The 'Golden Thread' of Continuity: Aboriginal Customs at Common Law and under the Constitution Act, 1982" (1999) 44:3 McGill LJ 711.

But if the sovereignty-without-a-doubt passage from *Sparrow* is read not as an assertion of *historical fact*, but as an assertion of *law* informed by *present fact*, one might say that it has some merit. Leaving aside for the moment McEachern CJ's erroneous conclusion that Indigenous claims to ownership and jurisdiction challenge Crown sovereignty, is there not something to be said for his basic assumption that a court of law cannot "undo" the "reality" of the state and its constitution? Do not judges have to accept the sovereignty of the state from which they derive their judicial authority? And, finally, are not the answers to these questions determined, in part at least, by the "absolute" nature of sovereignty – its essential character as plenary, untrammelled, and unchecked political authority – that forces upon judges duties of undivided allegiance?

The answers to these questions depend upon how one views the theoretical nature of law. As a conceptual matter, legal positivists tell us that the very foundation of the state's legal order is a supra-legal fact – a "sovereign," as they used to say, or, as they now tend to say, a customary rule evidenced by official state practice – and that this supra-legal fact defines the criteria of validity for laws in the system, but it cannot be, itself, either legally valid or legally invalid.[30] Alternatively, it has been argued that the European legal discourse on sovereignty, properly interpreted, *does* recognize that the sovereign foundations of the modern state are based not on fact alone but on a kind of law or juridical norm – a public law immanent within the very idea of sovereignty securing public good and human dignity – but that this *constitutive* law of the sovereign state is entirely separate from, and out of reach of, the ordinary laws *constituted* by the sovereign state.[31] The legality of states may be questioned by outside laws – by international law or natural law or, of course, Indigenous law – but not, according to such theories of law that trace ordinary law back in a linear way to a supra-legal fact or supra-legal juridical norm, by the internal laws of the state. Finally, it may be argued that these conceptual claims about the separation of ordinary law from its sovereign foundations find their expression doctrinally within the common law in the "act of state" doctrine, which posits that no municipal court can question assertions of Crown sovereignty over new lands or foreign peoples.

---

30 HLA Hart, *The Concept of Law* (Oxford: Clarendon, 1961).
31 Martin Loughlin, *Foundations of Public Law* (Oxford: Oxford University Press, 2010).

If the view of law and sovereignty is understood according to one or other of the various linear theories of law that puts sovereignty beyond ordinary law is right, then, we must say, Vitoria's claim that we can look for knots in the bulrush must be rejected. Certainly, it is fair to say that the idea that European sovereignty over the Indigenous peoples of the Americas was open to legal examination became increasingly difficult to defend during the centuries after Vitoria wrote. Juridical thought became more compartmentalized: writers like Grotius encouraged the conceptual separation of the law of nations from the law within nations, and writers like Hobbes encouraged the conceptual separation of the law of sovereigns from the law of nature. At the height of the British Empire, in the eighteenth and nineteenth centuries, it was a given that *law* – meaning the common law of the British Empire – would never question the sovereign claims of the Crown over new territories or foreign peoples.

In articulating this "act of state" doctrine, common law judges were careful not to say that assertions of Crown sovereignty were necessarily lawful and just. An act of state might be "just or unjust, politic or impolitic, beneficial or injurious," but, so the judges concluded, *domestic* courts had no means of forming an opinion on such matters, or no right to express such an opinion if they had formed one; when it came to the existence of Crown sovereignty over a territory or a people, and the manner in which it was asserted, "[i]t is sufficient to say that, even if a wrong has been done, it is a wrong for which no municipal court of justice can afford a remedy."[32] An act of state was thought to be "a catastrophic change, constituting a new departure," but that municipal law had "nothing to do with the act of change by which this new departure is effected," its "duty" being "simply to accept the new departure; and its power and its duty to adjudicate upon, and enforce rights of individuals, or of the Government, in the future."[33]

---

32 *Secretary of State for India in Council v Kamachee Boye Sahaba* (1859), 13 Moo PC 22, 15 ER 9 at 86, and cited in *Doss v Secretary of State for India in Council*, (1875) LR 19 Eq 509 at 534, 32 LT 294, and quoted with approval in *Calder v AG of British Columbia* (1970), 13 DLR (3d) 64 at 70–71, 74 WWR 481 (BCCA), Tysoe JA; see also *Calder, supra* note 9 at 405, Hall J.
33 *Salaman v Secretary of State for India*, [1906] 1 KB 613 at 640 (CA), Fletcher Moulton LJ [*Salaman*].

There are at least two ways to interpret the act of state doctrine. One way is to say that judges were, in effect, acknowledging the basic premise of those linear theories of law, like legal positivism, that separate the sovereign foundations of law from ordinary law, such that sovereignty is, from the perspective of ordinary law, neither legally valid nor legally invalid, but is just *there*, and the ordinary law is deemed to flow from it. Another way, however, is to say that judges declined to intervene to question the formation of sovereign authority in new places, not for conceptual reasons relating to the theoretical nature of law, but rather for more pragmatic reasons relating to institutional competence and capacity. The act of state doctrine may be, in other words, consistent with a *circular* or interpretive theory of law that *denies* the separation of ordinary law from its sovereign foundations.

Interpretive theories of law, in which the resolution of difficult legal points is thought to involve an interpretive oscillation between specific rules of law and the underlying principles of political morality that they presuppose in the search of a reflective equilibrium between rules and principles that is normatively coherent and compelling, cannot draw boundary lines that mark off some but not other foundational principles as beyond the interpretive exercise.[34] Hard constitutional cases may take ordinary legal analysis all the way to the structure of principle that the system presupposes. But when we get to this structure (or skeleton) of principle, to the sovereign foundation of the state, no supra-legal fact of the matter exists (certainly this is true, as we have seen, if we search for a historical fact of the matter in support of Crown sovereignty in Canada); instead, all we find is "a whole set of shifting, developing and interacting standards" that we could not, even if we tried, "bolt" together into some kind a sovereign rule.[35] The sovereign foundation of Canada, in other words, is an interpretive concept open to ordinary legal analysis just like any other legal concept. The task of "looking for a knot in a bulrush and for wickedness in the abode of the righteous" is one that may be undertaken through ordinary legal discourse today, just as it could in Vitoria's day. However, it is important to acknowledge that, for institutional reasons regarding the appropriate relationship between courts, executives, and legislatures, there may be sound reasons for ordinary courts to defer to the Crown in its exercise of foreign relations and so to

---

34 See, e.g., Ronald Dworkin, *Law's Empire* (Cambridge, MA: Belknap, 1986).
35 Ronald Dworkin, "The Model of Rules" (1967) 35:1 U Chicago L Rev 14 at 41.

accept assertions of sovereignty abroad, and presumably there will be sound reasons of principle, relating to legitimate expectations and the rule of law, for why an ordinary court might be reluctant to declare a long-established state to be illegal. Both institutional constraints and the normative impact of time will mean that judges who find themselves in wicked legal systems will confront challenging legal and moral dilemmas on how best to discharge their judicial duties. However, so long as the abode has a claim to righteousness – so long, that is, that the legal system still has pretensions of being a real legal system – then the identification and expunging of wickedness through the interpretive techniques of ordinary legal discourse will always be the responsibility of ordinary lawyers and judges. In the common law tradition, at least, it is through ongoing interpretation that, according to the old saying, the law works itself pure.[36]

Indeed, the most famous defender of circular or interpretive theories of law Ronald Dworkin states that such theories are exemplified by "the traditional common law method."[37] Returning to the act of state doctrine, then, the argument that it is consistent with circular or interpretive rather than linear or positivist theories of law – that it is, in other words, consistent with the idea that law encircles sovereignty and not with the idea that law hangs on a line held up by sovereignty – is supported by two points. First, we should recall that although the orthodox view is that municipal courts did not question "acts of state" relating to the assertion of sovereign authority over foreign peoples or places, the common law did *not* recognize a general "law of state" that exempted the King or Queen or their ministers from legal controls for *any* reason of state that they might wish to invoke; the area of unreviewable discretion in areas like foreign affairs was enveloped within the disciplining web of the common law.[38] Second, as a result, common law judges

---

36 See, e.g., *Omychund v Barker* (1744), 1 Atk 21, William Murray, solicitor general (later Lord Mansfield CJ) ("the common law works itself pure by rules drawn from the fountain of justice" at 32–33).

37 Ronald Dworkin, *Justice in Robes* (Cambridge, MA: Harvard University Press, 2006) at 251.

38 The fallout from *Darnel's Case* or *Case of the Five Knights* (1627) 3 St Tr 1 is illustrative. In defending the imprisonment of five knights who refused to make loans to the King, the attorney general Sir Robert Heath and Sir Francis Ashley attended a parliamentary conference to argue the King's position. Ashley submitted that there was a "Law of State" that governed in areas where "the common law extends not," giving the King power to act "when the necessity of state requires it," the King's power to

insisted that *they* would decide whether a Crown act was indeed an act of state, and, furthermore, the municipal courts would "consider the *results* of acts of State, *i.e.*, their *effects* on the rights of individuals, and *even of the Government itself*," for "Acts of State are not all of one kind; their nature and consequences may differ in an infinite variety of ways, and these differences may profoundly affect the position of municipal Courts with regard to them."[39] So even if the courts might not undo sovereign authority once established, they would indeed inquire into its justness and fairness to determine how to interpret the essence of the new legal regime.

We need look no further than Canada and the *Royal Proclamation of 1763* for an example. The *Proclamation* established the constitution for the new British province of Quebec and, on its face, introduced English law, making no mention of the continuity of existing French-Canadian law. But common lawyers did not interpret the *Proclamation* as abrogating the local legal system, at least in non-criminal matters. "There is not a *Maxim* of the *Common Law* more certain," the law officers of the Crown stated in 1766 in arguing that French-Canadian law survived the *Proclamation*, "than that a Conquer'd people retain their ancient Customs till the Conqueror shall declare New Laws."[40] This was considered a point of principle, of justice. Attorney General Edward Thurlow was blunt, stating in 1774 that if the *Royal Proclamation of 1763* "is to be considered as importing English laws into a country already settled, and habitually governed by other laws,

---

commit "acts of state" upon subjects in virtue of his "supreme power in matters of state" being a power "too high to be determined by any legal direction" ("Proceedings in Parliament Relating to the Liberty of the Subject" [1628] 3 St Tr 59–234 at 149–51). Sir Edward Coke and his fellow parliamentarians in the House of Commons objected, Coke stating that although the prerogative is "highly tendered and respected ... it hath bounds set unto it by the laws of England," for "the common law has admeasured the king's prerogative" (at 68, 78, 81–82). Indeed, they were so offended that Ashley was briefly taken into custody after making his point. As Lord Camden would put it in *Entick v Carrington* (1765) 19 St Tr 1029 at 1073, "Serjeant Ashley was committed to the Tower ... only for asserting in argument, that there was a "law of state" different from the common law." See generally Mark D Walters, "Is Public Law Ordinary?" (2012) 75:5 Mod L Rev 899.

39 *Salaman, supra* note 33 at 639, Fletcher Moulton LJ.

40 Charles Yorke, attorney general, and William de Grey, solicitor general, to the Lords of Trade, 14 April 1766, in Adam Shortt & Arthur G Doughty, eds, *Documents Relating to the Constitutional history of Canada, 1759–1791*, vol 1 (Ottawa: SE Dawson, 1907) 251 at 255–56.

I take it to be an act of the grossest and absurdest and cruelest tyranny, that a conquering nation ever practiced over a conquered country."[41] Here, then, was an interpretation by the common law that sought to expunge wickedness from the abode of the righteous by questioning the consequences of an assertion of sovereignty and by insisting upon recognizing the continuity of a pre-existing legal system, even in the face of a constitutional document that, on its express terms, provided for a different result. Within this common law perspective, sovereignty is not, as McEachern CJ thought it was, some absolute and unyielding thing to be questioned, if at all, only upon philosophical and never upon legal grounds. Sovereignty's justice *is* open to common law testing, and the results of that testing may affect the constitutional status of people, rights, and laws in places over which the Crown claims to have sovereignty.

To summarize, then, perhaps there are sound reasons of principle for the existential fears that judges have expressed about challenges to Crown sovereignty, but it does not follow that law cannot question sovereignty. The common law interpretive perspective did not draw a sharp line between law and sovereignty, and nor should we. Of course, this entire discussion has been undertaken from the perspective of European-based conceptions of law and sovereignty. I am not well placed to speak of Indigenous conceptions of sovereignty, but I wonder whether they might share at least some commonalities with circular theories of legal discourse. From my reading of the covenant chain treaty relationship in the Great Lakes region, it seems to me that, for a long time, nations in that region exercised sovereignty in the following sense: they denied that absolute political authority vested in a single entity, insisting instead upon a conception of multiple and interlocking centres or nodes of normativity – family lineages, clans, villages, nations, confederacies, colonies, their "father" the King and his representatives, and even the spiritual forces within their lands and waters – centres of interlocking normativity, that is, that were each independent but also inseparable from the others, all of them being subject to an overarching requirement to enhance coherent or harmonious relationships through honouring duties of care but also by honouring each group's field of

---

41 Sir Henry Cavendish, *Debates of the House of Commons in the Year 1774, on the Bill for Making More Effectual Provision for the Government of the Province of Quebec* (London: J Wright, 1839) at 29.

equal freedom.[42] If we are ever to integrate Indigenous legal traditions into our understanding of Canadian law,[43] the very conception of sovereignty must be open to reinterpretation – and a circular or interpretive theory of legal discourse may assist in that process.

III

In considering what the Supreme Court of Canada meant in 2004 when it distinguished between Crown sovereignty and Aboriginal sovereignty, it is helpful to return to the concept of Crown sovereignty as that idea has been employed in Canadian law generally and within cases involving Aboriginal peoples in Canada in particular. Sir Edward Coke once described the "Crown" as a "hieroglyphic" – a symbol or metaphor.[44] Reference to the Crown in Canadian legal discourse is rarely meant as a reference to the Queen personally, though sometimes it is a reference to the office she occupies. More often than not, however, "Crown" is used metaphorically to refer to something else – and this is invariably true when the words "Crown" and "sovereignty" are employed together.

The "sovereignty of the Crown" was an expression used to describe the geographical and juridical extent and identity of the British state proper,[45] as well as the geographical and juridical extent and identity of British dominions and colonies forming part of the British Empire.[46] But it is important to recall that, from the internal or domestic legal perspective, the expression "sovereignty of the Crown" or "Crown sovereignty" was just a short-form expression for a set of constitutional

---

42 Mark D Walters, "'Your Sovereign and Our Father': The Imperial Crown and the Idea of Legal-Ethnohistory" in Shaunnagh Dorsett & Ian Hunter, eds, Law and Politics in British Colonial Thought: Transpositions of Empire (Houndmills, UK: Palgrave Macmillan, 2010) 91.

43 See, e.g., John Borrows, Canada's Indigenous Constitution (Toronto: University of Toronto Press, 2010).

44 Calvin's Case (1608), 7 Co Rep 1a at 12a, 77 ER 377. See also Frederick Maitland, The Constitutional History of England (Cambridge: Cambridge University Press, 1911) at 418 ("There is one term against which I wish to warn you, and that term is 'the crown.' You will certainly read that the crown does this and the crown does that. As a matter of fact we know that the crown does nothing but lie in the Tower of London to be gazed at by sight-seers. No, the crown is a convenient cover for ignorance: it saves us from asking difficult questions").

45 See, e.g., R v Keyn (1876), 2 Ex D 63 at 197.

46 See, e.g., Lyons (Mayor of) v East India Co (1836), 1 Moo Ind App 175 at 282, 12 ER 782.

propositions that were actually fairly complex. In describing the basic principles of the British constitution, Dicey did not speak of the "sovereignty of the Crown," because, as a matter of British constitutional law, the Crown was *not* sovereign. Instead, he spoke of the "sovereignty of Parliament" (or, more accurately, the "King [or Queen] in Parliament").[47] Parliamentary sovereignty, not Crown sovereignty, was the rule of constitutional law. This was true in relation to British colonies too. "A country conquered by the British arms becomes a dominion of the King in the right of his Crown," wrote Lord Mansfield in 1774, "and, therefore, necessarily subject to the Legislature, the Parliament of Great Britain"; in other words, whatever power the King had in such colonies, it was "subordinate to his own authority, as a part of the supreme Legislature in Parliament."[48] Finally, it is worth recalling that, according to the orthodox view of things, the sovereignty of Parliament throughout Britain and its overseas dominions was a point of constitutional *law* because it was a principle that the ordinary courts enforced.[49] The sovereignty of Parliament was a "rule of common law."[50] From the idea of Crown sovereignty over colonial territories, then, we come very quickly to the conclusion that the Crown, acting alone, was *not* sovereign, but rather the Crown-in-Parliament was – and, even then, only by virtue of principles secured by a *common law* constitution.

Turning to Crown sovereignty in Canada today, we may say that, strictly speaking, in law, no such thing exists. "Crown sovereignty" is, again, just a short-form expression for a complex set of constitutional propositions. The position of the Crown in Canada is defined by the terms of the Constitution of Canada, which by section 52(1) of the *Constitution Act, 1982* is the "supreme law." By section 9 of the *Constitution Act, 1867* the "Executive Government" over Canada is "vested in the Queen," and by sections 17 and 91 federal legislative power is vested in a "Parliament for Canada" consisting of the Queen, the Senate, and the House of Commons, and, as in Britain, the principle of parliamentary supremacy ensures that the Crown's executive power in Canada is subordinate to the power of Parliament. But even the Crown-in-Parliament

---

47 AV Dicey, *Introduction to the Study of the Law of the Constitution*, 8th ed (London: Macmillan, 1915) at 37 [Dicey].
48 *Campbell v Hall* (1774), Lofft 655 at 741–42, 1 Cowp 204.
49 Dicey, *supra* note 47 at 22–23.
50 Sir Ivor Jennings, *The Law and the Constitution*, 2nd ed (London: University of London Press, 1938) at 38–39.

is not sovereign in Canada. Its powers are, of course, limited by the Constitution of Canada in a variety of ways, most notably by provisions securing rights and powers for the provinces. Federal and provincial legislatures in Canada are, technically, "non-sovereign" bodies "subordinate" to the Constitution from which they obtain their powers.[51]

So who is, as a matter of law, sovereign in Canada? We could say that sovereignty lies with the body or bodies of people capable of amending the Constitution of Canada according to the amendment procedures set forth in Part V of the *Constitution Act, 1982*. However, as Dicey observed, amending bodies have "only a potential existence"; as a result, he concluded that, in federal systems with written constitutions, it is the judiciary that is "at a given moment the master of the constitution."[52] Perhaps, then, in Canada the Constitution of Canada, as judicially interpreted, is sovereign. But this seems like an awkward use of the idea of sovereignty, which is typically associated with people, not documents or laws. Perhaps it is best, in the end, to concede that as a matter of Canadian constitutional law there is no such thing as sovereignty in Canada in the sense of an office or institution vested with absolute and untrammelled authority. The legal powers that do exist are all subject to law and open to ordinary legal interpretation.

The expression "Crown sovereignty" is not often used by judges outside of the field of Aboriginal rights law in Canada. The brief discussion above suggests why: strictly speaking it is legally incoherent. Although we may refer to "Crown sovereignty" as a metaphor for "Canadian sovereignty" or "the sovereignty of the Canadian state" when defining Canada's geographical and juridical extent and identity vis-à-vis the outside world, from the perspective of Canadian domestic constitutional law the term "Crown sovereignty" is deeply problematic, for at best it is a metaphor for juridical ideas that are highly dependent upon the context within which the term is invoked. A brief review of how judges employ the term "Crown sovereignty" in relation to Aboriginal peoples is instructive.

The first category of cases involve Indigenous claims that are actual attacks on the very existence of Canada as a sovereign state – or what we might call *existential threat* cases. When it was argued that an interlocutory injunction against protesters from the Lilwat people was invalid "because the Lilwat People constitute a sovereign nation to

---

51 Dicey, *supra* note 47 at 83–109, 146.
52 *Ibid* at 171.

which the laws of Canada do not apply and over which the Courts have no jurisdiction,"[53] the response from provincial lawyers, that this "Indian sovereignty argument challenges the basic constitutional framework of Canada,"[54] was probably fair, in the sense that the Aboriginal sovereignty claim was made against, not under or pursuant to, the Constitution of Canada. Arguments of this kind are characterized by judges as attacks on the "sovereign integrity" of the "state"[55] or on "the sovereignty of the Crown over ... Canada."[56] It is fair to characterize the claims this way, because, in these cases, challenging the very existence of the Canadian state, at least over them, is what the Indigenous claimants have in mind (though such claims are not necessarily inconsistent with the view that there might exist a complex set of legal relationships between Canada and the relevant Indigenous nation established by treaty). Often Indigenous claimants in these cases invoke international law as well as the laws of their own Indigenous nation against the validity of the Canadian state.[57] In general, judges respond

---

53 *British Columbia (AG) v Mount Currie Indian Band*, [1991] BCJ No 208 (CA), per Macfarlane JA (in chambers refusing leave to appeal an interlocutory injunction).

54 *British Columbia (AG) v Mount Currie Indian Band*, [1991] 4 WWR 507, 54 BCLR (2d) 129 at para 22 (Sup Ct), Macdonald J.

55 *R v Jones*, [2000] 10 WWR 116, 83 Alta LR (3d) 103 at para 26 (QB) Johnstone J [*Jones*]. See also *RO:RI:WI:IO v Canada (AG)* (19 September 2006), 06-630 (Ont Sup Ct), (Pelletier J), affirmed by the Ontario Court of Appeal, in an endorsement dated 15 February 2007, quoted at *R v Francis*, [2007] 85 OR (3d) 45 at para 8, 3 CNLR 294 (Sup Ct), Hackland J [*Francis*] (rejecting the "challenge to Canada's sovereignty").

56 *R v Wayne Kahpeechoose*, [1997] 4 CNLR 215 at 217 (Sask Prov Ct) [*Kahpeechoose*]. See also *R v Noltcho*, 2000 SKQB 223 at para 6, 196 Sask R 221; *R v Chief*, [1997] 4 CNLR 212 (Sask QB). See also cases in which Aboriginals accused of criminal acts committed during protests over land claims argue that the courts lack jurisdiction over them: *R v Williams*, [1995] 2 CNLR 229 (BCCA), Hollinrake JA, leave to appeal to SCC refused [1994] SCCA No 566 ("no aboriginal jurisdiction superior to laws intended to govern all inhabitants of this Province survived the assertion of sovereignty"; "[t]here is no residual aboriginal sovereignty capable of displacing the general jurisdiction of the Provincial Court to try persons, whether aboriginal or non-aboriginal" at 233); *R v Clark*, [1997] BCJ No 618, 88 BCAC 213, leave to appeal to the SCC refused, [1997] SCCA No 260; *R v Ignace*, [1998] BCJ No 243, 156 DLR (4th) 713 (CA), leave to appeal to SCC refused, [1998] SCCA No 92.

57 *R v Yellowhorn*, [2006] AJ No 491, [2006] 10 WWR 722, 62 Alta LR (4th) 143 (QB), Langston J [*Yellowhorn*] (a woman charged under provincial law with driving in the City of Lethbridge in an unregistered and uninsured vehicle claimed that as a "member of the Independent Sovereign Blackfoot Nation" she had acted in the good faith belief, supported by "scholars of international law," that she was not subject to any of the laws of Canada or the province "but only to the laws of the Blackfoot nation" at paras 1, 44).

to existential threat cases by quickly denying the claims, often by citing the sovereignty-without-a-doubt passage from *Sparrow*[58] and/or the act of state doctrine.[59]

It is, however, not always clear whether an indigenous claim is meant to be an existential threat to Canada as a state. The accused in *R v Francis*, a Mohawk man who was charged with a number of offences related to a drug-related armed robbery on the Akwesasne Mohawk reserve, argued that the court had no jurisdiction over him in light of the sovereignty of the Mohawk nation and the acts of genocide committed by Canada upon Aboriginal peoples contrary to international law, as well as Aboriginal rights under sections 25 and 35 of the *Constitution Act, 1982*, prompting the judge to observe that he was arguing for "the sovereignty of the Mohawk nation and the denial of the sovereignty of the Crown and the denial of both the applicability of the Constitution of Canada and the jurisdiction of the Canadian Courts" while also "somewhat incongruously" arguing that section 35 guarantees "the indigenous right of sovereignty and self-determination."[60] Whether in fact these propositions are incongruous is, of course, open to question: there is nothing illogical about the idea that the domestic constitutional law of one sovereign nation might recognize the existence of another sovereign nation, or about the idea that a member of that other nation might raise this point of constitutional law in the courts of the first nation.

In other cases, judges have suggested that the development of a Canadian legal conception of Aboriginal rights has somehow encouraged the denial of Canadian state authority. The accused in *R v David* was charged with cigarette smuggling between Canada and the United States and argued that as a member of the Mohawk or Kanienkeha:ka nation he was under Haudenosaunee law, the "Keyanerekowa" or Great Law of Peace, and that, as he said, "[I] cannot subject myself to foreign legal process, for to do so would be going against the very law by which I live by: The Great Law."[61] The judge cited the sovereignty-without-a-doubt passage from *Sparrow* and the act of state doctrine and rejected this argument, but he then observed,

---

58 *R v Jones, supra* note 55 at para 24; *R v Yellowhorn, supra* note 57 at para 27; *R v David*, [2000] OJ No 561 (QL) at para 15 [*David*].

59 *Wayne Kahpeechoose, supra* note 56 at 217–18; *David, ibid* at para 16.

60 *Francis, supra* note 55 at para 5.

61 *David, supra* note 58 at para 10.

While the laws of Canada must be shaped to recognize the rights and free-doms guaranteed in the *Constitution Act, 1982*, such shaping and moulding by the integrated actions of the legislative and judicial branches of government is, nonetheless, the exercise of Canada's sovereignty. It seems probable that some observers have misconstrued this shaping of certain laws to accord with treaty or other aboriginal rights ... as deference on the part of the government of Canada to another sovereign authority. To construe the process that way is wholly erroneous and has been the root of much trouble and frustration.[62]

The response by lower court judges to the existential threat cases is not surprising, but the reasoning employed by judges is unsatisfactory. It would perhaps be beneficial for the Supreme Court of Canada to grant leave to appeal in an appropriate case of this kind so that the deeply complex and morally troubling aspects of the relationship between sovereignty and Aboriginal rights might be explored and explained. As an interpretive legal concept, the sovereignty of the Canadian state is not beyond ordinary legal analysis, and, in the end, it must be explained in a manner that fits the aspirations for legality and legitimacy that underlie the Constitution of Canada – even if the wrong of including an Indigenous nation within the bounds of Canada cannot be remedied through a judicial order that dismantles Canada.

We may now turn from the existential threat cases to the leading deci-sions of the Supreme Court of Canada on section 35 – none of which (even *Delgamuukw*, despite the opinions of the lower court judges in that case) involved Indigenous claims that represented existential threats to the Canadian state. In these cases, the expression "Crown sovereignty" features prominently, but its meaning varies according to context, and the Supreme Court of Canada is not at all clear about when and why it uses the expression in different ways. Two main senses of "Crown sovereignty" may be identified in the cases.

The first sense in which the leading section 35 cases use the expres-sion "Crown sovereignty" seems to track closely the use of the expres-sion in the existential threat cases. In *Van der Peet*, Lamer CJ, writing for a majority of the Court, stated that section 35 "provides the consti-tutional framework for reconciliation of the pre-existence of distinc-tive aboriginal societies occupying the land with Crown sovereignty."[63]

---

62 *Ibid* at para 18.
63 *Van der Peet, supra* note 9 at para 42.

He explained that although the Aboriginal perspective must be taken into account in the articulation of Aboriginal rights, "that perspective must be framed in terms cognizable to the Canadian legal and constitutional structure," for Aboriginal rights must "exist within the general legal system of Canada," a requirement that flows from the objective of reconciling Aboriginal societies "with the assertion of Crown sovereignty."[64]

The requirement that Aboriginal rights be consistent with Crown sovereignty and therefore fit within the "Canadian legal and constitutional structure" is, of course, an unclear one. It might mean that Aboriginal rights must not threaten the existence of the Canadian state or the viability of the Constitution of Canada, or it might mean that they must comply with substantive constitutional and legal standards, or even public interests more generally, that are unrelated to what we have called *existential* issues. The former, narrower reading of Crown sovereignty seems to be supported by comments from the 2001 *Mitchell* case, in which a majority of the Court referred to the old rule of colonial common law according to which "aboriginal interests and customary laws were presumed to survive the assertion of sovereignty, and were absorbed into the common law as rights, unless ... they were incompatible with the Crown's assertion of sovereignty."[65] And in his concurring opinion, Binnie J, joined by Major J, explained that this sovereign compatibility rule should be used, at the definitional phase of section 35 analysis (i.e., in the first phase of defining the scope and content of a section 35 right, which takes place before the second phase of the analysis, which involves a consideration of whether limitations on the right are justified), only "sparingly," and his examples of Aboriginal practices ruled out by Crown sovereignty – use of military force or interfering with Canada's control of its international borders – suggest that he had in mind matters very closely related to the existence of Canada as a sovereign state (or existential matters).[66] However, as we shall see, other passages in his reasons suggest that he may have had a broader sense of "Crown sovereignty" in mind when thinking about the sovereign incompatibility limit to section 35.

---

64 *Ibid* at para 49.
65 *Mitchell, supra* note 9 at para 10.
66 *Ibid* at para 154.

The second sense in which the leading section 35 cases use "Crown sovereignty" extends the meaning of that term well beyond the basic idea of the existence of Canada as a sovereign state. After Aboriginal rights have been defined and proven, the Court holds that they may be limited by legislatures, so long as the limitation meets a justification test. The first step in this test is to ensure that the legislative infringement fulfils some constitutionally legitimate objective. In *R v Gladstone*, it was held that the requirement that Aboriginal rights be reconciled with Crown sovereignty means that Aboriginal rights may be limited to account for the fact that Aboriginal societies "exist within, and are a part of, a broader social, political and economic community, over which the Crown is sovereign."[67] In *Delgamuukw v British Columbia*, Lamer CJ explained that this meant that Aboriginal rights could be limited to allow for "the development of agriculture, forestry, mining, and hydroelectric power, the general economic development ... protection of the environment or endangered species, the building of infrastructure and the settlement of foreign populations to support those aims."[68] These are all possible public policy objectives, of course, but they are not obviously linked to the very existence of the Canadian state; they are, rather, simply things that the Canadian state may wish to do. Crown sovereignty, in this context, simply means general legislative authority, exercised pursuant to the domestic Constitution of Canada, to pursue whatever is deemed to be in the general public interest.

The Court never explains explicitly when or why it shifts between the two very different senses of Crown sovereignty at work within the section 35 jurisprudence. One concern is that, as a result of using the same expression for different purposes, the broader public interest sense of Crown sovereignty will be used when only the narrower existential sense of Crown sovereignty is appropriate. This happened in the recent decision of the British Columbia Court of Appeal in *Tsilhqot'in Nation v British Columbia* when the Court reasoned that Aboriginal title cannot be a broad territorial or national right to ancestral lands but only a narrow property right to patches of land intensively used, a conclusion it justified not by reference to any principled argument about the nature of rights to territory or property, but purely on the basis of the political goal of wanting to avoid "placing unnecessary limitations on

---

67 *R v Gladstone*, [1996] 2 SCR 723 at para 73, 137 DLR (4th) 648.
68 *Delgamuukw v British Columbia*, [1997] 3 SCR 1010 para 165, 153 DLR (4th) 193.

the sovereignty of the Crown or on the aspirations of all Canadians, Aboriginal and non-Aboriginal."[69] It is unclear how recognition of a territorial conception of Aboriginal title would threaten the existence of the Canadian state. It seems, then, that Crown sovereignty here was used in its broader public interest sense, as synonymous with the "aspirations of all Canadians," rather than in the narrower existential sense. The previous cases suggest, however, that this kind of Crown sovereignty is not supposed to circumscribe the initial definition of Aboriginal rights; rather, it is limited to providing a justification for legislative limitations of Aboriginal rights, which must then be shown by governments to meet other tests of proportionality and Crown honour to be valid. On appeal, however, the Supreme Court of Canada in *Tsilhqot'in* rejected the narrow conception of Aboriginal title in favour of a broader territorial right and seemed, in the process, to reject the idea that Crown sovereignty might be invoked to limit the scope of lands subject to Aboriginal title.[70]

Slippage between the two uses of Crown sovereignty under section 35 was perhaps foreshadowed in Binnie J's concurring reasons in the *Mitchell* case. Binnie J sought to address the moral problem arising from the fact that Crown sovereignty was imposed upon Indigenous peoples unilaterally by reassuring them that, properly interpreted, Crown sovereignty is not the power of some "entity across the seas," but it is an "updated concept of Crown sovereignty" according to which "aboriginal and non-aboriginal Canadians *together* form a sovereign entity with a measure of common purpose and united effort," and it is with this concept of "merged" or "shared" sovereignty that Aboriginal rights under section 35 must be reconciled.[71] How this merger was achieved, except through the unilateral assertion of Crown sovereignty or judicial fiat, is unclear. However, with this updated and supposedly inclusive concept of Crown sovereignty as the new thing against which Aboriginal rights must be reconciled, there is a danger that the broader sense of public interest sovereignty will creep into the analysis at the definitional stage of Aboriginal rights analysis. As Binnie J stated, the conclusion that the scope of Aboriginal rights must be narrowed at the definitional

69 *Tsilhqot'in Nation v British Columbia*, 2012 BCCA 285, [2012] 3 CNLR 333 at para 219, Groberman JA.
70 *Tsilhqot'in Nation v British Columbia*, 2014 SCC 44.
71 *Mitchell, supra* note 9 at para 129.

stage out of respect for Crown sovereignty will be one reached when the specific claim in question "relates to national interests that all of us have in common."[72] The scope of Aboriginal rights may, in other words, be limited at the definitional stage by the interests of "our collective sovereignty."[73] Of course, national interests often extend far beyond existential concerns.

Perhaps the most curious thing about Binnie J's discussion of sovereignty in *Mitchell* is that he drew the idea of shared or merged sovereignty from the *Report of the Royal Commission on Aboriginal Peoples*, which linked the idea explicitly to the recognition that "Aboriginal governments" are, or should be, like federal and provincial governments, i.e., "sovereign" within the spheres established, or to be established, for them under the Constitution of Canada.[74] Binnie J even compared this idea with the idea of "residual aboriginal sovereignty" acknowledged in the old Marshall cases from the United States.[75] But then Binnie J observed that it was "unnecessary, for present purposes, to come to any conclusion about these assertions."[76] In effect, the Royal Commission on Aboriginal Peoples presented a package deal: if internally sovereign Aboriginal governments are acknowledged, then it will be possible to say that, collectively, Canadian sovereignty is a merged or shared sovereignty, and legitimacy will be restored to the Canadian constitutional order. Binnie J took one part of the package, the idea of merged or shared sovereignty, without the other part, sovereign Aboriginal governments, and as a result any claim to moral coherence to his argument collapsed. Of course, he left open the possibility that arguments for residual Aboriginal sovereignty might be judicially accepted, and so, in effect, he invited future courts to rectify the moral asymmetry he created.

IV

From this account of how "Crown sovereignty" was invoked by the Supreme Court of Canada in its leading decisions on section 35, at least prior to *Haida Nation* and *Taku River*, several observations can be

72 *Ibid* at para 164.
73 *Ibid*.
74 *Ibid* at para 130, quoting *Report of the Royal Commission on Aboriginal Peoples*, vol 2, 240–41.
75 *Ibid* at para 165, citing *Cherokee Nation v Georgia*, 30 US (5 Pet) 1 (1831) at 17.
76 *Ibid* at para 135.

made. First, only rarely does the Court invoke Crown sovereignty in the existential sense, i.e., as a metaphor for the existence of a sovereign Canadian state. More often, Crown sovereignty is used as a metaphor for either general legislative authority or the national or public interest. Second, in relation to both uses, Crown sovereignty appears to be treated as a legal concept open to ordinary legal analysis; indeed, Crown sovereignty in the public interest sense is purely a judicial construct – it is, we may say, a sui generis concept designed for the Aboriginal rights context. Third, the reasons that might exist for suggesting that sovereignty cannot be questioned by ordinary legal analysis (the act of state doctrine) apply, if at all, only to the first, existential sense of Crown sovereignty, and not to the second, public interest sense of Crown sovereignty. Finally, although we may say that there may be good reasons of principle for why ordinary courts would not question the existence of the Canadian state, or Crown sovereignty in the existential sense, the justice or lack of justice underlying the founding of the Canadian state can never be treated as out of bounds for ordinary legal analysis; indeed, the injustice of the assertion of Crown sovereignty in the course of establishing the existence of the Canadian state may find its remedy, as a matter of domestic constitutional law, through the questioning and limiting of the legality of Crown sovereignty in the second, public interest sense.[77] In the end, it would be best if the Court ceased using the expression "Crown sovereignty" altogether in Aboriginal rights cases, in either the existential or the public interest sense. It would be interesting to see how the law in this area would develop if judges employed, instead of the incantation of Crown sovereignty, phrases like "the existence of the Canadian state" and "public interest." In this respect, the Court's recent decision on Aboriginal title in *Tsilhqot'in* is promising: references to Crown sovereignty seem to give way to references to the need to show a "compelling and substantial public interest" in order to limit an Aboriginal right – and also the need to show that "the broader public goal asserted by the government ... further[s] the goal of reconciliation, having regard to both the Aboriginal interest and the broader public objective."[78]

---

77 For a broadly similar line of reasoning, see Hoehn, *Reconciling Sovereignties, supra* note 11.
78 *Tsilhqot'in, supra* note 70 at paras 88, 82.

What the Supreme Court of Canada really meant by the idea that Aboriginal sovereignty is de jure and Crown sovereignty is de facto must await further analysis. Clearly, the legality of Crown sovereignty has been questioned and found wanting – a remarkable conclusion in light of the long history of judicial concern and anxiety about the sensitive subject of sovereignty. Even if the legality of Crown sovereignty in the existential sense has not really been drawn into question, and even if the legality of the Constitution of Canada has been left intact, the conclusion that Crown sovereignty in other senses – like the ability of legislatures to pursue the national or public interest – is merely a de facto power that must be reconciled with pre-existing Aboriginal sovereignty through honourable negotiation, is significant. Certainly, as Professor Lyon observed, new rules of the game are needed. However, the methods of the obsequious law student – in particular the ordinary interpretive discourse of the common law – may serve this end well, especially if we are interested in the incorporation of Indigenous legal traditions into our evolving conception of sovereignty in Canada.

3 We Are Still in the Age of Encounter: Section 35 and a Canada beyond Sovereignty

JEREMY WEBBER*

This chapter examines whether Canada's recent grappling with Indigenous rights, under section 35 and in relations between Indigenous and non-Indigenous governments generally, has begun to unsettle the longstanding assumption that Canadian institutions are sovereign in a manner that excludes Indigenous sovereignty. It investigates the particular attributes of sovereignty – the particular claims often associated with the concept of sovereignty – that are placed in issue by the encounter between Indigenous peoples and the legal and political institutions of Canada, and it explores the specific form that the recomposition of sovereignty should take.

In particular, it suggests that we may be observing a bracketing of the question of sovereignty, not in a way that ignores the question, but that suspends its final determination, allowing multiple assertions of sovereignty to exist in a continual, unresolved – perhaps never resolved – tension. If the question of sovereignty is being reconstructed in this way, then it represents a substantial change in our understanding of what is necessary to sustain a constitutional order. It represents the emergence of what might be called an "agonistic

* My thanks to Catherine George, Maegan Hough, and Vivian Lee for their able research assistance; and to Robert Gibbs, Martin Loughlin, Val Napoleon, Heidi Kiiwetinepinesiik Stark, Jim Tully, and the participants in the Conference, "35@30: Reflecting on 30 Years of Section 35 of the Constitution Act, 1982," University of Toronto, October 2012, and the reading group on legal pluralism and Indigenous peoples, University of Victoria, fall 2013, for their many useful comments on previous versions of this chapter.

constitutionalism," in which a constitutional order is characterized by divergent, perhaps even contradictory, assertions of fundamental principle, held in continual tension. Such a constitutionalism is especially evident in the Indigenous dimensions of Canadian constitutional practice, but it is also apparent elsewhere. Indeed, it may turn out to be a more common feature of constitutional orders than we have ever suspected.[1]

Now, it is unusual to speak of "the existing aboriginal and treaty rights" that are protected by section 35 in terms of sovereignty. The dominant language of Indigenous rights in Canada has been proprietary. The jurisprudence has been preoccupied with the recognition of Aboriginal title to land, the nature and incidents of that title, how Aboriginal title must be proven, regulated, or extinguished, and the possibility of Indigenous peoples holding lesser rights to resources (chiefly hunting and fishing rights). Distinctly governmental rights have not been wholly absent from the debate. A few Canadian judicial decisions have addressed rights of self-government, although they have done so cautiously, confining the issues posed.[2] Some Canadian scholars have argued that a right of sovereignty or self-government persists unextinguished, in a manner very similar to the persistence of

---

1 For approaches to constitutionalism that have close affinities to that presented here, see James Tully, *Strange Multiplicity: Constitutionalism in an Age of Diversity* (Cambridge: Cambridge University Press, 1995); and Jean Leclair, "Le fédéralisme comme refus des monismes nationalistes" in Dimitrios Karmis and François Rocher, eds, *La dynamique confiance / méfiance dans les démocraties multinationales: Le Canada sous l'angle comparatif* (Quebec: Presses de l'Université Laval, 2012) 209.

2 See *R v Pamajewon*, [1996] 2 SCR 821 (where the Supreme Court of Canada declined to address a general right of self-government and instead focused on a more narrow right to control gambling activities); *Delgamuukw v British Columbia*, [1997] 3 SCR 1010 at paras 170–71 (where the Court suggested that the plaintiffs' claim to jurisdiction over their traditional lands was framed in excessively broad terms, but left it to a subsequent trial, which never occurred, to examine that claim in depth); and *Campbell v British Columbia (AG)*, 2000 BCSC 1123 at paras 180, 183 (perhaps the most germane discussion, although a trial decision, where Williamson J of the BC Supreme Court held that the Nisga'a retained reduced powers of government after the assertion of colonial sovereignty, although he did not accept that these were "sovereign powers"). For discussion of these cases, see Kent McNeil, "Judicial Approaches to Self-Government since Calder: Searching for Doctrinal Coherence" in Hamar Foster, Heather Raven, & Jeremy Webber, eds, *Let Right Be Done: Aboriginal Title, the Calder Case, and the Future of Indigenous Rights* (Vancouver: UBC Press, 2007) 129.

Aboriginal title itself.[3] Moreover, attention to questions of sovereignty has been common internationally. In the United States, the Marshall judgments – a series of judgments of Chief Justice John Marshall of the US Supreme Court in the early nineteenth century, which form an important source of the Canadian as well as US law of Aboriginal title – recognize a restricted form of Indigenous sovereignty (although this aspect of the Marshall decisions has never been embraced by the Canadian courts).[4] In this highly qualified form, sovereignty remains a foundational element of US Indian law. And at the international level, the related notion of self-determination has become a central concept of the *United Nations Declaration on the Rights of Indigenous Peoples*.[5]

Furthermore, it is a great mistake to think that constitutional law is the exclusive province of the courts. Beyond the judiciary, assertions of Indigenous self-government, occasionally invoking the concept of

---

3   See, for example, Bruce Clark, *Native Liberty, Crown Sovereignty: The Existing Aboriginal Right of Self-Government in Canada* (Montreal & Kingston: McGill-Queen's University Press, 1990); Brian Slattery, "Aboriginal Sovereignty and Imperial Claims" (1991) 29 Osgoode Hall LJ 681; Michael Asch & Patrick Macklem, "Aboriginal Rights and Canadian Sovereignty: An Essay on *R v Sparrow*" (1991) 29 Alta L Rev 498; John Borrows, "A Genealogy of Law: Inherent Sovereignty and First Nations Self-Government" (1992) 30 Osgoode Hall LJ 291; Mark Walters, "British Imperial Constitutional Law and Aboriginal Rights: A Comment on *Delgamuukw v. British Columbia*" (1992) 17 Queen's LJ 350; Patrick Macklem, "Distributing Sovereignty: Indian Nations and Equality of Peoples" (1993) 45 Stan L Rev 1311; John Borrows, "Constitutional Law from a First Nation Perspective: Self-Government and the Royal Proclamation" (1994) 28 UBC L Rev 1; John Borrows, "Tracking Trajectories: Aboriginal Governance as an Aboriginal Right" (2005) 38 UBC L Rev 285; Felix Hoehn, *Reconciling Sovereignties: Aboriginal Nations and Canada* (Saskatoon: Native Law Centre, University of Saskatchewan, 2012).

4   See *Johnson v McIntosh*, 5 US (8 Wheat) 543 (1823) at 574; *Cherokee Nation v State of Georgia*, 8 US (5 Pet) 1 (1831) at 17–20; *Worcester v Georgia*, 31 US (6 Pet) 515 (1832) at 520. For the limitations of the sovereignty recognized in these cases, see Joanne Barker, "For Whom Sovereignty Matters" in Joanne Barker, ed, *Sovereignty Matters: Locations of Contestation and Possibility in Indigenous Struggles for Self-Determination* (Lincoln: University of Nebraska Press, 2005) 1 at 12–16; N Bruce Duthu, *Shadow Nations: Tribal Sovereignty and the Limits of Legal Pluralism* (Oxford: Oxford University Press, 2013). For the authority of the Marshall decisions in Canada, see *R v Van der Peet*, [1996] 2 SCR 507 at para 35, although Lamer CJ notes that their relevance is at the level of general principles rather than specific holdings.

5   United Nations General Assembly, *United Nations Declaration on the Rights of Indigenous Peoples*, art 3, UN Doc. A/RES/61/295 of 13 September 2007, online: <undesadspd. org/IndigenousPeoples/DeclarationontheRightsofIndigenousPeoples.aspx>.

Ind. peoples themselves are carving out self-determination on the outside of the treaty ground.

sovereignty, have been pervasive in Canada. From the very beginning of colonization, Indigenous peoples have strongly defended their legal and political autonomy. That autonomy is exemplified in today's invocation of a "nation-to-nation relationship," reflected in the practice of treaty-making.[6] The existence of an inherent right of self-government became the central focus of Indigenous leaders' representations in the four constitutional conferences of the mid-1980s that sought to define the content of the rights affirmed by section 35, and the recognition of an inherent right of self-government has remained a principal demand in treaty negotiations and constitutional talks ever since.[7] Indeed, there is a strong argument that Indigenous advocates adopted the language of property itself because it had the best chance of being accepted; Aboriginal title has always been claimed not just to establish a property right but as the foundation for an autonomous sphere of Indigenous law and governance.[8]

Kent McNeil, "Territory Sovereignty" The entitlement of Indigenous peoples to govern their own societies, then, has been an important dimension of the debate over Indigenous rights in Canada. That debate has generally avoided the concept of sovereignty, however. For one thing, sovereignty is likely to generate as many questions as it answers.[9] What matters fall within Indigenous

6   See, among many examples, John Bird, Lorraine Land, & Murray MacAdam, *Nation to Nation: Aboriginal Sovereignty and the Future of Canada* (Toronto: Irwin Higher Education, 2002). See also Royal Commission on Aboriginal Peoples, *Report of the Royal Commission on Aboriginal Peoples, Volume 2: Restructuring the Relationship* (Ottawa: Minister of Supply and Services Canada, 1996) at 107; *R v Sioui*, [1990] 1 SCR 1025 at 1052–53.

7   Bryan Schwartz, *First Principles, Second Thoughts: Aboriginal Peoples, Constitutional Reform and Canadian Statecraft* (Montreal: Institute for Research on Public Policy, 1986); David C Hawkes, *Aboriginal Peoples and Constitutional Reform: What Have We Learned?* (Kingston: Institute of Intergovernmental Relations, 1989); Kent McNeil, "The Decolonization of Canada: Moving toward Recognition of Aboriginal Governments" (1994) 7 Western Legal History 113; Jeremy Webber, *Reimagining Canada: Language, Culture, Community and the Canadian Constitution* (Montreal & Kingston: McGill-Queen's University Press, 1994) at 122–25 and 170–72; Peter Russell, *Constitutional Odyssey: Can Canadians Become a Sovereign People?* 3rd ed (Toronto: University of Toronto Press, 2004), chs 10–12.

8   Webber, *ibid* at 72–73; Kent McNeil, "Aboriginal Rights in Canada: From Title to Land to Territorial Sovereignty" (1998) 5 Tulsa J Comp & Int'l L 253.

9   See, for example, the comments of Lamer J when faced with a general claim to self-government in *Delgamuukw, supra* note 2 at para 171:

The broad nature of the claim at trial also led to a failure by the parties to address many of the difficult conceptual issues which surround the recognition of aboriginal

peoples' sovereign jurisdiction? Through what institutions is Indigenous sovereignty exercised? What if those institutions fail to respect rights – would Canadian governments retain any continuing responsibility? Sovereignty tends to promise an easy answer to these questions, implying that whoever is sovereign can simply decide. But if these questions cannot be decided unilaterally – if they are inevitably the subject of negotiations – talk of sovereignty may only complicate, not aid, their resolution.

Moreover, for the people who make decisions within Canadian institutions – members of governments, members of legislatures, judges – the recognition of Indigenous sovereignty has the additional, visceral disadvantage of restricting their freedom of action, subjecting their decisions about what is right, what is politically sound, what is in the interest of Canadians, and what is economically required to a process of decision-making that is still largely unspecified and certainly beyond their unencumbered control. They have thus had their own interest to resist any talk of Indigenous sovereignty.

Of course, even now, the power of decision-making of Canadian institutions is not unencumbered. Indeed, sovereignty is not about a claim to unencumbered decision-making in fact but (to take the example of Sovereignty 1, defined below) about a claim to be *entitled* to decide matters in any way one wants. Moreover, Canadian institutions' claims of entitlement, and their power in fact to decide matters however they want, has been more constrained than a simple invocation of sovereignty would suggest. The evolution of Indigenous rights over the last sixty years has been driven not by Canadian institutions but by Indigenous peoples' insistence that the relationship be reconceived in a manner that accords substantial respect to their

---

self-government The degree of complexity involved can be gleaned from the *Report of the Royal Commission on Aboriginal Peoples*, which devotes 277 pages to the issue. That report describes different models of self-government, each differing with respect to their conception of territory, citizenship, jurisdiction, internal government organization, etc. We received little in the way of submissions that would help us to grapple with these difficult and central issues.

In the BC Court of Appeal in *Delgamuukw v British Columbia* (1991), 79 DLR (4th) 470, the judges who acknowledged a right of self-government suggested that its modalities were best determined through negotiations: see the reasons of Lambert JA & Hutcheon JA at paras 1030, 1098, and 1171.

normative traditions.[10] Canadian institutions have been in reactive mode, searching for a way to respond that escapes the charge of colonial domination by establishing terms that are mutually acceptable or that at least have some claim to be just. The fact that Indigenous peoples have asserted their position largely from outside Canadian institutions, with some real effect, plays a very important role in the argument that follows. Coming to terms with the assertion of Indigenous political agency, finding some way to accommodate the role of Indigenous peoples within one's understanding of the constitutional order, is an important reason for re-examining the question of Indigenous sovereignty.

But why, the reader might ask, is *sovereignty* the appropriate concept through which to explore those issues? Sovereignty does indeed have the disadvantages listed above, namely that it poses a series of questions without furnishing sufficient resources for their resolution. It may in fact be positively unhelpful, for it seems to promise that those who possess it will have a unilateral power of decision-making, freed from the need to compromise. If many of the issues that face us have to be resolved ultimately through negotiations – through co-determination rather than self-determination – the language of sovereignty might point us in exactly the wrong direction. Nevertheless, there is good reason to believe that the question of sovereignty is inescapable – good reason why governments, legislatures, and courts have found themselves driven to reopen the question, however tentatively.

First, as we shall see, sovereignty is used to capture several claims that can be teased apart. At least one of these claims is undeniably part of the debate over Indigenous rights, but other claims associated with sovereignty often run interference with that element, obscuring precisely what is in issue. Distinguishing the claims associated with sovereignty can therefore clarify the debate, reducing misunderstanding and, I hope, preparing the way for better solutions. Second, it is not as though claims of sovereignty are radically absent from the statements

---

10 And of course there was a long history before this recent period. See, e.g., Paul Tennant, *Aboriginal Peoples and Politics: The Indian Land Question in British Columbia, 1849–1989* (Vancouver: University of British Columbia Press, 1990); Robert Galois, "The Indian Rights Association, Native Protest Activity and the 'Land Question' in British Columbia, 1903–1916" (1992) 8:2 Native Studies Rev 1; Hamar Foster, "We Are Not O'Meara's Children: Law, Lawyers, and the First Campaign for Aboriginal Title in British Columbia, 1908–28" in Foster et al, *supra* note 2 at 61.

of Canadian institutions on Indigenous rights. On the contrary, those institutions have tended to presuppose, at least in the modern era, a complete and untrammelled sovereignty for themselves. There is real doubt whether Canadian institutions can achieve a more satisfactory relationship with Indigenous peoples without some reconsideration of their claims of Canadian sovereignty. This chapter seeks to lay the foundation for that reconsideration. Third, many Indigenous advocates (but by no means all) themselves embrace the language of sovereignty – not surprisingly, given Canadian institutions' reliance on the concept to justify their own right to have the last word.[11] The terminology is, then, already part of the debate, directly and through such associated concepts as self-determination and the inherent right to self-government. It is time that one clarified what a reconceived sovereignty might mean.

Some might object that it is quixotic to resurrect discussion of sovereignty just at the time that the term is falling out of favour in the international relations literature. But not only have many participants in that literature demonstrated convincingly that accounts of its death have been greatly exaggerated, but there is good reason why the term refuses to die.[12] At the foundation of sovereignty lies a concern with political agency: a desire to be clear about who can make what decisions, by what means, so that people can participate effectively in their own governance, without having their social relations determined by a law over which they have no control. At bottom, questions about sovereignty are questions about self-government. Those questions can and should be given more complex answers than they are usually given. But if one cares about self-government, one must pose questions of sovereignty.

This chapter begins by reviewing the ways in which those questions have re-emerged, as questions, both in decisions under section 35 of the *Constitution Act, 1982* and, most directly, in negotiations between

---

11 See the instructive discussion in Heidi Kiiwetinepinesiik Stark, "Nenabozho's Smart Berries: Rethinking Tribal Sovereignty and Accountability" (2013) Michigan State Law Review 339; Heidi Kiiwetinepinesiik Stark, "Invoking Creation, Inheriting Earth: Anishinaabe Expressions of Sovereignty" (Paper delivered at the Canadian Historical Association, Victoria, BC, 5 June 2013) [unpublished].

12 This is of course a voluminous literature, but for sovereignty's persistence see, e.g., Jack Donnelly, *Universal Human Rights in Theory and Practice* (Ithaca: Cornell University Press, 2002) at 35 and 67, where, in an argument devoted to affirming universal rights in international law, he nevertheless concedes the continued centrality of states.

Indigenous peoples and Canadian governments. It then goes on to distinguish four claims often associated with sovereignty, showing their relative independence from one another. Finally, it analyses which of those claims are in issue in the Canadian debate and what steps might achieve more satisfactory resolutions in Indigenous/non-Indigenous relations.

Indigenous Sovereignty in post-1982 Constitutional Debate

The orthodox position, during the last hundred years or so, has been that the colonial powers obtained sovereignty upon discovery, completed by their taking of possession of the territory, either by symbolic acts or by symbolic acts backed by actual occupation.[13] Indeed, for many years, imperial decision-makers doubted whether Indigenous peoples were capable of exercising sovereignty at all: Indigenous peoples were commonly considered to be "uncivilized peoples or savages" who lacked the ability to exert political control over or maintain legal orders within their territories, or, more charitably, who possessed forms of social organization that lacked the characteristics of states and therefore, in decision-makers' eyes, lacked sovereignty.[14] Those arguments are rarely voiced today; they are considered to be the product of the discriminatory denigration of Indigenous peoples. But although Canadian governments and courts have generally abandoned the doctrines on which the absence of Indigenous sovereignty was based – the simplest versions of the doctrine of discovery, and the belief that Indigenous societies lacked systems of law and government – they still tend to presume that

---

13 Brian Slattery, *The Land Rights of Indigenous Canadian Peoples, as Affected by the Crown's Acquisition of Their Territories* (Saskatoon: University of Saskatchewan Native Law Centre, 1979).

14 *R v Syliboy*, [1929] 1 DLR 307 at 313 (1928), 50 CCC 389 at 396 (NS Co Ct). The opinions expressed in this case are an example of "classic colonial thinking about the historical place of First Nations peoples in North America." Doug Moodie, "Thinking Outside the 20th Century Box: Revisiting 'Mitchell' – Some Comments on the Politics of Judicial Law-Making in the Context of Aboriginal Self-Government" (2003–04) 35 Ottawa L Rev 1 at 3. Some Indigenous commentators have also criticized the use of sovereignty to describe Indigenous governance. See the arguments of Taiaiake Alfred, *Peace, Power, Righteousness: An Indigenous Manifesto* (Don Mills, ON: Oxford University Press Canada, 1999) at 55–69; and Alfred, "Sovereignty" in Barker, *supra* note 4, although he would challenge the entire value of sovereignty, including on the part of the state.

Canadian institutions are sovereign in a manner that excludes Indigenous sovereignty. Canadian sovereignty is taken to be a fact of history, no longer open to doubt in a Canadian court. The Supreme Court of Canada's 1990 decision in *R v Sparrow* is characteristic: "[T]here was from the outset never any doubt that sovereignty and legislative power, and indeed the underlying title, to such lands vested in the Crown."[15] However, in recent years, some judges have begun to soften their assertions, allowing doubt to creep in where it was once excluded. While the Supreme Court of Canada has not directly recognized the existence of a continuing Indigenous sovereignty, majority judgments now generally speak of the need to reconcile "the pre-existence of aboriginal societies" or "prior Aboriginal occupation" with the Crown's sovereignty.[16] Indeed, those or like phrases have become almost a mantra in recent Supreme Court decisions on Indigenous rights. In *Haida Nation*, the Court took another step, noting that treaties "serve to reconcile pre-existing Aboriginal *sovereignty* with assumed Crown sovereignty."[17] The Court has repeatedly said that the requirement of reconciliation is the driving force underlying section 35.[18]

Moreover, the Court has begun to qualify its references to Crown sovereignty. It has, for example, spoken of that sovereignty as "asserted" or "assumed."[19] This qualification is open to two possible interpretations. First, the Crown's "assertion of sovereignty" may simply refer to its

---

15 [1990] 1 SCR 1075 at para 49; Asch & Macklem, *supra* note 3. See also *Calder v British Columbia (AG)*, [1973] SCR 313; *Guerin v Canada*, [1984] 2 SCR 335; and the majority's decision in *Delgamuukw* (BCCA), *supra* note 9, which held that the division of legislative authority in the *Constitution Act, 1867* excluded Indigenous sovereignty (the Supreme Court of Canada in *Delgamuukw* declined to address this issue: *supra* note 2). The issue was squarely raised in relation to Australia – and rejected summarily as disclosing no cause of action, even with respect to the limited sovereignty in the Marshall judgments – in *Coe v Commonwealth* [1979] HCA 68; (1979) 24 ALR 118. There, Gibbs J stated (at para 12), "The contention that there is in Australia an aboriginal nation exercising sovereignty, even of a limited kind, is quite impossible in law to maintain."

16 *Van der Peet, supra* note 4 at para 31; *Delgamuukw, supra* note 2 at para 186; *Haida Nation v British Columbia (Minister of Forests)*, 2004 SCC 73, [2004] 3 SCR 511 at para 17; *Taku River Tlingit First Nation v British Columbia (Project Assessment Director)*, 2004 SCC 74, [2004] 3 SCR 550 at para 42.

17 *Haida Nation, ibid* at para 20 [emphasis added].

18 This purpose was first put forward in *Van der Peet, supra* note 4 at para 31. See also *Haida Nation, ibid; Taku River, supra* note 16 at para 42; and *Delgamuukw, supra* note 2 at para 137.

19 See, for example, *Taku River, ibid* at para 24; *Haida Nation, ibid* at paras 20 and 26.

acquisition of sovereignty. On this view, the assertion of sovereignty generates the need for reconciliation simply because the government has taken responsibility for Indigenous peoples, much as a fiduciary assumes an obligation upon taking responsibility for another's interests. On this view, the use of "asserted" involves no acknowledgment that Crown sovereignty is in any way impaired. There is, however, a second possibility, namely that the assertion of Crown sovereignty, being unilateral, is incomplete or diminished. On this view, Canada's claim to exercise legitimate authority over Indigenous peoples is impaired because Indigenous peoples have not consented to that authority.[20] Canadian institutions may rest upon some conception of popular sovereignty when it comes to non-Indigenous Canadians, but the same cannot be said of Indigenous peoples. It is this diminished character that requires reconciliation with Indigenous peoples so that Canadian sovereignty can be perfected. This latter view is supported by the Court's use of the adjective "*de facto*" to describe the Crown's sovereignty when speaking of the need for reconciliation in *Taku River Tlingit First Nation v British Columbia (Project Assessment Director)*:

> The purpose of s. 35(1) of the *Constitution Act, 1982* is to facilitate the ultimate reconciliation of prior Aboriginal occupation with *de facto* Crown sovereignty. Pending settlement, the Crown is bound by its honour to balance societal and Aboriginal interests in making decisions that may affect Aboriginal claims.[21]

This reading is also consistent with *Haida Nation*, which speaks of "sovereignty claims [being] reconciled through the process of honourable negotiation."[22]

---

20 Borrows, "Tracking Trajectories," *supra* note 3 at 309–10; Brian Slattery, "Aboriginal Rights and the Honour of the Crown" (2005) 29 SCLR (2d) 433 at 437–38; Mark Walters, "The Morality of Aboriginal Law" (2005) 31 Queen's LJ 470 at 515–16. The language of "consent" itself often hides more than it reveals. Some common uses of "consent" – those that emphasize consistency with one's tradition, custom, and usage – harmonize closely with Sovereignty 3 below. See Jeremy Webber, "The Meanings of Consent" in Jeremy Webber & Colin M Macleod, eds, *Between Consenting Peoples: Political Community and the Meaning of Consent* (Vancouver: UBC Press, 2010) 3.
21 *Taku River, supra* note 16 at para 42. *Haida Nation, supra* note 16 at para 32 speaks of the Crown's "*de facto* control of land and resources."
22 *Haida Nation, ibid* at para 20 (see also para 25).

The Court has expressly acknowledged the existence of Indigenous sovereignty only in *Haida Nation,* and then without clear recognition of that sovereignty continuing today.[23] Rather, it has generally spoken of "prior Aboriginal occupation" or "the pre-existence of aboriginal societies." On at least one occasion, however, two members of the Court have suggested that Indigenous sovereignty not only pre-existed Canadian sovereignty but may continue to exist, albeit in modified form. In *Mitchell v Canada (Minister of National Revenue)* (2001), Binnie J (supported by Major J in a judgment concurring with the majority in result) discusses at length the question of Indigenous sovereignty, notes that internal self-government on the model of the Marshall judgments would not be incompatible with an overarching Crown sovereignty, and expressly leaves open the question of whether Indigenous peoples might be said to have some kind of "shared" or "merged" sovereignty within the framework of the Canadian state.[24] He draws the language of "merged" or "shared" sovereignty from the final *Report of the Royal Commission on Aboriginal Peoples.* "Merged sovereignty" suggests that "aboriginal and non-aboriginal Canadians together form a sovereign entity," while "shared sovereignty" describes something akin to federalism.[25] While Binnie J does not come to any conclusions on the point, even the suggestion that Indigenous sovereignty has some continuing force in Canada represents a new position for the Court.[26]

There have also been important developments outside the courts. Canadian governments have acknowledged an Indigenous right of self-government in constitutional negotiations, although those negotiations did not lead to constitutional amendments, and the term "sovereignty" was not used to describe the right. The clearest example is

---

23   *Ibid.*
24   2001 SCC 33, [2001] 1 SCR 911. The discussion of sovereignty is found at paras 125–35. McLachlin CJ, writing the majority decision, expressly declines to discuss questions of sovereignty: paras 63–64.
25   *Ibid* at paras 129–34. See Royal Commission, *supra* note 6 at 228–32, and the criticisms of Binnie J's use of merged sovereignty in Gordon Christie, "The Court's Exercise of Plenary Power: Rewriting the Two Row Wampum" (2002) 16 SCLR 285 at 294–95; and Walters, *supra* note 20 at 511–12.
26   There has been some disagreement following *Mitchell* as to the significance of Binnie J's reasons, especially as he relied on shared or merged sovereignty to underpin his acceptance of the "sovereign incompatibility" doctrine. See Moodie, *supra* note 14 at 29–31, summarizing the varying points of view; Moodie himself takes the view that Binnie J's judgment represents progress, suggesting that the approach in *Mitchell* could ease the way for the recognition of an Indigenous right to self-government.

found in the 1992 Charlottetown Accord, which would have recognized that "[t]he Aboriginal peoples of Canada have the inherent right of self-government within Canada."[27] The prime minister of the day, all provincial premiers, the two territorial leaders, and the leaders of four national Aboriginal organizations all agreed to that bundle of constitutional amendments, although it was ultimately abandoned after a majority of voters rejected the package in a national referendum. The accord's description of the right as "inherent" could be seen as an acceptance of Indigenous sovereignty, at least in one of the senses described below. Moreover, the accord stated that the right was to be interpreted "in a manner consistent with the recognition of the governments of the Aboriginal peoples of Canada as constituting one of three orders of government in Canada," clearly drawing an analogy between Indigenous governments and the federal and provincial governments, which are generally described as being sovereign in their jurisdictions.[28] The accord called for further negotiations to determine the mode of exercising the right, with those negotiations supervised by the courts.[29] The accord as a whole was rejected in the referendum and so, of course, never came into effect. Nevertheless, it is a striking example of non-Indigenous governments' willingness to contemplate the recognition of a constitutionally entrenched right of self-government.

In 1995, the federal government issued a policy document recognizing an Aboriginal right to self-government; although not rising to the level of law (let alone constitutional recognition), the policy affirms many of the concepts from the accord. It notes that "the Aboriginal peoples of Canada have the right to govern themselves in relation to matters that are internal to their communities, integral to their unique cultures, identities, traditions, languages and institutions, and with respect to their special relationship to their land and their resources."[30]

---

27 *Draft Legal Text: October 9, 1992* [Charlottetown Accord], proposed s 35.1(1) to be enacted by s 29. For a full discussion of the Charlottetown Accord, see Webber, *supra* note 7 at 162–75.

28 *Ibid*, proposed s 35.1(2).

29 *Ibid*, proposed ss 35.1(4), 35.2, and 35.3.

30 Minister of Indian affairs and northern development, *Aboriginal Self-Government: The Government of Canada's Approach to Implementation of the Inherent Right and the Negotiation of Aboriginal Self-Government* (Ottawa: Public Works and Government Services, 1995) at 3. See further discussion of this and other federal acknowledgments of the inherent right of self-government in royal commission, *supra* note 6 at 202–05.

The final report of the Royal Commission on Aboriginal Peoples in 1996 specifically adopted the language of sovereignty when recommending that all governments in Canada recognize Indigenous peoples as one of three orders of government, in which each order "operates within its own distinct sovereign sphere, as defined by the Canadian constitution, and exercises authority within spheres of jurisdiction having both overlapping and exclusive components" (although this recommendation too had no force of law).[31]

In addition, some of the provincial governments – especially British Columbia – have shown a willingness to agree to disagree, expressly, on the location of sovereignty. The most striking (but not the only) example is the *Haida Gwaii Reconciliation Act* of 2010,[32] an act of the BC Legislature. The recitals in the *Act's* preamble declare that the agreement of the Haida Nation and British Columbia to the Kunst'aa guu – Kunst'aayah Reconciliation Protocol is "an incremental step in the process of the reconciliation of the Haida and Crown title" and a framework "to guide joint decision-making regarding land and natural resource management on Haida Gwaii." But the most remarkable recital is the following:

> WHEREAS the Kunst'aa guu – Kunst'aayah Reconciliation Protocol provides that the Haida Nation and British Columbia hold differing views with regard to sovereignty, title, ownership and jurisdiction over Haida Gwaii, under the Kunst'aa guu – Kunst'aayah Reconciliation Protocol the Haida Nation and British Columbia will operate under their respective authorities and jurisdictions.

Here, in an enactment of the BC legislature, we see that legislature acknowledging that there is a competing view on the location of sovereignty and accepting that its rival claimant to sovereignty will act according to its own conception of due authority. The legislature then proceeds to implement an agreement with its rival on "joint decision-making respecting lands and natural resources on Haida Gwaii" (which involves, among other things, changing the name of the Queen Charlotte Islands to Haida Gwaii and establishing a special collaborative land-management regime for the Islands).

---

31 Royal Commission, *supra* note 6 at 228–32 and 310 (quotation at 232).
32 SBC 2010, c 17.

The Kunst'aa guu – Kunst'aayah Reconciliation Protocol itself is even more striking.[33] It begins by stating, "The Parties hold differing views with regard to sovereignty, title, ownership and jurisdiction over Haida Gwaii," and then it sets out those views in two parallel columns:

The Haida Nation asserts that:	British Columbia asserts that:
Haida Gwaii is Haida lands, including the waters and resources, subject to the rights, sovereignty, ownership, jurisdiction and collective Title of the Haida Nation who will manage Haida Gwaii in accordance with its laws, policies, customs and traditions.	Haida Gwaii is Crown land, subject to certain private rights or interests, and subject to the sovereignty of her Majesty the Queen and the legislative jurisdiction of the Parliament of Canada and the Legislature of the Province of British Columbia.

Like the statute, the protocol makes clear that "the Parties will operate under their respective authorities and jurisdictions."

This is the most obvious example of a Canadian legislature acknowledging an Indigenous claim to sovereignty and being willing to work, at least to some degree, with that claim. Most references to Indigenous governmental authority avoid the language of sovereignty, speaking instead of self-government or eschewing any conceptual framing and simply accepting, in practice, the autonomous decision-making authority of Indigenous peoples. Developments such as Binnie J's judgment in *Mitchell* and the *Haida Gwaii Reconciliation Act* are tentative, experimental, groping – certainly not definitive. But how should we understand them? What are they groping for?

Four Meanings of Sovereignty

Sovereignty is one of those concepts that harbour disparate but frequently combined claims. In the context of non-state societies, and especially when dealing with the relations between those societies and the states into which they have been incorporated, one must distinguish

---

33 Kunst'aa guu – Kunst'aayah Reconciliation Protocol (14 December 2009), between the Haida Nation and Her Majesty the Queen in Right of the Province of British Columbia, online: <www.llbc.leg.bc.ca/public/pubdocs/bcdocs2010/462194/haida_reconciliation_protocol.pdf>. See also the preamble to the Strategic Land Use Planning Agreement (27 June 2006) between the Heiltsuk First Nation and the BC Government, online: <www.for.gov.bc.ca/tasb/slrp/lrmp/nanaimo/central_north_coast/docs/Heiltsuk_FN_Signed_SLUPA.pdf>.

among these claims, for they have significantly different implications that may be differentially in issue.

Here I explore four such claims. There is a fifth that will not figure in the discussion that follows: the role of a sovereign in providing a unified, often personalized, representation of a political community as a whole, in the sense that one might say that one's monarch is one's "sovereign." This is perhaps the oldest signification of sovereignty. It has been relevant to Indigenous/non-Indigenous relations – for example, to treaty peoples' insistence that their treaties are with the British monarch in a sense strongly identified with the person of that monarch, not a governmental abstraction (though perhaps still with a symbolic dimension attached to the monarch's person, expressed as fatherhood or motherhood).[34] It is also an important aspect of the conceptions of sovereignty associated with the political theorists Thomas Hobbes and Carl Schmitt, other aspects of which will feature in the argument that follows.[35] But it has little impact on the contemporary self-government debate. I shall therefore leave it aside.

Sovereignty 1: Final Power of Decision

First, sovereignty is commonly used to denote the final power of decision – ultimate authority over the existence and application of rights

---

34 See *R v Secretary of State for Foreign and Commonwealth Affairs, ex parte Indian Association of Alberta* [1982] 2 All ER 118 (CA) (where First Nations objected to patriation on this basis). For fatherhood, see Richard White, *The Middle Ground : Indians, Empires, and Republics in the Great Lakes Region, 1650–1815* (Cambridge: Cambridge University Press, 1991); for motherhood, Aimée Craft, *Breathing Life into the Stone Fort Treaty: An Anishnabe Understanding of Treaty One* (Winnipeg: Purich, 2013); and for the continuing role of the monarch as a symbolic focus of unity, Jeremy Webber, "Constitutional Poetry: The Tension between Symbolic and Functional Aims in Constitutional Reform" (1999) 21 Sydney L Rev 260 at 275–76. See also royal commission, *supra* note 6 at 228–29, where the Crown is said to symbolize "the association of the various political units that make up the country."

35 Thomas Hobbes, *Leviathan*, ed by CB Macpherson (London: Penguin, 1968) at 227; Carl Schmitt, *The Concept of the Political* (New Brunswick, NJ: Rutgers University Press, 1976); Ulrich K Preuss, "Political Order and Democracy: Carl Schmitt and His Influence" in Chantal Mouffe, ed, *The Challenge of Carl Schmitt* (London: Verso, 1999) 155; Jeremy Webber, "National Sovereignty, Migration, and the Tenuous Hold of International Legality: The Resurfacing (and Resubmersion?) of Carl Schmitt" in *Of States, Rights, and Social Closure: Governing Migration and Citizenship* (New York: Palgrave Macmillan, 2008) 61. Here, I will draw on Hobbes's and Schmitt's conceptions of sovereignty through the work of Martin Loughlin rather than directly.

and obligations, the entitlement to make or unmake any right whatever.[36] This sense of sovereignty as the entitlement to utterly "supreme power" – which I shall call Sovereignty 1 – has long historical roots.[37] It plays a very prominent role in the treatment of Indigenous rights. It is on this basis, for example, that discussions of Aboriginal rights often presume that the Crown has the right to infringe, limit, or extinguish those rights. I also suspect that it is the principal reason that Canadian decision-makers have been reluctant to concede the existence of an Indigenous sovereignty. It is highly doubtful that Canadian courts and governments would ever accept that Indigenous peoples have a unilateral power to determine their legal relations with the rest of Canada.[38] At most, one might imagine that something like this ultimate power might be conceded with respect to internal Indigenous concerns[39] (although the definition of "internal" would no doubt elicit considerable debate). Some Indigenous peoples – notably the Mohawk – have claimed this form of sovereignty.[40] If Canadian authorities ever acknowledge a form of Indigenous sovereignty, however, it is almost certain to be something other than an ultimate power of decision, at least with respect to intercommunal matters.

It may be that developments in Aboriginal rights have nevertheless reshaped Sovereignty 1 in one particular way: they have, to some degree, limited the Canadian governments' assertion of this form of sovereignty. The conditions imposed on any attempt to infringe or extinguish Indigenous rights in *Delgamuukw v British Columbia* and *Tsilhqot'in Nation v British Columbia* (requiring either Indigenous consent or justification for the incursion, in which latter case "the government must show: (1) that it discharged its procedural duty to consult

---

36 The latter phrase is adapted from Dicey's famous formulation of parliamentary sovereignty: AV Dicey, *Introduction to the Study of the Law of the Constitution*, 8th ed (London: Macmillan, 1915) at 3–4.

37 Martin Loughlin, *Sword & Scales: An Examination of the Relationship between Law & Politics* (Oxford: Hart, 2000) at 125.

38 In the United States, where Indigenous peoples are recognized as holding a limited form of sovereignty, the courts have imposed strict limitations on external exercises of sovereignty: see *supra* note 4.

39 In *Delgamuukw* (BCCA), *supra* note 9 at paras 709–16, Lambert J, in his dissenting reasons, concludes that Indigenous peoples retain power to govern internal matters, although he accepts that "sovereignty" (apparently Sovereignty 1) resides with Canadian institutions.

40 Royal commission, *supra* note 6 at 109.

and accommodate, (2) that its actions were backed by a compelling and substantial objective; and (3) that the governmental action is consistent with the Crown's fiduciary obligation to the group")[41] represent an auto-limitation, by the Canadian legal order, on its exercise of Sovereignty 1. While the scope of that limitation is not fully clear, it seems clear that certain forms of infringement or extinguishment by unilateral parliamentary action – infringements that were not supported by a sufficiently compelling and substantial objective, for example – would be prohibited without Indigenous consent. Of course, it might be that, even if they are interpreted at their most demanding level, the *Delgamuukw* and *Tsilhqot'in* tests would still allow even those forms of extinguishment by constitutional amendment. Or, if an amendment of this kind were attempted, might we encounter the limits to Canadian constitutional legitimacy, so that the Canadian courts develop something equivalent to the "basic structure doctrine" of the Supreme Court of India, which bars the state from making constitutional amendments that alter the "essential features" of the constitution?[42] Or, more likely, might we see the simple rejection by Aboriginal peoples of any claim whatever of the Canadian constitution to authority? Might we encounter, in other words, sovereignty's dependence upon some minimal acquiescence on the part of those who are subject to it (as Gandhi saw in relation to pre-Independence India, when he argued that Indians simply refuse to cooperate in the exercise of British authority)?[43] Without some acceptance, the exercise of governmental authority ceases, with respect to its subjects, to have any dimension of right. It ceases to be sovereignty and becomes sheer domination.

In any case, the more that the power to make or unmake any right whatever is hedged about by restrictions and conditions – the more that

---

41 *Supra* note 2 at paras 168–69; *Tsilhqot'in Nation v British Columbia*, 2014 SCC 44, quotation at para 77. But note that in these judgments the restriction appears to be an *auto*-limitation, ultimately presuming the sovereign right of the non-Indigenous legal order to determine whether to limit itself. For a critique, see John Borrows, "Sovereignty's Alchemy: An Analysis of *Delgamuukw v British Columbia*" (1999) 37 Osgoode Hall LJ 537.

42 Sudhir Krishnaswamy, *Democracy and Constitutionalism in India: A Study of the Basic Structure Doctrine* (New Delhi: Oxford University Press, 2009).

43 MK Gandhi, *Hind Swaraj and Other Writings* (New Delhi: Cambridge University Press, 1997) at 39–41 and 72. Indeed, one might imagine a similarly conclusive rejection by Canadians if the United Kingdom were to seek to repeal the *Canada Act 1982* (UK), 1982, c 11: see Brian Slattery, "The Independence of Canada" (1983) 5 SCLR 369.

the infringement of Aboriginal rights is made dependent on conditions of justification, prior negotiations, or Indigenous consent – the more Sovereignty 1 recedes into the background, no longer a dominant feature of the parties' relationship.

Sovereignty 2: Status as a State in International Law

Second, sovereignty can refer to the exclusive ability to represent a specific population and territory in international law – to the possession, in other words, of the distinctive international legal personality accorded to states. This is Sovereignty 2. Like Sovereignty 1, Sovereignty 2 has been at issue in discussions of Indigenous rights. It has, for example, bedevilled the discussion of the status of Aboriginal treaties, with the question ultimately being fudged by considering Aboriginal treaties to be sui generis: genuine treaties, but treaties that are not dependent on their Indigenous signatories having full international personality as states.[44] Scholars have also, in one specific way, invoked the international form of sovereignty in the self-government debate: Indigenous peoples are often said to have had international sovereignty before the coming of the colonists, a sovereignty that, in the transactions with the newcomers, was never surrendered or extinguished.[45]

It does not appear, however, that Sovereignty 2 plays much role in the current debate over the scope and foundation of Indigenous governance. At some point, Indigenous peoples may concertedly advance a claim for full international statehood; certainly, they already want to be considered "peoples" in international law, possessing the right of self-determination.[46] But at least for now, with the possible exception of the Mohawk, most appear to be content with an international role that does not reach the level of full statehood. What they seek is recognition of substantial autonomous jurisdictions with respect to their people, their lands, and relations with non-Indigenous governments.

---

44 *Simon v R*, [1985] 2 SCR 387 at para 33; *R v Sioui, supra* note 6 at 1037–43.
45 *Supra*, note 3. Sovereignty 2 is also the jumping-off point of Asch's argument in Michael Asch, *On Being Here to Stay: Treaties and Aboriginal Rights in Canada* (Toronto: University of Toronto Press, 2014), although Asch then suggests that we reject that form of sovereignty and move to a position having close affinities with the argument in this chapter.
46 See, generally, royal commission, *supra* note 6 at 108–10, 161–75, and 202; Jeff Corntassel & TH Primeau, "Indigenous 'Sovereignty' and International Law: Revised Strategies for Pursuing 'Self-Determination'" (1995) 17:2 Hum Rts Q 343.

It is those autonomous jurisdictions, not international statehood, that appear to be in issue in the developments noted above. The analogy to the sovereignty of the provinces in the Charlottetown Accord, for example, suggests a focus on internal, not international, relations.

Sovereignty 3: The Originating Source of Law

Third, sovereignty can refer to the idea that law and the associated governmental rights originate from within the particular people's own traditions. They have their own autochthonous origin, their own autochthonous legitimacy; they are not the result of a grant of authority from any other entity (other than, in some traditions, a supernatural entity). This might be said to be Sovereignty 3. It has certainly been in issue in Indigenous rights. Indeed, it is the most natural meaning of the "inherent right of self-government."[47] It aligns closely with the concept of sovereignty that the Royal Commission on Aboriginal Peoples understood Indigenous peoples to be using:

> For many Aboriginal people, this is perhaps the most basic definition of sovereignty – the right to know who and what you are. Sovereignty is the natural right of all human beings to define, sustain and perpetuate their identities as individuals, communities and nations.

After a review of comments made by Indigenous representatives, the commission continued:[48]

> From this perspective, sovereignty is seen as an inherent attribute, flowing from sources within a people or nation rather than from external sources such as international law, common law or the Constitution. Herb George of the Gitksan and Wet'suwet'en stated:
>
> > ... If this issue is to be dealt with in a fair way, then what is required is a strong recommendation from this Commission to government that the source of our rights, the source of our lives and the source of

---

47 Webber, *supra* note 7 at 265–66.
48 Royal commission, *supra* note 6 at 105 and 107 (see also 201–02). See also Stark, "Nenabozho's Smart Berries" *supra* note 11 at 342–44; Wallace Coffey & Rebecca Tsosie, "Rethinking the Tribal Sovereignty Doctrine: Cultural Sovereignty and the Collective Future of Indian Nations" (2001) 12 Stan L & Pol'y Rev 191.

our government is from us. That the source of our lives comes from
Gitksan-Wet'suwet'en law.

This concept of sovereignty is at the core of the developments noted
above. The recitals in the preamble to the *Haida Gwaii Reconciliation
Act*, for example, refer specifically to the separate origin of each party's
claims inhering in their own legal traditions. Interestingly, those recitals
do not exclude the other party's claims or insist that its claims must be
subjected to one's own; they do not, in other words, extend to Sovereignty 1. They expressly contemplate each party operating "under their
respective authorities and jurisdictions."

This self-authorization – this grounding of governmental authority in
one's own institutions and traditions – is also the vision of sovereignty
inherent in the recent move by several First Nations simply to exercise
their jurisdictions without waiting for Canadian institutions to recognize
their authority through treaty or legislation. Indeed, the Haida were one
of the first peoples to adopt this approach. The reliance on self-authorization has limits; without agreement, Indigenous authority is liable to
be contested by Canadian institutions (although there are also instances
of toleration of Indigenous claims, as the *Haida Gwaii Reconciliation Act*
makes clear). Self-authorization alone leaves many dimensions of the
relationship yet to be defined. But the compelling force of this conception
to Indigenous peoples – the sense that the starting point of one's own
political action should be one's own traditions of governance – is clear.

The expressions used by the Supreme Court in the more recent
case law can also be seen as adverting to this kind of sovereignty.
The court explicitly affirms the need to reconcile Crown sovereignty
with the prior presence of the Aboriginal peoples, thereby emphasizing the separate origin of each people's understanding of governmental legitimacy. The suggestion that Canadian sovereignty is somehow
imperfect – merely "asserted" or "de facto" – until it is completed
by some form of legitimacy conferred by Indigenous peoples also
appears to emphasize the separate stems of normativity that exist
in the Canadian context. It implies that the legitimacy of Canadian
institutions vis-à-vis Indigenous peoples must be based on arguments that can appeal to, can engage with, Indigenous traditions –
that arguments of legitimacy that are deployed for non-Indigenous
Canadians do not automatically suffice for Indigenous peoples. The
invocations of "shared" and "merged" sovereignty in the report of the
Royal Commission on Aboriginal Peoples and in Binnie J's judgment

in *Mitchell* also carry this implication; they seek, above all, to conceive of Canadian sovereignty as the product of powers flowing from both Indigenous and non-Indigenous sources.[49]

This understanding of sovereignty also harmonizes well with two of the dominant theories of Aboriginal title, the first of which holds that Indigenous land rights originate in the Indigenous societies themselves, before colonization, and that those rights then survive the assertion of colonial sovereignty and are recognized by the newly imposed order; and the second that holds that the law of Aboriginal title is inter-societal law, emerging from the interaction of Indigenous and non-Indigenous peoples.[50] If either of these theories is sustained, Indigenous legal traditions continue to be an operative force in the post-contact period. On the first theory, they are essential, even to the determination of who is entitled to hold the title today – who is the rightful descendant of the original holder of the lands. At the very least, some conception of a collective agent, able to make decisions with respect to the land, must continue, together with a set of principles to govern rights of succession and powers of decision-making. On the second theory, Aboriginal title is the result of a mediation between Indigenous and non-Indigenous forms of legality. The law of Aboriginal title, then, implicitly acknowledges that Indigenous peoples retain at least some powers of law and governance, and that these find their origin in the people's own traditions.[51]

---

49 Royal commission, *supra* note 6 at 228–32; *Mitchell, supra* note 24 at para 129.

50 For the first, see Slattery, *supra* note 3 at 10–62; *Mabo v Queensland (No 2)* (1992) 107 ALR 1 at 20–42 (Brennan J). For the second, see Brian Slattery, "Understanding Aboriginal Rights" (1987) 66 Can Bar Rev 751; Jeremy Webber, "Relations of Force and Relations of Justice: The Emergence of Normative Community between Colonists and Aboriginal Peoples" (1995) 33 Osgoode Hall LJ 623; Royal Commission on Aboriginal Peoples, *Report of the Royal Commission on Aboriginal Peoples, Vol 1: Looking Forward, Looking Back* (Ottawa: Minister of Supply and Services Canada, 1996) at 99–132.

51 See Jeremy Webber, "Beyond Regret: Mabo's Implications for Australian Constitutionalism," in Duncan Ivison, Paul Patton, & Will Sanders, eds, *Political Theory and the Rights of Indigenous Peoples* (Cambridge: Cambridge University Press, 2000) 60 at 62–74; Webber, "The Public-Law Dimension of Indigenous Property Rights" in Nigel Bankes & Timo Koivurova, eds, *The Proposed Nordic Saami Convention: National and International Dimensions of Indigenous Property Rights* (Oxford: Hart, 2013) 79. Some courts have, however, stumbled over the definition of the scope of these powers, a stumbling generated directly by courts' desire to see non-Indigenous governments as exercising an exclusive sovereignty. This is especially true of Australia, where the majority of the High Court in *Members of the Yorta Yorta Aboriginal Community v Victoria* [2002] HCA 58 at para 43 insisted, "Upon the Crown acquiring sovereignty, the normative or law-making system which then existed could not thereafter

Unlike Sovereignty 1, Sovereignty 3 does not require that either party possess a final power of decision, capable of being forced upon the other. It is, at least in theory, consistent with the acceptance of co-determination. That fact may lead some people to suspect that Sovereignty 3 is not sovereignty at all and that it is unidiomatic and a potential source of confusion to apply the term "sovereignty" to it. It is tempting to respond that then one should choose whatever term one wants; my concern is not lexicography but how we might live together. But the objection to Sovereignty 3 is nevertheless misconceived. Consider "popular sovereignty" (which it would be a challenge – to say the least – to expel from the idiom of political theory). Popular sovereignty has always been concerned, above all, with the grounding of governmental authority and only tangentially with the final legal power of decision. Indeed, Dicey's distinction between legal and political sovereignty, where Parliament holds the former and the people the latter, can be understood only when one distinguishes the power to make a decision from the political grounding of that power.[52] Popular sovereignty is a subset of Sovereignty 3.

An embrace of Sovereignty 3, and a corresponding reluctance to insist on Sovereignty 1, may well be implicit in a remarkable aspect of the courts' treatment of Indigenous rights, at least until *Tsilhqot'in Nation*, namely their signal reluctance to issue definitive determinations of Aboriginal title and their strong exhortations to the parties to negotiate.[53] This may result simply from the courts' belief that the complexity of Aboriginal title requires that parties settle any outcome

---

validly create new rights, duties or interests," and yet went on to acknowledge a range of ways in which the Indigenous legal order must continue to operate after the Crown's acquisition of sovereignty, including (at para 44): "Nor is it to say that account could never be taken of any alteration to, or development of, that traditional law and custom that occurred after sovereignty. Account may have to be taken of developments at least of a kind contemplated by that traditional law and custom. Indeed, in this matter, both the claimants and respondents accepted that there could be 'significant adaptations.'" It is difficult to see how there could be such adaptations without some law-making power remaining in the community.

52 Dicey, *supra* note 36 at 26ff.

53 See in particular *Delgamuukw*, *supra* note 2 at para 186; *Sparrow*, *supra* note 15 at 1119. One suspects that the trial decision in *Tsilhqot'in Nation v British Columbia*, 2007 BCSC 1700, like the SCC's decision in *Delgamuukw*, seized upon a perceived defect of pleading to encourage the parties to negotiate, while nevertheless saying enough about the substance of the right to guide the outcome. In *Haida Nation*, *supra* note 16 at para 20, the Court emphasizes "the process of honourable negotiation" as the mode by which "sovereignty claims" are reconciled.

among themselves.[54] I suspect, however, that there is more going on here – that the Court believes that any durable solution cannot simply be imposed by a non-Indigenous institution but should instead be a negotiated resolution between two competing orders of right, two traditions of law and governance. It constitutes, in other words, an implicit recognition of Sovereignty 3. In *Tsilhqot'in Nation*, the court has stepped beyond this reticence to make the first modern declaration of title. I suspect that governments' shirking of their obligations to address these claims forced the issue. But even here, the Court declares that section 35 – especially the process by which incursions onto Aboriginal title might be justified – "provides a framework to facilitate negotiations and reconciliation of Aboriginal interests with those of the broader public."[55] Co-definition remains the Court's desired objective.

Sovereignty 4: A Unified and Rationalized Order of Law

Finally, a fourth conception of sovereignty lurks in Indigenous/non-Indigenous relations, namely the presumption that any society must be organized in a comprehensive fashion, in conformity to a consistent set of legal principles, with mechanisms for adjudicating disagreements so that the legal order as a whole is coherent and rationalized. This notion of sovereignty, Sovereignty 4, emphasizes the unity and consistency of a sovereign order. In the past, it has led some theorists to doubt the viability of any form of divided sovereignty, including federalism – although contemporary theorists of sovereignty interpret federalism as being consistent with Sovereignty 4, for it is the federal order as a whole, not its component parts, that is sovereign.[56] At any rate, this form of sovereignty presumes a need for rationalized state-like structures of authority, with mechanisms

---

54 This is one of the considerations suggested in *Delgamuukw* (SCC) when the court declines to address the issue of self-government: *supra* note 2 at paras 170–71.

55 *Tsilhqot'in Nation, supra* note 41 at para 118. See also para 82, where the court cites Lamer CJ's exhortation to reconciliation on the basis that we are all "here to stay."

56 For an account of these debates at the time of the creation of the United States, see Alison LaCroix, *The Ideological Origins of American Federalism* (Cambridge, MA: Harvard University Press, 2010). For a statement of the modern position, see Martin Loughlin, *The Idea of Public Law* (Oxford: Oxford University Press, 2003) at 84–85.

for definitive decision, so that the order can achieve the normative coherence required.

Sovereignty 4's emphasis on state-like structures may clash with the highly decentralized nature of many Indigenous orders, in which different units – clans, families, other lineage groups, villages, the people as a whole – often have their own spheres of authority and indeed their own distinctive variants of the tradition. These variants may not be consistent with those of other units and may be reconciled only in a partial and provisional way, when and to the extent necessary, through a process of discussion and deliberation.[57] Taiaiake Alfred has argued against the use of sovereignty to refer to Indigenous societies precisely because he believes it includes Sovereignty 4, which may then serve to remake Indigenous institutions in the image of the state.[58] Seeking sovereignty, he writes, pushes Indigenous peoples "towards acceptance of forms of government that more closely resemble the state than traditional systems" and requires that they accept (and therefore adopt) an "adversarial and coercive Western notion of power."[59] Note that this objection is specific to Sovereignty 4 and perhaps Sovereignty 1 (given Sovereignty 1's insistence on someone having the final power of decision-making). One can accept Sovereignty 3 without accepting Sovereignty 4. As Patrick Macklem says in response to Alfred's argument, "Nothing inherent in the concept of sovereignty dictates a particular institutional form." He argues that the focus should instead be on "influencing how sovereignty is exercised once Aboriginal peoples are viewed as sovereign within their spheres of authority" (which sounds something like a focus on Sovereignty 3).[60] Not all Indigenous peoples

57 There is a very large literature on the decentralized character of Indigenous orders. For a contribution that explores the process of open and allusive discussion and deliberation that adjudicates and reconciles conflicting traditions among the Gitksan people, see Val Napoleon, "Living Together: Gitksan Legal Reasoning as a Foundation for Consent" in Webber & Macleod, *supra* note 20 at 45.

58 Alfred, *supra* note 14 at 55–69. See also Alfred, *supra* note 4 at 33; Royal Commission, *supra* note 6 at 107–08; and Menno Boldt & J Anthony Long, "Tribal Traditions and European-Western Political Ideologies: The Dilemma of Canada's Native Indians" in Boldt & Long, eds, *The Quest for Justice: Aboriginal Peoples and Aboriginal Rights* (Toronto: University of Toronto Press, 1985) 333.

59 Alfred, *supra* note 14 at 57, 59.

60 Patrick Macklem, *Indigenous Difference and the Constitution of Canada* (Toronto: University of Toronto Press, 2001) at 112.

reject Sovereignty 4.[61] State-like structures have gained a measure of legitimacy in many Indigenous communities, and the challenge then becomes how to reconcile traditional and band structures internally, not the simple rejection of state-like forms. Nevertheless, one should not fall into Sovereignty 4 without realizing that it may not fit with Indigenous structures of authority.

To many non-Indigenous jurists, Sovereignty 4 goes without saying. They have a hard time imagining a species of law that does not conform to this demand for coherence. One suspects that this demand accounts, at least in part, for the old authorities that Indigenous peoples had no law, or for many contemporary decisions that, faced with multiple accounts of an Indigenous tradition, end up rejecting any right based on those traditions. The problem may not lie with the forms of social ordering in Indigenous societies, however. It may lie with non-Indigenous jurists' failure to understand those forms of ordering as law and to explore how law and governance function in societies in which decision-making power is widely distributed.[62]

Sovereignty's Unanswered Questions

This account strongly suggests, then, that the demand for self-government relates, above all, to Sovereignty 3, not the other forms of sovereignty. Moreover, it suggests that one can pursue Sovereignty 3 without settling Sovereignty 1 – that one can bracket the latter while pursuing the former. But is this marginalization of Sovereignty 1 a problem? Does it sidestep a tough form of sovereignty that remains operative in Canadian law? After all, even if Sovereignty 1 has been limited, it has certainly not disappeared and, to the extent it remains, the parties are positioned in acutely asymmetrical ways with respect to it. There has never been even a shadow of an acknowledgment in Canadian law

---

61 At the very least, many peoples combine traditional institutions with state-like institutions descended from band governments under the *Indian Act*. The Royal Commission on Aboriginal Peoples placed considerable emphasis on the consolidation of Indigenous bands into nations precisely so that they could exercise a range of governmental functions: Royal Commission, *supra* note 6 at 169ff. That recommendation apparently contemplates at least a partial embrace of Sovereignty 4.

62 Napoleon, *supra* note 57, would be a good place to start. See also Val Napoleon, *Ayook: Gitksan Legal Order, Law and Legal Theory* (PhD Thesis, University of Victoria, 2009) [unpublished].

that Indigenous peoples might possess Sovereignty 1 with respect to their interactions with non-Indigenous people and interests. On the contrary, the Canadian courts have consistently maintained that, prior to the enactment of section 35, the Canadian Parliament could do anything it wanted with Indigenous interests, as long as its intention were sufficiently "clear and plain."[63] To the extent that that ability has been constrained by section 35, the constraint has been constructed, at least formally, through the actions of Canadian institutions using the vehicle of Canadian law. At least in theory, it could be deconstructed by the same means. Moreover, the self-imposed constraint on Sovereignty 1 is by no means complete; the power to initiate infringements of Indigenous interests clearly remains with non-Indigenous governments. They can and do authorize the extraction of resources from lands subject to Aboriginal title and can and do exercise governmental authority over Indigenous people, for purposes ranging from "the development of agriculture, forestry, mining, and hydroelectric power" to "the settlement of foreign populations to support those aims."[64] Thus, much of the value of Aboriginal title – indeed, the very continuation of Indigenous traditions and interests with respect to the land and people more generally – is being whittled away by the provincial and federal governments, with Indigenous peoples able to do little, in Canadian law, to prevent it. The proposed Enbridge pipeline may be the ultimate test of whether there are any real constraints, in Canadian law, on governments' capacity to infringe Indigenous interests without Indigenous consent.

I do not claim, then, that Sovereignty 1 has been rendered irrelevant. Rather, I argue that our preoccupation with Sovereignty 1 has not been helpful, that there are good reasons why it has come to be questioned or bracketed in recent attempts to address Indigenous/non-Indigenous relations, and that we would do well to question it more vigorously and bracket it more concertedly, focusing instead on the heart of the matter, Sovereignty 3. In the attempt to fashion a more satisfactory relationship between Indigenous peoples and the Canadian state, the solution lies not in the recognition that Indigenous peoples have Sovereignty 1, but rather the attenuation of Sovereignty 1 for *both* the Canadian government and Indigenous peoples, so that neither is considered

---

63 See *Sparrow, supra* note 15 at para 37.

64 *Delgamuukw, supra* note 2 at para 165, repeated in *Tsilhqot'in Nation, supra* note 41 at para 83.

to have an unencumbered ultimate power of decision. Arguably, this has been the dominant approach taken by Indigenous peoples themselves in their emphasis on the sharing of the land and their reliance on treaty as the mode of organizing coexistence among peoples. It also resonates with the distributed nature of political authority typical of many Indigenous societies, as Alfred's work makes clear. One can also argue that this approach is implicit, in embryonic form, in the Supreme Court's reluctance to be drawn into the specification of detailed self-government arrangements or even final determinations of title, but instead to exhort the parties to settle these matters by negotiation.[65]

But can the issue of the ultimate power of decision ever be sidelined? Does the attempt to do so simply veil an underlying power that must be inherent in any viable political order? First, the power of decision would not be completely eliminated; at the very least, it would still be possible, at least in theory, to decide anything by the joint concurrence of the parties. It is really the vesting of the ultimate power of decision in either of the parties acting alone that would be constrained. But beyond this clarification, it may well be that the emphasis in many theories of sovereignty on an ultimate power of decision is itself exaggerated.

The most insightful discussion of sovereignty of our times, that of Martin Loughlin, emphasizes the relational nature of sovereignty: the fact that sovereignty inheres – not just ideally but also practically – in a relationship between the citizenry and their government, in which the former accept government acting on their behalf in maintaining and consolidating the social order, while the structures of government themselves contribute to the definition of the people, specifying its boundaries and determining how it fashions and expresses a coherent collective voice.[66] Sovereignty, in his conception, "is the name given to express the quality of the political relationship that is formed between the state and the people."[67] The extent of government's capacity to act depends on its ability to build and maintain the general support of the populace for the overall structure of the society and of its institutions, a process that is, of course, a continual work in progress given the need to work with – Loughlin says "manage" – the diverse

---

65 See *supra* note 53.
66 Loughlin, *supra* note 56 at 72–98.
67 *Ibid* at 83.

attitudes expressed within society.[68] This relational focus dovetails well with Lon Fuller's emphasis upon the way in which the existence of law, even in non-democratic societies, is a function of a relationship between the government and the governed, rather than simply a unilateral relation of command.[69] It also resonates with the political theory literature on trust, which emphasizes the role of the citizenry's trust in their institutions in sustaining well-ordered societies; if trust is lacking and a government has to rely on coercion alone, the very effectiveness of its pronouncements is curtailed, for their effectiveness is wholly dependent on the state's capacity to bring power to bear at any moment – a capacity that is both limited and expensive to deploy.[70] If sovereignty is fundamentally relational, then the significance of an ultimate, unilateral power of decision becomes attenuated, because the struggle to build and maintain legitimacy is itself a condition of government's ability to act. What government can "decide" is a function of that legitimacy.

It may well be, then, that Sovereignty 3 ends up being the more significant of the two concepts, for it speaks directly to the foundation of legitimacy, emphasizing the grounding of law and government in the specific normative traditions, the specific normative languages, of the populace that will be subjected to any decision. Reaching for mechanisms by which governmental decisions can draw upon those traditions – Indigenous traditions themselves in areas of Indigenous autonomy, or Indigenous traditions combined with non-Indigenous traditions of governance when dealing with relations across the Indigenous/non-Indigenous divide – may be precisely the way to build the capacity for effective government on these matters.

But can Sovereignty 3 be pursued in a political community marked by deep cultural difference without some notion of Sovereignty 1 in the background, specifying which side wins in case of a conflict? Even Loughlin emphasizes the necessity of a unified, undivided locus of sovereignty, and indeed continues to speak of sovereignty involving an "ultimate"

---

68 *Ibid* at 82.
69 See, e.g., Lon Fuller, *The Morality of Law*, rev'd ed (New Haven, CT: Yale University Press, 1964) at 48.
70 Robert Putnam, *Making Democracy Work: Civic Traditions in Modern Italy* (Princeton: Princeton University Press, 1993). See also Stephen Holmes, *Passions and Constraint: On the Theory of Liberal Democracy* (Chicago: University of Chicago Press, 1995) at 113ff.

power of decision.[71] He goes so far as to say, "[S]overeignty divided is sovereignty destroyed."[72] He does acknowledge that sovereignty inheres in the relationship between the people and the entire governmental structure, so that it is compatible with the separation of governmental powers or a federal system of government.[73] His emphasis on the necessary unity of sovereignty essentially comes down to the argument that the structure of government must be coherent and rationalized across the whole of government – ultimately, Sovereignty 4.

Yet that very rationalization is one of the things that is put into question by a recognition of Indigenous sovereignty, even if only in the form of Sovereignty 3. One might imagine Canada one day finding a federal structure that orders and allocates governmental authority to all parties, Indigenous and non-Indigenous, in a manner essentially acceptable to all. But that seems a very big task at the present moment, given the profound and frequently inconsistent stakes that all parties have in heavily overlapping territories; the very different traditions of normative ordering in relation to those territories; the different traditions of political authority, extending even to the highly distributed forms of decentralized government typical of many Indigenous peoples; and the existence of highly contested areas in which the parties do not agree on how whose contests are to be decided. Accepting some incoherence, some persistence of conflicting ultimate claims, may be a necessary concomitant of any real movement on these issues, as indeed the *Haida Gwaii Reconciliation Act* and other comparable developments have expressly accepted.

I am not convinced that there is a need to attain, now or ever, the level of coherence that Loughlin expects. The ultimate question of who gets to decide, once and for all, is seldom posed; indeed, there is a real issue whether, in the life of a society, one might succeed in never posing it. Most of the time we work within modes of social ordering in which those issues lie well in the background, so that they might effectively be bracketed. Is there anything wrong or fundamentally incoherent, for example, in the Haida and the BC legislature each approving the land-management structures within the *Haida Gwaii Reconciliation Act*, each using its own autonomous traditions of decision-making, as indeed

---

71 Loughlin, *supra* note 56 at 94.
72 *Ibid* at 84.
73 *Ibid*.

they expressly say they are doing? In fact, in societies generally, even culturally homogeneous societies, fundamental questions of legitimacy have frequently been bracketed in a manner that looks not that different from the Haida situation, with that bracketing often persisting for a very long time. Think, for example, of the question of the ultimate grounding of Canadian sovereignty prior to the *Statute of Westminster*. Did it reside in the Canadian structures of government or did it reside in the UK Parliament? Indeed, that same question remained unanswered after the passing of the *Statute of Westminster*, given that Canada's constitution remained, at least in form, a statute of the UK Parliament up until 1982. The *Statute of Westminster* could always, at least in theory, be repealed. The same is true of the *Canada Act 1982*.[74] One might also cite the long contest over the respective authority of the monarch and Parliament in Britain. That contest was ostensibly decided by the English Civil War, pushed in the opposite direction by the Restoration, then decided yet again by the Glorious Revolution; but couldn't those issues have remained bracketed for a much longer time, had the Stuarts been more adept and subtle?[75] Indeed, in some particulars, the relationship between monarch and Parliament did remain an open question long after 1688.

One of the consequences of Loughlin's emphasis on legitimacy as a continual work in progress – an idea implicit in his relational conception of sovereignty – is that, in any constitutional order, fundamentals are constantly open to a measure of disagreement, different parties advancing different theories, so that those fundamentals undergo a continual evolution, although that evolution may be so subterranean that the shifts are discernible only in retrospect. We exist in a situation in which the ultimate resolution of those fundamentals is, in effect, bracketed. It is necessary to ask questions of sovereignty – to ask who gets to decide, to debate what legal order should be brought to bear upon the task of land management in Haida Gwaii, for example. But it may not be necessary to conclusively resolve these questions. It may be possible to acknowledge, explicitly or implicitly, the existence of contending answers and to find some acceptable work-around, precisely as

---

74 See Slattery, *supra* note 43. The repeal of the Statute of Westminster was contemplated but dismissed as a practical possibility in *British Coal Corporation v The King* [1935] AC 500 at 520.

75 See, among many others, Steve Pincus, *1688: The First Modern Revolution* (New Haven, CT: Yale University Press, 2009).

the parties did in the *Haida Gwaii Reconciliation Act*. Indeed, Loughlin's relational theory suggests precisely why it is necessary to reach out to previously excluded populations in a way that may require this bracketing of Sovereignty 1: if there is no real effort to justify government to Indigenous peoples, it is hard to see what separates Canadian institutions today from a simple relationship of colonial domination. If Indigenous peoples are truly to be integral participants in a Canadian legal and political order, we have no alternative but to engage Indigenous peoples' traditions of legitimacy, even if we cannot yet find any stable reconciliation between those traditions and those of non-Indigenous Canadians.

Such issues arise outside Indigenous contexts, too. Consider the *Secession Reference*, which involved comparable questions of legitimacy and sovereignty. In that case the Supreme Court took the kind of approach contemplated here.[76] The Court declined to address the amending formula at all, so as not to insist upon a final means by which Quebec could secede. It acknowledged that tension could arise between the conceptions of political legitimacy held by differently structured democratic communities (Quebec, Canada as a whole, First Nations), and it exhorted the parties to address these tensions through negotiations, not through reliance on an ultimate power of decision.[77] Indeed, it suggested that the ultimate power of decision ought to be shared among the parties:

> The negotiation process precipitated by a decision of a clear majority of the population of Quebec on a clear question to pursue secession would require the reconciliation of various rights and obligations by the representatives of two legitimate majorities, namely, the clear majority of the population of Quebec, and the clear majority of Canada as a whole, whatever that may be. *There can be no suggestion that either of these majorities "trumps" the other.*[78]

Although this was not made express in the judgment, the Court took this approach precisely because it did not want to insist that the expression of democratic decision within the province of Quebec

---

76 *Reference Re Secession of Quebec*, [1998] 2 SCR 217.
77 *Ibid* at paras 88–95.
78 *Ibid* at para 93 [emphasis added].

would be utterly subjected to the will of the rest of Canada (or, if a secession in accordance with the amending formula would require unanimity, as is likely the case,[79] the will of any one province). To act otherwise would have communicated that Quebec was locked within Canada – perhaps even that the relationship was, fundamentally, colonial. The Court's decision renounced any such conclusion, and it did so by emphasizing that the terms of Quebec's participation in Canada had to be open to continued deliberation, with no one position presumed to trump the other.

If all of this is right, then the courts' and governments' willingness to reopen the question of Indigenous sovereignty (however gingerly) creates space to consider how the institutions of Canadian law and government might be defined in complex relationship to both Indigenous and Canadian assertions of sovereignty, without choosing between them. Now, to open those issues is not to settle them. Indeed, we may be groping for some considerable time before we find an adequate response. Moreover, we should never forget, in that search for answers, that there remains an asymmetrical relationship of power among the parties. That fact alone may require action by the courts to ensure that governments take the questions seriously – as the Supreme Court of Canada did in *Haida Nation* when it insisted that governments must consult with Indigenous peoples about potential infringements to their rights prior to a judicial determination of Aboriginal title, and in *Tsilhqot'in Nation* when it made the first modern declaration of Aboriginal title.[80] The courts may be compelled, in other words, to intervene in order to ensure that these issues are grappled with, not ignored, even if the courts are reticent to impose their own definitive solutions. But the questions of sovereignty must nevertheless be asked if we care at all about the justification of Canadian governance to Indigenous peoples. It may be that our practical relations are so complex, burdened by so much history, and still so fraught in conflicting aims that asking the questions, engaging in partial experiments like the *Haida Gwaii Reconciliation Act,* and, when possible, negotiating agreements is the best we can do. But if we are clear on what is fundamentally in issue, we are much more likely to devise responses that are adapted to the real challenges that we face.

79 Jeremy Webber, "The Legality of a Unilateral Declaration of Independence under Canadian Law" (1997) 42 McGill LJ 281.
80 *Haida Nation, supra* note 16; *Tsilhqot'in Nation, supra* note 41.

Moving Forward

In this chapter, my principal aim has been to explore the claims associated with sovereignty, assess their contribution to contemporary debates over self-government, and suggest the general form that progress on these issues should take. It will now be clear that I consider Sovereignty 3 to lie at the heart of the debates. Sovereignty 2 and 4 are much less central. Indeed, they tend to confuse rather than illuminate. To the extent that they are discussed, they are likely to be addressed in attenuated form: in the case of Sovereignty 2, by the recognition of Indigenous peoples as peoples but not as states, having an internal but not an external right of self-determination; and in the case of Sovereignty 4, through the development of mediating institutions between state-like and non-state structures of decision-making so that Indigenous and Canadian institutions can relate productively to one another. Sovereignty 1, on the other hand, has certainly been a constant, though not helpful, presence in our discussions – often unexpressed but hovering in the background nevertheless. Its insistence on always asking who holds the trump card has bedevilled the debate, for we end up stumbling over who should ultimately prevail before we have even begun to talk. This preoccupation is unfortunate and unnecessary. If we wish to build Canada on a foundation broadly acceptable to members of all peoples, the question of who gets to impose their will recedes and the crucial questions become those associated with Sovereignty 3, in particular how the framework of governance can be restructured so that it draws upon all sources of normativity in Canada. We should bracket questions of ultimate determination and get on with the relationship. Indeed, this chapter suggests that, at our best moments, this is precisely what we have begun to do, albeit haltingly.

What difference would it make to privilege Sovereignty 3 in our development of Indigenous self-government? A complete answer lies outside the scope of this chapter, but in conclusion let me suggest three possibilities.

First, once one realizes that the reconciliation in issue is between sovereignties – between legal and governmental orders understood in the light of Sovereignty 3 – then one must pay attention not just to the ultimate terms of settlement but also to the institutions and procedures through which those terms are decided. Many of the courts' pronouncements on reconciliation, for example, suggest that section 35 serves as the framework for reconciliation, which no doubt connotes, for many lawyers, that the interpretation of that provision by the courts, and governments' exercise of their fiduciary obligations, are the principal means by which reconciliation occurs. But don't we need to take Indigenous institutions themselves seriously? Those institutions have their own modes of reasoning, narrative sources, principles of order, norms of interaction embodied in ceremonial and rhetorical forms, and ways of sifting and weighing the diverse opinions on right conduct that exist in decentralized societies.[81] If Sovereignty 3 means anything, it means that Canadian governance must draw on these stems of legitimacy as well. It was once commonly held that the sovereignty of settler nations could not be challenged in the very courts that owe their authority to that sovereignty.[82] The Canadian courts now rightly resile from such a stark position, but there is some logic in the view that the courts are poorly placed to determine challenges to the very legal order from which they derive their authority. At the very least, they cannot be the exclusive forum in which legitimacy and law are adjudicated. Rather than seeking to bring, for example, Indigenous customary law into the courts exclusively via the testimony of a few expert witnesses, who provide their testimony from the witness stand and are then cross-examined by lawyers, we may need to bring non-Indigenous actors into the Indigenous institutions – the feast halls, the long houses – in which Indigenous law is articulated, challenged by other members, refined, and thereby obtains its definition.[83]

This approach does not negate the need for non-Indigenous institutions to get their act together through adjudication under section 35. In large measure, in this task of reconciliation, each party will have to work through the institutional processes that it understands and accepts (as the *Haida Gwaii Reconciliation Act* expressly contemplates). But it is important to realize that section 35 is not the single vehicle through which these issues are reconciled. It is, at most, half of the institutional story. The other half is the process internal to each Indigenous people. This is what it means to surrender one's attachment to Sovereignty 1, or at least to de-emphasize Sovereignty 1 in favour of Sovereignty 3.

---

81 Jeremy Webber, "The Grammar of Customary Law" (2009) 54 McGill LJ 579.
82 See, e.g., *Coe v Commonwealth, supra* note 15 at para 3. See also *Yorta Yorta, supra* note 51 at para 37.
83 See also James Tully, "Reconsidering the BC Treaty Process" in Law Commission of Canada, ed, *Speaking Truth to Power: A Treaty Forum* (Ottawa: Minister of Public Works, 2000) 3 at 11–12. For feasts among the Gitksan, see Napoleon, *supra* note 57.

Second, we have to be more concerned with Indigenous legal traditions themselves. The experiments in reconciling sovereignties will draw from both sets of traditions, not simply from an adaptation of common-law forms. This in turn means that Indigenous legal traditions have to be engaged with the same seriousness of purpose that lawyers bring to non-Indigenous law. Students need to be trained in the specific traditions of particular peoples, the variations among Indigenous institutions, and the contrast between Indigenous and non-Indigenous modes of legality. They need tools for working across traditions, creating mediating practices of law and governance and constructing hybrid institutions at the community/government interface. Students must also attend to the traditions' capacity for criticism and correction. Indigenous traditions, like any system of law, have mechanisms for dealing with tensions and change; they too need careful study.[84]

Now, in emphasizing the adaptation of legal education, I am not suggesting that law schools should displace the learning and deliberation that occurs within communities. On the contrary, any true study of Indigenous law must involve engagement with those processes. But as it stands now, law schools generally ignore these traditions and, in doing so, they fail to provide their students – even Indigenous students – with the tools to reason with them. It is an education of displacement, where students receive wonderful training in the common or civil law but only the briefest introductions to Canada's other legal traditions. We are not equipping ourselves and our students for the challenging task of manoeuvring among traditions. Nor are we equipping governments with satisfactory models of reconciliation.

Third, in allowing for the persistence of conflicting understandings of sovereignty, we must also keep in mind the need for action, for agency. One of the reasons Sovereignty 1 is so pervasive – so attractive, even – is that it does emphasize the capacity to make decisions. If the ultimate power of decision is bracketed, there is a risk that the system might drift towards the path of least resistance: no decision at all. We have to look for ways to make decisions prior to an ultimate resolution (indeed, there may be no "ultimate" resolution). This might, for example, be achieved by lessening the pressure placed on negotiations over fundamental interests. One way to do this – which also protects Indigenous

---

84 See, therefore, the proposal for training in Indigenous law in John Borrows, *Canada's Indigenous Constitution* (Toronto: University of Toronto Press, 2010) at 228ff.

title that has not yet been subject to judicial determination – is by shifting the focus of negotiations from final settlements to interim measures. Interim measures are expressly provisional; possible solutions can be tried without matters having to be decided once and for all, although it would be important for courts to supervise those negotiations to temper imbalances of power. For these reasons, interim measures constituted a principal recommendation of the Royal Commission on Aboriginal Peoples, and court-supervised negotiations were an integral element of the Charlottetown Accord's provisions on self-government. Arguably, the Supreme Court of Canada's decision in *Haida Nation* points towards a similar combination of strategies.[85] Not only did the Court find that the government had a duty to consult with Indigenous people on decisions that could affect "as yet unproven Aboriginal rights and title claims" – a step towards interim measures – but it also affirmed (although without providing detail) that the courts would assess the processes through which such interim measures were devised.[86]

In short, one great challenge of a constitutionalism based on the reconciliation of sovereignties is how to maintain the capacity for change, for movement. A key element in that process may be a turn towards the negotiation of provisional rather than final outcomes – to processes that allow decisions to be made even when full agreement is lacking. Those are features, after all, of decision-making through democratic institutions.[87] Our challenge now is to achieve those characteristics in interactions among societies.

This argument has departed markedly from the way in which some of the literature addresses issues of Indigenous sovereignty – namely, by rewinding the question to the period of early interaction, accepting that Indigenous peoples were sovereign, and tracing the history to see whether a sufficient act took place to transfer or extinguish sovereignty.[88] Instead, it has taken Indigenous and Canadian legal and political orders as established in this land, and has then explored

---

85 Royal Commission, *supra* note 6 at 540–42 and 562–64; *Draft Legal Text, supra* note 27, proposed sections 35.1(4), 35.2, and 35.3; *Haida Nation, supra* note 16.

86 *Haida Nation, ibid* at paras 50, 11, 60–63.

87 Jeremy Webber, "Democratic Decision Making as the First Principle of Contemporary Constitutionalism" in Richard Bauman and Tsvi Kahana, eds, *The Least Examined Branch: The Role of Legislatures in the Constitutional State* (New York: Cambridge University Press, 2006) 411.

88 *Supra* note 3.

the potential for treating those persisting, contemporaneou
eign orders as engaged in common constitutional processes, in which
neither need be taken as definitive. That approach declines to make a
choice between orders. It keeps contending claims in play. But isn't it
truer to our predicament? Our country is made up of overlapping societies, which hold deep significance for their members and for which
the only homeland is right here. Our task is to think through the inter-
relation of those societies as going concerns, not argue as though that
history didn't exist. The approach suggested in this chapter, which contemplates the interaction of contesting sovereignties, is best placed to
capture that predicament.

In his 2012 Hugh Alan Maclean lecture, the eminent Canadian legal
historian Philip Girard examined the first stages of French and English
colonization in what became Canada, when governance was exercised
through the framework of chartered commercial enterprises. He found
it difficult to say much about the location of sovereignty in those early
years because, it seemed to him, the assertion of governmental authority was provisional, experimental, not hard-edged.[89] But isn't the same
true of our contemporary interactions across the Indigenous/non-
Indigenous divide? Aren't we still seeking forms of relationship that
are adequate to our lives together? We are still in the age of encounter.

89 Philip Girard, "Beginnings: Chartered Enterprises and Canadian Legal History"
   (Hugh Alan Maclean Lecture in Legal History, University of Victoria, 22 October
   2012).

4   The Generative Structure of Aboriginal Rights

BRIAN SLATTERY*

Introduction

Are Aboriginal rights historical rights – rights that gained their basic form in the distant past? Or are they generative rights – rights that, although rooted in the past, have the capacity to renew themselves, as organic entities that grow and change? Section 35(1) of the *Constitution Act, 1982*, provides little guidance on the point, referring ambiguously to "existing aboriginal and treaty rights." In the *Van der Peet* case,[1] decided in 1996, the Supreme Court of Canada character- ized Aboriginal rights primarily as historical rights, moulded by the customs and practices of Aboriginal groups at the time of European contact, with only a modest ability to evolve. However, as a brief review of the Court's reasoning reveals, this approach left much to be desired.

In his majority opinion, Antonio Lamer CJ holds that section 35(1) is animated by two main purposes: recognition and reconciliation.[2] With respect to the first, he argues that the doctrine of Aboriginal rights exists because of one simple fact: when Europeans arrived in North America, Aboriginal peoples were already here, living in communities on the land and participating in distinctive cultures, as they had done for centuries. It is this fact that distinguishes Aboriginal peoples from all other groups in Canadian society and mandates their special legal

---

* Adapted with permission of the publisher from vol. 38, *Supreme Court Law Review* (2nd series) (LexisNexis Canada, 2007).

1 *R v Van der Peet*, [1996] SCJ No. 77, [1996] 2 SCR 507.
2 *Ibid* at paras 26–43.

and constitutional status. So a major purpose of section 35(1) is to recognize the prior occupation of Aboriginal peoples.[3]

However, recognition is not the sole purpose of the section, which also aims to secure reconciliation between Indigenous peoples and the Crown. Chief Justice Lamer notes that the essence of Aboriginal rights lies in their bridging of Aboriginal and non-Aboriginal cultures, so that the law of Aboriginal rights is neither entirely English nor entirely Aboriginal in origin: it is a form of inter-societal law that evolved from long-standing practices linking the various communities together.[4]

In light of these two fundamental goals, Lamer CJ proceeds to craft the following test for Aboriginal rights. In order for an activity to qualify as an Aboriginal right, it must be an element of a practice, custom, or tradition that was integral to the distinctive culture of a particular Aboriginal group in the period prior to European contact.[5] If a practice arose only after the critical date of contact, it cannot be an Aboriginal right. Although pre-contact practices are capable of evolving and adapting somewhat to modern conditions, they must maintain continuity with their ancient roots.[6] Applying this test to the case at hand, Lamer CJ holds that the pre-contact practice of fishing for food and ceremonial purposes, with limited exchanges of fish in the familial and kinship context, cannot evolve into a modern Aboriginal right to exchange fish for money or other goods.[7]

Several features of this approach merit comment. First, the *Van der Peet* test assumes that Aboriginal rights are shaped entirely by factors particular to each Indigenous group – that they are specific rights rather than generic rights. Chief Justice Lamer rejects the notion that Aboriginal rights make up a range of abstract legal categories with normative underpinnings, opting instead for the view that Aboriginal rights assume myriad particular forms, as moulded by the distinctive customs of the specific groups in question.[8] In effect, the test suggests that identifying

---

3 *Ibid* at paras 30, 32.
4 *Ibid* at para 42, quoting Mark D Walters, "British Imperial Constitutional Law and Aboriginal Rights: A Comment on *Delgamuukw v British Columbia*" (1992) 17 Queen's LJ 350 at 412–13; and Brian Slattery, "The Legal Basis of Aboriginal Title" in F Cassidy, ed, *Aboriginal Title in British Columbia: Delgamuukw v R* (Lantzville, BC: Oolichan Books, 1992) at 120–21.
5 *Van der Peet, supra* note 1 at paras 44–46, 55–56, 60–62.
6 *Ibid* at paras 63–64, 73.
7 *Ibid* at paras 76–91.
8 *Ibid* at para 69.

Aboriginal rights is a largely descriptive matter – an exercise in historical ethnography. The judge plays the role of ethno-historian, attempting
to discern the distinctive features of Aboriginal societies in the distant
reaches of Canadian history. He need not trouble himself with normative
questions – such as whether these features merit recognition as constitutional rights and, if so, what basic purposes they serve.

Second, the *Van der Peet* test looks exclusively to conditions prevailing in the remote past – the era prior to the critical date of European
contact – which may be as much as 500 years ago.[9] The test excludes
many activities that became central to the lives of Aboriginal peoples in
the post-contact period and that linked them socially and economically
to neighbouring settler communities. Not surprisingly, it tends to yield
rights that have a limited ability to serve the modern needs of Aboriginal peoples and may also fit uneasily with third-party and broader
societal interests.

Third, the test makes no reference whatever to the extensive relations
that developed between the Indigenous peoples and incoming Europeans in the post-contact period, or to the legal principles that informed
those relations. While the Court pays lip service to the view that Aboriginal rights are grounded in an inter-societal law that bridges Aboriginal and non-Aboriginal cultures, it does not assign this idea any real
role in the *Van der Peet* test, which looks entirely to the period before
settlers arrived and inter-societal relationships were formed.

So, while Lamer CJ identifies both recognition and reconciliation as
the underlying goals of section 35(1), in practice he focuses mainly on
the goal of recognition – that is, the identification of the central attributes of Aboriginal societies in the period before European contact. He
does not take into account the historical modes of reconciliation that
occurred when the Crown established relations with Indigenous peoples, nor does he consider the need for new modes of reconciliation
today. The result is that Aboriginal rights are identified in an almost
mechanical manner, without regard to the contemporary needs of Aboriginal peoples, the rights and interests of other affected groups, or the
welfare of the body politic as a whole.

---

9 This would be true of the portions of Eastern Canada encountered by early English
and French explorers and adventurers. See, e.g., Brian Slattery, "French Claims in
North America, 1500–59" (1978) 59 Canadian Historical Review 139.

Nevertheless, in the decade since the *Van der Peet* case was decided, the Supreme Court has shown mounting signs of discomfort with the test laid down there. In a series of important decisions, it has quietly begun reshaping the test's basic tenets. This process has taken place on three fronts. First, the Court has relaxed its exclusive focus on specific rights – rights distinctive to particular Aboriginal groups – and allowed for the existence of generic rights – uniform rights that operate at an abstract level and reflect broader normative considerations. Second, the Court has recognized that the date of European contact is not an appropriate reference point in all contexts and looked increasingly to the period when the Crown gained sovereignty and effective control. Finally, the Court has placed ever-greater emphasis on the need for Aboriginal rights to be defined by negotiations between the parties, tacitly signalling that Aboriginal rights are flexible and future-oriented, rather than mere relics of the past. Here I take stock of the matter and argue that these trends presage the birth of a new constitutional paradigm, in which Aboriginal rights are viewed as generative and not merely historical rights.[10]

Specific and Generic Rights

As just noted, in *Van der Peet* the Supreme Court expressed the view that all Aboriginal rights are specific rights – rights whose nature and scope are determined by the particular circumstances of each individual Aboriginal group.[11] However, this generalization proved to be premature. No more than a year was to pass before it was quietly discarded by the Court. The occasion was the *Delgamuukw* case,[12] in which the Gitksan and Wet'suwet'en peoples claimed Aboriginal title over their traditional homelands in northern British Columbia. In contesting the claim, the governmental parties maintained that there was no such thing as Aboriginal title in the sense of a uniform legal estate with fixed attributes. Rather, Aboriginal title was just a bundle of specific

---

10 The following sections draw on Brian Slattery, "Making Sense of Aboriginal and Treaty Rights" (2000) 79 Can Bar Rev 196 at 211–15; and Slattery, "A Taxonomy of Aboriginal Rights" in Hamar Foster, Heather Raven, & Jeremy Webber, eds, *Let Right Be Done: Calder, Aboriginal Title, and the Future of Indigenous Rights* (Vancouver: University of British Columbia Press, 2007) 111.

11 *Supra* note 1 at para 69.

12 *Delgamuukw v British Columbia*, [1997] SCJ No 108, [1997] 3 SCR 1010.

rights, whose contents varied from group to group. Each component in a group's bundle had to be proven independently. In effect, the group had to show that the particular activity in question was an element of a practice, custom, or tradition integral to its culture at the time of European contact. This argument was a logical extension of the approach taken in *Van der Peet*. Nevertheless, the Supreme Court rejected the argument and held that Aboriginal title gives an Indigenous group the exclusive right to use and occupy its ancestral lands for a broad range of purposes, which do not need to be rooted in the group's historical practices.[13] So a group that originally lived by hunting, fishing, and gathering would be free to farm the land, raise cattle on it, exploit its natural resources, or use it for residential, commercial, or industrial purposes, subject to the limitation that the group cannot ruin the land or render it unusable for its original purposes.

The crucial point to note is that *Delgamuukw* treats Aboriginal title as a uniform right, whose dimensions do not vary significantly from group to group according to their historic patterns of life. Aboriginal title is not a specific right of the kind envisaged in *Van der Peet*, or even a bundle of specific rights. It is a generic right – a right of a standardized character that takes the same basic form wherever it occurs. The fundamental contours of the right are determined by the common law rather than the distinctive circumstances of each group.

How can this discrepancy in approach between *Van der Peet* and *Delgamuukw* be explained? As we shall now see, the conflict is more apparent than real.

The Panoply of Generic Rights

Recall that in *Van der Peet* the Court holds that Aboriginal groups have the right to engage in practices, customs, and traditions that are integral to their distinctive historical cultures. To be "integral" to a particular culture, a practice must be a central and significant part of the culture, one of the things that make the society what it is. If we consider this holding in the light of *Delgamuukw*, we can see that *Van der Peet* also recognizes a generic right – namely the right of Aboriginal peoples to maintain and develop the central and significant elements of their ancestral cultures.

---

13 *Ibid* at paras 116–32.

In the abstract, this right has a fixed and uniform character, which does not change from one Aboriginal group to another. Each and every group has the same right – to maintain and develop the central elements of its ancestral culture. Of course, what is "central and significant" varies from society to society in accordance with its particular circumstances, so that at the concrete level the abstract right blossoms into a range of distinctive rights – a matter to be discussed later. The point to grasp here is that the abstract right itself is uniform. Like Aboriginal title, it constitutes a generic right – what we may call the right of cultural integrity.[14]

So now we have two generic rights: Aboriginal title and the right of cultural integrity. Are there still others? A little reflection shows that the answer is yes.[15] Here is a tentative list of generic Aboriginal rights, which includes the two just considered:

- the right to an ancestral territory (Aboriginal title);
- the right of cultural integrity;
- the right to conclude treaties;
- the right to customary law;
- the right to honourable treatment by the Crown; and
- the right of self-government.

While this list is not necessarily definitive or complete, it represents a fair estimate of the current state of the jurisprudence. I shall say a few words about the last four rights, not yet discussed.

It has long been recognized that Aboriginal peoples have the right to conclude binding treaties with the Crown, a right reflected in the wording of section 35 itself.[16] Under Canadian common law, the treaty-making capacity of Aboriginal groups has a uniform character, which does not vary from group to group. The capacity of the Saanich Nation is the same as that of the Huron Nation. As such, the right to conclude treaties qualifies as a generic Aboriginal right.

---

14 For discussion of the right of cultural integrity in international law, see S James Anaya, *Indigenous Peoples in International Law* (New York: Oxford University Press, 1996), 98–104.

15 For fuller discussion, see Slattery, "Taxonomy of Aboriginal Rights," *supra* note 10, which the following account summarizes.

16 The treaty-making power is reviewed in *R v Sioui*, [1990] SCJ No 48, [1990] 1 SCR 1025 at paras 16–41.

Aboriginal peoples also have the right to maintain and develop their systems of customary law.[17] The introduction of French and English laws did not supersede Indigenous laws, which continued to operate within their respective spheres. As McLachlin J observed in *Van der Peet*,

> The history of the interface of Europeans and the common law with aboriginal peoples is a long one ... Yet running through this history, from its earliest beginnings to the present time is a golden thread – the recognition by the common law of the ancestral laws and customs [of] the aboriginal peoples who occupied the land prior to European settlement.[18]

The right of Aboriginal peoples to maintain their own laws is a generic right, whose basic scope is determined by the common law doctrine of Aboriginal rights. The abstract right does not differ from group to group, even though the particular legal systems protected by the right obviously differ in content.

Aboriginal peoples also have the right to honourable treatment by the Crown. As the Supreme Court stated in the *Sparrow* case,

> [T]he Government has the responsibility to act in a fiduciary capacity with respect to aboriginal peoples. The relationship between the Government and aboriginals is trust-like, rather than adversarial, and contemporary recognition and affirmation of aboriginal rights must be defined in light of this historic relationship.[19]

Although the Court was referring here to section 35(1) of the *Constitution Act, 1982*, subsequent Supreme Court decisions have confirmed that the Crown's responsibility is not confined to this context but

---

17 See *Connolly v Woolrich* (1867), 17 RJRQ 75 (Que SC); *Casimel v Insurance Corp of British Columbia*, [1993] BCJ No 1834, 106 DLR (4th) 720 (CA); *Van der Peet, supra* note 1 at paras 38–40; *Delgamuukw, supra* note 12 at paras 146–48; *Campbell v British Columbia (AG)*, [2000] BCJ No 1524, 189 DLR (4th) 333 at paras 83–136 (SC); *Mitchell v Canada (MNR)*, [2001] SCJ No 33, [2001] 1 SCR 911 at paras 9–10, 61–64, 141–54.

18 *Van der Peet, supra* note 1 at para 263. Justice McLachlin was dissenting, but not on this point.

19 *R v Sparrow*, [1990] SCJ No 49, [1990] 1 SCR 1075 at para 59. See also *Guerin v Canada*, [1984] SCJ No 45, [1984] 2 SCR 335; *Van der Peet, supra* note 1 at paras 24–25; *Wewaykum Indian Band v Canada*, [2002] SCJ No 79, [2002] 4 SCR 245.

accompanies and controls the discretionary powers that the Crown historically has assumed over the lives of Aboriginal peoples.[20]

At the most abstract level, the right to honourable treatment by the Crown is a generic right, which vests uniformly in Aboriginal peoples across Canada. The point was underlined in the *Haida Nation* case,[21] where McLachlin CJ held that the honour of the Crown is always at stake in its dealings with Aboriginal peoples. The Court explained that the Crown has the general duty to determine, recognize, and respect the rights of Aboriginal peoples over whom it has asserted sovereignty. This binds the Crown to enter into treaty negotiations in order to reconcile Aboriginal rights and achieve a just settlement. Pending the conclusion of such treaties, the Crown is obliged to consult with Aboriginal peoples before doing things that may affect their asserted rights, and to accommodate these rights where necessary. In situations where the Crown has assumed discretionary control over specific Aboriginal interests, the honour of the Crown gives rise to fiduciary duties, which require the Crown to act with reference to the Aboriginal group's best interests in exercising its discretion.[22] In effect, then, the abstract right to honourable treatment gives rise to a range of more precise rights and duties that attach to specific subject matters in particular contexts.

Finally, Aboriginal peoples have the right to govern themselves as a third order of government within the federal constitutional framework of Canada.[23] This right finds its source in the Crown's recognition that it could not secure the amity of Indigenous nations without acknowledging their right to manage their own affairs. As Lamer J noted in the *Sioui* case,[24] the Crown treated Indian nations with generosity and respect out of the fear that the safety and development of British colonies would otherwise be compromised:

---

20 *Mitchell v Canada (MNR)*, [2001] SCJ No 33, 1 SCR 911 at para 9; *Wewaykum Indian Band, ibid* at paras 79–80.

21 *Haida Nation v British Columbia (Minister of Forests)*, [2004] SCJ No 70, [2004] 3 SCR 511 at paras 16–25.

22 *Ibid* at para 18. See also *Wewaykum Indian Band, supra* note 19 at paras 72–85.

23 Royal Commission on Aboriginal Peoples, *Report of the Royal Commission on Aboriginal Peoples*, vol 2 (Ottawa: Minister of Supply and Services Canada, 1996), 163–244; *Campbell, supra* note 17; Brian Slattery, "First Nations and the Constitution: A Question of Trust" (1992) 71 Can Bar Rev 261 at 278–87.

24 *Sioui, supra* note 16 at paras 71–74.

The British Crown recognized that the Indians had certain ownership rights over their land, it sought to establish trade with them which would rise above the level of exploitation and give them a fair return. It also allowed them autonomy in their internal affairs, intervening in this area as little as possible.[25]

It is submitted that the right of self-government is a generic right, which recognizes a uniform set of governmental powers held by Aboriginal peoples as a distinct order of government within the Canadian federal system. At the same time, it allows Aboriginal groups to establish and maintain their own constitutions, which take a variety of forms. There are parallels here with the provinces, which are vested with a uniform set of governmental powers, but also have distinctive constitutions, which they have the power to amend.[26]

It might be argued that the Aboriginal right of self-government is not a generic right but a collection of specific rights, each of which has to be proven separately under the *Van der Peet* test.[27] In the *Pamajewon* case,[28] the Supreme Court viewed the question through the lens of *Van der Peet* and held that the right of self-government would have to be proven as an element of specific practices, customs, and traditions integral to the particular Aboriginal society in question. According to this approach, the right of self-government would be a collection of specific rights to govern particular activities rather than a generic right to deal with a range of abstract subject matters. However, the *Pamajewon* case was decided prior to the Court's decision in *Delgamuukw*, which expanded the horizons of Aboriginal rights and recognized the category of generic rights. In light of *Delgamuukw*, it seems more sensible to treat the right of self-government as a generic Aboriginal right, on the model of Aboriginal title, rather than as a bundle of specific rights. On this view, the right of self-government is governed by uniform principles laid down by Canadian common law. The basic scope of the right does not vary from group to group; however, its concrete application differs, depending on the circumstances.

---

25 *Ibid* para 74.
26 See s 92, *Constitution Act, 1867* (UK), 30 & 31 Vict, c 3, reprinted in RSC 1985, App II, No 5; and s 45 of the *Constitution Act, 1982.*
27 The following discussion draws on Slattery, "Making Sense of Aboriginal and Treaty Rights," *supra* note 10 at 213–14.
28 *R v Pamajewon*, [1996] SCJ No 20, [1996] 2 SCR 821 at paras 23–30.

The Universality of Generic Rights

Generic rights are not only uniform in character; they are also universal in distribution. They make up a set of fundamental rights held by all Aboriginal groups in Canada. There is no need to prove in each case that an Aboriginal group has the right to occupy its ancestral territory, to maintain the central attributes of its way of life, to conclude treaties with the Crown, to enjoy its customary legal system, to benefit from the honour of the Crown, or to govern its own affairs. It is presumed that every Aboriginal group in Canada has these fundamental rights, in the absence of treaties or valid legislation to the contrary. This situation is hardly surprising, given the fact that the doctrine of Aboriginal rights applies uniformly throughout the various territories making up Canada, regardless of their precise historical origins or their former status as French or English colonies.[29]

The generic rights held by Aboriginal peoples resemble the set of constitutional rights vested in the provinces under the general provisions of the *Constitution Act, 1867*. Just as every province presumptively enjoys the same array of rights and powers, regardless of its size, population, wealth, resources, or historical circumstances, so also every Aboriginal group, large or small, presumptively enjoys the same range of generic Aboriginal rights.

However, this conclusion could be disputed. For example, it could be argued that the generic right of Aboriginal title is not a universal right. Some Aboriginal peoples, it is said, never had sufficiently strong or stable connections with a definite territory to hold Aboriginal title, as opposed to specific rights of hunting, fishing, and gathering. Certain musings of the Supreme Court seem to entertain such a possibility.[30] However, the better view is that every Aboriginal group holds Aboriginal title to an ancestral territory, the only question being its location and scope.

---

29 See *R v Côté*, [1996] SCJ No 93, [1996] 3 SCR 139 at paras 42–54; *R v Adams*, [1996] SCJ No 87, [1996] 3 SCR 101 at paras 31–33; Brian Slattery, "Understanding Aboriginal Rights" (1987) Can Bar Rev 727 at 736–41.

30 See *Adams, ibid* at paras 27–28; *R v Marshall*; *R v Bernard*, [2005] SCJ No. 44, [2005] 2 SCR 220 at paras 58–59, 66. For full discussion, see *Tsilhqot'in Nation v British Columbia*, [2014] SCJ No 44, [2014] 2 SCR 256 at paras 24–50.

A Hierarchy of Rights

What is the relationship between generic and specific rights? The answer should now be clear. Specific rights are concrete instances of generic rights. So, for example, the generic right to honourable treatment by the Crown operates at a high level of abstraction and harbours a range of intermediate generic rights relating to various subject matters, such as the creation of new Indian reserves, or the protection of existing ones. These intermediate generic rights, in turn, engender myriad specific fiduciary rights, whose precise scope is determined by the concrete circumstances. Similarly, the abstract right of cultural integrity fosters a range of intermediate generic rights relating to such matters as language, religion, and livelihood. These intermediate rights give birth to specific rights, whose character is shaped by the practices, customs, and traditions of particular Aboriginal groups.

The interplay between generic and specific rights is reflected in the terms of treaties concluded by Aboriginal peoples with the Crown. Consider, for example, the following document signed by Brigadier General James Murray in 1760, which provides:

> THESE are to certify that the CHIEF of the HURON tribe of Indians, having come to me in the name of His Nation, to submit to His BRITANNICK MAJESTY, and make Peace, has been received under my Protection, with his whole Tribe; and henceforth no English Officer or party is to molest, or interrupt them in returning to their Settlement at LORETTE; and they are received upon the same terms with the Canadians, being allowed the free Exercise of their Religion, their Customs, and Liberty of trading with the English: – recommending it to the Officers commanding the Posts, to treat them kindly.[31]

In the *Sioui* case,[32] Lamer J held that the document constituted a treaty and that it gave the Hurons the freedom to carry on their customs and religious rites over the entire territory that they frequented in 1760, so long as this freedom was not incompatible with the particular uses of the territory made by the Crown.

---

31 Reproduced in *Sioui, supra* note 16 at para 5.
32 *Ibid*, esp. at paras 89, 116.

What is interesting about this brief treaty is its reference to a large array of generic and specific rights. It opens by recognizing the Hurons as an autonomous people under the protection of the British Crown. So doing, it endorses their right to honourable treatment by the Crown, and perhaps also by implication recognizes their right to govern themselves under the Crown's aegis. The treaty allows the Hurons the free exercise of their religion, which, as just noted, is an intermediate generic right falling under the right of cultural integrity. The treaty also guarantees Huron customs, thus reflecting the generic right to a distinct legal system. The document further promises the liberty of trading with the English, which is a specific application of the intermediate generic right to gain a livelihood, which, as we shall see shortly, falls under the right of cultural integrity. Finally, of course, the very existence of the document bears witness to the generic right to conclude treaties.

The precise nature of the relationship between generic and specific rights varies with the generic right in question. Consider, for example, the generic right of self-government. This right arguably confers the same set of governmental powers on all Aboriginal peoples in Canada. Nevertheless, this abstract homogeneity does not mean that Aboriginal peoples possess the same internal constitutions or that they exercise their governmental powers up to their full theoretical limits. The generic right of self-government gives an Aboriginal group the power to establish and amend its own constitution within the overarching framework of the Canadian federation. So the abstract right engenders a range of specific governmental powers detailed in particular Aboriginal constitutions.

Likewise, the generic right to conclude treaties empowers Aboriginal groups to enter into binding agreements with the Crown. As such, the right spawns an array of particular agreements differing in subject matter and scope. Of course, it does not follow that each such treaty is a "specific right" or that the rights embodied in the treaty are "specific rights." Rather, the generic right gives the Aboriginal parties to a treaty a specific right to its performance, and the nature and scope of that right and the remedies it engenders are shaped by the overarching generic right. Similarly, the generic right to customary law harbours a host of distinct legal systems enjoyed by particular Aboriginal groups. Although these systems are concrete manifestations of the overarching generic right, it would seem an excess of legal logic to characterize them as "specific rights." Rather, we may say that an Aboriginal group has a specific right to possess its own legal system to the extent determined by the generic right that governs it.

Just as all generic rights give birth to specific rights, all specific rights are the offspring of generic rights. There are no "orphan" specific rights. In effect, generic rights provide the fundamental normative structure governing specific rights. This structure determines the existence of specific rights, their basic scope, and their potential for evolution. The significance of these points is illustrated by the right of cultural integrity, which we shall now consider in detail.

The Right of Cultural Integrity

As noted earlier, the right of cultural integrity shelters a host of specific rights that differ from group to group in accordance with their particular ways of life, such as the right to hunt in a certain area, the right to fish in certain waters, the right to harvest certain natural resources, the right to conduct certain religious rites, the right to speak a certain language, and so on. Despite their differences, these specific rights fall into a number of broad categories relating to such subjects as religion, language, and livelihood. These categories constitute cultural rights of intermediate generality – for short, intermediate generic rights.

For example, the right to practise a religion arguably qualifies as an intermediate generic right, because spirituality and the performance of religious rites have always been central to Indigenous societies, a matter acknowledged in relations between the Crown and Aboriginal peoples, notably in the ceremonies attending diplomacy and treaty-making. As Professor Oren Lyons, a peace-keeper with the Six Nations, has written,

> The primary law of Indian government is the spiritual law. Spirituality is the highest form of politics, and our spirituality is directly involved in government. As chiefs we are told that our first and most important duty is to see that the spiritual ceremonies are carried out. Without the ceremonies, one does not have a basis on which to conduct government for the welfare of the people. This is not only for our people but for the good of all living things in general. So we are told first to conduct the ceremonies on time, in the proper manner, and then to sit in council for the welfare of our people and of all life.[33]

---

33 Oren Lyons, "Spirituality, Equality, and Natural Law," in Leroy Little Bear, Menno Boldt, & J Anthony Long, eds, *Pathways to Self-Determination: Canadian Indians and the Canadian State* (Toronto: University of Toronto Press, 1984) 5–6.

Viewed in the abstract, the right to practise a religion has a uniform scope, which does not vary from one Aboriginal people to another. However, the particular activities, rites, and institutions protected by the right differ from group to group, depending on their specific religious outlook. In effect, then, the generic right of cultural integrity harbours an intermediate generic right to religion, which in turn shelters a range of specific religious rights vested in particular Aboriginal groups.

Consider another example. Aboriginal peoples arguably have the right to use and develop their ancestral languages and to enjoy the educational and cultural institutions needed to maintain them. Language is normally an integral feature of a group's ancestral culture and an important means by which that culture is manifested, nurtured, and transmitted. As Elder Eli Taylor from the Sioux Valley First Nation explained,

> The Aboriginal languages were given by the Creator as an integral part of life. Embodied in Aboriginal languages is our unique relationship to the Creator, our attitudes, beliefs, values and the fundamental notion of what is truth. Aboriginal language is an asset to one's own education, formal and informal. Aboriginal language contributes to greater pride in the history and culture of the community: greater involvement and interest of parents in the education of their children, and greater respect for Elders. Language is the principal means by which culture is accumulated, shared and transmitted from generation to generation. The key to identity and retention of culture is one's ancestral language.[34]

So the right to use and develop an Aboriginal language has a strong claim to qualify as an intermediate generic right. The abstract dimensions of this right are identical in all Aboriginal groups; however, it gives rise to a spectrum of specific rights relating to particular languages and linguistic institutions.

Another important intermediate right is what may be called the right of livelihood. A fundamental principle informing the Crown's assumption of sovereignty was that Aboriginal peoples could continue to gain their living in their accustomed ways. Justice McLachlin identified

---

34 Assembly of First Nations, *Towards Rebirth of First Nations Languages* (Ottawa: AFN, 1992), 14; quoted in Canada, Task Force on Aboriginal Languages and Cultures, *Towards a New Beginning: A Foundational Report for a Strategy to Revitalize Indian, Inuit and Métis Languages and Cultures* (Ottawa: Department of Canadian Heritage, 2005) 21.

this right in her dissenting opinion in the *Van der Peet* case.[35] Citing the
terms of treaties and the *Royal Proclamation of 1763*,[36] she observed,

> These arrangements bear testimony to the acceptance by the colonizers of
> the principle that the aboriginal peoples who occupied what is now Can-
> ada were regarded as possessing the aboriginal right to live off their lands
> and the resources found in their forests and streams to the extent they
> had traditionally done so. The fundamental understanding – the *Grund-
> norm* of settlement in Canada – was that the aboriginal people could only
> be deprived of the sustenance they traditionally drew from the land and
> adjacent waters by solemn treaty with the Crown, on terms that would en-
> sure to them and to their successors a replacement for the livelihood that
> their lands, forests and streams had since ancestral times provided them.[37]

A similar viewpoint subsequently attracted the Supreme Court's
support in the *Marshall* case.[38] In the course of interpreting a Mi'kmaq
treaty of 1760, Binnie J referred to the objectives of the British and
Mi'kmaq in their negotiations, which were aimed at reconciliation and
mutual advantage.[39]

> It is apparent that the British saw the Mi'kmaq trade issue in terms of
> peace, as the Crown expert Dr. Stephen Patterson testified, "people who
> trade together do not fight, that was the theory." Peace was bound up with
> the ability of the Mi'kmaq people to sustain themselves economically. Star-
> vation breeds discontent. The British certainly did not want the Mi'kmaq
> to become an unnecessary drain on the public purse of the colony of Nova
> Scotia or of the Imperial purse in London, as the trial judge found. To
> avoid such a result, it became necessary to protect the traditional Mi'kmaq
> economy, including hunting, gathering and fishing.[40]

In light of this policy, Binnie J interpreted the treaty as recognizing the right of the Mi'kmaq parties to continue to obtain necessaries

---

35 *Supra* note 1.
36 RSC 1985, App II, No 1. The most accurate printed text is found in Clarence
    S Brigham, ed, *British Royal Proclamations Relating to America* (Worcester, MA:
    American Antiquarian Society, 1911) 212.
37 *Van der Peet, supra* note 1 at para 272 [italics in original].
38 *R v Marshall*, [1999] SCJ No 55, [1999] 3 SCR 456.
39 *Ibid* at para 3.
40 *Ibid* at para 25.

through hunting and fishing and by trading the products of those traditional activities. What the treaty contemplated, he emphasized, was not a right to trade generally for economic gain, but rather a right to trade for "necessaries." The concept of "necessaries" was equivalent to what may be described as a "moderate livelihood," which extends to such day-to-day needs as food, clothing, and housing, supplemented by a few amenities, but not the accumulation of wealth.[41]

To recapitulate, the generic right of cultural integrity forms a pyramid with three levels. At the top is the abstract right itself, which takes the same form in all Aboriginal groups. Beneath this summit lies a tier of intermediate generic rights that relate to distinct subject matters such as religion, language, and livelihood. At the bottom rests a broad range of specific rights that differ from group to group in accordance with their particular cultures and ways of life.

In many respects, the middle tier of the pyramid is the most important of the three. Intermediate generic rights serve several crucial functions. First, they determine which concrete aspects of Aboriginal societies rise to the level of constitutional significance and merit recognition as specific cultural rights. In other words, they speak to the *identity* of Aboriginal rights. Second, intermediate rights determine the way in which specific practices are characterized for constitutional purposes, speaking to the *scope* of Aboriginal rights. So doing, intermediate rights also determine the *generative potential* of these rights. We shall consider these points in turn.

The Identity of Rights

One of the shortcomings of the *Van der Peet* test is that it does not provide a reliable basis for distinguishing between Indigenous practices that are constitutionally significant and those that are not.[42] In its ethnohistorical bias, the test obscures the fact that identifying Aboriginal rights cannot simply be a descriptive exercise, that it has deep normative dimensions. The court's role is not to reconstruct the internal dynamics of long-vanished Aboriginal lifestyles. Rather it is to determine what general constitutional norms underpin section 35, and the kind of modern rights these norms support.

---

41 *Ibid* at paras 56–59.
42 See McLachlin J's apt remarks in *Van der Peet, supra* note 1 at para 242.

Recall that, in *Van der Peet*, Lamer CJ says that Aboriginal rights represent practices that are truly "integral" to an Aboriginal society, in the sense of being "central and significant." However, "integrality" is an unsure guide to constitutional import. There are certain practices that obviously cannot qualify as Aboriginal rights, no matter how "integral" they may be from a purely anthropological perspective. Otherwise there might be Aboriginal rights to sleep, to flirt, to tell jokes, to gamble, to make love, and so on. Chief Justice Lamer struggles with this fact in observing that "eating to survive" does not qualify as an Aboriginal right because it is "true of every human society" and so is not sufficiently "distinctive."[43] However, with respect, this puts the emphasis in the wrong place. The question is not what is distinctive but what is constitutionally significant. And indeed, later in his opinion, Lamer CJ obliquely concedes the point in recognizing that "fishing for food" can constitute an Aboriginal right, notwithstanding the fact that it is practised by most societies around the world.[44] So, near-universal prevalence is no bar to recognition as an Aboriginal right.

The reason why such practices as eating, joking, and gambling fail to qualify as Aboriginal rights is not because they are not integral features of Aboriginal societies (they may well be) but because they do not rise to the level of constitutional significance. How do we know that? The answer, in part, lies in the historical relations between Aboriginal societies and the Crown and the principles that underpin those relations – what we have called inter-societal law.[45] There is little evidence that inter-societal law ever supported a right to sleep or joke, but much that attests to a right to gain a livelihood. Take another example. From a purely ethnographic point of view, the practice of bearing arms was a central feature of most Aboriginal societies in early times, because it was essential to their ability to defend themselves and ultimately to survive. However, that fact does not support a modern Aboriginal right to bear arms. The reason does not lie in any paucity of ethno-historical evidence but in the fact that fundamental constitutional norms do not support such a right.

---

43 *Ibid* at para 56.
44 *Ibid* at para 72.
45 For the sources of this law, see Slattery, "Making Sense of Aboriginal and Treaty Rights," *supra* note 10 at 198–206.

The Scope and Generative Potential of Rights

Intermediate generic rights play another function, closely related to the first. Not only do they determine the range of practices capable of constituting Aboriginal rights, they also shape the way those practices are characterized. This in turn influences the extent to which the concrete rights are capable of evolving and adapting to modern conditions without breaking the link to their historical progenitors – in effect determining the extent to which these rights are generative.

The *Van der Peet* test assumes that the character and scope of Aboriginal rights are matters determined simply by the historical and anthropological evidence. However, such evidence does not speak for itself. Social practices may be characterized in any number of different ways and at varying levels of abstraction. Ultimately, the question of characterization is normative as well as factual. The trick is to strike the right balance between the two.

The point is illustrated by the argument advanced by McLachlin J, in her dissenting opinion in *Van der Peet*. She maintains that, under section 35(1), Aboriginal peoples have the right to sustain themselves from the land or waters upon which they have traditionally relied for sustenance. In her view, this includes the right to trade in the resource to the extent necessary to maintain traditional levels of sustenance.[46] So where an Aboriginal group can show that traditionally it sustained itself by fishing in the river or sea, then it has the right to continue to do so today. And if it further demonstrates that the modern trade in fish is the only way to gain the equivalent of what it traditionally took, it has the right to trade in the resource to the extent necessary to provide replacement goods and amenities. In this context, she says, "trade is but the mode or practice by which the more fundamental right of drawing sustenance from the resource is exercised."[47]

Nevertheless, McLachlin J argues that such a right to trade is not unlimited. It does not extend beyond what is required to provide reasonable substitutes for what was traditionally obtained from the resource – in most cases, basic housing, transportation, clothing, and amenities, in addition to what is needed for food and ceremonial purposes. In effect, where the Aboriginal group historically drew a

---

46 *Supra* note 1 at para 227.
47 *Ibid* at para 278.

moderate livelihood from the fishery, it would have an Aboriginal right to obtain a moderate livelihood from the fishery today. However, there is no automatic entitlement to a moderate or any other livelihood from a particular resource. The right exists only to the extent that the Aboriginal group can show historical reliance on the resource. For example, if the evidence indicates the group used the fishery only for occasional food and sport fishing, it would not have a right to fish for the purposes of sale, much less to provide a moderate livelihood.

There is, on this view, no generic right of commercial fishing, large-scale or small. There is only the right of a particular Aboriginal people to take from the resource the modern equivalent of what by Aboriginal law and custom it historically took.[48]

In McLachlin J's view, the Aboriginal right of traditional sustenance is subject to two limitations. First, it must be exercised in a manner that respects the need for conservation, because use of the resource cannot be sustained over the long term unless the product of the lands and adjacent waters is maintained. Second, any right by its nature carries with it the obligation to use it responsibly. So, for example, the right cannot be used in a way that harms people, Aboriginal or non-Aboriginal.[49]

In effect, then, McLachlin J holds that Aboriginal peoples have an intermediate generic right to sustain themselves from the land or waters upon which they traditionally relied for sustenance, subject to the requirements of conservation and responsible use. The existence and basic scope of this intermediate generic right are matters of law. However, the specific resources to which the right attaches and the level to which the right rises are determined, not by general norms governing the generic right, but by the particular historical practices of each group. So, for example, there is no generic right of commercial fishing as such; the matter turns on the evidence relating to the specific group in question. Nevertheless, where a group can show that traditionally it drew a moderate livelihood from the fishery, it has a specific Aboriginal right to do so today, and this right includes the right to trade in fish in order to obtain the equivalent of what it traditionally got, even where there is no evidence of significant trade at the critical historical date. Justice McLachlin's approach, then, represents an effort to strike the balance between normative and historical considerations in a way that

---

48 *Ibid* at para 279.
49 *Ibid* at para 280.

favours the generative potential of livelihood rights, so as to support the modern welfare and prosperity of Aboriginal peoples.

Compare this approach with that taken by the Supreme Court in the recent *Sappier/Gray* decision.[50] The case concerns a claim by members of the Maliseet and Mi'kmaq peoples of New Brunswick to an Aboriginal right to harvest timber for personal uses. In a seminal judgment, the Court unanimously adopts the view that section 35(1) protects the means by which an Aboriginal society traditionally sustained itself.[51] So doing, the Court effectively accepts the existence of an intermediate generic right of livelihood. Speaking for the majority, Bastarache J holds that section 35 seeks to protect the integral elements of the way of life of Aboriginal societies, including their traditional means of survival.[52] He cautions, nevertheless, that there is no such thing as an Aboriginal right to sustenance as such, the right being confined to traditional means of sustenance, namely the pre-contact practices relied upon for survival.[53]

As for the precise characterization of the right, Bastarache J holds that the respondents' claim of "a right to harvest timber for personal uses" is too general. The practice should be characterized as the "harvesting of wood for domestic uses," including such things as shelter, transportation, tools, and fuel.[54] He notes that, so characterized, the right has no commercial dimension. The harvested wood cannot be sold, traded, or bartered to produce assets or raise money, even if the purpose is to finance the building of a dwelling. In other words, although the right permits the harvesting of timber to be used in the construction of a dwelling, the wood cannot be sold to raise money to purchase or build a dwelling.[55]

Turning to the generative potential of the right, Bastarache J holds that "[l]ogical evolution means the same sort of activity, carried on in the modern economy by modern means."[56] So, the right to harvest wood for the construction of temporary shelters may evolve into a right to harvest wood by modern means for the construction of a modern

---

50 *R v Sappier; R v Gray*, [2006] SCJ No 54, [2006] 2 SCR 686.
51 *Ibid* at paras 37–40, 45. Justice Binnie dissented on the precise scope of the Aboriginal right in question, however otherwise he agreed with the majority reasons.
52 *Ibid* at para 40.
53 *Ibid* at para 37.
54 *Ibid* at para 24.
55 *Ibid* at para 25.
56 *Ibid* at para 48; quoting McLachlin CJ in *Marshall/Bernard*, *supra* note 30 at para 25.

dwelling. Any other conclusion would freeze the right in its pre-contact form. Justice Bastarache notes the Crown's argument that the construction of large permanent dwellings from multidimensional wood, obtained by modern methods of extraction and milling, could not constitute an Aboriginal right or a proper application of the "logical evolution" principle. However, he rejects this argument in strong terms, noting that under the established jurisprudence Aboriginal rights must be interpreted flexibly so as to permit their evolution over time.[57] In a striking passage, he explains,

> In *Mitchell*, McLachlin C.J. drew a distinction between the particular aboriginal right, which is established at the moment of contact, and its expression, which evolves over time (para. 13). L'Heureux-Dubé J. in dissent in *Van der Peet* emphasized that "aboriginal rights must be permitted to maintain contemporary relevance in relation to the needs of the natives as their practices, traditions and customs change and evolve with the overall society in which they live" (para. 172). If aboriginal rights are not permitted to evolve and take modern forms, then they will become utterly useless. Surely the Crown cannot be suggesting that the respondents, all of whom live on a reserve, would be limited to building wigwams. If such were the case, the doctrine of aboriginal rights would truly be limited to recognizing and affirming a narrow subset of "anthropological curiosities," and our notion of aboriginality would be reduced to a small number of outdated stereotypes.[58]

In summary, then, in *Sappier/Gray*, the Supreme Court effectively recognizes what we have described as an intermediate generic right of livelihood. The existence and basic scope of the right are established by general legal norms – so that, for example, the Court construes the right as extending to traditional means of sustenance, rather than to sustenance generally. However, in other respects, the character of the right is governed by the evidence relating to the particular group in question – such as, for example, the question whether a resource can be sold in order to raise money. The specific right at issue in the case is characterized at a fairly high level of generality, which in turn allows

---

57 *Ibid* at para 49; quoting Dickson CJ in *Sparrow, supra* note 19 at para 27; and Slattery, "Understanding Aboriginal Rights," *supra* note 29 at 782.
58 *Sappier/Gray, supra* note 50.

considerable scope for its evolution over time. However, the Court does not explore in any depth the normative underpinnings of the generic right of livelihood. Had it done so, it might have adopted a position closer to that of McLachlin J in *Van der Peet*.

The point to be drawn from this analysis is simple. The assessment of claims to Aboriginal rights has two complementary dimensions: historical and normative. A court has to consider not only the historical evidence mounted to support the specific claim, but also the underlying rationale of the generic right invoked. While the Supreme Court has finally acknowledged the normative dimensions of the question, it still has some distance to go.

The Critical Date

As a matter of Anglo-Canadian law, Aboriginal rights came into existence when the Crown gained sovereignty over an Indigenous people. Before that time, the relations between an Indigenous people and the Crown were governed by international law and the terms of any treaties. Although Aboriginal peoples held rights under international law prior to the change of sovereignty (and continue to hold such rights today), it was only upon the advent of the Crown that Aboriginal rights arose in Anglo-Canadian law.[59]

Consider for a moment the generic right of honourable treatment by the Crown. This right clearly did not come into existence at the point of European contact, for mere physical interaction could not vest an Aboriginal group with rights under Anglo-Canadian law, any more than it could burden the Crown with duties. The Crown's honour was engaged only when the Crown assumed sovereignty over the Aboriginal group in question. As McLachlin CJ says in *Haida Nation*,

> The historical roots of the principle of the honour of the Crown suggest that it must be understood generously in order to reflect the underlying realities from which it stems. In all its dealings with Aboriginal peoples, from the assertion of sovereignty to the resolution of claims and the implementation of treaties, the Crown must act honourably. Nothing less is

---

59 For the status of Indigenous rights in international law, see Anaya, *supra* note 14.

required if we are to achieve "the reconciliation of the pre-existence of aboriginal societies with the sovereignty of the Crown."[60]

In other words, under Anglo-Canadian law (as distinct from international law), the Crown has no legal responsibilities for Indigenous peoples until such time as it assumes sovereignty over them. At that point, the principle of the honour of the Crown takes hold and imposes basic standards governing the Crown's conduct. However, the same observation holds true of the other generic Aboriginal rights. It seems implausible that any one of them could come into force simply at the point of contact. As a matter of Anglo-Canadian law, they all accompany and control the Crown's assumption of governmental responsibility over Indigenous peoples. So it seems natural to think that the critical historical date for establishing the existence of Aboriginal rights is the time of sovereignty. However, the matter is not so straightforward. We have to distinguish between generic and specific rights.

As seen earlier, when an Aboriginal people passes under the Crown's sovereignty, it automatically gains a basic set of generic rights – the right to an ancestral territory, the right of cultural integrity, and so on – as well as a range of intermediate generic rights arising under their auspices. These rights come into existence at the time of sovereignty and possess a uniform character. Nevertheless, generic rights have specific aspects or applications, many of which originate at later dates and change over time. For instance, the principle of the honour of the Crown takes effect at the date of sovereignty; however, specific fiduciary rights and duties generally arise from events occurring well after sovereignty, such as the negotiation of treaties or the creation of reserves. In such cases, the critical date for proving the specific fiduciary right is clearly the date of the event that triggered it, not the date of sovereignty.

Likewise, the generic right to customary law arises at the time of sovereignty; however, the particular bodies of customary law protected by the right are not static but continue to evolve and adapt to keep pace with societal changes. It follows that the relevant date for determining the existence of a particular rule of customary law is not the date of

---

60 *Supra* note 21 at para 17; the quotation is from *Delgamuukw, supra* note 12 at para 186, which quotes, in turn, *Van der Peet, supra* note 1 at para 31.

sovereignty but the date of the activity or transaction whose legality is in question. So, for example, the validity of a customary adoption that took place in southern Quebec in 1980 would be governed by the customary rules prevailing at that date, rather than in the year 1763, when New France was ceded to the British Crown. Of course, while the customary rules must have existed for an appreciable period of time before they can gain the status of law, there is no need to show they existed at the time of sovereignty.

The right of cultural integrity poses more difficult and complex questions. As with other generic rights, the abstract right comes into existence at the time of sovereignty, and the same holds true of the intermediate generic rights that shelter under its auspices, relating to such subjects as language, religion, and livelihood. What, then, of the specific rights that occupy the bottom tier in the pyramid? In principle these cannot date from a period earlier than the time of sovereignty, because Anglo-Canadian law (as distinct from international law or Indigenous law) did not apply prior to that date. So presumably they must arise at the time of sovereignty or at some later period, depending on the precise nature of the right in question.

The question is bedevilled by the fact that Indigenous cultures (like all cultures) are organic entities that change constantly over time. After Europeans arrived in North America, Aboriginal societies responded in dynamic and creative ways to the new opportunities, circumstances, and influences that presented themselves.[61] Just as European cultures quickly adopted many products of American origin, such as tomatoes, corn, and potatoes (to say nothing of tobacco), so also Native American cultures swiftly absorbed many items of European origin, such as horses, metal artefacts, and firearms. Trade in furs, skins, and fish transformed the economies of Aboriginal societies and helped sustain the economies of settler colonies. Religious ideas born in the crucible of the Middle East had a notable impact on Aboriginal spirituality, as did Aboriginal conceptions of personal freedom and federalism on European political thought. On the negative side, European-borne diseases such as smallpox decimated many Aboriginal societies and caused important changes in lifestyle, political organization, and outlook,

---

61 For a good survey, see Colin G Calloway, *New Worlds for All: Indians, Europeans, and the Remaking of Early America* (Baltimore, MD: Johns Hopkins University Press, 1997).

while venereal syphilis (often thought to be of American origin) took a lesser toll in Europe.[62]

So the question arises: given the dynamic nature of Aboriginal cultures and the fact that they underwent significant changes both before and after sovereignty, what date is "critical" for determining the existence and content of specific cultural rights? The answer has two facets. First, the critical date cannot normally be *earlier* than the date of Crown sovereignty, because, except in unusual situations, it does not make sense for the content of a right to be fixed by reference to a period prior to the time that the right itself came into existence. Second, it seems possible that the critical date may vary, depending on the kind of cultural right at issue and the underlying purposes it serves. The date appropriate for language rights may not serve well for livelihood rights. It follows that the matter should be determined on a category-by-category basis, so that the considerations appropriate to each context may be thoroughly assessed.

Nevertheless, as seen earlier, the Supreme Court held in *Van der Peet*[63] that the critical date for determining the content of specific cultural rights was the time of initial European contact – normally well before Crown sovereignty – and that this date held true for Aboriginal rights across the board. The Court apparently thought that the right of cultural integrity was designed to preserve the central aspects of Aboriginal cultures as these existed in their "pristine" form, prior to the advent of European influence. So while Aboriginal rights themselves came into existence only at the time of sovereignty (for they could not arise earlier under Anglo-Canadian law), the concrete content of these rights was determined by social conditions prevailing at a much earlier period, when Europeans first arrived. This means, for example, that, when the Indigenous nations of New France fell under British rule in 1763, they gained the right to maintain their antique way of life as it existed as much as three centuries previous, when French adventurers sailed up the St Lawrence River. The result is somewhat puzzling, since it is not clear why the Crown or Indigenous nations would have any interest in reviving or protecting long-vanished modes of life.

---

62 See Bruce G Trigger & William R Swagerty, "Entertaining Strangers: North America in the Sixteenth Century" in Bruce G Trigger & Wilcomb E Washburn, eds, *The Cambridge History of the Native Peoples of the Americas*, vol 1 (Cambridge: Cambridge University Press, 1996) at 363. Syphilis was probably carried back to Europe as early as 1493.

63 *Supra* note 1.

Van der Peet was not to be the last word on the matter. When the question of Aboriginal title came up in the *Delgamuukw* case, the Supreme Court beat a partial retreat. It held that the critical date for establishing the existence of Aboriginal title (as distinct from other Aboriginal rights) was the time the Crown asserted sovereignty rather than the date of first contact.[64] The Court said that this difference was justified for three reasons.

It did not make sense, argues the Court, to speak of a burden on the underlying title before that title existed. So Aboriginal title crystallized only at the time sovereignty was asserted.[65] The Court's reasoning, with respect, is impeccable. However, the underlying logic is not limited to Aboriginal title but extends to other generic Aboriginal rights. Like Aboriginal title, they all pose legal limitations or burdens on the Crown's sovereign rights under Anglo-Canadian law – limits that arose only at the time of sovereignty. Consider the right of cultural integrity, which binds the Crown to respect the integral elements of an Indigenous culture. In the Court's words, it does not make sense to speak of such a limit on the Crown's sovereignty before sovereignty itself existed.

The Court mounts a second argument. Aboriginal title "does not raise the problem of distinguishing between distinctive, integral Aboriginal practices, customs and traditions and those influenced or introduced by European contact." Under common law, it says, the act of occupation or possession is sufficient to ground Aboriginal title, and it is not necessary to prove that the land was an integral part of the Aboriginal society before the arrival of Europeans.[66] With respect, this reasoning is somewhat self-serving. Aboriginal title does not raise the problem of distinguishing between pre-European Aboriginal practices and those introduced by European contact, because the Court has (correctly) defined Aboriginal title as a generic right, whose character and scope are not determined by the practices of specific Aboriginal groups, either before or after contact. However, the same observation holds true of all the other generic rights. For example, the right of cultural integrity does not itself arise from Aboriginal cultures, nor is the scope of the abstract right shaped by traditional Aboriginal practices. The right

---

64 *Delgamuukw, supra* note 12 at para 144.
65 *Ibid* at para 145.
66 *Ibid.*

arises from an inter-societal body of law governing relations between the Crown and Aboriginal peoples. As such, it comes into existence at the point of sovereignty, just like Aboriginal title.

The Court gives a third reason for choosing a distinctive critical date for Aboriginal title. From a practical standpoint, it says, the date of sovereignty is more certain than the date of first contact. It is often very difficult to determine "the precise moment that each aboriginal group had first contact with European culture."[67] However, once again, the Court's logic has a broader application. The difficulty of determining the date of contact is no greater or less for Aboriginal title than for Aboriginal rights generally. What is sauce for the Aboriginal goose is sauce for the Aboriginal gander.

Carried to its natural conclusions, then, *Delgamuukw* makes a convincing case for rejecting the time of European contact as the critical date for Aboriginal rights and for choosing a date no earlier than the time of sovereignty. However, this conclusion does not take us much further than the position arrived at earlier. As we have seen, generic Aboriginal rights arise at the time of Crown sovereignty, and specific rights often come into existence at later dates or have aspects that change over time. So the critical date for determining the existence and scope of a specific right varies, depending on the kind of generic right at issue and its underlying rationale. In effect, as suggested earlier, the courts ought to deal with each generic right separately, so that the appropriate considerations may be weighed in their context.

The need for an incremental approach is shown by the *Powley* decision,[68] where the Supreme Court determined the critical date governing the Aboriginal rights of the Metis people.[69] As entities of mixed European and Indigenous descent, Metis groups came into existence only in the post-contact period, so a critical date of European contact is clearly problematic for determining their rights. Realizing this difficulty, Lamer CJ in *Van der Peet* explicitly postponed the question to a later day.[70] In *Powley*, the Court finally grasped the nettle and held that the critical date for the Metis is the time when Europeans established effective political and legal control in a particular area – what we may

---

67 *Ibid.*
68 *R v Powley*, [2003] SCJ No 43, [2003] 2 SCR 207.
69 Section 35(2) of the *Constitution Act, 1982*, provides: "In this Act, 'aboriginal peoples of Canada' includes the Indian, Inuit and Métis peoples of Canada."
70 *Van der Peet, supra* note 1 at para 67.

call the date of effective control. The Court rejected the argument that the rights of Metis groups must be grounded in the pre-contact practices of their Aboriginal ancestors, arguing that this approach would deny to Metis their full status as distinctive rights-bearing peoples.[71]

Once again, the Court's logic is persuasive, and once again it undermines the approach taken in *Van der Peet*. Take the case of two modern Aboriginal groups – one Metis, the other Indian – that live side by side in a certain area. The groups have common ancestors on the Indigenous side; they are both the descendants of an Indian nation that occupied the area when Europeans first arrived. By the time the Crown gained effective control over the area, a Metis community had grown up alongside the Indian one, and both groups had become heavily involved in the commercial fur trade – something absent from the culture of their Indian forebears at the time of contact. Under the *Powley* test, the Metis group would gain an Aboriginal right to trade in furs, while under the *Van der Peet* test the Indian group would not. The rights of the Metis would be ascertained by reference to their practices at the time of effective control, while the rights of their Indian neighbours would be determined by their practices at the time of contact. The result, needless to say, is paradoxical. The group of mixed Aboriginal-European descent is credited with an Aboriginal right that is denied to their Indian neighbours, despite the fact that both groups were engaged in the fur trade at the time of effective control, and both are the descendants of an Indian nation that did not trade in furs at the time of contact. A similar problem arises in dealing with claims to Aboriginal title advanced by the two groups, because, at the time of sovereignty, the Indian group may well have occupied lands that, by the time of effective control, were occupied by the Metis. What these conundrums show is the need for uniform critical dates for all Aboriginal peoples, at least in the context of livelihood rights and Aboriginal title.

From Recognition to Reconciliation

At the start of this chapter, we noted that in the *Van der Peet* case Lamer CJ held that section 35(1) was animated by the twin goals of recognition and reconciliation. However, in practice, the test he enunciated gave almost exclusive priority to the goal of recognition: it mandated that

---

71 *Powley, supra* note 68 at paras 15–18, 36–38.

Aboriginal rights should be identified on a purely descriptive basis, by reference to Indigenous customs and practices existing in remote historical periods. No thought was given to the question of how far these primordial practices, reified as rights, might serve the cause of reconciliation at the present day. The doctrine of generic rights goes a long way towards resolving this deficiency. In focusing attention on the underlying rationales of various categories of Aboriginal rights, it provides a bridge between the historical groundings of Aboriginal rights and their modern-day incarnations, as living rights that serve the ongoing needs of Indigenous peoples.

Reconciliation is a complex and multifaceted objective. While the doctrine of generic rights gives Aboriginal peoples a strong legal basis for achieving reconciliation with the larger society, it may in certain cases be insufficient to attain that goal. In focusing (necessarily) on the rights of Aboriginal groups, the doctrine has difficulty taking proper account of the competing interests of third parties and indeed the body politic as a whole. So, for example, while the new approach supports a broader interpretation of Aboriginal livelihood rights regarding resources such as fish, game, and timber, it does not provide an adequate basis for determining how these limited resources should be shared with other user groups, whose welfare may be gravely affected. Again, the straightforward application of the legal criteria governing recognition of Aboriginal title may have far-reaching effects on the interests of innocent third parties and indeed society as a whole – interests that the law may have trouble accommodating.

In certain cases, of course, the resolution of such problems may safely be left to legislation, which in turn is subject to judicial review under section 35(1).[72] In other instances, the external interests affected by Aboriginal claims may be so important or deep-seated that the mere fact of judicial recognition may risk precipitating a crisis in relations between Aboriginal and non-Aboriginal peoples, thus setting back the cause of reconciliation. On the other hand, for a court to give routine priority to third-party interests would be to ignore the promise of section 35(1) and the demands of historical justice. What is the way out of this dilemma?

The answer, interestingly enough, is suggested by the wording of section 35(1) itself. The provision states that the existing Aboriginal and treaty rights of the Aboriginal peoples of Canada are hereby "recognized

---

72 See *Sparrow, supra* note 19 at paras 46–83.

and affirmed." The use of two terms – "recognized" and "affirmed" – is an obvious but little-discussed feature of the section. Indeed, at first blush, the two words may seem to say more or less the same thing. Yet closer examination suggests that their orientation is actually somewhat different. In saying that Aboriginal rights are "recognized," the section seems to focus on rights in their original, historically based forms. The word "affirmed," by contrast, seems more concerned with the way these rights are to be treated in contemporary times – as living rights that serve the modern interests of Aboriginal peoples and at the same time promote reconciliation with the larger society.

What this suggests, then, is that the process of identifying Aboriginal rights under section 35(1) is governed by two distinct but complementary sets of constitutional principles, which we may call principles of recognition and principles of reconciliation.[73] Principles of recognition govern the identification of generic Aboriginal rights and the specific rights that arise under their auspices, on the basis of a mix of historical and normative considerations. In a word, they encompass the set of basic principles discussed in earlier sections of this chapter. These principles provide the point of departure for any modern inquiry into the existence of Aboriginal rights and a benchmark for assessing the historical scope of Indigenous dispossession and deprivation. By contrast, principles of reconciliation govern the legal effects of Aboriginal rights in modern times. They take as their starting point the historically based rights of the Aboriginal group concerned, as determined by principles of recognition, but they also take into account a range of other factors, such as the modern condition of the lands or resources affected, the Aboriginal group's contemporary needs and interests, and the interests of third parties and society at large. So doing, principles of reconciliation posit that certain Aboriginal rights cannot be implemented in their entirety by the courts but require the negotiation of modern treaties.

Unless we distinguish between these two sets of principles, we may fall into the trap of assuming that historical Aboriginal rights automatically give rise to modern rights, without regard to societal changes that have occurred in the interim. Such an assumption fosters twin judicial tendencies. The courts may be led to identify historical Aboriginal rights in a highly restrictive way – as by imposing an artificially early

---

73 See Brian Slattery, "The Metamorphosis of Aboriginal Title" (2006) 85 Can Bar Rev 255 at 281–86, from which the following discussion draws.

critical date – in the effort to minimize conflicts with third-party interests. Alternately, a restrictive view may be taken of the ability of an
Aboriginal right to evolve and adapt, so as to curtail its modern effects.
These tendencies, if left to operate unchecked, will diminish the possibility of reconciliation ever occurring. The successful settlement of
Aboriginal claims must involve the full and unstinting recognition of
the historical reality of Aboriginal rights, the true scope and effects
of Indigenous dispossession and exclusion, and the continuing links
between an Aboriginal people and its traditional culture, lands, and
resources. By the same token, the recognition of historical rights, while
a necessary precondition for modern reconciliation, is not always in
itself a sufficient basis for reconciliation, which may have to take into
account a range of other factors. So, for example, to suggest that historical Aboriginal rights give rise to modern rights that automatically
trump third-party interests represents the attempt to remedy one injustice by committing another.

The point is nicely captured in the *Mikisew* case, where Binnie
J affirms that the "fundamental objective of the modern law of aboriginal and treaty rights is the reconciliation of aboriginal peoples
and non-aboriginal peoples and their respective claims, interests and
ambitions."[74] Nevertheless, he observes, the management of these
relationships takes place in the shadow of a long history of grievances
and misunderstanding. These comments remind us that the process
of reconciliation requires the courts to take account of the claims and
interests of both Aboriginal and non-Aboriginal peoples. Neither side
can be left out of the equation. However, the process takes place in the
wake of historical injustices and grievances that cannot be minimized
or ignored. In effect, reconciliation must strike a balance between the
need to remedy past injustices and the need to accommodate the full
range of contemporary interests. On the one hand, unless the modern
law provides appropriate standards (in the form of principles of recognition) for understanding the true nature and scope of historical Aboriginal rights, there can be no proper basis for modern reconciliation.
On the other hand, if historical rights are taken to give rise to modern
rights tout court, without regard to their effects in present-day society,
the cause of reconciliation will be equally ill-served.

---

74 *Mikisew Cree First Nation v Canada (Minister of Canadian Heritage)*, [2005] SCJ No 71,
[2005] 3 SCR 388 at para 1.

What form do principles of reconciliation take? It would be a mistake to attempt an answer on the basis of a priori reasoning. The matter can be settled only by detailed discussion in the context of actual cases. Indeed, it seems likely that these principles take a variety of forms, depending on the kind of Aboriginal right in question. Subject to this caution, nevertheless, I suggest that principles of reconciliation must have the following basic features:

- They should acknowledge the historical rights of Aboriginal peoples, as determined by principles of recognition, as the essential starting point for any modern settlement.
- They should take account of how historical Aboriginal rights have been affected by changes in the circumstances of Indigenous peoples and the rise of third-party and other societal interests.
- Where appropriate, they should distinguish between the "inner core" of Aboriginal rights, which may be implemented by the courts without need for negotiation, and a "penumbra" or "outer range" that needs to be defined in treaties negotiated between the Aboriginal people concerned and the Crown.[75]
- They should provide guidelines governing the accommodation of rights and interests held by other affected groups, both Aboriginal and non-Aboriginal.
- Where appropriate, they should create strong incentives for negotiated settlements to be reached within a reasonable period of time.[76]
- They should provide for judicial remedies where negotiations fail to yield a settlement.

---

75 For the distinction between an inner core and a negotiated penumbra as applied to Aboriginal governmental rights, see Royal Commission on Aboriginal Peoples, *Partners in Confederation: Aboriginal Peoples, Self-Government, and the Constitution* (Ottawa: Minister of Supply and Services Canada, 1993) 36–48; *Report of the Royal Commission on Aboriginal Peoples, supra* note 23, vol 2, 213–24.

76 For helpful discussion, see Sonia Lawrence & Patrick Macklem, "From Consultation to Reconciliation: Aboriginal Rights and the Crown's Duty to Consult" (2000) 79 Can Bar Rev 252, esp. at 270–72; Shin Imai, "Sound Science, Careful Policy Analysis, and Ongoing Relationships: Integrating Litigation and Negotiation in Aboriginal Lands and Resources Disputes" (2003) 41 Osgoode Hall LJ 587; Imai, "Creating Disincentives to Negotiate: *Mitchell v MNR*'s Potential Effect on Dispute Resolution" (2003) 22 Windsor YB Access Just 309.

The constitutional basis for this approach has already been identified by the Supreme Court in the path-breaking *Haida Nation* and *Taku River* decisions.[77] The Court effectively portrays section 35 as the basis of a generative constitutional order – one that mandates the Crown to negotiate with Indigenous peoples for the recognition of their rights in a form that balances their contemporary needs and interests with those of the broader society.

According to these decisions, when the Crown claimed sovereignty over Canadian territories, it did so in the face of pre-existing Indigenous sovereignty and territorial rights. The tension between these conflicting claims gave rise to a special relationship that requires the Crown to deal honourably with Aboriginal peoples. The fundamental principle of the "honour of the Crown" obliges the Crown to respect Aboriginal rights, which in turn requires it to negotiate with Aboriginal peoples with a view to identifying those rights. It also obliges the Crown to consult with Aboriginal peoples in all cases where its activities affect their asserted rights and, where appropriate, to accommodate these rights by adjusting the activities.[78] Chief Justice McLachlin sums up the matter as follows:

> Put simply, Canada's Aboriginal peoples were here when Europeans came, and were never conquered. Many bands reconciled their claims with the sovereignty of the Crown through negotiated treaties. Others, notably in British Columbia, have yet to do so. The potential rights embedded in these claims are protected by s. 35 of the *Constitution Act, 1982*. The honour of the Crown requires that these rights be determined, recognized and respected. This, in turn, requires the Crown, acting honourably, to participate in processes of negotiation. While this process continues, the honour of the Crown may require it to consult and, where indicated, accommodate Aboriginal interests.[79]

The chief justice emphasizes that the Crown has the legal duty to achieve a just settlement of Aboriginal claims by negotiation and treaty.

---

77 *Haida Nation, supra* note 21; *Taku River Tlingit First Nation v British Columbia (Project Assessment Director)*, [2004] SCJ No 69, [2004] 3 SCR 550. For fuller discussion, see Brian Slattery, "Aboriginal Rights and the Honour of the Crown" (2005) 29 SCLR (2d) 433.
78 *Haida Nation, supra* note 21 at para 32; *Taku River, supra* note 77 at para 24.
79 *Haida Nation, supra* note 21 at para 25.

So doing, she attributes a generative role to section 35. In effect, she holds that the Crown, with judicial assistance, has the duty to foster a new legal order for Aboriginal rights, through negotiation and agreement with the Aboriginal peoples affected. This approach views section 35 as serving a dynamic function – one that does not come to an end even when treaties are successfully concluded. As she states,

> The jurisprudence of this Court supports the view that the duty to consult and accommodate is part of a process of fair dealing and reconciliation that begins with the assertion of sovereignty and continues beyond formal claims resolution. Reconciliation is not a final legal remedy in the usual sense. Rather, it is a *process* flowing from rights guaranteed by s. 35(1) of the *Constitution Act, 1982.*[80]

In other words, section 35 does not simply recognize a body of historical rights whose contours are ascertained by the application of general legal criteria to particular historical circumstances. Rather, the section envisages Aboriginal rights as flexible and future-oriented rights that need to be adjusted and refurbished from time to time through negotiations with the Indigenous peoples concerned.

Conclusion

Over the past two decades, the Supreme Court has reshaped the *Van der Peet* test in several important respects. First, the Court has moved towards accepting the fact that Aboriginal rights are not just specific rights, particular to each individual group, but rather are grounded in a range of generic rights recognized by the common law of Aboriginal rights. Second, in certain contexts, the Court has adopted critical dates that effectively undermine the view that Aboriginal rights crystallized at the time of European contact, pointing rather to the time of Crown sovereignty and effective control. Third, the Court has increasingly emphasized the fact that Aboriginal rights are not just historical in character; they are also generative rights that need to accommodate the full range of modern interests, both Aboriginal and non-Aboriginal, and as such may require articulation in agreements with the Crown.

---

80 *Ibid* at para 32 [emphasis added].

This evolution in the jurisprudence should come as no surprise. It is a distinctive feature of common law systems to shun absolute principles conceived a priori in favour of flexible principles fleshed out in concrete cases. The *Van der Peet* decision was handed down at a time when there was a dearth of judicial authority on the Aboriginal rights recognized in section 35(1). The Supreme Court set out a comprehensive approach to the matter, with the aim, no doubt, of providing guidance to lower courts that were struggling to apply the section's somewhat enigmatic terms. While the test served its purpose at the time, inevitably it has needed revision and amendment. As McLachlin J observed in *Van der Peet*, there is much to commend the pragmatic approach adopted by the common law – reasoning from the experience of decided cases and recognized rights – all the more so, given the complexity and sensitivity of the task of defining Aboriginal rights.[81] The Court's jurisprudence in the decade since *Van der Peet* shows the wisdom of this approach.

---

81 *Van der Peet, supra* note 1 at para 262.

PART TWO

Contesting Methodologies

5 A Common Law Biography of Section 35

P.G. MCHUGH

Barely a generation ago, anthropology was the lead discipline in the academic study of Indigenous peoples, but during the 1980s law became the more prominent. This prominence and the rise of the academic field known generally as "Aboriginal rights" were linked to the appearance of a court-based jurisprudence with which section 35 has been closely associated in Canada. Those "breakthrough" court judgments are usually identified as *Calder* (Canada), *Te Weehi* and the *Maori Council* cases (New Zealand), and *Mabo No 2* (Australia), this era spanning the years 1972–92. These cases became the platforms for a mushrooming academic field in which law dominated. The term "Aboriginal rights" encompassed not only an emergent corpus of legal doctrine, much of it with a busy transjurisdictional flavour, but also what soon became a vast interdisciplinary academic field. Anthropology remained important; however, the surging field of "Aboriginal rights" also attracted historians, human geographers, and political scientists, as well as lawyers.

Those of us who have lived through the rise of this academic field, from niche and specialist in the late 1970s and early 1980s to its immense, sprawling form today, know that law became so important because it had suddenly acquired profound bearing upon the pursuit of Aboriginal claims against the state. The major court judgments transformed what had been the received legal position, which effectively blockaded court action, and suddenly catapulted Aboriginal claims up the national political agenda. The judgments announced the courts' newfound willingness to monitor the conduct of Crown relations with tribes. The judgments represented not merely a U-turn in legal terms but also a fundamental revision of the politics of Crown relations. In keeping with a wider trend in the nature of Anglo public law in the last quarter of the twentieth century by which courts became more willing to monitor executive discretion, the embedded principle of non-justiciability in Crown-tribe relations was undone. In that sense the inauguration of a court-centred jurisprudence of Aboriginal rights chimed with the general tenor of legal development of the time. As I shall argue, it was wholly consistent with contemporary public law values that were stressing the reviewability of discretion vested in the executive branch. Nonetheless in reversing the long-standing supposition of non-justiciability, those judgments were highly controversial then and, in terms of what they unleashed, remain so today, without much, if any, reduction in temperature.

Section 35 was born at a time in the early 1980s when the common law corpus was highly unformed and prospective, the court judgments then no more than suggestive of a jurisprudence yet to come. In consequence it has become associated with the major Anglo-Commonwealth trend that ripened through the 1980s and after, by which Aboriginal claims acquired a legal and therefore a political imperative and texture they previously lacked.

This transformation of the political landscape sparked widespread debate as well as the intensifying academic discourse as a nascent and, in many eyes, promising jurisprudence was beginning its faltering steps. Indeed, from the outset all three dimensions – the legal, academic, and more populist – surged and crisscrossed into the other. Quickly the notion of Aboriginal rights described fields of popular, legal, and more general academic discourse that necessarily overlapped. The very idea of Aboriginal rights thus became a conflation and confluence of all kinds of thought and, indeed, arguing (given that rights-talk usually entails ongoing debate over the nature, extent, and balancing of rights). By the early 1980s rights-talk was coming to dominate the conduct of state relations with its tribal peoples. It was a transition that academic scholarship had promoted, that the courts had authoritatively and irreversibly endorsed, and that continuing scholarship, legalism, and public discourse intensified.

These ways of thought have attempted to incorporate the perspective of Indigenous peoples, and certainly the Aboriginal voice has presence; however, when one talks of "Aboriginal rights" as a field of academic enquiry, it has to be said that this activity has been mostly inside the house of whitefella's thought. That is to say, discussion, rumination, and disputation within the vast academic field of Aboriginal rights that emerged from the early 1980s have been conducted largely through the terminology, conceptual machinery, and protocols of the whitefella. The rise of "Aboriginal rights" may have changed the nature of thought and encouraged interdisciplinarity within the academy, but the very nature of the academy as well as the political consequences of the court-based pursuit of those Aboriginal rights has also shaped those rights. Numerous contributors to this collection were veterans of a journey going back, for some, to the 1970s, long before section 35 was envisaged. We old-timers recall well that section 35 was not part of the original patriation package (1980) but appeared essentially, and rather suddenly, as a Trudeau concession to pressure from First Nations, jurists, and other sources worried by the potential impact of his initial proposal upon the nascent Aboriginal rights jurisprudence. For some of us, the omission of an Aboriginal rights clause from the initial proposal had signalled the prime minister's return to pre-*Calder* rights-scepticism of the kind associated with the notorious White Paper (1969). Before the *Calder* case, Prime Minister Trudeau had famously dismissed common law Aboriginal rights as a "historical might-have-been." Section 35 was therefore seen as placatory, an afterthought inserted in order to rebuff any such semblance. It betokened as much the prime minister's deference to the rule of law – an acknowledgment that courts were giving credence to the untested legal arguments for Aboriginal rights arising from *Calder*, process that the dominion government's proposals for constitutional reform should not abridge – rather than a willingness to recognize, much less initiate, substantive new rights. At the time, those of us watching this aspect of the patriation controversy realized that the prime minister was intending to show that the political branches were taking the formative jurisprudence and courts' new role seriously whilst, by insertion of the key word "existing," signalling also that section 35 was not meant to confer or enlarge Aboriginal rights beyond those that the courts had recognized anyway. Section 35 would not have been inserted without the impact of the *Calder* case, stirrings from which by the early 1980s were beginning to resurge as the expected outcome – a pattern of negotiated settlements – failed to materialize. By 1980 the James Bay Agreement had in many respects become an emblem of what had not happened in the decade after *Calder*, rather than heralding the start of a new agreement-based phase in Crown–First Nations relations. To be sure, there had been in that decade a lot of talk about negotiation and land claims settlements, but this was not translating into political will or substantial progress. This meant that by the late 1970s and into the early 1980s the Canadian courts were being drawn back and more increasingly into the frame of those relations, this at the time the patriation package was being conceived.

Notably by the time of the patriation controversy, the *Guerin* litigation was in train,[1] the first-instance *Baker Lake* case (1978)[2] was drawing attention, and Brian Slattery's ground-breaking Oxford doctoral dissertation (1979) in reprinted form was a bestseller for the Native Law Centre, Saskatoon. These were tangible signs of legal possibilities and prospects that the Trudeau government agreed to accommodate, or at least not to subvert, by way of the assurance to First Nations that became section 35. To some of us, the insertion of section 35 signalled a statement as to what constitutional reform was *not* doing (aborting a very new and unformed jurisprudence) rather than a conferral of new rights or conscious reframing of Crown–First Nations relations. During the 1980s, as the Constitutional Conferences wended their irresolute way, and the Meech Lake (1987) and Charlottetown (1990) Accords became footnotes in Canadian constitutional history, section 35 stood largely unattended by the courts.[3] This was not to be its continuing fate, of course, but at the time it suggested that its role in the framing of Aboriginal rights was symbolic and confirmatory rather than formative and foundational. There seemed to be a constitutionalism that was about to happen without the courts, but this was not to be.[4]

Meanwhile, inside the academy, the field of Aboriginal rights grew enormously during the 1980s and so into the new century. This fervid intellectual activity has gone every which way. Since its rise in the early 1980s, the pattern of rights-talk about the situation of Aboriginal peoples has now had such longevity as to have its own history. Often, and for a long while now, this activity has, in my view, seemed to take forms

---

1 *Guerin v R* [1984] 2 SCR 335; see [1982] 2 FC 385 (FCTD); [1983] 2 FC 656 (FCA). Also James I Reynold, "The Impact of the *Guerin* Case on Aboriginal and Fiduciary Law" (2005) 63:3 Advocate 365–72.

2 *Hamlet of Baker Lake v Minister of Indian Affairs and Northern Development* (1978) 87 DLR (3rd) 312 (FCTD). For instance, Catherine Bell and Michael Asch, "Challenging Assumptions: The Impact of Precedent on Aboriginal Rights Litigation" in Asch, ed, *Aboriginal and Treaty Rights in Canada: Essays on Law, Equity, and Respect for Difference* (Vancouver: University of British Columbia Press, 1997) 38–75 at 59–62.

3 The one major Supreme Court judgment between *Guerin* (1984) and *R v Sparrow* [1990] 1 SCR 1075 was *Kruger and Manuel and Dick v R* [1985] 2 SCR 309. This case dealt with section 88 of the *Indian Act* (provincial laws of general application) rather than section 35.

4 Jeremy Webber captured this brief era and its lost promise poignantly (as it reads today) in *Reimagining Canada: Language, Culture, Community, and the Canadian Constitution* (Montreal & Kingston: McGill-Queen's University Press, 1994).

in which the core concern – the position of Aboriginal peoples – has been subordinated to the performance of the activity itself. This is not to claim any high ground with regard to my own position, though it is to claim some seniority as a long-time participant with a strong sense of how this rights-talk has fared. This personal sense of intellectual journey and a dash of scepticism about what it has been achieving for Aboriginal peoples has been a theme of my work in the past decade. In this time the titles of many of my publications have shown that concern with the temporality of the Aboriginal rights discourse and the shapes or patterns that it has taken through modern times. There have been titles like "New Dawn to Cold Light,"[5] "A Retrospect and Prospect,"[6] and "Relations inside a Conservative Jurisprudence,"[7] whilst my latest book was written entirely as contemporary legal history. Such retrospection is also a theme of the chapters in this volume.

Since the early 1990s, my work has been concerned not only with the changes that have occurred within my own professional lifetime but also, more generally, with the temporality of legalism through the history of the British Empire and the rise of the Anglo settler nation states. This point might seem obviously axiomatic, yet its realization has been especially slippery in the Canadian jurisprudence of Aboriginal rights: law is a human activity, and as such it occurs in time. This means that this activity necessarily changes over time. Law has historicity. I shall return to this point by way of coda to this paper, to show how section 35 has acquired a role not only in terms of the formation of contemporary legal doctrine but also as an interpretative tool for past Crown conduct. The Canadian jurisprudence of Aboriginal rights uses section 35 to obfuscate the past and the present. The courts have been collapsing law's historicity into a timeless present, where Crown officials of a generation that had no idea of a section 35 must bear the blame for the contemporary failings of the executive branch. This is valid legal policymaking through the courts, but it is not an account of the past as its actors experienced it and shaped their own contemporaneity. Please excuse the sarcasm oozing through the following sentence: strangely enough, Crown officials in

---

5 "New Dawn to Cold Light: Courts and Common Law Aboriginal Rights" (2005) NZLR 485.
6 PG McHugh, "Aboriginal Title in New Zealand: A Retrospect and Prospect" (2004) 2 New Zealand Journal of Public and International Law 139.
7 PG McHugh, "'Treaty Principles': Constitutional Relations inside a Conservative Jurisprudence" (2007) 39 VUWLR 39.

the late nineteenth century and early twentieth did not set their conduct according to the requirements of section 35 and the Supreme Court's interpretation of it. Legalism that would materialize decades later, a legalism that its own publicity hailed at the time as highly revisionist,[8] could hardly have shaped conduct decades before it occurred.

Quite evidently, this chapter is raising the themes of the temporality as well as the constructedness of legal thought. They underlie this account of section 35 and the pathway surrounding the Canadian jurisprudence of Aboriginal title/rights.

I

In Canada, New Zealand, and Australia, court intervention in Crown relations with the tribes was a response to political stalemate. In the breakthrough judgments, we see the judicial branch prodding the political branches towards an accommodation of Aboriginal peoples that had seemed in the offing (particularly during the 1980s) but after years of avowal was failing to occur. By that time Aboriginal peoples had strenuously rejected the post-war intensification of state policies of assimilation proposed and being implemented by national governments, especially during the 1960s and into the 1970s. These policies were predicated upon the liberal principle of a culturally undifferentiated citizenry enjoying equal rights and protection from discrimination. In all jurisdictions, governments saw this as requiring the dismantling of the colonialist regimes of protection and legal distinction embedded in the creaky statutory structures that had surrounded the national management of Aboriginal affairs for over a century. For all their deep-seated ambivalence about these regimes, tribal peoples grasped that they had at least permitted a continuance of tribal identity and landholding (albeit misshapen by those laws). They rejected these state policies of assimilation and countered them with an insistence upon the maintenance, if not enhancement, of special legal status alongside state measures for redress of land claims. Common law Aboriginal title was to embed this claim to legal distinctiveness with a special claim upon the ear of the Crown. Indeed, it enhanced it by reauthorizing and

---

8 See the essays in Hamar Foster, Heather Raven, & Jeremy Webber, eds, *Let Right Be Done: Aboriginal Title, the Calder Case, and the Future of Indigenous Rights* (Vancouver: University of British Columbia Press, 2007).

rigidifying historical forms of Aboriginal political organization – the tribal polity that had held land title and "owned" the claim to it.

During this period prior to court intervention (roughly, the 1970s), assimilation disappeared as the paramount state policy for tribal relations. Aboriginal rejection of this policy was so thorough that continued state subscription was not viable. The centre of political gravity and discussion moved increasingly through the 1970s towards the establishment of land claims bodies. All three key jurisdictions (Canada, Australia, New Zealand) debated their establishment as the state cautiously accepted a political obligation to address these land claims. The reasoning, certainly by most politicians, was that, once the grievances surrounding the depleted Aboriginal asset-base had been addressed and ameliorated, the state and its Aboriginal peoples could move forward. Historical discrimination needed to be addressed and corrected, so that Aboriginal peoples might merge into an undiscriminating future. Even before the courts intervened, many politicians saw land claims resolution as a precondition to assimilation. This unspoken expectation had a softening effect upon political attitudes towards the establishment of land claims mechanisms. Court intervention in the breakthrough period (1972–92) prodded political indecision and low prioritization of such measures, which, even then, were becoming electorally – and, the omens were wailing, financially – costly. In an era of rising civil rights consciousness, these land claims absorbed the language of non-discrimination and unfair negative treatment and turned it back against the state, meshing it with the more traditional language of contract and property. Land claims resolution thus acquired the flavour of unattended social justice and the state's addressing of its acts of dispossession under colour of its own (self-interested) constitutional might on which its national wealth had been based.

As they appeared in all key jurisdictions (Canada, Australia, and New Zealand) during the 1970s, these land claims had both a contemporary and a historical dimension. Tribal peoples called for the legal protection of their current use and occupation of traditional lands whilst also demanding state redress and restitution for lands taken from them by colourable means, including breach of treaty, Crown conflict of interest, and condoning of settler usurpation. The twofold orientation of these claims, contemporary and historical, placed the focus squarely on the Crown's present-day and past exercise (and alleged misuse) of its executive discretion and legislative authority. Land claims were thus framed primarily in constitutional terms that challenged the past and present exercise of settler-state authority. In that regard, politicians had long been accustomed to the courts' stance that these relations were non-justiciable, that is to say incapable of adjudication and enforcement through the courts, except to the (very limited) extent they had received statutory recognition. The cautious and initial acceptance of a state obligation to address land claims was undertaken during the 1970s, therefore, on a supposition that the courts would not be involved. It was driven by a vague political commitment informed loosely by emergent norms of human rights – shaky and unreliable as this was – rather than a legal imperative. Some partial statutory experiments were put in place, as in Australia's Northern Territory, where the process that followed the Woodward Report was conceived as a pilot for a national preferred model (that failed ultimately to eventuate when the electoral cost became clear). New Zealand established the Waitangi Tribunal with recommendatory powers limited to contemporary claims, excluding the historical claims that formed the bulk of Maori grievance. Canada also experimented with claims-resolution bodies and rather rested on the laurels, such as they were, of the James Bay Agreement (which, as noted already, for many years was a portent of less rather than more to come). Nonetheless the political stalemate remained, in that governments flirted with and avowed their commitment to national land rights mechanisms without legislating comprehensive regimes. In all jurisdictions those inconclusive politics waged over many years, in Canada even after the Supreme Court judgment in *Calder* (1972). The political branches were certainly willing to talk about addressing land claims through specialist statutory bodies but without translating that into any substantial national form. Increasingly and by the end of the 1970s, politicians' talk of commitment to land-claims resolution was seen as empty.

As that political debate stuttered on fitfully during the 1970s and into the early 1980s and with increasing lameness, a handful of lawyers (mainly) began exploring other avenues by which the Crown might be prodded into meaningful action on land claims. Initially these lawyers were based mostly in central and western Canada (Berger, Sanders, Slattery, McNeil, Lester, Morse, Jackson), but they pulled into their orbit some in Australia (Hocking, Reynolds [a historian], Bartlett [relocated from the prairies]) and New Zealand (Hookey, myself). I have bracketed the academics whose work has often been regarded as key and formative, but of course there were others involved in what then seemed a niche form of scholarship, such as the now-classic work by Cumming and Mickenberg, *Native Rights in Canada* (1972 and 1978). It was at this juncture that section 35 was born. As observed earlier, there had been the *Calder* case (which raised more questions about the common law argument than it answered), the *Guerin* litigation had commenced, and there was a sprinkling of lower court judgments; however, the argument for common law foundation of rights was then concentrated in the legal academy. Certainly there was rumbling in the courts, and it was this that the prime minister took more seriously than the mutterings of his erstwhile colleagues in the law schools. Nonetheless court intervention would never have occurred without this scholarship, as became demonstrated by the frequent citation in the Supreme Court of Brian Slattery and, later in the 1980s, Kent McNeil.

Section 35 was born of a prospective jurisprudence rather than a formed one. The intellectual focus of that yet-to-be jurisprudence was on the judicial branch and primarily upon contemporary claims for the recognition of current Aboriginal use and occupation of traditional lands through what was then becoming known as the common law doctrine of Aboriginal title. The point is that, even as the political branches failed to deliver, there commenced what was primarily (though, of course, not entirely) a scholarly attempt to persuade the courts to reverse their refusal of competence. This scholarship invoked what in retrospect we can see as essentially conservative legal tools for all the radicalism of the legal change they exhorted and the inspiration drawn from the public law values of the time: they drew on the reasoning logic of the common law and, especially though highly suggestively, its language of property rights. Section 35 was, therefore, a response to what was then a suggestive jurisprudence of common law intervention, including the uncertainty surrounding the status of the *Royal Proclamation* eastward of the Rockies.

The latent conservatism of the common law doctrine's recourse to property was barely acknowledged at the time. Even today, the downstream consequences have been rarely faced. From the mid-1980s some critical legal scholars decried the appearance of common law Aboriginal title and court-centred rights-talk, but this was as a political stance suspicious of courts as a state instrumentality.[9] They saw that the doctrine

---

9 For instance, Jane Kelsey, "Legal Imperialism and the Colonization of Aotearoa" in P Spoonley, C MacPherson, D Pearson, & C Sedgwick, eds, *Tauiwi: Racism and Ethnicity in New Zealand* (Palmerston North: Dunmore, 1984) 20. See the discussion in Andrew Sharp, *Justice and the Maori: The Philosophy and Practice of Maori Claims in New Zealand Political Argument since the 1970's*, 2nd ed (Oxford: Oxford University Press, 1997), in ch 5.

carefully distinguished Crown *imperium* from *dominium* and slated its deference to the former. Without realizing it, they were implicitly identifying a structural feature (or was that flaw?) in its method – the use of private law means (the law of property) to a public law end (the constitutional adjustment of Crown-tribe relations). The critical legal scholars did not delve into the epistemic qualities of the common law style that would later become so problematic and, as I shall explain, crippling. It is only in retrospect that we can see how this recourse to deep, one might say traditional, common law reasoning shaped and, I suggest here, inadvertently straitened the jurisprudence and the surrounding legal politics that emerged faintly during the 1980s but more distinctly during the 1990s. Most of the scholars who wove the common law argument that the courts were to accept were not seriously concerned with the question of advanced rights-design. The literature of the time suggested in no more than in very general terms how the Aboriginal property right might be constructed, assuming mostly that this would be achieved consensually and textually in claims settlements. There was in the late 1970s and into the 1980s a more basic problem, and that was of justiciability. Most scholarly effort went into convincing the courts that the common law recognized in principle (and therefore might enforce) an Aboriginal title against the Crown, despite a history that showed decidedly otherwise. The huge political controversy that surrounded those key judgments reflected a strong and far from receptive national consciousness of the major change the courts were suddenly engineering. Some hailed this as overdue correction of long-standing over-deference to executive discretion, whilst others were horrified that an unelected judiciary could activate such profound political change. Propelled by court judgment, Aboriginal land claims raced to the top of the national agenda, and as this occurred, the debate became intense and rancorous. To repeat, the fierce intensity of this national debate showed that common law Aboriginal title was ground-shifting legal revisionism.

It need hardly be said that we are dealing with a jurisprudence generated through litigation. Common law Aboriginal title did not spring into the world fully formed. Indeed, through most of the 1980s and early 1990s, it remained more an idea that the courts had accepted in principle than a jurisprudence that had progressed onto post-recognition matters of detailed rights-design. It appeared initially as an announcement by the courts that they were prepared to embark upon the exercise of rights-building, starting from the reversal of the long-standing and now discarded principle of non-justiciability. Most of those who had contributed to the scholarship that enabled these court judgments had expected implicitly that once the principle of justiciability was accepted, Crown and tribe would set about serious negotiation and claims-settlement. Courts absorbed that expectation and often spoke in those terms. They still speak in those terms of the preferability of negotiated settlement to protracted zero-sum litigation. Rights-design was regarded as a matter for the parties rather than for the courts, who, it was expected, would monitor and facilitate those processes through the procedural framework and other tools of public law that had been developed (and were still being shaped) by courts in the new age of administrative law. Restoration of the Aboriginal land base was to be founded primarily on contract rather than adversarialism.

As I have been stressing, it was into this world of a beckoning rather than a formed jurisprudence of rights that section 35 was born. Through most of the 1980s the constitutional conferences diverted First Nations attention from the courts so that through this decade the role and scope of section 35 remained largely unexplored. There thus appeared a hiatus between the groundbreaking judgment in *Calder* and the First Nations realization that the political roadway was not opening as much as promised. The hiatus proved to be nearly a twenty-year one, between *Calder* and *Sparrow*. Reluctantly and into the mid-1990s the peak courts of Canada and Australia were being dragged into the business of rights-design through cases like the *Van der Peet* trilogy and *Delgamuukw* in Canada, and *Ward* and *Yorta Yorta* in Australia.

During the mid-1990s, as this judicial attention to the shape of the Aboriginal title property right became necessary and more pointed, the courts' willingness to proclaim it a common law mission ebbed considerably. Perhaps the judges were spooked by the political ferocity of the media and public attention excited by the key judgments. The courts now invoked other legal foundation for their judgments downplaying the role of the common law.

In Canada, section 35, largely untouched and symbolic during its first decade, became the hook for the Aboriginal title/rights jurisprudence. Yet for all its invocation, the actual impact of section 35 at that key evolutionary juncture – the title/rights period of *Van der Peet* (1996)[10] and

---

10 The trilogy comprises *R v Van der Peet*, [1996] 2 SCR 507; *R v NTC Smokehouse Ltd*, [1996] 2 SCR 672; *R v Gladstone* [1996] 2 SCR 723.

Delgamuukw (1997)[11] – remains, in my view, mysterious. Certainly the presence of section 35 enabled judges to chime with the Royal Commission on Aboriginal Peoples (1996) and talk of reconciling Crown sovereignty with First Nations' Aboriginal presence and bringing an "Aboriginal perspective" to judicial reasoning. These were judicial platitudes that, frankly in my estimation, had little perceivable impact upon the shape of the title/rights doctrine as the Supreme Court judges were then articulating it. Section 35 did not itself at this stage become the platform for a jurisprudence of rights/title any more expansive than what might have eventuated anyway. It was essentially hollow.

This abnegation of the common law mission was not just a Canadian trend. In Australia section 223 of the *Native Title Act* became treated not as accommodation of the common law, as most agree it was originally intended, so much as its replacement.[12] The New Zealand courts were faced with claims that were more historical than contemporary, though there were some crucial contemporary claims mostly with regard to the coastline (notably commercial sea fisheries). They matched the trend of the fraternal jurisdictions by downplaying the common-law originating and amplification of rights and focused instead upon "treaty principles" extrapolated from the sustained policy of Parliament embodied in key statutes. The New Zealand *Treaty of Waitangi* (1840) involved a cession of sovereignty rather than (as in Canada) land, and so judges used the trail of statutory recognition from the mid-1980s as licence for their constitutional mission of rehabilitating the treaty.[13]

By the late 1990s then, judges were not invoking the common law to justify their efforts at rights-design in which they were now being drawn, so much as portray it as activity ensuing from initiatives of the political branches. It was almost as if they were disowning or at least downplaying the momentousness of their earlier "activism." The revisionism of the breakthrough cases now took a decidedly conservative hue.

---

11 *Delgamuukw v British Columbia* [1997] 3 SCR 1010.
12 Simon Young explains this trenchantly in *Trouble with Tradition: Native Title and Cultural Change* (Leichardt, NSW: Federation, 2008). More recent lower Federal Court judgments in Australia, however, suggest a very cautious rediscovery of the mission: *Akiba on Behalf of the Torres Strait Islanders of the Regional Seas Claim Group v Queensland (No 2)* [2010] FCA 643.
13 McHugh, "Treaty Principles," *supra* note 7.

The late 1990s saw courts pulled seriously into the advanced territory of giving doctrinal substance to Aboriginal title. Again, and as with the breakthrough cases, this development was an outcome yet again of a continuing political stalemate – the failure of the breakthrough cases to generate meaningful political advancement in claims resolution. As they were pressed reluctantly into this activity, the means by which they did so were quintessentially (and predictably, though now less avowedly) of the common law. The epistemic properties of the judgments of this period were building and carried hallmarks of common-law property reasoning, despite the courts' shying away from acknowledging this as the source. As this activity progressed, there emerged in Canada and Australia what can only be termed disfigured jurisprudences. From the mid-1990s, the high expectation with which Aboriginal peoples and their supporters had greeted those earlier turnaround cases deflated into consternation and bewilderment. We went, as I have said elsewhere, from a new dawn to the cold light of day.

So what was it about the common law itself that produced the messy and unhelpful shape that the national jurisprudences of Canada and Australia took from the mid-1990s? This was an eventuality unforeseen in the scholarship that earlier had swayed the courts. It cannot be explained away by reference to our intellectual concentration on reversing the principle of non-justiciability and implicit expectation of a significant and resultant rise in negotiated settlements. At this distance of time, I believe that it can be seen that there was something inherent in the common law form itself that spawned these messy jurisprudences. This was something more than the incremental and accretive nature of the way in which the common law takes shapes, going from case to case, a process in which the articulation of rules and principles is conditioned by the facts giving rise to the case, not to say the willingness of parties to go all the way to peak courts. That incrementalism certainly did not help; however, the national jurisprudences of Aboriginal title are far from the only instances of the common law working itself into highly awkward and contorted doctrinal shapes that serve the legal profession well, whilst not necessarily making its pathway explicable to others. Yet that jerking incrementalism alone does not explain the disfigured national jurisprudences. Other elements of common-law reasoning contributed, most especially its subscription to a private law concept – the proprietary one – to address what have always remained at heart public law issues concerning the nature and management of Crown relations with tribes.[14]

Common law Aboriginal title was presented in a manner that navigated carefully around Crown sovereignty by distinguishing *imperium* from *dominium*. The argument was that the Crown's assumption of the former did not entail the suspension of local property rights. Whilst the tenets of feudal tenure were introduced into the white settlement colonies of Canada and Australasia, the reasoning went (and remains), this operated only with regard to non-Indigenous land ownership, the legal foundation of which required Crown grant. Whilst technically the Crown was the legal owner of land occupied by tribal peoples, its customary use and occupation acted as a burden that courts could (now) recognize and enforce. Thus the doctrine invoked the proprietary paradigm, a private law device, to transform (domesticate) relations that previously had been characterized as inherently political. It went from one juridical extreme – the "moral" or political trust beyond any judicial purview – to the other – the most revered and intensely respected of common law notions, that of property based on possession. This re-characterization of the key type of Aboriginal land claim was, of course, a technique to make the courts' intervention palatable in its appeal to the most conservative of common law paradigms – the property one. It chimed also with public law values of the time, dressed though they were in the garb of property law. These were the values of non-discrimination, public interest litigation, and judicial indisposition towards untrammelled executive authority and dominance.

Thus, the important contemporary and historical Aboriginal land claims were repackaged as not primarily about a political relationship with the Crown. They were about ownership. Ownership claims thereby became sectioned off from self-government, this lasting for a good while in Canada, where initially the federal government treated Aboriginal title and self-government claims as separate – a separation that the Australians still largely make.

The core distinction between *imperium* and *dominium* was one against which some railed (the critical legal scholars from the beginning, but, as

---

14 There is the deeper-seated aspect of common law thought, its core notion of immanence (by which law is treated presentistly as always having "been there" in its past(s), which I do not address here other than in the context of the proprietary paradigm.

already observed, as a political reaction rather than analytical critique). Aboriginal representatives certainly were uncomfortable with it and as it dug in. They saw it as depicting the nature of their claims only incompletely and as creating an artificial distinction that bore little relation to their view of their claims against a colonialist settler-state. Thus as the promise of the 1980s turned into the contorted jurisprudence of the late 1990s, many Aboriginal representatives turned closer attention to the suddenly reanimated sphere of international law as more likely to give their claims the kind of traction they sought.

Within the academy many historians and political theorists failed to see that the distinction between *imperium* and *dominium* was even there, but the courts knew, and that supposition was fundamental to the (dis)figuring that occurred from the late 1990s, as they got seriously into the job of advanced rights-design. Thus Prime Minister John Howard of Australia was clear that Aboriginal communities could have self-management (what owners do) but not self-government (nations). Some leading legal scholars tried to dissolve the distinction. They argued that *dominium* of the kind claimed by Aboriginal peoples necessarily had elements of *imperium*, such that the settlement of land claims necessitated arrangements for self-government.[15] The courts kept away from any such suggestion. Nonetheless a lot of the other scholarship (the non-legal especially) continued in a vein blithely unaware that this crucial distinction was there, much less with realization of the practical, not to say increasingly debilitating, impact it was having.

Having anticipatively pitched the Aboriginal title as a property right, albeit in the setting of litigation that had a clear if not overriding public law concern with the nature and exercise of executive branch discretion, courts had then to use the conceptual machinery of property law to substantiate that right. This meant that when the day came, they necessarily dug into the *dominium* aspect, and it was in the very nature of this exercise that the problems arose. The courts literally dug themselves into holes out of which they have struggled to emerge.

Many attending this conference will know very well what became the "problem with property" as the juridical axis of Crown-tribe

---

15 Notably Kent McNeil, "Self-Government and the Inalienability of Aboriginal Title" (2002) 47 McGill LJ 473–510; McNeil, "Aboriginal Title and the Supreme Court: What's Happening?" (2006) 69 Sask L Rev 281; and McNeil, "Judicial Approaches to Self-Government since *Calder*: Searching for Coherence" in Foster, Raven, & Webber, *supra* note 8, 129–54.

relations in the legal landscape of the late 1990s and early millennium. The stakes, of course, had always been more than merely intellectual, but by then their sheer scope was so huge as to be (for courts anyway, I suspect) very sobering. The claims usually involved territory with natural resources of immense if not incalculable value. Grasping this, the once-adventurous courts of Canada and Australia blinked and, to some extent, choked. They developed tests of authenticity that put the highly various and often overlapping forms of Indigenous attachment under legal microscope. There was the "integral to a distinctive culture at the time of contact" test given by the *Van der Peet* trilogy in Canada (1996). This test drew immediate criticism,[16] some of which tried politely to nudge the Court out of its corner by informing it that this was an Aboriginal "rights" case and that a less constrictive test for "title" might be devised.[17] The Court took that help soon after in *Delgamuukw* (1997), but it meant the embedding of an unhelpful distinction between Aboriginal "rights" and "title." Moreover the notion of "rights" was so broad as to include those with a non-proprietary dimension. Also, although the test for "title" was presented in seemingly generous garb that spoke of sensitivity to Aboriginal perspectives and evidence, the reality has since been one of extreme difficulty of bringing successful claims (as well as high contestation of such litigation). As those who have followed the *Tsilhqot'in* case in the British Columbia Supreme Court (2007)[18] and recent Court of Appeal judgment (2012)[19] know well, there remain major problems for the courts in trying to substantiate the nature of a common law Aboriginal title. In Canada it seems that the "harder" the outcome (i.e., an Aboriginal title with attendant rights of exclusivity), the harder it is for the courts to render it. Likewise in Australia the courts developed a continuity test that gives Aboriginal custom little dynamism and that effectively penalizes those communities that have been more proximate – and therefore, necessarily, more adaptive – to white settlement and encroachment.

---

16 John Borrows, "Frozen Rights in Canada: Constitutional Interpretation and the Trickster" (1997) 22 Am Indian L Rev 37: Russell Barsh & James Youngblood Henderson, "The Supreme Court's *Van der Peet* Trilogy: Naive Imperialism and Ropes of Sand" (1997) 42 McGill LJ 993.
17 McNeil, "Aboriginal Title and Aboriginal Rights: What's the Connection?" (1997) 36:1 Alta L Rev 117.
18 2007 BSCS 1700 (Vickers J).
19 *William v British Columbia* 2012 BCCA 285.

There came in the late-1990s highly essentialist tests of authenticity that supposed an inner and unique "core" of "Aboriginality." Authenticity became the conceptual threshold for the property right. It also became the inherent limitation of the property right, the nature and function of which was literally conservative – to conserve an ancient right rather than enable a living one. The property right(s) were recognized by the courts in order to conserve a pre-contact or pre-sovereignty (but certainly not contemporary and commercially oriented) tribal culture. The prefacing of the rights being claimed with the adjective "Aboriginal" doubtless invited this essentialism, and it has so pervaded the jurisprudence and its attendant evidentiary foundations as to be ineradicable. It is not only the lawyers, historians, and anthropologists who have been drawn into this authenticity game but also scientists (as with the rise of DNA profiling of claimant groups), linguists, curators, and what seems an ever-widening range of experts able to give credibility to or undermine a core (though somehow always slippery) notion of authenticity. Most Aboriginal groups stand puzzled and nervous on the sideline, increasingly aware of how courts and their experts are capable of characterizing some of them as more "Indigenous" than others. And a notion of authenticity riddles the public sphere, as well as in the (American) episode of Kennewick Man, the bizarre biography of Ward Churchill (as a latter-day politicized Grey Owl), and frequent populist invocations of blood percentages – that is to say, of a Western paradigm of "race" – as indicative of "real" indigeneity. Thus one can sympathize with Indigenous peoples' embrace during the 1990s of international law (the Draft Declaration), not least because it put much less stress upon historical authenticity as a kind of juridical threshold. International law spoke mostly in the present tense of self-defining practices, rather than constructing tribal nations rights as a polity defined bewilderingly by reference to some bygone historical moment (contact/sovereignty) somehow defined by courts and lawyers as pivotal for their contemporary status.

    This is not to say that the situation has been wholly bleak, but it is to emphasize the braking effect that judicial elaboration of the proprietary paradigm has had on the pace of settlement (in Canada especially). The key difficulty with property lies in the awkward relationship it builds with the Crown, a stickiness that is reflected in the movement in the second decade of this century away from it towards a more relational and public law oriented form of jurisprudence. In Canada the Supreme Court has recently turned more consciously onto a road that perhaps in retrospect should have been the one from the start – the essentially public law road of the "honour of the Crown."[20] The title/rights distinction remains and is still being elaborated by the Canadian courts, but where these claims are made, there seems presently to be a distinct effort to loosen the strictures of the overly proprietary approach of the mid-1990s.[21] This is a direction that uses section 35 more consciously as a positive tool in its own right rather than as a mere accommodation of rights derived from some other legal source.

Again, the trend away from the late-twentieth-century fixation with property is not only a Canadian one. In Australia patches of blue sky have come from the rise in tempo of the consensual mechanisms of the *Native Title Act*, an essentially extra-judicial pathway rather belatedly but perhaps blessedly more taken.[22] The only major New Zealand case after the landmark late-1980s series, the Court of Appeal's judgments in *Ngati Apa* (2003), kept to the proprietary paradigm, albeit no more than highly suggestively, in recognizing the possibility of residual customary property rights around the coastline.[23] The government then set about pre-empting court-led rights design by legislating a regime (the *Foreshore and Seabed Act* 2004) that replicated and combined all the awkward elements and rigid tests of authenticity recently manufactured by the Canadian and Australia courts. The *Marine and Coastal Area (Takutai Moana) Act* 2011 replaced it with a purposefully more relational approach to Maori interests around the coastline. Though it facilitates such processes, the new Act is less concerned with translating Maori coastline interests into hardened territorial or non-territorial proprietary form than with putting in place mechanisms of coastline management that include the *tangata whenua*. Again it does not preclude the proprietary approach so much as soften it with more relational mechanisms. Even the freshwater controversy that engaged the country

---

20 *Haida Nation v British Columbia (Minister of Forests)*, 2004 SCC 73, [2004] 3 SCR 511.

21 *Lax Kw'alaams Indian Band v Canada (AG)*, 2011 SCC 56, giving a four-stage test for Aboriginal rights. The *Tsilhqot'in* Aboriginal title case is on appeal to the Supreme Court.

22 The National Native Title Tribunal (NNTT) maintains the Register of Indigenous Land Use Agreements (ILUA). Importantly, once an ILUA is registered with the NNTT it has the same status as a legal contract, binding all Native title parties to the terms of the agreement – including those who may not have been identified at the time the agreement was made. As of 12 August 2013 there were 787 registered ILUAs, of which 652 were area agreements and 134 body corporate agreements.

23 *AG v Ngati Apa* [2003] 3 NZLR 643.

through 2012 – the question of Maori rights in relation to freshwater resources – was pitched (to my distant eye) less in the more absolute terms of ownership than in the more relational terms of management.[24] Certainly in the developments of current legal frameworks for Crown–tribe relations one sees the more overt appearance of what I have been terming the public law values[25] that underpinned the origination of the common law scholarship and breakthrough judgments. The proprietary paradigm has been less discarded than put to one side, as other less all-or-nothing legal mechanisms are brought to bear upon the Crown–tribe relationship. These values include modern juridical assumptions about the nature and feasibility of proceedings against the Crown, the justiciability of executive discretion, and dissatisfaction with a lack of judicial check where distinct interests are affected by official activity, the relevance of anti-discriminatory norms derived from international and municipal human rights instruments, the foundation of representative actions, respect for the particularities and variability of context, procedural regularity and consistency (on both sides and incorporating third parties, if needs be), and appreciation of the role of public interest litigation. These are important values of late-twentieth-century public law, but at the time when the courts were taking tribal nations into a rights-based position in national constitutions they were packaged into the conservative mould of the proprietary paradigm.

---

24 At date of this rough draft *iwi* were dissatisfied with the Crown's short consultation with them about the sale of government assets (up to 49 per cent of its shareholding) in Mighty River Power (hydroelectric). On the table at the moment are "shares plus" (a concept that has strong echoes, Canadians will see at once, of the early 1970s concept of "citizens plus"). Shares plus involve special classes of shares which could provide Maori with:

• Financial dividend every year;
• Power to appoint some company directors;
• Enhanced voting rights on shareholder decisions such as approving major transactions; and
• Voting or decision rights over the management or strategic decisions of the company, including its use of water.

25 This was a term used by Professor Michael Taggart to describe the shift of outlook as well as doctrine that was occurring from the early 1970s as the common law busily developed the field known as "administrative law." Its provenance is more than Michael's, but he was a major public law thinker whose influence on me was considerable and who was taken from us at a tragically early age.

I have spoken parenthetically about the current trend away from the strictures of the proprietary paradigm towards more relational forms of legalism that take a more context-based orientation emphasizing the public law machinery of dialogue rather than a boxed fixity of outcome of the kind represented, not always helpfully, by the law of property. Maybe now legal thought is beginning to think outside the proprietary box? Maybe we are seeing the more explicit recourse to and judicial validation of those public law values with section 35 as its foundation in Canada? Perhaps we shall eventually look back on the late 1990s to the end of the 2000s as the "high proprietary" phase – a necessary playing and spluttering out of the rationale that enabled the courts to intervene in Crown–tribe relations in the first place.

II

In this high proprietary phase not only has legal doctrine become straitened and contorted. Other disciplines have been drawn into litigation, and the requirements set by the courts have affected, infected even, the method of the anthropologist, historian, and other professionals drawn into supplying or challenging the evidentiary platform for proprietary claims. These experts have been commissioned to present evidence shaped by the dictates of the adversarial pleadings and the legal tests set by the case law. Much of the expert evidence I have seen in Aboriginal rights litigation has a tendentiousness formed from and framed by the evidentiary requirements and criteria of the courts. It is not only legal thought that has been boxed in by the proprietary paradigm. Aboriginal communities have found the court door opened, or shut, according to bewildering notions of authenticity that, being oriented about the court-built proprietary paradigm, validate or compromise their legitimacy within the national legal system.

The proprietary paradigm has gripped historical as well as contemporary claims. Being put in the language of property and its past dispossession, those historical claims have also been framed by the legal necessities and attendant politics of present-day claim-making. A recent and excellent New Zealand dissertation puts that tendency this way:[26]

---

26 Lindsey Te Ata o Tu MacDonald, *The Political Theory of Property Rights* (PhD Thesis, University of Canterbury, New Zealand, 2009).

In the language of aboriginal claims, to claim historical injustice on the basis of the partial or complete dispossession of indigenous people would be to claim, amongst other things, that indigenous property rights were understood and able to be incorporated into the colonial government system of property law. Assessing historical claims of this nature presents some difficulties since the mass of literature on colonial dealings is a kind of scholarly hunt for the moral and legal failings of colonisation based on the belief that it was possible to assimilate indigenous property into the colonial administration. The need to identify moral failings, as Judith Shklar has noted,[27] lies in following the "normal model of justice" in which agents are generally only responsible for their "active misconduct." In the literature reviewing colonisation, such a prosecutorial model has become dominant and it tends to find a particular administration or government who is responsible for dispossessing indigenous peoples. This makes it more difficult to perceive the troubles of indeterminate property that indigenous and colonial governments faced; such difficulties are forgotten in the search for agents of dispossession, and that search relies on there not being an indeterminacy problem.

That is to say, the overlay of the proprietary paradigm onto the past can produce a crude and binary typology of dispossessor and dupe. The agency of the historical actors is removed, reduced certainly, as they are depicted and caricatured almost entirely by reference to their conduct with regard to a clutch of proprietary rights built mostly by late-twentieth century legal doctrine. Major historical figures like George Grey, James Douglas, and Alexander Morris (to identify some of the bigger names) become boxed as dispossessors rather than as more complex political actors. Tribal chiefs become naive well-meaning facilitators of white acquisitiveness and rapaciousness. The grim spectre of land loss overshadows their transacting with officialdom and efforts to lead their people positively and proactively into an intensifying intercultural economy.

That rather brutal historiography was probably a necessary one in giving historical (specific) claims an initial impetus and traction inside the national political systems (Canada and New Zealand). It entailed the

---

27 The author cites Judith N Shklar, *The Faces of Injustice* (New Haven, CT: Yale University Press, 1990) 41. For a discussion of this point, see Paul Muldoon, "Thinking Responsibility Differently: Reconciliation and the Tragedy of Colonization" (2005) 26:3 Journal of Intercultural Studies 240.

transposition into past Crown dealings with Aboriginal land, not only of the modern-day proprietary paradigm but also the wrapping of it in contemporary public law values surrounding the exercise of executive discretion. These were neither legal doctrines nor values that pervaded or even animated official relations with tribes through the nineteenth century or most of the twentieth. This was an era in which Crown proceedings were highly problematic. The cultural attitude towards the exercise of public authority was vastly more deferential and inclined to work inside the internal modes of discipline (rather than challenging it laterally through the courts). Nonetheless the presentist projection of contemporary legalism back into those earlier times and onto historical episodes of loss has served an important goal of bringing historical claims before current systems (however flawed) of redress. The presentation of historical claims before Canadian courts especially says more of the contemporary politics of claims-making (and First Nations frustrations with specific claims processes) than it does accurately and with historical sensitivity of the past at the centre of such claims. A "whiggish" approach towards the past depicts it in terms of the demands and agenda of the present.[28] It has persisted in the depiction of the history of Crown relations to the tribes in Canada because of the bottleneck in specific claims and First Nations perception of the lack of Crown will to settle. In the face of such reluctance, recourse to the courts is now an established tactic to spur the pace of settlement.

Again an overseas parallel can be made. This whiggish depiction of the past (which one might term a historiography, or "style" of historical writing) had its moment in New Zealand during the second half of the 1980s. Like the common law doctrine of Aboriginal rights on which it consciously drew, this historiography was born of political purpose. Since 1985 the New Zealand Waitangi Tribunal has been concerned mostly with historical claims. The statutory framing of this jurisdiction over historical claims requires the tribunal to give a contemporary expression to principles derived from the 1840 Treaty. In its early days it adopted a historiography of this good guy / bad guy type, albeit tinged also with a "golden age" element suggestive of the possibilities

---

28 More fully, PG McHugh, *Aboriginal Title: The Modern Jurisprudence of Tribal Land Rights* (Oxford: Oxford University Press, 2011) ch 5; also McHugh, "The Politics of Historiography and the Taxonomies of the Colonial Past: Law, History and the Tribes" in C Stebbings and A Musson, eds, *Making Legal History: Approaches and Methodology* (Cambridge: Cambridge University Press, 2012) 164–95.

for Crown and tribe before and beyond the life of the claim itself.[29] But those days have gone, and a vastly more sophisticated and textured historiography has emerged in tribunal deliberation of the past twenty years, one that acknowledges and respects (though not uncritically at times) the agency of officials and *iwi*. In large part this has been an outcome of the involvement of major historians in tribunal processes,[30] all of whom have brought a sharp appreciation of *tangata whenua* agency to tribunal deliberation and resisted simplistic caricature of the historical actors. It has also been encouraged by a new generation of historians, some of whom have also been involved in contemporary claims-making and, seeing complexity in their own experience, have likewise understood it in the past.[31] If absorption of this complexity brought a pause to the pace of claims settlement during the late 1990s and early 2000s, it has more recently been its motor, enabling more numerous and fluid settlement frameworks. In New Zealand, historical claims settlements are now being reached at a good, healthy pace and this, I venture, has been oiled by the sophisticated historiography and the disappearance of a facile good-guy / bad-guy one. Casting the Crown as an eternal oppressor does not create a working environment for progress towards settlement. A historiography of multiple agency is also one that matches the cut of the country's national politics in the new century with its proportional representation system, one wherein Maori have proved to be the most adept players of the highly fluid interest-based forms and occasions of engagement.[32]

This is not to say that an identical historiography could or should apply in Canada, because there are important differences, not least those arising from a federal constitutional system. It is, however, to make the point that a simplistic good-guy / bad-guy typology towards the past can never be an accurate depiction of that past any more than it

---

29 WH Oliver, "The Future behind Us: The Waitangi Tribunal's Retrospective Utopia" in Andrew Sharp and PG McHugh, eds, *Histories, Power and Loss: Uses of the Past – A New Zealand Commentary* (Wellington, NZ: Bridget Williams Books, 2001).

30 These leading historians include Don Loveridge, Alan Ward, Judith Binney, Anne Salmond, and Richard Boast.

31 Notably Mark Hickford, Damen Ward (both of whom hold Oxford PhDs in imperial legal history and have published academically as well as acting as legal counsel for the Crown), and Samuel Carpenter.

32 McHugh, "Sovereignty in Australasia: Comparatively Different Histories" (2009) 13:1 Legal History 57.

~ can be of our present. When the past is being depicted brutishly in that way, it will be as a manifestation of a contemporary agenda more interested in propaganda and embarrassing the Crown than truth. Much of this propaganda has been aimed rather bluntly against the Crown, the same Crown that represents us all and whose advisors (its Ministers) face ultimate accountability to the electorate.

The declaratory theory of the common law itself encourages this approach towards the past. By this approach, present-day legalism can be transposed unproblematically into a past that this law is declared always to have inhabited. The legal argument for common law Aboriginal title did that. It described the doctrine as immanent in the past, as always having been there as a positive law, intellectually available to the actors in the past who had shunned, overlooked, or unwittingly (and unevenly) followed it. So long as this depiction of the past was designed to justify contemporary legal doctrine, it was an instance of lawyers marshalling precedent, albeit using past episode with a sprinkling of past (and very equivocal) case law. That is to say, common law Aboriginal title was a legal argument built from past concatenations of facts and occasional selective judicial statements. It was not historical truth (for had it been, *Calder* would not have been the truly momentous case that it was). Nonetheless many historians take the position that the law as it was post-*Calder* was also the law in the nineteenth and early twentieth century. Most of them have absorbed the position taken by the courts and legal scholars of the modern era without any matching inquiry into the nature of legal culture and conceptualization of legal and other obligation in the past. Everything about the contemporary law – its mode of thought and values as well as its actual doctrine – became immanent in the past. The lack of any robust enquiry into the history of the legal status of the *Royal Proclamation 1763* is symptomatic of the whiggish, and, to be frank, lazy supposition that legal doctrine of today applied also in the past.

There is a new version of this ahistorical thinking derived from the common law mode of reasoning and the declaratory theory's unquestioning transposability of present into the past. It is linked directly to the new role that courts have been giving section 35. In the *Manitoba Metis Federation* case the Supreme Court applied the doctrine of the honour of the Crown as though it were also legal doctrine in that past.[33] That is, it

---

33 *Manitoba Métis Federation Inc v Canada (AG)* 2013 SCC 14.

collapsed present and past into an enduring legal doctrine of Crown honour (derived from a constitutional provision enacted in 1982). Of course, we are able to and should make judgments about the past, but this must occur as a conscious act of legal policymaking, knowing it is our present-day values that are being deployed. We are on thin ice when we conclude that the Crown officials charged with administering section 31 of the *Manitoba Act* 1870 in the late nineteenth century were acting unlawfully because they did not know how the Supreme Court in 2012 would apply section 35 of the *Constitution Act, 1982*. The honour of the Crown is anyway not an exacting or principled standard. It is a means by which the Court can characterize Crown conduct as inadequate or falling short of contemporary standards set by the judges. The doctrine has been applied in both contemporary and historical settings without much differentiation between a past where section 35 was in force and one where it was not. As it has been articulated, the doctrine rubs closely against the constitutional foundation of the executive's role in the management of relations with First Nations. We await its further elaboration, and this needs much more careful judicial delineation than it has been receiving to date. ￢

III

I have identified two major features of common law thought that have shaped the thirty-year history of section 35: first, the proprietary paradigm of the Aboriginal title jurisprudence that was emerging at the time section 35 was born, and, second, the common law notion of immanence that encourages depiction of the past in terms of the requirements of the present.

In focusing on those dimensions I have given section 35 a biography that tracks my pathway as an academic common lawyer born in New Zealand whose career commenced at much the same time as it – section 35 – was born. This has been a history informed by my own intellectual agenda as it has evolved over the past thirty years shaped by my graduate study in western Canada during the patriation controversy (essentially the birthplace of the common law doctrine) and Cambridge (and its association with the "Cambridge school" of the history of political thought[34]). This biography of section 35 has been written in terms of its

---

34 See the discussion in Ian Hunter, "Natural Law, Historiography, and Aboriginal Sovereignty" (2007) 11 Legal History 137. Also on my "Pocockian turn" see Mark

relation to Aboriginal title as a common law property right and, more latterly, in terms of how the common law, as a human activity, lives in time and acknowledges – or obfuscates – its historicity. This biography is in many respects my own. The past is a selective place.

This has also been a common law biography in its focus upon section 35 as an adversarial device, a role it must inevitably perform as a constitutional provision amenable to interpretation by the courts. But that is not necessarily the whole of its life, even allowing for the solipsism of its biography in this chapter. Surrounding that history is a broader contemporary one – or series of histories – of First Nations experience(s) inside the Canadian federal system, including each Nation's history of claim-making –resolution and implementation (matters of governance not least) as well as their relations with federal and provincial governments. The modern constitutional history of First Nations inside the Canadian confederation raises issues of comprehensive and specific claims settlement. In July 1997 there were twelve comprehensive claims settlements of the post-*Calder* era.[35] Fifteen years later, this number had risen to twenty-six.[36] Meanwhile the federal government has avowed its commitment to progress under the Kelowna Accord (2005), as each year a clutch of specific claims are resolved alongside underlying issues of First Nations education, health, and economic development.[37] The federal government insists upon its commitment to negotiated settlement, but important historical claims are also before the courts.

Hickford, *Lords of the Land: Indigenous Property Rights and the Jurisprudence of Empire* (Oxford: Oxford University Press, 2012) at 19; DV Williams, "Judges and Judging in Colonial New Zealand: Where Did Native Title Fit In?" in P Brand and J Getzler, eds, *Judges and Judging in the History of the Common Law and Civil Law* (Cambridge: Cambridge University Press, 2012) at 308–9; and my own account in "A History of the Modern Jurisprudence of Aboriginal Rights: Some Observations on the Journey So Far" in D Dyzenhaus, M Hunt, and G Huscroft, eds, *A Simple Common Lawyer: Essays in Honour of Michael Taggart* (Oxford: Hart Publishing, 2009) at 209.

35 Auditor General of Canada, *1988 September Report of the Auditor General* at para 14.10.
36 Aboriginal Affairs and Northern Development Canada, "Fact Sheet: Implementation of Final Agreements" (June 11 2014), online: <www.aadnc-aandc.gc.ca/eng/1100100030580>.
37 Aboriginal Affairs and Northern Development Canada, "Sustaining Momentum: The Government of Canada's Fourth and Final Report in Response to the Kelowna Accord Implementation Act 2011–12" (28 May 2012), online: <www.aadnc-aandc.gc.ca/eng/1338220678979/1338220793751>.

As an academic common lawyer, it is possible to render, as here, a history of section 35 by reference to its use by Canadian courts linked also to the pathway of my career. It is more difficult to gain a sense of section 35's role in the other constitutional venues that it inhabits, as well as its influence upon First Nations' strategizing of their claims. The federal government has recognized the inherent right to self-government as part of section 35, whereas the Supreme Court has studiously avoided a similar position. The royal commission (1996) gave section 35 breadth and possibility never matched by the dominion, any province, or court at trial or appellate level. This shows that as a constitutional provision it lives – and therefore carries a history (or series of them) – other than in the churning adversarial jurisprudence. Section 35 lives not only in the courtroom but incalculably and symbolically in the experiences, frustrations, and hopes of First Nations in long-room and negotiating room. This symbolism is important, but it is also elusive. Section 35 has also suggested courses of action to governments and officials that might never become public, much less tested or scrutinized by a court or written into the institutional histories of these sites. Section 35 has biographies inside First Nations, governments, and their bureaucracies other than the court-centred one essayed here.[38]

I close on the sceptical note similar to that with which the birth of section 35 was witnessed during the patriation controversy. The New Zealand experience suggests that historical and contemporary claims settlements would have occurred without such constitutional provision as section 35 and that their achievement, fitful and uneven as these have been, has been an outcome of political will more than court-driven imperative. In the end, then, section 35's measurable achievement might have been no more than prophylactic, to have saved Aboriginal and treaty rights and entitlements from executive, implied, or unjustified extinguishment. This was the first real meaning that the Supreme Court gave section 35 in *Sparrow* (1990). For all the symbolism that it has attracted and which has given it imaginative and historical life beyond the compass of court judgment, in substantive legal terms this may turn out to be its most enduring impact.

---

38 As Jeremy Webber portrays in *Reimagining Canada, supra* note 4.

6 Indigenous Knowledge and the Reconciliation of Section 35(1)

DALE TURNER

The purpose of the constitutional entrenchment of Aboriginal rights has been characterized as the reconciliation of Aboriginal practices, customs, and traditions with the assertion of Crown or state sovereignty.[1] In this chapter, I reflect on this idea of constitutional reconciliation in the context of Indigenous knowledge. I show that Indigenous knowledge can be articulated in two ways: in the language of the common law tradition and as a form of knowledge that is embedded in Aboriginal homelands. The first approach characterizes Aboriginal rights as a form of cultural right. In order for an Aboriginal right to be recognized and protected as a constitutional right, Aboriginal peoples must demonstrate, and ultimately prove in a court of law, a causal connection with pre-contact Aboriginal cultural practices. In the second approach, Aboriginal rights are rooted in Aboriginal nationhood, and therefore the laws, customs, and traditions of Aboriginal peoples constitute a form of knowledge, and way of thinking about the world, that is embedded in Aboriginal homelands.

My discussion follows in three sections. In the first section, I begin with Trudeau's idea of a Just Society in 1968 and show how this vision of Canadian society affected Indian politics in the 1970s to the creation of Aboriginal rights in 1982. In the second section, I discuss how the *Van der Peet* decision in 1996 has characterized the meaning of Aboriginal rights as a form of constitutional reconciliation.[2] In the final section, I recast *Van der Peet*'s idea of reconciliation and argue that if constitutional reconciliation is to recognize and respect Indigenous ways of

---

1 *R v Van der Peet*, [1996] 2 SCR 507.
2 *Ibid.* See *R v Kapp*, [2008] 2 SCR 483, 2008 SCC 41; *R v Sappier, R v Gray*, [2006] 2 S.R 680; *R v Powley*, [2003] 2 SCR 207, 2003 SCC 43; *Mitchell v MNR*, [2001] 1 SCR 911, 2001 SCC 33; *R v Sundown*, [1999] 1 SCR 393.

thinking about the world, then Indigenous knowledge must be understood in its proper context – as a form of embedded knowledge on Aboriginal homelands.[3]

Aboriginal Rights and a Just Society

By the late 1960s, Canadian political identity, especially the question of Canadian unity, had become a national, publicly debated issue in Canada.[4] The possibility of Quebec separating from the rest of Canada was very real, the western provinces were becoming increasingly agitated with Quebec and Ontario politics, and the east coast fisheries industry was on the brink of major environmental and economic change. Canadians, especially younger Canadians, were looking for a way out of the growing political tensions. In 1968, Pierre Elliott Trudeau and his Liberal Party swept into power on the platform that Canada was destined to be a "Just Society."[5] This political vision of Canada was grounded in two strongly held beliefs. First, Trudeau believed that a unified Canada required a strong centralized federal government. Second, a unified, independent Canadian state needed its own constitution that could guarantee and protect the fundamental rights and freedoms of all citizens.

Indians were included in Trudeau's Just Society. However, federal Indian policies were clearly an obstacle to achieving a society built upon the freedom and equality of all citizens. The fact was, Indians were treated differently from ordinary citizens, and the miserable living conditions on reserves were, in large part, caused by an outdated,

---

3 A few words on terminology. Pre-1982, with the repatriation of the Canadian Constitution, I refer to the Indigenous peoples of Canada as "Indians." Post-1982, I use the term "Aboriginal" to refer to the Indigenous peoples of Canada, especially in a legal and political context. The term "'Indigenous' is used to refer broadly to peoples of long settlement and connection to specific lands who have been adversely affected by incursions by industrial economies, displacement, and settlement of their traditional territories by others" "Terminology," University of British Columbia, online: <indigenousfoundations.arts.ubc.ca/home/identity/terminology.html>. For the most part, "Aboriginal" and "Indigenous" are interchangeable, though I prefer to use the more global term "Indigenous" in a philosophical context.

4 For example, see George P Grant, *Lament for a Nation: The Defeat of Canadian Nationalism* (Ottawa: Carleton University Press, 1982).

5 Pierre Elliott Trudeau, *The Essential Trudeau*, ed by Ron Graham (Toronto: McClelland and Stewart, 1998).

unjust, and oppressive *Indian Act*. It had become painfully obvious to the federal government that the costs of administering the *Indian Act* were growing out of control.[6] It made sense, then, that Trudeau's approach to solving the Indian problem was that they needed to be part of mainstream Canadian society:

> The Just Society will be one in which our Indian and Inuit population will be encouraged to assume full right of citizenship through policies which will give them both greater responsibility for their own future and more meaningful equality of opportunity.[7]

Not all Liberals believed that assimilation was the answer. The 1966–67 government-funded Hawthorn Report documented the dismal living conditions on Indian reserves and concluded that, contrary to assimilation, Canada needed to recognize and respect the political distinctiveness of the treaty relationship *and* the fact that Indian peoples had been deprived of the full benefits of Canadian citizenship. As a way of levelling the political playing field, the report recommended that Indians be recognized as "citizens plus."[8] The report stated, "Indians should be regarded as 'citizens plus' ... in addition to the normal rights and duties of citizenship, Indians possess certain additional rights as charter members of the Canadian community."[9] According Indians "additional" or "special" rights, especially when Trudeau's political goal was to bring home a charter of universally held *individual* rights, was unacceptable to his vision of Canada as a Just Society.

This Liberal view of Canadian society guided the federal government's infamous "Statement of the Government of Canada on Indian Policy, 1969," now known simply as "the White Paper." The goal of the White Paper was clear:

---

6 The total expenditures for Indian Affairs in 1968–69 rose to over $165 million. See Sally Weaver, *Making Canadian Indian Policy: The Hidden Agenda 1968–70* (Toronto: University of Toronto Press, 1981) at 25.

7 Trudeau, *supra* note 5 at 16.

8 *A Survey of the Contemporary Indians of Canada: A Report on Economic, Political, Educational Needs and Policies*, 2 vols (Ottawa: Indian Affairs Branch, 1966–67). Recommendations are found at 13–20.

9 *Ibid* at 13.

The Government believes that its policies must lead to the full, free, and nondiscriminatory participation of the Indian people in Canadian society. Such a goal requires a break with the past. It requires that the Indian people's role of dependence be replaced by a role of opportunity and responsibility, a role they can share with all other Canadians.[10]

This form of equality could be achieved by assimilating Indians into mainstream Canadian society. Indians would be stripped of their special political status, their lands turned into private property and, most importantly, opened up for economic development. In the process, Canadians would welcome and facilitate Indians' assimilation into mainstream Canadian society. Everyone would win. The federal government could get out of the Indian business and save taxpayers billions of dollars, and Indians could, once and for all, join the modern world and reap the full economic benefits of Canadian citizenship.

Indians from across Canada reacted swiftly, loudly, and publicly. Two Indian groups in particular published formal responses to the White Paper. The first response came from the Indian Chiefs of Alberta, whose counterproposal was titled "Citizens Plus," now referred to as the "Red Paper." The chiefs began,

To us who are Treaty Indians there is nothing more important than our Treaties, our lands and the well being of our future generation. We have studied carefully the contents of the Government White Paper on Indians and we have concluded that it offers despair instead of hope. Under the guise of land ownership, the government has devised a scheme whereby within a generation or shortly after the proposed Indian Lands Act expires our people would be left with no land and consequently the future generation would be condemned to the despair and ugly spectre of urban poverty in ghettos.[11]

Alberta was home to Treaties 6, 7, 8, and 10, and therefore the chiefs made it very clear that any political vision of Canada needed to recognize and honour the treaty relationship. The chiefs added,

---

10 Canadian Government, *Statement of the Government of Canada on Indian Policy 1969* (Ottawa: Queen's Printer, 1969).

11 Indian Chiefs of Alberta, *Citizens Plus* (Edmonton: Indian Association of Alberta, 1970) at 189, online: <ejournals.library.ualberta.ca/index.php/aps/article/view/11690>.

The Government must admit its mistakes and recognize that treaties are historic, moral and legal obligations. The redmen signed them in good faith, and lived up to the treaties. The treaties were solemn agreements. Indian lands were exchanged for the promises of the Indian Commissioners who represented the Queen. Many missionaries of many faiths brought the authority and prestige of whiteman's religion in encouraging Indians to sign.

In our treaties of 1876, 1877, 1899 certain promises were made to our people; some of these are contained in the text of the treaties, some in the negotiations and some in the memories of our people. Our basic view is that all these promises are part of the treaties and must be honored.

Essentially, the chiefs insisted that Indians were citizens like every other Canadian, and therefore entitled to full rights of citizenship, but also Indians possessed additional rights of citizenship – citizens plus – in virtue of their historical and ongoing treaty relationship with Canada.

The second response came from the Union of British Columbia Indian Chiefs (UBCIC), an organization that represented BC Indians, and therefore (for the most part) were not from treaty nations. The union's response came in the form of a declaration, the Brown Paper, which, like the Red Paper, called upon the federal government to recognize, respect, and facilitate Indians' rightful place in Canadian society. The chiefs wrote,

[T]he federal government seems intent on raping our culture and unique status, on wanting to destroy our identity as Indians. We reject this philosophy and demand our rightful place in society as INDIANS. We demand the right to determine our own destiny without jeopardizing our aboriginal rights and our special relationship with the Federal government.[12]

Like the Red Paper, the Brown Paper demanded that the federal government recognize both the political distinctiveness of Indian nationhood and that Indians were citizens of Canada. The Brown Paper insisted that

new legislation must reflect the real intent of past government obligations. It must guarantee Government commitments to its treaties, to its

---

12 Union of BC Indian Chiefs, "A Declaration of Indian Rights: The B.C. Indian Position Paper" (17 November 1970), online: <www.ubcic.bc.ca/files/PDF/1970_11_17_DeclarationOfIndianRightsTheBCIndianPositionPaper_web_sm.pdf>.

legislative commitments, and to verbal promises. It must provide the basis for equality and opportunity and reflect mutual trust and understanding. It must provide consideration for all people of Indian ancestry regardless of bureaucratic classification, and we must play a major role in defining these new commitments.

The Red and Brown Papers provided Indians a much-needed political spark that brought Indian voices to the forefront of national news, and set the tone for Trudeau's goals of achieving constitutional reform. The White Paper may not have been adopted as a matter of federal policy, but its political vision of Canada as a Just Society is very much alive in contemporary Aboriginal politics. The White Paper's commitment to the equality and freedom of individuals, coupled with the assumption that the sovereignty of the state is supreme and non-negotiable, are fundamental to a liberal theory of justice. Indians fit into the Just Society but had to be respected and treated like every other citizen. However, there are profound differences between treating individual Indians equally, and treating *with* Indians as equal nations. The Indians of Alberta and BC defended the position that the federal government had to protect individual rights *alongside* the rights that flowed out of the nation-to-nation political relationship between Indian peoples and the Canadian state.

The White and Red/Brown Papers embodied two fundamentally different approaches to understanding the nature of the political relationship between Indian nations and the Canadian state; and consequently, they entailed different understandings of the meaning and source of Indian rights. Defenders of the White Paper believed that, as a matter of justice, Indians should not possess any special form of political recognition – in other words, in a constitutional democracy, there are no special Indian rights. The Red and Brown Paper advocates, on the other hand, embraced the view that Indians possessed special rights over and above the rights of ordinary citizens. Indians, though, did not possess special *individual* rights, they possessed special *political* rights. The Chiefs of Alberta argued that the mutually binding treaty relationship justified the "plus" in "citizens plus." It is important to point out that these two disparate ways of understanding the nature of the political relationship, and therefore characterizing the nature of Indian rights, is that both approaches articulated and negotiated the legal and political relationship in the discourse of rights. In other words, if Indian rights existed in Canadian common law, then their meaning and content would be articulated in the language of rights.

One of the highlights of Trudeau's illustrious political career came in 1982 when Parliament finally ratified its own Constitution.[13] The first part of the Constitution, the *Charter of Rights and Freedoms*, protected the individual rights that liberals argued were foundational to a Just Society.[14] The innovative addition to the Canadian Constitution is Part II, which is dedicated to Aboriginal rights:

> 35. (1) The existing aboriginal and treaty rights of the aboriginal peoples of Canada are hereby recognized and affirmed.
>
> (2) In this Act, "aboriginal peoples of Canada" includes the Indian, Inuit and Métis peoples of Canada.
>
> (3) For greater certainty, in subsection (1) "treaty rights" includes rights that now exist by way of land claims agreements or may be so acquired.
>
> (4) Notwithstanding any other provision of this Act, the aboriginal and treaty rights referred to in subsection (1) are guaranteed equally to male and female persons.[15]

The fact that a separate part of the Constitution is devoted to Aboriginal rights demonstrated that the government recognized that Aboriginal peoples possessed some form of distinctive political identity. Aboriginal rights were manufactured on the constitutional foundation of individual rights and Crown sovereignty, and therefore their source could not lie outside of Canadian common law.

Aboriginal rights, then, became another part of the Canadian legal and political landscape. The fact that the Constitution "recognized and affirmed" a group right was innovative but counter-intuitive for most Canadians who believed that individual rights were foundational to a theory justice. The reality was that the constitutional recognition of Aboriginal rights was peripheral to the more serious political problem in Canada: the pervasive threat of Quebec separation. Trudeau refused to recognize the political distinctiveness of Quebec society, and he was certainly not willing to embed any form of special political recognition for Quebec in the new constitution. To push this idea further, if Trudeau was not willing to accommodate the political distinctiveness of Quebec

---

13 *Constitution Act 1982*, being Schedule B to the *Canada Act 1982* (UK), 1982, c 11.
14 *Canadian Charter of Rights and Freedoms*, s 2(b), Part I of the *Constitution Act, 1982* (UK), 1982, c 11.
15 Section 35 was amended by the Constitution Amendment Proclamation, 1983, SI/84-102 (which added subsections 35(3) and 35(4)).

in the constitution, why would he do so for Indians? The answer is simple: he wouldn't – and he didn't.

Section 35(1) may have created Aboriginal rights, but it concomitantly raised a complex philosophical and political question: how can the Court recognize the political integrity of the treaty relationship within a constitutional framework that preserved and privileged individual rights and the unquestioned superiority of state sovereignty? Since 1982, the Supreme Court of Canada has recognized and affirmed Aboriginal rights as a form of cultural right, at the expense of discounting the nation-to-nation political relationship. Essentially, the Supreme Court of Canada misrecognized Aboriginal rights by locating their source in the context of Aboriginal cultures – in their "Aboriginality" – and not in the political context of Indigenous nationhood.

The meaning of Indigenous nationhood, however, can be approached in two different ways. The first approach recognizes Indigenous nations as distinctive *cultural* groups that happen to occupy Crown lands. The second approach recognizes Aboriginal nations as distinctive *political* groups and therefore constitute self-determining nations. The 1996 *Van der Peet* decision embodied the first approach by locating section 35(1) rights in Indigenous cultures. In the next section, I discuss *Van der Peet*'s approach to characterizing Aboriginal rights as a form of reconciliation between pre-contact Aboriginal societies and contemporary Crown sovereignty. In the final section, I recast the idea of constitutional reconciliation in the context of the second approach: characterizing Aboriginal rights as a form of political reconciliation.

The Legacy of *Van der Peet*[16]

Dorothy Van der Peet, a member of the Stó:lō Nation in British Columbia, was charged with selling salmon in violation of section 27(5) of the British Columbia Fisheries Regulations. The Superior Court judge held that the Stó:lō had a licence to fish for sustenance and ceremonial purposes, but the Fisheries Regulations did not allow the Stó:lō to sell fish for commercial purposes. Van der Peet countered that the restriction violated the Stó:lō section 35(1) right to fish. At the level of the Supreme Court, "the constitutional question … queried whether s. 27(5) of the Regulations was of no force or effect in the circumstances

---

16 *R v Van der Peet*, [1996] 2 SCR 507.

by reason of the aboriginal rights within the meaning of s. 35 of the *Constitution Act, 1982.*"[17]

Since the *Van der Peet* decision, the Court has characterized Aboriginal rights as a form of reconciliation between the special political status of Aboriginal societies and mainstream Canadian society. Chief Justice Lamer acknowledged the "special" rights of Aboriginal peoples:

> In my view, the doctrine of aboriginal rights exists, and is recognized and affirmed by s. 35(1), because of one simple fact: when Europeans arrived in North America, aboriginal peoples *were already here*, living in communities on the land, and participating in distinctive cultures, as they had done for centuries. It is this fact, and this fact above all others, which separates aboriginal peoples from all other minority groups in Canadian society and which mandates their special legal, and now constitutional, status.[18]

He added,

> What s. 35(1) does is provide the constitutional framework through which the fact that Aboriginals lived on the land in distinctive societies, with their own practices, traditions and cultures, is acknowledged and reconciled with Crown sovereignty. The substantive rights that fall within the provision must be defined in light of this purpose; the Aboriginal rights recognized and affirmed by s. 35(1) must be directed towards reconciliation of the pre-existence of Aboriginal societies with the sovereignty of the Crown.[19]

The Court has manufactured a constitutional theory of Aboriginal rights, guided by the unquestioned and uncontroversial assumption that Aboriginal rights exist definitively within Canadian common law. Aboriginal nations have been around for thousands of years; nevertheless, post-1982, whatever the political status of Aboriginal societies – that is, whatever Aboriginal rights mean – they will be de facto subsumed within the existing legal and political practices of the state – legitimated by the unilateral assertion of Crown sovereignty.

---

17 *Ibid* at 508.
18 *Ibid* at para 30.
19 *Ibid* at para 31.

In addition to the unquestioned superiority of Crown sovereignty, *Van der Peet*'s form of constitutional reconciliation associated Aboriginal rights with Aboriginal "practices, customs and traditions"; in other words, Aboriginal rights flowed out of the distinctiveness of Aboriginal cultures. The Court stated,

> The task of this Court is to define aboriginal rights in a manner which recognizes that aboriginal rights are *rights* but which does so without losing sight of the fact that they are rights held by aboriginal people because they are *aboriginal*.[20]

In order to cordon off Aboriginal rights in the context of culture, the Court invoked the "integral to a distinctive culture test":

> To be an aboriginal right an activity must be an element of a practice, custom or tradition *integral to the distinctive culture* of the aboriginal group claiming the right.[21]

The Stó:lō had to prove to the Court that selling fish as a commercial enterprise was "integral to their culture" – to their culture *as it existed* before the arrival of Europeans.[22] To assist the Court in determining the distinctiveness of a particular practice, the Court listed ten criteria that the practice in question must meet to warrant constitutional protection.[23] The Court listened to Stó:lō legal arguments, weighed the evidence, and decided whether the practice of selling fish was integral "enough" to Stó:lō culture to warrant constitutional protection under section 35(1). In ruling against the Stó:lō, the Court stated,

---

20 *Ibid* at para 20 [emphasis in original].
21 *Ibid* at para 46 [emphasis added].
22 "The practices, customs and traditions which constitute aboriginal rights are those which have continuity with the practices, customs and traditions that existed prior to contact." *Ibid* at para 59.
23 *Factors to Be Considered in Application of the Integral to a Distinctive Culture Test. Ibid* at paras 48–75. For example, "Courts must take into account the perspective of aboriginal peoples themselves, In order to be integral a practice, custom or tradition must be of central significance to the aboriginal society in question, and, for a practice, custom or tradition to constitute an aboriginal right it must be of independent significance to the aboriginal culture in which it exists."

The appellant failed to demonstrate that the exchange of fish for money or other goods was an integral part of the distinctive Sto:lo culture which existed prior to contact and was therefore protected by s. 35(1) of the *Constitution Act, 1982.*[24]

In addition, the Stó:lō had to demonstrate – prove – that fishing was a commercial community practice before the arrival of Europeans *in the language of the common law*:

As had already been noted, one of the fundamental purposes of s. 35(1) is the reconciliation of the pre-existence of distinctive Aboriginal societies with the assertion of Crown sovereignty. Courts adjudicating Aboriginal rights claims must, therefore, be sensitive to the Aboriginal perspective, but they must also be aware that Aboriginal rights exist within the general legal system of Canada. The definition of an Aboriginal right must, if it is truly to reconcile the prior occupation of Canadian territory by Aboriginal peoples with the assertion of Crown sovereignty over that territory, take into account the Aboriginal perspective, *yet do so in terms cognizable to the non-Aboriginal legal system.*[25]

The *Van der Peet* decision entrenched three requirements in the evolving constitutional theory of Aboriginal rights: first, Aboriginal rights are characterized as a form of constitutional reconciliation; second, there are definitive criteria for what counts as a section 35(1) right; and, finally, Aboriginal communities must assert and defend their rights in the normative language of the common law. Aboriginal rights have constitutional significance only to the extent that Aboriginal peoples can explain their cultural distinctiveness in Canadian courts, in the language of the common law, and in ways that do not undermine the integrity of the Canadian legal system. In other words, the source of Aboriginal rights cannot entail a form of political identity that lies outside or beyond the authority of Crown sovereignty.

By locating the source of Aboriginal rights in Aboriginal cultures, the Court need not consider that Aboriginal "practices, customs and traditions" have political significance. If we characterize Aboriginal rights as a form of reconciliation between Aboriginal societies and mainstream

24 *Ibid* at 512.
25 *Ibid* at para 49 [emphasis added].

Canadian society, then I argue that the "forms of difference" between the two distinctive societies are cultural *and* political.

Indigenous Forms of Difference and the Idea of Reconciliation

The concept of reconciliation in *Van der Peet* dictates that Aboriginal "practices, customs and traditions" be understood as *cultural* practices, customs, and traditions. I contend that Aboriginal "practices, customs and traditions" ought to be understood in their proper context – within Indigenous philosophical traditions. Articulating Aboriginal cultural practices within Indigenous ways of thinking about the world recasts the idea of constitutional reconciliation. However, what are "Indigenous ways of thinking about the world"?

Although Indigenous ways of thinking about the world vary, the belief that everything in the world is "interconnected" is central to almost all Indigenous world views. This interconnectedness is most often expressed as "spiritual." Indigenous spirituality highlights profound differences between Indigenous and Western European ways of thinking about the world. Understandings of this interconnectedness are expressed as Indigenous knowledge and therefore are spiritual, manifested in the everyday practices, customs, and traditions of Indigenous cultures. Most importantly, Indigenous knowledge is a form of embedded knowledge, rooted in Indigenous homelands. Indigenous knowledge, then, reveals the forms of difference that legitimate Indigenous ways of thinking about the world.

Taken in its rightful context, Indigenous knowledge is organic and phenomenological and is experienced on Indigenous homelands. For example, hunting is more than simply going out on the land and killing an animal. For many Indigenous communities, hunting is a sacred practice that affirms a community's complex set of relationships between land, animals, people, and the spirit world. It is worth noting that Indigenous spirituality is one of the key concepts that has evolved in international Indigenous politics. For example, Article 12 of the recently ratified *United Nations Declaration on the Rights of Indigenous Peoples* states, "Indigenous peoples have the right to manifest, practice, develop and teach their spiritual and religious traditions, customs and ceremonies." Article 25 ties Indigenous spirituality to the land, and therefore to governance:

> Indigenous peoples have the right to maintain and strengthen their distinctive spiritual relationship with their traditionally owned or otherwise

occupied and used lands, territories, waters and coastal seas and other resources and to uphold their responsibilities to future generations in this regard.[26]

From a Western European philosophical perspective, using terms like "spirituality" and "interconnectedness" to define Indigenous knowledge is deeply problematic, if not untenable. When these concepts are used in a court of law, they fail to be understood *in terms cognizable to the non-Aboriginal legal system*. However, within Canadian common law, a concept like "spirituality" does not need to be understood in the context of Indigenous knowledge. What is important to the Court is whether Indigenous spirituality justifies the distinctiveness of particular Aboriginal cultural practices. For the Supreme Court of Canada, then, Aboriginal rights are a form of constitutional right tethered to distinctive Aboriginal practices, customs, and traditions, articulated in the language of the common law, and reconciled within the legal and political framework of the sovereign Canadian state.

For example, in the *Delgamuukw* decision, the Court stated,

> At trial, the appellants' claim was based on their historical use and "ownership" of one or more of the territories. The trial judge held that these are marked, in some cases, by physical and tangible indicators of their association with the territories. He cited as examples totem poles with the Houses' crests carved, or distinctive regalia. In addition, the Gitksan Houses have an "adaawk" which is a collection of *sacred oral tradition* about their ancestors, histories and territories. The Wet'suwet'en each have a "kungax" which is a *spiritual song* or dance or performance, which ties them to their land. Both of these were entered as evidence on behalf of the appellants.[27]

The Court recognized the cultural significance of the *adaawk* and *kungax*, but only to the extent that they justify the distinctiveness of Gitksan and Wet-suwet'en cultures. The *adaawk* and *kungax*, however, are exemplars of Indigenous knowledge and are properly understood in the context of Gitksan and Wet'Suwet'en world views.

---

26 UNGA, *United Nations Declaration on the Rights of Indigenous Peoples*, 2 October 2007, online: <www.refworld.org/cgi-bin/texis/vtx/rwmain?docid=471355a82>.
27 *Delgamuukw v British Columbia*, [1997] 3 SCR 1010, para 10 [emphasis added].

I argue that Aboriginal "practices, customs and traditions" – properly understood – are inextricably woven into Indigenous knowledge. Aboriginal rights still entail a form of constitutional right, but the distinctive Aboriginal "practices, customs and traditions" are revealed within a view of Indigenous knowledge as organic, phenomenological, and spiritual. The form of constitutional reconciliation is not constrained by the normative language of the common law, or for that matter, Western European philosophy; rather, reconciliation embraces forms of difference that justify and authenticate Aboriginal world views. There are two contemporary examples that embody this approach to Indigenous knowledge.

The first example is the Dechinta Centre for Research and Learning, located on Denendeh traditional lands in the Northwest Territories. Dechinta, an institution of higher learning, affiliated with the University of Alberta, is committed to teaching Indigenous knowledge. Learning takes place on Denendeh territories, is community-centred, and is taught by the appropriate traditional knowledge keepers. Students experience hunting, fishing, and harvesting in addition to learning Dene political theory, history, and environmental sustainability. Dechinta's mission is to produce "a new generation of leaders and researchers by providing accessible and practical learning and development experiences, respectful of traditional ways, in a taiga bush environment."[28] These leaders will be better placed to understand the complex legal, political, and economic issues that face Aboriginal and non-Aboriginal people who live in the north.

The second example is the recently ratified Constitution of the Anishinaabek Nation – Anishinaabe Chi Naaknigewin.[29] Chi Naaknigewin is divided into two parts. The first part – Ngo Dwe Waangizid Anishinaabe [One Anishinaabe family] – "drafted" by the clan mothers, outlines the fundamental teachings of the Anishinaabe, and is written in Anishinaabemowin.[30] The second part of Chi Naaknigewin shifts to English, which consists of the eleven Articles that outline the principles of the relationship between the Anishinaabek Nation and the Canadian

---

28 Mission Statement, Dechinta homepage, online: <dechinta.ca/>.
29 See Anishinabek Nation, "Restoration of Jurisdiction" online: <www.anishinabek. ca/roj/index.asp>.
30 These are the Seven Grandfather teachings: *zaagidwin, debwewin, mnaadendmowin, nbwaakaawin, dbaadendiziwin, gwekwaadziwin miinwa aakedhewin* [love, truth, respect, wisdom, humility, honesty, and bravery].

state. The shift from Anishinaabemowin and English, a kind of "Anishinaabek linguistic turn," highlights moral, constitutional, political, and spiritual forms of difference that creates a kind of dialogical space that allows Anishinaabe voices to speak for themselves. Chi Naaknigewin is a complex philosophical text that respects both Anishinaabe and Western European ways of thinking about moral and political relationships. Indigenous knowledge, in both Dechinta and Chi Naaknigewin, constitutes an authentic way of thinking about the world.

For many, the idea of authenticating Indigenous knowledge is as untenable philosophically as it is to define Indigenous spirituality. However, characterizing Aboriginal rights as a form of reconciliation between pre-contact Aboriginal cultures and the unilateral assertion of state sovereignty *is not cognizable to Aboriginal ways of understanding the world*. If Aboriginal rights distinguish the unique constitutional place that Aboriginal peoples have within Canadian society, then *part* of understanding this uniqueness requires us to listen to Aboriginal ways of thinking about the meaning of their rights. This approach to reconciliation is offered in the same spirit as the Red and Brown Papers: Aboriginal peoples constitute nations, the state recognized and continues to recognize this fact, and Aboriginal peoples are calling upon Canadian society to live up to its obligations.

I have shown that Indigenous knowledge can be articulated in two contexts: in the language of the common law tradition and as a form of embedded knowledge in Aboriginal homelands. Indigenous knowledge defines distinctive Aboriginal cultural practices, and the rightful place to understand them is on Aboriginal homelands, taught by the appropriate knowledge keepers. If we characterize Aboriginal rights as a form of reconciliation between Aboriginal practices, customs, and traditions and the unilateral assertion of Crown sovereignty, then we ought to use the appropriate understanding of Aboriginal cultural practices. This requires us to recognize the legitimacy of Aboriginal ways of thinking about the world; and, if we take Aboriginal knowledge seriously, it requires us to listen to Aboriginal voices.

7 Military Historiography, Warriors, and Soldiers: The Normative Impact of Epistemological Choices

JEAN LECLAIR

L'impossibilité de trancher, à la guerre, entre le poids de l'action collective et l'héroïsme d'un seul, la mouvante imprécision de leur équation, fut l'une des leçons de ces quatre années de combats.

Andrei Makine (1957–)[1]

En effet, que répliquer à celui qui vous dit: Quelle que soit la somme des éléments dont je suis composé, je suis un: or, une cause n'a qu'un effet; j'ai toujours été une cause une: je n'ai donc jamais eu qu'un effet à produire; ma durée n'est donc qu'une suite d'effets nécessaires.

Denis Diderot (1713–1784)[2]

More than a precautionary compassion is needed if we are to help decolonized peoples; we must also acknowledge and speak the truth to them, because we feel they are worthy of hearing it ... Telling the truth to one's people, even if others can hear it and make use of it, does not add to their misery but, on the contrary, is a sign of respect and assistance. The bad faith of groups is more damaging than that of individuals; it is essential, therefore, that their more farsighted and courageous members attempt to enlighten them. If no one is willing to take the trouble to do this, then those groups can only look forward to a loss of credibility and authority.

Albert Memmi (1920–)[3]

---

1 *La vie d'un homme inconnu* (Paris: Éditions du Seuil) 148.
2 *Jacques le Fataliste et son maître* (1771; Paris: Gallimard, 1973) 235.
3 *Decolonization and the Decolonized*, translated by Robert Bononno (Minneapolis: University of Minnesota Press, 2006), originally published in 2004 as *Portrait du décolonisé arabo-musulman et de quelques autres* at xiii–xvi and 32.

For many years, I have been reflecting upon the manner in which a contextualized normative and constitutional federal theory[4] could be devised to accommodate Aboriginal political communities and their members within Canada. Initially, my interest in federalism had been sparked by issues relating to Quebec's place within the Canadian federation. In the course of such studies, I was struck by the impact of the often unstated epistemological assumptions of constitutionalists and political scientists – whether Aboriginal or non-Aboriginal, French- or English-Canadian – on the avenues of coexistence they offered. Some of these assumptions, I realized, often had the potential to disqualify federalism as a meaningful path to more harmonious relationships. Furthermore, as I shall try to demonstrate, many of the accounts devoted to the recognition and reconciliation of Aboriginal peoples with Canadian sovereignty share unstated assumptions that each of the various communities implicated by these accounts – Aboriginal and non-Aboriginal – possesses a unitary "identity" and speaks in one voice.

In this chapter, I intend to show that the epistemological lens[5] through which one examines reality entails momentous normative

---

4 This theory is the subject of a book I am writing. It also forms the intellectual underpinning of the following articles: "Les droits ancestraux en droit constitutionnel canadien: quand l'identitaire chasse le politique," in Alain Beaulieu, Stéphan Gervais, & Martin Papillon, eds, *Les Autochtones et le Québec. Des premiers contacts au Plan Nord* (Montreal: Les Presses de l'Université de Montréal, 2013) 299; "Le fédéralisme: un terreau fertile pour gérer un monde incertain," in Ghislain Otis & Martin Papillon, eds, *Fédéralisme et gouvernance autochtone / Federalism and Aboriginal Governance* (Quebec: Les Presses de l'Université Laval, 2013) 21; "Le fédéralisme comme refus des monismes nationalistes," in Dimitrios Karmis & François Rocher, eds, *La dynamique confiance-méfiance dans les démocraties multinationales: Le Canada sous l'angle comparatif* (Quebec: Presses de l'Université Laval, 2012) 209; "'Il faut savoir se méfier des oracles.' Regards sur le droit et les autochtones" (2011) 41:1 Recherches amérindiennes au Québec 102; and Réplique 41:1 Recherches amérindiennes au Québec 110; "Les périls du totalisme conceptuel en droit et en sciences sociales" (2009) 14 Lex Electronica; "'Vive le Québec libre!' Liberté(s) et fédéralisme" (2010) 3 *Revue québécoise de droit constitutionnel*; "Federal Constitutionalism and Aboriginal Difference" (2006) 31 Queen's LJ 521; Leclair J, "Le droit et le sacré ou la recherche d'un point d'appui absolu," in Jean-François Gaudreault-Desbiens, dir, *Le droit, la religion et le "raisonnable" – Le fait religieux entre monisme étatique et pluralisme juridique* (Montreal: Éditions Thémis, 2009) 476; Leclair J, "Forging a True Federal Spirit: Refuting the Myth of Quebec's 'Radical Difference,'" in André Pratte, ed, *Reconquering Canada: Quebec Federalists Speak Up for Change* (Toronto: Douglas & MacIntyre, 2008), 29.

5 Epistemology addresses issues of knowledge. It concerns itself with the question of how we know what we know. It refers to the constitutive conditions that must be

consequences[6] and that, quite often, these are not fully appreciated – or else they are wilfully ignored – by intellectuals interested in finding political and constitutional solutions to the Aboriginal/non-Aboriginal or Quebec/Canada conundrums.

More specifically, I wish to demonstrate that the source of the "monocular outlook"[7] of many of the normative and constitutional theories devoted to the accommodation of Quebec's or of the Aboriginal peoples' "difference" within Canada's political organization and constitutional framework is often to be found in such monocular outlooks' unstated epistemological assumptions. In other words, after reading many of the authors propounding such theories, I felt like saying, "Tell me how you *see* the world, and I will tell you what you intend to *prescribe*."

Granted, a normative theory – political or constitutional – does not have for a prime purpose the description of reality. Its vocation is always aspirational. It invariably advocates a particular mode of being. However, for it to be relevant for human beings of flesh and blood, the prescriptions it commands must, in some fashion, have some resonance with the reality as experienced by these individuals.

Some constitutionalists or political theorists, reflecting upon the place of Quebeckers or of Aboriginal peoples within the Canadian state, often take for granted the ontological materiality of abstractions such as "nations," "peoples," and "cultural communities." These are implicitly conceptualized as endowed with a subjectivity of their own and their constituent members ideated as immersed in a sea of homogeneity and unanimity. These communal abstractions are depicted as having one centre only, the locus of a single all-dominating culture, as if one heart palpitated in all and every community member's breast.

---

satisfied for a belief or a theory to be held true. An epistemology aims at providing a systematic and truthful understanding of reality. For example, "scientific knowledge" is an expression generally confined to discourses made up of a coherent ensemble of statements themselves based on empirically verifiable facts. Finally, all epistemologies have ontological ramifications, for methods of inquiry will determine the facts perceived as being part of reality. Ontology is concerned with the nature of the constituent elements of reality.

6 By "normative" I do not refer exclusively to legal normativity, but rather to any process implying a value judgment between, for instance, how things are and how they should or ought to be, between what is good and what is evil, what is right and what is wrong.

7 An expression I borrow from John Keegan, *The Face of Battle: A Study of Agincourt, Waterloo and the Somme* (London: Pimlico, 1976) 25.

From this perspective, not only are double allegiances anathema, but cultures end up being painted with a Manichean brush. Although much is valuable in their work, Marie Batiste and James (Sa'ke'j) Youngblood Henderson's very influential *Protecting Indigenous Knowledge and Heritage: A Global Challenge*[8] provides an excellent example of this binary approach. In it, "Eurocentric" cognitive theories are depicted as "unreliable ... as means for arriving at truth about the natural world"; they are said to provide categories that are "arbitrary" and whose sole object is "to measure, predict or control," never, it seems, to explain and understand. In addition, "desire" is said to be the Eurocentric thought's only impetus. Consequently, "[p]eople are subject to arbitrary desires and accept certain assumptions about the natural world. Based on their desires and assumptions, they use reason to explain and structure the world around them." On the contrary,

> Indigenous ways of knowing hold as the source of all teachings caring and feeling that survive the tensions of listening for the truth and that allow the truth to touch our lives. Indigenous knowledge is the way of living within contexts of flux, paradox, and tension, respecting the pull of dualism and reconciling opposing forces. In the realm of flux and paradox, "truthing" is a practice that enables a person to know the spirit in every relationship.[9]

Truth, by the way, is inaccessible by way of Eurocentric thought.[10] Aboriginals are, fortunately for them, genetically endowed with the ability to commune with truth. One question – out of many – comes to mind when reading Batiste and Henderson: what allows them to speak on a realist mode of Aboriginal concepts, while in the very same breath, they depict Western concepts as mere illusions?[11] Mary Ellen Turpel's celebrated article "Aboriginal Peoples and the Canadian Charter: Interpretive Monopolies, Cultural Differences" provides another eloquent example. In it, she claims that cultures are incommensurable. Ironically,

---

8 Saskatoon: Purich, 2000.
9 *Ibid* at 27–28, 42; see also 36–37.
10 *Ibid* at 27.
11 For an equally Manichean perspective, see Taiaiake Alfred, *Peace, Power and Righteousness: An Indigenous Manifesto* (Don Mills, ON: Oxford University Press, 1999); and, best of all, Claude Denis, *We Are Not You: First Nations and Canadian Modernity* (Peterborough, ON: Broadview, 1997).

her argument is based on the opinion of a non-Aboriginal, i.e., Ruth Benedict's totalist understanding of "culture": "[C]ultures are oriented as wholes in different directions. They are travelling along different roads in pursuit of different ends, and these ends and these means in one society cannot be judged in terms of those of another society because essentially they are incommensurable."[12]

Other authors, at the other end of the spectrum, conceptualize "individuals" as isolated monads capable of making significant choices in cultural vacuums and impervious to any primordial attachments.[13] Such atomized individuals can therefore, it is presumed, flutter about from one community to another without undergoing any pain or hardships.

Each time I read a new book or article on the place of Aboriginal peoples or Quebeckers within the Canadian federation, I keep asking myself, What kind of person does the author have in mind when proposing such and such normative theory? What anthropological assumptions do these theories imply? On closer examination, it struck me that while structural and communitarian theories underestimated human agency, their individualistic counterparts overestimated it. In both cases, we end up with an impoverished understanding of humanity. The latter always seems irretrievably lost in those theories' epistemological blind spots. As individuals, we are either conceived as pre-programmed to pursue a culturally fixed agenda defined by an enlightened vanguard or, contrariwise, we are presumed able to act out any motivation whatsoever, notwithstanding the circumstances in which the lottery of life has cast us.

---

12 Quoted in Mary Ellen Turpel, "Aboriginal Peoples and the Canadian Charter: Interpretive Monopolies, Cultural Differences" (1989–90) Can Hum Rts YB 3, at 35. As for Quebec scholars, I have described elsewhere the methodological nationalism of legal scholars Andrée Lajoie and Eugénie Brouillet and that of political scientists Guy Laforest and Patrick Fafard, François Rocher and Catherine Côté in Leclair J, "Forging a True Federal Spirit," supra note 4 and "Le fédéralisme comme refus des monismes nationalistes," supra note 4, an ontological and epistemological perspective according to which the Québécois nation has but one soul and, therefore, but one way of envisaging the world. Quebeckers failing to embrace that perspective are, sad to say, still colonized or ill informed.

13 Tom Flanagan's *First Nations? Second Thoughts* (Montreal & Kingston: McGill-Queen's University Press, 2000); and Melvin H Smith's *Our Home or Native Land: What Government's Aboriginal Policy Is Doing to Canada* (Toronto: Stoddard, 1996) are paradigms of such perspectives.

The mono-conceptualism, or conceptual "totalism,"[14] embraced by many social sciences and legal theoretical perspectives, does not allow for a realistic depiction of the complexity of our individual identities. By mono-conceptualism, I refer to the attempt to pigeonhole the entirety of reality in a single concept that admits no contradiction, or the tendency to anchor a theory on the belief that humans are driven by a single dominating motivation. Or again, the trend, in some historical circles, to depict a community's trajectory through time as "incomparable." Such monocular perspectives generate concepts that feed on incommensurability.

Marcel Detienne, a staunch and iconoclastic advocate of a comparative anthropology, has for many years now criticized the proponents of "a national and unique type of history"[15] "autistic" historians,[16] who defend such nationalistic history as superior to all others and who, imbued with their conviction of its uniqueness, rebel against the idea of any form of comparative approach: "The belief that [a nation's] identity has been unique in its unbroken continuity ever since the beginning rules out the slightest mention of anything that might cast doubt upon this incomparable phenomenon." He underlines that "what is central to any nation-with-historians-of-its-own is a mythology, a *myth-ideology*, in short, whatever possesses the power to generate belief in a 'national history' of unique and incomparable nature":[17] an understanding of nationality designed to "mar[k] out foreigners."[18] Detienne "suggest[s] that the reasons why the framework of 'nationalism' is so solid and so resistant is that it is constructed from excellent materials and put together by highly qualified workmen."[19] Fernand Braudel's passionate appeal to his fellow historians, according to which "[w]e must not allow our history to be expropriated" could have been written by many Aboriginal, Quebec, or English Canadian intellectuals. As Detienne says, instead of immuring ourselves in our own national

---

14 A term I borrow from Bernard Valade, "De l'explication dans les sciences sociales: holisme et individualisme," in Jean-Michel Berthelot, ed, *Épistémologie des sciences sociales* (Paris: PUF, 2001) 385.
15 *The Greeks and Us*, translated by Janet Lloyd (Cambridge: Polity, 2007), originally published in 2005 as *Les Grecs et nous*, at 4; from the same author, see *Comparer l'incomparable: Oser expérimenter et construire* (Paris: Éditions du Seuil, Paris, 2009).
16 *Ibid* at 100.
17 *Ibid* at 86–87.
18 *Ibid* at 88.
19 *Ibid* at 89.

histories, much more interesting would be to "compare various species of the 'national history genre' and analyse in context the elements that compose the myth-ideologies of nationalism [of various nations]."[20] We must, he pleads, "draw attention to the stupidity of incomparability."[21]

Warriors, be they Taiaiake Alfred's "new warriors"[22] or Dale Turner's "word warriors,"[23] are potent figures in Aboriginal universes,[24] as is the pipe-smoking, musket-carrying *Patriote* for many staunch independence-seeking Québécois. And so, to illustrate my claim that epistemological choices carry normative consequences, and that this reality holds sway in all disciplines, I intend to focus on military historiography. I mean to describe the manner in which military history has been – and still is, in many instances – written, and depict its normative impact, i.e., its influence on the training given to those who put their very lives in the service of the state.

In his masterpiece *The Face of Battle: A Study of Agincourt, Waterloo and the Somme*,[25] the military historian John Keegan's object is to answer the following questions: How do soldiers behave during a battle? Why do they keep on marching even in the face of absolute horror? When and why do they flee? Strangely enough, the voluminous military literature at the time of his writing (1976) provided next to no answer to such questions. Why was that so?

---

20 *Ibid* at 92.

21 *Ibid* at 129.

22 *Wasàse: Indigenous Pathways of Action and Freedom* (Peterborough, ON: Broadview, 2005) 19.

23 Dale Turner, *This Is Not a Peace Pipe: Towards a Critical Indigenous Philosophy* (Toronto: University of Toronto Press, 2006).

24 For an in-depth attempt – based on archival and documentary evidence, and also on Indigenous oral traditions – at explaining the phenomenon of war in terms of the "cultural logic" of the – diverse – Indigenous peoples themselves, see Gilles Havard, *Empire et métissages: Indiens et Français dans le Pays d'en haut, 1660–1715* (Sillery & Paris: Septentrion & Presses de l'Université Paris-Sorbonne, 2003) at 126–79 and 184–203. Although Havard defends a fonctionnalist understanding of the war phenomenon (at 147–48), such understanding does not, however, completely smother individual agency under the heavy mantle of inexorable and univocal cultural forces (see, for instance, 150–51, 169).

25 *Supra* note 7.

Naturally, where ancient battles were concerned, evidence was an issue (only official documentation and generals' memoirs – Caesar's *Commentaries* for example – were available). But the main reason had to do with the "strategocentric"[26] format of the historical narratives. Let's examine the latter's epistemological features.

Such a narrative is characterized, in the first instance, by a "'win' or 'lose'" perspective.[27] Because historians are concerned with the *outcome* of battles, they envisage the latter as rational mind games fought by opposing generals. Plans of attack, available material, limits of daylight are all-important. Thus the entire focus is on leadership and constraints imposed on it.

This leads to a second fundamental feature of that narrative: the "reduction of soldiers to pawns."[28] The commander is envisaged as a chess player moving "large, intellectually manageable blocks of human beings" from here to there.[29] Human and even animal behaviour is always depicted as unbelievably uniform.[30] The "French cavalry" is advancing; the "British artillery" retaliates. Nobody flinches; all obey. Very rarely are we made aware of individuals refusing to advance, casting themselves to the ground trying to shield themselves behind the corpses of their comrades. When one recollects that a horse does not like to tread on a living object,[31] one is left to wonder how a mass of 15,000 horsemen can be said to storm over a battlefield littered with bodies. Soldiers are also reduced to the names of their officers ("Marshall Ney led the attack") or lost in anonymous concepts such as "the hardiest veterans," the "struggling multitude," or the "mighty mass." The narrative is replete with such collective images.[32]

Third, these battle-pieces are often characterized by abrupt unexplained discontinuities. For example, at the battle of Albuera, on 18 May 1811, the French were, for a time, on the verge of winning the day when, according to General Sir William Napier's account, the British Fusilier Brigade "suddenly and sternly recovering, … closed on their terrible enemies, and then was seen with what strength and majesty

---

26 *Ibid* at 74.
27 *Ibid* at 47.
28 *Ibid* at 62.
29 *Ibid* at 47.
30 *Ibid* at 39.
31 *Ibid* at 45.
32 *Ibid* at 36.

the British soldier fights."[33] What happened exactly? Why did these soldiers regroup and attack? It is worth reminding that at the end of the battle only 1,800 out of 6,000 British infantrymen were left standing. The *normative* consequences of such a "monocular" outlook[34] on the phenomena of war was the establishment of a system of military education designed for would-be officers where the conduct of war was reduced to a set of rules and a system of procedures. Command and control could be achieved, it was thought, only if officers and soldiers obeyed rules of procedure. The whole system rested on a belief that it was possible "to make orderly and rational what is essentially chaotic and instinctive." Although not entirely incorrect, this view of the conduct of war was premised on the erroneous belief that the ordinary soldier's *sole* motivation for combat was respect for discipline and for hierarchy.

In fact, as demonstrated by military historians such as Keegan and his disciples – and some pioneers before them – and as popular series such as *Brothers in Arms* or *The Pacific* have made common knowledge, "it will not be because of his or anyone else's leadership that the group members will begin to fight and continue to fight. It will be, on the one hand, for personal survival, which individuals will recognize to be bound up with group survival, and on the other, for fear of incurring by cowardly conduct the group's contempt."[35] Putting the ordinary soldiers in the spotlight of research also revealed some bewildering – and, from my point of view – comforting facts about human nature, the most interesting one being that, during the Second World War, in the Pacific theatre and in the battle for France that ensued after D-Day, "no more than about a quarter of all [American] 'fighting' soldiers [used] their weapons against the enemy."[36] Beyond the horizons of collective abstractions one can get a glimpse of real humanity (or inhumanity).

Most modern armies have now integrated into the traditional organization of their fighting units what is called the "small group dynamics." However, as underlined by Keegan, military historians, in large numbers, continue to hold on to the ancient strategocentric paradigm and essentially ignore events contradicting it. Keegan's explanation for such resistance deserves to be quoted in full:

---

33 Quotation reproduced at *ibid* at 37.
34 *Ibid* at 15.
35 *Ibid* at 53.
36 *Ibid* at 73.

The introduction of the concept of "small groups" ... deals a body blow to the assumptions underlying the "win/lose" approach. For if one once admits that the behaviours of a group of soldiers on any part of the battlefield ought to be understood in terms of their corporate mood, or of the conditions there prevailing at the time, indeed in terms of anything but their willingness to do as duty, discipline and orders demand, then the whole idea of the outcome of a battle being determined by one commander's defter manipulation of his masses against his opponent's crumbles.[37]

Researchers in the field of Aboriginal issues or Quebec nationalism also fall prey to the temptation of focusing on leadership, be that of provincial or federal heads of government, band chiefs, elders, "word warriors," or the "new indigenous intelligentsia"[38] called forth by Alfred. Furthermore, as military historians content with seeing combat units where there are soldiers, many researchers see only communities where, in fact, there are persons. Abstract notions of "non-Aboriginals" as opposed to "Aboriginals," "nations," "peoples," although most pertinent, nevertheless occupy the whole of the intellectual horizon. Implicit in these intellectuals' discourses is the empirically unverified belief in these abstract collective entities' perfect homogeneity, and the unanimity of their members on fundamental issues.

No one will be surprised to hear that Quebeckers are anything but unanimous in their understanding of the "nation." As for Aboriginals, unsurprisingly, they too are divided on fundamental issues of identity. For example, in its October 2007 report entitled *A Review of the Kahnawá:ke Membership Law*,[39] the Mohawk Council of Kahnawá:ke's Membership Department underlined how difficult it was to circumscribe what counts as culture or tradition:

> When it comes to Membership, the Kahnawá:ke community has many conflicting opinions. Each family has its own idea of what being a member of the community really means. Few of our community would actually fit into the strictest mode of lineage calculation as evidenced by the application of strict blood quantum consideration, clan association and ties to the community. Our oral history and tradition often contradict the actions

---

37 *Ibid* at 52.
38 Alfred, *Peace, Power and Righteousness, supra* note 11, at 135, 142–43.
39 At 18, online: <www.kahnawake.com/org/docs/MembershipReport.pdf>.

taken during the history of membership administration in that if the community were truly traditional, not many would be refused through the Council of Elders or Chief and Council's past methods. There has been a regeneration of culture in our community. More have begun learning about our language and traditions. Efforts are being made to incorporate this in our identity defining practices (i.e. the Membership Law). Yet, with the current Membership Law, we are stressing administrative processes as well as hard and fast rules based on blood quantum over tradition and culture. To continue to survive in the face of Canada's attempts to completely assimilate or extinguish the Indians of this country through the Indian Act and other "programs," we must find ways to better incorporate our traditional values and practices with the procedural requirements of a modern law.

A striking feature of the nationalist or holistic epistemological perspective is the often implicit presumption of the "natural" as opposed to the "artificial" character of the "nation" or the "community." In other words, the latter is envisaged as originating from some kind of transcendent authority, at once ontologically prior and superior to individuals, and as deriving its existence from a quasi-natural historical process where individual wills play no significant part. Of course, in that perspective, community members emerge as mere pawns. And, in fact, proponents of methodological nationalism and methodological holism rarely inquire about whether the members of the communities to which they refer agree on the nation's or the community's essence or, more fundamental still, whether they place the interest of the nation or of the community at the top of their multiple identitary referents (gender, sexual orientation, social class, profession, place of residence, religion, etc.) at all times and in all circumstances.[40]

---

40 The temptation of explicate all phenomena by way of the simplest possible generalization is a trap in which many intellectuals fall. Donald Kagan, another military historian, cautions his colleagues against such peril (*On the Origins of War and the Preservation of Peace* [New York: Anchor Books, 1995], at 8–9):

What, then, is the best method for gaining an understanding of how and why states and nations go to war? Since honor, fear, and interest are at issue, a grasp of the particular ways in which these were appreciated and related to one another in the outbreak of each war is essential, for these may differ in different societies and at different times. The well-known lines of the ancient Greek poet Archilochus present the two fundamental choices: "The fox knows many tricks, the hedgehog only one; / one big one." Philosophers and most social scientists are the hedgehogs; they seek

Furthermore, in presuming the consubstantiality of the nation and society, and by presuming the members' unanimity, such nationalistic and holistic intellectuals confer great authority to those who speak in the nation's or the community's name. The attention of researchers is thus focused on the official discourses of governments and political parties where Quebec scholars are concerned, and on the discourses of band chiefs, elders, or word warriors where Aboriginal scholars are concerned. Although of great importance, these discourses do not necessarily reflect the sentiments and beliefs of the totality of the community's or nation's members.

The figure of the elder is prominent in Aboriginal scholarship. However, very often, in the scholarship of Marie Batiste, James (Sa'ke'j) Youngblood Henderson, Taiaiake Alfred, Claude Denis, Dale Turner, and others, the identity of such elders is presumed to be uncontroversial. In fact, and again unsurprisingly, such is not always the case. In its April 2008 report entitled *Council of Elders: Operational Review*,[41] a report following its October 2007 report entitled *A Review of the Kahnawá:ke Membership Law*,[42] the Mohawk Council of Kahnawá:ke's Membership Department had this to say about the identification of elders:

> Traditionally Kanien'kehá:ka ways indicate that "everyone has a voice," yet the name "Council of Elders" does not support everyone having a voice. Many respondents indicated maturity as an essential quality for a

---

to explain a vast range of particular phenomena by the simplest possible generalization. But in the world of human affairs, wildly complicated by the presence of individual wills, and of particular ideas of what produces or deprives people of honor, in what does interest consist, and even of what is there to fear, extremely general explanations are neither useful nor possible. Historians should, in the first instance, be foxes, using as many tricks as they can to explain as many particular things as accurately and convincingly as possible. Then, they should try to find revealing examples from the wide variety of human experiences to support generalizations of varying breadth. They should not expect to find the one big trick that will explain everything, but the lesser generalizations, to be tested by other understandings of the evidence and by new human experiences as they arise, which can still be interesting and useful. It is this mixed path taken by the historian, chiefly of the fox but with a necessary element of the hedgehog, that I believe promises the best results.

See also Leclair J, "Les périls du totalisme conceptuel en droit et en sciences sociales," *supra* note 4.

41 Online: <www.kahnawake.com/org/docs/CoEReport_May08.pdf>.
42 *Supra* note 39.

CoE member, noting a bias for people 50 and over, making the assumption that people under 50 are not mature enough for the work. It is the experience of the project team (based on extensive work on governance) that this is far from the truth in this community. Age does not guarantee maturity or wisdom and it is the youth of the community that will have to live with the results of the KML [Kahnawá:ke Membership Law]. Also for consideration, opinions (from community consultation) *may not always be sufficient* to establish all the criteria needed for committees, councils or boards. It requires *concrete assessment* of the knowledge, skill sets and attitudes essential to the work. There are clear indicators of racism existing within the CoE. Comments made during interviews indicate blood quantum is still entrenched in the thinking and attitudes of those involved in decision making. Lineage is not well understood and is strongly based on blood quantum and not affiliation. Racism seems to be prevalent in the community so the question arises, how does the selection of those who will be determining membership ensure that the decisions made are not racist? Or what can be built into the CoE that will counteract racist influence. The answer is clear criteria and definitions that allow no room for subjective opinions of decision makers.[43]

Finally, as these nationalistic and holistic perspectives seek the identification of a unique essence, one that radically distances the Other from ourselves, they tend to favour an adversarial understanding between cultural communities or nations. However, where Aboriginal peoples are concerned, it must be admitted that, through its interpretation of section 35 of the *Constitution Act, 1982*, the Supreme Court of Canada has done everything in its power to encourage Aboriginal parties to congeal in constitutional concrete a most essentialized understanding of their identity.[44] Notwithstanding its effort at imposing a duty to consult on the Crown where constitutional Aboriginal interests are at stake, the radical "red vs white" cultural demarcation forming the basis of the Court's reasoning makes it extremely difficult to envisage a solution emphasizing the manner in which a federal spirit could infuse

---

43 *Supra* note 41, at 61–62 [emphasis in the original].
44 For an eloquent critique of the Court's reasoning, see Leonard I Rotman, "Creating a Still-Life out of Dynamic Objects: Rights Reductionism at the Supreme Court of Canada" (1997) 36 Alta L Rev 1; Russel Lawrence Barsh & James [Sa'ke'j] Youngblood Henderson, "The Supreme Court's *Van der Peet* Trilogy: Naive Imperialism and Ropes of Sand" (1997) 42 McGill LJ 993.

a new dynamic to the *relationships* of Aboriginals and non-Aboriginals, both as individuals and as members of political communities.

Intellectuals in the social sciences and the normative disciplines naturally think in terms of ensembles and therefore tend to distance themselves from the individual attitudes making up the structures of the social entities they theorize. The more abstract the structures, the greater will be the tendency to lose sight of the world in all its complex configurations. The historian or the philosopher convinced that human events obey a specific telos, or the sociologist or anthropologist reducing social reality to a few general concepts, all run the risk of dispossessing individuals of their own selves by denying any relevance to either their individual decisions or actions or to their individual strategies and aims. Conceptual oversimplifications generally end up depersonalizing human beings.[45] On the other hand, such depersonalization can also occur when social scientists put too great an emphasis on an individual's agency, thus forgetting the historically contingent context that constrains that individual's ability to choose and as such contributes to his life's tragic patina.

When blinded by the illusion of their Promethean capacity to explicate the world through a few abstract concepts, intellectuals forget that, for a theory to be valid, the macroscopic representations it generates must eventually be broken up into their microscopic components. Conceptual realism, or the belief that our provisional theories have become true social facts, veritable material entities, awaits those who fail to water down their abstractions with a few millilitres of empirical data.[46] Prudence is even more appropriate when a concept is mobilized to shape future political behaviour, as opposed to enabling a retrospective understanding of a particular phenomenon. Especially where political theories are concerned, too rigid a conceptualization is bound to clash with the aporetic essence of politics.

As an "individual" member of such a "nation," "people," or "cultural community," I have never found communitarian or individualistic approaches to be in harmony with the reality of my own life and, in truth, with that of anyone I ever met – whether Aboriginal, non-Aboriginal, French, Belgian, Spanish, Brazilian, etc. Although, contrary to what individualists of strict obedience pretend, our range of choices

---

45 Valade, *supra* note 14, at 376 and 383–86.
46 *Ibid* at 393–94.

is indeed limited by context, we still are all motivated and called upon to act by infinitely more sophisticated and multifarious motivations than the ones proposed by holistic or nationalistic approaches.

Being a constitutionalist by profession, I see with diffidence any and all attempts at institutionalizing such normative proposals in legal concrete. Law, it is worth reminding, is always implicitly structured by the manner in which humans and societies are depicted in the social sciences, and today's legists are always the children of some of yesterday's philosophers, be they aware of it or not.

I also believe that, if studies of federalism are subordinated to these proposals' implicit or explicit anthropological postulations, the potential of federalism will be weakened both in terms of the values it could help to promote and in terms of its capacity to structure human interactions in a manner that honours the complexity of those free agents' individual and collective lives.

Following in the footsteps of others before me,[47] I therefore thought that a more nuanced and contextualized normative and constitutional federal theory needed to be devised. At bottom, the thesis developed has the following departure point: if we substitute to a highly abstract understanding of human beings the minimalist anthropological premise that human beings are neither superhuman nor constantly shepherded around by invisible structural or cultural forces, then we shall be compelled to choose an epistemological perspective that does not deny either our inevitable socialization or our agency. As such, in invoking concepts – whether descriptive, normative, or legal – to make sense of the world, we should be careful to resist the temptation of conceptual totalism, that is, of trying to crush and to compress reality into the confined space of monocular concepts such as "nations," "peoples," cultural communities," "culture," "identity," "rights," and "sovereignty." If a single concept is to be resorted to, it should bring to light and reckon with the partially unsettled nature of our identities, of our convictions, of our beliefs, and of our knowledge of the world. It

---

47 Dimitrios Karmis & Jocelyn Maclure, "Two Escape Routes from the Paradigm of Monistic Authenticity: Post-Imperialist and Federal Perspectives on Plural and Complex Identities" (2001) 24 Ethnic and Racial Studies 361; Dimitrios Karmis & Wayne Norman, "The Revival of Federalism in Normative Political Theory" in Karmis & Norman, eds, *Theories of Federalism: A Reader* (New York: Palgrave Macmillan, 2005) 1; Tim Schouls, *Shifting Boundaries: Aboriginal Identity, Pluralist Theory, and the Politics of Self-Government* (Vancouver: University of British Columbia Press, 2003).

should entail a search not so much for elusive essences as for the networks of relations that make up our world. A non-monocular normative approach would involve facing up to the challenge of the unequal distribution of power between *and within* collective abstractions such as "nations," "peoples," and "cultural communities."[48] It would call for a normative perspective going beyond learned discussions of abstract values and probing the historical context that made possible the institutionalization of such values (a process, by the way, that always fails to meet the ideal pursued).

I underline that such an approach does not lead ineluctably to an asocial or antisocial form of individualism, for it does not deny the influence on an individual of the different forces and powers at play in a given community. On the contrary, deprived of "cultural competence,"[49] a person could not develop her own individuality. The individual is therefore not here conceptualized as an abstract atomized entity, but rather as a subject engaged in a constant process of individuation in the course of which he fathers himself with the assistance of others and not simply in opposition to them. Furthermore, this approach hypothesizes that, in the course of such a self-generating process, a person might very well develop and cultivate multiple belongings whose prioritization is not fixed in advance. The flow of our humanity does not issue from a single source.

The monist, however, whether of a communautarian or of an individualistic obedience, interprets all social phenomena on a fact assumed to be dominant and permanent. He bluntly affirms that one particular dimension of reality, one specific activity of humankind, determines all others.[50] The monistic conceptual outline therefore presumes that social

---

48   On the subject of the unequal distribution of power *within* communities, see Val Napoleon, "Aboriginal Discourse: Gender, Identity, and Community" in Benjamin Richardson, Shin Imai, & Kent McNeil, eds, *Indigenous Peoples and the Law: Comparative and Critical Perspectives* (Portland: Hart Publishing, 2009) 233; and Schouls, *supra* note 47.

49   Marcel Detienne defines cultural competence as "the body of representations that any individual, as a member of a society, must possess in order to think and act": *supra* note 15, at 39–40.

50   Schouls, *supra* note 34, at 84: "By 'reifie,' I mean the tendency to grant an aspect of identity a permanency that it either does not possess or possesses only temporarily. By 'absolutize,' I mean the assumption that one or another aspect of Aboriginal identity (in this case, the cultural nation) is primary and therefore has greater significance than any other potential aspect." See also Leclair, "Les périls du totalisme conceptuel en droit et en sciences sociales," *supra* note 4.

actors are spurred into action by a single dominating motivation. Such conceptual totalism allows, for instance, some social scientists (whether a historian, sociologist, or anthropologist, etc.) to ascribe to an entire community one sole dimension and intent. Some economists, on the other hand, will often depict human beings as concerned primarily, if not solely, with consumerist preoccupations.

Monistic conceptualization often reconstructs reality from the perspective of the *spectator*, rather than from that of the *actor*. Because the former is capable of making intelligible what could not have been predicted at the time, he tends to depict social and political evolutions as necessary rather than as the result of choices. In so doing, he fails to face up to the plurality of considerations existing at the time decisions were taken and presumes that these were the result of "necessity" rather than choice.[51] Because the spectator knows the outcome, he satisfies himself with one single explanation.

This *spectator* perspective entails other epistemological, ontological, and normative consequences. First, at the epistemological level, even if one admits the existence of a dominating trait in a specific community, should not one allow for the possibility of *interactions* between that trait and other less important features? For instance, if "culture" is held to be all-dominant, might not the importance of say, "economic efficiency" recognized by the same community, transform or at least influence the concept of culture itself? The same question can be asked about more individualistic approaches. What interactions exist between an individual's consumerist preferences and her other multifarious identitary referents?

Second, monistic explanations often treat individual states of mind as either immaterial or – worse – as illusions. This is the result of their often postulating a world complete in itself, already given, and that, well before we enter in relations with it[52] – a world made up, as I said earlier, of static ultimate realities (nation, tradition, sovereignty, for instance)

51 Raymond Aron, *The Opium of the Intellectuals*, introduction by Harvey C Mansfield, foreword by Daniel J Mahoney and Brian C Anderson (New Brunswick: Transaction, 2011) originally published in 1955 under the title *L'opium des intellectuels*, at 168–69. At 184: "Every human act is a choice between several alternatives – a response solicited, but not chained to a contingency: the succession of acts is intelligible without being premeditated."
52 William James, *Some Problems of Philosophy. A Beginning of an Introduction to Philosophy* (1911; New York: Greenwood, 1968) at 139 and 221–22.

antecedent to our very existence and where the whole determines the role of each and every part. Therefore, such a conceptualization, as I said, envisages the world as one where necessity predominates. However, if necessity denies relevancy to individual states of mind, how do changes and novelty come about? How do the huge monistic tectonic ensembles (nations, proletariat, Aboriginal peoples, etc.) grow from one state to another? There is something much too mechanical and univocal in the depiction of these structural transformations. If human choice is removed from the equation, how do structures evolve? If reality truly matters for the monists, on what ground can they ignore individual states of mind that are, after all, part and parcel of that reality? And where is the place of luck and of accidents in such conceptualizations? In addition, and if human choice is an essential part of reality, it is not the only one. What about the context in which it is exercised?

If the monist's "'through-and-through' philosophy ... seems too buttoned-up and white-chokered and clean-shaven a thing to speak for the vast slow-breathing unconscious Kosmos with its dread abysses and its unknown tides,"[53] then what? If the blatant and undisputed complexity of our historically situated individual lives makes risible the naive claim that we, as individuals, or the collective entities encompassing us, are driven forward by a unique principle, how should we envisage conceptualization?

If our lives are not driven by necessity, if our world is unfinished, if nothing is entirely predetermined, then we must conclude that individuals are necessarily called upon to make decisions, to choose among a plurality of possible avenues. We thus partly create ourselves as well as our world. We add something to that world. We forge history, at least in part. We choose ourselves and find ourselves at the same time. Our agency and our ability to reason reflexively make these choices possible. But our volition is never exercised in a vacuum. Our choices are constrained, although not determined, by the particular context in which we find ourselves and by the limits of the knowledge upon which they feed.

At an epistemological level, pluralism's rejection of necessity stems from its recognition that the impossibility of pinning down one single motivation or one single fact as the basis of a total explication is not the

---

53 William James, "Absolutism and Empiricism" in *Essays in Radical Empiricism* (1912; Lincoln: University of Nebraska Press, 1996) 266–79, at 277–78.

result of intellectual failure, but rather of the multiplicity of reasonable meanings that can be attached to an action or fact.[54] For an intellectual to recognize the limits of his or her knowledge and the complexity of reality is no defeat; it is a moral imperative.

The academic intellectual's vocation is not that of the politician. The search for objectivity must remain the former's ultimate ambition, objectivity being here understood as an horizon rather than as an ultimate reality,[55] as an obligation to submit one's observations and thoughts to constant criticism. No intellectual will ever fully succeed in this endeavour, but some critical analysis is certainly better than none. The straightforward statement of one's personal preferences in the introduction of a scientific work is also to be encouraged.[56] The impossibility of embracing the totality of reality and the undeniable limits of any form of knowledge are no excuse to abandon our effort to achieve objectivity.

Raymond Aron suggests a methodology that, while not aiming at neutrality – for it does not prevent value judgments – nonetheless guarantees a minimum of objectivity.[57] He gives as an example the manner in which a sociologist can assess the problem of social classes. First, she should not arbitrarily select facts. For instance, she

---

54 Aron, *supra* note 51, at 138 and 157; at 145–46: "But the whole will only be grasped by reference to a multiplicity of viewpoints as long as man refuses to be defined entirely by a single question, as long as societies are not planned in accordance with a global system."

55 Dominique Schnapper, *Providential Democracy: An Essay on Contemporary Equality*, translated by John Taylor (New Brunswick: Transaction, 2009); originally published in 2002 under the title *La démocratie providentielle – Essai sur l'égalité comtemporaine*, at 7: "[T]he research scientist's efforts to keep universality in sight and to strive for objectivity – conceived as a goal, an ambition, as well as a limit, not as a reality – continue to distinguish 'academic' sociologists from intellectuals popularized in the mass media; that is, where both kinds of thinkers are taken as social types "

56 For an excellent example of such an admonition, see Wayne Warry, *Unfinished Dreams: Community Healing and the Reality of Aboriginal Self-Government* (Toronto: University of Toronto Press, 1998) at 7–13; and Warry, *Ending Denial: Understanding Aboriginal Issues* (Toronto: University of Toronto Press, 2009) at 23–31. In the words of historian Yvan Lamonde, *Historien et citoyen. Navigations au long cours* (Montreal: Fides, 2008) at 72, "The object is not so much to evacuate subjectivity as to know and recognize it" [my translation]. Original text: "L'objectif est moins d'évacuer la subjectivité que de la connaître et la reconnaître."

57 What follows is taken from Raymond Aron, *Les sociétés modernes*, collection "Quadrige" (Paris: PUF, 2006) 49–76, at 62–71.

should abstain from emphasizing the factors at the root of a society's homogeneity to the detriment of an examination of the grounds of its heterogeneity. She ought to resist the temptation to judge an entire regime on the sole basis of a few selected merits or demerits. Second, she should avoid jumbling together theoretical definitions and definitions generated by empirical research. For instance, one can define social classes as possessing their own values or as being impermeable to the global society's influence, but evidence must be submitted to sustain that claim: "[S]uch a definition can only be the outcome of empirical research and not a way to designate the object itself."[58] Third, she should abstain from pretending to know with certainty and precision phenomena that, by their very nature, are ambiguous. She can certainly study, for instance, the "class consciousness" of a particular group, but she should not ascribe to such states of conscience a density and consistency they do not possess. Fourth, the researcher should not arbitrarily distinguish what are "important" facts and what are "trivial" ones. Forceful reasons should be at the source of such differentiations. Finally, the researcher, in her assessment of the merits and demerits of a particular social or political order, should not cast her personal preferences upon reality.[59]

Aron concludes by emphasizing that methodological "equity" does not imply or require that researchers abstain from making value judgments:

> I will not draw the conclusion that the sociologist must avoid making value judgments, but rather that he at once clarify those, diffuse and implicit, of his *milieu* and, so far as possible, his own ...
>
> The sociologist studying classes must not ignore value judgments spontaneously passed by his readers. But such generally partial spontaneous judgements fail to recognize the implications of a phenomenon desirable in itself or the necessary price of attaining a goal on the surface required

---

58 *Ibid* at 62, footnote 1 [my translation]. Original text: "une telle définition ne peut être que le terme de l'étude empirique et non un mode de désignation de l'objet."

59 After his review of several examples of disastrous high-modernist authoritarian state planning, Scott prescribes four "rules of thumb" to make development planning less prone to disaster: "*Take small steps ... Favor reversibility ... Plan on surprises ... and Plan on human inventiveness.*" James C Scott, *Seeing Like a State: How Certain Schemes to Improve the Human Condition Have Failed* (New Haven, CT: Yale University Press, 1998) at 345 (author's emphasis). It seems to me that any form of conceptualization, not just development planning, could find inspiration in those rules.

by our ideal. The sociologist is not different from the politician or from the man on the street in that he would harbour no preferences or opinions. His difference should be his consideration of the whole, his refusal systematically to exalt or to denigrate, his admission of the flaws of his system, and his acknowledgment of the merits of the one he opposes. The sociologist strives to be scientific, not through neutrality, but through equity.[60]

Aron therefore concedes that an academic intellectual cannot escape passing judgment. Olympian detachment is not of this world. However, as this quotation makes clear, he believed a distinction had to be made between the realms of action and that of knowledge.

Aron rejected any form of historical determinism[61] – or historical necessity – and so did not believe that the future was mechanically secreted by the past. Nor did he hold conceptual totalism as possible or desirable. Rather, he was convinced that scientific knowledge – nay, any knowledge – could not dictate political solutions. It could certainly help in the choice of the more reasonable paths to follow or in providing information as to the probable consequences of such or such action, but no more. However, it could, at the very least, help judge "those who arbitrarily abandon themselves to the fascination of one aspect of

---

60 Raymond Aron, "Science et conscience de la société," *supra* note 57, at 66 [my translation]. Original text:

Je n'en tirerai pas la conclusion que le sociologue doit éviter les jugements de valeur, mais qu'il doit tirer au clair ceux, diffus et implicites, de son milieu et, autant que possible, préciser les siens propres. Le sociologue qui étudie les classes ne doit pas ignorer les jugements de valeur que portent spontanément ses lecteurs. Mais ces jugements spontanés, généralement partiaux, méconnaissent les implications d'un phénomène en lui-même souhaitable ou le prix qu'il faudrait payer pour atteindre un but, en apparence appelé par notre idéal. Le sociologue ne diffère pas de l'homme politique ou de la rue en ce sens qu'il n'aurait pas de préférences ou n'exprimerait pas d'opinions. Il devrait en différer par la considération de l'ensemble, par le refus d'exalter ou de dénigrer systématiquement, par l'aveu de défauts inséparables du régime qu'il choisit, par la reconnaissance des mérites propres au régime qu'il combat. Le sociologue s'efforce d'être scientifique, non par la neutralité mais par l'équité.

61 Aron, *supra* note 57, at 195: "[H]istory is the tragedy of a humanity that makes its own history, but knows not which history it makes" [my translation]. Original text: "Oui, l'histoire est la tragédie d'une humanité qui fait son histoire, mais qui ne sait pas l'histoire qu'elle fait."

reality, and whose fanaticism inclines them to sacrifice everything to *one* value only."[62]

Many Aboriginal intellectuals have been resorting to the methodology advocated here. I am thinking of scholars such as John Borrows[63] and especially Val Napoleon.[64] Instead of multiplying examples, a brief examination of Justin B. Richland's *Arguing with Tradition: The Language of Law in Hopi Tribal Court*[65] will serve as an illustration of how the prudential approach advocated here can be applied in studies dealing with Aboriginal law.

Richland's study aims at analysing "tradition and culture as discourses in and of contemporary tribal law by considering the microdetails of face-to-face communication in one tribal legal context: that of property hearings held before the Hopi Tribal Court."[66] The author felt that the need for such an ethnographic and ethno-linguistic study of tribal courts was necessary, because "few efforts ha[d] yet been made to explore precisely how notions of tribal custom, tradition, and culture, are invoked by tribal legal actors in tribal courtroom proceedings."[67] Much too often, the whole debate about the role of custom, tradition, and culture ended

---

62 Aron, *supra* note 57, at 70 [my translation]. Original text: "[C]eux qui, arbitrairement, se laissent fasciner par un aspect du réel, enclins par fanatisme à tout sacrifier à *une* valeur."

63 Whereas some books are premised on an Aboriginal epistemology completely devoid of even the slightest trace of reflexive critique, Borrows's eloquent plea in favour of an integration of Indigenous legal traditions within our understanding of the Canadian constitution is replete with cautionary comments about the danger of oversimplification and about the need not to discard human agency. John Borrows, *Canada's Indigenous Constitution* (Toronto: University of Toronto Press, 2010). Furthermore, his willingness to compare, not only reinforces his arguments, it enables the building of epistemological bridges between Aboriginals and non-Aboriginals. For instance, after having described the historical evolution of both the civil law and the common law traditions, he states (at 113; see also 56), "This brief examination of the civil and common law illustrates the importance of history and culture in the development of legal traditions. Without such understanding, some people might not recognize that the development of civil and common law traditions is based on specific historical and cultural circumstances. Choice and moral agency both played a role in the adoption and adaptation of these traditions. Choice and agency will be as important to the adoption and continued adaptation of Indigenous legal traditions. Since legal traditions are subject to human intervention, they can change, grow, and develop."

64 Her article "Aboriginal Discourse: Gender, Identity, and Community," *supra* note 48, is a remarkable example of courageous and constructive criticism.

65 Chicago: University of Chicago Press, 2008.

66 *Ibid* at 22.

67 *Ibid* at 6–7.

up being a "perpetuation of the divide between a demonization and valorization of that role."[68] He goes on to underline the epistemological underpinnings of this all-or-nothing approach. What he describes is basically what I referred to as methodological holism:

> [T]he field of tribal legal study generally is informed by a largely structuralist theoretical orientation to tribal jurisprudence. The notions of tribal law, politics, culture, and tradition in such an orientation are imagined as whole, homogenous systems that operate in and on the world in ways that impinge on but remain mostly unaffected by the actions of particular tribal members in particular contexts ... Thus we lack the knowledge of the interactions of those tribal peoples who are engaged with and contribute to the construction of these institutions at the moments of their making, as well as a proper consideration of the political implications of their contributions. Missing is the measure of human agency that, while necessarily shaped by the nature of preexisting material, political, and semiotic systems, nonetheless accrues to tribal social actors at particular moments of tribal social life when they confront each other in proper political ways.[69]

Rejecting such holistic approaches that lead to all-encompassing definitions of custom, tradition, and culture, Richland chose to commit himself to the following path of investigation:

> [T]he analyses in this study subsume questions of what tradition "is" under the more general questions of what tradition "does" and "means" for the tribal actors who engage each other in these legal contexts. This study thus suggests that striking a balance between tribal notions of law and tradition – notably including moments where tradition is constructed by differently situated Hopi legal actors in multiple and even contradictory orientations to perceived Anglo-American legal practices – is an ongoing negotiation for Hopi legal actors that not only reaches the finest details of Hopi tribal court praxis but is central to the ways in which Hopi people constitute their tribal jurisprudence, its sociopolitical force, and the tribal lives that it affects.[70]

---

68 *Ibid* at 21. See the detailed account he gives at 148–53 of this "demonization and valorization" divide.
69 *Ibid*.
70 *Ibid* at 23.

Upon the basis of this prudential methodology, the author then proceeds to examine how different Hopi legal actors mobilize the notions
of custom, tradition, and culture in the context of tribal courtroom
proceedings. He found that, in many cases, the Hopi people shared
"quite regular understandings regarding what is or is not Hopi tradition and culture."[71] However, in many cases, radically divergent views
were entertained. The "Hopi property proceedings ... constituted as
collaborative, sense-making activities" nevertheless proved to be a
milieu where "discourses of tradition and culture [were] not treated
as essentialized or homogeneous notions, but emerge[d] as thoroughly
negotiated discourses, made meaningful primarily in light of their contributions to the larger story of contemporary Hopi jurisprudence."[72] In
addition, his study revealed how tradition was

> constructed in relation to what are seen as the Anglo-American juridical
> practices of the [Hopi] court. Sometimes tradition is constructed in oppo-
> sition to adversarial practices and norms of contemporary Hopi tribal law,
> while other times Hopi tradition is talked about in ways that are consistent
> (or at least no in inherent conflict) with that law and court procedures.[73]

Finally, and most interestingly, Richland shows that, even within
Aboriginal communities, knowledge is power. As he explains,
"[K]nowledge of tradition – whether sacred or secular – is often inte-
grally tied to the legitimate authority of the possessor and is an essential
element of that person's efficacy in the world."[74] Therefore, for instance,
elders were infuriated at the Hopi judges' requests that they limit their
testimony to a description of tradition as if it was "merely some cohe-
sive body of inert information, easily detachable from its source and
[capable of being] transferred to new carriers and new contexts."[75]
For elders, their authority over tradition should have allowed them to
"control ... the purposes to which it [would] be put."[76]

   In short, Richland meticulously avoids arbitrarily selecting facts. He
resists the temptation to judge an entire regime on the sole basis of a

---

71 *Ibid* at 161.
72 *Ibid*.
73 *Ibid* at 66.
74 *Ibid* at 83.
75 *Ibid*.
76 *Ibid* at 84.

few selected merits or demerits. He abstains from pretending to know with certainty and precision phenomena that, by their very nature, are ambiguous, and he does not arbitrarily distinguish what are "important" facts and what are "trivial" ones. And, most importantly, he never forgets that generals and leaders, however important they might be, are not the ones who win battles; soldiers and warriors do.

Conclusion

The whole purpose of this chapter, if I try to sum it up in one sentence, is to recall to memory the virtues of doubt and the danger of totalist understandings of the world, understandings that imprison us in conceptual silos making mutual understandings impossible. We face each other over the chasm of tradition/modernity, Aboriginal/non-Aboriginal identities, condemned to reciprocal solitudes. Doubt, I strongly believe, can be the catalyst not only for tolerance, but also for collective action. Doubts constitute, in the words of René Sève,

> the guarantee of our openness to the world, of our capacity to evolve with it and to adapt to it. Furthermore, doubt is certainly a guarantee of our openness to others. It is sometimes said that while human beings are brought together by certitudes, the search for the remedy to their incertitudes makes them work together and accept choices other than their own.[77]

Our uncertainties, our doubts, impel us to collaborate. At least, such is the hope of the pluralist whose faith might be said to hinge on both our capacity to reason together and the choice of sociability. Epistemological humility might be the price to pay for true reconciliation.

In other words, Aboriginal and non-Aboriginal scholars should look over their shoulder once in a while; they might see the Trickster, perched in the Tree of Knowledge, laughing at them.

---

77 "Douter c'est décider: nature et caractère constructifs du doute," in François Terré ed, *Le doute et le droit* (Paris: Dalloz, 199) at 124 [my translation]. Original text: "la garantie de notre ouverture au monde, de notre capacité à évoluer avec lui et de nous adapter à lui. Et j'ajouterai que le doute est certainement aussi une garantie de notre capacité d'ouverture aux autres. On dit parfois que ce sont les certitudes qui rassemblent les hommes, on peut aussi dire que ce sont leurs incertitudes, leurs incertitudes qui les font travailler ensemble pour y remédier mais qui font aussi accepter les choix différents des autres."

PART THREE

Constitutional Consultations

8 Consultation and Economic Reconciliation

DWIGHT NEWMAN*

Introduction

Section 35 Aboriginal rights case law is obviously framed in terms of a rights discourse rather than in terms of, for instance, an economic distributive discourse. That said, there are also hints in the jurisprudence that the shape of the rights themselves is subject to development by the courts in light of some broader theory and not simply in terms of any natural rights theory of rights.[1] For example, the Court early on affirmed that section 35 did not simply entrench rights in some historical formation but in terms of a broader set of considerations, such as a "just settlement," that could reshape the rights themselves.[2] In more recent case law, section 35 has transmuted into a section not about rights to be applied

---

* I thank Lorelle Binnion for research assistance on some points in the chapter and for reading and commenting on a draft version. I thank John Borrows, Sari Graben, Patrick Macklem, Brian Slattery, and others for their comments on the conference version.
1 For such a theory in the resource/territorial context, see Cara Nine, *Global Justice and Territory* (Oxford: Oxford University Press, 2012); and Nine, "Resource Rights" (2012) Political Studies 1. Nine advances an account involving collective rights held by communities explained significantly in terms of natural law theory. A predecessor of sorts in terms of a theoretical account similarly grounding Indigenous rights to land in a natural law theory of property would, to the surprise of many, be Robert Nozick, *Anarchy, State, and Utopia* (New York: Basic Books, 1974). Nozick's framework would support enduring Indigenous rights, whether or not they furthered other policy objectives, in contrast to a Rawlsian approach that would arguably support certain Indigenous rights only if Indigenous communities remained economically worse off than other communities.
2 See *R v Sparrow*, [1990] 1 SCR 1075 at 1105, quoting Noel Lyon, "An Essay on Constitutional Interpretation" (1988) 26 Osgoode Hall LJ 95 at 100 that "the context of 1982 is surely enough to tell us that this is not just a codification of the case law on aboriginal rights that had accumulated by 1982. Section 35 calls for a just settlement for aboriginal peoples."

by the courts but a vehicle of "reconciliation."[3] An ethical account prioritizing a "just settlement" or "reconciliation" that then determines the shape of rights is not actually, in the traditional distinctions, a "right-based" theory but is a "goal-based" theory.[4] That is to say, the courts have adapted the language of section 35 into a constitutional imperative in support of certain goals, from which certain Aboriginal rights and other legal consequences (including the duty to consult) then follow. Potentially deontological rights are interpreted in accordance with the courts' present teleological theory of Aboriginal-state relations.[5]

There are, it bears noting, indications that part of what the courts see section 35 as geared to achieving arises from a responsiveness to the historically dire wealth gaps between Aboriginal and non-Aboriginal communities. For example, in *Delgamuukw*,[6] while acknowledging "an important non-economic component" to Aboriginal title,[7] Chief Justice Lamer also emphasizes that "lands held pursuant to aboriginal title have an inescapable *economic component*,"[8] with that economic component arguably serving as a partial subtext to ongoing Aboriginal title determinations.[9] In some cases, the courts have explicitly referred to the background of past inequalities as part of the reason for their approach to Aboriginal rights today.[10] The courts have not, of course, readily granted Aboriginal title claims, but they have spoken of foreseeing negotiation

---

3 See, e.g., *Mikisew Cree First Nation v Canada (Minister of Canadian Heritage)*, [2005] 3 SCR 388, 2005 SCC 69 at para 1 (Binnie J stating, "The fundamental objective of the modern law of aboriginal and treaty rights is the reconciliation of aboriginal peoples and non-aboriginal peoples and their respective claims interests and ambitions").

4 On the distinction, see Ronald Dworkin, *Taking Rights Seriously* (London: Duckworth, 1978) 171ff; JL Mackie, "Can There Be a Right-Based Moral Theory?" (1978) 3 Midwest Studies in Philosophy 350.

5 Cf also Michael Ilg, "Culture and Competitive Resource Regulation: A Liberal Economic Alternative to Sui Generis Aboriginal Rights" (2012) 62 UTLJ 403 at 405. Ilg's important (and potentially controversial) article begins from what I respectfully see as an overstated interpretation that the courts currently apply a deontological model, with Ilg then arguing for a shift to teleological considerations. Ilg advances his interpretation more on the basis of the Aboriginal rights test in *R v Van Der Peet*, [1996] 2 SCR 507 than on the Aboriginal title test.

6 *Delgamuukw v British Columbia*, [1997] 3 SCR 1010.

7 *Ibid* at para 129.

8 *Ibid* at para 166 [emphasis in original].

9 But see, e.g., *Lax Kw'alaams Indian Band v Canada (AG)*, 2011 SCC 56 (Court rejecting arguments of general rights to engage in wealth creation activities).

10 See, e.g., *Mikisew Cree, supra* note 3 at para 1.

processes "reinforced by the judgments of this Court."[11] Without any economic reductionism, it is also possible to note that litigation by Aboriginal communities will sometimes be an attempt to overcome dire economic circumstances, and the litigated rights may be affected by economic considerations.[12] However, the fact that courts have not explicitly recognized this dynamic also means that they have often developed doctrines without any sophisticated analysis of the prospective effects of the doctrines for the future.[13] The focus on retrospective considerations is perhaps inevitable in the context of what have to be framed as rights claims,[14] but the consequences are no less real.[15]

In this chapter, I take up the specific section 35 doctrine that has taken on so much prominence in recent years, and on which I have written previously,[16] this being the doctrine of the duty to consult,[17] and I examine the ways in which it has become a springboard for explicit

11 *Delgamuukw, supra* note 6 at para 186.
12 See generally Jacob Levy, "Three Perversities of Indian Law" (2008) 12 Texas Rev L & Pols 329.
13 *Ibid.*
14 Cf Dworkin, *supra* note 4, at 87ff (discussing the view that a decision based on rights must be based on existing entitlements rather than desirable future effects). This retrospective dimension of the rights analysis is a major concern of Ilg's as well: *supra* note 5.
15 For some recent beginnings of attention to the economic consequences of Aboriginal rights doctrines, see especially Levy, *supra* note 12; Ilg, *supra* note 5; Ian Keay & Cherie Metcalf, "Aboriginal Rights, Customary Law and the Economics of Renewable Resource Exploitation" (2004) 30 Cdn Public Pol'y 1; Cherie Metcalf, "Compensation as Discipline in the Justified Limitation of Aboriginal Rights: The Case of Forest Exploitation" (2008) 33 Queen's LJ 385; Ian Keay & Cherie Metcalf, "Property Rights, Resource Access, and Long-Run Growth" (2011) 8 J Empirical Leg Sts 792; Tom Flanagan, Christopher Alcantara, & André Le Dressay, *Beyond the Indian Act: Restoring Aboriginal Property Rights* (Montreal & Kingston: McGill-Queen's University Press, 2010).
16 See Dwight G Newman, *The Duty to Consult: New Relationships with Aboriginal Peoples* (Saskatoon: Purich, 2009); Newman, *Revisiting the Duty to Consult Aboriginal Peoples* (Saskatoon: Purich, 2014).
17 I refer particularly to the modern doctrine mandating a duty to consult based on actual or constructive Crown knowledge of an Aboriginal or treaty rights claim, even prior to final settlement of that claim in negotiations or final adjudication of that claim in the courts. The original trilogy of cases developing this doctrine were: *Haida Nation v British Columbia (Minister of Forests)*, [2004] 3 SCR 511, 2004 SCC 73; *Taku River Tlingit First Nation v British Columbia (Project Assessment Director)*, [2004] 3 SCR 550, 2004 SCC 74; and *Mikisew Cree First Nation, supra* note 3. The Court re-engages significantly with the doctrine and its underlying purposes in *Rio Tinto Alcan Inc v Carrier Sekani Tribal Council*, 2010 SCC 43, [2010] 2 SCR 650.

discussions of Aboriginal economic accommodation but also how the orientation of such a legal doctrine may end up generating problematic policy outcomes. The duty-to-consult doctrine has supported new discussions in some contexts of Aboriginal economic participation, economic accommodation of potential Aboriginal and treaty rights claims, and what could more generally be thought of as an economic dimension of reconciliation. However, I argue that any economic reconciliation outcomes from the duty to consult will be complex. I argue that the doctrine has the potential, realized in some instances, of contributing to economic accommodation relatively effectively, but I also show that there are risks that it may contribute to certain unstable policy outcomes, accentuate some policy challenges, and pose an obstacle to certain highly desirable policy outcomes. In the concluding section, I suggest that some, but not all, of these issues arise from the rigidity of consultation as a legal doctrine and I suggest some paths forward on the policy front for making consultation and economic reconciliation interact as harmoniously as possible in actually furthering optimal policy outcomes.

There is no doubt that section 35 has made major contributions to economic accommodation and reconciliation that are still underway. However, I shall argue, major work may be ahead for lawyers and legal scholars to overcome an economic and policy amateurism that I shall argue section 35 has risked inviting. To be clear, this challenge applies to my own past work on the duty to consult,[18] on reconciliation,[19] and on other Indigenous rights topics. Like other legal scholars, focused on law and a rights-oriented framework, my own work has likely fallen into the pattern of describing the law, identifying possible incremental changes by which the law can help fulfil Indigenous rights, and then assuming that positive outcomes will follow.[20] The challenge this chapter tentatively issues and tentatively begins to pursue is to bring to the section 35 Aboriginal rights context some analytical approaches concerned with more complex chains of economic and political interactions

---

18 Newman, *supra* note 16.
19 Dwight G Newman, "Reconciliation: Legal Conception(s) and Faces of Justice," in John Whyte, ed, *Moving toward Justice: Legal Traditions and Aboriginal Justice* (Saskatoon: Purich, 2008); Dwight Newman & Danielle Schweitzer, "Between Reconciliation and the Rule(s) of Law: *Tsilhqot'in Nation v British Columbia*" (2008) 41 UBCL Rev 249.
20 Alan Cairns rightly critiques this and other dimensions of legal scholarship on Aboriginal rights.

arising from the section 35 discourse. If the legal approach to section 35 is to be goal-oriented, then lawyers and legal scholars need to be more attentive to effects on the achievement of the goals it embodies.

The Duty to Consult and Economic Accommodation

The duty-to-consult doctrine, one should recall, actually originated in its modern form (that mandating the duty to consult even in the context of claims not yet proven in the courts or definitively settled) in a case in which the possible alternative appeared to be the granting of injunctions as a more routine occurrence.[21] The duty-to-consult doctrine thus keeps consultation with Aboriginal communities in the hands of government (with potential delegations to industry)[22] rather than under constant judicial supervision (though that judicial supervision is available for alleged breaches of the duty to consult).[23] That latter possibility of judicial supervision, however, represents a significant change from a prior regime in which governments could more easily infringe upon rights, subject to facing a rights claim afterward. Now, the decision to act in ways that may infringe upon a right is subject to prior restraint through a consultative process or, if that is not carried out in accordance with applicable standards, judicial supervision. Those wishing to pursue a resource development project that may affect Aboriginal rights or Aboriginal title interests are thus tasked with finding prospective ways of respecting those rights and, in cases where accommodation is appropriate, the outcome of consultation should include accommodation. As McLachlin CJC put this point in her decision in *Haida Nation*, "[T]he effect of good faith consultation may be to reveal a duty to accommodate."[24]

Where the applicable accommodation is economic in form, the duty-to-consult doctrine may, in principle, directly mandate different forms of economic accommodation, which might include outright compensation or might include other forms of economic accommodation, such as Aboriginal stakes in a project or Aboriginal economic participation in some form. In an admittedly limited set of cases, the courts have pronounced directly as to this principle. Drawing upon

---

21 *Haida Nation, supra* note 17 at paras 13–15.
22 *Ibid* at para 53.
23 For this role of judicial supervision, see the discussion of remedies for breaches of the duty to consult in *Rio Tinto, supra* note 17.
24 *Haida Nation, supra* note 17 at para 47.

the passage rendered by McLachlin CJC in *Haida*,[25] courts have discussed accommodation with an "economic component"[26] and even the possibility of "revenue sharing" as a form of interim accommodation,[27] with the guidance that a Crown facing a strong Aboriginal position and not making "reasonable concessions" will violate the requirement of meaningful consultation.[28] Economic accommodation obviously does not arise in every case in which it is argued,[29] and a well-reasoned government decision not to provide economic accommodation may well win out.[30] Indeed, the courts have recognized the complex regulatory environment and various complexities attaching to economic accommodation issues.[31] Under the duty-to-consult doctrine, there is thus a legal mandate for economic accommodation in appropriate cases.

The duty-to-consult doctrine has also opened conversations on related matters that one surely would not have seen under such serious discussion without the doctrine.[32] For example, that resource revenue sharing has become as much a part of the public discourse as it has is no doubt significantly attributable to the development of this doctrine.[33] Moreover, significant governmental policies have in fact developed to attempt to offer interim economic accommodation in some contexts, again surely motivated significantly by the duty-to-consult doctrine.

25 See, e.g., *Wii'litswx v British Columbia (Minister of Forests)*, 2008 BCSC 1139, [2008] 4 CNLR 315 at paras 10, 178 (both paraphrasing statements of McLachlin CJC from *Haida Nation, supra* note 17 at para 47).

26 *Ibid* at para 208.

27 *Ibid* at paras 207–08.

28 *Ibid* at para 243. See also *Klahoose First Nation v Sunshine Coast Forest District (District Manager)*, [2009] 1 CNLR 110 (stating the need for accommodation that addressed economic interests of the community in the watershed at issue).

29 See, e.g., *Louis v British Columbia (Minister of Energy, Mines and Petroleum Resources)*, [2011] 4 CNLR 252.

30 *Ka'a'Gee Tu First Nation v Canada (AG)*, 2012 FC 297 at para 127 ("the reasons given by Canada to refuse to provide economic accommodation for the KTFN's asserted infringement of Aboriginal title were not capricious").

31 *Ibid* at para 126.

32 See discussion in Newman, *supra* note 16.

33 See, e.g., Sam Adkins, Kristyn Annis, Thomas Isaac, & Rob J Miller, "Recent Developments in Resource Revenue Sharing with First Nations" (23 June 2009), online: McCarthy Tetrault <www.mccarthy.ca/article_detail.aspx?id=4576>; Newman, *supra* note 16 at 61–62.

The Province of British Columbia has some ninety extant Forest Consultation and Revenue Sharing Agreements, the first of these signed 9 December 2010, and more on through the time since.[34] The typical text of many of these agreements provides for a specific sum to be transferred annually to the First Nation to reflect an interim economic accommodation of Aboriginal interests in forestry resources.[35] Some Economic and Community Development Agreements have included percentage shares of resource revenues. The McLeod Lake Indian Band Economic and Community Development Agreement of 25 August 2010 provides for payment of 15 per cent of *Mineral Tax Act* taxes paid by the mine proponent to devolve to the First Nation.[36] The Stk'emlúpsemc of the Scwepemc Nation Economic and Community Development Agreement of 24 August 2010 provides for payments of 37.5 per cent of *Mineral Tax Act* taxes paid by the mine proponent to devolve to the First Nation.[37] Thus, government policies have also provided for economic accommodation.

Moreover, in some instances, industry proponents themselves have been ready to negotiate economic accommodation arrangements pre-emptively so as to avoid later legal uncertainties concerning the duty to consult.[38] These have sometimes taken the form of

---

34 For the developing list, see Forest Consultation and Revenue Sharing Agreements, online: The New Relationship with First Nations and Aboriginal People <www2. gov.bc.ca/gov/topic.page?id=5633DE296BAC46098E130A382AAF9D03>.

35 See, for example, Si a'new First Nation Forest & Range Consultation and Revenue Sharing Agreement of 11 March 2013, section 3.2, online: The New Relationship with First Nations and Aboriginal People <www2.gov.bc.ca/gov/DownloadAsset?assetId= 969182CC7D554C35842199B8BDCCD52E>.

36 McLeod Lake Indian Band Economic and Community Development Agreement of 25 August 2010, section 3.1(c), online: The New Relationship with First Nations and Aboriginal People <www2.gov.bc.ca/gov/DownloadAsset?assetId=A26A692EA897 43409648D98FC6BF8A52&filename=ecda_mcLeod_lake.pdf>. An additional 12.5 per cent is payable under the Nak'azdli First Nation Economic and Community Development Agreement of 12 June 2012, online: The New Relationship with First Nations and Aboriginal People <www2.gov.bc.ca/gov/DownloadAsset?assetId=FD4F200D8 B9A4C72BCAC26E6F52465CA&filename=ecda_nakazdli.pdf>.

37 Stk'emlupsemc of the Secwepemc Nation Economic and Community Development Agreement of 24 August 2010, section 3.1(c), online: The New Relationship with First Nations and Aboriginal People <www2.gov.bc.ca/gov/DownloadAsset?assetId= 63B4A3C1428949F7B8EF8ED7645ECA8C&filename=ecda_secwepemc.pdf>.

38 Sandra Gogal, Richard Riegert, & JoAnn Jamieson, "Aboriginal Impact and Benefit Agreements: Practical Considerations" (2005) 43 Alta L Rev 129 at 156.

lump sum payments.[39] In some prominent instances, corporations
have even offered equity stakes in development projects to Aboriginal communities along, for instance, the route of a pipeline.[40] These
industry policies would seem unlikely to have developed on their
own independently of the legal framework provided by the duty-to-
consult doctrine.

Although courts have themselves been relatively reluctant to offer
precise interventions on economic accommodation questions, they have
provided sufficient legal benchmarks to motivate economic accommodation processes by governments and even by industry, many of which
will take the effect of resource revenue streams (or something equivalent, such as an equity stake in a resource venture). The court decisions
themselves arguably offer a mixture of reflections on the general goals
to be pursued and legally prescribed attention to the very specific rights
of a particular Aboriginal community.[41] Governments and industry take
these general prescriptions forward in specific contexts, no doubt with
a possibly mixed approach in terms of the exact bases underlying each
agreement. Indeed, once resource shares are put up for more individu-
alized negotiations, there is the potential for governments to pursue
various program and policy objectives, so long as they can fit within
the constraints of the overall legal framework.[42] Moreover, factors other
than the strict legal claims of the parties will potentially come into play
because the negotiation environment adds a set of broader considerations related to the bargaining position of the parties.[43]

---

39 Such a provision is present in many impact benefit agreements (IBAs). For a discussion of some such agreements, see Dwight Newman, *Natural Resource Jurisdiction in
Canada* (Toronto: LexisNexis, 2013).
40 For example, Enbridge made such an offer along the route of the Northern Gateway
Pipeline.
41 For an interesting example, see *Huu-Ay-Aht First Nation v British Columbia (Minister of Forests)*, [2005] 3 CNLR 74 at paras 125–27. In this case, the Court identifies
some approaches as likely being more effective policy approaches but then indicates that others must be those that are more responsive to the "specific interests"
(para 127) of the First Nation involved. The Court is attentive to general policy
goals but then compelled by the rights discourse in which it does ultimately operate into a more specifically oriented accommodation than would be most efficient
on policy grounds.
42 Cf William Ascher, *Why Governments Waste Natural Resources: Political Failures in
Developing Countries* (Baltimore, MD: Johns Hopkins University Press, 1999) at 25ff.
43 See Dwight Newman, "Negotiated Rights Enforcement" (2006) 69 Sask L Rev 119.

Problematic Policy Outcomes from the Doctrine's Approach to Economic Accommodation

Legal structures that affect natural resource development, natural resource ownership, and the ways in which natural resource development is governed have major implications for economic outcomes for communities.[44] But the implications reach beyond the direct economic consequences of resource sales themselves, as the effects of resource development also end up pervading the broader economic context and political structures of a society.[45] Counter-intuitively, some literature suggests that countries with greater natural resource wealth have tended to have lower economic growth rates than countries not so similarly endowed, manifesting the "resource curse."[46] The causal chains supporting this correlation are complex and contested (and by no means so simplistic as one Canadian politician's musings about the "Dutch disease").[47] What is important is to realize that there are more complex dynamics arising from natural resource development and complex challenges in terms of making natural resource wealth effectively support economic development.

---

44 See, e.g., Paul Collier, *The Plundered Planet: Why We Must – and How We Can – Manage Nature for Global Prosperity* (Oxford: Oxford University Press, 2010).

45 See, e.g., Naazneen Barma, Kai Kaiser, Tuan Minh, & Lorena Vinuela, *Rents to Riches?* (Washington: World Bank, 2011) (examining the political economy of natural resource development and its effects on governance).

46 See, e.g., Richard M Auty, *Sustaining Development in Mineral Economies: The Resource Curse Thesis* (London: Routledge, 1993); Jeffrey M Sachs & Andrew M Warner, "Natural Resource Abundance and Economic Growth" (1999) 59 J Development Economics 43. See also Marcia Langton & Odette Mazel, "The Resource Curse Compared: Aboriginal Australian Participation in the Resource Extraction Industry and the Distribution of Impacts," in Marcia Langton & Judy Longbottom, eds, *Community Futures, Legal Architecture: Foundations for Indigenous Peoples in the Global Mining Boom* (London: Routledge, 2012) 23 (showing the "resource curse" in action within Australia and examining why Aboriginal Australians in resource-rich parts of the country have not benefited from natural resource development).

47 Federal New Democratic Party Leader Thomas Mulcair offered musings on "Dutch disease" as a phenomenon behind a temporarily high Canadian dollar. On the broader question, see, e.g., Ciaran O'Faircheallaigh, "Curse or Opportunity? Mineral Revenues, Rent Seeking and Development in Aboriginal Australia" in Langton & Longbottom, eds, *supra* note 46, 45 (discussing the highly circumstantial character of the correlations and the resulting need for complex chains of causality to explain different outcomes).

If the duty-to-consult doctrine and its results in terms of economic accommodation in the natural resource context specifically are simply assumed to have positive outcomes on the basis that they further some form of economic redistribution (and I do think this is an underlying assumption for some), then matters are more complicated than they first appear. Indeed, I wish to suggest three specific causal chains that at least complicate any simple assumptions about positive outcomes arising from duty-to-consult-motivated economic accommodation, particularly in the form of resource revenue streams. I shall pose the possibilities that the economic accommodations resulting may give rise to certain unstable policy outcomes, may accentuate certain policy challenges, and may actually pose an obstacle to potentially more desirable policy approaches. The point of this argument, I should be clear, is *not* to argue against economic accommodation but, rather, to challenge any simplistic assumption that relatively rigid legal doctrines can foster the policy outcomes that might be sought by those thinking of them in certain teleological frameworks. In the next (and last) section of the chapter, I shall turn to consider some possible ways of trying to overcome these challenges.

First, as suggested already above, one tendency of the consultation-related economic accommodation discourse has been a real awakening of discussion on resource revenue sharing.[48] These calls have no doubt been heightened by periods in which resource revenues have been strong, and the calls have arguably been strongest in regions where resource revenue streams had larger rather than smaller possible contents. Resource revenue sharing may appear to be entirely to the benefit of the Aboriginal communities receiving a share, especially if developed on a percentage basis, as commonly urged and as is arguably implicit in the concept. However, if one assumes that Canadian governments will not make unlimited concessions to Aboriginal communities, then resource revenue shares will to some degree crowd out other government transfers that were being made or would have been made in lieu of the resource revenue share. The challenge that arises is that resource revenue shares offer an unstable or volatile revenue stream. The boom-bust cycles of resource-dependent economies are of course well known. Indeed, the Economic and Community Development Agreements signed with several British Columbia Aboriginal

---

48 See discussion in Newman, *supra* note 16.

communities include a clause requiring acknowledgment of the instability of resource revenue streams.[49] Establishing the revenue streams of Aboriginal communities based on resource shares has the effect of transferring to Aboriginal communities the risk of resource price volatility from governments more able to bear that risk in place of other revenue streams that would be less volatile. The result is that rights discourses that lead towards this kind of policy approach may actually create a policy approach less beneficial to the Aboriginal communities involved than some other approach would have been.

A second challenge related to transfers of resource revenue streams – and quite possibly arising with other policies that the current section 35 discourse also promotes – pertains to the possibility that the policy outcomes generated in the context of professed concerns about inequality may actually promote new, albeit possibly different inequalities. Who benefits in what ways from resource revenue sharing is often undefined in discussions of the concept. To begin with just one manifestation, a political party that advanced a resource revenue proposal in a recent provincial election had at one stage had discussions of a policy proposal related to First Nations and Metis communities but during the election campaign suddenly came forth with a proposal referring only to First Nations communities.[50] There will of course be complex legal arguments concerning the scope of Metis rights and whether the lack of prior Metis occupancy implies an inability to make rights claims to resources. In any event, the proposal could arguably work awkward effects as between First Nations and Metis communities.[51]

Perhaps more significantly, however, the proposal under discussion was silent as to how resource revenues would be split as between different First Nations communities. Specifically, are resource revenues to be divided on a site-specific basis corresponding to the possible resource rights of a particular Aboriginal community in relation to its own traditional territory? One could of course imagine the development of a

---

49 Compare the various agreements at Forest Consultation and Revenue Sharing Agreements, online: The New Relationship with First Nations and Aboriginal People <www2.gov.bc.ca/gov/topic.page?id=5633DE296BAC46098E130A382AAF9D03>.

50 See Dwight Newman, "Revenue Sharing Proposal Divisive, Unwise," [Saskatoon] Star-Phoenix (27 October 2011), online: <www2.canada.com/saskatoonstarphoenix/news/forum/story.html?id=aa61b894-4093-48c8-8884-8686ef735297&p=1>.

51 Of course, were the Metis communities to later achieve some other revenue stream, they might actually end up better off with a less volatile revenue stream.

more centralized pool. However, the duty-to-consult discourse is clearly oriented towards an approach based on the rights of particular rights-bearing communities. Cases that have touched upon economic accommodation options as between more centralized pools and those based on specific historical Aboriginal interests of a particular community have suggested that the latter approach corresponds to the legal doctrine. Such will also be the result under a decentralized and/or privatized negotiation process, particularly one where corporate stakeholders enter into negotiations with particular communities whose best alternative to a negotiated agreement (BATNA) will depend upon their particularized resource interests.[52] The result is that one should likely foresee a very meaningful possibility of resource revenue sharing benefiting some Aboriginal communities and not others, with the effect of accentuating inequality at least as between Aboriginal communities rather than lessening it and, in the process, quite possibly generating a powerful set of interest groups no longer pushing for equality for other Aboriginal communities.

A third causal chain of concern arising from the allocation of resource revenue streams pertains to the broader and perhaps not entirely well understood phenomenon of the "resource curse."[53] Two possible causal chains potentially contributing to this problem merit particular attention. First, resource wealth has particular effects on governance insofar as the presence of resource wealth may alter power bases and be used to further alter power bases.[54] This much more complex phenomenon of course merits further discussion elsewhere, but for present purposes, one might note, for instance, the possibility that a greater attachment of Aboriginal communities' revenues to resource streams based on their traditional territories may well further entrench the political power of on-reserve individuals relative to off-reserve individuals, with the effect of favouring the rural over the urban at the very time when many Aboriginal community members are moving to urban areas for economic reasons. Second, resource wealth also has the potential of altering the economic incentives applicable to economic activities separate from the resource wealth and, for instance, discouraging other entrepreneurialism and investments that may contribute to long-term growth.[55] All of

---

52 On negotiations concerning rights claims generally, see Newman, *supra* note 43.
53 M Ross, "The Political Economy of the Resource Curse" (1999) 51 World Politics 297.
54 Cf, e.g., *ibid.*
55 See, e.g., Langton & Mazel, *supra* note 46, at 29–30.

these claims depend significantly, of course, on the management of the resource wealth in question. But the latter possibility again raises the risk that resource revenue streams may not be all that one might hope.

These complex causal chains and their applicability or inapplicability in particular circumstances could face objections and would of course merit further discussion. However, that is precisely my point. Although the courts try to be non-prescriptive concerning the form of economic accommodation to which their doctrines give rise, the very shape of their legal doctrines has certain implications beyond those that would arise from a pure goal of "economic reconciliation." The doctrines imply more community-specific approaches that, in the process, risk taking away from some of the goals initially to be pursued. Section 35 itself takes a deontological form, stating the existence of certain historical rights, but the courts have wanted to interpret it in light of certain teleological goals. In doing so, they can take it only so far, however, and the deontological structure remains as a constraint on the more straightforward pursuit of the teleological goals at issue. The resulting paradox is a deontological structure that undermines the teleological goals at which it purportedly aims.

Conclusions and Paths Forward

There remains, of course, a tentative character to the argument advanced, and I welcome counterarguments, as life would be simpler if there were a more straightforward alignment between deontology and teleology, between entrenched rights and worthwhile goals, and between natural rights and egalitarian impulses. However, the continued development of section 35 on the sort of path it follows – one of stating a set of background rights, stating goals such as reconciliation, and stating that courts will seek to avoid being involved and prefer to leave matters to negotiation in light of the background entitlements applicable[56] – is quite possibly not one geared to establishing an optimal policy environment for Aboriginal communities.

An objection to this whole chapter might, of course, run as follows. Complaining at the outset of lawyers' and legal scholars' policy and

---

56 All of these dimensions are to the fore in Lamer CJC's judgment in *Delgamuukw*, *supra* note 6. But they continue in later cases and are equally present in consultation cases like *Mikisew Cree*, *supra* note 3.

economic amateurism, I have gone on to try to develop several very formal economic arguments in non-formal ways that undermine the precision of the concepts at issue. I have gone on to make empirical claims without definitive empirical evidence. Guilty as charged. However, I suggest that these performative problems with the argument just reinforce the main argument, which says that better approaches to the questions at stake may well depend upon drawing upon richer disciplinary resources in larger ways, with philosophy, politics, and economics, among other areas, having much to contribute to the analysis of the legal doctrine at issue.

My comments, then, on ways forward are subject to possible qualification. However, one possibility to emerge might be the development of a separation between section 35 claims that are principally cultural and section 35 claims that are principally economic. This division will not be easy to establish, for the very nature of many Aboriginal rights claims is precisely that they present the claims of a holistic culture that, like any, is not easily divisible into different categories. Nonetheless, it may be possible for the courts to develop a test that attempts to draw the distinction. To some degree, there are already some such distinctions insofar, for instance, as Aboriginal title doctrine, though purporting to be grounded in a more general Aboriginal rights test,[57] actually has a different test whose underlying principles diverge at several key junctures from what the more general Aboriginal rights test might have seemed to imply.[58]

I might note in passing that drawing such a distinction more clearly would arguably actually liberate the Aboriginal rights test applicable in cultural contexts from certain constraints under which it operates because of courts' worries about the precedent set in economic contexts by decisions in cultural contexts. The *Van der Peet* test has been subject to an ongoing concern that it appears to adopt a "frozen rights" model that fixed cultural rights essentially in place on the basis of a certain moment of settler-Indigenous encounter.[59] However, it arguably does

---

57 *Delgamuukw, supra* note 6 expresses itself as being based on *Van der Peet, supra* note 5.
58 See the distinctions referenced in *ibid.*
59 This has been raised over time. See, e.g., Russell Barsh & James Youngblood Henderson, "The Supreme Court's Van der Peet Trilogy: Naïve Imperialism and Ropes of Sand" (1997) 42 McGill LJ 3; Avigail Eisenberg, "Reasoning about Identity: Canada's Distinctive Culture Test," in Avigail Eisenberg, ed, *Diversity and Equality* (Vancouver: UBC Press, 2006) 34.

so in large part because to have adopted a test that operated otherwise would have adopted consequences for economic rights that the courts were not willing to accept. The *Van der Peet* test serves as an effective check on certain economic and political rights that would, in the courts' view, otherwise be inconsistent with the animating themes of reconciliation and justice between communities.

On this model, section 35's implications for economic reconciliation would then potentially become less precise, with policymakers and Aboriginal communities having more scope to develop flexible policy frameworks that better achieve the teleological purposes at issue. The objection, of course, is that this approach risks making Aboriginal economic rights claims non-justiciable. I have several responses. First, the very reason for undertaking the division is to reduce the role of the courts in seeking to define precisely Aboriginal economic claims, out of concern that the rights framework with which they inevitably operate is in fundamental tensions with policy approaches. Second, it is not obvious that a governmental duty to develop terms of economic reconciliation cannot be justiciable in some manner. It may simply be subject to review on different bases, such as reasonableness-type analyses, rather than the frameworks associated with deontological rights analyses. That this is so may well be a good thing. Governments currently contemplating broad frameworks for economic reconciliation with Aboriginal communities are as apt to be paralyzed by legal considerations as to be supported by them, and a distinction between section 35 cultural and economic claims, the development of a section 35 duty to pursue an economic reconciliation program, and the adoption of a reasonableness review of that program could well better foster better policy that gets things done.

The best paths forward together are not simple to discern. In this chapter, I have presented a somewhat tentative argument. I have argued, first of all, that courts have underlying teleological ideas for what needs to be achieved under section 35 that become entangled in their inevitably deontologically affected analyses. Second, I have argued that section 35 has supported significant economic reconciliation policies. However, third, I have argued that the section 35 analysis has had no room for consideration of more complex considerations applicable to something like policies following on the duty to consult in the natural resource context. Indeed, I have argued that there are possible chains of causality that may significantly undermine the effects one initially envisions from certain policies that may appear to flow directly from the underlying section 35 rights framework and the doctrines developed from it. Fourth, I have argued that the policy analyses to be pursued need analyses that lawyers and legal scholars alone cannot offer. In addressing these issues, I have argued for the possibility of a different path forward on section 35. The chapters collected in this volume can be an occasion for deep reflection and dialogue together, and I welcome further dialogue.

9 The State of the Crown–Aboriginal Fiduciary Relationship: The Case for an Aboriginal Veto

MICHAEL J. BRYANT

The Crown–Aboriginal relationship in Canada is a legal construction, arising from the ingenious mind of Professor Brian Slattery,[1] and adopted by the late Chief Justice Brian Dickson in the heady, early days of post-patriation constitutional jurisprudence. As a young law student around that time, I learned about fiduciary law not only from Aboriginal rights scholar Professor Slattery, but also from restitution and contract law scholar Professor John D. McCamus.[2] It led me to believe that Aboriginal rights were an odd fit for fiduciary law, a "phantom of fiduciary law."[3] Since then I have had experience as an Aboriginal rights litigator, consultant, legislator, and teacher, and still conclude that the Crown–Aboriginal relationship may be fiduciary *de lege lata*, but de facto it's something else entirely.

Put another way, if the relationship between governments and Aboriginal peoples in Canada is truly one belonging to the law of equity – the stuff of Chancery, trust, escrow and restitution – then the Crown in right of Canada is without a doubt the most notorious miscreant of a legal entity known to fiduciary law. So too of the Crown in right of our provinces.

---

1 "Understanding Aboriginal Rights" (1987) 66 Can Bar Rev 727.
2 John D McCamus is a professor of law and university professor at Osgoode Hall Law School of York University (dean 1982–87). He is also chair of Legal Aid Ontario; a member of the Ontario Bar, associated with Davies Ward Phillips & Vineberg LLP; a member of the American Law Institute Advisory Committee for the Restatement of Restitution and Unjust Enrichment 3d; former chair of the Ontario Law Reform Commission; and author of numerous books and articles, including texts on contracts and restitution.
3 Michael J Bryant, "Crown–Aboriginal Relationships in Canada: The Phantom of Fiduciary Law" (1993) 27 UBC L Rev 19.

Systemic poverty, addiction, and overrepresentation in prisons and morgues, the systemic underrepresentation among the professions and the prosperous, the squalid housing conditions on many reserves are all unquestionable facts of life for too many Aboriginal peoples in Canada and surely constitute a 24/7 breach of the Crown's fiduciary duty.

But the Crown–Aboriginal relationship is *not* the stuff of Chancery, trust, escrow and restitution. Nor is it adequate to call the relationship "sui generis."[4] There are elements of the relationship that can borrow from fiduciary law. Accordingly, the Supreme Court of Canada may have left the nature of the Crown–Aboriginal fiduciary relationship too undefined for too long, just as governments have been skittish about advancing beyond the constitutional minimums set forth by the Court. As such, another of my professors at Osgoode Hall, Michael Mandel, was quite right to lament the legalization of politics with the advent of section 35 of the *Constitution Act, 1982*.[5] It's just that without that legalization, the result would have been even more abysmal.

The caution to be exercised in applying fiduciary law to the Crown–Aboriginal relationship is legal and practical. Legally, the doctrines of undue influence, unconscionability, and fiduciary should not be lumped into one.[6] Moreover, the Crown–Aboriginal relationship is sui generis and so too is the Crown-Aboriginal fiduciary law sui generis, such that non-Aboriginal fiduciary law ought not borrow from its Aboriginal cousin. And the jurisprudence has strained to clarify Crown-Aboriginal fiduciary law to the point of inventive formulation, rendering just results for the case at bar, but also rendering confusing jurisprudence for the parties to apply in practice. Nowhere is this more true that the duty to consultation and accommodation arising from the Crown–Aboriginal fiduciary relationship.

Thus, the practical concern: consultation is easy to identify as a duty but impossible to fulfil as a standard of care, without more. Identifying a breach of the duty is too onerous, too nebulous, and has unhelpfully consumed the parties, often overwhelming the parties in consultative process, since the courts named the duty to consult as a hurdle for

---

4 *Guerin v R* [1984] 2 SCR 335.
5 Michael Mandel, *The Charter of Rights and the Legalization of Politics in Canada*, rev ed (Toronto: Thompson, 1994).
6 "[W]hereas undue influence focuses on the sufficiency of consent and unconscionability looks at the reasonableness of a given transaction, the fiduciary principle monitors the abuse of a loyalty reposed": *Hodgkinson v Simms*, [1994] 3 SCR 377 at 406, per La Forest J.

private and public sector parties to cross, in doing business with Aboriginal peoples. The better approach, in my view, is to require consent, not consultation, for major projects with Aboriginal communities. Nevertheless, the jurisprudence need not be an impediment to reforming the fiduciary duty. In fact, section 35 of the *Constitution Act, 1982* has been primarily the creature of jurisprudence, not statute or government policy. Ordinarily, constitutional jurisprudence is the cart that follows the horse. People act, the government regulates, and the courts arbitrate. Then the government implements the jurisprudence, and life goes on, under the new legal regime, but it goes on with full participation of all parties, including governments, which often have to manage issues not contemplated by the courts. There is an evolution, from action, litigation, jurisprudence, to application, public policy, and private practice. Professor Peter Hogg refers to this evolution as a dialogue between branches of the state, and the citizenry.[7] Some scholars take issue with that description,[8] but the Court has agreed,[9] and governments could care less. Governments just keep on moving.

Except when it comes to Aboriginal rights and this fangled fiduciary duty. Governments tend to await word from the courts on Aboriginal affairs, then apply the jurisprudence like a nervous sous-chef following a sacred recipe. Then when something new develops in Aboriginal affairs, governments enter a public policy coma until further appeal. Governments are so timid when it comes to section 35. The Crown-Aboriginal fiduciary doctrine was never intended as a straitjacket, yet that's exactly what has happened, in no small part because of that doctrine's so-called duty of consultation and accommodation.

Crown as Fiduciary: One Perspective

From an insider's perspective, the Crown in right of Ontario does take its fiduciary duties seriously, more often than not, based on my own observations during a decade in the Ontario Legislative Assembly and six years on the Executive Council. During that time I was Official

---

7 PW Hogg & AA Bushell, "The Charter Dialogue between Courts and Legislatures (or Perhaps the Charter of Rights Isn't Such a Bad Thing after All)" (1997) 35 Osgoode Hall LJ 75.
8 See discussion in Kent Roach, "A Dialogue about Principle and a Principled Dialogue: Justice Iacobucci's Substantive Approach to Dialogue" (2007) 57 UTJ 449.
9 *Vriend v Alberta*, [1998] 1 SCR 493 at 562–67 (per Iacobucci J).

Opposition attorney-general critic (1999–2003) and energy critic (2002–3), attorney general (2003–7), minister responsible for Aboriginal affairs (2003–5), minister for Aboriginal affairs (2007–8), and minister of economic development (2008–9). All those portfolios saw me engaged on issues of Aboriginal peoples and rights, working with civil servants, Cabinet ministers, Premier's Office and various ministry officials; chiefs and councillors for Ontario First Nations; Metis leaders; pan-Aboriginal stakeholder leaders (e.g., Native Friendship Centres); non-Aboriginal business leaders, and plenty of lawyers: agents of the Crown, private sector litigators and solicitors. My interaction with the federal Crown was primarily through federal-provincial-territorial collaboration efforts, but this experience was more vicarious than direct, except for the period between 2007 and 2008 when I had at least monthly contact with the federal minister for Indian and northern affairs.

This experience leads me to make several general observations.

1 *The Fiduciary Duty Itself Is Taken Seriously by All Concerned, Even If Its Content Remains Elusive* To the extent that the Supreme Court of Canada sought to provide an umbrella concept that would guide the activities of the Crown, the jurisprudence brought some order to a relationship lacking any trust between the parties. By invoking a legal concept of significant gravitas, lawyers have successfully intervened to ensure that government officials and Aboriginal leaders are fully aware that a unique, actionable, constitutional duty hovers over their dealings. Today, the concept of a special relationship existing between the provincial government and Aboriginal peoples is omnipresent in the halls of government. This was hardly a phenomenon of the Ontario Liberal government in which I served; it clearly predated my tenure in Cabinet. That the relationship is characterized as a "fiduciary" one is not unknown, but that technical term is considered the stuff of legalese.

And that is the point: the government officials, Aboriginal leaders, and non-Aboriginal actors all saw the fiduciary duties as being in the domain of lawyers. This phenomenon is played out in corporate boardrooms as well, wherein the role of the general counsel has evolved, having languished for too long as the "Dr No" of corporate executives.[10] Lawyers can either be problem-solvers, harbingers of solutions, or they can be mindless criers of "Wolf."

---

10 Deborah DeMott, "The Discrete Roles of General Counsel" (2005) 74 Fordham L Rev 1.

Within governments, lawyers are pervasive, more so than you might imagine. In the government of Ontario, there are agents of the attorney general, hundreds of them, scattered throughout the government, in pretty much every ministry. That means that every policy or action typically gets vetted by that lawyer. Because these lawyers are technically still part of the Ministry of the Attorney General, they are sometimes viewed as outsiders, meddlers. Sometimes these agents of the attorney team up with their host ministry officials to fend off questions from the attorney's senior managers and staff. But in most cases, the system works well: somebody is there in the various ministries to advise government officials about, for instance, the Crown's fiduciary duty to Aboriginal peoples.

2 The Fiduciary Duty May Be an Effective Shield against Crown Oppression, but It Can Be an Impediment to Innovation, in the Public Sector, and Increasingly in the Private Sector The legal bear hug provided by the federal Department of Justice, for instance, often leaves ministries reticent to engage with Aboriginal communities, for fear of running afoul of the fiduciary duty. It just takes one government lawyer, invoking his role as agent of the attorney, to unnecessarily stall a positive initiative within a ministry.

"One of *your lawyers* said we can't do that" were words I heard sometimes as attorney general, from the mouths of Cabinet colleagues. Sometimes, I was relieved: counsel had slowed something down that would have been harmful. Sometimes, the speaker of those words was exaggerating. But occasionally it was true: a Crown law officer was wielding the Crown fiduciary duty like a sledgehammer where none was needed. I was fortunate to have a team of senior managers at the Ministry of the Attorney General who did their jobs extremely well. There are over a thousand lawyers, a thousand attorney agents, in the government of Ontario. An indivisible Crown legal position is the goal of every attorney general, but practically speaking, this requires give and take, forgiveness and hard lessons.

The Crown-Aboriginal fiduciary duty could stifle innovation within First Nations, in that some Aboriginal leaders assess the fiduciary duties as a threshold question before engaging with governments, in any fashion, no matter the issue.

An example by way of contrasts would be as follows. When visiting Six Nations of the Grand River for the first time in 2007, as the newly minted minister of Aboriginal affairs, I spoke with Councillor Ava Hill about how the province could warm relations with Six Nations. Détente seemed better than confrontation, from my perspective. She immediately listed off five things that the government of Ontario could do to assist Six Nations: provide long-promised funding, through a youth engagement fitness program, to complete repairs to a hockey rink; fund MRI machines, through the Health Ministry, at the Six Nations wellness clinic, which would serve both the Six Nations community and its non-Aboriginal neighbours in Caledonia; and fill potholes – repair an infamous provincial road. (Chief William Montour helpfully drove me up and down that bumpy road several times, to underscore the point.) The remaining requests were highly technical, I recall. In less than a year, all of those requests were fulfilled. We were two governments, working together, for the betterment of Six Nations and the surrounding area. It allowed us to discuss the intractable issues, like land claims and contraband cigarettes.

Without that positive relationship, those discussions could not take place. There were times of high tension, when relations between the Aboriginal and non-Aboriginal communities was volatile. This required careful discussions between the parties, and a level of trust. In this sense, Six Nations and Ontario were *exemplifying* the special relationship between Aboriginal peoples and the Crown, rather than analysing or testing it.

I touted the practical efforts of détente to other First Nation communities around the province. When I mentioned the hockey rink repairs at a gathering of northern First Nation chiefs, one took the microphone and lectured me on the Crown's fiduciary duty to his First Nation. It seemed a non sequitur to me: "Forget about the legalese, the fiduciary duties. Let's fix your community's hockey rink. Let's get some things done together." Some Ontario First Nations chiefs could not agree. Allowing hockey rink repairs seemed to them to miss the point of the fiduciary relationship. To me, that misses the point of governing altogether.

3 The Crown–Aboriginal Fiduciary Relationship Is Less Well Known to Corporate Managers in the Private Sector To senior global corporate managers new to Canadian resource and energy markets, the duty is a conundrum. As ever, a tension often develops between one corporate manager responsible for advancing the project in question, and the corporation's general counsel. Sometimes, the community relations branches tend to bump up against general counsel concerned with global anti-bribery restrictions.[11]

11 Aisha Anwar & Gavin Deeprose, "The Bribery Act 2010" (2010) 125 Scots Law Times 23; E Spahn, "Multi-Jurisdictional Bribery Law Enforcement: The OECD Anti-Bribery Convention" (2012) 53 Va J Intl L 34.

Even companies familiar with doing business in Canada still see the "duty to consult" as a risk and a delay, similar to environmental regulations. If the company resorts to litigation, the courts inevitably send the parties back to the negotiation table, and practically never order that the First Nation must stand aside and allow for a project to proceed.[12] But it's too late to renegotiate post-injunctive relief. In my view, if the courts are asked to resolve a disagreement between parties over the duty to consult Aboriginal peoples, then the relationship has unravelled, trust is lost, and the project is doomed.

Increasingly, companies in the natural resource and energy sectors have senior positions within the company devoted to Aboriginal affairs. Companies that treat Aboriginal affairs as equivalent to stakeholder relations are in for a rude surprise: this is insulting to a First Nation, which rightly considers itself as more than a local Chamber of Commerce. Companies wise enough to hire Aboriginal people themselves into these positions are off to an excellent start, however, and this is a trend worth pursuing.

4 *The Crown Plays Arbiter, More Than Mediator or Facilitator, When It Comes to Corporations Doing Business with Aboriginal Communities* That the fiduciary relationship is between Crown and Aboriginal peoples does not mean that the fulfilment of that duty is the Crown's doing. The government action subjected to the constitutional duty usually turns on a regulatory decision that is the culmination of the negotiations between a First Nations community and a business. But along the way, governments in Canada are inconsistent in developing programs to build capacity for Aboriginal communities, with some notable exceptions.[13]

Accordingly, corporations either wait for the government to magically deliver a consultation process, or governments wait for the consultation to happen, without government involvement. Corporations

---

12 See Penelope Simons & Lynda Collins, "Participatory Rights in the Ontario Mining Sector: An International Human Rights Perspective" (2010) 6 JSDLP 177 (2010).

13 In Ontario, we tried to anticipate the capacity deficit within First Nation communities, by creating a fund to which Aboriginal communities could apply to get help assessing a potential business project on or near their traditional lands. Establishing this fund was a key recommendation of the Report of the Ipperwash Inquiry. The fund was developed with input from First Nation and Metis partners: Ministry of Aboriginal Affairs, Ontario. Online: New Relationship Fund, <www.ontario.ca/business-and-economy/new-relationship-fund>.

are wise to simultaneously negotiate an agreement with an Aboriginal community, while constantly pressuring government to deliver assistance. Companies should develop a realistic wish-list for the three levels of government implicated by a project, since often the governments themselves will be unaware as to the specific needs of the parties.

5 Increasingly, in Ontario, the Victor Diamond Mine Project Is Seen as the Industry Standard for a Proponent Partnering with a First Nation on a Natural Resources or Energy Project De Beers Canada Inc worked with Attawapiskat First Nation for several years, eventually executing an impact benefit agreement that was ratified by the First Nation in 2005. As Attawapiskat Chief Mike Carpenter put it, "De Beers Canada's diamond mine is the first and only opportunity our community has ever had to break free of our soul-destroying poverty."[14] So enmeshed did De Beers Canada become in fulfilling the Crown's fiduciary duty, it even bejewelled the sovereign's ceremonial mace.[15] Nice symbolism, but impossible without an agreement between the parties. Not consultation – consent. Companies seeking the Crown jewels with Aboriginal communities will find no treasure through consultation alone.

The Crown-Aboriginal Fiduciary Duty to Consult

The linchpin to every fiduciary relationship is the undertaking, express or implied, between parties. This establishes whether there is a fiduciary relationship, for ad hoc fiduciaries, and scopes the duty of care, for both ad hoc and per se fiduciary relationships.[16] Any re-examination of the fiduciary duty of the Crown to Aboriginal peoples ought to return to an analysis of the undertaking, real or constructed, by the Crown, to Aboriginal peoples. On this front, there are two approaches: articulate an omnibus undertaking, arising out of the time of European contact, and evidenced by the *Royal Proclamation of 1763*. Alternatively, identify

---

14 Norm Tollinsky, "Victor Mine a Game Changer for Far North," *Sudbury Mining Solutions Journal* (1 December 2009).

15 "From Mine to Mace to Mine: Ceremonial Mace from Ontario Legislature Makes Historic Visit to De Beers Canada Victor Mine," *Canada Newswire* (8 July 2011): when it came time for Ontario to perform maintenance of its 1867 ceremonial mace, the very symbol of the Crown's authority in Ontario, displayed prominently in the chamber of the Legislative Assembly (when in session), De Beers Canada supplied new diamonds through its Mine to Mace program.

16 *Galambos v Perez*, [2009] 3 SCR 247.

different undertakings for different activities, as well as an undertaking respecting Aboriginal title. Although I was originally a proponent of the omnibus undertaking, the alternative may be preferable, as it avoids straining to match the omnibus undertaking with a particular Aboriginal activity or property.[17]

As it turns out, section 35 Aboriginal rights in Canada might be summarized into two categories: activities and title.[18] There are Aboriginal rights and treaty rights to particular activities that are integral to an Aboriginal society.[19] Protected activities include fishing or hunting for sustenance and for trade, and could include Aboriginal management of lands, resources, economy, health, education, and welfare.[20] In addition, there is Aboriginal title, as distinct from the protected activities, albeit nothing prevents overlap of protected activities on protected lands. Aboriginal title is the only property right entrenched in Canada's Constitution, and, as such, has a test distinct from Aboriginal activities, both to establish the right and to determine whether that it had been extinguished prior to the passing of the *Constitution Act, 1982*. Regardless, all Aboriginal rights infringements are subject to a limitations test akin to that required under section 1 of the *Charter of Rights*.

At some point in the juridic interpretation of this phantom of fiduciary law, more phantoms were rendered. The duty to consultation and accommodation is one such phantasmic offspring of the Crown-Aboriginal fiduciary duty. "There is always a duty of consultation," stated Chief Justice Lamer in *Delgamuukw v BC*. That apparently self-evident duty was said to vary from mere discussion to a strict veto.[21] I obviously support the government-to-government, or nation-to-nation, engagement between the Crown and Aboriginal peoples, so consultation is a self-evident proposition. However, to frame something as

---

17 See the discussion on this point in Tom Allen, *The Right to Property in Commonwealth Constitutions* (Cambridge: Cambridge University Press, 2000) 26–27.
18 Michael Bryant & Lorne Sossin, *Public Law* (Toronto: Carswell, 2002) ch 1.
19 The SCC in *Van der Peet* put much emphasis on two elements of the test: first, whether the activity was integral to the Aboriginal society, and, second, whether that society was distinctive. But upon closer consideration, the distinction between integral and distinctive unravels, such that the test boils down to whether the Aboriginal activity in question is integral to the Aboriginal society in question: Bryant & Sossin, *supra* at 13.
20 See *R v Sparrow*, [1990] 1 SCR 1075; *R v NTC Smokehouse Ltd*, [1996] 2 SCR 672; *R v Gladstone* [1996] 2 SCR 723.
21 *Delgamuukw v British Columbia*, [1997] 3 SCR 1010 at para 168.

amorphous as "consultation" as a "duty" proves problematic, when it comes to governmental operations.

In any event, in deciding when the duty to consult arises, the Supreme Court of Canada recently summarized its 2004 test[22] in *Rio Tinto Alcan Inc v Carrier Sekani Tribal Council* (2010),[23] in a unanimous decision by Chief Justice Beverley McLachlin. The duty to consult is ongoing and prospective, rather than retrospective. The duty is triggered when: (1) the Crown has knowledge, actual or constructive, of a potential Aboriginal claim or right; (2) there is contemplated Crown conduct; and (3) the contemplated conduct may adversely affect an Aboriginal claim or right. For the second element, McLachlin CJ wrote that the impugned government action does not need to have an immediate impact on lands and resources: "A potential for adverse impact suffices ... Thus the duty to consult extends to 'strategic, higher level decisions' that may have an impact on aboriginal claims and rights." The challenge with that prong of the test is that lawyers' imaginations have no limit, when it comes to advising on adverse impacts rather than speculative ones. One person's speculation is another's *res ipsa loquitur*.

Consultation *Ad Absurdum*

On more than one occasion, upon announcing a consultation process for an issue raised by Aboriginal leaders, a First Nations chief would complain publicly that the government of Ontario had breached its duty to consult, by consulting without pre-consultation on the consultation process. So within government, before establishing a consultation process, we would approach the affected Aboriginal leaders, to consult about the consultation process. This approach did not lend itself to decisive or timely government action.

But who could be blamed for insisting on consultative rights, when the Supreme Court of Canada said "the duty to consult extends to 'strategic, higher level decisions' that may have an impact on aboriginal claims and rights"? Strategic, higher level decisions are made every day in the Ontario Ministry of Aboriginal Affairs, and almost every day at Ministry of Natural Resources, and the Ministry of Energy and its generation, transmission, and regulatory agencies and corporations. And

---

22 *Haida Nation v British Columbia (Minister of Forests)*, 2004 SCC 73, [2004] 3 SCR 511.
23 2010 SCC 43.

there are "strategic, higher level decisions" contemplated regularly at Cabinet committees and "four corners" meetings between a relevant ministry's top officials, the minister's office (i.e., political staff), the Premier's Office, and the Cabinet Office (central senior civil service). That's the practice in Ontario, and I doubt it's much different in other Canadian governments. If interpreted too narrowly, the Court's findings on when the duty to consult is triggered would paralyse the government, and often it does just that.

In the private sector, even in cases where a fiduciary relationship governs, there is typically a fluidity to the practical arrangements made by the parties to a contract. Not so the duty to consult Aboriginal peoples by the natural resource and energy industry. In my experience and observation, the Supreme Court of Canada got it wrong, with respect to the "duty to consultation and accommodation" arising from the Crown's fiduciary duty to Aboriginal peoples. Unintended consequences have sprung from the Court's efforts to avoid unjustified infringement of Aboriginal rights through this aspect of the Crown's fiduciary duty.

For example, as a consultant, we once spent weeks negotiating the protocol for non-disclosure around the protocol for the duty to consult. In other words, was there any limit on the transparency necessary to meet the duty to consult? To be sure, an Aboriginal community requires full disclosure by the proposed project leaders, a fulsome risk analysis, and quantification of potential economic benefit for the community. The duty to consult was established by the courts to avoid an injustice; to ensure that that process was not skipped. But consulting is not the objective, by itself, when it comes to projects on or near Aboriginal territory.

An Aboriginal community is often underserved by the professions – either they have a vulture of an attorney or consultant who has moved into the community with sketchy or exaggerated credentials, or they have good counsel whom they can ill afford and don't fully trust yet, or they must rely upon funding from the project leaders for legal and other counsel. As if a history of shameful treatment by outsiders isn't enough, this capacity deficit leaves the Aboriginal community feeling as if there is an imbalance of power as between the parties. Some of the delay in project development is caused by the capacity deficit, by an awareness of the power imbalance, some by inherent cynicism about outsiders, and some by the ever increasing "duty to consult" process that becomes the one thing that all parties can obsess over because consultation requires no tough decisions, only endless disclosure, analysis, over-analysis, procedural wrangling, and then more discussion.

Beyond this personal perspective on the "duty to consult," the law on point rests on shaky ground. Besides its questionable juridic foundation,[24] it renders a *reductio ad absurdum*: if there is a never-ending requirement to consult, then there is no end to the consultation. Under the current law, it follows that, at some point, a decision must be made, by a proponent of a mining project, for instance, to either proceed with or without the consent of Aboriginal peoples.

However, if the fundamental objective is consultation, rather than the means, then that decision cannot happen. If consultation is the means to an end, then what is the end? The answer is a fully consultative process. That makes the legal test circular in practice. Consider this telling finding by the Court in *Rio*:

> The duty to consult embodies what Brian Slattery has described as a "generative" constitutional order which sees section 35 as serving a dynamic and not simply static function" ("Aboriginal Rights and the Honour of the Crown" (2005), 29 S.C.L.R. (2d) 433, at p. 440). This dynamism was articulated in Haida Nation as follows, at para. 32:
>
> > ... the duty to consult and accommodate is part of a process of fair dealing and reconciliation that begins with the assertion of sovereignty and continues beyond formal claims resolution. Reconciliation is not a final legal remedy in the usual sense. Rather, it is a process flowing from rights guaranteed by s. 35(1) of the Constitution Act, 1982.
>
> As the post-Haida Nation case law confirms, consultation is "[c]oncerned with an ethic of ongoing relationships" and seeks to further an ongoing process of reconciliation by articulating a preference for remedies "that promote ongoing negotiations": D.G. Newman, *The Duty to Consult: New Relationships with Aboriginal Peoples* (2009), at p. 21.

Unintentionally, the Court has established process as the Holy Grail, rather than the methodology. The goal is "to further an ongoing process ... to promote ongoing negotiations." That renders the *reductio ad absurdum*, in the context of a single transaction. A transaction requires process and a negotiation, but surely not ongoing ad infinitum. At some point the process should complete, the negotiation has to conclude, and the parties have to agree or disagree; to execute an agreement, or not.

---

24 See Bryant, *supra* note 3.

On the one hand, the Court has rightly identified a laudable goal for the Crown–Aboriginal relationship: reconciliation. On the other hand, achieving reconciliation requires a conciliation: a decision, uniting the parties. As such, reconciliation is (typically) achieved via negotiation and consultation and accommodation. But reconciliation is not the same thing as consultation. In theory, reconciliation could be unilateral in deed, even if it is ideal in result.

On behalf of the Crown, in late 2007, I offered to return Ipperwash Provincial Park to the Chippewas of Kettle and Stony Point First Nation, on the basis of a brief conversation, and a handshake, with Chief Thomas Bressette and Councillor Sam George. The ensuing process took years to finalize, but the reconciliation was achieved that December morning, not by consultation alone, but through a meaningful agreement between the parties. A drum ceremony on Kettle and Stony Point First Nation traditional lands would later follow. It was a long time coming.[25] If we had entangled ourselves in fiduciary minutia, the relationship would not have been furthered. There would have been no reconciliation, no deal, no drums.

The better view, as long as we're relying upon fiduciary law, is to be found in the jurisprudence and practice governing shareholder rights under circumstances of a merger or asset sale. Shareholders' default rights are to ratify or reject such a radical change to their shareholdings,[26] and so it ought to be with Aboriginal peoples' traditional lands facing an industrial upheaval. The fiduciary duty to shareholders is not consultation, but consent (at a minimum, where directors invite shareholder ratification, notwithstanding debate over shareholder rights and director primacy, especially for hostile takeovers).[27] First Nations, Inuit, and Metis communities need to have to the right to reject major projects on their traditional lands.[28] In my experience, without Aboriginal consent, there is no project to be had.

---

25 Chinta Puxley, "Indians Get Ipperwash Park," *Toronto Star* (20 December 2007), online: <www.thestar.com/news/ontario/2007/12/20/indians_get_ipperwash_park.html>.

26 See, e.g., Model Bus Corp Act Ann s 11.04(b) (1999).

27 See George Bittlingmayer, "The Market for Corporate Control (Including Takeovers)" (2000) III Encyclopedia of Law & Econ 725; Julian Velasco, "Taking Shareholder Rights Seriously" (2007) 606 UC Davis L Rev 605.

28 But note that chief and council for First Nations may have the democratic equivalent of director primary in corporate law, albeit my experience is the chief and council seek ratification votes, regardless.

As such, the incentive matches the goal for all concerned. Just do a deal. The Supreme Court of Canada tiptoed back from that pronouncement, in fashioning the terms of our elusive Crown-Aboriginal fiduciary requirements. No doubt they were wary of the implications of an Aboriginal veto, fearing its potential impact upon the economy, particularly in remote regions of Canada. As it turns out, Aboriginal communities are more innovative and entrepreneurial than the Court gave them credit for, even if a few communities needed the confidence that comes with a veto power. As it turns out, the duty to consult created heaps of process, delays, and uncertainty; it has done more harm than good. As it turns out, the only project worth doing is done with Aboriginal consent.

10 Administering Consultation at the National Energy Board: Evaluating Tribunal Authority

SARI GRABEN AND ABBEY SINCLAIR*

I. Introduction

Over the course of the last thirty years, section 35(1) of the *Constitu-tion Act, 1982* has shifted governmental engagement with Aboriginal peoples from a matter of executive discretion to a matter of legal right.[1] While there are differences over the scope, content, and protections of those rights, the jurisprudence has first and foremost clarified that dis-putes over competing uses can be settled in law. Nevertheless, if past jurisprudence has focused on the duty of the executive, the authors argue here that there has been little clarity surrounding the duty of administrative tribunals to adhere to the legal requirements of sec-tion 35(1) in regulating resource use.[2] The Supreme Court of Canada has affirmed the authority of tribunals to administer Aboriginal rights

* Thank you to the Social Sciences and Humanities Research Council and Fulbright Canada for the funding that supported this project. The views expressed in this chap-ter are exclusively the views of the authors.
1 *Constitution Act, 1982*, being Schedule B to the *Canada Act 1982* (UK), c 11 [*Constitution Act, 1982*].
2 For discussion, see Janna Promislow, "Irreconcilable? The Duty to Consult and Administrative Decision Makers" (2013) 22:1 Constitutional Forum 63–79; Nigel Banks, "Who Decides if the Crown Has Met Its Duty to Consult" ABlawg.ca (6 December 2012), online: <ablawg.ca/2013/10/24/constitutional-questions-and-the-alberta-energy-regulator/> [Banks]; Kirk N Lambrecht, *Aboriginal Consultation, Environmental Assessment and Regulatory Review* (Regina: University of Regina Press, 2013); Zena Charowsky, "The Aboriginal Law Duty to Consult: An Introduction for Administrative Tribunals" (2011) 74 Sask L Rev 213–230 [Charowsky]; Keith B Bergner, "The Crown's Duty to Consult and the Role of the Energy Regulator" Energy

and to evaluate the Crown's duty to consult.[3] Moreover, the courts are willing to treat tribunal proceedings as part of a larger framework for achieving consultation.[4] Yet, even though courts have implicated tribunals in the task of ensuring that rights are respected, key decisions have seemingly released tribunals from the legal strictures of the jurisprudence on section 35(1). As a consequence, it is unclear whether tribunals can use their own methods of evaluation or whether they are required to assess consultation in accordance with the legal criteria established by the Supreme Court.[5]

Drawing on the treatment of Aboriginal consultation by the National Energy Board (NEB), the authors argue that its approach to evaluating proponent engagement has led to an untenable situation – a situation where the Crown is permitted to rely on panel findings made in the absence of legal criteria for the purposes of fulfilling its own legal duties. The NEB decisions reviewed in a study by the authors show that NEB panels draw conclusions about the Aboriginal engagement activities of applicant proponents but that the NEB does not evaluate the adequacy of Crown or proponent consultation on the basis of any established legal criteria. Analysis of NEB decisions since 2000 reveals that of the forty-two applications where the adequacy of consultation was considered, forty-one applications were approved.[6] Despite legal authority to approve projects where consultation remains outstanding, the authors argue that an approval rate of almost 100 per cent provides some indication that the duty to consult, whether carried out by the Crown or delegated to the proponent, is not a determinative factor in the NEB's regulatory approval process. This quantitative indicator is substantiated by a qualitative analysis of the reasons provided by the NEB in avoiding a legal evaluation of consultation in these forty-one applications. The authors found that the NEB overwhelming relied on three justifications for approving or recommending the approval of an application where

Regulation Quarterly (2014), online: <www.energyregulationquarterly.ca/articles/the-crowns-duty-to-consult-and-the-role-of-the-energy-regulator>.

3 R v Paul 2003 SCC 55, [2003] 2 SCR 585 [Paul]: Haida Nation v British Columbia (Minister of Forests) 2004 SCC 73, [2004] 3 SCR 511 [Haida].

4 Brokenhead Ojibway Nation v Canada (AG) 2009 FC 484, [2009] FCJ No 608 [Brokenhead Ojibway].

5 2004 SCC 74, [2004] SCJ No 69 [Taku]; Haida, supra note 3.

6 These statistics are based on an analysis of the approximately 100 applications heard by the NEB, either individually or as part of a joint review panel between 2000 and June 2014, for which it had issued written "Reasons for Decisions."

the issue of consultation remained outstanding or unresolved: (1) that it lacks the jurisdiction to consider the consultation at issue, (2) that it believes outstanding consultation can be addressed through ongoing consultation, and/or (3) that the absence or mitigation of impact(s) on Aboriginal rights equated to an absence of "adverse effects" on rights. This chapter proceeds in three parts. Part II provides background on the development of the Supreme Court jurisprudence on administrative authority to consider constitutional questions such as duty to consult, over the last thirty years. Part III explains the empirical study of the NEB decisions and explores how the tribunal has addressed consultation by discussing the three main reasons the NEB has used to justify the approval or recommended approval of applications where Crown consultation is insufficient or incomplete. Part IV concludes the chapter by summarizing the central issues raised by the research findings.

II. The Background on Thirty Years of Administrative Jurisdiction

The duty to consult and accommodate Aboriginal peoples is a legal duty that rests with the federal and/or provincial governments where a right will be infringed as a result of Crown action.[7] Arising from the protection of Aboriginal and treaty rights recognized in section 35(1) of the *Constitution Act, 1982* and grounded in the honour of the Crown, the purpose of the duty as articulated by the Supreme Court is the reconciliation of the pre-existence of Aboriginal societies with the sovereignty of the Crown.[8] The authority and responsibilities of tribunals for consultation was raised in the landmark consultation cases of *Haida* and *Taku*.[9] In *Haida*, the Supreme Court recognized the power of the Crown to delegate the processes of consultation and clarified that it is "open to governments to set up regulatory schemes to address the procedural requirements appropriate to different problems at different stages."[10] However, the Supreme Court confirmed that the Crown was not required to establish a separate consultation process to address Aboriginal concerns, instead leaving it to the government to decide whether to create or expand

---

7   The Crown has a duty to consult with Aboriginal groups when it has knowledge of a potential or existing Aboriginal right or title, and contemplates conduct that might adversely affect it. *Haida, supra* note 3 at para 35; and *Taku, supra* note 5 at para 25.

8   *Haida, supra* note 3 at para 38.

9   *Ibid; Taku, supra* note 5.

10 *Haida, supra* note 3 at para 51.

existing regulatory regimes.[11] The Supreme Court subsequently clarified that, where appropriate, the Crown could rely on these regulatory proceedings to fulfil all or part of the duty to consult.[12]

Based on this jurisprudence, the role of tribunals in addressing Aboriginal rights is most often sourced to the court's reasoning in *Haida*. However, it is useful to recognize that the delineation and rationalization of tribunal authority originated in the companion cases of *Paul v British Columbia (Forest Appeals Commission)*[13] and *Nova Scotia (Workers' Compensation Board) v Martin*.[14] In these two cases the Supreme Court explained the authorization of tribunal authority to consider constitutional questions. The Supreme Court held that administrative tribunals with the authority to consider questions of law are generally presumed to possess the authority to consider constitutional issues. Most importantly, it clarified that the authority to consider questions of law includes the authority to decide questions concerning the Crown's duty to consult with Aboriginal peoples.[15]

The Supreme Court further refined the test for administrative authority in *Rio Tinto Alcan Inc. v Carrier Sekani Tribal Council*.[16] Although it ultimately reaffirmed the test set out in *Paul* and *Martin*, it rejected the notion that every tribunal with jurisdiction to consider a question of law has a constitutional duty to consider whether adequate consultation has taken place, and if not, to fulfil that duty itself.[17] Writing for the majority, Chief Justice McLachlin distinguished between the authority to determine whether consultation is adequate and the authority to engage in consultation itself. She stressed the importance of a tribunal's statutory mandate and remedial powers in determining its authority to consider consultation.[18] A tribunal must have the statutory authority to grant the *particular* remedy sought.[19] In the Aboriginal context, this

---

11 *Taku, supra* note 5 at para 40.
12 *Brokenhead Ojibway, supra* note 4.
13 *Paul, supra* note 3.
14 2003 SCC 54, [2003] 2 SCR 504 [*Martin*].
15 *Ibid.*
16 2010 SCC 43 [*Rio Tinto*].
17 *Ibid.*
18 *Ibid* at para 58.
19 *R v Conway*, 2010 SCC 22, [2004] 3 SCR 511 [*Conway*]. In considering whether the Ontario Review Board was capable of granting remedies under section 24(1) of the *Charter*, the Supreme Court stated that a tribunal's jurisdiction to grant a particular remedy depends on its mandate, structure, and function.

means that in addition to whether it possesses the power to consider questions of law, a tribunal must be able to meaningfully address the specific concerns raised.[20]

A decade after the Supreme Court first set out this role for administrative tribunals, federal and provincial tribunals continue to wrestle with their obligations with respect to section 35(1). The confusion stems in part from the lack of specific jurisprudential guidance on how tribunals are to interpret their statutory and remedial powers with respect to section 35 rights, and in part from the Federal Court of Appeal's reasoning in *Standing Buffalo Dakota First Nation v Enbridge Pipelines Inc*.[21] As one of the first courts to apply the Supreme Court's jurisprudence on the administrative authority to consider the duty to consult, the Federal Court of Appeal set a precedent by adopting a strict interpretation of the role of the NEB in assessing the adequacy of Crown consultation. The Federal Court of Appeal held that the NEB's enabling statute does not prevent it from recommending the approval of a pipeline without first undertaking a *Haida* analysis, nor did it explicitly empower the NEB to order the Crown to undertake consultations. Conflating the notion of assessing and conducting consultation, it also determined that as a result of the NEB's independent and quasi-judicial nature it was incapable of acting as a Crown agent and therefore could not be expected to undertake a *Haida*-style analysis. Most significantly, the three-judge panel noted that the application for a Certificate for Public Convenience and Necessity to construct a pipeline is focused on the applicant, in this case a private proponent, suggesting that any of the tribunal's constitutional duties related to section 35(1) could be satisfied by a proponent's Aboriginal engagement activities.[22] Therefore it determined that the NEB's process was consistent with its obligations under section 35(1) and that it provided a "practical and efficient framework within which the Aboriginal group can request assurances."[23]

The reasoning in *Standing Buffalo* has gained some currency with courts and tribunals, particularly where the enabling statute of the

---

20 The presumption of administrative authority is not easily overcome and the Crown's intention to exclude the authority to consider constitutional questions – such as the duty to consult – must be clear.

21 *Standing Buffalo Dakota First Nation v Enbridge Pipelines Inc*, 2009 FCA 308, [2009] FCJ No 1434 [*Standing Buffalo*].

22 *Ibid* at para 40.

23 *Ibid* at para 44.

administrative body at issue does not explicitly require it to engage in consultation,[24] or where tribunals have drawn a formal distinction between the Crown's public duty to consult and the proponent's private consultation activities.[25] Regarding the former circumstance, Zena Charowsky notes that the Federal Court of Appeal's reasoning is difficult to reconcile with the Supreme Court jurisprudence on tribunal authority.[26] The notion that a tribunal, with authority to consider constitutional questions, is not obligated to consider consultation because the legislation does not explicitly require it, conflicts with the Supreme Court's clear reasoning on the administrative authority to consider constitutional questions.[27] Similarly, distinguishing tribunal duties based on whether the proponent or the Crown brings an application raises serious questions about whether tribunals can limit their obligations to undertake a full *Haida* analysis because the Crown has assigned the tasks of consultation. As Nigel Banks has noted, this interpretation effectively exempts the duty to consult from a tribunal's purview, because only very rarely is the Crown a project applicant. Moreover, irrespective of whether those tasks have been formally delegated to the proponent or undertaken as a condition of permitting, it is the Crown's decisions and or actions permitting the given activity that trigger the duty. The Crown relies on proponent engagement to fulfil its legal duties to Aboriginal peoples, which helps to explain the increasingly comprehensive consultation requirements placed on proponents. If tribunals are not using the test set out in *Haida* to determine whether the Crown's duty has been triggered and fulfilled by the proponent, it is unclear against what standards that affect Aboriginal and Treaty rights are being assessed in the regulatory process.

---

24 See, e.g., *Fond du Lac Denesuline First Nation v Canada (AG)*, 2010 FC 948, [2010] FCJ No 1182; *Yellowknives Dene First Nation v Canada (AG)*, 2010 FC 1139, [2010] FCJ No 1412; and *Union Gas Ltd (Re)*, Decision with Respect to Preliminary Questions and Final Decision and Orders (25 July 2011) 2011 LNONOEB 201 (EB-2011-0040, EB-2011-0041, EB-2011-0042).

25 For discussion of this approach by the Energy Resources Conservation Board, see Banks, *supra* note 2.

26 Charowsky, *supra* note 2.

27 *Ibid.*

III. An Empirical Study of the National Energy Board

A. The NEB as a Case Study

The NEB provides an apt illustration of an administrative body with the authority to consider questions of law that also has significant remedial powers and regularly faces issues of Aboriginal rights in its day-to-day decisions. Established by Parliament in 1959, the NEB is the independent federal agency responsible for regulating the international and interprovincial aspects of pipelines and transmission lines, energy development, and trade in the Canadian public interest.[28] It also hears applications for offshore oil and gas exploration as well as drilling and exploration activity north of 60° (in the Northwest Territories, Nunavut, and Hudson Bay).[29] As a federal tribunal with the authority to approve large projects of national importance, it regularly reviews applications for large infrastructure, transmission, and pipeline projects that span traditional and disputed treaty lands and that have the potential to affect wildlife habitats and natural resources important to Aboriginal peoples.

The *National Energy Board Act*[30] is silent with respect to the duty to consult. However, the Act expressly allows the NEB to consider questions of law. Section 12(2) of the Act gives the Board "full jurisdiction to hear and determine all matters, whether of law or of fact."[31] While the NEB lacks the broad remedial powers of a court, it does possess significant powers allowing it to attach conditions to its recommendations and approvals. In reviewing applications the NEB acts in a quasi-judicial capacity. It is a court of record, with the powers, rights, and privileges of a superior court and has broad authority to compel and consider a wide range of evidence, including impacts on Aboriginal

---

28 National Energy Board, "Who We Are," online: NEB <www.neb-one.gc.ca/clf-nsi/rthnb/whwrndrgvrnnc/whwrndrgvrnnc-eng.html>.

29 For more information, see *ibid.*

30 RS, c n-6, s 1 at ss 11, 12 [Act]. Note that the legislative scheme in force during the period in which the majority of these decisions were issued has been altered by recent amendments to the Act created by the *Jobs, Growth and Long-term Prosperity Act*, SC 2012, c 19. The NEB's role in the regulatory review for large projects has shifted from a decision-making role to an advisory role; and the Governor-in-Council now has the ultimate authority for approving or denying a project.

31 *Ibid.*

peoples when making its decisions.[32] It can also delay and/or refuse to approve a given project until outstanding legal requirements have been satisfied. Most importantly, its orders and decisions are enforceable.[33] The NEB maintains that it cannot engage directly in one-on-one consultation on behalf of the Crown, but it does hear and consider Aboriginal issues in its hearing process.[34] This information forms the basis of the NEB's evaluation of the applicant's Aboriginal engagement activities.[35]

B. Quantitative Findings

In order to evaluate what impact consultation has on the NEB's decisions, the authors analysed written decisions issued by the NEB between January 2000 and June 2014.[36] The authors identified that out of the approximately one hundred application decisions released by the NEB during this period, the adequacy of Aboriginal consultation was considered in forty-two applications.[37] The NEB issued approvals in forty-one of the forty-two decisions (albeit most with conditions), giving it an almost 100 per cent approval rate.[38] However, the authors found that in

---

32 *Act, supra* note 30, s 11.

33 *Ibid* s 17.

34 See, e.g., *Re Suma Energy 2 Inc*, Reasons for Decision (March 2004), LNCNEB 1 at 344 (EH-1-2000) [*Sumas Energy 2 Inc*]. The basis for the NEB's position is based on the Supreme Court's statements that direct engagement in consultation would be contrary to the independent nature of quasi-judicial bodies in *Quebec (AG) v Canada (NEB)*, [1994] 1 SCR 159 [*Quebec*].

35 See National Energy Board, "Filing Manual: Chapter 3 Common Information Requirements" Subsection 3.4 (30 December 2014), online: NEB <www.neb-one.gc.ca/bts/ctrg/gnnb/flngmnl/fmch3-eng.html#s3_4> – which describes the detailed information that applicants are required to submit on their Aboriginal engagement activities. Note: the referenced Filing Manual is being updated to comply with the changes to the Act created by the recent *Jobs, Growth and Long-term Prosperity Act*, SC 2012, c 19.

36 The cut-off year for inclusion was set at 2000 in order to capture and differentiate trends in decision-making both before and after the Supreme Court issued its foundational decisions on consultation in *Haida* and *Taku*. The resulting analysis indicated that these decisions had relatively little impact on how the NEB addressed consultation issues in its decision-making process.

37 These statistics are based on written decisions released between January 2000 and June 2014.

38 In one application the NEB denied approval, *Sumas Energy 2 Inc, supra* note 34, on the basis of general concerns that the project was not in the public interest and not due to consultation concerns raised by the affected First Nations.

thirty out of the forty-two cases in which the issue of Aboriginal consultation was raised, consultation issues remained outstanding.[39]

Although the NEB does not explicitly declare itself to be in the business of evaluating or assessing the adequacy of Crown consultation, the decisions indicate that it does draw conclusions about the sufficiency of consultation by applicants with Aboriginal peoples.[40] This is evidenced by the sections of its written reasons dedicated to the issue of Aboriginal consultation as well as statements explicitly stating that "engagement is sufficient" or that "sufficient opportunities for participation or the voicing of concerns have been provided."

The authorization in *Standing Buffalo* to approve projects prior to the fulfilment of Crown consultation might predict that consultation would not be settled in all applications. But if tribunals are vested with the authority to evaluate consultation as part of the regulatory process and purport, through written reasons that account for Aboriginal engagement, to have done this evaluation, one should be asking whether a near-perfect approval rate is an indicator that the NEB understands its duties regarding the consultation as perfunctory or secondary to regulatory approval.

On the basis of these questions, the authors undertook a qualitative analysis of the thirty cases where consultation was raised as an issue and remained outstanding. The authors set out to identify the reasons provided by the NEB as to why consultation did not appear to significantly affect its decisions to approve and/or recommend the approval of the applications in question. Each decision was parsed for one or

---

39 On the basis of the NEB's comments, the authors identified that consultation was considered and deemed satisfied by the Aboriginal group(s) in only twelve out of forty-two cases. Of the twelve cases where consultation was deemed sufficient or settled, the Aboriginal group had either withdrawn as an intervener, submitted a letter of support, failed to raise any concerns, or was noted by the NEB to support the project. The authors determined that consultation was outstanding, on the basis of the NEB's failure to address the specific concerns raised by the Aboriginal group; express comments by the panel that it believed consultation was incomplete or ongoing; and/or comments that it understood Aboriginal interveners to believe that consultation was insufficient. Because the NEB did not apply any known legal test to determine the adequacy of consultation, the authors' characterization of "outstanding" consultation is based solely on the written reasons provided by the tribunal and is not suggestive of conclusions based on a judicial standard.

40 For the purposes of inclusion, Aboriginal groups included First Nations, Métis, and Inuit as well as other interest groups and associations.

more rationales provided in support of the NEB's treatment of consultation. Each rationale was charted in order to determine which rationales the NEB most commonly relied upon to justify approval. In many cases, the authors noted that multiple rationales were used, and charted each rationale separately.[41] Through this exercise the authors expected to obtain a quantitative understanding of which rationales have had the strongest persuasive value for the NEB. By linking the frequency of reliance on these rationales to the outcome of the decisions, the authors expected to identify how these rationales pertain to the NEB's responsibilities to evaluate consultation.

C. Qualitative Findings

In the thirty cases where the adequacy of consultation was considered, the NEB generally provided one of three justifications for its decision to approve or recommend the approval of projects where consultation was outstanding or unsettled, namely that (1) it lacked jurisdiction to consider the consultation matter at issue, (2) outstanding consultation could be addressed through ongoing consultation, and/or (3) that the absence or mitigation of impact(s) on Aboriginal rights equated to an absence of "adverse effects" on Aboriginal rights.

I. LACK OF JURISDICTION

In ten out of thirty cases, the NEB cited lack of jurisdiction as a justification for approving projects with outstanding consultation. As a creature of statute the NEB is confined to the matter before it and the powers expressly or implicitly conferred by its enabling legislation. As may be expected, the NEB interprets the scope of the application and its implied jurisdiction to consider consultation narrowly where (1) the NEB shared approval authority with other regulatory bodies over large infrastructure projects, (2) the consultation involved larger overarching rights issues, such as land and treaty claims, and/or (3) where the issues raised pertained to the relationship of the parties and not the application. In each case the NEB found the consultation questions to be outside its jurisdiction and concluded that it could not consider the issues as part of its decision-making process. However, concerns about

---

41 This results in some overlap, as some decisions are counted in more than one of the three justification categories.

the NEB's authority to rule on consultation in these circumstances were intimately tied to the tribunal's limited remedial powers. The NEB lacked the authority to grant the particular remedy sought and meaningfully address the specific Aboriginal concerns and therefore failed to exercise its powers to address deficiencies in consultation.[42]

For example, in *Sumas Energy 2, Inc*[43] the NEB relied on shared approval authority to find a lack of jurisdiction. In this case, Sumas made an application for leave to construct and operate the Canadian portion of an international power line. The Stó:lō Nation argued that the environmental impacts of the project on their Aboriginal rights and title had not been adequately or meaningfully addressed.[44] Concerns regarding the environmental impacts of the project included impacts on air quality, waterways, wetlands and fish habitat, resource access, and water usage and effluent discharge from the proposed power plant.[45] The NEB ultimately denied the application. However, insofar as there were consultation concerns arising from the construction and operation of the power plant, the NEB drew a jurisdictional line separating the potential impacts on rights arising from the international power line and those of the US power plant, which had already received US approval.

Concerns about the NEB's authority to rule on land claim and treaty related consultation matters are illustrated by the NEB's reasons in the related pipeline cases of *TransCanada Keystone Pipeline GP Ltd*,[46] *Enbridge Southern Lights LP*,[47] and *Enbridge Alberta Clipper Expansion*,[48] which were appealed to and upheld by the Federal Court in *Brokenhead Ojibway*.[49] These cases involved seven First Nations who claimed that the Crown had failed to fulfil its duty to consult and that the proposed

42 *Conway, supra* note 19.
43 *Sumas Energy 2, Inc, supra* note 34.
44 *Ibid* at para 7.2.4.
45 *Ibid* at para 7.2.
46 Reasons for Decision (September 2007), OH-1-2007, NEB, online: <https://docs. neb-one.gc.ca/ll-eng/llisapi.dll/fetch/2000/90464/90552/418396/446070/478070/ 477791/A1A4H2_%2D_Reasons_for_Decision_OH%2D1%2D2007.pdf?nodeid=477856 &vernum=-2> [*TransCanada Keystone*].
47 Reasons for Decision (February 2008), OH-3-2007, NEB, online: <publications.gc.ca/ collections/collection_2008/neb-one/NE22-1-2008-1E.pdf> [*Southern Lights*].
48 Reasons for Decision (February 2008), OH-4-2007, NEB, online: <publications.gc.ca/ collections/collection_2008/neb-one/NE22-1-2008-2E.pdf> [*Enbridge Alberta Clipper Expansion*].
49 *Brokenhead Ojibway, supra* note 4.

pipeline projects would limit the Crown lands available to meet the terms of its flood compensation and any treaty claim. The NEB dismissed their arguments, finding that the root of consultation related to the Treaty One First Nations' outstanding land claims and were outside the scope of the applications being considered.[50]

Lastly, the decisions reveal a tendency on the part of the NEB to find a lack of jurisdiction where the consultation pertained to the relationship of the parties rather than the project application. In *Maritimes and Northeast Pipeline Management Ltd (Re)*,[51] the Union of New Brunswick Indians (UNBI) argued that the applicant had failed to conduct good faith consultations with its people and that it had misrepresented its consultation process and long-term agreement with the UNBI.[52] Rejecting the UNBI's requests for conditional approval, the NEB found that consultation related to the implementation of an impact benefit agreement between the applicant and an affected First Nations group were outside the scope of the application, despite the fact that it was related to the proposed project.[53] Instead it suggested that the parties seek a more appropriate forum or court.[54] This type of reasoning indicates that the NEB will consider the existence of an impact benefit agreement as evidence of consultation, but that disputes as to the content or application of the agreement are generally considered beyond the NEB's jurisdiction, as the NEB lacks the authority to provide parties with any of the remedies typically requested in contractual disputes.[55]

Taken together, these varied decisions indicate the NEB's discomfort with the scope of panel review relative to its jurisdiction.[56] Rights claims

---

50 *TransCanada Keystone, supra* note 46. The Federal Court affirmed the NEB's decision in *Brokenhead Ojibway* and noted that although the NEB process could be used to fulfil the Crown's duty to consult, it did not appear to be designed to address unresolved land claims.

51 Reasons for Decision (November 2002), GH-3-2002, NEB, online: <https://docs.neb-one.gc.ca/ll-eng/llisapi.dll/fetch/2000/90464/90550/90705/156802/252834/252947/A0G4U1_-_Reasons_For_Decision.pdf?_gc_lang=en&nodeid=252948&vern um=0> [*Maritimes and Northeastern*].

52 *Ibid* at para 111.

53 *Ibid* at 42.

54 *Ibid*.

55 See, e.g., Kent Roach, "Aboriginal Peoples and the Law Remedies for Violations of Aboriginal Rights" (1992) 21 Man LJ 498–543 at para 2, discussing the panoply of possible remedies courts provide for Aboriginal litigants.

56 *Brokenhead Ojibway, supra* note 4 at para 27.

or claims regarding impacts on rights forwarded by Aboriginal groups required the NEB to identify adverse effects experienced as a result of the entirety of a project and to use its remedial powers to address the overall impacts on rights. Generally, when the NEB was faced with such claims, it declined to exercise its authority over the specifics of the application that was contributing to those impacts.

II. ONGOING CONSULTATION IS SUFFICIENT TO
CURE INADEQUACIES OF CROWN CONSULTATION

Even more than lack of jurisdiction, the NEB has relied on the justification that section 35 rights issues can be resolved through ongoing consultation. In twenty-one out of the thirty cases where consultation was raised as an issue, the NEB determined that ongoing consultations between the applicant and affected Aboriginal groups would address any outstanding consultation. The NEB has adopted the position that consultation need not be complete prior to approving or recommending the approval of a project. Thus, irrespective of whether consultation has addressed impacts, evidence of a commitment to ongoing consultation and/or applicant efforts to mitigate the project's impact on Aboriginal rights is usually deemed sufficient.[57]

The notion that approval may precede consultation is summed up in *Enbridge Southern Lights*, where the NEB explicitly rejected the argument that it must consider the strength of Aboriginal claims and assesses the adequacy of Crown consultation *before* assessing the substantive merits of an application.[58] The NEB explained that while it is the sole body with the ability to impose conditions on a Certificate of Public Convenience and Necessity, other government authorities may have their own regulatory responsibilities pertaining to specific aspects of a federal pipeline.[59] Given that the process for these approvals may be carried out parallel to, or independently of, the NEB process, it determined

---

57 See, e.g., *EnCana Corp (Re)*, Reasons for Decision (September 2007), 2007 LNCNEB 8 (GH-2-2006), where the NEB maintained that meaningful consultation need not take place before operations commence; *New Brunswick Power Corp. (Re)*, Reasons for Decision (May 2003), 2003 LNCNEB 8 (EH-2-2002); *EnCana Ekwan Pipeline Inc (Re)*, Reasons for Decision (September 2003), 2003 LNCNEB 7 (GH-1-2003); *SemCAMS Redwillow ULC (Re)*, Reasons for Decision (March 2009), 2009 LNCNEB 3 (GH-2-2008); and *Vantage Pipeline Canada ULC (Re)*, Reasons for Decision (January 2012), 2012 LNCNEB 1 (OH-3-2011).

58 *Southern Lights, supra* note 47.

59 *Ibid* at para 62.

that they are often irrelevant to the NEB's decision-making process.[60] Thus, the fact that consultation by these other government agencies or departments is incomplete should not prevent the NEB from moving ahead with its own approval processes.

Reliance on continuing consultation is also evident in the recent *Enbridge Northern Gateway Project* decision.[61] The joint review panel expressly noted that "in keeping with its mandate ... it has not made any determinations regarding Aboriginal rights, including Métis rights, treaty rights, or the strength of an Aboriginal group's claim respecting Aboriginal rights."[62] It went on to state that in order for the project to proceed, the company would be required to report on its ongoing consultation activities with Aboriginal groups, including consultations in developing a number of operational plans and employment related programs.[63] Overall the joint panel concluded that the "company could effectively continue to engage and learn from Aboriginal groups that choose to engage throughout the project's operational life."[64] Again, tribunal decision-makers appear confident that any outstanding adverse impact on traditional lands and uses can and will be addressed through continued involvement of affected Aboriginal groups in the construction and operation stages of the project.

The only exception to a trend towards recommending approval on the basis of ongoing consultation is the NEB's decision in *Georgia Strait Crossing Pipeline Limited* (on behalf of *GSX Canada Limited Partnership*).[65] It appears to be the only case in which the NEB refused to schedule an oral hearing until it was satisfied that adequate Crown consultation

---

60 *Southern Lights, supra* note 47.
61 Enbridge Northern Gateway Project Joint Review Panel, "Considerations: Report of the Joint Review Panel for the Enbridge Northern Gateway Project," vol 2, 4 Aboriginal Interests and Consultation with Aboriginal Groups, NEB, online: <gatewaypanel. review-examen.gc.ca/clf-nsi/dcmnt/rcmndtnsrprt/rcmndtnsrprt-eng.html>.
62 *Ibid* at s 4.7.
63 *Ibid*.
64 *Ibid*.
65 Reasons for Decision (November 2003), 2003 LNCNEB 13 (GH-4-2001) at 39–40 [*GSX Canada*]. In this case, the panel was "encouraged" by the fact that the applicant had reached an agreement with the Cowichan Tribes, Tseycum First Nation, and Sencot'en Alliance on the project. However, it admitted that it was unable to address the concerns of the Snuneymuxw First Nation as the result of specific concerns about the Vancouver Island Generation Project, which it did not have the ability to approve or regulate.

had taken place.[66] Over an eight-month period, the NEB engaged in a number of creative tactics to encourage the applicant and both levels of government to initiate and carry out proper consultative processes with affected First Nations groups.[67] It proceeded with approving the project only once some of the First Nations had expressed satisfaction with the project and/or the ongoing consultation activities.

Although the NEB's reliance on future consultations is consistent with the reasoning in *Standing Buffalo*, it raises concerns that Aboriginal concerns will not be accommodated once the planning and project design phases of the project have been completed. Absent any conditions imposed by the NEB, a proponent has no legal obligation or duty to maintain ongoing consultations with affected Aboriginal groups once a project and or application is approved. Only the Crown has a constitutional duty to consult and accommodate. The conditions imposed do not serve as a safeguard for ensuring the Crown's duty to consult is fulfilled. While the Crown may continue to have a duty for ongoing consultation following approval, it is not clear what would trigger that duty in law if the Crown relies on the regulatory process to fulfil its consultation obligations.

III. AN ABSENCE OF "IMPACT" EQUATES TO AN ABSENCE OF "ADVERSE EFFECTS"

Finally, in twenty of the thirty cases where adequacy of consultation was raised as an issue, the NEB reasoned that if there is no impact on Aboriginal rights or the impact can be mitigated, then consultative processes are either unnecessary or satisfied. Like many tribunals, the NEB is directed by its enabling statute, guidelines, and policies to consider the "harm" or

---

66 *Ibid* at para 127. In March 2002 the panel issued a letter to the applicant stating that in accordance with its *Memorandum of Guidance regarding Consultation with Aboriginal Peoples*, it expected that prior to the commencement of the oral hearing it would provide evidence that consultations had been carried out. Then in May 2002, after considering a round of comments on consultation, the panel issued another decision, which revised the schedule for the proceeding and did not set a date for the oral hearing until after a further round of comments on consultations.

67 For example, the NEB issued multiple information requests to the federal and provincial Crown intervenors and the applicant inquiring about the activities undertaken to meet any duty the Crown may have to consult. The panel also attended two sessions to hear presentations regarding First Nations issues as part of its consultation with the public on the information required and the issues that should be considered during the hearing.

"impact" of a proposed project. The Act allows it to consider "any public interest that may be affected" when deciding whether to grant or refuse permission for a project in the form of a Certificate of Public Convenience and Necessity.[68] Furthermore, in exercising its powers to evaluate environmental impacts, the NEB must now also determine whether there are biophysical impacts that effect Aboriginal peoples, as defined in the *Canadian Environmental Assessment Act*.[69] The NEB determines whether a project is in the "public interest" by balancing the economic, environmental, and social interests and then weighing the positive and negative impacts of a project. This includes Aboriginal interests.[70]

Generally, the NEB has found that there can be an "impact" on historical, archaeological, and sacred sites, as well as on traditional land use triggering a need for consultation. However, it tends to find little or no "impact" on land where it has been previously disturbed in some way, suggesting that the duty to consult is not triggered in these circumstances. In *Enbridge Pipelines (Westspur) Inc*,[71] the NEB found that the project would have little to no impact, given that it was located on an existing right of way and the fact that no claims had been raised during the fifty years of operation of the pipeline over the existing right of way. In the *Enbridge Bakken Pipeline Co.*[72] application, the NEB focused on the fact that the right of way for the Bakken Pipeline would be occupied Crown lands and privately held lands used for agriculture and ranching.[73] On this basis, the NEB found no impacts on rights and declined the requests of the Treaty Four Council of Chiefs, White Bear First Nation, Carry the Kettle First Nation, and Federation of Saskatchewan Indian Nations, to require Enbridge Bakken to fund a traditional land use study and an impact benefit agreement.[74]

---

68 Act, *supra* note 30, s 51.
69 SC 2012, c 19, s 52 [CEAA]. Recent amendments to the CEAA as a result of the *Jobs, Growth and Long-Term Prosperity Act*, SC 2012, c 19, collapsed the review process from a two-stage review into a single review, giving the NEB authority for reviewing both the regulatory merit and environmental impacts of a project.
70 See also National Energy Board, "Safety & Environment" (26 September 2014), online: NEB <https://www.neb-one.gc.ca/sftnvrnmnt/nvrnmnt/index-eng.html>.
71 Reasons for Decision (June 2007), 2007 LNCNEB 4 (OH-2-2007).
72 Reasons for Decision (December 2011), 2011 LNCNEB 6 (OH-1-2011).
73 *Ibid.*
74 *Ibid* at 50.

Likewise, where there are environmental impacts but they can or will be mitigated, the NEB tends to find that there are no adverse effects. This is illustrated in the *NOVA Gas Transmission Ltd*[75] decision where the NEB determined that, on the basis of the site-specific mitigation strategies and procedures proposed by the applicant, the project's impacts on lands and resources used for traditional purposes would be effectively mitigated.[76] The NEB specifically relied upon the applicant's commitment to consult with trappers regarding the construction schedule, willingness to consult with Aboriginal groups regarding monitoring, and involvement of Aboriginal businesses in clearing and construction activities for the project. [77]

Given these factors, the NEB reasoned that there would not be any negative impacts on the traditional use of lands and resources. Nevertheless, while a biophysical approach can identify physical impacts to the resources and lands in which rights are exercised and determine the need for mitigation, it would be erroneous to wholly equate this process with consulting on rights. The fallacy of using a biophysical approach to evaluate rights is that it may not reflect the extent of damage experienced by Aboriginal peoples. As author Zena Charowsky explains, the meaning of "adverse effect" in *Haida* and the meaning of "harm" or "impact" used by the NEB represent different standards[78] when considering whether the duty has been triggered. The meaning of "adverse effect" as articulated in *Haida* is a much broader test than that of "impact" and "harm" used by the NEB. Unlike the "impact" or "harm" tests, the "adverse effects" test does not need to have an immediate or tangible impact on lands and resources.[79] It can flow from abstract Crown conduct such as high-level managerial, organizational, or policy changes that have the potential to limit the Crown's power to ensure that development takes place in a way that respects Aboriginal rights.[80] The substitution of "impact" for "adverse effect" can result in the oversight of Crown or delegated conduct that triggers the duty to consult, thereby failing to address or accommodate early in the process. For example,

---

75 Reasons for Decision (March 2010), 2010 LNCONE 1 (GH-2-2010).
76 *Ibid* at 45.
77 *Ibid* at 46.
78 Charowsky, *supra* note 2.
79 *Rio Tinto*, supra note 16 at para 44.
80 *Ibid* at para 87.

contrary to the approach employed by NEB, the Supreme Court in *Haida* noted that a "previous disturbance" is not determinative.[81] In that case, a duty to consult was found to exist, despite the fact that the Crown was renewing or transferring an existing tree farm licence, illustrating that the application of a narrow "impact" test can lead to different outcomes for Aboriginal peoples.

IV. Conclusions

The reasons given for approval by the NEB in the forty-two decisions analysed by the authors indicate that while the NEB considers the Aboriginal engagement activities of applicant companies or proponents, it typically does not evaluate the adequacy of Crown consultation against any legal criteria related to rights. With the exception of the *GSX Canada* case, the NEB has not concerned itself with applying a legal analysis to determine whether a duty to consult was triggered, the scope of the duty, and/or whether it had been fulfilled in any of the cases studied. More tellingly, the three rationales for avoiding evaluation indicate that the NEB does not assume meaningful authority for assessing Crown or proponent consultation.

Although the NEB's approach to addressing consultation is consistent with the Federal Court of Appeal's reasoning in *Standing Buffalo*, the findings presented here raise questions as to whether it is possible to reconcile the concerns about tribunal capacity raised by the court, with the call for tribunal authority as expressed by the Supreme Court. The development of the test in *Haida* was initially developed to address the fact that the Crown was undertaking public decision-making without regard to the impacts on Aboriginal peoples' rights. Consultation was expected to identify impacts to rights in cooperation with Aboriginal governments and to generate accommodations to address them. If the NEB merely documents proponent efforts to engage with communities but does not evaluate the effect of consultation on rights, then it effectively does what the Crown may not: play a role in authorizing conduct that infringes rights. It is possible that some administrative tribunals are ill-suited to the job of evaluating the requirements of consultation and should not be authorized to undertake such a task. However, until such time that project proponents,

---

81 *Haida, supra* note 3.

the Crown, and the courts begin to distinguish between tribunal practice and the duty to consult, greater attention must be paid to its processes. Ultimately, this means that if the last thirty years have been focused on bringing section 35(1) to bear on executive decision-making, the next thirty years should be focused on the more difficult task: bringing it to bear on its administration.

PART FOUR

Recognition and Reconciliation in Action

11 Non-Status Indigenous Groups in Canadian Courts: Practical and Legal Difficulties in Seeking Recognition*

SÉBASTIEN GRAMMOND, ISABELLE LANTAGNE,
AND NATACHA GAGNÉ

One major aspect of the recognition of Indigenous claims brought about by section 35 of the *Constitution Act, 1982* is the declaration, in paragraph 2 of that constitutional provision, that "'aboriginal peoples of Canada' includes the Indian, Inuit and Métis peoples of Canada." The Constitution thus recognizes the wrongfulness of past policies whereby certain Indigenous groups were excluded from the purview of colonial laws regulating the lives of the Indigenous peoples, such as the *Indian Act*.[1] It also mandates a process of reconciliation whereby Indigenous groups that currently lack official recognition are identified and granted rights similar to those of other groups whose Indigenous identity has never been challenged.[2] In this connection, the Royal Commission on Aboriginal Peoples suggested, in its 1996 final report, the creation of a body that would study such claims for recognition against the backdrop of predefined criteria and make recommendations to the federal government.[3] However, such a process never materialized. As

---

* This chapter is a translated and revised version of Sébastien Grammond, Isabelle Lantagne, and Natacha Gagné, "Aux marges de la classification officielle: les groupes autochtones sans statut devant les tribunaux canadiens" (2012) 81 *Droit et société* (France) 321–42; reproduced with permission.
1 See, among others, Sébastien Grammond, *Identity Captured by Law: Membership in Canada's Indigenous Peoples and Linguistic Minorities* (Montreal & Kingston: McGill-Queen's University Press, 2009).
2 See, e.g., Robert K Groves, "The Curious Instance of the Irregular Band: A Case Study of Canada's Missing Recognition Policy" (2007) 70 Sask L Rev 153; Paul LAH Chartrand, "The 'Race' for Recognition: Toward a Policy of Recognition of Aboriginal Peoples in Canada" in Louis A Knafla and Haijo Westra, eds, *Aboriginal Title and Indigenous Peoples: Canada, Australia, and New Zealand* (Vancouver: UBC Press, 2010) 125.

a result, the only option that remained open to non-status groups was to bring their claims to the courts and to ask judges to recognize that they were "Aboriginal peoples" within the meaning of section 35, even though the governments refused to admit it.

We have undertaken the study of the trial transcripts of cases in which non-status individuals are charged with regulatory offences against wildlife conservation laws and assert, in defence, that they were exercising Aboriginal rights protected by section 35. We examine the conceptions of Indigenous identity conveyed by different participants in the process (the accused and the defence witnesses, the prosecution witnesses, and the judge). Using this analysis as a basis, this chapter seeks to identify the obstacles faced by the accused in these cases. Obstacles stem from the structure of the judicial process, the resources available to the participants in this process, the intellectual environment of these claims, and the legal tests adopted by the courts. As we pinpoint some of these obstacles, it becomes clear that the law and the courts have difficulty understanding the social reality of marginalized groups who do not correspond to the popular image of these groups – who are, in other words, socially invisible.[4] This chapter reviews the preliminary results of our research project.

One original feature of our project is that we focus on trial decisions, whereas the attention of researchers is more often directed at appellate or Supreme Court decisions, which establish legal principles that will be applicable in other cases. However, in the Canadian judicial system, witnesses are heard by the trial courts, who analyse the evidence and give a ruling based on the facts. When trial judgments are appealed, appellate judges are generally interested in questions of law and not questions of fact. The findings of fact of the trial judges are almost definitive, unless it can be shown that they are tainted by a "palpable and overriding error."[5] This is particularly important in Indigenous rights cases, since crucial questions such as the existence of an Indigenous community or an Aboriginal right are considered to be questions of fact. Thus, it is

3 Royal Commission on Aboriginal Peoples, *Report, vol. 2, Restructuring the Relationship* (Ottawa: Canada Communications Group, 1996), recommendation 2.3.27.
4 Marie-Ève Sylvestre, Céline Bellot, Philippe Antoine Couture Ménard, & Alexandra Tremblay, "Le droit est aussi une question de visibilité: l'occupation des espaces publics et les parcours judiciaires des personnes itinérantes à Montréal et à Ottawa" (2011) 26 CJLawS 531.
5 See, e.g., *R v Van der Peet*, [1996] 2 SCR 507 [*Van der Peet*] at 564–66, paras 80–82.

especially important to analyse the work of the trial judges in order to understand the concrete application of principles of Indigenous rights, and how they contribute to the process of reconciliation between unrecognized or non-status groups and the Canadian state.

Since the early 2000s, nearly thirty judgments have been rendered across Canada in cases where non-status Indigenous groups invoked their Aboriginal rights as a defence to prosecutions based on hunting, fishing, or forestry legislation. We have obtained official transcripts of the testimonies from fifteen of these trials and have analysed them using qualitative content analysis. This method allows us to identify the different elements put forward by the accused and the witnesses that support their cases as markers of Indigenous identity – and more precisely, a Métis identity in most of the cases studied – as well as the elements that define a community and give proof of its existence. We also analysed the elements that are put forward by the Crown in order to deny the claims of the accused, and those that are retained in the end by the judge. This chapter is founded upon a preliminary analysis of a subgroup of these trials, including the *Powley*,[6] *Hopper*,[7] *Chiasson*,[8] *Breau and Brideau*,[9] *Castonguay*,[10] *Lavigne*,[11] *Acker*,[12] *Kelley*,[13] *Willison*,[14] and *Howse*[15] cases. On the basis of a summary comparison of the elements emphasized by the accused and the witnesses they call and the patterns of the judgments, this chapter describes the aspects of the judicial process that, according to our observations, pose an obstacle to the claims of non-status groups.

---

6 *R v Powley*, [1999] 1 CNLR 153 (Ont Prov Ct); aff'd [2000] 2 CNLR 233 (Ont SCJ); aff'd (2001), 196 DLR (4th) 221 (Ont CA); aff'd [2003] 2 SCR 207. For detailed results of our analysis of this trial, see Sébastien Grammond & Lynne Groulx, "Finding Métis Communities" (2012) 32 Can J Native Studies 33.

7 *R v Hopper* (2004), 275 NBR (2d) 251 (NB Prov Ct); aff'd (2005), 295 NBR (2d) 21 (NBQB); aff'd [2008] 3 CNLR 337 (NBCA).

8 *R v Chiasson* (2004), 270 NBR (2d) 357 (NBQB), aff'd (2005), 291 NBR (2d) 156 (NBCA).

9 *R v Brideau*, 2008 NBQB 74.

10 *R v Castonguay and Faucher* (2003), 271 NBR (2d) 128 (NB Prov Ct); (2006), 298 NBR (2d) 31 (NBCA).

11 *R v Lavigne*, [2005] 3 CNLR 176 (NB Prov Ct); [2007] 4 CNLR 268 (NBQB).

12 *R v Acker* (2004), 281 NBR (2d) 275 (NB Pro. Ct).

13 *R v Kelley*, [2006] 3 CNLR 324 (Alberta Prov Ct); [2007] 2 CNLR 332 (Alberta QB).

14 *R v Willison*, [2006] 4 CNLR 253 (BCSC).

15 *R v Howse*, [2000] 3 CNLR 228 (BC Prov Ct); [2002] 3 CNLR 165 (BC Prov Ct); leave to appeal granted: 2003 BCCA 152; it seems that the appeal was never heard.

This chapter begins with an examination of the emergence of non-status Indigenous groups in Canada and the legal basis of their claims. Next, we identify the practical difficulties that confront these groups when they wish to present their cases in court. Finally, we consider how the legal tests adopted by the courts render recognition of these groups' Indigenous identity highly improbable.

Non-Status Indigenous Groups and Their Claims

The emergence of non-status Indigenous groups is a by-product of the Canadian government's long-standing colonial policies. Since the mid-nineteenth century, these policies have been based on the idea that it is the government's job to define who is Indigenous and who is not. The legalization of identity in a colonial context had several unfortunate consequences. Indigenous peoples' assimilation into the majority society very quickly became the principal long-term objective of Canadian governmental policy. To this end, the *Indian Act* provided for several situations in which an Indigenous person might lose status, in particular by way of the procedure of enfranchisement, or after the marriage of an Indian woman to a non-Indian man.

There were periods when the Canadian government chose not to treat certain groups as Indigenous, even though they clearly were.[16] For example, in 1870, legislation was adopted that would grant land individually to Métis in the western part of the country. The *Indian Act* was then modified to state that those Métis who accepted such land (or "scrip") could not also hold Indian status.[17] At the beginning of the twentieth century, the federal government also decided that the *Indian Act* did not apply to the Inuit. It has maintained this exclusion, despite a Supreme Court ruling that the Inuit do fall under federal jurisdiction.[18] And in 1949, after Newfoundland joined Canada, the two governments

---

16 Sébastien Grammond, *Identity Captured by Law: Membership in Canada's Indigenous Peoples and Linguistic Minorities* (Montreal & Kingston: McGill-Queen's University Press, 2009); Grammond, "Equality between Indigenous Groups" (2009) 45 Sup Ct L Rev (2d) 91; Grammond, "L'identité autochtone saisie par le droit" in Pierre Noreau and Louise Rolland, eds, *Mélanges Andrée Lajoie* (Montreal: Éditions Thémis, 2008) 285; also online: <www.lex-electronica.org/docs/articles_260.pdf>.

17 *Indian Act*, SC 1876, c 18, s 3(3)(e).

18 *Re Eskimos*, [1939] SCR 104; see, on this subject, Constance Backhouse, *Colour-Coded: A Legal History of Racism in Canada 1900–1950* (Toronto: University of Toronto Press, 1999).

agreed that the *Indian Act* would not apply to the Indigenous population of the new province.[19] In addition to these situations, which stem from political decisions, there are numerous cases in which, because of administrative errors or decisions made on a case-by-case basis, official recognition was refused to groups who claimed to be Indigenous.[20] These decisions were often based on government officials' perception that the groups in question were "less Indigenous" than First Nations governed by the *Indian Act* and thus would be more easily assimilated. These policies of exclusion had the effect of creating a subgroup of the Indigenous population – one whose identity was not legally recognized in terms of status or specific rights. In an era when the government believed that assimilation was in the best interest of Indigenous peoples, one might have found some merit in those policies. Today, however, policies of exclusion perpetuate the idea that people who are denied status are not "genuinely Indigenous," that their identity does not deserve recognition, and that they should not be permitted to exercise the same rights as First Nations members who are recognized as status Indians under the *Indian Act*.

Federal policies regarding the Indigenous peoples began to change in 1970, when the 1969 White Paper (which proposed to eliminate Indian status) was scrapped. Following the Supreme Court's *Calder* decision, delivered in 1973, the federal government began to recognize the existence of Aboriginal rights and announced its intention to negotiate "modern treaties" with Indigenous peoples who possessed such rights. Following this change in policy, Indigenous groups whose members did not formerly have Indian status brought forward claims in order to gain the same recognition as "Indian bands" governed by the *Indian Act*.

---

19 Adrian Tanner, "The Aboriginal Peoples of Newfoundland and Labrador and Confederation" (1998) 14 Newfoundland Studies 238; David Mackenzie, "The Indian Act and the Aboriginal Peoples of Newfoundland at the Time of Confederation" (2010) 25 Newfoundland and Labrador Studies 161; Sébastien Grammond, "Equally Recognized? The Indigenous Peoples of Newfoundland and Labrador" (2014) 51 Osgoode Hall LJ 469.

20 Groves, *supra* note 2; John Giokas & Robert K Groves, "Collective and Individual Recognition in Canada: The *Indian Act* Regime" in Paul LAH Chartrand, ed, *Who Are Canada's Aboriginal Peoples? Recognition, Definition and Jurisdiction* (Saskatoon: Purich, 2002) 41.

264 Sébastien Grammond, Isabelle Lantagne, and Natacha Gagné

The federal government's response was to maintain that non-status Indigenous peoples did not fall under its constitutional responsibility, according to article 91(24) of the *Constitution Act, 1867,* but rather fell under the jurisdiction of the provinces. The federal government thus refused to negotiate with these groups with respect to their potential Aboriginal rights. Nevertheless, it agreed to fund a political organization to represent non-status or off-reserve Indigenous peoples. And so the Native Council of Canada, which later became the Congress of Aboriginal Peoples, was born, as well as its provincial member organizations, such as the New Brunswick Aboriginal Peoples Council, which we shall discuss further on.[21]

This gradual recognition of non-status groups culminated in the adoption of section 35 of the *Constitution Act, 1982,* which states, "The existing aboriginal and treaty rights of the aboriginal peoples of Canada are hereby recognized and affirmed." In the second paragraph, article 35 also states, "In this Act, 'aboriginal peoples of Canada' includes the Indian, Inuit, and Metis peoples of Canada." This sentence was apparently added at the request of the Native Council of Canada.[22] When we read these two paragraphs, the difficulty is immediately apparent: how is it possible to recognize the rights of a category of persons who possess no legal status, whose political organizations have no status defined by law, and who are not recognized by the government as holders of Aboriginal rights? Non-status groups are thus, in a sense, left to fend for themselves.

After 1982, a split occurred among organizations representing non-status Indigenous groups. The Alberta, Saskatchewan, and Manitoba provincial chapters decided to separate from the other provincial organizations in order to form the Métis National Council. This organization represents members of the Métis Nation of Western Canada, a well-known Indigenous group, descended from mixed marriages between European fur-traders and Indigenous women, that twice took up arms to resist territorial dispossession – first in 1869–70 during the Red River

---

21 Larry N Chartrand, "Métis Identity and Citizenship" (2001) 12 Windsor Rev Legal Soc Issues 5; Joe Sawchuk, "Negotiating an Identity: Métis Political Organizations, the Canadian Government and Competing Concepts of Aboriginality" (2000) 24 Am Indian Q 73.
22 Harry W Daniels, "Foreword" in Paul LAH Chartrand, ed, *Who Are Canada's Aboriginal Peoples? Recognition, Definition and Jurisdiction* (Saskatoon: Purich, 2002) 11.

"Rebellion" and again in 1885 during the Northwest "Rebellion."[23] The Congress of Aboriginal Peoples continues to federate provincial organizations representing non-status or off-reserve Indigenous people who do not identify with the Métis Nation.

After the adoption of the *Constitution Act, 1982*, various non-status Indigenous groups tried to negotiate with the federal and provincial governments in order to obtain concrete recognition of their rights. Without going into the details, there were various reasons why these discussions produced little result. One justification often cited by the government for rejecting the claims of non-status groups was the difficulty of identifying, with any precision, groups who held Aboriginal rights, and counting their members.[24] So, despite their constitutional recognition, non-status groups remained marginalized. For example, when Ontario came to an agreement with its First Nations about sharing revenue from a casino on an Indian reserve, non-status groups were excluded from this agreement. The Supreme Court ruled that this exclusion was not discriminatory.[25]

Faced with the government's refusal to recognize them, non-status groups turned to the courts. But what was their strategy? Certain members of these groups engaged in conduct that constituted offences to hunting, fishing, or forestry legislation, often with the specific intention of being caught. Once they were before the judge, they invoked their Aboriginal rights in defence. If the process were successful, a precedent would be set for other trials. Such a verdict would establish them as recognized Indigenous groups, within the meaning of section 35 of the *Constitution Act, 1982*, even if they did not constitute "bands" under the *Indian Act*. This could considerably shift the balance of power between the government and the group in question and potentially accelerate discussions in order to come to an agreement. This type of strategy is not fundamentally different from ones that various First Nations communities across the country have used in the past few decades.

---

23 For details on these events, see Douglas N Sprague, *Canada and the Métis, 1869–1885* (Waterloo, ON: Wilfrid Laurier University Press, 1988); George FG Stanley, *The Birth of Western Canada: A History of the Riel Rebellions* (Toronto: University of Toronto Press, 1960); Joe Sawchuk, *The Metis of Manitoba: Reformulation of an Ethnic Identity* (Toronto: Peter Martin Associates, 1978).
24 See, for example, *R v Powley* (2001), 196 DLR (4th) 221 (Ont CA) at 230.
25 *Lovelace v Ontario*, [2000] 1 SCR 950.

Non-Status Aboriginal Groups and Access to Justice

In the majority of cases, the courts have refused to recognize that non-status groups were either "Métis" or "aboriginal" within the meaning of section 35 of the *Constitution Act, 1982*. An analysis of trials and judgments has allowed us to outline the main obstacles that prevent non-status groups from obtaining legal recognition of their identity.

On a pragmatic level, studies about access to justice have shown that lack of resources constitutes one of the most significant obstacles preventing disadvantaged people from presenting their case before the courts.[26] Our study has led us to identify two types of resources that are lacking for certain non-status groups, in particular those in Canada's eastern provinces: financial resources and expertise.

The Imbalance of Financial Resources

Let us begin with what seems obvious. An Aboriginal rights case is usually quite complicated. The facts necessary to carry out the legal tests established by the Supreme Court are extremely complex. Proving these rights requires long days of hearings – the cases we analysed lasted an average of ten days. Adequate preparation beforehand requires even more time and money.

Under such conditions, it seems almost impossible for individuals acting alone to present sufficient evidence, even if they are represented by a legal aid lawyer. The support of an organized group seems to be vital. On this subject – although the analysis of trial transcripts does not usually give an indication of financial arrangements – the difference between the cases we have analysed is striking. The accused in *Powley* received support from associations that represent the Métis Nation. The president of the Métis Nation of Ontario was a witness at trial and the accused were represented by a lawyer with a strong national reputation in Indigenous rights. The accused also hired two academics who wrote expert reports and testified at the hearing. In contrast, in most of the cases judged in New Brunswick, the accused represented themselves or

---

26 For an overview, see Roderick A Macdonald, "Access to Justice in Canada Today: Scope, Scale and Ambitions" in Julia Bass, WA Bogart, & Frederick H Zemans, eds, *Access to Justice for a New Century: The Way Forward* (Toronto: Law Society of Upper Canada, 2004) 19.

were represented by a legal aid lawyer[27] – in other words, a lawyer who did not specialize in Indigenous rights. Testimonies were often disorganized, and several people who were allowed to testify as expert witnesses had no university degree or professional certification, or were amateur genealogists. The associations to which the accused belonged were marginal and did not receive government subsidies, in contrast with the Western Métis Nation associations.

We might assume that the presence of a lawyer is essential to the efficient presentation of a claim and its success. The *Howse* case, however, requires us to qualify this assertion. In this trial, the accused retained the services of a lawyer only for the closing argument. They represented themselves throughout the major part of the trial – notably, during the examination of the witnesses. Paradoxically, this situation allowed them to address certain aspects of their identity that were not touched upon in other cases – in particular, the fact that the Western Métis remain very mobile, while still maintaining their family and community bonds. We can assume that lawyers have a tendency to prepare clients to testify on subjects that, in their opinion, are relevant to the legal tests established by the Supreme Court. The presence of a lawyer in *Howse* would have had the effect of framing or even formatting the "identity narrative" of the accused. For example, a lawyer might have warned clients against placing too much emphasis on mobility, since he or she might think that geographical concentration and stability of the community would be key factors in the judge's decision.[28] The absence of a lawyer thus allowed the accused, who happened to be the directors of the newly formed British Columbian chapter of the Métis National Council, to present a very articulate vision of their identity, free from any legal constraint. Still, this is an exception – most cases heard in New Brunswick show that the absence of a lawyer results only in the case being poorly organized and researched, and that testimonies often lack focus and precision.

---

27 It is not always possible to determine whether the lawyer representing the accused is paid by legal aid, but we know that this was the case in both the *Hopper* and the *Vautour* cases. Moreover, the accused were not represented by a lawyer in the *Lavigne, Breau and Brideau* and *Castonguay* cases.

28 Natacha Gagné, Claudie Larcher, and Sébastien Grammond, "La communauté comme sujet et objet du droit: implications pour les Métis du Canada" (2014) 38:2 Anthropologie et sociétés, 151.

Desperately Seeking Expert

The facts relevant for the legal tests established by the Supreme Court to determine whether a group is an Aboriginal community are not generally within the accused's personal knowledge, and the accused would not be allowed to testify on them. When proof must be made of the existence of a historical Indigenous community, of the importance of specific cultural practices to the identity of a group, or of the relationships between different Indigenous groups, an expert witness is generally called to testify – whether it be a historian, an anthropologist, a sociologist, or other qualified professional. Courts have indeed a tendency to require what they consider the best evidence. This has the effect of "professionalizing" Aboriginal rights litigation. The preliminary results of our analysis show that this situation has several types of consequences.

First, the length and the cost of the trial increase. The preparation of an expert report requires a considerable amount of work, for which the author must be remunerated. For example, in *Powley*, the accused hired two university professors, each of whom wrote a fifty-page report citing a wide range of primary and secondary sources. They also testified over several days. In a trial of this scope, lawyer and expert fees can rise to several thousand (or even several hundred thousand) dollars.[29] The possibilities for public funding of such a trial are slim, especially if it involves individuals or groups that the government does not recognize as Indigenous.[30] The inequalities that we mentioned earlier in terms of financial resources available to various non-status groups are thus exacerbated.

Second, an Indigenous group may have difficulty finding an expert who is willing to testify in its favour. As a general rule, an expert should agree to testify only on subjects that he or she has studied in depth.

---

29 It is difficult to obtain information on the cost of a trial. In *Daniels v Canada*, 2011 FC 230, a case that was clearly more complex than the trials we are studying and in which the hearing lasted nearly two months, the cost was estimated at $1.8 million.
30 The Department of Indian and Northern Affairs in Canada can grant financial aid to Indigenous groups who bring test cases that are judged to be of sufficient interest. Moreover, in the past few years, the courts have been willing, in exceptional cases, to order the state to pay litigation costs in a public interest case: *British Columbia (Minister of Forests) v Okanagan Indian Band*, [2003] 3 SCR 371; *R v Caron*, [2011] 1 SCR 78; *Daniels v Canada*, 2011 FC 230.

Certain disadvantaged groups – who have been kept to the margins of official history and have limited access to financial resources (as well as limited social and cultural capital[31]) – can have a hard time finding qualified expert witnesses. Once again, the contrast between groups belonging to the Western Métis Nation and non-status groups in New Brunswick is striking. Even if the Western Métis do not have the same rights as First Nations, they have nevertheless been the subjects of research and of a considerable number of publications. There is a pool of potential experts available in the West. In *Powley, Goodon,*[32] and *Belhumeur,*[33] the well-known historian Professor Arthur Ray[34] of the University of British Columbia testified in favour of the Métis. The judges hearing these cases drew heavily upon his testimony. In contrast, there are (to our knowledge) very few university studies about non-status Indigenous communities in New Brunswick – particularly about their present-day realities.

It may well be that the development of "Métis studies" under the leadership of a group of intellectuals from the Métis Nation has contributed to the construction of an identity narrative accentuating the distinctive character of the Métis Nation – particularly in relation to other unrecognized Indigenous groups. In certain cases, this identity narrative may go so far as to deny these other Indigenous groups the right to use the label "Métis."[35] This distinctive character would stem from the fact that unions between men of European origin and Indigenous women in Western Canada in the eighteenth century formed a largely endogamous group, which would have quickly acquired a distinct collective identity. Their collective identity would have been cemented through the Métis "rebellions" of the end of the nineteenth century, the establishment of a provisional government, and the negotiation of the terms

31 See Pierre Bourdieu, "Les trois états du capital culturel" (1979) 30 Actes de la recherche en sciences sociales 3; Pierre Bourdieu, "Le capital social" (1980) 31 Actes de la recherche en sciences sociales 2.
32 *R v Goodon,* [2009] 2 CNLR 278 (Man Prov Ct).
33 *R v Belhumeur,* [2008] 2 CNLR 311 (Sask Prov Ct).
34 Arthur J Ray, *Telling It to the Judge: Taking Native History to Court* (Montreal & Kingston: McGill-Queen's University Press, 2011), tells the story of his experience as an expert witness.
35 See, for example, Paul LAH Chartrand and John Giokas, "Defining 'The Métis People': The Hard Case of Canadian Aboriginal Law" in Chartrand, ed., *Who Are Canada's Aboriginal Peoples? Recognition, Definition and Jurisdiction* (Saskatoon: Purich 2002) 268.

of union with Canada. According to some, such as Métis law professor Paul Chartrand,[36] this process (called "ethnogenesis" by anthropologists and sociologists[37]) could have taken place only in Western Canada, where specific economic factors favoured the emergence of a Métis people. As Macdougall showed, the economy of the fur trade – as well as family values and the Catholic Church – was central to the formation of a Métis community in the West.[38] In contrast, historian Olive Dickason maintains that the process of colonization in the Maritimes did not lead to the emergence of a Métis group that was distinct from both the non-Indigenous population and First Nations.[39] This conclusion is often cited to deny non-status groups in Eastern Canada the possibility of claiming Aboriginal rights, since the framework of analysis established by the Supreme Court in *Powley* requires proof of the existence of such a distinct community. The way in which Métis studies have been developed and the political objectives underlying them add to the difficulties of the claims of unrecognized groups in the Atlantic Provinces.

Consequently, the defence evidence in trials held in the Atlantic Provinces is a motley assortment in which university experts figure hardly at all. The main "expert" witness is often an amateur genealogist who attempts to establish the Indigenous ancestry of the accused (notably in *Hopper, Breau and Brideau,* and *Chiasson*). In some cases, the accused tries to have a non-academic self-taught in matters of Indigenous culture qualified as an expert. In *Hopper,* for example, the accused had his cousin, "Doctor" Williams, qualified as an expert witness. The latter teaches martial arts and was the founder of an association representing "Acadian Métis." He testified for a long time on his perception of Acadian history and the impact of colonization on Aboriginal communities in the Maritimes. In particular, on the basis of his personal research, he maintained

---

36 *Ibid.*
37 Louis-Pascal Rousseau, "Les études sur l'ethnogénèse au Canada: enjeux et horizons de recherche pour le Québec" (2006) 36:1 Recherches amérindiennes au Québec 49.
38 Brenda Macdougall, *One of the Family: Metis Culture in Nineteenth-Century Northwestern Saskatchewan* (Vancouver: UBC Press, 2010).
39 Olive P Dickason, "From 'One Nation' in the Northeast to 'New Nation' in the Northwest: A Look at the Emergence of the Metis" in Jacqueline Peterson and Jennifer SH Brown, eds, *The New Peoples: Being and Becoming Métis in North America* (Winnipeg: University of Manitoba Press, 1984) 19; Gerhard Ens, *Homeland to Hinterland: The Changing Worlds of the Red River Metis in the Nineteenth Century* (Toronto: University of Toronto Press, 1996) 13; Devrim Karahasan, *Métissage in New France and Canada 1508 to 1886* (Frankfurt: Peter Lang, 2009).

that the French colonization in Acadia gave rise to numerous mixed unions between French colonists and Indigenous women, which led to the emergence of Métis communities. But his testimony – which lasted more than eight days – carried little weight in the judge's decision.[40] Even when an expert with university credentials testifies in favour of the accused, as in *Vautour*,[41] the theory put forward – the existence, in New Brunswick, of a Métis community that has become "invisible" since the deportation of the Acadians – seems to contain so few documented historical facts to support this theory that the judge prefers the evidence of Crown expert witnesses who maintain that the contact between Acadians and Mi'kmaq did not lead to the emergence of a distinct ethnic group, in contrast to what happened in western provinces.[42] In these cases, it is easy for the judge to give credit to the testimony of the Crown expert who denies the existence of such a community.

Academic expert testimony has been instrumental in the successes of the Western Métis in several cases, in particular in *Goodon* and *Laviolette*, as well as in *Powley* in Ontario. Non-status groups in New Brunswick, however, have had all their claims rejected. The only case where the courts in this province ruled in favour of a non-status Indigenous individual was when he was able to prove his de facto membership in a First Nations band (the *Lavigne* case). Hence, requiring an expert testimony may contribute to reinforcing the invisibility of non-status groups who have not been the subject of academic attention. This compounds the fact that the *Powley* test seems to have been established with the particular situation and history of the Western Métis Nation in mind, and does not necessarily reflect the reality of non-status Indigenous groups in the East.

Non-Status Indigenous Groups and the Legal Test for Aboriginal Rights

The above analysis shows that non-status groups who have financial resources and, in our words, "expert capital," are able to present their

---

40 In his reasons, the trial judge stated that no evidence of the existence of a Metis community had been presented: *R v Hopper* (2004), 275 NBR (2d) 251 (NB Prov Ct); this conclusion was explicitly confirmed by the Court of Appeal: [2008] 3 CNLR 337 (NBCA) at para 11.
41 *R v Vautour*, [2011] 1 CNLR 283 (NB Prov Ct).
42 *Ibid* at paras 58 and 81.

case in a much more convincing manner than non-status groups who lack these resources. The obstacles that stem from this lack of resources can be linked to those that have been identified in studies on access to justice. The difficulties the courts have in comprehending the social reality of non-status Indigenous groups may also stem from the substance of the legal rules that they apply. In the cases under review, the relevant criteria (or "legal test") were defined by the Supreme Court in *Powley* and focus on proof of the existence of a "community," defined as "a group of Métis with a distinctive collective identity, living together in the same geographic area and sharing a common way of life."[43] Given the emphasis it places on the concept of "community," the Supreme Court's decision seems to have been made with the situation of the Western Métis Nation in mind. Also, the way in which *Powley* was interpreted by parties and trial judges in subsequent cases emphasizes two concepts: ancestry and territory, which correspond to the popular image of First Nations Indigenous communities – an image that is the product of the colonial policies of the *Indian Act*. But this image does not generally apply to non-status groups, who are, in a sense, obligated to conform to a social structure and a cultural model that are not their own if they want their claims to be taken seriously.

Indeed, one of the pitfalls of any process of recognition is the risk of perpetuating a stereotyped image of Indigenous cultures.[44] Thus, in Canada, the courts have not hesitated to recognize hunting and fishing rights – activities that, in the popular imagination, are associated with a traditional Indigenous way of life. But the reasoning adopted by the courts leaves little room for claims that are at odds with the popular image of the Indigenous peoples. Despite good intentions, the legal system does not always succeed in separating out the dominant

---

43 *R v Powley*, [2003] 2 SCR 207 at para 12.
44 See in particular Ronald Niezen, *The Rediscovered Self: Indigenous Identity and Cultural Justice* (Montreal & Kingston: McGill-Queen's University Press, 2009); Joanne Barker, *Native Acts: Law, Recognition and Cultural Authenticity* (Durham, NC: Duke University Press, 2011); Michael Asch, "The Judicial Conceptualization of Culture after *Delgamuukw* and *Van der Peet*" (2000) 5 Rev Constitutional Studies 119; Neil Vallance, "The Misuse of 'Culture' by the Supreme Court of Canada" in Avigail Eisenberg, ed, *Diversity and Equality: The Changing Framework of Freedom in Canada* (Vancouver: UBC Press, 2006) 97; Michael Murphy, "Prisons of Culture: Judicial Constructions of Indigenous Rights in Australia, Canada and New Zealand" (2009) 87 Can Bar Rev 357; Sébastien Grammond, *Terms of Coexistence: Indigenous Peoples and Canadian Law* (Toronto: Carswell, 2013) at 9–10, 12–13, 236–37.

society's social representations of the Indigenous peoples from the prejudices that these representations carry. This differentiation is all the more difficult, given that these popular representations are carried by non-governmental organizations and global governance institutions that work in favour of Indigenous rights.[45]

The risk is particularly acute when the issue is the identification of previously unrecognized groups. This is borne out by the example of the United States, where similar claims were treated through administrative channels. The federal government established the Federal Acknowledgment Process (FAP) in 1978, which would enable groups to request recognition as Indigenous groups, with all the advantages and legal consequences that flow from it – particularly in regards to access to certain governmental programs. Studies on this process have shown that the groups who obtain recognition correspond to the traditional image of Indigenous groups in the eyes of mainstream society. A group has a better chance of being recognized if its members have Indigenous traits, if they engage in cultural practices generally associated with Indigenous peoples, and if the group constitutes a homogeneous and geographically isolated community.[46] In short – it will be difficult, under policies aimed at the protection of marginalized groups, to separate the reality of these groups from the mainstream society's image of them. What makes this all the more ironic is that this image stems from forms of social organization imposed upon Indigenous peoples by colonial policies – in particular, through settlement policies and the imposition of elective local governments.

The Persistence of Colonial Concepts: Ancestry

One of the most striking aspects of the trials we studied is the importance placed by the accused on genealogical evidence. In the majority of these cases, the accused put great effort into establishing that they have Indigenous ancestors.

---

45 See, e.g., Ronald Niezen, *Public Justice and the Anthropology of Law* (Cambridge: Cambridge University Press, 2010).

46 Mark E Miller, *Forgotten Tribes: Unrecognized Indians and the Federal Acknowledgement Process* (Lincoln: University of Nebraska Press, 2004) esp at 10–11, 54–57; Renée A Cramer, *Cash, Color and Colonialism: The Politics of Tribal Acknowledgement* (Norman: University of Oklahoma Press, 2005); Mark D Myers, "Federal Recognition of Indian Tribes in the United States" (2001) 12 Stan L & Pol'y Rev 271.

274 Sébastien Grammond, Isabelle Lantagne, and Natacha Gagné

This obsession with ancestry allows us to see the way in which the judicial process reinforces pre-existent social norms. The prevalence of racial conceptions of Indigenous identity in the popular imagination is well known. The emphasis placed on "blood" in the definition of Indigenous identity was reinforced by Canadian and American laws that based Indian status upon ancestry. In certain cases, these laws required a certain "blood quantum," which gave weight to the idea that people in whom this "blood" was too "diluted" were not authentically Indigenous. The internalization of these conceptions by Indigenous people themselves is well documented[47] and has led numerous Indigenous groups to define their membership criteria according to "Indian blood" or similar concepts.[48] It can be said that the present *Indian Act*, in particular the "second generation cut-off rule," whereby Indian status depends upon the number of Indian grandparents a person has, perpetuates a racial conception of Indigenous identity.[49]

In most of the trials we studied, this fixation on ancestry resulted in extensive genealogical evidence. In such cases, the initiative comes from the accused and not from the Crown or the judge. In each of the *Acker*, *Chiasson*, *Hopper*, and *Lavigne* cases, the modus operandi was similar. The accused present to the court a genealogical chart in order to prove that they have Indigenous ancestry. This demonstration is very complex and involves the filing of the birth and marriage certificates of each ancestor on the accused's chart. The genealogist called to the bar by the accused confirms the authenticity of the documents. During the testimony, the genealogist establishes, often by way of ancestors' family names, who was and who was not Indigenous. When there is no original document available to support the testimony, the genealogist presents genealogy collections or archives that served as secondary sources.

---

47 Circé Sturm, *Blood Politics: Race, Culture and Identity in the Cherokee Nation of Oklahoma* (Berkeley: University of California Press, 2002); Eva M Garroutte, *Real Indians: Identity and the Survival of Native America* (Berkeley: University of California Press, 2003); Bonita Lawrence, *"Real" Indians and Others: Mixed-Blood Urban Native Peoples and Indigenous Nationhood* (Vancouver: UBC Press, 2004); Caroline Dick, "The Politics of Intragroup Difference: First Nations' Women and the Sawridge Dispute" (2006) 39 Can J Pol Sci 97.
48 For example, the membership codes of numerous Indian Bands in Canada: Grammond, *Identity Captured by Law*, 135–44.
49 Sébastien Grammond, "Discrimination in the Rules of Indian Status and the *McIvor* Case" (2009) 35 Queen's LJ 421.

In some cases, to support this evidence, the accused also calls an official representative from the association in which he or she is a member
to testify, whether from the New Brunswick Aboriginal Peoples Council (recognized by the federal government for funding purposes) or
an unrecognized association. This witness confirms that the accused
is recognized as an Indigenous or Métis person by the association in
question. The witness also establishes that one of the requirements for
a new member is to submit a genealogical chart proving that his or her
ancestors really were Indigenous. This was the case in *Hopper, Chiasson,
Lavigne,* and *Acker,* among other cases.

Judges tend to have an ambiguous reaction to this type of evidence.
We have observed that successful claims usually include proof of a
relatively "close" Indigenous ancestry, at the fifth (*Lavigne*) or seventh
(*Powley*) generation. However, proof of "close" ancestry is not sufficient
in and of itself to obtain recognition of Indigenous status and the rights
that flow from section 35 of the *Constitution Act, 1982.* Thus, in the *Acker*
case, the grandmother of the accused is described by the judge as being
a "full-blooded Indian,"[50] but the fact that the accused paid no attention
to his Mi'kmaq origins until he was forty was, in the judge's thinking,
a more decisive factor. Cases in which the accused did not succeed in
showing more than "distant" Indigenous ancestry, such as at the tenth
or twelfth generation, were nearly always unsuccessful. The judge's
remarks in the *Hopper* case illustrate this type of reasoning:

> The defendant's genealogy chart marked as Exhibit D-18 shows branches
> leading to ancestors purporting to be aboriginals. According to that chart,
> he would be between the 10th and 12th generation in each of these branch-
> es. Assuming that these branches, there are six of them at the most, cor-
> rectly trace the defendant to aboriginal ancestors, the percentage of his
> aboriginal ancestry would amount to very little of his entire ascendance.
> Assuming that these treaties are valid, I cannot envision that the mere fact
> of being a descendant of a treaty signer entitles the latter to the rights con-
> tained in that treaty. These chiefs or grand chiefs, as the case may be, did
> not acquire more rights than the members of their tribes or bands which
> they were representing. From the other perspective, it follows that the de-
> scendants of each member of these tribes or bands did not acquire less
> rights than those of the signer. But it does not necessarily follow that all

---

50 *R v Acker* (2004), 281 NBR (2d) 275 (NB Prov Ct) at para 44.

descendants of the signers of the treaties or those of their tribe or band are beneficiaries of those treaties.[51]

What seems to be emerging from these observations is that a relatively close Indigenous ancestry is an essential condition – but not sufficient in and of itself – for recognition of Indigenous status under the *Constitution Act, 1982*. Still, certain judges adopt a discursive strategy that minimizes the importance of ancestry: they accept the validity of genealogical evidence, or the legitimacy of the self-identification that it supports, while denying that legal consequences or constitutional rights flow from such self-identification. For example, in *Chiasson*, the trial judge writes,[52] in reference to the genealogical evidence,

> On this issue, the evidence is persuasive. Indeed, I am of the opinion that Roseline Guitard's genealogical research was done with great care and according to the criteria established by her profession. A court cannot ask for more unless contrary evidence is presented. Moreover, works by Monique Thériault-Léger, Fidèle Thériault as well as by researchers at the Société Historique Nicholas Denys describe what seems to be all of the current information on the period in which the defendant's family tree is included. (para 9)
>
> ...
>
> It is obvious that we do not have the same kind of evidence here as was the case in *Fowler* and *Harquail*. The gap in this case, between the defendant and his Indian origins, is 280 years and only closes 8 generations removed from Mr Chiasson. This, in my opinion, does not bring this case within the caselaw nor any law that could have been relied upon. The conclusion is therefore easy and clear in my opinion: the connection with Mr Chiasson's Indian ancestry is neither solid nor substantial enough to ensure him rights to any protection under any treaty. (para 12)

In *Castonguay and Faucher*, the Court of Queen's Bench judge (the first level of appeal) asserted that "an aboriginal genetic connection that was formed ten generations ago and has no continuity with the present cannot give rise to a constitutional right."[53] The same idea is expressed in the Court of Appeal's decision in the *Hopper* case:

---

51 *R v Hopper* (2004), 275 NBR (2d) 251 (NB Prov Ct).
52 *R v Chiasson* (2001), 239 NBR (2d) 1 (NB Prov Ct) at 6–9.
53 *R v Castonguay and Faucher* (2003), 271 NBR (2d) 128 (NBQB) at para 74; this passage was approved by the Court of Appeal: (2006), 298 NBR (2d) 31 (NBCA).

I am satisfied Mr Hopper has proven, by birth, a connection to an historic Indian community. However, given my opinion regarding the territorial reach of the Treaty ... and the conclusions of the trial judge concerning the lack of connection to an historic rights-bearing community, this observation of connection by birth to an Indian community is of no assistance to Mr Hopper in his effort to prove a treaty exemption.[54]

In *Hopper*, the accused attempted to take this further. In addition to proving his ancestor's affiliation with an Indigenous community, he also presented evidence of this ancestor's social status and political role in Canadian history, explaining that he was the chief of a tribe and signatory of a treaty. This attempt also failed. The conclusive character of an Indigenous ancestry that is too "distant" is striking when we compare the weight given to other kinds of identity markers. In *Breau and Brideau*, the accused spoke about how important it was for them to have an intimate relationship with nature and the land; they also emphasized the importance of spirituality in the definition of Indigenous identity. The judgment remains silent about these factors and rejects the claim. The *Hopper* case, too, is informative in this regard, in terms of how the testimony from the accused's mother was received. Her testimony lasted only a few moments, compared to the testimony of "Doctor" Williams on history and genealogy, which lasted more than eight days. And yet the explanation of family life given by Ms Hopper seems particularly significant:

Q. Okay, can you give me some – some background into family life?
A. Family life – we've lived our life as Indians off reservation.
Q. Okay, in what sense?
A. In what sense – that we hunt, we fish, we do all the things that Indians do – okay – but we live in a white man's world.
Q. And for how long has this been going on?
A. All my life. I've never lived on a reservation. My father did. My aunts and uncles did, but I didn't.

No further questions were asked of the witness on this subject. The defence lawyer did not attempt to pursue the line of questioning. Even if the judge took note of this exchange in the establishment of

---

54 *R v Hopper*, [2008] 3 CNLR 337 (NBCA) at para 16; see also *R v Vautour*, [2011] 1 CNLR 283 (NB Prov Ct) at para 63.

278 Sébastien Grammond, Isabelle Lantagne, and Natacha Gagné

the accused's Indigenous identity, it did not have an impact in terms of recognition of the existence of a community or constitutional rights. In short, the importance of genealogy in the popular conception of Indigenous identity, as what underlies legislation related to Indian status, leads the accused to spend considerable effort preparing genealogical evidence. It also means that ancestry is taken into account in the judge's decision. However, our analysis of trials leads us to believe that Indigenous ancestry is a necessary condition, but not a sufficient one, for the recognition of rights.

The Persistence of Colonial Institutions: The Reserve

Since Aboriginal rights are collective rights – they belong to Indigenous *peoples*, according to the constitutional text – one of the elements that the accused must show is the historical and contemporary existence of an Indigenous community that holds such rights. The Supreme Court's *Powley* decision is often interpreted as having required proof of the existence of a very localized Indigenous community[55] – rather like an Indian reserve.[56] But in the trials we have analysed, this requirement (especially if strictly applied) does not necessarily reflect the testimonies (of the accused or the witnesses) about the relationship of the accused to a specific territory.

These testimonies are varied. The notion of "territory" seems to be used differently from one case to the next. Emphasis is placed either on the territory where a group practises hunting or fishing activities, or else on the territory where members of the same community live. We have noted that issues around territory are different from one province to another. These differences likely stem from history, especially from

---

55 This requirement may be reinforced by the fact that, on the subject of Indigenous rights, the courts have generally required evidence related to very specific territories. It is generally accepted that the majority of Aboriginal rights recognized by the courts, such as hunting and fishing rights, are site-specific. When a claim is presented by non-status Indigenous peoples, it is possible that the judge will have a tendency to mix up the community's geographic range with the place where it exercises its rights. See, however, *R v Goodon*, [2009] 2 CNLR 278 (Man Prov Ct) at para 16, where the difference between the two geographical sites is recognized.

56 An Indian reserve is a plot of land, the exclusive possession of which is attributed to an Indigenous community (an "Indian band"), according to the terms of the *Indian Act*. In most cases, the members of the community live in a village situated on a reserve. Non-Indigenous people cannot reside there.

the forms of ethnogenesis of Métis groups and the political situation of the Métis in the province in question, but also from the accused's relationship to a specific community and the cultural particularities of the latter. This said, certain similarities can still be observed between the conceptions of relationship to a territory that are put forward by the accused in different regions of the country.

In many of the New Brunswick cases, the accused called experts to the bar to describe the ways of life of their Indigenous ancestors. According to historical or anthropological evidence, the Mi'kmaq were nomads, occupying the territory that covers the region from the Maritimes to the Great Lakes as well as a portion of the Northeastern United States. These Indigenous peoples lived in small groups and communicated between groups via messengers. Still according to these witnesses, the territory occupied by these groups was divided into seven districts, and the chief of each district was part of an assembly called the Grand Council.[57] Each small group assembled annually and according to the seasons. Marriage was a central form of alliance between these groups. The anthropologist who testified in *Acker* underlined territorial mobility and family bonds as characteristic elements of the Mi'kmaq way of life:

> Q. Okay, you say "these people," What do you mean, who do you mean, just be specific?
>
> A. The whole, this is a family, and they're moving around. So when you say this is a family, you mean the, the family tree on Exhibit, on Exhibit D – But you can't see them all in one community, in one place. This fellow's on Sable Island, Sable River, not only on the Sable River, but he moves down to Cap Sable, he's following animals, he's following wildlife, he's following migrating birds, he's following fish, he's moving, season by season. He's fishing the cod when they come to shore.

The creation of reserves in the early 1920s led to the reduction and parcelling of Mi'kmaq territory. The increasing presence of colonists forced Indigenous peoples to choose between settling on reserves – pieces of land put aside by the government for the exclusive use of status Indians – or to "wander" on the territory that was still largely unoccupied. This process, initiated by the government, created two

---

57 *Acker* case, hearing of 25 August 2003.

categories of Indigenous peoples: those who had accepted to live on the reserves and were thus granted Indian status, and the rest, who were without status.

However, the recent establishment of associations representing non-status Indigenous peoples would, according to the representative of one of these organizations (who testified in the *Acker* case), allow people to maintain community links in a situation where community members are scattered over the territory:

> The New Brunswick Aboriginal Peoples Council covers the province of New Brunswick and, and in order to maintain communication between the head office and the people, there are community Locals established around the province. And to give you an example, there would be one here in – because, because our people don't live in, in areas like the Indians who live on-reserve, because you can't go and say, okay this is where the Miramichi Local is and they're on one reserve, they're spread out all over the place, they're spread out in rural areas, in towns and villages, so to make it easier in, in different areas, people have gotten together and, and formed these community Locals where they have meetings.[58]

A somewhat similar conception of the relationship to territory was put forward by the accused in the *Howse* case, which took place in British Columbia. In this case, the accused emphasized the importance of the concept of "homeland."[59] According to them, this concept, which would include all of the western provinces, shows the importance of nomadism (associated with the fur-trade era) and of this mode of life for their community. The concept of "homeland," for them, is stronger than an attachment to a clearly defined and precisely located territory. As one witness stated, "I think I've covered it all. I mean, I can be here all day if I was to tell every place I've been and, you know, I've hunted from all four provinces. I've been in all four provinces. I'm a typical Métis. That's about all."[60] This concept comes up again in the *Willison* case, which was also judged in British Columbia. In his closing argument, the accused's lawyer stated,

---

58 *Acker* case, hearing of 10 February 2003.
59 A similar conception of community and its links with territory can be found, for example, in Brenda Macdougall, *One of the Family: Metis Culture in Nineteenth-Century Northwestern Saskatchewan* (Vancouver: UBC Press, 2010).
60 *Howse* case, hearing of 29 September 1999.

There were strong family connections between the core community at Red River and this Métis community that existed in the Pacific Northwest, that this Pacific Northwest Métis community rose from, in conjunction with, the fur trade economy and culture, if I can put it that way. I've said in that region as elsewhere and that – so B follows directly from A. This whole fur trade economy, you know, it's impossible to isolate it. It's the Pacific Northwest. It's part of a larger picture of – it encompasses the entire – what are now the entire four western provinces and the province of Ontario, or at least the western part of the province of Ontario, if I can put it that way.

The judges' reaction to such propositions is mixed. In some cases in the western provinces, the court accepted a broad definition of community. For example, the trial judge in *Goodon* described the accused's community as "a large inter-related community that included numerous settlements located in present-day southwestern Manitoba, into Saskatchewan and including the northern Midwest United States."[61] This was also the case with the trial judge in *Howse*, who agreed to recognize the existence of a Métis community according to the concept of "homeland." This decision, however, was reversed on appeal, on the basis that "[t]here was not sufficient evidence upon which the learned trial judge could conclude that any of the defendants had the necessary territorial connection to the Kootenay area."[62] Similarly, the trial judge in *Kelley* refused to accept the existence of a Métis community in Hinton, Alberta, where the offence took place. In particular, he pointed out the fact that the parents of the accused were originally from Manitoba – suggesting that their rights, if any, were in relation to that province.[63]

All the New Brunswick cases had a similar outcome, with the exception of the *Lavigne* case, in which the accused convinced the judge that he was a de facto member of an Indian band, even if he did not have Indian status. In several rulings, the judges have emphasized that communities that are specifically Métis do not exist in New Brunswick. These rulings are often delivered in English, and the term "community," in this language, signifies not only a group of people, but also a localized area such as a village or small town. In certain cases, such as

---

61 *R v Goodon*, [2009] 2 CNLR 278 (Man Prov Ct) at para 46.
62 *R v Howse*, [2002] 3 CNLR 165 (BCSC) at para 34.
63 *R v Kelley*, [2006] 3 CNLR 324 (Alberta Prov Ct) at paras 32–35.

the *Chiasson* case, the accused or the witnesses are forced to admit that a Métis community, in this sense, does not exist.

Q. Now, are there, are there any communities, like Métis communities in New Brunswick? defined, you know, that you can define?

A. Well, Metis, ninety per cent of the Metis in New Brunswick are people like you and I that live in different villages and, and – Yes. – and there's no Metis living on a reserve and it's the last thing in the world we want. No, no. Okay. I'm not talking – Okay. – exclusively – Okay. – about a reserve. But there's no, there's no Metis Villages, okay. No. As we know, like I know what you might refer to do we have a, a, a small enclave where all Metis lives in. No, we don't have that. Metis are people that, that go to church, go to church, go shopping every day and, and you would – Right. And, they can be in Moncton. – you would – They can be in Saint-John, Fredericton. You wouldn't know a Metis if you saw one walking the street.[64]

This absence of "communities" resembling Indian reserves is fatal for their claims. The courts' conclusion is clear and was expressed in a particularly direct manner by the Court of Queen's Bench in *Castonguay and Faucher*, in a passage approved by the Court of Appeal: "There is no evidence, historical or otherwise, of a Métis community in our province."[65]

Some accused parties have explicitly invited New Brunswick courts to move away from a "localized" vision of community and to accept that community can be founded on factors other than the exclusive possession of a territory – such as family ties that are maintained through frequent or occasional visits, and communal cultural practices. In other words, they've asked the courts to stop looking for "quasi-reserves." But the trial judge in *Vautour* rejected this argument as being incompatible with the guidelines given by the Supreme Court in *Powley*.[66] It is still surprising to note that certain judges in the western provinces (as in the *Howse* trial or in *Goodon*) were more amenable to such an argument, and that they did accept the existence

---

64 *Chiasson* case, hearing of 3 February 2000.
65 *R v Castonguay and Faucher* (2003), 271 NBR (2d) 128 (NB Prov Ct) at para 77; (2006), 298 NBR (2d) 31 (NBCA) at para 6.
66 *R v Vautour*, [2011] 1 CNLR 283 (NB Prov Ct) at paras 82–85.

of Métis communities that were never concentrated in a specific, circumscribed territory.

Thus, the preliminary results of our research tend to show that the judicial process poses particular obstacles to the claims of non-status Indigenous groups. Many of these obstacles stem from the fact that the reality of these groups does not align with the stereotypical image of Indigenous peoples. Non-status groups are, in a way, invisible, and their claims are often met with a degree of incredulity. Especially if they do not live in specific localities that look like reserves and do not have close Indigenous ancestry, it is difficult for the members of these groups to convince the judges that they truly are part of Aboriginal rights–holding "communities." The struggle to find credible experts who could establish the existence of such a community, together with the cost of a complex trial, also adds to the challenges faced by many of these claimants.

More generally, these results suggest that it is challenging for the courts to respond to the claims of individuals or groups whose marginal or disadvantaged condition is not known to the larger public – in short, groups that are socially and legally invisible. Since the characteristics of these groups cannot be compared to those of groups that are known and have already been identified by law or the government, there is a strong risk that they will remain in oblivion.

In fact, to recognize the claims of these individuals, it may even be necessary to question the collective nature of Aboriginal rights and to find alternatives to the concept of "community," which dominates the post-*Powley* case law. After all, the dislocation and dispersion of Indigenous communities was one of the consequences of the assimilationist and paternalistic policies of the Canadian state. As Justice Todd Ducharme puts it, we must not forget "the broader historical reality that Aboriginal assimilation and cultural displacement is the result of conscious policies pursued by past Canadian governments."[67] Thus, true reconciliation might require concepts that more accurately reflect the patterns of oppression and colonialism suffered by the Indigenous peoples.[68]

---

67 *R v Prevost*, 2008 CanLII 46920 (Ont SCJ) at para 47.
68 Jean Leclair, "Les périls du totalisme conceptuel en droit et en sciences sociales" (2009) 14 Lex Electronica, online: <www.lex-electronica.org/docs/articles_233.pdf>.

The concept of "community," often understood as the search for a "quasi-reserve," might capture the realities of those groups whose bonds have survived the onslaught of colonial policies. Ironically, where these policies were most successful and destroyed such bonds, the descendants of the original groups would not be entitled to any form of recognition or assistance in affirming and reviving their identity and culture.

These conclusions are, of course, preliminary, and could be enriched by the analysis of several more trials. We can already discern a dichotomy between the West and the East of Canada – Métis claims are more likely to be successful in the West. This contrast puts us on the trail of potential explanations other than those outlined above. We could speculate that the degree of organization and political experience in Métis communities is stronger in the West. The proportion of the Indigenous peoples in the provincial population and the public perception of Métis claims, and of Indigenous claims in general, are indisputably different in the western provinces, which could also explain the greater receptivity of the judges there.

Whatever the case, it is clear that the process of legal recognition of non-status Indigenous groups does not function in a vacuum, according to purely objective norms. Our results show that numerous external factors influence the process and the result. This suggests that social change cannot result solely from a legal strategy, but that the legitimacy of a claim is constructed on several fronts at once, including but not limited to law.

12 Liberal and Tribal Membership Boundaries: Descent, Consent, and Section 35

KIRSTY GOVER[1]

In the western settler states of Canada, Australia, New Zealand, and the United States, the contemporary law of non-discrimination has co-evolved with mechanisms to accommodate Indigenous claims and rights. Human rights frameworks draw on the fundamental liberal principle of inherent human equality and offer only limited accommodation of laws that confer benefits on ascriptive groups, because such laws appear to discriminate between individuals on the basis of immutable personal characteristics. Consequently, in the Western settler states, a range of legal and policy-based adaptations have been developed to insulate the logics of human and Indigenous rights from one another to the degree necessary to maintain a just state–indigenous relationship. Approaches include agreement-making between states and Indigenous communities (which can appear as forms of "contracting out" of human rights frameworks), the inclusion in human rights instruments of provisions protecting the cultural rights of Indigenous minorities, the modification of "reasonable limits" tests in human rights jurisprudence to accommodate Indigenous governance, and the development of special property-based common law doctrines, including the doctrines of Aboriginal title, associated fiduciary responsibilities,

---

1 This chapter draws substantially on a related article: "When Tribalism Meets Liberalism: Human Rights and Indigenous Boundary Problems in Canada" (2014) 64:2 UTLJ 206. The author is grateful for comments received from participants at the "35@30" Conference, hosted by the Faculty of Law, University of Toronto, 27–29 October 2012. Special thanks to Robert Goodin, Miranda Johnson, Morris Litman, Kent McNeil, Lael Weis, and anonymous reviewers for comments on earlier drafts. Thanks also to the Melbourne Law School Research Service. All errors and opinions are my own.

and the principle of the "honour of the Crown." Only Canada, however, has enacted a special Indigenous rights provision that operates alongside a constitutional bill of rights: section 35 of the Canadian *Constitution Act 1982*.

I begin with the premise that these adaptations of human rights norms are expressions of a developing settler-state political theory and that they usefully show where existing liberal democratic theories "run out" and must be modified to accommodate the particular circumstances of settler societies. In particular, the move from the recognition of Indigenous "collective rights" to the operationalization of Indigenous jurisdiction reveals the limits of human rights methodologies. Self-governing Indigenous communities are no longer only rights-bearers but are also responsible for the protection of the human rights of persons subject to their jurisdiction, acting through their representative institutions. Nowhere is this shift from rights-recognition to reconciliation more essential than in the contestation of Indigenous membership boundaries. In this chapter I consider the capacity of section 35 and associated judicial methodologies to assist in the resolution of Indigenous membership disputes, when the *Charter*'s non-discrimination provisions are brought to bear on First Nations' membership rules. Given the evolving controversy in Canada over gender discrimination in First Nations' membership governance, and the striking persistence of descent-based differentiation in the *Indian Act* and in First Nations' membership codes, it seems timely to take a step back from the positive law on this issue and ask a broader question: why are disputes about Indigenous membership so difficult to resolve in a human rights framework? In this chapter I suggest that some insight on this question can be gained by framing Indigenous membership disputes as democratic boundary problems.

Disputes about descent-based Indigenous membership rules arise from competing claims for limited resources and status, but they are also ideological struggles over the constitutive premises of tribal and liberal democracies and the boundaries of those demoi. The "boundary paradox" is one of the most intractable puzzles of democratic theory. If a demos is necessarily bounded, so that some people are excluded, what normative principle could justify these exclusions? The answer cannot be found within democratic theory itself, since the identification of a demos logically precedes democratic decision-making. When Indigenous boundaries are contested, as they are in membership disputes, human rights adjudication provides the theatre within which these deep constitutive and theoretical questions are debated. But non-discrimination law is firmly premised in the liberal tradition, and liberalism is not neutral on the question of boundaries. Applied to expressly kinship-based polities like tribes, it potentially denies to tribes the capacity to distribute membership by reference to characteristics listed as "prohibited grounds" in human rights law, including, most problematically, race or "national or ethnic origin."[2] Because non-discrimination principles identify prohibited grounds of exclusion (gender, for example), but do not usually provide a positive theory of permissible grounds, there is a danger that the application of unmodified non-discrimination law to Indigenous communities could progressively divest them of their means of self-constitution.

Part I of this chapter considers political theories of boundary problems and discusses their possible application in the tribal context. Part II examines the distinctive role to be played by section 35 of Canada's *Constitution Act 1982* in tempering non-discrimination logics, along with sections 1 (the "reasonable limits" test) and 25 (the "aboriginal rights savings provision") of the *Canadian Charter of Human Rights and Freedoms*. In order to show the effect of using unmodified human rights norms to evaluate indigenous boundaries, in Part III I consider the efforts of the UN Human Rights Committee in *Lovelace v Canada* to apply the *International Covenant on Civil and Political Rights* to an Indigenous membership dispute. I conclude in Part IV that a distinctive but precarious methodology can be discerned in Canadian law and policy, in which the "reasonableness" of Aboriginal descent-based exclusions is assessed relative to the characteristics of a free and democratic *Aboriginal* community. I suggest that this adaptation of liberal non-discrimination norms is much more than just a concession to Indigenous communities as interest groups. It is an expression of the continuing importance of kinship and descent boundaries in settler-state constitutionalism, originating in the colonial encounter of Indigenous and non-Indigenous populations, understood (problematically) in settler law as a meeting of two races, as well as of multiple bodies politic.

---

2 In this article I use the words "tribe" and "tribal" advisedly, as generic terms to describe historic, Indigenous, kinship-based communities in the Western settler states. I acknowledge that it is not a word used to describe Aboriginal peoples in Canada (as it is in New Zealand and the United States). I use "First Nation" or "Aboriginal" as appropriate when discussing Canadian law and policy.

I. The Comparative Backdrop: Why the Canadian Experience Is Uniquely Instructive

Recognized self-governing tribes are increasingly influential actors in the Western settler states of Canada, New Zealand, Australia, and the United States. Across all four countries there are now nearly 1500 officially recognized tribal institutions exercising various forms of jurisdiction, and the vast majority of these exercise primary jurisdiction over membership governance.[3] At the time of writing, Canada had recognized 24 self-governing Aboriginal communities and 617 "Indian Act" First Nations. Of these, 241 "Section 10 First Nations" now govern their own membership, having opted out of the Act's Indian status provisions. My 2008 survey of 535 current tribal constitutions and membership codes from all four countries shows that tribes use descent (not birthplace) to identify persons who are members by birthright.[4] Most also admit qualifying non-descendants under certain conditions, by processes recognizably similar to the naturalization procedures used by states.[5]

To evaluate any aspect of tribal membership governance, it is necessary to first ask what an optimally inclusive tribe might look like. It seems clear, at least, that a tribe cannot be expected to admit all comers (such a community would not be a tribe at all, nor, arguably, would it be a "community"). In the public law of the Western settler states, the tribal exclusion of *legally non-Indigenous* applicants is accepted, notwithstanding the fact that it appears on its face, and as a matter of legal doctrine, to discriminate on the basis of race,[6] or on one of the race cognates used in settler-state non-discrimination law: national or ethnic origin,[7] nationality,[8] or descent.[9] Distinctions made *between* legally Indigenous applicants are much more controversial, especially rules

---

3 Kirsty Gover, *Tribal Constitutionalism: States, Tribes and the Governance of Membership* (Oxford: Oxford University Press, 2010).
4 *Ibid* ch 2.
5 *Ibid* at 36–39.
6 For judicial views on aboriginality (and non-aboriginality) as "race," see *R v Kapp*, [2008] 2 SCR 483 [*Kapp*], especially paras 29, 56, and 114, also *R v Drybones*, [1970] SCR 282, at 298.
7 *Canadian Human Rights Act*, RSC 1985, c H-6, s 3(1); Racial Discrimination Act 1970 (Au), s 9(1); *New Zealand Human Rights Act 1993 (Human Rights Act (NZ))*, s 21(1)g.
8 *Human Rights Act (NZ)*, s 21(1)g.
9 *Racial Discrimination Act 1970* (Au), s 9(1).

that measure "degrees" of descent, corresponding to the number of a person's recognized Indigenous ancestors. Qualitative descent rules of this kind are used by tribes and settler governments in Canada and the United States, but not in Australia and New Zealand. These rules are a long-standing feature of public law in North America. They are used to regulate entitlements for Indigenous persons, are accepted as legitimate forms of tribal self-constitution in federal law and policy, and have not yet been successfully challenged in court. In the United States, however, the necessity of evaluating tribal descent-based exclusions has been postponed by the doctrine of tribal sovereign immunity, which shields tribal membership rules from scrutiny in federal court.[10] This means effectively that of the four Western liberal settler democracies, substantive legal disputation about the compatibility of non-discrimination law and qualitative descent rules in the law of indigeneity, is possible only in Canada.

Part of the puzzle of the Canadian status quo, however, is that while gender discrimination in the allocation of Indian status and Aboriginal membership has proved a source of heated debate and litigation,[11] qualitative measures of *descent* have not been the subject of a direct legal challenge.[12] Similarly, while in the post-*Charter* era the gender-discriminatory aspects of the *Canadian Citizenship Act* and the *Indian Act* (including the Act-dependent aspects of First Nations membership codes) have been removed by legislative amendment, qualitative descent-rules remain in place in those statutes. The persistence of these distinctions in Canadian law thus seems to require justification.

The latest amendments to the *Canadian Citizenship Act* restrict citizenship by descent to the first generation born abroad, meaning that a foreign-born child of a Canadian citizen cannot pass citizenship to his or her foreign-born child.[13] In other words, Canada deploys a membership rule that discriminates against some descendants by reference to their "degree" of descent from a Canadian-born ancestor. In addition to the *jus sanguinis* use of descent rules in the allocation

---

10 *Santa Clara Pueblo v Martinez* (1978), 436 US 49.
11 *Sawridge Band v Canada*, [1996] 1 FC 3 [*Sawridge* 1996], and ensuing litigation. See also the helpful analysis in Caroline Dick, *The Perils of Identity: Group Rights and the Politics of Intragroup Difference* (Vancouver: University of British Columbia Press, 2011).
12 For a thorough treatment of the likelihood of such a challenge, see Pamela D Palmater, *Beyond Blood: Rethinking Indigenous Identity* (Saskatoon: Purich, 2011).
13 *Ibid* s 3(3).

of citizenship, Canada, like other liberal democracies, also deploys the principle of *jus soli* to assign birthright citizenship to any person born in Canada, except if that person's parents were non-Canadian foreign diplomats.[14] In addition, qualifying permanent residents may apply to be naturalized as Canadian citizens. In this way, restrictions on the eligibility of some foreign-born descendants are supplemented by the possibility that some persons who do not descend from Canadian citizens are nonetheless able to acquire citizenship. In contrast, while a majority of "Section 10 First Nations" in Canada also allow naturalization of persons who do not acquire membership at birth, none allocates birthright membership to a non-descendant by reference to that person's birthplace.[15] The *Indian Act* is likewise a purely *jus sanguinis* regime, in which status is allocated only to descendants, regardless of their birthplace, and no person can be "naturalized" as an Indian.[16] The Act retains a "second-generation cut-off rule" that denies Indian status to persons with only one Indian grandparent.[17] Across all four CANZUS countries, the *jus sanguinis* rules used by tribes are not supplemented by *jus soli* principles.[18] Thus both states and tribes use qualitative descent-based rules, and both admit persons as members who did not acquire citizenship at birth, but only states allocate citizenship to persons born in the territory who are not the descendant of a member.

14 *Ibid* s 3(1)a and s 2.
15 The 2008 study considers "first iteration" membership codes only. First Nations are obliged to receive the approval of the minister of Aboriginal and northern affairs for the initial code, but thereafter are free to amend the code's provisions without federal oversight.
16 Adopted children are arguably an exception, but it is probably more accurate to say that they obtain their Indianness "by descent" rather than through naturalization. See *Indian Act*, RSC 1985, c I-5 [*Indian Act*], s 2(1), "'child' includes a legally adopted child and a child adopted in accordance with Indian custom."
17 Provisions restricting Indian status to persons with a sufficient "degree" of descent first appeared in the Act in 1951. Bradford W Morse, Robert Groves, D'Arcy Vermette, & Canadian Human Rights Commission, *Balancing Individual and Collective Rights: Implementation of Section 1.2 of the Canadian Human Rights Act* (Ottawa: Canadian Human Rights Commission, 2010) at 47.
18 This is typical of tribes in Australia, New Zealand, and the United States. My 2008 study indicates that some US tribes assign birth-right membership only to persons whose parent or parents were born on the reservation, but only one refers to the birthplace of the applicant. Gover, *supra* note 3 at 40.

While Canada's allocation of *citizenship* by qualitative descent rules has been thoroughly "naturalized," and the *Indian Act*'s second-generation rule remains intact for the time being, "blood quantum" rules used by First Nations are widely regarded as a paradigmatic expression of illiberalism.[19] In fact, all of these forms of descent-based membership are difficult to defend in a liberal democracy, since they all appear to distribute status and resources arbitrarily by reference to the circumstances of a person's birth, and to discriminate against ineligible persons on the basis of immutable characteristics. In the case of Indigenous peoples, descent from pre-colonial ancestors has allowed them to be rendered in settler state law collectively as an Indigenous "race," so that some descent-based exclusions also appear on their face to be racially discriminatory. In addition, tribes are obliged to defend their membership criteria in a way that states are not, because they lack the sovereign prerogatives that allow states very wide discretion to determine their membership in international law. The International Convention on the Elimination of All Forms of Racial Discrimination, for example, preserves the authority of state parties to discriminate on the basis of race in law governing citizenship and nationality.[20] What tools exist in political theory to make sense of the apparently discriminatory effects of human boundaries, especially those that enclose kinship groups?

---

19 Canada, Royal Commission on Aboriginal Peoples, *Report of the Royal Commission on Aboriginal People* (Ottawa: Canada Royal Commission on Aboriginal Peoples, 1996) at 239; Will Kymlicka, "American Multiculturalism and the 'Nations Within'" in Duncan Ivison, Paul Patton, & Will Sanders, eds, *Political Theory and the Rights of Indigenous Peoples* (Cambridge: Cambridge University Press, 2000) at 216n23; Patrick Macklem, *Indigenous difference and the Constitution of Canada* (Toronto: University of Toronto Press, 2001) at 56; Duncan Ivison, "The Logic of Aboriginal Rights" (2003) 3 Ethnicities 321 at 334n15. Also, more generally, Sebastien Grammond, *Identity Captured by Law: Membership in Canada's Indigenous Peoples and Linguistic Minorities* (Montreal & Kingston: McGill-Queen's University Press, 2009); Grammond, "Discrimination in the Rules of Indian Status and the McIvor Case" (2009) 35 Queen's LJ 421; and Palmater, *supra* note 12.

20 Convention on the Elimination of All Forms of Racial Discrimination (1965) UNTS vol 660 at 195. Art 1(2) provides that the convention "shall not apply to distinctions, exclusions, restrictions or preferences made by a State Party to this Convention between citizens and non-citizens," and art 1(3) provides that "[n]othing in this Convention may be interpreted as affecting in any way the legal provisions of States Parties concerning nationality, citizenship or naturalization, provided that such provisions do not discriminate against any particular nationality."

II. The Boundary Problem in Democratic Theory: Implications for Tribal Democracies

Democratic theorists do not usually investigate the principles on which a demos is constituted, tending overwhelmingly to assume the pre-constitution of such a community, and then to turn their attention to the values and processes by which that demos should govern itself. Ian Shapiro and Casiano Hacker-Cordon have called this lacuna an "enduring embarrassment of democratic theory," one that reveals "a chicken-and-egg problem [that] lurks at democracy's core."[21] The problem of "constituting the demos" arises because the identification of the membership of a demos seems necessarily to precede any decision made collectively by that demos.[22] We cannot, as Robert Goodin has observed, have an election without an electorate.[23] Accordingly, in the constitution of any demos there occur exclusions that confront liberal democratic principles of equality and non-discrimination, and would likely be indefensible were they to be made between *members* of a demos.[24] It may be, as Robert Dahl has argued, that wherever boundary problems arise in democratic reasoning, "there is no theoretical solution to the puzzle, but only pragmatic ones."[25] Likewise Frederick Whelan has suggested that where exogenous principles "fail, like democracy, to provide clear guidance, it appears that our only choices are to abide by the arbitrary verdicts of history or war, or to appeal on an ad hoc basis to other principles, none of which commands general respect."[26] Even if this is true, the positive political theory of these principles must still

---

21 Shapiro and Hacker-Cordon, "Outer Edges and Inner Edges" in Shapiro and Hacker-Cordon, eds, *Democracy's Edges* (Cambridge: Cambridge University Press, 1999) 1.

22 Robert E Goodin, "Enfranchising All Affected Interests, and Its Alternatives" (2007) 35 Philosophy and Public Affairs 40 at 41. See also Robert A Dahl, *Democracy and Its Critics* (New Haven, CT: Yale University Press, 1989) at 109; Genevieve Nootens, "Democracy and Legitimacy in Plurinational Societies" (2009) 8 Contemporary Political Theory 276 at 278–79; Shapiro and Hacker-Cordon, *ibid*; and generally, Frederick G Whelan, "Prologue: Democratic Theory and the Boundary Problem" in J Roland Pennock and John W Chapman, eds, *Liberal Democracy* (New York: New York University Press, 1983) 13.

23 Goodin, *supra* note 23 at 43; Whelan, *supra* note 23 at 13.

24 Goodin, *supra* note 23 at 43, Whelan, *supra* note 23 at 22.

25 Robert A Dahl, *After the Revolution: Authority in a Good Society* (New Haven, CT: Yale University Press, 1970) [Dahl, *After*] at 59.

26 Whelan, *supra* note 22 at 40.

be evaluated when they are contested. In the current context, because non-discrimination law is firmly premised in the liberal tradition, it has a logic that favours some "pragmatic" solutions over others (and therefore benefits some people more than others). I am concerned in this chapter to draw attention to the consequences of this logic for tribes, particularly the consequences of the liberal "all-affected principle" that seems dominant in current thinking on boundary problems. I discuss this principle and its alternatives below.

Broadly speaking, liberal social contract theories suggest that any group of consenting individuals can form a demos, and members need not be linked together by any pre-political values or affiliations. In answer to the normative question of who *should* be included in an optimally inclusive demos, consent theorists tend to advance a version of the "all-affected" principle, a corollary of the liberal principle that no person should be governed without consent, arguing that the basis of a person's membership in a demos should be the exercise of governance authority over that person.[27] In practice, the all-affected principle favours territorially bounded communities, because it is the coincidence of territory and compulsory jurisdiction inherent in sovereign statehood that renders a group of individuals similarly affected by the exercise of political authority.[28] As some commentators have pointed out, however, the utility of the all-affected principle is undermined by constraints of logic, because the identity of those "affected" by a decision cannot easily be determined in advance of the decision itself.[29] Perhaps more significantly in the context of this article (which is concerned fundamentally with state–tribal relationships), it is subject to the powerful empirical claim that it does not reflect the actual practice of any existing state, because all states assert authority over persons who are present in their territories, even if those persons are not citizens and have no right to participate in that community's political processes. The fact is that all liberal democratic states assign citizenship primarily

---

27 Dahl, *supra* note 26 at 122; Ian Shapiro, *Democratic Justice* (New Haven, CT: Yale University Press, 1999) at 37. See Nasstrom for the argument that the principle is better understood as the "all-subjected" principle: Sofia Nasstrom, "The Challenge of the All-Affected Principle" (2011) 59 Political Studies 116.

28 Whelan, *supra* note 22 at 21.

29 Gustaf Arrhenius, "The Boundary Problem in Democratic Theory" in Folke Tersman, ed, *Democracy Unbound: Basic Explorations I* (Stockholm: Filosofiska Insitutionen, Stockholm University, 2005) 14 at 20–21.

by birthright, not by consent and not by reference to an "all-affected" principle.[30] Accordingly, as Ayelet Shachar has pointed out, unchosen birthright membership rules "clearly represent ... an exception to the basic tenets of liberal political theory."[31] Critiques that highlight the failure of liberalism to provide an adequate explanatory or justificatory theory of boundaries have been given normative purchase by a group of scholars who can be loosely categorized for present purposes as "communitarians." Might communitarian thinking yield an alternative or supplement to the "all-affected" principle that could inform liberal engagement with the boundaries of tribes?

The key communitarian contribution to (and critique of) liberal theory is that individuals are situated in and constituted by their communities, and that liberal social contract models (most acutely, Rawls's model) over-emphasize individual agency and autonomy in a way that degrades the importance of community in constructing a person's choices and preferences. In communitarian thinking, an ideal demos is one structured by close civic relations and "common sympathies,"[32] especially of the kind derived from unchosen pre-political attributes, such as kinship.[33] These, they say, provide the "high degree of mutual understanding, trust, and commitment" that is necessary for effective democratic governance.[34] Michael Walzer, for example, has argued that that "[s]tates are like families rather than clubs, for it is a feature of families that their members are morally connected to people they have not chosen."[35] The analogy he draws between states and families supports a sharp distinction between the moral obligations of members

30 Whelan, *supra* note 22 at 26.
31 Ayelet Shachar, "The Thin Line between Imposition and Consent: A Critique of Birthright Membership Regimes and Their Implications" in Martha Minow & Nancy L Rosenblum, eds, *Breaking the Cycles of Hatred: Memory, Law, and Repair* (New Jersey: Princeton University Press, 2002) 200 [Shachar *Thin*] at 210.
32 John Stuart Mill, *Considerations on Representative Government* (New York: Harper and Brothers, 1862) at 546.
33 Susan Moller Okin, *Justice, Gender and the Family* (New York: Basic Books, 1989); Clarissa Rile Hayward, "Binding Problems, Boundary Problems: The Trouble with 'Democratic Citizenship'" in Seyla Benhabib, Ian Shapiro, & Danilo Petranovic, eds, *Identities, Affiliations, and Allegiances* (Cambridge: Cambridge University Press, 2007) 119 at 181.
34 Charles Taylor, "The Dynamics of Democratic Exclusion" (1998) 9 J Democracy 143 at 148.
35 Michael Walzer, *Spheres of Justice: A Defense of Pluralism and Equality* (New York: Basic Books, 1983) at 41.

to one another, and those owed by members to non-members. The family is constructed by obligations of "kinship and love"[36] and "[k]inship ties and sexual relations are commonly thought to constitute a domain beyond the reach of distributive justice."[37] According to Walzer then, membership in a kinship group (be it a state, tribe, or family) is a good, and in fact may be "the primary good we distribute to one another,"[38] but one that cannot be distributed in accordance with general principles of justice. Instead the allocation of membership, however arbitrary, establishes a community within which other goods can be distributed justly. In Walzer's communitarian paradigm, then, liberal concepts of equality and non-discrimination are irrelevant to the constitution of kinship-based communities, and, it seems, exclusions based on gender or race are no more normatively suspect than others.

An alternative argument is vividly asserted in a body of scholarship broadly positioned (as I understand it) within feminist political theory, that reclaims and emphasizes the correlation between family, nationhood, and the state. Building on the efforts of feminist theorists to draw attention to the politics and political importance of family relationships, these scholars suggest that the liberal state has not succeeded in differentiating itself from the family and in fact relies on arbitrary measures of genealogy and race to constitute itself in ways that are not distinguishable from the kinship ties that constitute families and other pre-political or "primitive" societies.[39] If these communities are arbitrarily and unjustly constituted, so too are liberal democratic states. Jacqueline Stevens, for example, suggests that social contract theories not only exclude the family from normative theory in ways that excuse and perpetuate injustice, but also obscure the kinship-based structure of liberal democratic states, and render invisible the non-consensual distribution of citizenship by birthright. "The fact is," says Stevens, "that the paradigmatic membership structure for all political societies derives from invocations of birth and ancestry."[40] Even in the liberal

---

36 *Ibid* at 52.
37 *Ibid* at 227.
38 *Ibid* at 31.
39 Particularly Ayelet Shachar, Jacqueline Stevens, & Nira Yuval-Davis.
40 Jacqueline Stevens, *Reproducing the State* (Princeton: Princeton University Press, 1999) at 51. See also Ayelet Shachar, *Children of a Lesser State: Sustaining Global Inequality through Citizenship Laws* (Jean Monnet Working Paper 2/03, EU Jean Monnet Chair NYU School of Law, 2003) at 21.

democracies, birthright rules have, as Shachar observes, "an immensely powerful hold on our imagination" and considerable "staying power," notwithstanding the fact that they distribute public goods arbitrarily, in accordance with the "accident of birth" [41] and the "sheer luck of descent."[42] By emphasizing the equivalency of family and state organizational forms, critiques of birthright citizenship help to complicate the polarization of states and tribes as ideal types, and point to the distinctive theoretical challenges posed by birthright membership rules in both liberal and tribal democracies.

There is something of relational (and therefore jurisdictional) significance in the observation that both liberal and tribal democracies allocate membership by birthright to descendants, and exclude some descendants from the class of eligible members. If the liberal democracies are no less liberal or democratic for their reliance on descent rules, then this seems to support, in principle, an argument that these rules impose reasonable limits on the rights of excluded persons. In other words, membership rules are a distinctive form of law-making, because political societies are not voluntary organizations (despite the liberal theoretical insistence on the principle of consent and the possibility of naturalization), and because membership is a good that is inherited, as well as distributed. Membership laws, then, seem unavoidably to impose arbitrary limits on the rights of ineligible persons. Whatever standard of reasonableness can be devised from within human rights methodologies to assess the validity of membership laws, it cannot be one that wholly dismantles kinship by insisting that descent not be used to discriminate between individuals, unless the concept of statehood itself is to be undone, along with the international order it constitutes.

If they are to ensure the legitimacy of their institutions, settler societies must find a way to express a form of statehood that includes ascriptive, kinship-based polities within a liberal, consent-based constitutional order, and this necessitates the adaptation of liberal principles, including those that underpin non-discrimination law. One major challenge, then, lies in the way that *international* human rights norms are brought to bear on Indigenous membership disputes in the settler states. Can universal norms and methodologies accommodate

---

41 Shachar, *supra* note 33 at 210–11.
42 *Ibid* at 7.

the specific circumstances of settler societies, and navigate the tension between principles of non-discrimination and tribal self-constitution? In Part 3 of this article, I consider the potential of section 35 to curb the logic of non-discrimination in order to support the reconciliation of Indigenous and liberal forms of political organization in Canada. In Part 4 I consider the ways in which the United Nations' Human Rights Committee has struggled to apply an "unmodified" human rights instrument, the *International Covenant on Civil and Political Rights*, to disputes involving indigenous membership boundaries.

III. Constitutional Rights and Aboriginal Boundaries in Canada

Aboriginal boundary problems raise complicated and as yet unanswered questions of Canadian constitutional law. These turn on whether membership governance, or particular acts of membership governance, could be rights protected by section 35 of the *Constitution Act 1982*, and if so, whether and to what degree those rights are shielded from *Charter*-based discrimination claims and legislative infringement. In this section I argue that using section 35 to defend Aboriginal membership rules against section 15 claims engages questions of jurisdiction and requires a methodology that can address the reasonableness of Aboriginal law-making on membership. A section 35 claim to membership governance is not the assertion of a collective right, so much as a defence of that community's capacity to reach reasonable compromises on boundary questions by enacting laws in the tribal public interest. The *Charter*'s section 1 "reasonable limitations" provisions provides a way to reconcile tribal and liberal approaches to membership governance, by allowing a court to take account of the particular methods and values of Aboriginal communities, including the significance of descent as a constitutive rule of kinship-based polities.

The application of section 35 to First Nations' membership codes or the *Indian Act*'s status provisions has not yet been fully argued in litigation, but several membership disputes have begun to percolate through the court system, and these will shape the way Indigenous boundary disputes are conceived and approached in Canadian public law and policy. As the British Columbia Court of Appeal observed in *McIvor*,

The interplay between statutory rights of Indians and constitutionally protected aboriginal rights is a complex matter that has not, to date, been thoroughly canvassed in the case law. It seems likely that, at least for some purposes, Parliament's ability to determine who is and who is not an Indian is circumscribed.[43]

This indeterminacy is compounded by the fact that while First Nations exercise authority that has been conferred on them by the *Indian Act*, they may also exercise authority that does not derive from that Act, or from any other statute.[44] Where First Nations exercise law-making powers that either do not have a basis in legislation,[45] are legislatively recognized but not mandated,[46] or do not otherwise "originate" from other Canadian governments, they may be exercising powers of inherent self-government.[47] It is clear that where a First Nation exercises decision-making power pursuant to the *Indian Act*, including in the enactment of membership codes under section 10, it is a "federal board, commission of other tribunal," and so subject to the jurisdiction of the federal court.[48] Aboriginal governments are not, however, specifically mentioned in section 32 of the *Constitution Act*, which specifies that the *Charter* applies to "the Parliament and government of Canada" and "the legislature and government of each province."[49]

---

43 *McIvor v Canada (Registrar of Indian and Northern Affairs)* 2009 BCCA 153 at para 66.
44 Debates about the extent to which the decisions of First Nation band councils can be said to have been made "under or pursuant to" the *Indian Act* have been furthered in jurisprudence on the scope of section 67 (now repealed) of the Canadian *Human Rights Act* (that exempted from the purview of the CHRA "any provision of the *Indian Act* or any provision made under or pursuant to that Act"). Not all decisions made by First Nation band councils were immunized by section 67. See, for example, *Canada (Human Rights Commission) v Gordon Band Council*, [2001] 1 FC 124 [*Gordon*]; *Desjarlais v Piapot Band No 75* [1989] 3 FC 605; and *Shubenacadie Indian Band v Canada (Human Rights Commission) (TD)* [1998] 2 FC 198.
45 See, for example, *R v Pamajewon* [1996] 2 SCR 821 [*Pamajewon*].
46 McNeil suggests, for example, that the *Indian Act* recognizes that Indian bands retain some unextinguished customary governance powers beyond the Act's express "declaratory" references of by-law-making power. Kent McNeil, "Aboriginal Governments and the Canadian Charter of Rights and Freedoms" (1996) 34 Osgoode Hall LJ 61 at 87; also McNeil, *The Jurisdiction of Inherent Right Aboriginal Governments* (Ottawa: National Centre for First Nations Governance, 2007) at 3.
47 See discussion in *Campbell v British Columbia (AG)* [2000] 79 BCLR (3d) 122, esp para 86.
48 *Federal Courts Act* RSC 1985, c F-7, s 18; *Grismer v Squamish Indian Band* [2006] FC 1088 [*Grismer*], para 32; *Scrimbitt v Sakimay Indian Band Council* (TD) [2000] 1 FC 513 [*Scrimbitt*], para 22.
49 *Constitution Act, 1982*, being Schedule B to the *Canada Act 1982* (UK), 1982, c 11 [*Constitution Act*], s 32. See discussion in McNeil, *supra* note 47 at 68–69.

Arguably, Aboriginal governments exercising authority that is not delegated by a non-Aboriginal government do not fall within the scope of entities identified in section 32.[50] In addition, acts of self-governance may derive from "aboriginal and treaty rights" protected by section 35, if other evidentiary requirements are satisfied, calling into question the application of the *Charter* to those acts.

The relationships between section 32, section 35, and the *Charter* in respect to Aboriginal self-government has not yet been determinatively considered by a Canadian court. Meanwhile, the federal government has recognized, since 1995, "the inherent right of self-government as an existing aboriginal right under s. 35" and embarked on negotiating self-government agreements with Aboriginal communities.[51] Federal policy specifies that self-government agreements will "have to provide that the [*Charter*] applies to Aboriginal governments and institutions."[52] Of the twenty-four self-government agreements in effect at the time of writing, however, only four refer expressly to the *Charter*, specifying either that the Aboriginal government is "bound by the provisions of the Charter,"[53] or that the *Charter* applies in the exercise of "all matters within its authority."[54] At least some of the rights contained in self-government agreements are protected as "treaty rights" by section 35, and others may be protected as section 35 Aboriginal rights, but the application of the *Charter* to self-government agreements and their implementing statutes remains to be debated in court.[55]

The inclusion in section 35(1) of an Aboriginal right of self-government has been assumed, although not determinatively confirmed, however,

---

50 McNeil, *ibid* at 68.
51 McNeil, *ibid*.
52 *Ibid*.
53 *Westbank First Nation Self-Government Agreement*, 2003 s 32. None of the implementing Acts associated with self-government agreements contains reference to the *Charter*, but all specify that in the event of conflict, the agreement takes precedence over the legislation.
54 See, e.g., *Nisga'a Final Agreement*, 1999 s 9 "The Canadian Charter of Rights and Freedoms Applies to Nisga'a Government in Respect of All Matters within Its Authority, Bearing in Mind the Free and Democratic Nature of Nisga'a Government as Set Out in This Agreement." Also *Tsawwassen First Nation Final Agreement*, 2007 s 9; *Tlicho Land Claims and Self-Government Agreement*, 2003 s 2.15.
55 Brad Morse, "Twenty Years of Charter Protection: The Status of Aboriginal Peoples under the Canadian Charter of Rights and Freedoms" (2002) 21 Windsor YB Access Just 385 at 423–24.

in at least one Supreme Court case.[56] The evidentiary difficulty of proving the existence of an Aboriginal right is substantial. If argued as an Aboriginal right (as distinguished from Aboriginal title or treaty rights), a right to self-government must be proved to be an "element of a practice, custom or tradition integral to the distinctive culture of the aboriginal group claiming the right" in accordance with the "Van der Peet test."[57] Whether and how the *Charter* applies to an Aboriginal community in the exercise of a proven section 35 right turns on the meaning and effect given to section 25 of the *Constitution Act*, which specifies that *Charter* rights "shall not be construed as to abrogate or derogate from any aboriginal, treaty or other rights or freedoms that pertain to the aboriginal peoples of Canada," a category of rights that would include, but is not limited to, rights protected by section 35.[58] Jurisprudence on section 25 is sparse. Current debates turn on the degree to which section 25 "shields" section 35 rights from *Charter* provisions.[59] In the 2008 Supreme Court case of *R v Kapp*, without relying on section 25, the majority indicated that the question is still live, querying the claim that in a relevant case, the provision "would constitute an absolute bar" to a *Charter*-based claim, "as distinguished from an interpretive provision informing the construction of potentially conflicting Charter rights."[60]

For present purposes, one outstanding question that arises from debates about section 25 is whether and to what extent that provision might shield a section 35 right to Aboriginal *membership self-governance* from claims based on section 15 of the *Charter*, which prohibits discrimination on the basis of enumerated and analogous grounds, including race.[61] This engages deep controversies about how the concept of equality applies when Aboriginality and Aboriginal difference is in question. Some commentators have argued that since the purpose of

---

56 *Pamajewon, supra* note 46, paras 24 and 25. Kent McNeil, "Challenging Legislative Infringements of the Inherent Aboriginal Right of Self-Government" (2003) 22 Windsor YB Access Just 329 at 338.

57 *Van der Peet, supra* note 5 at para 46.

58 *Corbiere v Canada (Minister of Indian and Northern Affairs)*, [1999] 2 SCR 203 [*Corbiere*] at para 52.

59 *R v Agawa*, (1988), 28 OAC 201, at para 11; and *Campbell v British Columbia (AG)* [2000] 79 BCLR (3d) 122 *supra* note 48, at para 156.

60 *Kapp*, supra note 6 at para 64.

61 Canada, Royal Commission on Aboriginal Peoples, *Partners in Confederation: Aboriginal Peoples, Self-Government and the Constitution* (Ottawa: Royal Commission on Aboriginal Peoples, 1993) at 39.

section 35 is to protect the unique constitutional status of Aboriginal Canadians, differences between Aboriginal and non-Aboriginal persons are not "discriminatory" in the terms of the *Charter*, and a section 35 right to membership should be entirely insulated by section 25 from the application of section 15.[62] For a time, questions about the connection between *Charter* provisions (sections 15 and 25), the *Indian Act*, and section 35 seemed likely to be resolved in the *Sawridge Band* litigation, which has been the major vehicle for the assertion of section 35 rights in First Nations membership governance.[63] After twenty-three years of convoluted litigation, however, the band's claim against Canada finally ground to a halt in 2009.[64] Nonetheless, the *Sawridge Band* case provides some indication of how a similar claim might be structured in the future.

The Sawridge Band is a small First Nation in Alberta.[65] Along with other "Section 10 First Nations," it elected in 1985 to take control of its membership governance, and subsequently sought to exclude a number of persons who were legislatively entitled to band membership (mostly Indian women reinstated in accordance with the 1985 "Bill C-31" amendments to the *Indian Act*).[66] The Sawridge Band is not alone in its resistance to the C-31 *Indian Act* status and membership provisions. A number of First Nations strenuously object to the reinstatement of persons who had lost or been denied membership under the old *Indian Act* regime, arguing variously that the influx of new members places unsustainable pressure on land and services on the reserves,[67]

---

62 See, e.g., Macklem, *supra* note 49, at 227 and 229.
63 The plaintiffs at first instance were the Sawridge, Sarcee, and Ermineskine Bands. *Sawridge* 1996, *supra* note 11.
64 *Sawridge Band v Canada* [2008] FC 322; *Sawridge Band v Canada* [2009] FCA 123 [*Sawridge* 2009], leave denied [2009] SCCA No 248.
65 Statistics Canada reported that the 2006 national census showed the Sawridge reservation was home to forty-five people, of whom thirty-five identified as Aboriginal. Statistics Canada, 2006 Community Profiles, "Sawridge 150G," online: Statistics Canada <www12.statcan.ca/census-recensement/2006/dp-pd/prof/92-591/details/page.cfm?Lang=E&Geo1=CSD&Code1=4817832&Geo2=PR&Code2=48&Data=Count&SearchText=sa>. Other information provided by the AANDC records a 2011 band population of 379: Aboriginal and Northern Affairs Canada, "Registered Indian Population by Sex and Type of Residence by Group, Responsibility Centre and Region 2011 – Alberta," online: <https://www.aadnc-aandc.gc.ca/eng/1351794569236/1351794633025>.
66 *Indian Act, supra* note 17 at ss 10(4) and 10(5).
67 See, for example, *Six Nations of the Grand River Band Council v Henderson*, [1997] 1 CNLR 202 at paras 6–7.

disrupts the cultural integrity of on-reserve communities, interferes with existing members' freedom of association, and violates the rights of those communities to self-govern and to apply customary membership norms.[68] Some First Nations have refused to provide services to reinstated women,[69] denied them the right to vote,[70] or have otherwise discriminated against "C-31" members in reserve governance.[71] At least one First Nation has expressed its opposition to the Bill C-31 amendments in a communication to the Human Rights Committee of the UN, ironically, the same body that heard Sandra Lovelace's claim in 1981, the determination of which lead to enactment of Bill C-31 in 1985.[72]

The Sawridge Band's central argument was that the relevant provisions of the *Indian Act* (sections 8 to 14) contravened their section 35 right to determine their own membership, either as a "standalone" Aboriginal right, or as an incident of a right to self-governance.[73] The judge at first instance found that even if a right to control membership could be shown to be protected by section 35, the right to discriminate on the basis of gender in the governance of membership had conclusively been extinguished by section 35(4), which guarantees section 35 rights equally to male and female persons.[74] Likewise, any infringement of their freedom of association claim, based on section 2(d) of the *Charter*, was justified by section 28, guaranteeing *Charter* rights equally to male

---

68 *Sawridge* 1996, *supra* note 11, at 147; *Canadian Charter of Rights and Freedoms*, s 2(b), Part 1 of the *Constitution Act, 1982*, being Schedule B to the *Canada Act 1982* (UK), 1982, c 11 [*Canadian Charter*], s 2(d).

69 See, e.g., *Gordon, supra* note 45.

70 *Scrimbitt, supra* note 49. The judge held that persons entitled to be reinstated under Bill C-31 could not be denied membership consistently with section 10 of the Act, and the denial of voting rights to reinstated members constituted a violation of the guarantees in section 77 of the *Indian Act*.

71 Megan Furi, Jill Wherett, & Parliament of Canada, Political and Social Affairs Division, *Indian Status and Band Membership Issues* (Ottawa: Library of Parliament, 1996, revised 2003), online: Parliament of Canada <www.parl.gc.ca/Content/LOP/ResearchPublications/bp410-e.pdf> at 7.

72 *RL et al v Canada, Communication No. 358/1989 (1 April 1989)*. UN Doc CCPR/C/43/D/358/1989 at para 3.3, in which members of the Whispering Pines Band of British Columbia claimed that the *Indian Act* amendments infringed their freedom of association under article 22 of the *International Covenant of Civil and Political Rights*.

73 The difference between these two approaches was litigated in a series of cases between 2003 and 2009. See discussion in *Sawridge Band v Canada*, [2006] FCJ No 1525.

74 *Constitution Act, supra* note 50 at s 35(4); *Sawridge* 1996, *supra* note 11 at 60.

and female persons.[75] Much depends, then, on the characterisation of the Sawridge Band's membership code as one that discriminates on the basis of gender and therefore attracts the express prohibitions contained in *Charter* and in section 35(4) in a way that other prohibited grounds (including race and its analogues) would not. In 1997 the band obtained an order for the retrial of the first instance decision, successfully arguing that they had a reasonable apprehension of judicial bias.[76] That retrial has not yet taken place. However, the Crown was able to secure a mandatory interlocutory injunction in 2004, compelling the band to comply with the *Indian Act* and enrol the excluded persons.[77] Despite the band's efforts to appeal this decision and marshal evidence to continue the section 35 challenge in retrial, at the time of writing they had been unable to comply with applicable evidentiary rules and their case had been dismissed.[78]

The Sawridge Band's claim, then, is a defence of its efforts to govern its membership inconsistently with the *Indian Act* by asserting an inherent section 35 right, which it claims was unjustifiably infringed by the 1985 amendments. The logic of this argument is in keeping with the dominant understanding of section 35 as a measure that protects collective Aboriginal and treaty rights against legislative interference. However, the justificatory tests developed by the Supreme Court to assess federal infringement of section 35 rights have concerned Aboriginal title and property-based Aboriginal rights (especially fishing rights), so that the concept of a "substantial and compelling" legislative objective first identified in *R v Sparrow* has so far been elaborated in reference to the use and regulation of land and natural resources.[79] Claims to self-governance rights explicitly engage the relationship between Aboriginal governments and persons subject to their jurisdiction, in a way that jurisprudence on collective Aboriginal property rights so far has not.[80]

---

75 *Canadian Charter, supra* note 69 at s 28; *Sawridge* 1996, *supra* note 11 at 147.
76 First instance, *Sawridge* 1996, *supra* note 11; *Sawridge* 1997, *supra* note 19; *Sawridge Band v Canada* 2001 FCA 338; appeal: *Sawridge Band v Canada* [2002] 2 FC 346.
77 *Sawridge Band v Canada*, [2003] 4 FC 748; *Sawridge Band v Canada* [2004] 3 FCR 274.
78 *Sawridge* 2009, *supra* note 65.
79 *R v Sparrow*, [1990] 1 SCR 1075 [*Sparrow*] at 40. See also *Delgamuukw v British Columbia*, [1997] 3 SCR 1010 [*Delgamuukw*], discussing infringement tests for Aboriginal title.
80 See *Campbell v British Columbia (AG)* [2000] 79 BCLR (3d) 122 at para 114. "On the face of it, it seems that a right to aboriginal title, a communal right which includes occupation and use, must of necessity include the right of the communal ownership to make decisions about that occupation and use, matters commonly described as governmental functions. This seems essential when the ownership is communal."

Communal title and inherent self-governance are, however, as Duncan Ivison has pointed out, "difficult to keep apart for very long."[81] The idea that a right of self-governance may be a concomitant of Aboriginal title is the subject of much academic commentary and may yet shape the evolution of section 35 jurisprudence. Such a concept of self-governance would not need to be framed as an Aboriginal right and defended against the restrictive "integral to the distinctive culture" *Van der Peet* test. However, the right to govern membership is most likely to be litigated, as it was in *Sawridge Band*, as a standalone Aboriginal right, rather than as a corollary of Aboriginal title.[82] The application of a justificatory test to evaluate interference with such a right raises other, even more complex normative questions about the application of the *Charter* and the possibility of *Charter*-based discrimination claims.

As complex as the *Sawridge Band* litigation was, it did not, as argued, require a court to consider an individual's *Charter*-based challenge to a section 35 right exercised by an Aboriginal government. This is significant, because the closer the proximity of the complainant to an Aboriginal government, and the greater the impact on that person of the law in question, the more difficult it is to conceive of that *Charter* challenge as one that threatens Aboriginal "collective rights." Instead, claims brought by persons directly affected by First Nations' membership rules would resemble the "ordinary" assertion of an individual right against the legislative act of a public government. This is especially true if the right asserted is not based on a legislative entitlement of the kind in question in the *Sawridge Band* and *McIvor* litigation.[83] If and when such a dispute is heard in these terms by a Canadian court, the argument that a collective right to self-governance should enjoy absolute immunity from the *Charter*, by virtue of section 25, will be much harder to sustain. A new approach to reconciliation would be required. Fundamentally, this is because membership disputes call into question the composition of the collective purporting to exercise collective rights, that is, they directly

81 Duncan Ivison, *Postcolonial Liberalism* (Cambridge: Cambridge University Press, 2002) at 149.
82 See for persuasive commentary on the governance component of communal Aboriginal title, see Jeremy Webber, "Beyond Regret: Mabo's Implications for Australian Constitutionalism" in Duncan Ivison, Paul Patton, & Will Sanders, eds, *Political Theory and the Rights of Indigenous Peoples* (Cambridge: Cambridge University Press, 2001); and Kent McNeil, "Self-Government and the Inalienability of Aboriginal Title" (2002) 47 McGill LJ 473 at 486.
83 See also, e.g., *Scrimbitt, supra* note 49.

implicate an Aboriginal boundary problem. They accordingly confound the idea that collective section 35 rights are in some way inherently and necessarily opposed to individual *Charter* rights, such that section 25 should form an impermeable bulwark between them. This unique feature of *Charter*-based membership disputes also ensures that they are most likely to arise between Aboriginal peoples, who in the case of First Nations may stand on either side of the "status Indian" boundary or the "band membership" boundary (or both). Membership disputes may thus involve more than one Indigenous community, each of which might assert a section 35 right to establish a membership boundary. In inter-Indigenous disputes, the guidance offered by the Supreme Court to the effect that the underlying purpose of section 35 is to reconcile the pre-existence of Aboriginal societies with the sovereignty of the Crown would be far less instructive.[84]

There is a danger, then, that the existing jurisprudence on section 35, focused on recognizing collective Aboriginal rights opposable to non-Aboriginal governments, may work to downplay the jurisdictional capacities and responsibilities of Aboriginal and First Nations governments. Decision-makers who focus on the external protective function of section 35 and its section 25 "shield" may fail to take account of the ways in which First Nations governments themselves resolve the competing claims of persons subject to or affected by their jurisdiction.[85] Put another way, if it is accepted that not all would-be members can be included in a First Nation, and in fact not all would-be members can be included in any political society, properly so-called, then individual human rights are unlikely to supply a defensible boundary on their own. Instead, the task of governments faced with boundary problems is to develop a persuasive justification for limitations imposed on the rights of non-members. This is particularly so for groups, like tribes and states, that are constituted primarily through the arbitrary mechanisms of birthright membership. Reconciliation in this context would

---

84 *Delgamuukw, supra* note 80 at 1123–24, per Lamer J; *Van der Peet, supra* note 5, especially at para 31, per Lamer CJ; see also *Taku River Tlingit First Nation v British Columbia (Project Assessment Director)* 2004 SCC 74 at para 42: "The purpose of s. 35(1) of the Constitution Act, 1982 is to facilitate the ultimate reconciliation of prior Aboriginal occupation with de facto Crown sovereignty."

85 Canada, Royal Commission on Aboriginal Peoples, *supra* note 102 at 39, drawing a distinction between "the *right* of self-government proper and the *exercise* of governmental powers flowing from that right" [emphasis in original].

require that liberal principles of membership (consent and non-discrimination) should reasonably accommodate tribal principles (descent and kinship). Crucially, then, the adjudication of any *Charter*-based membership claim should take due account of the agency exercised by Aboriginal governments in conducting their *own* balancing exercises as part of their right and responsibility to manage the competing claims of group members (and aspirant members) in the tribal public interest.

Given these features, if and when section 35 is argued as part of an Aboriginal government's defence to a section 15 non-discrimination claim brought by a person affiliated with that community, in substance this would look not so much like an assertion of a collective right, as a defence of that community's jurisdiction, encompassing its law, legal and political theory, institutions, and decision-making processes. What would be required in such a case is a plausible way to assess the *reasonableness* of an exclusionary rule by considering a First Nation government's reasons for enacting it. Along with consideration of the material circumstances and histories of the community, an inquiry of this kind should consider the distinctive features of Aboriginal political societies, including the central importance of descent as the constitutive principle of Aboriginal communities, and the connection of values and law that comprises that group's particular political theory.[86] This seems to invite the application of a section 1 "reasonable limits" test to First Nations law-making, but doctrinally at least, section 1 cannot be brought to bear directly on the exercise of a section 35 right.[87] It also seems to invite the possibility that Aboriginal membership laws that have an ameliorative purpose should be saved by section 15(2).[88] If sections 1 and 15(2) cannot be used to defend Aboriginal membership

---

86 See the report of the AFN Focus Group on Registration and Membership, recording participants' views on membership: AFN-INAC Joint Technical Working Group, *First Nations Registration (Status) and Membership Research Report* (Ottawa: Assembly of First Nations and Indian and Northern Affairs, 2008) at 12, online: National Centre for First Nations Governance <fngovernance.org/resources_docs/First_Nations_Registration_and_Membership_Research_Report.pdf>. "All participants agreed that kinship ties are and have always been the foundation of First Nations societies ... Participants were clear that the kinship ties do not end with a specific blood quantum. Blood quantum was rejected by all groups as a basis for establishing identity, citizenship, Indian status or band membership. Rather, participants saw lineage as providing the linkage between the generations."

87 *Sparrow, supra* note 120 at 29.

88 *Kapp, supra* note 6, especially para 40. See also *Grismer, supra* note 49 at para 51.

rules that would otherwise be found to discriminatory, what concept of "reasonableness" could be applied to an Aboriginal community's membership rules when they are challenged by excluded applicants? In other words, how is the boundary proposed by an aboriginal government to be evaluated?

To this extent, there remains a jurisprudential (and conceptual) gap. Some guidance, however, can be taken from *Charter* cases that involve First Nations membership codes, but do not engage section 35, the most centrally relevant of which is *Grismer v Squamish Indian Band*.[89] In this case, the Squamish Indian Band (now the Squamish Nation) had denied membership to two applicants in accordance with its membership code, which did not allow the enrolment of adopted children who had only one enrolled parent.[90] The applicants argued that the challenged provision was invalid because it violated rights protected by section 15 of the *Charter*. Unlike *Sawridge Band, McIvor,* and other "C-31" cases that turned on gender discrimination,[91] *Grismer* involved a challenge to a descent-based membership rule, although in this instance, one distinguishing between biological descendants and descendants by adoption. Nothing in the *Indian Act* required the inclusion (or exclusion) of the applicants, since the Squamish Nation governed its own membership under section 10, and the applicants were not among the category of persons who were deemed eligible for band membership by the 1985 amendments to that Act.[92] While the adopted children of persons with Indian status inherit *Indian Act* status from their adoptive parents (providing they otherwise are eligible in accordance with the second-generation cut-off rule), "Section 10 First Nations" are entitled to exclude such persons from *membership*. The question in this case was whether that exclusion was constitutionally valid.[93]

The judge found that the challenged provision did indeed discriminate against the applicants because they were treated less favourably than the biological children of an enrolled member would have been, and their adopted status constituted an analogous ground for

---

89 *Grismer, supra* note 49.
90 *Ibid* at paras 6–8 and 37–40.
91 *Scrimbitt, supra* note 49.
92 In contrast to *McIvor, supra* note 29, and *Scrimbitt, supra* note 49.
93 Grismer, the adopted child of McIvor, was also a clamant in the 2009 McIvor case, as a person registered as an Indian under section 6(2) of the *Indian Act. McIvor, supra* note 29.

the purposes of section 15.[94] Because of the distinction drawn between adopted and biological children, the judge was of the view that the code amounted to "legislation based on blood quantum,"[95] and that this (among other factors) had the effect on the applicants of "demeaning their dignity," so satisfying the definition of discrimination prescribed by the Supreme Court in *Law v Canada*.[96] Applying section 1, however, the judge concluded that the limitation imposed on the rights of the applicants was nonetheless a reasonable and justifiable one, and rationally connected to the code's objective, as "[r]estricting membership to persons who have a bloodline connection to the Squamish Nation is [a] rational way of preserving and protecting the unique Squamish culture and identity."[97] Because the First Nation had made allowance for the discretionary enrolment of some adopted children (albeit not those who, like the applicants, had only one enrolled parent), the code gave effect to a "compromise arrangement" that "minimally impair[ed] any rights that may exist for non-Squamish adoptees, while still achieving the objective of protecting Squamish culture and identity through traditional means."[98] Crucially, although the Squamish Nation argued that their right to exclude the claimants was protected by section 35, the judge declined to make findings on the respondent's section 35 defence, because the evidentiary record could not support a declaration of Aboriginal rights, and because this broader question remained to be determined in the (then) ongoing *Sawridge Band* litigation. Resort to section 35 was in any case unnecessary, given the finding:

> [I]n view of the conclusion I have reached above, it is not necessary that I decide in this case whether the respondent's right to control membership is an "aboriginal right" within the meaning of subsection 35(1) of the Constitution Act, 1982, or alternatively, an "other right" as contemplated by section 25 of the Charter, that cannot be abrogated or derogated from by subsection 15(1) of the Charter."[99]

---

94 *Grismer, supra* note 49 at paras 36 and 46.
95 *Ibid* at para 55.
96 *Ibid* at para 58. Applying the "Law test" set out in *Law v Canada (Minister of Employment and Immigration)*, [1999] 1 SCR 497 at para 70.
97 *Grismer, supra* note 49 at paras 64–65.
98 *Ibid* at para 74.
99 *Ibid* at para 85.

In a different case, where the section 1 test could not be satisfied by a First Nation, a section 35 defence might be determinative. Importantly, however, in *Grismer*, the judge was able to apply the section 1 reasonable limits test to examine the policymaking process deployed by the Squamish Nation, noting that the nation had adequately "sought to balance the potential rights of persons with no Squamish blood against the Squamish tradition and the need to preserve the unique Squamish culture and identity"[100] and that the compromise reached in the nation's code was intended "to preserve the collective Squamish culture and identity, particularly in the face of an overwhelming non-Native and non-Squamish population, in a manner consistent with Squamish heritage, culture and values."[101] The judge also noted, without further comment, that section 15(2) was a relevant contextual factor, and that "[a]ccording to the Squamish Nation, the ameliorative purpose and effect of the Membership Code is to preserve Squamish culture and identity."[102] The significance of the court's reasoning, then, lies in the emphasis given to the nation's efforts to balance the rights of adopted children against the rights of other individuals, and the opportunity provided to the Squamish Nation to defend the content of its membership law by reference to the community's values, history, and context.

There may well be better forums in which to further the kind of deep constitutional dialogue that *Grismer* suggests is possible. The judge himself wondered whether "judicial review applications are perhaps not the best vehicle for resolving the complex constitutional issues involving alleged discriminatory actions involving members of First Nations."[103] Nonetheless, by bringing section 1 to bear on First Nations law-making, the court was able to consider the vulnerability of the Squamish Nation as a distinctive cultural minority, and the importance of heritage and tradition to such a community, including the central significance of descent lines in the constitution of the tribal body politic.[104] In its broadest sense, the reasoning in *Grismer* suggests that the "reasonableness" of Indigenous membership law in a "free and democratic"

---

100 *Ibid* at para 77.
101 *Ibid* at para 61.
102 *Ibid* at para 51.
103 *Ibid* at para 83.
104 Other cases suggest that socio-economic justifications may in some circumstances form a part of s1 analysis. See, for example, *Six Nations, supra* note 67 at paras 6–7; and *Scrimbitt, supra* note 49 at para 69.

settler society must be understood in the context of settler-state history, which is, crucially, a history of colonization.[105] More specifically, exclusions that are reasonable in a free and democratic *Aboriginal* society, predominantly constituted by kinship and descent, may differ substantially from those that can be justified in other Canadian jurisdictions, where additional constitutive principles (especially *jus soli* and residency rules) determine the legal relationship between governments and individuals.

It seems probable that as Indigenous polities become more embedded in the constitutional framework of the settler states, the concept of Indigenous self-governance will move from a "collective rights" based framework to a jurisdictional one. This may well track a move from rights-based recognition to governance-based reconciliation. The method adopted in *Grismer* seems to reflect the increasing nuance of inter-governmental relations involving Aboriginal communities, and the capacity of constitutional and "quasi-constitutional" human rights mechanisms to adapt to these changes.[106] The development of a "reasonable limits" test that can do justice to Indigenous legal and political theories expressed in Indigenous law-making, is a primary challenge for settler-state constitutionalism. Brought to bear on Indigenous membership governance, such an approach would amount not only to an important adaptation of settler human rights law, but would also be an important move towards to the reconciliation of tribal and liberal constitutive principles within settler societies.

The promise of these adaptive methodologies as distinctive settler-state responses to tribal boundary problems is further illustrated by the limits of human rights–based approaches that do not or cannot take account of tribal interests in boundary-setting, because they do not account for Indigenous governance, or Indigenous governments. In these circumstances, decision-makers tend instead to resort to the rubric of minority rights to address claims involving Indigenous membership disputes. Because of the nexus between descent and race, I suggest, minority rights provisions are inadequate to the task of

---

105 The application of this test may be an example of what Lorne Sossin has recently referred to as an emergent body of "Aboriginal administrative law." Lorne Sossin, "Indigenous Self-Government and the Future of Administrative Law" (2012) 45 UBC L Rev 595.

106 The CHRA has been described as having a "quasi-constitutional" character. See, e.g., *Canada (House of Commons) v Vaid*, [2005] 1 SCR 667 at para 81.

assessing the reasonableness of exclusions from kinship-based communities. These shortcomings are evident in the approach taken by the Human Rights Committee (HRC), the body tasked with administering the *International Covenant on Civil and Political Rights (ICCPR)*, and with adjudicating individual complaints under the Optional Protocol of that treaty. In the following section I consider the approach taken by the HRC, and its consequences, in the landmark case of *Lovelace v Canada* (1981).[107]

IV. Lovelace and the Tobique First Nation in the Human Rights Committee

International human rights bodies struggle to adjudicate disputes that involve decisions made by sub-state groups, especially where those groups are ascriptively constituted (and so are not voluntary associations) or exercise forms of jurisdiction not delegated by a national government. Importantly, in accordance with the logic of international human rights law, the HRC can consider only the performance of a state party to the *ICCPR*, and has no capacity to consider individual claims brought against tribes as sub-state actors. In the HRC a self-governing Indigenous community is effectively a third party in a dispute between an applicant and the state, and if its interests are to be brought to bear in the committee's reasoning, they must form part of the state's defence.

Significantly, the *ICCPR* has no general provision equivalent to the "reasonable limits test" of the *Canadian Charter's* section 1, although some provisions of the treaty expressly describe permissible restrictions on particular rights,[108] and the HRC has also developed limited "proportionality" and "necessity" tests in respect to rights not expressly subject to these tests. The HRC's decisions on the admissibility of claims under the individual complaints mechanisms of the *ICCPR* Optional Protocol have also limited its ability to engage with the interests of sub-state groups, by removing from its jurisdiction the capacity to hear communications on the right to self-determination

---

107 Lovelace v Canada, Comm. 24/1977, U.N. Doc. CCPR/C/OP/1, at 10.

108 See, for example, UN General Assembly, International Covenant on Civil and Political Rights, 16 December 1966, United Nations, Treaty Series, vol. 999, p. 171, article 19, protecting freedom of expression. See also General Comment No. 34 on article 19 of the ICCPR; UN Human Rights Committee (HRC), General comment no. 34, Article 19, Freedoms of opinion and expression, 12 September 2011, CCPR/C/GC/34.

protected by the *Covenant*'s article 1.[109] As a result, while the right to self-determination informs the interpretation of the other articles of the *ICCPR*, it cannot itself be the basis of an individual communication.[110] Indigenous claims premised on article 1 are routinely displaced onto article 27, and heard as cultural claims, rather than as collective claims to property, resources, and political autonomy.[111] Thus in the Human Rights Committee, Indigenous collective interests are usually debated in the course of assessing a state's responsibility to protect the individual rights of persons "belonging to" minorities, to enjoy the right to "enjoy their own culture" in "community with the other members of their group."[112] Article 27 has provided the only plausible basis for Indigenous membership claims brought to the HRC by excluded individuals, as well as claims brought by members seeking to defend exclusions against state intervention.[113] The HRC's jurisdictional constraints have the effect of obscuring the inter-Indigenous elements of membership disputes, along with the interests of tribes in membership governance, and in fact, most of what is most normatively pressing about Indigenous boundary problems. To illustrate these shortcomings, in the section that follows I consider the methodology used by the HRC in *Lovelace v Canada*.

Sandra Lovelace is a Canadian Maliseet Indian and a member of the Tobique First Nation of New Brunswick. She acquired Indian status at birth in accordance with the *Indian Act*, but was divested of that status, and so also her band membership, along with her right to live

---

109 Lubicon Lake Band v. Canada, Communication No. 167/1984 (26 March 1990), U.N. Doc. Supp. No. 40 (A/45/40) at 1 (1990), UN Human Rights Committee (HRC), CCPR General Comment No. 23: Article 27 (Rights of Minorities), 8 April 1994, CCPR/C/21/Rev.1/Add.5, para 3.1.
110 UN Human Rights Committee (HRC), CCPR General Comment No. 12: Article 1 (Right to Self-determination), The Right to Self-determination of Peoples, 13 March 1984.
111 See for example: Lubicon Lake Band v. Canada, Communication No. 167/1984 (26 March 1990), U.N. Doc. Supp. No. 40 (A/45/40) at 1 (1990); Ivan Kitok v. Sweden, Communication No. 197/1985, CCPR/C/33/D/197/1985 (1988), para 6.3. R.L. v. Canada (358/1989), ICCPR, A/47/40 (5 November 1991) 358 (CCPR/C/43/D/358/1989). Apirana Mahuika et al. v. New Zealand, Communication No. 547/1993, U.N. Doc. CCPR/C/70/D/547/1993 (2000). UN Human Rights Committee (HRC), CCPR General Comment No. 12: Article 1 (Right to Self-determination), The Right to Self-determination of Peoples, 13 March 1984.
112 International Covenant on Civil and Political Rights, *supra* note 109, article 27.
113 See, for example, Human Rights Committee, 1991, R.L. v Canada, *supra* note 112.

on the Tobique Reserve, when she married a non-Indian in 1970. In her 1977 communication to the HRC, she successfully argued that the denial of her right to live on the reserve, effected by the federal *Indian Act*, constituted an infringement of rights protected by article 27 of the *ICCPR*. In its reasoning, the committee focused on the parts of the Act that resulted in her loss of status, not on the powers conferred on First Nations to determine the consequences of such a loss, including their power to exclude non-status Indians from the reserve, or, importantly, to allow them to reside there.[114] The decisions actually made by the Tobique First Nation in accordance with the powers conferred by the *Indian Act* were entirely absent from the committee's reasoning, as was any reference to the interest of the Tobique First Nation in Lovelace's claim and the *Indian Act* regime, let alone the possibility that the First Nation exercised governance authority not derived from the Act. These are important elisions, because when Lovelace's marriage came to an end, and she returned to the Tobique Reserve to live with her parents, the band council did not exclude her from the reserve as it was entitled to do.[115] The council did, however, decline Lovelace's request for a house of her own, consistently with its power to pass by-laws allotting reserve land, apparently because it was the council's policy to give priority to members in the allocation of on-reserve housing.[116] The council's decisions would necessarily have been constrained by the quantity of housing funding made available to First Nations, a resource limited (unless housing was funded by the nation's own capital or revenue moneys[117]) by the federal government's insistence at that time, that band funding quantums be calculated by reference to the on-reserve population of

---

114 This point was raised by Canada in its submissions on sections 30 and 31 of the Indian Act dealing with trespassing persons; see *Lovelace, supra* note 108 at paras 9.3 and 9.4.

115 *Indian Act* 1985, s 81(p), (p.1) and (p.2). Possibly Lovelace was permitted to stay because (as she submitted), her supporters on the reserve had promised to physically protect her from eviction, but whatever the rationale, it did not feature in the evaluation performed by the HRC.

116 *Indian Act* 1985, s 81 and 20. See also Corbiere, *supra* note 59, discussion in paras 77 and 78. For an example of a similar dispute, see *Laslo v Gordon Band Council*, 1996 CHRT 12, at 16–17, containing a discussion of the 1987 Housing Policy of the Gordon Band Council, which ranked applicants in accordance with the duration of their residency on the reserve and specified that "[p]ersons living with a non-Treaty person" were not likely to be given priority in awarding houses on the reserve.

117 See sections 62 and 64 of the *Indian Act*, discussed in *Corbiere, supra* note 59 at para 77.

status Indians, regardless of who else was living there.[118] In any case, while Lovelace had lost her legislative *right* to live on the reserve, she continued to live there in band housing allocated to her parents, with the acquiescence of the band council, albeit while being denied a house of her own.[119]

Because of the HRC's focus on the *Indian Act*, the reasonableness of the First Nation's decisions (to allow Lovelace to stay but to deny her federally funded housing) did not form part of the committee's reasoning.[120] Nor, consequently, did the material constraints operating on First Nations, including the lack of economic opportunities and housing on reserves, and the restrictive service-provision and funding policies of the federal government.[121] More generally, the committee did not consider the economic advantages that the *Indian Act*'s restrictive status provisions might secure for First Nations under conditions of scarcity, along with by-law-making powers that permit First Nations to limit the on-reserve population and prioritize in the allocation of limited resources. The committee found, rather, that "[w]hatever may be the merits of the Indian Act in other respects, it does not seem to the Committee that to deny Sandra Lovelace the right to reside on the reserve is reasonable, or necessary to preserve

---

118 Since 2001, funding formulas increasingly rely on First Nations' membership, not their status Indian population. See Annex 4, Funding Formula, in band funding policy 2004; also AFN-INAC Joint Technical Working Group First Nations Registration (Status) and Membership Research Report (2008), at 7 and 25, suggesting that (in 2008) "[t]here are only two federal programs that currently rely exclusively on 'status' to determine funding eligibility: Non-Insured Health Benefits, funded by Health Canada; and the Post-Secondary Education Program funded by INAC."

119 *Lovelace, supra* note 108, para 13.1

120 *Lovelace, supra* note 108 at paras 9.6 and 9.7. Contrast *Kitok, supra* note 112: "In this context, the Committee notes that Mr. Kitok is permitted, albeit not as of right, to graze and farm his reindeer, to hunt and to fish" para 9.8.

121 See discussion in *Corbiere, supra* note 59 at para 62 explaining that the lack of housing on the reserve is one reason why many First Nation members cannot or do not live on reserves; "In addition, because of the lack of opportunities and housing on many reserves, and the fact that the *Indian Act*'s rules formerly removed band membership from various categories of band members, residence off the reserve has often been forced upon them, or constitutes a choice made reluctantly or at high personal cost," para 62, per L'Heureux-Dubé, Gonthier, Iacobucci and Binnie JJ.

the identity of the tribe."[122] Thus while some exclusions might be reasonable or necessary, this one was not, and there was consequently no need to "determine in any general manner which restrictions may be justified under the Covenant ... because the circumstances are special in the present case."[123] Whether or not the HRC's decision can be thought of as just, there is no room in its methodology for the Tobique Nation Band Council's view of what might be a "reasonable" compromise in the circumstances of Lovelace's claim. It is not difficult to imagine, however, that the situation Lovelace found herself in was a product of exactly that, a balancing of the rights and interests of individuals with the tribal public interest, that is, an act of democratic governance. In principle however, the HRC's findings required the Canadian state to restrain the powers exercised by the Tobique First Nation, in order to make it impossible for the band council to prevent Lovelace from enjoying her culture in community with its members. This is, in fact, what the Canadian government proceeded to do, by amending the *Indian Act* in 1985. Viewing the Lovelace claim as a boundary problem, then, what principles might be extracted from the HRC's reasoning?

The committee was obliged to at least *consider* the boundaries of Lovelace's community in order to determine whether she "belonged" to a minority. It did so, broadly speaking, by insisting that article 27 offers protection to persons who, like Lovelace, are ethnically Indian, whether or not they are or were also legally Indian. Several considerations are apparent in the committee's reasoning, reflecting a complicated mix of objective and subjective criteria. First, the committee referred to principles consistent with the concept of birthright; Lovelace had been "born and brought up on a reserve" and was "ethnically a Maliseet Indian." Second, it drew on evidence that seems to support a consent-based concept of community; she had "kept ties with [her] community and wish[ed] to maintain these ties," and had not been absent from the Tobique Reserve for more than a few years.[124] Significantly, however, while finding that Lovelace belonged to "a" minority,[125] the committee did not then expressly identify that minority. In the judgment, it

---

122 *Lovelace, supra* note 108, para 17.
123 *Ibid* at para 16.
124 *Lovelace supra* note 108, para 14.
125 *Ibid.*

is equally possible that the committee refers to the minority of "Canadian Indians" (persons who are ethnically Indian) or to one of the other groups referenced in the decision, namely, "Maliseet Indians," the Tobique First Nation, or that part of the Tobique First Nation resident on the Tobique Reserve.[126] Some indication of the boundaries of the minority to which Lovelace belongs, however, can be garnered from the committee's characterization of the article 27 breach. According to the committee, Lovelace's "access to her native culture and language in community with the other members of her group" had been infringed precisely "because there is no place outside the Tobique Reserve where such a community exists."[127]

On the face of reasoning, then, it seems that the committee has identified two boundaries, one enclosing Lovelace as a member of an ethnic minority for the purpose of establishing her standing as a beneficiary of article 27, and another locating the breach of article 27 in the provisions of the *Indian Act* that deny her a legal right to live on the reserve. Whatever minority Lovelace belongs to, the relevant *cultural* group, to which Lovelace should be guaranteed access, is the community resident on the Tobique Reserve. This is important, because the ethnic, legal, and cultural *human* boundaries of the Tobique Reserve community do not coincide with its territorial ones. The reserve is home to some (but not all) members of the Tobique First Nation,[128] along with some persons who are status Indians but not members of the Tobique First Nation,[129] some ethnically Indian persons who are not status Indians,[130] and some

---

126 Aboriginal Affairs and Northern Development Canada, "First Nation Profiles" (23 January 2015), online: <pse5-esd5.ainc-inac.gc.ca/FNP/Main/Search/FNRegPopulation.aspx?BAND_NUMBER=16&lang=eng>.

127 *Lovelace, supra*, note 108, para 15.

128 "Tobique Band," Indian Affairs and Northern Development (31 December 2011), online: <www.aadnc-aandc.gc.ca/eng/1100100017100/1100100017101>.

129 2015 AANDC data suggest there are at least six such persons on the Tobique Reserve: "Registered Population: Tobique," Indian Affairs and Northern Development (23 January 2015), online: <pse5-esd5.ainc-inac.gc.ca/FNP/Main/Search/FNRegPopulation.aspx?BAND_NUMBER=16&lang=eng>.

130 2011 Census data suggest there are at least five such persons on the Tobique Reserve. Statistics Canada, "NHS Profile, Tobique 20, IRI, New Brunswick, 2011" (28 April 2014), online: <www12.statcan.gc.ca/nhs-enm/2011/dp-pd/prof/details/page.cfm?Lang=E&Geo1=CSD&Code1=1312007&Data=Count&SearchText=tobique&SearchType=Begins&SearchPR=13&A1=All&B1=All&Custom=&TABID=1>.

non-Indians.[131] If these people form a cultural community in terms of article 27, it is likely by virtue of their shared residence on the reserve, not their kinship ties and not their common ethnicity. Is territory the determinative factor in the committee's solution to the boundary problem implicated by Lovelace's claim? This would seem to equate to an application of the "all-affected rule," so that all residents should be members because they are similarly affected by the jurisdiction of the Tobique First Nation Council, and that jurisdiction is coextensive with the nation's reserve lands. This approach seems compatible with the HRC's emphasis on Lovelace's choice to affiliate with the Tobique community and reside on the reserve (consent) but not with its emphasis on her objective "ethnicity" (birthright). Further, even if a territorially defined "all-affected principle" were offered by the HRC, and even if it could be agreed that the reserve boundaries were the appropriate measure of territoriality, one additional complication would have to be noted. In Canada, some First Nations occupy more than one reserve, and some reserves are occupied by more than one First Nation. As at January 2015, there were 617 recognized First Nations in Canada, occupying 863 reserves.[132] Lovelace's community, the Tobique First Nation, currently exercises jurisdiction over two non-contiguous reserves: a "mainland" reserve of approximately 2724 hectares, and a much smaller reserve located on two islands in New Brunswick's Kennebecasis Bay, which it shares with three other First Nations.[133] Furthermore, many members of First Nations do not live on a reserve, whether their own or that governed by another nation.

---

131 2011 Census data suggest there are at least sixty-five persons without Aboriginal ancestry on the Tobique Reserve. *Ibid.* (An additional twenty residents have Aboriginal identity but do not have Aboriginal ancestry, including five persons who have First Nations (North American Indian) identity but no First Nations ancestry.

132 Aboriginal Affairs and Northern Development Canada (23 January 2015), online: <pse5-esd5.ainc-inac.gc.ca/fnp/Main/index.aspx?lang=eng>. See also Statistics Canada, "List of Indian Band Areas and the Census Subdivisions They Include" (13 November 2013), online: <www12.statcan.gc.ca/nhs-enm/2011/dp-pd/aprof/help-aide/a-tab.cfm?Lang=E> which lists 601 "band areas." For the number of inhabited reserves, see Statistics Canada, "Aboriginal Peoples in Canada: First Nations People, Métis and Inuit, National Household Survey, 2011," online: <www12.statcan.gc.ca/nhs-enm/2011/as-sa/99-011-x/99-011-x2011001-eng.pdf> p 6, fn 1.

133 Aboriginal Affairs and Northern Development Canada, "Reserves/Settlements/Villages" (23 January 2015), online: <pse5-esd5.ainc-inac.gc.ca/FNP/Main/Search/FNReserves.aspx?BAND_NUMBER=16&lang=eng>.

In January 2015 for example, the Tobique First Nation had a total registered population of 2,240 people, of whom 1,486 lived on the Tobique (mainland) Reserve.[134] The complicated demographies of contemporary tribal communities seem to vastly reduce the prospects of developing a single overarching principle, directing settler governments in the fulfilment of their human rights obligations in Indigenous membership disputes, in the absence of attention to the particular circumstances, preferences, and interests of the tribe(s) in question. It may well be that the best state-Indigenous political compromise that can be reached on matters of principle is the one that so far has survived in Canada; Indianness is a measure of descent, First Nations are Indian communities, and given the need for tribal demoi to be bounded, descent-based exclusions are reasonable limitations on the rights of excluded persons. Such an approach can be sustained only by resort to the adaptive methodologies described in Part III, making use of the section 1 "reasonable limits" test to evaluate decisions made by an Aboriginal community exercising a governance right protected by section 35. This approach engages the relationship between Canadian and Aboriginal governments as a jurisdictional one, engaging Aboriginal law and law-making as well as Aboriginal rights.

V. Conclusion

I conclude by offering a sketch of what may be a distinctive settler-state response to the tribal boundary problem, evidenced in Canadian law and policy. First, in the law and policy of all four CANZUS states, some Indigenous communities are expressly recognized as self-governing kinship-based polities organized by shared descent, and the tribal exclusion of non-descendants is accepted (for now) as a reasonable limitation on the rights of those persons, justified in a free and democratic *settler* society. This general principle depends for its coherence on the characterization of tribes as the successors of pre-contact communities, whose continuity with those historic communities is demonstrated in large part by their shared descent from common ancestors. Consequently the liberal democratic frameworks of settler states must

---

134 Aboriginal Affairs and Northern Development Canada, "Registered Population" (23 January 2015), online: <pse5-esd5.ainc-inac.gc.ca/FNP/Main/Search/FNRegPopulation.aspx?BAND_NUMBER=16&lang=eng>.

work around the existence of tribes as kinship-based political societies that predate the state, and so also must accommodate descent and race as sources of legal status. Because of these particular features of settler-state constitutionalism, then, in those societies, race is not a remnant of pre-modernism, but a constitutive principle of settler statehood itself. In effect, racial difference marks the boundaries between the descent-based polities of tribes and the descent-based polity of the settler state. Second, while discrimination against non-descendants can be justified as a concomitant of tribalism, distinctions made *between* tribal descendants are suspect to the extent that they are based on immutable personal characteristics *other than descent*. Accordingly, in principle a descendant should not be treated less favourably than other descendants on the basis of gender, or the gender of Indigenous ancestors (or in fact any other prohibited ground). However, distinctions made between descendants on the basis of the number of their Indigenous ancestors or "blood quantum" may be justified as reasonable limitations on the rights of excluded persons, given the necessity of boundaries, the nature of tribes as kinship-based polities, and the histories and experiences of tribal communities in the settler states.

If we are to conclude that in settler societies, qualitative descent-based membership rules are simply not susceptible to non-discrimination principles in the same way that other laws are, this suggests that qualitative descent rules can be accommodated within the political theories of the settler societies, and can be defended by tribes as reasonable limits on the rights of non-members, and so justified in terms compatible with the concepts of proportionality and "reasonable limits" used in human rights law. The resulting accommodations may well be "pragmatic," as Dahl has suggested, but they need not be "ad hoc," as Whelan anticipates.[135] In fact they may yield a new conceptual language that mediates tribal and liberal political theories.

---

135 Dahl, *supra* note 23 at 59; Whelan, *supra* note 22 at 40.

13 Overlapping Consensus, Legislative Reform, and the Indian Act*

DOUGLAS SANDERSON†

[T]he *Indian Act* [should be] retained [*not*] because it is a good piece of legislation. It isn't. It is discriminatory from start to finish. But it is a lever in our hands
and an embarrassment to the government, as it should be. No just society and
no society with even pretensions to being just can long tolerate such a piece of
legislation, but we would rather continue to live in bondage under the inequitable *Indian Act* than surrender our sacred rights.

Harold Cardinal[1]

Introduction

In 1969, when Harold Cardinal penned these words, the federal government had just tabled a White Paper on Indian policy in Canada.[2]
The White Paper proposed eliminating the *Indian Act*, the abolition of
treaties, and the assimilation of Indigenous people into the broader
Canadian society, such that Indigenous people would be reduced to
the status of every other ethnic minority. Cardinal opposed this abrogation

---

* This chapter was first published in (2014) 39:2 Queen's LJ 511–50.
† I am grateful for the tremendous research efforts of Avery Au, the editorial assistance
of Patrick Healy, and the thoughtful revisions suggested by the anonymous referees
obtained by the *Queen's Law Journal*. This chapter greatly benefited from the insights
provided to me by John Borrows, Patrick Macklem, Kent Roach, Bryce Edwards, and
Adam Dodek.
1 *The Unjust Society: The Tragedy of Canada's Indians* (Edmonton: MG Hurtig, 1969) at 140.
2 Indian Affairs and Northern Development, *Statement of the Government of Canada on
Indian Policy* (Ottawa: Indian Affairs and Northern Development, 1969).

of the Crown's constitutional responsibility to respect treaties and to deal with Indigenous people as a founding people. In this chapter, I too argue against calls to abolish the *Indian Act*. Like Cardinal, I believe that the *Indian Act* is an embarrassment, but nevertheless, it exists in part to set out the terms of the relationship between First Nations and the government of Canada (the Crown). That the current *Indian Act* is neither reflective of the Crown's historic commitments to Indigenous people nor adequate to sustain contemporary First Nation communities is no reason to cast aside the Act; rather, the current dismal and racist state of the *Indian Act* is necessary and sufficient reason for reform.

My concern is with both the substance and the process of reform to the *Indian Act*.[3] I believe that legislation can and must set out a rightful relationship between First Nations and the settler people – though I do not here propose a full vision of that relationship.[4] Instead, drawing on the work of John Rawls, I propose a process through which First Nations and the Crown can find consensus on *Indian Act* reform, despite very different understandings of the relationship between them. The process builds on Rawls's concept of "overlapping consensus" by asking First Nations and the Crown to seek consensus on the things they are likely to agree on, and more importantly, on the principles that underlie those areas of agreement. In other words, we must not only identify areas where there happens to be agreement, but also the crucial subject of those areas where the agreement comes about because the parties agree *on the underlying principles*. Such an agreement on principles forms the basis of overlapping consensus, and, I shall argue, is what permits productive discussion about reform to take place. In specific terms, I believe there is already a consensus on certain critically important areas of government responsibility: accountability, and the economic and political integration of (and within) First Nation communities.

---

3 RSC 1985, c I-5.
4 The meaning of a right relationship is beyond the scope of the chapter for several reasons. First and foremost, the particulars of a right relationship will change over time, and the appropriate relationship must therefore be specified by political representation and negotiation. Second, and connected to the first, the "right relationship" is not something that is discovered as a matter of truth by the academy; rather, it is an artefact of interacting cultures and peoples – it is something built with the effort of both sides. That said, the underlying principles of a right relationship, from now to the foreseeable future, are set out in my article "Redressing the Right Wrong: The Argument from Corrective Justice" (2012) 62:1 UTLJ 93.

I do not here advocate the abolition of the *Indian Act*, or its replacement with a sweeping new legislative regime, though in time this too may be possible and advisable. Instead, I argue for change within the existing framework of the Act in areas that are capable of generating political consensus among First Nations, Canadians generally, and Parliament in particular. I do not take this position because I believe that incremental change is best, but because there is at present little chance of agreement between settler and Indigenous people on the fundamental issue of how to define the relationship between First Nations and the Crown. Indeed, we have been seeking that consensus since the arrival of the settler people, and we are no closer to a broad agreement about how we are to live side by side. Instead, for the past seven generations the Crown has imposed its vision of the proper relationship between itself and First Nations through the *Indian Act*.[5] Given this history, we may not be able to come any time soon to a grand bargain where everything is on the table and a new relationship is sealed, but we can advance towards that end by taking principled steps every time First Nations and the Crown meet to negotiate some aspect of their relationship. This chapter is concerned with a rightful relationship, reciprocity of opportunity, and the need to finance our communities with the human resources available to us.

The elders tell us that things take time, that actions have consequences, and that we must think through these consequences not only for this generation and the next, but for seven generations down the line. This chapter is my argument for a better *Indian Act*, and for a process to get us there. In part I, I shall make my argument for the existence of some form of *Indian Act*. In part II, I shall outline Rawls's theory of "overlapping consensus." In part III, I shall identify the areas of reform in which I believe an overlapping consensus can be achieved: accountability and integration. By accountability, I refer to the common sense meaning of the word as appropriate transparency in financial decision-making.[6]

---

5 See John Borrows, *Seven Generations, Seven Teachings: Ending the Indian Act* (Vancouver: National Centre for First Nations Governance, 2008), online: Scholars Portal Books <books1.scholarsportal.info/viewdoc.html?id=372332> [Borrows, *Seven Generations*]. I am particularly indebted to Professor Borrows, both for his many years of mentorship, and for the seeds of some of the ideas found in this chapter.
6 Shin Imai's definition of accountability includes accountability in the sense that I am using the term, but also "some form of community participation in the making of laws" and "a policy that distinguishes routine decisions, which do not require

By integration, I mean the right of First Nation communities to choose to enter into the broader Canadian economy, and the right to encourage the adoption of non-status Indians as citizens of those communities. Finally, I shall put the idea of overlapping consensus into practice by proposing an income tax reform that builds on the shared interests of Aboriginal and settler people.

I. An Argument for Some Form of the *Indian Act*

The *Indian Act*, for all its trappings of colonial thinking and clear paternalistic intent, does important work. Among many other things, the Act sets out the powers of Indigenous governments,[7] creates a system of land holdings and property interests,[8] provides for the education of Indigenous children (because provincial legislation does not extend to Indian reservations),[9] establishes programs for financial assistance,[10] provides for the legal authority to issue warrants in Indigenous communities to maintain peace and order,[11] determines who is and is not legally an Indian person,[12] and sets out the electoral process in Indigenous community elections.[13]

Of course, the *Indian Act* does all of these things badly. The powers of Indigenous governments under the Act are few and of little consequence if the goal is to govern modern communities. The system of education

---

consultation, from important decisions should involve the whole community." Shin Imai, "The Structure of the Indian Act: Accountability in Governance" (Paper delivered at the National Centre for First Nations Governance, 30 July 2007) at 2, online: Centre for First Nations Governance <fngovernance.org/publications/research/the_structure_of_the_indian_act_accountability_in_governance>. Imai demonstrates that the accountability and transparency regimes in First Nation communities are imposed by the structure and legal framework of the *Indian Act*. Alcantara, Spicer, and Leone further demonstrate that First Nation communities *not* constrained by the *Indian Act* can readily create successful regimes of accountability and transparency. Christopher Alcantara, Zachary Spicer, & Roberto Leone, "Institutional Design and the Accountability Paradox" (2012) 55:1 Canadian Pub Ad 69.

7 *Supra* note 3, ss 81–86.
8 *Ibid*, ss 20–30.
9 *Ibid*, ss 114–22.
10 *Ibid*, s 70 (providing that the minister of finance may authorize loans to Indian bands).
11 *Ibid*, ss 103(4), 105.
12 *Ibid*, ss 5–17.
13 *Ibid*, ss 74–80.

enabled by the *Indian Act* is today set out in the very same language that established the residential school system and its well-documented horrors. Maintenance of peace and order is impossible because there are not enough resources to fund police services and attend court hearings. The criteria for who is an "Indian" are anachronistic at best and racist at worst.[14] The system of property rights in Indigenous communities stymies rather than promotes economic development. The statutory framework governing the electoral process in Indigenous communities imposes what is, in effect, a foreign system of governance on an unwilling people. And so, the *Indian Act* is in many ways a terrible piece of legislation: racist, backwards, inefficient, and colonial in both scope and intent. It is no wonder so many cry out for abolition of the *Indian Act*.[15]

All that said, the *Indian Act* is a *necessary* statute, because some legislation must govern the settler–Indigenous relationship.[16] If the *Indian*

---

14 See Pamela D Palmater, "An Empty Shell of a Treaty Promise: *R v Marshall* and the Rights of Non-Status Indians" (2000) 23:1 Dal LJ 102; Palmater, *Beyond Blood: Rethinking Indigenous Identity* (Saskatoon: Purich, 2011) [Palmater, *Beyond Blood*].

15 See, e.g., Shawn A-in-chut Atleo, "Breaking Free of Tattered Indian Act," *Toronto Star* (18 November 2010), online: Toronto Star <www.thestar.com/opinion/editorial-opinion/2010/11/18/breaking_free_of_tattered_indian_act.html>; Phil Ambroziak, "Rob Clarke in Hot Water over Indian Act," *Northern Pride* (14 February 2012), online: Northern Pride <northernprideml.com/2012/02/14/rob-clarke-in-hot-water-over-indian-act/>; Ambroziak, "Indian Act to Be Modernized: PM," *Northern Pride* (31 January 2012), online: Northern Pride <northernprideml.com/2012/01/31/indian-act-to-be-modernized-pm/>; Peter O'Neil, "'An aboriginal uprising is inevitable' If Harper Doesn't Listen, Chief Threatens," *National Post* (23 January 2012), online: National Post <news.nationalpost.com/2012/01/23/canada-could-face-aboriginal-uprising-if-harper-doesnt-listen-chief-threatens/>; Herb George Satsan, "Aboriginal Crises Are Symptoms of a Deep-Rooted Problem," *Toronto Star* (25 January 2012), online: Toronto Star <www.thestar.com/opinion/editorialopinion/2012/01/25/aboriginal_crises_are_symptoms_of_a_deeprooted_problem.html>; Lorne Gunter, "The Indian Act Sustains the Problems on Our Reserves," *National Post* (6 December 2011), online: National Post <fullcomment.nationalpost.com/2011/12/06/lorne-gunter-the-indian-act-sustains-the-problems-on-our-reserves/#__federated=1>; Tom Flanagan, "First Nations Property Rights: Going beyond the Indian Act," *Globe and Mail* (22 March 2010), online: Globe and Mail <www.theglobeandmail.com/globe-debate/first-nations-property-rights-going-beyond-the-indian-act/article1209790/>; Matthew Pearson, "Abolish Indian Act, Elijah Harper Says: Legislation Treats First Nations People like 'Children,' Says Man Who Killed Meech Lake Accord," *Ottawa Citizen* (27 January 2012), online: Ottawa Citizen <www.cfne.org/modules/news/article.php?storyid=13236>.

16 In the words of my research assistant, Avery Au, "We need a productive debate on what the *Indian Act* should contain; not a futile debate about whether settler and Indigenous people together could live without an *Indian Act*."

Act were abolished today, some other piece of legislation would simply spring up to take its place.[17] Nevertheless, in its present form, the *Indian Act* is not a piece of legislation that any of us wants to live under. Surely we can do better.[18]

It is helpful to contrast the approach I am advocating with the current proposed alternatives. On one hand, Indigenous peoples tend to advocate for the wholesale replacement of the *Indian Act* with a different statutory

---

17 Even the call for a return to the treaty relationship is, tacitly, a call for a legislative relationship. International treaties between nations (i.e., bodies in a nation-to-nation relationship) provide no cause of action to Canadian citizens (i.e., they cannot sue the Crown) unless those treaties are implemented through domestic legislation. So to call for a nation-to-nation relationship or a return to the treaty relationship is necessarily to call for a relationship that is set out in legislation.

18 On the subject of improving the *Indian Act*, there is a paucity of literature. Save for a few targeted reforms around the taxation and membership provisions, there are almost no articles on the constructive reformation of the *Indian Act*. Even the *Report of the Royal Commission on Aboriginal People*, which charts out an extensive history of the Act, has virtually nothing to say about its reform. Its recommendations with respect to the Act begin with its wholesale abolition and replacement with an Aboriginal parliament. *Report of the Royal Commission on Aboriginal Peoples: Renewal – A Twenty-Year Commitment*, vol 5 (Ottawa: Supply and Services Canada, 1996) at 172–73, recommendations 2.3.45, 2.3.51 [*RCAP*].

With regards to the present government's stance on *Indian Act* reform, Prime Minister Stephen Harper has said,

To be sure, our government has no grand scheme to repeal or to unilaterally rewrite the *Indian Act*. After 136 years, that tree has deep roots. Blowing up the stump would just leave a big hole. However, there are ways, creative ways, collaborative ways, ways [involving consultation], ... ways that provide options within the *Act*, or outside of it, for practical, incremental, and real change.

So that will be our approach, to replace elements of the *Indian Act* with more modern legislation and procedures, in partnership with provinces and First Nations.

Stephen Harper, "Statement by the Prime Minister of Canada at the Crown- First Nations Gathering" (Statement delivered in Ottawa, 24 January 2012), online: Prime Minister of Canada <pm.gc.ca/eng/node/14983>.

While I agree that we cannot simply repeal the *Indian Act*, it is clear that the current federal government has not developed any creative or collaborative proposals for amendments to the *Act*. Reforms by previous governments are few and far between, as are the introduction of legislative instruments dealing with Indigenous-Crown relations. One notable exception is the *First Nations Land Management Act*. This legislation makes it possible for First Nation reserve communities who develop and approve land-use management plans to bypass the need for federal approval to lease reserve lands. SC 1999, c 24.

or government-to-government relationship based on historical and contemporary treaties. The *Report of the Royal Commission on Aboriginal Peoples*
(*RCAP*) represents the most comprehensive of these proposals.[19] More
recently, Bill S-212 (a private member's Senate bill) has proposed moving First Nations out of the Act by transforming *Indian Act* communities
into self-governing nations, replete with constitutions, law-making powers, jurisdiction over lands and resources, and powers of taxation over
lands and citizens.[20] On the other hand, the federal Crown has proposed
a variety of legislative changes to various aspects of its relationship with
First Nations people, including changes to the *Indian Act*, virtually all of
which are vociferously opposed by First Nations' political leadership.
These proposed reforms have either demanded too many concessions
on issues of fundamental disagreement between First Nations and the
Crown, or the proposals have been too narrow and poorly developed,
such that there is little or no agreement between the parties about how or
whether to proceed. I should note that reforming the *Indian Act* involves
a special kind of political process because the Act sets out the terms of
the relationship between First Nations people, the government of Canada, and its settler citizens. Reforming the Act involves more than the
sorts of policy considerations that affect all Canadians in the way that,
for example, reforming the *Criminal Code* or the process of conducting
environmental assessments affects all Canadians. Reforming the *Indian
Act* has consequences that fall primarily on one group of people: Indians, as defined by Act. Thus, proposals for reform must be attentive to
the special relationship between First Nations and the Crown and to the
fact that First Nations are likely the only people who will bear the consequence of those reforms (or lack thereof). One way to be attentive to
that special relationship, and to create the space for principled and fair
agreements, is by identifying an overlapping consensus.

II. Rawls and the Overlapping Consensus

John Rawls was concerned with how a diversity of communities and
individuals could come to consensus on political questions central to the
governance of a state. Rawls accepted as given that citizens come to the
political process with a range of comprehensive (though not necessarily

---

19 See discussion of the *RCAP*, *supra* note 24.
20 *An Act providing for the recognition of self-governing First Nations of Canada*, 1st Sess,
    41st Parl, 2012 (first reading 1 November 2012).

fully formed or considered) doctrines that by their very nature generate different answers to political questions about the organization of the state and its relationship to citizens. In light of this disagreement on fundamental questions (and even disagreement on the facts of our current situation – which he termed the "burdens of judgment"[21]), Rawls sought a process by which persons with starkly different (though necessarily reasonable) comprehensive doctrines could still come to agreement on political questions.[22] One means to that end, and the one that I shall draw on in this chapter, is the idea of an "overlapping consensus"[23] – a set of ideas that can garner consensus among reasonable persons on a particular topic, despite the parties' differing comprehensive doctrines. Rawls wrote, "[T]here can, in fact, be considerable differences in citizens' conceptions of justice provided that these conceptions lead to similar political judgments. And this is possible, since different premises can yield the same conclusion. In this case there exists what we may refer to as overlapping rather than strict consensus."[24]

In the context that I am using Rawls's ideas and terminology, I mean not so much a comprehensive moral doctrine as a comprehensive view about the nature of the appropriate relationship between First Nations, the Crown, and the settler citizens of Canada. It is the vast divergence between these comprehensive starting positions on the appropriate relationship between First Nations and the Crown that can make impossible negotiation to a principled middle ground.[25] In this chapter, I want to use the idea of an overlapping consensus to facilitate both the process and the

---

21 John Rawls, *Political Liberalism* (New York: Columbia University Press, 2005) at 54.
22 Rawls imagines that citizens actually have two views: one political and one comprehensive. Where persons argue from their comprehensive doctrines, consensus is difficult or impossible. Instead, Rawls asks us to argue from our political views by referring back to our comprehensive doctrines and tempering these views with principles such as public reason, justice, political and civil liberty, and other fundamental concepts. These comprehensive views, suitably tempered, enable a discussion of and consensus on political questions. *Ibid* at 133–40, 143–44.
23 A similar approach to constitutionalism is presented by James Tully in *Strange Multiplicity: Constitutionalism in an Age of Diversity* (Cambridge: Cambridge University Press, 1995). Tully's account is directed to the ideals of constitutionalism in socially, politically, culturally, and economically diverse societies. He argues for a constitutionalism based on conventions of mutual recognition, consent, and continuity.
24 John Rawls, *A Theory of Justice*, rev ed (Cambridge, MA: Belknap, 1999) at 340.
25 For further critique, see Jeremy Webber, "The Meanings of Consent" in Jeremy Webber & Colin M Macleod, eds, *Between Consenting Peoples: Political Community and the Meaning of Consent* (Vancouver: UBC Press, 2010).

substance of reform. To the extent that First Nations and the Crown have comprehensive starting positions on the appropriate nature of their relationship, my proposal does not ask that the parties abandon their principled and reasonable positions. Rather, my strategy is to ask that parties approach negotiation on questions of reform by aligning their comprehensive starting position with the more narrow questions of legislative reform. Let me provide two examples of how this might be done.

First, imagine that the federal government has proposed a bill to modernize water safety and sewage standards for First Nation communities. The bill would create new standards and regulations, transfer authority for water and waste systems to First Nation governments, and absolve the Crown of any future liabilities arising from this arrangement. First Nation representatives agree on the fundamentals of water safety, and gaining jurisdictional authority over water in their communities is consistent with their views on self-determination. This is a form of overlapping consensus: both parties can agree on certain issues without compromising their comprehensive starting positions. But, the First Nations may reasonably ask, "Given that the water and sewage systems are in decay, how can we be expected to modernize them without new resources to ensure that the work is done properly and that safety standards can be met in the years and decades to come?" Raising these concerns does not ask the Crown to move from its position of wanting to modernize water systems, or even from its position of wanting to absolve itself of future liabilities. It only asks the Crown to continue to work with First Nations on marshalling the resources to achieve what both parties agree are principled and necessary reforms.

Second, imagine that First Nation and government representatives come together to discuss land reforms under the *Indian Act*. But the First Nation refuses to discuss reforms to land tenure, instead asserting that a discussion about self-determination is more appropriate. The Crown could then reasonably ask, "Given your desire to talk about self-determination, what would the land regime look like under your proposed vision of self-governance?"[26] This approach has the potential to

---

26 I am grateful to the members of the University of Western Ontario's Kawaskimhon Moot team (Maeve Mungovan, Devin Fulop, & Michelle Manning), who provided me with this example. Although the context in which this question was raised was not a hypothetical discussion between the Crown and a First Nation, the nature of the question has been extremely valuable to me in thinking through the idea of overlapping consensus on relations between First Nations and the Crown.

move the First Nation towards discussing land reforms that are consistent with its comprehensive doctrine, and does not require the Crown to abandon its own comprehensive starting position. The fact that the parties have principled starting positions is not a barrier to achieving overlapping consensus of this sort, because neither is asked to give up on its principles.[27]

Consider an example of a proposed reform that lacked overlapping consensus to show how and why failure to reform the *Indian Act* is inevitable if parties are unable to align the proposed reforms with their comprehensive starting positions. The *First Nations Governance Act* (*FNGA*) of 2002 sought to overhaul several sections of the *Indian Act* dealing with electoral codes, band administration, and financial management.[28] The

---

27 An example of this kind of commitment is set out in the Kunst'aa Guu-kunst'aayah Reconciliation Protocol, signed by the Haida Nation and the Province of British Columbia on 11 December 2009. Kunst'aa guu – Kunst'aayah Reconciliation Protocol (2009), online: <www.haidanation.ca/Pages/Agreements/pdfs/Kunstaa%20guu_Kunstaayah_Agreement.pdf>, as referred to in *Haida Gwaii Reconciliation Act*, SBC 2010, c 17.

The Protocol begins:

The Parties hold differing views with regard to sovereignty, title, ownership and jurisdiction over Haida Gwaii, as set out below.

The Haida Nation asserts that:

Haida Gwaii is Haida lands, including the waters and resources, subject to the rights, sovereignty, ownership, jurisdiction and collective Title of the Haida Nation who will manage Haida Gwaii in accordance with its laws, policies, customs and traditions.

British Columbia asserts that:

Haida Gwaii is Crown land, subject to certain private rights or interests, and subject to the sovereignty of her Majesty the Queen and the legislative jurisdiction of the Parliament of Canada and the Legislature of the Province of British Columbia.

Notwithstanding and without prejudice to the aforesaid divergence of viewpoints, the Parties seek a more productive relationship and hereby choose a more respectful approach to coexistence by way of land and natural resource management on Haida Gwaii through shared decision-making and ultimately, a Reconciliation Agreement.

Ibid.

28 Bill C-7, *An Act respecting leadership selection, administration and accountability of Indian bands, and to make related amendments to other Acts*, 2nd Sess, 37th Parl, 2003 [Bill C-7]. For commentary on the *FNGA*, see John Borrows, "Stewardship and the First Nations Governance Act" (2003) 29:1 Queen's LJ 103; John Provart, "Reforming the *Indian Act*: First Nations Governance and Aboriginal Policy in Canada" (2003) 2 Indigenous LJ 117.

motivation for these revisions is tidily summarized in the preamble to the Act, which stated, "Whereas representative democracy, including regular elections by secret ballot, and transparency and accountability are broadly held Canadian values ..."[29] First Nations rejected the *FNGA* in part because the proposed legislation was developed through a flawed consultative process, but more importantly, the proposed legislation failed to recognize that while First Nations value transparent financial information and accountable governments, First Nations have a different understanding of where and how those values should apply in their own communities. Reform of the *Indian Act* requires us to focus on the things on which we do agree and on finding common ground about those shared values. These are difficult topics, reconciling as they must the wide range of political and economic structures of more than six hundred First Nations with those of the dominant settler state. But we need not find a precise alignment of the relevant values and principles. In that vein, our goal in amending the *Indian Act* should never be to impose "broadly held Canadian values" on Indigenous peoples. Rather, we should seek to identify policies and principles that can form the core of an overlapping consensus between First Nations and the Crown, thereby identifying subjects capable of consensual legislative reform.

Some readers may object to the use of liberal political philosophy as a methodology for guiding agreements on legislative reform of the *Indian Act*.[30] I do not here take issues with these objections; my point

---

29 Bill C-7, *supra* note 25, preamble.
30 Some argue that liberalism is incapable of incorporating uniquely Indigenous views of community. See Gordon Christie, "Law, Theory and Aboriginal Peoples" (2003) 2 Indigenous LJ 67. Others argue more broadly that the paradigm of liberal philosophy sets out the terms of the debate such that Indigenous political philosophies or rights to self-determination are subsumed at the outset. See, e.g., Dale Turner, *This Is Not a Peace Pipe: Towards a Critical Indigenous Philosophy* (Toronto: University of Toronto Press, 2006); Robert Nichols, "Indigeneity and the Settler Contract Today" (2013) 39:2 Philosophy & Social Criticism 165. A different tack is taken by Jean Leclair, who argues that the "constitutionalization of aboriginal rights has led to an unfortunate and unsatisfactory reification of aboriginal identity by *all* concerned, natives and non-natives alike." Jean Leclair, "Federal Constitutionalism and Aboriginal Difference" (2006) 31:2 Queen's LJ 521 at 522 [emphasis in original]. Leclair asserts that the better way of conceptualizing the relationship is to recognize Aboriginal people as "federal actors" who should be able to assert their claims of nationalism within the existing federal constitutional order. *Ibid* at 532. I am not certain that this approach is in any way at odds with the methodology that I set out in this chapter for negotiating such an order.

in this chapter is not to argue against the legitimacy of the Canadian state's assertions of sovereignty over Indigenous people, or to spell out what a rightful relationship looks like from the vantage point of legal or political theory. My goal is more modest: to acknowledge that whatever the legitimacy or otherwise of the current relationship between Indigenous people and the Canadian state, the two are indeed in a relationship, and that fact requires us to work together to improve the lives of Indigenous people. This is true whether we are talking about the need for safe water, adequate funding for schools, fixing the broken child welfare system, or any number of real world issues that First Nations people themselves want addressed in their communities. To make principled progress on these issues, First Nation and settler government representatives must come to principled agreements, and to do that they must hash out their differences through negotiations. This is not to say that we Indigenous people should give up and accept colonization, or forget about the importance of self-determination, or abandon the wisdom of our elders in negotiating the historic treaties: it is simply to say that we can, and must, negotiate principled agreements on a wide range of topics while maintaining fidelity to our principles and beliefs.

III. Some Essential Background

Later in this chapter, I shall to focus on two key areas for reform – accountability and integration – each of which is, I think, capable of being the object of overlapping consensus between First Nations and the Crown. But I shall first set out some brief background on the socioeconomic context in which First Nation communities find themselves and on how these communities are funded. This background is necessary to understand the perspective of First Nation communities on matters such as accountability and integration.

First Nations people face poorer outcomes in health,[31] education, wealth, and social status when compared to those of their settler

---

31 See Brian Postl, Catherine Cook, & Michael Moffatt, "Aboriginal Child Health and the Social Determinants: Why Are These Children So Disadvantaged?" (2010) 14:1 Healthcare Quarterly 42; Janet Smylie & Paul Adomako, *Indigenous Children's Health Report: Health Assessment in Action* (2009), online: St Michael's Hospital <www.stmichaelshospital.com/pdf/crich/ichr_report.pdf>; J Reading, "The Crisis of Chronic Disease among Aboriginal Peoples: A Challenge for Public Health, Population Health and Social Policy Centre for Aboriginal Health Research," *Centre for Aboriginal Health*

counterparts. More specifically, First Nation communities are statistically more prone to teen suicide,[32] experience higher rates of crime,[33] suffer an endemic lack of housing[34] and clean water,[35] and have little

---

Research (2009), online: <www.uvic.ca/research/centres/cahr/knowledge/publications/chronicdisease.pdf>; Malcolm King, Alexandra Smith, & Michael Gracey, "Indigenous Health Part 2: The Underlying Causes of the Health Gap" (2009) 374:9683 Lancet 76; Chantelle AM Richmond & Nancy A Ross, "Social Support, Material Circumstance and Health Behaviour: Influences on Health in First Nation and Inuit Communities of Canada" (2008) 67:9 Social Science & Medicine 1423.

32 In general, Aboriginal rates of teen suicide are five to six times higher than for non-Aboriginal Canadians. The rates vary between large and small, northern and southern communities, such that small northern communities suffer more than others. Laurence J Kirmayer, Gregory M Brass, Tara Holton, Ken Paul, Cori Simpson, & Caroline Tait, *Suicide among Aboriginal People in Canada*, Aboriginal Healing Foundation (2007) at 22, online: Aboriginal Healing Foundation <www.ahf.ca/downloads/suicide.pdf>.

33 Aboriginal people are three times more likely than non-Aboriginals to experience a violent victimization. On-reserve crime rates were three times higher than off-reserve crime rates, and violent on-reserve crime rates were eight times higher. Jodi-Anne Brzozowski, Andrea Taylor-Butts, & Sara Johnson, "Victimization and Offending among the Aboriginal Population in Canada," *Statistics Canada* (2006) at 1, online: Statistics Canada <publications.gc.ca/Collection-R/Statcan/85-002-XIE/85-002-XIE2006003.pdf>.

34 INAC estimates the *current* backlog of housing needs for the on-reserve Aboriginal population as 20,000 to 35,000 new housing units, 17,000 existing units in need of major repair, and 5,200 existing units in need of replacement. Aboriginal Affairs and Northern Development Canada, *Evaluation of INAC's On-Reserve Housing Support*, online: Aboriginal Affairs and Northern Development Canada <https://www.aadnc-aandc.gc.ca/eng/1325099369714/1325099426465>. The authors of this report note that the *growing* backlog is especially troubling for two reasons: the Aboriginal demographic is exploding and, over the last five years, INAC has built only 1,500 new units and serviced 6,000 existing units. *Ibid.*

35 As early as 1995, Health Canada determined that 25 per cent of on-reserve water systems posed health and safety risks. Between 1995 and 2001, $1.9 billion was spent to improve these systems. However, in 2001, INAC found that 75 per cent of on-reserve water systems posed a safety risk. In 2003, $600 million over five years was budgeted for further improvements. Office of the Auditor General of Canada, "Report of the Commissioner of the Environment and Sustainable Development to the House of Commons: Chapter 5 – Drinking Water in First Nations" at 6, online: Office of the Auditor General of Canada <www.oag-bvg.gc.ca/internet/docs/c20050905ce.pdf>. Consider these statements from an INAC expert panel in 2006:

[T]he federal government has never provided enough funding to First Nations to ensure that the quantity and quality of their water systems was comparable to that of off-reserve communities.

access to education beyond the primary years.[36] First Nations people are overrepresented in prisons[37] and underrepresented in the economy.[38] It is not possible to summarize the precise manner in which First Nation communities are funded. To start with, there is no legislative basis for existing funding formulae.[39] The formula applied to any given

---

For example, in the five-year capital plan covering 2002–07, INAC officials acknowledge that the federal government's initial estimates of the capital needed to invest in First Nations water and wastewater systems turned out to be *one-third to one-half* of what was actually needed. The estimates were *not based* on detailed engineering analysis. As well, they did not take into account increases in construction ... and the impact of increasing water-quality standards.

Harry Swain, Stan Louttit, & Steve Hrudey, "Report of the Expert Panel on Safe Drinking Water for First Nations" Indian and Northern Affairs Canada (2006), online: Safe Drinking Water Foundation <www.safewater.org> at 22 [emphasis added].

36 In 2006, educational attainment among First Nations persons aged twenty-five to sixty-four was composed of 38 per cent having less than high school, 20 per cent having no more than high school, and 42 per cent having more than high school. Only 8 per cent of the Aboriginal population had university degrees, compared with 23 per cent of the non-Aboriginal population. Statistics Canada, *Educational Portrait of Canada, 2006 Census,* at 21, online: Statistics Canada <www12.statcan.ca/census-recensement/2006/as-sa/97-560/pdf/97-560-XIE2006001.pdf>.

37 In 2008, Aboriginal adults composed 22 per cent of the prison and temporary custody population while representing only 3 per cent of the Canadian population. Samuel Perreault, "The Incarceration of Aboriginal People in Adult Correctional Services" *Statistics Canada* (2009) at 5, online: Statistics Canada <www.statcan.gc.ca>. To help with the technicalities of this document, see Statistics Canada, "Definitions," online: Statistics Canada <www.statcan.gc.ca/pub/85-002-x/2009003/definitions-eng.htm>.

38 *House of Commons Debates,* No 184 (23 November 2012) at 34 (Michelle Rempel), online: <www.parl.gc.ca/content/hoc/House/411/Debates/184/HAN184-E.PDF> [emphasis mine].

39 The source of AANDC's mandate is vague. It stems from the Constitution, the *Indian Act,* and modern legislation, none of which sets out the basis of any principled funding relationship. AANDC explains that its mandate is essentially to maintain continuity with the current structures and to respond to judicial decisions when necessary: "[Besides legislation, the] Department's mandate is also derived from policy decisions and program practices that have been developed over the years; it is framed by judicial decisions with direct policy implications for the Department; and it is structured by funding arrangements or formal agreements with First Nations and/or provincial or territorial governments." Treasury Board of Canada Secretariat, "2012–13 Part III: Reports on Plans and Priorities (RPP)" *Aboriginal Affairs and Northern Development Canada and Canadian Polar Commission* (2012) at 4, online: Treasury Board of Canada Secretariat <www.tbs-sct.gc.ca/rpp/2012-2013/inst/ian/ian-eng.pdf>.

First Nation community is based not on legislation, but is instead based on the policies of the Department of Aboriginal Affairs and Northern Development Canada (AANDC).[40] Small communities are funded according to formulae that are different from those for large ones, and more northern and remote communities according to formulae different from those for urban ones. Internal AANDC policy documents go so far as to state that there is no coherence to the funding formulae, and even the department itself does not know the long-term goals of these labyrinthine arrangements.[41]

The current system of transfer payments to First Nation communities is not tied directly to the number of members in a community, and increases to social program and band administration spending for the communities has been capped by AANDC at 2 per cent growth per year since 1998, even when inflation exceed the 2 per cent rate.[42] Thus, as more members are born into a community (First Nations are the fastest

40 See Emmanuel Brunet-Jailly, "The Governance and Fiscal Environment of First Nations' Fiscal Intergovernmental Relations in Comparative Perspectives," *National Centre for First Nations Governance* (March 2008), online: Centre for First Nations Governance <fngovernance.org/ncfng_research/emmanual_brunet-jailley.pdf>.
41 For example, a report entitled "Special Study on INAC's Funding Arrangements" states,

> Funding arrangements are the primary instrument through which INAC implements its policies and programs ... Despite the centrality of funding arrangements to the Department and their importance in terms of INAC's relationship with First Nations ... [i]t is not clear what the overall objective is in terms of funding arrangements, there is a lack of coherence among programs and funding authorities that make up the arrangements, and there is no clear leadership at Headquarters to coordinate the management and implementation of funding arrangements.
>
> Responsibility for the design, negotiation, and monitoring of funding arrangements is split between INAC HQ and the regions, and across Finance, Programs and Regional Operations. There is no centre of expertise on grants and contributions... and no single point of contact for coordination with other federal departments ... Policy and program officials are often not familiar with the details of funding arrangements and funding authorities, and program terms and conditions can conflict with broader policy objectives or be inconsistent with each other.

Aboriginal Affairs and Northern Development Canada, "Special Study on INAC's Funding Arrangements" at 30–31, online: Aboriginal Affairs and Northern Development Canada <https://www.aadnc-aandc.gc.ca/DAM/DAM-INTER-HQ/STAGING/texte-text/fass_1100100011585_eng.pdf> ["Special Study"].
42 Inflation was only 2.3 per cent during this period, effectively freezing funding for more than a decade. For the response of AANDC ministry officials, see House of

growing demographic in Canada[43]) and as inflation negates the 2 per cent per annum increase in funding, First Nation communities face increasing financial constraints, even as the challenges and populations of their communities grow.

Commons Standing Committee on Aboriginal Affairs and Northern Development, 40th Parl, 2nd sess, No 006 (26 February 2009). Neil Yeates, associate deputy minister of AANDC, noted, "[T]he 2% cap … has been in place for a long time. It has placed a significant amount of pressure on the whole array of programming. It's not just education; it is social programming, and so on, more broadly … I would say, however, that the government has made investments [elsewhere constituting funding] above and beyond the 2% cap." *Ibid.* The 2 per cent cap applies to what AANDC calls the "core funding envelope" comprising fifteen programs, including post-secondary education and band support, the latter aiming to "provide a stable funding base to facilitate effective community governance." The 2 per cent cap is not applied to each community, but rather to each of AANDC's regional offices. This funding arrangement is explained and criticized in two internal audits. The first stated,

Since 1998/99, a global funding methodology has been employed that allocates core budget funds to [INAC regional offices] annually, with no breakdown of the core funds by program. National budget increases (currently 2% annually) are allocated to each [regional office] in proportion to their existing budgets … Internal Audit is of the view that the allocation methodologies currently in place do not ensure that eligible students across the country have equitable access to post-secondary education.

Indian and Northern Affairs Canada, "Audit of the Post-Secondary Education Program" (23 January 2009) at 11–12, online: Aboriginal Affairs and Northern Development Canada <https://www.aadnc-aandc.gc.ca/eng/1100100011661/1100100011663>.

The second stated,

The [regional offices] determine how the core funding is to be allocated within the fifteen programs based on the greatest needs of their [recipient communities] … [Though t]he core funding envelope increases 2% each year … where the total year-over-year increase in [band support] commitments is greater than 2%, regions are forced to re-allocate funds from other areas of their core funding envelope to meet [band support] commitments.

Indian and Northern Affairs Canada, "Audit of the Band Support Funding Program." (25 September 2009) at 11, 16, online: Aboriginal Affairs and Northern Development Canada <https://www.aadnc-aandc.gc.ca/eng/1100100011357/1100100011359>.

43 The present Indigenous population in Canada is 1.2 million and, by 2026, will number 1.5 million. The Indigenous population is growing at an average annual rate double that of the general Canadian population. Also, the Indigenous population is much younger, with a median age of twenty-seven, compared to a median

The *Indian Act* provides few meaningful powers of taxation[44] and little ability to raise money, so a community's decisions about its fiscal and capital priorities are subject to the spending authority of the minister of Aboriginal affairs and the policy directives of AANDC. The taxation powers of an Indian band are very limited and do not provide First Nation communities with significant revenues, certainly insufficient compared to those of other levels of government. Section 83 of the *Indian Act* prescribes the bylaw-making authority of First Nation governments. Section 83(1)(f) is so vague that it might authorize income taxes, but this has never been tested in court.[45] The *First Nations Goods and Services Tax Act* provides definitive authority to collect sales tax on reserve,[46] but the national unemployment rate of status Indians living on reserve is almost 25 per cent, and the median household income has remained unchanged for over ten years at an astonishingly low $26,000 per year.[47] Under these circumstances, sales taxes and income taxes, even if fully deployed, simply cannot yield significant revenue.

---

age of forty for the general Canadian population. Aboriginal Affairs and Northern Development Canada, *Aboriginal Demography: Population, Household and Family Projections, 2001–2026* at 5, online: Aboriginal Affairs and Northern Development Canada <www.aadnc-aandc.gc.ca/eng/1309463897584/1309464064861>; "Aboriginal Peoples in Canada in 2006: Inuit, Métis and First Nations, 2006 Census" *Statistics Canada* (2006) at 14, online: Statistics Canada <www12.statcan.ca/census-recensement/2006/as-sa/97-558/pdf/97-558-XIE2006001.pdf>.

44 I should note here that communities that negotiate their own self-government agreements are free to negotiate for themselves new or augmented powers to tax. Further, communities opting into the *First Nations Fiscal and Statistical Management Act*, *First Nations Goods and Services Tax Act*, and *First Nations Land Management Act* have augmented powers of taxation such as sales tax and real property tax. The otherwise limited powers of taxation under the *Indian Act* are enumerated in section 83.

45 *Indian Act, supra* note 2, 83(1)(f). It should be noted that s 83(1)(f) is so vague it seems to authorize "almost any means of taxation of band members, including income taxes"; Jack Woodward, *Native Law*, loose leaf (Toronto: Carswell, 2012) at 12:350. To my knowledge, 83(1)(f) has never been utilized by a First Nation to impose personal income taxes on its members.

46 S 3(1).

47 See Indian and Northern Affairs Canada, *Comparison of Socio-economic Conditions 1996 and 2001: Registered Indians, Registered Indians Living on Reserve and the Total Population of Canada* at 15, online: Library and Archives Canada <www.collections-canada.gc.ca/webarchives/20071206083536/http://www.ainc-inac.gc.ca/pr/sts/csc/csc_e.pdf>. In comparison, during this period the median Canadian household income grew from $44,000 to $47,000 (constant 2000 dollars).

IV. Financial Accountability

Funds that flow from the federal government to First Nation communities are supposed to be spent for the benefit of the community and its members, and proof that funds are spent in this way is typically what is meant by "accountability." There has been no shortage of calls for accountability of this kind. Politicians and the press regularly seek to make First Nation communities more accountable, and to that end the *First Nations Financial Transparency Act* was passed in March 2013.[48] This Act is just thirteen sections long and purports to "strengthen first nations governance by increasing accountability and transparency, *giving first nations community members the information they need to make informed choices about their leadership.*"[49] The Act requires the preparation and public disclosure of annual consolidated financial statements and statements of remuneration paid to the chief and councillors. It also requires that those documents be provided to any community members who request them.

No one will argue with accountability in the abstract, and First Nations people share with the settler people a desire for their governments to be accountable to them as citizens. Similarly, the federal Crown has the right to ensure that funds transferred for a specific purpose are spent accordingly. But it is important to understand the context in which this statute was introduced. Even before the *First Nations Financial Transparency Act* was passed, First Nation communities were (and are still) required to file more than 150 reports each year on their spending,[50] and the *Indian Act* already requires the minister of Aboriginal affairs to approve such spending and ensure that expenditures are

---

48 *First Nations Financial Transparency Act*, SC 2013, c 7 (royal assent received 27 March 2013). For further analysis of the Bill, see Tonina Simeone and Shauna Troniak, "Legislative Summary, Bill C-27: An Act to enhance the financial accountability and transparency of First Nations" (Ottawa: Library of Parliament, 2013), online: <www.parl.gc.ca/Content/LOP/LegislativeSummaries/41/1/c27-e.pdf>.

49 *House of Commons Debates, supra* note 39.

50 The auditor general in 2011 reported,

In 2002 ... we estimated that [the] four [principal] federal organizations together required about 168 reports annually from each First Nations reserve. We found that many of the reports were unnecessary and were not in fact used by the federal organizations ... In our 2006 follow-up audit ... INAC's officials told us that the Department obtained more than 60,000 reports a year from over 600 First Nation communities.

to be "used for the best interest of the band."[51] Thus the federal government already has all of the information that it could possibly need on
First Nation spending.[52]

The main problem with the *First Nations Financial Transparency Act*
is that it goes beyond its stated purpose of giving First Nation members the "information they need to make informed choices."[53] The Act
specifies that the venue for disclosure is the band's website, and so the
information is available to many more people than simply First Nation
community members.[54] The requirement that consolidated financial
statements be published means that some aspects of confidential agreements made between First Nations and resource companies working
on the First Nations' traditional lands are now publicly available. This
undermines the negotiating power of First Nations, because everyone in the resource sector now has access to the details of previous

---

[In 2008 t]he Treasury Board of Canada Secretariat … [issued an] Action Plan to
Reform the Administration of Grant and Contribution Programs… commit[ing] the
government to reduc[e] recipients' administrative and reporting burden … [A]t the
time of our audit, INAC had yet to finalize a process … to determine the level of
reporting requirements most appropriate to each First Nation …

Despite many initiatives, we have not seen a significant reduction in the reporting
burden. We were able to track the number of reports [filed in the electronic transfer
payment system used regularly by 228 of 700 First Nations – DS]. The number
of … reports increased from 30,000 in the 2007–08 fiscal year to 32,000 in 2009–10 …
[Many] First Nations officials … indicated that the reporting burden has increased in
recent years …

Many initiatives with the potential to streamline reporting have been started but
have not resulted in meaningful improvement.

*Status Report of the Auditor General of Canada to the House of Commons – Chapter 4:
Programs for First Nations on Reserves* (2011), at 32–35, online: <www.oag-bvg.gc.ca/
internet/docs/parl_oag_201106_04_e.pdf> [*Auditor General's Status Report*].

51 *Indian Act, supra* note 3, s 61.
52 In 2011, the auditor general of Canada characterized the government efforts to streamline reporting requirements over the last *ten years* as "unsatisfactory" and having "not
resulted in meaningful improvement." Reporting requirements have since increased;
Auditor General's Status Report, supra note 51. See also, the Assembly of First Nations' own
report on this issue, *First Nations Accountability Fact Sheet – June 2011*, online: <www.afn.
ca/uploads/files/accountability/11-05-31_fs-accountability_fe.pdf>.
53 *Supra* note 52.
54 *First Nations Financial Transparency Act, supra* note 49, s 8. The *First Nations Governance Act* contained these same requirements for public disclosure of audited statements; *supra* note 32 at cl 9.3.

agreements. For these reasons, the *First Nations Financial Transparency Act* failed to gain the support of First Nations.

That said, I believe the issue of financial accountability in First Nation communities is capable of becoming an object of overlapping consensus: First Nations people want their governments to be accountable to them, and the federal government as funding agent wants to know that monies transferred to First Nation communities are being spent for their intended purposes. But coming to agreement on a suitable statutory framework for such accountability will be possible only if we can agree on who is to be accountable to whom. First Nation governments already have detailed requirements designed to ensure financial transparency to their members.[55] In that light, the trumpet calls for accountability appear not to be for the benefit of First Nation members, but rather to open the communities' books to a political base of sceptical non-Indian citizens who do not believe that "*you* are spending *our* money wisely."[56]

It may well be that First Nations would agree to legislation that embodied the department of AANDC's existing policy requirements, namely, the requirement to disclose detailed financial information to AANDC and to band members. When partisan political concerns such

---

55 Currently, Aboriginal Affairs and Northern Development Canada's *Year-End Financial Reporting Handbook* requires every First Nation receiving federal funds to disclose in its financial statements the salaries, honoraria, travel expenses, and other remuneration paid to or received by elected officials (and some employees). These statements must include funds from all sources from which the First Nation receives funding. According to AANDC's Model Funding Agreement for 2015–16, First Nations must also provide within 60 days a copy of the report to any band member who asks for one, and the band must complete the financial report within 120 days of its fiscal year end. See Aboriginal Affairs and Northern Development Canada, "First Nations and Tribal Councils National Funding Agreement Model for 2015–2016" (2014) online: s 6.3 <https://www.aadnc-aandc.gc.ca/eng/1412272593986/1412272658789>. These provisions specify that members can request, and must be provided, financial statements from all previous years, and that the band may not charge more than a modest fee to cover the cost of copying the documents.

56 It pains me to point out that First Nations people pay taxes. If Indians live off-reserve, they have no tax breaks, and pay income, property, and sales taxes at the same rates as every other Canadian. To those persons who believe that the filing of 150 financial reports and ministerial oversight are insufficient, I would argue that the ambit of their concern should be directed to reforming the existing and extensive financial reporting rather than demanding new and unnecessary levels of transparency and accountability.

as those reflected in the *First Nations Financial Transparency Act* trump just and principled reforms, the ambit of overlapping consensus shrinks and the goodwill necessary to support a process of reform disappears.

I shall return to the issue of financial accountability later in this chapter, and I hold open the possibility that new regulations or new legislation may be desirable for both First Nations and the Crown. However, if accountability is to become an area of overlapping consensus, reforms must be aimed truly at making First Nation governments accountable to their members rather than merely being window dressing reforms aimed at responding to the unfounded scepticism of non-Indigenous Canadians.

V. Integration

"Integration" is a word with a dark history in the context of First Nations–settler relations, tied as the term is to assimilation and the residential school system. I do not mean integration in this way. By "integration" I mean that First Nation communities should be able to choose the degree to which they will participate in the modern global economy. This includes the manner in which First Nation communities might wish to use their lands and resources: for commercial exploitation, for leasing, for security against loans, or for preservation in pristine natural form. But I also use the word "integration" in a second way: the incorporation of non-status Indians into First Nation communities should be encouraged to the extent that this is desired by, and beneficial to, communities and non-status Indians.[57] Below, I shall propose how and under what circumstances First Nation communities might consider opening their membership doors more widely to non-status Indians, Metis, and even non-Aboriginal people.

A. Bars to Economic Integration

Let me begin with integration in the first of the two senses: economic integration. First Nation people and communities must be able to choose for themselves the extent to which they wish to participate in

---

57 See also Borrows, *Indigenous Constitution*, *supra* note 29 at 155–64; John Borrows, *Drawing Out Law: A Spirit's Guide* (Toronto: University of Toronto Press, 2010) at 202–03.

the broader Canadian and global economy. I believe that there is a consensus among the settler people that First Nation people should be able to work and farm either on or off reserve,[58] and First Nations people also want to be able to make such choices for themselves. Some kinds of economic integration therefore have the potential to become the object of overlapping consensus and legislative reform of the *Indian Act*.

Several sections of the current *Indian Act* drastically and arbitrarily limit First Nation participation in the broader economy. For example, consider the *Indian Act*'s fixation on farming.[59] Section 71(1) provides that the minister may operate farms on reserves and may purchase and distribute pure seeds to Indian farmers without charge. As for the profits from these farms, section 71(2) says that the minister may apply profits to extend farming operations on reserves, make loans to Indians to enable them to farm, or in "any way that he considers to be *desirable to promote the progress and development of the Indians.*"[60] Further, section 71 must be read in conjunction with section 32(1) of the Act, which provides that any transaction of agricultural goods by a band or band member to a non-member is void unless the "superintendent approves the transaction in writing."[61] In other words, the Act allows the minister to promote farming, but restricts the sale to non-Indians of agricultural goods produced by Indians. Similarly, section 93 of the *Indian Act* prohibits, without ministerial approval, the removal from an Indian reserve the following items: minerals, stone, sand, gravel, clay, soil, trees, timber, cordwood, or hay.[62] Thus, Indians can sell neither

---

58 See John Borrows & Sarah Morales, "Challenge, Change and Development in Aboriginal Economies" in Joseph Eliot Magnet & Dwight A Dorey, eds, *Legal Aspects of Aboriginal Business Development* (Markham, ON: LexisNexis Butterworths, 2005) 137.

59 During the earliest incarnations of the *Indian Act*, and into the early twentieth century, farming was understood to be the ultimate means of assimilating Indigenous people into the labour market. To the extent these efforts were successful, the *Indian Act* was modified to make such participation more difficult. See Sarah A Carter, *Lost Harvests: Prairie Indian Reserve Farmers and Government Policy* (Montreal & Kingston: McGill-Queen's University Press, 1990); Tony Ward, "Reserve Farming on the Canadian Prairies 1870–1910" (Paper delivered at the Canadian Network for Economic History Conference, 3 October 2009), online: Canadian Network for Economic History <www.ibrarian.net/navon/paper/Reserve_Farming_on_the_Canadian_Prairies.pdf?paperid=16020531>.

60 *Indian Act, supra* note 2 at ss 71(1)–(2) [emphasis mine].

61 *Ibid*, s 32.1. These provisions apply only to Indians living on reservation in the Prairie Provinces where, of course, the best farmlands are to be found.

62 *Ibid*, s 93.

the produce of their farms, nor the naturally occurring wealth of their reserve lands without ministerial approval.

Another deterrent to economic participation created by the *Indian Act* for First Nation people living on reserve are restrictions on access to capital. Under sections 29 and 89 of the Act, the property of an Indian on reserve cannot be seized, and the Act specifically rules out the possibility of mortgaging reserve lands (with the exception of leasehold interests per section 89(1.1)). This means that First Nation people living on reserve cannot access capital through conventional means and cannot enjoy the intergenerational transfer of wealth through real estate that is common off reserve.

Recent proposals to amend the *Indian Act* to allow for the creation of real property interests have merit and should be considered on their own terms.[63] Some of those terms, however, include the very uneasy history that Indigenous people in the Americas have had with efforts to encourage economic integration through the privatization and commodification of Indigenous lands. Past efforts at privatization have resulted in Indigenous people losing vast portions of their communally held lands with virtually no benefit to the economies of Indigenous communities. In Canada in the 1870s, Métis people were issued "scrip" – a form of currency that could be used to purchase Crown lands. Most scrip ended up enriching unscrupulous settler representatives, including members of the federal government, a lieutenant governor, and even the chief justice of Manitoba.[64] Métis people, on the other hand, ended up with very little of the 1.4 million acres subject to scrip.[65] Similarly, in the United States, the *Dawes Act* carved Indian reservations into allotments of private property.[66] Between 1887 and 1934, Indian land holdings in the United States dropped from 138 million acres to just 48 million acres, and nearly 20 million of those remaining acres

---

63 See, for example, Tom Flanagan, Christopher Alcantara, & André Le Dressay, *Beyond the Indian Act: Restoring Aboriginal Property Rights* (Montreal & Kingston: McGill-Queen's University Press, 2010).

64 *Report of the Royal Commission on Aboriginal Peoples: Perspectives and Realities*, vol 4 (Ottawa: Supply and Services Canada, 1996) at 199–386.

65 See Linda Goyette, "The X Files" (2003) 123:2 Canadian Geographic 70; Nicole C O'Byrne, "'A Rather Vexed Question …': The Federal-Provincial Debate over the Constitutional Responsibility for Métis Scrip" (2007) 12:2 Rev Const Stud 215. See also *Manitoba Metis Federation Inc v Canada (AG)*, 2013 SCC 14, [2013] 1 SCR 623.

66 See DS Otis, *Dawes Act and the Allotment of Indian Lands (Civilization of American Indian)* (Norman: University of Oklahoma Press, 1973).

are desert or semi-desert lands. In other words, more than 80 per cent of Indian lands were transferred into the hands of non-Indians, with virtually no economic development for the Indian nations subject to the *Dawes Act*.[67]

Given that the history of privatizing Indigenous lands is largely the history of transferring those lands at low cost to non-Indigenous people, many First Nations are rightly sceptical of any such proposals. At the same time, however, I note that property reforms may be helpful to some First Nation communities. Some communities may wish to relocate entirely, and to do so, they would need to sell their lands and obtain new lands. While I do not expect private property reform to end poverty or even lead to substantial economic growth in First Nation communities,[68] I acknowledge that some communities might feel that they could benefit from the spirit of entrepreneurship that could be fostered by access to capital.

B. The Potential for Overlapping Consensus on Economic Integration

Thus, on the issue of economic integration, I shall suppose that there is generally broad, overlapping consensus on reform of at least some sections of the *Indian Act*. The prohibition on sales of natural resource and farmed produce, for example, cannot possibly be justified and is ripe for consensual reform. Revisions to the *Indian Act* that would make reservation lands private property are controversial, but such proposals should not be entirely off the table as a part of a suite of potential reforms. But at present, there is not a consensus among First Nations that would justify putting real property reform at the top of the reform agenda. This is just to say that to proceed with property reforms in

---

67 See United States, *The Purpose and Operation of the Wheeler-Howard Indian Rights Bill: Hearing before the House and Senate Committees on Indian Affairs* (1934) at 2–5 (John Collier), online: Connecticut State Library <cslib.cdmhost.com/cdm/singleitem/collection/p4005coll11/id/513/rec/1>. See also United States, *The Indian Reorganization Act 75 Years Later: Renewing Our Commitment to Restore Tribal Homelands and Promote Self-Determination Hearing before the Senate Committee on Indian Affairs* (2011) (G William Rice), online: Senate Committee on Indian Affairs <www.indian.senate.gov/sites/default/files/upload/files/062311CHRG-112shrg68389.pdf>.
68 Jamie Baxter & Michael Trebilcock, "Formalizing Land Tenure in First Nations: Evaluating the Case for Reserve Tenure Reform" (2009) 7:2 Indigenous LJ 45, assert that land tenure reform should be only one of a range of possible solutions to advance economic development in First Nation communities.

the absence of other significant reforms that are part of an overlapping consensus between First Nations and the Crown is to substitute the priorities of the Crown and a small group of First Nations (who do want private property on reserve lands) instead of beginning with reforms on which there is consensus. It is simply better policy to proceed first in areas where there is already broad consensus on the reforms that are needed.

C. Integration through Membership

I now turn to the question of membership in a First Nations community, and in particular the extension of membership to what are termed non-status Indians. Let me begin by saying that the *Indian Act* itself determines who is an Indian for the purposes of the Act. The rules are very complex and have changed a number of times in recent decades. Families and individuals have, over the generations, found themselves removed from the registration rolls in Ottawa and made into non-Indians, and then later found themselves considered Indians again after legislative reform.[69] Others who were removed from the rolls continue, along with their children and grandchildren, to be non-Indians. To assist the reader, I have compiled the many rules governing who, and under what circumstances, one is legally an Indian into one set of rules that are generally true. You can be an Indian for the purposes of the Act only if:

1 Your parents were both legally Indians, in which case you are a section 6(1) Indian, and your children will be section 6(1) Indians.
2 One parent was legally a 6(1) section Indian and the other was not a legally registered Indian, in which case your children will be section 6(2) Indians.
3 One parent was a section 6(2) Indian, and the other parent was a section 6(1) Indian, in which case your children are section 6(1) Indians.
4 Both parents were section 6(2) Indians, in which case your children are section 6(1) Indians.

To put this in still plainer language, if your grandmother held legal status as an Indian and had a child with a non-Indian, that child – your

---

69 See my own example recounted in Douglas Sanderson, reviews of *Tribal Constitutionalism: States, Tribes and the Governance of Membership* by Kirsty Gover and *Beyond Blood: Rethinking Indigenous Identity* by Pamela D Palmater (2013) 63:3 UTLJ 511.

mother or father – would be a section 6(2) Indian. And then if your mother or father also had a child with a non-Indian, that child – you – would not be legally recognized as an Indian. This is informally called the "two-generation rule," and while not explicitly using terminology like "blood quantum," the implicit effect is to categorize First Nations people as a race whose purity requires blood lineage that is traceable to the fetishistic ideal of a "pure" Indian.[70]

Without government recognition and registration attesting to your status as an Indian person, you cannot legally be an Indian in Canada, at least not for the purposes of the *Indian Act*. However, being an Indian for the purposes of the *Indian Act* – that is, being a status or treaty Indian – and being a member of a First Nation community are not the same things.[71] It is possible to be a member of a First Nations community without being recognized by the federal government as an Indian. The *Indian Act*'s membership provisions allow communities to develop their own membership codes and to admit new members as they please,[72] but the vast majority now have membership provisions patterned after the *Indian Act*.[73] To understand why this is so, one must consider the financial implications of membership for First

70 Sebastien Grammond, "Discrimination in the Rules of Indian Status and the McIvor Case" (2009) 35 QLJ 421.
71 For example, band members who are not registered as status Indians with the federal government may still be band members. Band members have the legal capacity to make claims with respect to certain kinds of community resources and processes such as accessing trust funds and voting in band elections, but do not have the right to other rights such as the federal health insurance provided to status Indians. See also, *McIvor v Canada (Registrar, Indian and Northern Affairs)*, 2009 BCCA 153, 91 BCLR (4th) 1. See also, Mary C Hurley & Tonina Simeone, "Bill C-3: Gender Equity in Indian Registration Act" *Library of Parliament Research Publications* (2010), online: Parliament of Canada <www.parl.gc.ca/About/Parliament/LegislativeSummaries/bills_ls.asp?Language=E&ls=c3&Parl=40&Ses=3&source=library_prb>.
72 While bands can create membership codes, and membership rules under section 10 of the Act, this does not make members "Indians" for purposes related to the federal registrar of Indians. Indians remain by definition persons registered as Indians under the *Indian Act*, s 5(1), *supra* note 2. For more on the virtues and risks associated with coupling and decoupling membership in Indigenous communities, see Kirsty Gover, *Tribal Constitutionalism: States, Tribes, and the Governance of Membership* (Oxford: Oxford University Press, 2011).
73 Indeed, some communities have membership provisions that are even more restrictive than the *Indian Act*'s blood quantum provisions. See Pamela Palmater, *Beyond Blood, supra* note 16.

Nation communities. Section 10 of the Act decouples membership from funding because funding depends to some degree on the number of status Indians in a community (as determined by the federal government), rather than on the number of recognized community members (as determined by the membership codes of the Indian band). Communities that avail themselves of section 10 to expand their membership receive no additional federal or provincial funding for new members. But all members, including non-status members, are entitled to certain benefits, including the right to be beneficiaries of trust funds,[74] compensation from expropriated lands,[75] a certificate of possession allowing for exclusive occupation of a plot of land on the reserve,[76] benefits from band revenue,[77] and the ability to receive benefits related to farming, among others.[78] Given that many of these rights draw on the resources of an Indian band, without any concomitant rise in the community's funding levels, it is no surprise that bands are unwilling to extend membership in a more generous fashion than does the *Indian Act*.

There is another, more troubling aspect of the *Indian Act*'s rules about who is and who is not an Indian. By setting out incentives to limit First Nations community membership only to those persons who are already legally status Indians, the federal government has created a whole class of persons – non-status Indians – who are by every appropriate measure First Nations people, but who can claim no legal recognition of their status, and for whom membership in a community is possible in theory, but not in practice.[79]

---

74 *Indian Act, supra* note 2, ss 61.1, 63.
75 *Ibid,* ss 18.2, 35.4, 65.
76 *Ibid,* ss 20, 22–25, 58.3.
77 *Ibid,* s 66.2.
78 *Ibid,* s 71. Other rights may include the right of residency (81.1), the right to buried on reserve (*ibid*), and to vote in or hold office in a First Nation community election.
79 On the issue of the two generation rule, and the creation of a class of persons deemed non-status Indians, the *RCAP* says, "Thus, it can be predicted that in future there may be bands on reserves with no status Indian members. They will have effectively been assimilated for legal purposes into provincial populations. Historical assimilation goals will have been reached, and the federal government will have been relieved of its constitutional obligation of protection, since there will no longer be any legal 'Indians' left to protect." *Report of the Royal Commission on Aboriginal Peoples: Looking Forward, Looking Back,* vol 1 (Ottawa: Supply and Services Canada, 1996) at 307.

I might best be able to explain the situation of non-status Indians by relating a story from my own past. One of the worst experiences that I have ever endured was a two-day workshop when I worked as a videographer for the Royal Commission on Aboriginal Peoples. I was hired as part of a small research project called the Urban Identity Project. We assembled small groups of young urban Indians between the ages of fifteen and twenty years. None were status Indians, but they were all clearly Indians. They looked like Indians, they talked like Indians, they knew who they were. And many of them had tried to go home. They had hitched to the reserves where they knew they were from, where they knew their parents or grandparents had lived, and they begged to come home, home to this place where they thought they could find themselves, their cultures, and their place in the world. But they were, each and every one, told to leave. There were no resources to feed these kids, let alone house them. There were no language classes or ways for them to connect with their culture, their heritage, or their sense of identity. And they cried. They cried and they cried in front of my camera. They just wanted to go home, they just wanted to be who they were, but they lacked all the social and geographic and linguistic tools to find strength in their identity because the source and place of that identity was and is their home community. For all their pitiable state, these teens were deemed not to be Indians. The *Indian Act* said they were not Indians, and so they were told to leave the very communities that they so desperately wanted to join.

In many ways, this situation – Indigenous children who want to reclaim a part of their culture but who have no access to the institutions of that culture – is emblematic of a serious problem affecting contemporary Indigenous communities. The problem is the lack of alignment between the incentives of membership and the appropriate resources that would allow First Nations to repatriate the non-status Indians who want to rejoin their home communities. First Nations people who are legally non-status Indians know where their home communities are located, and the communities know how to adopt these persons into their families and clans, because there are many ways of doing so, both under provincial and Indigenous law. The reintegration of non-status Indians back to their home communities is the kind of policy issue that could become an object of overlapping consensus between First Nation people and the broader Canadian public. In the next section, I shall demonstrate how to tie together the issues of financial and membership integration with the issues around financial accountability, leading to a package of reforms that is capable of being the object of an overlapping consensus.

VI. Creating Overlapping Consensus by Combining Accountability and Integration

The reason that First Nation communities cannot easily integrate non-status Indians into their communities is a lack of alignment between resources and membership. Because First Nation communities have few effective powers of taxation, the vast majority of all revenues coming into a First Nation community are federal transfer dollars, and these dollars pay for education, housing, child welfare, maintenance, salaries of public officials, and the maintenance of public infrastructure such as roads, bridges, and water treatment plants. These costs are borne by small and often remote communities who have no negotiating power with their primary funders[80] and whose distance from large urban centres can mean increased costs for all manner of projects, from the mundane acquisition of printer toner, to the construction of houses and the provision of groceries. So the reality is that while First Nations can determine their own membership, doing so means that a community's

---

80 *Special Study, supra* note 44 at 31–32:

There is no real negotiation of funding arrangements with [First Nations] and [Tribal Councils]. They are drawn up and delivered for approval by Chief and Council or the Tribal Council with very little discussion. [First Nations] and [Tribal Councils] perceive it as a "take it or leave it" proposition. Budgeting, allocations and formulae are not well understood and budgets may be cut without warning. For most recipients, there is little discussion of their plans or outcomes; little guidance on best practices; and little opportunity to network and share experiences with others in the same region or across the country ...

Funding arrangements as currently implemented do not promote the movement of First Nations, Tribal Councils and other Aboriginal recipients towards increasingly responsive, flexible, innovative and self-sustained policies, programs or services ... The profile of funding arrangements has been static over the past decade.

Amounts allocated to management and administration at the band and the Tribal Council level are low and attempts to gain additional funding in the past have failed. There is very little funding available for capacity building related to institutions or programs. The cap of 2 per cent on funding to the regions is putting pressure on any discretionary spending in an effort to protect income assistance and education spending.

already stretched resources become still further stretched because no new resources attach to new community members.

A. Linking Membership and Revenue through Federal Income Tax

To make the ability to determine their membership meaningful, First Nation communities must be granted the power to raise revenues to provide basic government services in conjunction with the ability to admit new members. Ideally, membership and revenue should be linked so that as membership or citizenship lists grow, so too grows the ability to provide government services. One way to do this is to allow every member of a First Nation to include a box on federal income tax forms that would, if checked, direct a First Nation community member's income tax to his or her home community regardless of whether the community member lived on or off reserve.[81] I do not believe that members' income taxes alone could ever eliminate the need for other funding sources, but I do believe that this tax base could meet at least some of the needs of First Nation communities. Moreover, the collection of members' federal income taxes, while not sufficient to replace existing revenue streams, is an example of a proper fiscal relationship between First Nations and the Crown that is itself capable of being the object of an overlapping consensus, because the proposed reforms advance both First Nations' goal of self-determination and the Crown's goal of promoting economic development and fiscal accountability among First Nations.

This linking of federal income tax of community members to band revenue via membership has several implications. First, it would mean that First Nation communities would have an opportunity to raise revenues independent of federal transfer payments or other grant programs. This in turn would mean that First Nation communities could

---

81 In principle, First Nations could negotiate with the federal government a tax abatement system similar to that used by the provinces and some large corporations. The federal government would be contracted to collect the tax revenue, and then the federal government would write annual checks to each of the communities taking part in the abatement agreement. For the seed of this idea, see Borrows, "Seven Generations," *supra* note 127 at 28. The ability to choose to direct tax monies to support a particular institution is not new in Canada. Ontario's *Assessment Act* allows individuals to direct a portion of their property taxes to support Catholic schools rather than the public school system. RSO 1990, c A31, s16.

begin to set their own ends: they could decide to build schools and houses, or they could choose to fix their broken water treatment plants or invest in language and cultural programs for their members. First Nation communities could, in other words, set priorities, and then set out to achieve ends of their own making, and with their own financial resources.[82]

A second implication of allowing First Nations to tax their members is that chiefs and councils would be accountable to their citizens rather than to the federal government. Because federal transfer payments are the primary source of income in an Indian community, leadership can be forced to spend all their time making sure that the money keeps flowing, and that means making sure the federal government's priorities are met. Band administration is required to do this because, without meeting Ottawa's priorities, the communities would not continue to receive funding, or their funding would become wholly managed by third-party entities appointed by the Crown. By collecting income tax from community members, chiefs and councils would find themselves more accountable to their own community members, because they would be spending the tax money collected from their own citizens.[83]

Third, by being empowered to determine membership, and being able to collect income tax from members, communities will realize the appropriate incentives to bring home all those non-status Indians who want to come home, who want to learn their language, and who want to live proudly as members of their communities. Communities will be able to bring home non-status Indians, to teach them their language and culture, and then to have them start making an income to contribute to their home communities, whether that means employment on or off reserve. Those teenagers who I filmed so long ago would not be turned away, they would be welcomed, and they would be embraced, because the incentives for doing so would be properly aligned.

A fourth implication of my membership proposal concerns reciprocity of opportunity. So, just as a member of the Nipissing First Nation can, if he or she wishes, leave his or her community, move to Vancouver, become a marine biologist, and never once think about or engender

---

82 Of course, the amount of money at issue here is relatively small, but it is not insignificant.
83 See Mariana Mota Prado & Michael J Trebilcock, *What Makes Countries Poor? Institutional Determinants of Development* (Northampton, MA: Edward Elgar, 2012).

his or her Anishinabek identity, it simply has to be the case that membership in a First Nation community can, in principle, be open to anyone. A Hungarian cab driver in Sudbury or a *National Post* columnist in Toronto should be able, in principle, to decide "I hate this life" and make the decision that he wants to move to Northern Quebec. And if after doing so, he learns Cree, acquires a Cree name, marries into a Cree family, and is adopted into a clan, then I cannot see any reason why that person should not be Cree.[84] Being Cree is, after all, a matter of culture, of language, of world view, and these things can be learned.[85] I do not think there is any set of objective tests that, if passed, makes you Cree, but there is certainly a subjective set of community standards, and if we allow these standards to develop within cultural norms, then we stand able to create a fluid boundary of identity and nationhood.[86] Indeed, the powers in section 10 of the *Indian Act* are already sufficient to allow communities to develop creative, community-based standards that could include length of residency in the community, fluency in the community's language, and other demonstrations of cultural integration such as adoption into a clan.

One might think that this could allow large numbers of settler people to declare their Indigenous identity and move to First Nation communities. But there are no tax advantages to doing so, no secret well of casino money that pours riches onto First Nation members, no special access to social resources of any kind. Indeed, as discussed above, most First Nation communities enjoy no socio-economic advantages whatsoever over their non-Indian counterparts. It is true that some First Nation communities are very wealthy as a result of their proximity to urban developments, or on lands rich in oil, or through good old-fashioned strong leadership over many years. But these communities have incentives to keep their membership rolls limited and are eager to do so. For example, the Sawridge Band, which is rich in oil revenues, had to be sued by the Crown and forced to admit new members after changes to the *Indian Act* allowed those people to be

---

84 Indeed the judicial test for identifying rights-bearing Metis persons has just three components: self-identification as a Metis person, and acceptance by a Metis community that is itself a historic rights-bearing community. *R v Powley*, 2003 SCC 43, [2003] 2 SCR 207.
85 For a related discussion, see Borrows, "Seven Generations," *supra* note 12 at 30.
86 See my *Argument from Corrective Justice, supra* note 5 at 121–25.

registered as legal Indians.[87] Thus, I do not think we need to worry that there would be a vast move of non-Indians into First Nation communities. Moreover, allowing more people to become members of First Nation communities and to support those communities with tax dollars allows those communities to better compete *as communities*.

Another way to spread the benefits of my proposed income tax redirection is to enable the funds collected to be used as collateral against loans for large infrastructure projects. Section 89(1) of the *Indian Act* restricts the seizure or mortgaging of "property on reserve." This means that secured transactions like loans are impossible when the assets of a person or business are located on reserve, because section 89(1) makes it impossible to collect any collateral that may have been offered to secure a loan. I propose that First Nation communities be able to opt out of this section of the Act with respect to the revenue stream generated by the income tax of band members. This would enable communities to borrow money for infrastructure and other projects and to secure those loans with future tax revenues, something that is currently impossible under the *Indian Act*.[88] A similar scheme already exists with respect to property taxes collected by communities that have opted into sections of the *First Nations Fiscal Management Act*.[89]

B. How These Reforms Facilitate Overlapping Consensus

A key part of my argument is about the alignment of incentives with legislative reforms that are capable of becoming the object of an overlapping consensus between First Nations and the broader Canadian public. By providing both a means and a motivation to identify community members who lack legal status as Indians, First Nations can grow their communities by welcoming home the current diaspora of

---

87 *Sawridge Band v Canada*, 2004 FCA 16, [2004] 3 FCR 274.

88 This proposal is different from other recent proposals such as the *First Nations Property Ownership Act*, which would allow, one presumes – the legislation is not yet drafted – First Nations to sell their lands to non-Indians, and to mortgage those same lands with banks and other lenders. My proposal is not tied to land, only to the future tax revenue streams.

89 *First Nations Fiscal Management Act*, RSC 2005, c 9. See also J Paul Salembier, Al Broughton, Jeffery Hutchinson, Andrew Beynon, & Karl Jacques, *Modern First Nations Legislation Annotated* (Markham, ON: LexisNexis Butterworths, 2012) at 65–71. Salembier et al note that, as of November 2011, there has yet to be an issue of bonds under this scheme.

non-status Indians. And in bringing home this diaspora and linking membership with the allocation of federal income tax, First Nation communities gain access to a stream of revenue that grows with the success of their communities: as more people become educated and employed, more money will flow back to their home communities, and one can hope to establish some sort of a virtuous circle with increasing membership leading to increased revenues. As the number of First Nation community members grows, and as more and more of those community members begin to pay income taxes to their home communities, community members themselves will have incentive to demand greater accountability between themselves as citizens and the chief and council who allocate the spending of community resources.

One way of ensuring this accountability is through legislation that is itself the object of overlapping consensus. To the extent that First Nations and the Crown agree on the proper ambit of that accountability – namely, that chiefs and councils are to be accountable to their members – an overlapping consensus on this issue can be achieved and enshrined in legislation such as an amendment to the *First Nations Fiscal Transparency Act*.

By tying together integration and accountability, my proposal aims at a broad core of overlapping consensus between First Nation and non-First Nations people. What is more, the changes I propose couple legislative change with the revenue necessary to sustain Indigenous communities. It is worth comparing the approach that I advocate with an alternative approach such as that proposed by the Kelowna Accord, a political agreement reached among the provinces, the federal government, and Aboriginal organizations from across the country. The Kelowna Accord promised five billion dollars in funds from the federal and provincial governments over five years, with the promise to renegotiate another five-year term once the first term had expired. The object of the accord was to invest in Aboriginal health, education, and housing, such that at the end of the ten-year term, Aboriginal people would be more or less on par with non-Aboriginal Canadians on a wide range of social outcomes, including education, health, and housing. Within months a minority Conservative government was elected to Parliament and refused to budget the resources to fund the accord.

Since then, some commentators have called for a return to the Kelowna Accord as a road map for the relationship between Aboriginal people and the Crown.[90] I have my doubts. Five billion dollars is a lot of money and provides for very significant investment in Aboriginal communities. I applaud that effort. But I cannot help but think about a story my mother once told me about a community centre that was built in one of the northern communities. The centre was built as part of some kind of a deal, the details of which I forget, but the point is that the centre was built. What was not considered in the negotiations to build the community centre, however, was the upkeep cost of maintaining the building over years and decades. Nor was there revenue available to staff the centre so that the building could be supervised and provide activities for community members. The building became underused, and then experienced the kind of physical deterioration one would expect without sufficient maintenance. The Kelowna Accord is like that community centre. I applaud the investment, but how are we First Nations people to fund our communities in the long term? Investments are important, but even ten-year investments do not alter the landscape of funding, but instead maintain the relationship of dependency and paternalism.

It is worth stating that, despite its shortcomings, the death of the Kelowna Accord was a tragedy, because enormous investments *are* required in First Nation communities. But we are remiss if all we do is mourn the loss of the Kelowna Accord and long for its return. Much can be learned from the accord's demise, and perhaps one of the clearest lessons is that the process of building and maintaining consensus must be strong enough to endure and deliver the reforms and resources outlined in the agreement. The Kelowna Accord died because the incoming minority government did not share the values of the previous government, and the opposition parties were unwilling to vote against a budget bill that did not include the Kelowna Accord funding, because doing so would have brought down the minority government. The overlapping political consensus identified by the accord may have been strong, but it was not strong enough to endure either the natural ebb and flow of power nor the raw politics of Ottawa.[91]

---

90 See, e.g., Christopher Alcantara, "Kelowna Accord Holds Key to Native Renewal" *Toronto Star* (3 January 2013), online: Toronto Star <www.thestar.com/opinion/editorialopinion/2013/01/03/kelowna_accord_holds_key_to_native_renewal.html>.

91 For a detailed critique of the Kelowna process, see Lisa L Patterson, "Aboriginal Roundtable to Kelowna Accord: Aboriginal Policy Negotiations" *Library of Parliament Research Publications* (2006), online: Parliament of Canada <www.parl.gc.ca/Content/LOP/researchpublications/prb0604-e.pdf>.

Conclusion

In this chapter I have tried to lay out a set of proposals that address some of the issues currently affecting First Nation communities: who is a citizen of a First Nation, what rights attach to that citizenship, and how do First Nation communities access revenues? I have done so in a manner that seeks to identify the shared priorities of both First Nations and the broader Canadian public. The Supreme Court of Canada has repeatedly stated that the purpose of section 35 of the *Constitution Act, 1982* is to "reconcile the prior presence of aboriginal peoples in North America with the assertion of Crown sovereignty,"[92] and to do this First Nations people and their settler counterparts must come to terms to which both parties can agree. The reconciliation promised by section 35 can never be achieved unless we have both the will and a process to identify shared priorities and to make substantive reforms.

The proposal I make in this chapter stands to alter many things about First Nations communities in Canada. I do not propose to end the *Indian Act*, but rather have proposed ways to improve the relationship between First Nations and the Crown. Of course, there are more than six hundred First Nations in Canada with a wide range of economic, cultural, and political aspirations that do not easily converge on blunt pan-Indian legislation such as the *Indian Act*.[93] The federal Crown, too, is composed of myriad ministries with competing interests. There is then no reason to suppose that the *Indian Act* alone can, or even should, be the sole legislative instrument for meeting the needs of the complex relationship between First Nations and the Crown. The principles of overlapping consensus that I have developed in this chapter can be usefully applied to the development of other legislative instruments that regulate the relationship between First Nations and the Crown.

I believe that an overlapping consensus can be achieved if we engage in a fair and respectful process and focus on the principles underlying the reforms. We need to focus on the right issues and pay attention to the very real need for adequate funding in First Nation communities. If we do these things, we can begin to come to terms with an *Indian*

---

92 See, for example, *Delgamuukw v British Columbia*, [1997] 3 SCR 1010 at para 141.
93 For an accounting of just some of the diverse legal traditions making up Canada's First Nations, see John Borrows, *Canada's Indigenous Constitution* (Toronto: University of Toronto Press, 2010).

Act that is not the subject of derision and does not stand for inequality and paternalism, but rather sets out the right relationship between First Nations and the Crown for generations to come. We can set this generation on the right path. What we owe the seven generations to come is not the abandonment of the *Indian Act*. We owe the next seven generations an *Indian Act* that sets out a proper relationship between themselves and the Crown and the settler people who live around and among us. We owe that to the next seven generations, just as we owe it to the seven generations who came before us and in whose shadow we walk today.

14 Walls and Bridges: Competing Agendas in Transitional Justice

COURTNEY JUNG[1]

The framework of transitional justice, originally devised to facilitate reconciliation in countries undergoing transitions from authoritarianism to democracy, is used with increasing frequency to respond to certain types of human rights violations against Indigenous peoples.[2] In some cases, transitional justice measures are employed in societies not undergoing regime transition. Transitional justice measures offer opportunities for reinscribing the responsibility of states towards their Indigenous populations, empowering Indigenous communities, responding to Indigenous demands to be heard, and rewriting history. Nevertheless, treating Indigenous demands for justice as a matter of "human rights" is an ethically loaded project that may reinforce liberal (and neoliberal) paradigms that Indigenous peoples often reject. Whether transitional justice measures will serve primarily to legitimate the status quo between post-colonial states, settler societies, and Aboriginal peoples, or whether they will have transformational capacity will depend in part on the political context in which they take place. The impact of such transitional justice measures as apologies, truth commissions, and reparations will be limited, or extended, by the wider policy environment in which they occur.

---

1 The author would like to thank Paige Arthur, Gina Cosentino, Eduardo Gonzalez, and Patrick Macklem for helpful comments and insight on this chapter. The analysis and conclusions are the sole responsibility of the author.
2 On the intellectual history of transitional justice, see Paige Arthur, "How 'Transitions' Re-shaped Human Rights: A Conceptual History of Transitional Justice" (2009) 31:2 Human Rights Quarterly 321.

This chapter outlines some of the potential complexities involved in processing Indigenous demands for justice through a transitional justice framework. It identifies three broad areas in which the interests and goals of governments and Indigenous peoples may clash, and where transitional justice itself may be the object of political wrangling. First, governments and Indigenous peoples may differ over the scope of injustices that transitional justice measures can address. Second, governments may try to use transitional justice to draw a line through history and legitimate present policy, whereas Indigenous peoples may try to use the past to critique present policy and conditions. Third, governments may try to use transitional justice to reassert their sovereign and legal authority, whereas Indigenous peoples may try to resist this strategy and even make competing claims to sovereignty and legal authority.

Developments in the relationship between the Canadian government and First Nations highlight the challenges and opportunities of addressing Indigenous demands for justice from the perspective of transitional justice. In May 2006, the government, the churches, and the Assembly of First Nations and other Aboriginal organizations reached agreement on a settlement to address the legacy of the Indian residential school system.[3] The agreement included reparations, a truth commission, and commemoration. In June 2008, Conservative Prime Minister Stephen Harper offered an official state apology to former students of Indian residential schools. Both the Harper government and First Nations leaders seemed keen to employ transitional justice measures to deal with the legacy of the residential school system. Nevertheless, they had different reasons for endorsing a transitional justice framework, and distinct perspectives on the work and goals of the apology, the Truth and Reconciliation Commission (TRC), and compensation.

---

3 The Assembly of First Nations is an organization of First Nations chiefs that acts as the national political representative of First Nations governments and their citizens in Canada. The AFN is funded by the government and has an office in Ottawa. The national chief is elected by the Assembly of Chiefs and plays a prominent role in responding to and shaping government initiatives that affect Aboriginal people.

I. The Scope of Injustice

Almost every dimension of Indigenous life has been shaped, and limited, by the colonial encounter and by a postcolonial history of dispossession, racism, exclusion, betrayal, and forced assimilation. The Indigenous experience is one of loss of land and sovereignty, the loss or devaluation of language and culture, loss of access to resources, and limited access to the socio-economic and political rights of citizenship. The scope of the wrongs that have been committed against Indigenous people is extensive. As a result, Indigenous demands for justice are wide-ranging.

But transitional justice measures are limited. In Canada, the apology, the TRC, and compensation are designed to address only the legacy of the residential schools system. Yet the residential school system is a narrow slice of the outstanding issues that bedevil the relationship between Aboriginal peoples, the Canadian government, and non-Aboriginal Canadians. Since 1990 two major government initiatives proposed serious and wide-ranging transformation of Canada–First Nations relations – the Royal Commission on Aboriginal Peoples and the Kelowna Accord. But both floundered, and the Conservative government entered office in January 2006 with little more than a controversial proposal to "extend human rights to First Nations" in a way that threatened to undermine Aboriginal collective rights. The government has attempted to use "human rights" as a strategy for limiting state obligation and as a wedge to undermine Indigenous collective rights to self-determination. Although the Conservative government did not initiate the transitional justice project that became the centrepiece of its Aboriginal policy, transitional justice extends the party's human rights agenda and is offered as an alternative to constitutional transformation and social justice.

In 1991, the government of Canada established the Royal Commission on Aboriginal Peoples (RCAP) to investigate the social, economic, and political conditions of the Aboriginal peoples of Canada, and to develop recommendations focused on the improvement of these conditions, and the overall relationship between First Nations and the Crown. The commissioners directed their consultations to one overriding and extremely broad question: What are the foundations of a fair and honourable relationship between the Aboriginal and non-Aboriginal people of Canada? The commission held 178 days of public hearings, visited ninety-six communities, consulted dozens of experts, commissioned scores of research studies, and reviewed numerous past inquiries and reports. Their central conclusion was that the main policy direction, pursued for more than 150 years, first by colonial then by Canadian governments, has been wrong.[4]

The royal commission released its final report and recommendations in November 1996. The report was five volumes long, including 4,000 pages and 440 recommendations. The first volume traces the history of the relationship between Aboriginal peoples and the state, details failed policies, including the Indian residential schools policy, and proposes a new path forward. Volume 2 lays out the laws that govern First Nations, including treaty rights, financial arrangements for Aboriginal governments, land provisions, and co-management agreements. Volume 3 recommends new directions in social policy in housing, education, language preservation, health, family and child welfare, arts and heritage, and museums. Volume 4 articulates the views of Aboriginal people themselves. It includes sections on the perspectives of elders, women, youth, Metis, and urban Aboriginal people. Volume 5 is titled *Renewal: A Twenty-Year Commitment*. The two central planks of the commitment are redressing economic and welfare disparity, and constitutional reform.

Fourteen months later, in January 1998, the government unveiled its response to the RCAP report: "Gathering Strength: Canada's Aboriginal Action Plan." The action plan had four components: renewing the partnership, strengthening Aboriginal governance, developing a new fiscal relationship, and supporting strong communities, people, and economies. Nevertheless, in April 1999 the Human Rights Committee of the United Nations High Commissioner for Human Rights released its concluding observations on Canada's observance of UN human rights covenants: "[T]he Committee is particularly concerned that the State party (Canada) has not yet implemented the recommendations of the Royal Commission on Aboriginal Peoples." In fact, more than fifteen years later it is generally acknowledged that, although the government launched a few minor initiatives based in part on RCAP recommendations, the transformational spirit and intent of the commission has been squandered.[5]

---

4 "Highlights from the report of the Royal Commission on Aboriginal Peoples," Aboriginal Affairs and Northern Development, online: <www.aadnc-aandc.gc.ca/eng/1100100014597/1100100014637>.
5 "Implement Kelowna Deal on Native Poverty: Fontaine" CBC News, 21 November 2006, online: <http://www.cbc.ca/m/touch/canada/story/1.572607>.

The next major Aboriginal initiative was the Kelowna Accord. The Kelowna Accord is a series of agreements between the government of Canada, first ministers of the provinces, territorial leaders, and the leaders of five national Aboriginal organizations in Canada, including the Assembly of First Nations. The agreements resulted from eighteen months of roundtable consultations culminating in a First Ministers' Meeting in Kelowna, British Columbia, in November 2005. The accord committed the government to spend five billion dollars over ten years to improve the education, employment, and living conditions of Aboriginal peoples, and it was welcomed by Aboriginal leaders for involving a process of cooperation and consultation. AFN leader Phil Fontaine identified the Kelowna agreement as a "comprehensive, practical approach" to "the single most important social justice issue facing the country," and Paul Martin singled out the agreement as the "crowning achievement" of his term as prime minister.[6]

Nevertheless, when the Liberal government of Paul Martin fell in January 2006, the Conservative incumbents insisted that the Kelowna Accord "did not exist," because funds had not been budgeted for its implementation.[7] Under the leadership of Prime Minister Stephen Harper, the Conservative government has ignored the Kelowna Accord, and in June 2006 it tabled a new budget that dedicated few new resources to First Nations. Two days later, Paul Martin introduced a private member's bill, calling on the government to follow through on the promises laid out in the Kelowna Accord. The bill passed by a vote of 176 to 126, but private member's bills cannot compel government to spend money, and the Conservatives ignored the vote.[8]

Instead, the Conservative government came into office with its own Aboriginal initiative, Bill C-44, an Act to amend the *Canadian Human Rights Act* by removing the exemption (section 67) that shields the federal government and First Nations governments "from complaints of

6 *Ibid.*
7 "'There Is No Kelowna Accord': Jim Prentice to the House of Commons" Four Arrows, 9 June 2007. Four Arrows is an online publication that identifies itself as an e-note. For example, see "AFN, Opposition Stiffen Resistance to C-44, Legal Experts Cite Grave Problems with Bill," Docstoc (9 June 2007), online: <www.docstoc.com/docs/32572907/AFN_-Opposition-Stiffen-Resistance-to-C-44_-Legal-Experts-Cite>.
8 "Tories to Ignore Parliament's Kelowna Accord Vote," CTV News (22 March 2007), online: <www.ctvnews.ca/tories-to-ignore-parliament-s-kelowna-accord-vote-1.234221>.

discrimination relating to actions arising from or pursuant to the Indian Act." While the proposal is often described as extending human rights to First Nations people living on reserves, in fact Aboriginal people already enjoyed the general protection of the *Canadian Human Rights Act*, except in special situations where their rights and status are governed by the *Indian Act*. What is more, the section 67 exemption had no effect on *Charter*-based equality rights.[9]

The amendment received first reading in the House of Commons in December 2006 and was referred to the House of Commons Standing Committee on Aboriginal Affairs and Northern Development. That committee deliberated on the bill in sixteen meetings between March and June 2007, and heard a number of expert witnesses who raised serious concerns about the process and substance of the legislation. In June 2007 the committee adopted an opposition motion recommending that debate on the repeal be suspended for up to ten months to allow the government to initiate a broad consultative process to include First Nations representatives. In July 2007 a majority of members were called back, by the Conservative Party, to an unusual midsummer meeting for a clause-by-clause consideration of the bill. Again, the opposition voted to suspend such consideration, pending consultations, and the bill died when Parliament was prorogued in September 2007. Two months later the government introduced Bill C-21, which was identical to Bill C-44. That bill was finally passed in June 2008, with five significant opposition amendments.[10]

First Nations representatives and expert non-governmental witnesses had five major concerns regarding Bill C-44. First, they argued that a human rights bill must include a non-derogation clause to protect Aboriginal and treaty rights. Second, they insisted that the bill include an interpretive provision to guide the Canadian Human Rights Commission, tribunals, and courts in balancing individual human rights

---

9 "Bill C-44: An Act to amend the Canadian Human Rights Act," prepared by Mary C Hurley, Law and Government Division, 16 January 2007, Legislative Summaries (Library of Parliament – Parliamentary Information and Research Service), online: <www.parl.gc.ca/Content/LOP/LegislativeSummaries/39/1/c44-e.pdf>.

10 "Bill C-21: An Act to amend the Canadian Human Rights Act," prepared by C Mary Hurley, Law and Government Division, revised 30 June 2008, Legislative Summaries (Library of Parliament – Parliamentary Information and Research Service), online: <www.parl.gc.ca/About/Parliament/LegislativeSummaries/bills_ls.asp?lang=E&ls=c21&Parl=39&Ses=2&source=library_prb>.

and the collective constitutional rights of First Nations. Third, they requested a thirty-six-month transition period to develop the critical capacity to implement CHRA provisions. Fourth, they requested funding to help First Nations governments respond to human rights complaints. Fifth, they recommended that complaints against First Nations governments be considered by independent First Nations institutions.

Specifically, while First Nations representatives insisted on their own commitment to ensuring the full range of human rights for their people, they were concerned that an equality framework would expose First Nations governments to allegations of preferential treatment towards band members. Several expert witnesses insisted that the repeal of section 67 "could cause the Indian Act to unravel, dispossessing hundreds of First Nation communities across Canada from their reserve lands."[11] One way it might do so is by allowing non-Aboriginal people to challenge health and education benefits provided to Aboriginal people alone.[12] Non-Aboriginal people may also have been able to challenge the special land, fishing, logging, and other rights that Aboriginal people have secured, in part through the *Indian Act.*

Under the circumstances, Aboriginal representatives had reason to be wary of the Conservative government's intentions in introducing Bill C-44. Harper's long-time advisor Tom Flanagan has written a book titled *First Nation? Second Thoughts,* in which he argues that Aboriginal people are immigrants who should be assimilated, and he has appeared as an expert witness against Aboriginal land claims. Harper's first minister of Indian affairs was Jim Prentice, a property rights lawyer who has argued for extending property rights to reserves, and is also known for his opposition to Native land claims.[13] Property rights are another way of extending individual rights to band members in a way that threatens collective rights and, Indigenous leaders fear, may ultimately lead to land alienation.

In the end, Bill C-21 was amended by opposition members on the committee to include some of the exemptions and caveats

---

11 "AFN, Opposition Stiffen Resistance to Bill C-44."

12 Testimony provided by William Black, professor of human rights law, Faculty of Law, University of British Columbia, cited in *ibid,* 2.

13 "Aboriginal Agenda Conflicts with Background of Harper Advisors: Lead Advisor Tom Flanagan Has Made a Career of Opposing Land Claims," Harper Index, 16 May 2007, online: <www.harperindex.ca/ViewArticle.cfm?Ref=0022>.

recommended by First Nations and expert witnesses. In particular the final bill stated,

> The repeal of section 67 of the *Canadian Human Rights Act* shall not be construed so as to abrogate or derogate from any Aboriginal, treaty or other rights or freedoms that pertain to the First Nations peoples of Canada, including: 1) any rights or freedoms that have been recognized by the Royal Proclamation of October 7, 1763; 2) any rights or freedoms that now exist by way of land claims agreements or may be so acquired; and 3) any rights or freedoms recognized under the customary laws or traditions of the First Nations peoples of Canada.

In addition,

> In relation to a complaint made under the *Canadian Human Rights Act* against a First Nation government, including a band council, tribal council or governing authority operating or administering programs and services under the *Indian Act*, this Act shall be interpreted and applied in a manner that gives due regard to First Nations legal traditions and customary laws, particularly the balancing of individual rights and interests against collective rights and interests.[14]

Nevertheless, conservative commentators hailed the bill as "a good first step toward solving the much bigger problem of treating Native people as though they are different from the rest of the country, clearing up any misunderstanding that some may have about Natives being a 'sovereign nation.'"[15] Notwithstanding the opposition amendments, the repeal of section 67 of the Constitution is significant. It remains to be seen how much weight courts will assign to the non-derogation and interpretive clauses the bill includes.

As the bill moved into the Senate, Indian Affairs Minister Chuck Strahl clarified the relationship between C-21 and the UN Declaration on the Rights of Indigenous Peoples, explaining, "Our government believes that delivering real human rights to First Nations peoples, as this Bill does, is much more important and tangible than

14 "Bill C-21," *supra* note 10.
15 "Bill Helps Dispel 'Sovereign Nation' Notion," jeffparkinson.ca (27 June 2008), online: <caledoniawakeupcall.wordpress.com/2008/06/27/bill-c-21-helps-dispel-%E2%80%9Csovereign-nation%E2%80%9D-notion/>.

any aspirational document."[16] The Harper government insisted that its commitment to human rights justified its refusal to ratify the UN Declaration.[17]

Against the backdrop of these other policy initiatives, successive Canadian governments have struggled to address the legacy of the Indian residential school policy. For roughly one hundred years, between the late nineteenth and late twentieth centuries, the government of Canada collaborated with various churches to operate a residential school system that forcibly removed Aboriginal children from their parents and communities and placed them in boarding schools.[18] Approximately 150,000 children were sent to residential schools. Starting from only two schools in operation when Canada was formed in 1867,[19] a total of 130 residential schools existed over time.[20]

The explicit purpose of the residential schools was to destroy Aboriginal language and culture, "to take the Indian out of the child." Students were not allowed to speak their own languages at school, and their cultures and heritages were debased. Children also suffered physical harm. Some schools had mortality rates of 35 to 60 per cent, due to malnutrition, abuse, and exposure to tuberculosis, and many children were victims of physical and sexual abuse. Through the residential school system, the government of Canada violated human rights to bodily integrity, equality, privacy, education, culture, family, and life.

---

16 "Statement by the Honourable Chuck Strahl in Relation to Bill C-21, an Act to Amend the Canadian Human Rights Act" (28 May 2008), online: <news.gc.ca/web/article-en.do?crtr.sj1D=&mthd=advSrch&crtr.mnthndVl=&nid=401839&crtr.dpt1D=&crtr.tp1D=&crtr.lc1D=&crtr.yrStrtVl=2008&crtr.kw=&crtr.dyStrtVl=26&crtr.aud1D=&crtr.mnthStrtVl=2&crtr.yrndVl=&crtr.dyndVl=>.

17 "Canada Taking 'Bold Steps' on Aboriginal Issues, Strahl Tells UN," CBCnews.ca (1 May 2008), online: <www.cbc.ca/news/canada/canada-taking-bold-steps-on-aboriginal-issues-strahl-tells-un-1.772002>. Along with the United States, Australia, and New Zealand, Canada refused to ratify the UNDRIP when it was passed in 2007. The Harper government finally endorsed the resolution in November 2010.

18 See Agnes Grant, No End of Grief: Indian Residential Schools in Canada (Winnipeg: Pemmican, 1996), 64; Report of the Royal Commission on Aboriginal Peoples, vol 1 (Ottawa: Minister of Supply and Services Canada, 1996), ch 10, "Residential Schools," 343 [RCAP Report]; Indian Residential Schools Resolution, "Backgrounder: Federal Representative to Lead Discussions toward a Lasting Resolution of the Legacy of Indian Residential Schools" (8 June 2005), on file with the author [IRSR Backgrounder]; Indian and Northern Affairs Canada, "Backgrounder: The Residential Schools System," (23 April 2004), on file with the author [INAC Backgrounder].

19 RCAP Report at 353.

20 INAC Backgrounder.

Injustices associated with residential schools grew steadily more visible in the late 1980s. Commencing in 1989–90, prosecutions against
former residential school staff began in British Columbia and the
Yukon, spurring additional police investigations and, in turn, further
prosecutions.[21] By 1992, most churches had apologized for their conduct, but also asserted "shared responsibility" with the federal government for the consequences of the residential school system.[22] The
RCAP report detailed widespread neglect, governmental underfunding, health-related problems, as well as sexual, physical, and emotional
abuse endured by students over many years, and called for a public
inquiry into the policy.[23]

In response to the RCAP report, Jane Stewart, minister for Indian
affairs and northern development, issued a "Statement of Reconciliation" in 1998, acknowledging the federal government's role in the development and administration of the residential schools, and expressing
regret to those students who experienced sexual and physical abuse.[24]
The "Statement of Reconciliation" was part of a four-part strategy that
included a commitment of $350 million for community-based healing

---

21 *RCAP Report* at 378.
22 *Ibid* at 379–80.
23 *Ibid* at 383. According to the report,

> The public inquiry's main focus should be to investigate and document the origins,
> purposes, and effects of residential school policies and practices as they relate to
> all Aboriginal peoples, with particular attention to the manner and extent of their
> impact on individuals and families across several generations, on communities, and
> on Aboriginal society as a whole. The inquiry should conduct public hearings across
> the country, with sufficient funding to enable those affected to testify. The inquiry
> should be empowered to commission research and analysis to assist in gaining an
> understanding of the nature and effects of residential school policies. It should be
> authorized to recommend whatever remedial action it believes necessary for govern-
> ments and churches to ameliorate the conditions created by the residential school
> experience. Where appropriate, such remedies should include apologies from those
> responsible, compensation on a collective basis to enable Aboriginal communities to
> design and administer programs that assist the healing process and rebuild commu-
> nity life, and funding for the treatment of affected people and their families.

24 Indian and Northern Affairs Canada, "Statement of Reconciliation: Learning from
the Past" (24 April 2004), online: <www.ainc-inac.gc.ca/gs/rec_e.html>. See also
Indian and Northern Affairs Canada, *Gathering Strength: Canada's Aboriginal Action
Plan* (Ottawa: Minister of Indian Affairs and Northern Development, 1997), online:
<www.ahf.ca/downloads/gathering-strength.pdf> [*Gathering Strength*].

for those suffering the effects of physical and sexual abuse in residential schools, a revision of litigation strategy, and the implementation of alternative dispute resolution (ADR) mechanisms to avoid lengthy and expensive litigation.[25] Nevertheless, by October 2002, more than 11,000 legal cases had been filed against the federal government and the churches.[26]

In March 2004 the Assembly of First Nations issued a scathing critique of the government's ADR process, arguing that it perpetuated racial stereotypes, treated survivors unequally, measured abuse in accordance with the "standards of the day," and failed to compensate for loss of language and culture.[27] The overriding complaint was that the government's framework for resolving residential schools claims was inadequate and too slow.

The government was also dissatisfied with the ADR framework, which had failed to stem the tide of lawsuits against the federal government and the churches. In May 2005, the government signed a political agreement, promising negotiations towards "a settlement package that will address a redress payment for all former students of Indian residential schools, a truth and reconciliation process, community based healing, commemoration, an appropriate ADR process that will address serious abuse, as well as legal fees."[28]

Fast on the heels of the political agreement, in August 2005, the AFN launched a class action lawsuit against the federal government on behalf of four proposed subclasses: survivors, deceased, Aboriginal, and family.[29] Chief Phil Fontaine, leader of the AFN and a residential school

25 Gathering Strength, *ibid.* See also Indian and Northern Affairs Canada and First Nations and Inuit Health Branch, *The Path to Healing* (February 1998), online: <https://web.archive.org/web/20010208233157/http://www.ainc-inac.gc.ca/gs/pth_e.html>.

26 Kaufman, Thomas and Associates, "Review of Indian Residential Schools Dispute Resolution Projects," Final Report, Executive Summary (11 October 2002), online: <www.collectionscanada.gc.ca/webarchives/20071115232539/http://www.rqpi.gc.ca/english/pdf/final_report_executive_summary.pdf>; Pamela O'Connor, "Squaring the Circle: How Canada Is Dealing with the Legacy of Its Indian Residential Schools Experiment" (2000) 28 International Journal of Legal Information 251.

27 Assembly of First Nations, *Assembly of First Nations Report on Canada's Dispute Resolution Plan to Compensate for Abuses in Indian Residential Schools* (Ottawa: Assembly of First Nations, 2004).

28 "Political Agreement," Federal Representative-Indian Residential Schools, online: <www.iacobucci.gc.ca/doc-eng.asp?action=20050530pa>.

29 *Larry Philip Fontaine et al v AG*, Ontario Court File No 05-CV-294716 CP (issued 5 August 2005).

survivor, was named as the proposed representative of the survivor and Aboriginal subclasses. In addition to various declarations, the AFN sought twelve billion dollars in general damages, twelve billion dollars in special damages for negligence, breach of fiduciary, statutory, treaty, and other common law duties, and twelve billion dollars in punitive damages.[30] The AFN further sought the establishment of a fund "whose objects are to create, support, develop, enhance and expand programs designed to mitigate the Cultural, Linguistic and Social Damage caused by the Crown's Residential Schools Policy."[31]

According to Chief Fontaine,

> Our action is not an attempt to impede the process, but rather a means to ensure that we are able to fully participate in the process, more effectively settle this to the benefit of all residential schools survivors and all First Nations citizens affected by the residential schools, and to ensure that all options remain open for them. The [political agreement] has provided a political vehicle to move forward, but a legal vehicle is required to finalize the process with the AFN in a central and representative role, which this action now provides.[32]

On 10 May 2006 the government announced the approval by all parties of the Indian Residential Schools Settlement Agreement (IRSSA), an out-of-court settlement that represents the consensus reached in discussions between the government of Canada, legal counsel for former students, the churches, the Assembly of First Nations, and other Aboriginal organizations. It is the largest, most complex class action settlement in Canadian history. The IRSSA was approved by the courts and came into effect on 19 September 2007. The settlement agreement includes five important components of transitional justice: a "common experience" payment, an independent assessment process, a truth and reconciliation commission, commemoration, and healing.

---

30 Statement of Claim, para 2(j)–(l).
31 Statement of Claim, para 2(i).
32 Assembly of First Nations, news release, "AFN National Chief Files Class Action Claim against the Government of Canada for Residential Schools Policy" (3 August 2005), online: <media.knet.ca/node/1528>. While Fontaine claimed he had few substantive reservations about the political agreement, he launched the class action suit in order to reshape the process. He wanted the final settlement to be negotiated among equals (parties to a legal case), and he wanted it to be legally binding, so that the government could not renege on an agreement.

Against this backdrop, the scope of transitional justice is likely to be highly politicized. When governments and Indigenous groups agree to employ a transitional justice framework to address a discrete segment of the historical injustices that have structured relations between them, they are likely to try to use that framework for different purposes. The government may try to use such measures as apologies and reparations to shut down other Indigenous demands, offering transitional justice in exchange for quiescence on other issues. In particular, a transitional justice framework may channel Indigenous politics into a human rights framework as a way to undermine Indigenous demands for collective rights, on the one hand, and social and economic rights on the other hand.[33]

Bill C-21, the apology, and the TRC have emerged as the most visible elements of the Harper government's First Nations policy. Yet all three of these policies fail to prioritize First Nations' own goals as they were laid out in the RCAP document and the Kelowna Accord: education, housing, social welfare, and health.[34] Instead, the government has taken a predictably neoliberal approach to economic development on reserves, focusing on resource exploitation and small business development.

In the context of this adversarial political environment, the success of transitional justice depends in part on its capacity to animate politics, and political accountability, beyond its limited mandate. Aboriginal leaders have tried to use the transitional justice framework to extend their definitions of injustice to include not only individual harms suffered by former students themselves, but also collective and cultural harms suffered by Aboriginal communities, languages, and cultures.

---

33 In the South African context, Mahmood Mamdani has argued eloquently that the legacy of colonialism concerned social suffering, not primarily individual human rights violations. Transitional justice, he argues, should be about the provision of social and economic rights, not truth and reconciliation. Mahmood Mamdani, "Beyond Settler and Native as Political Identities: Overcoming the Political Legacy of Colonialism" (2001) 43:4, 651–64 Comparative Studies in Society and History. It is relevant to bring his analysis into the context of transitional justice for Aboriginal peoples because the perception of a trade-off, and of a bifurcation of political claims and strategies, bedevils Indigenous politics in many parts of the world, including Canada. The background to the Canadian apology and TRC shows how governments may try to present human rights as an alternative, rather than a complement, to social and economic rights.

34 "Government of Canada and Aboriginal Advisory Board Working to Improve Economic Development" Aboriginal Affairs and Northern Development Canada (17 February 2009), online: https://web.archive.org/web/20110921181647/http://www.ainc-inac.gc.ca/aiarch/mr/nr/j-a2009/nr000000189-eng.asp.

While acknowledging the harms done to individuals, they have also placed significant weight on collective and intergenerational harms, trying to change dominant conceptions of who suffered the injustice (whole populations, not individual students) and what counts as an injustice (loss of culture and language, not only physical or sexual abuse).[35] Because the primary aim of the residential schools was to extinguish Aboriginal language and culture, with explicit and intended intergenerational effects, such harms are clearly identifiable as a major and lasting component of the legacy of the residential school system.

Aboriginal survivors have also tried to resist the logic of "individual-izing" the harm of residential schools by insisting on the forward-acting effects of the schools on subsequent generations. Research has shown that residential school survivors often suffer from drug and alcohol addictions, depression, higher rates of suicide, and poor relationship and parenting skills. Many are not only victims, but also perpetrators of sexual and physical abuse. The children and other family members of residential school survivors suffer the continuing effects of their parents' experience in the schools. They also suffer because parents have been unable to transmit their own language, culture, and moral framework to their children. It is to some extent the children of residential school survivors who have inherited the real long-term impact of the schools – the loss of culture and language, substance abuse, and family violence.[36]

In response to this intergenerational conception of harm, the IRSSA allocated $125 million for "community healing," funding "eligible projects" that

address healing needs of Aboriginal People affected by the Legacy of Indian Residential Schools, which could include the intergenerational impacts. Under the terms of the Settlement Agreement, eligible projects (a) focus on prevention and early detection of the effects of the Legacy of

---

35 Truth and Reconciliation Commission of Canada, *Interim Report* (July 2011).
36 The intergenerational effects of trauma have been well documented, in particular in studies of children of Holocaust survivors. Marinus H van IJzendoorn, "Are Children of Holocaust Survivors Less Well-Adapted? A Meta-analytic Investigation of Secondary Traumatization" (2003) 16:5 Journal of Traumatic Stress 459; George Halasz, "Children of Child Survivors of the Holocaust: Can Trauma Be Transmitted across the Generations?" (2004) 21 Pro Memoria 45; Danny Brom, "A Controlled Double-Blind Study on Children of Holocaust Survivors" (2001) 38:1 Israel Journal of Psychiatry 47.

Indian Residential Schools, including the intergenerational impacts on all generations; (b) include elements of research and of capacity building for communities, including Communities of Interest, to address their long-term healing needs; (c) include, where and when possible, and depending on local needs and circumstances, a holistic approach including medial and traditional methodologies; (d) address special needs of segments of the population, including those of the elderly, youth and women; and (e) be based on a community healing approach designed to address needs of individuals, families and communities, which may include Communities of Interest.[37]

The scope of transitional justice has also been extended beyond individual survivors alone through attention to the potential danger that individual compensation and a truth commission that focuses on the experience of survivors will generate divisions between survivors and Aboriginal people who were not sent to residential schools. Roughly 10 per cent of the Aboriginal population of Canada has received compensation for their residential school experience, which means that roughly 90 per cent are left out of the transitional justice framework, have received no apology, and were unlikely to participate in the main events of the TRC.[38] Part of the legacy of the residential schools is fractured communities. Transitional justice is in danger of reproducing that outcome.

The TRC has therefore taken seriously the claim that harms were done to families and communities as a whole, not only to individual survivors. This commitment is in keeping with Aboriginal teachings that everything is related, "often represented visually by placing individuals at the centre of a set of concentric circles that ripple outward to include family, community, nation, and the natural world."[39] Commissioners have reached out to Aboriginal people who are not

37 Indian Residential Schools Settlement Agreement, Schedule M, Funding Agreement between the Aboriginal Healing Foundation and Canada (8 May 2006), online: <www.residentialschoolsettlement.ca/Schedule_M.pdf>.
38 94,000 people applied for the common experience payments, and 1.3 million people reported at least some Aboriginal ancestry in the 2001 census. Statistics Canada, "Aboriginal Peoples of Canada," online: <www12.statcan.ca/english/census01/Products/Analytic/companion/abor/canada.cfm>.
39 Marlene Brant Castellano, Linda Archibald, & Mike DeGagne, "From Truth to Reconciliation: Transforming the Legacy of the Residential Schools" (Ottawa: Aboriginal Healing Foundation, 2008).

school survivors, to support the "community healing" dimension of the settlement agreement with outreach programs intended to draw whole communities, and not only survivors, into a common dialogue.

The Indian Residential Schools Settlement Agreement also extended the common conception of who was a victim by negotiating a "common experience payment" for all residential school survivors. Previous frameworks for addressing government responsibility for the residential school system allocated compensation only to those former students who suffered sexual or serious physical abuse at the schools. Jane Stewart's 1998 "Statement of Reconciliation" expressed regret not for the residential school system as a whole, but specifically to those students who had suffered physical or sexual abuse in the schools. Such a paradigm sustains the myth that the system itself was faultless by acknowledging only harms perpetrated by particular individuals (a few bad apples) within the system. A common experience payment that offers compensation to anyone who went through the residential school system, regardless of the experience within the system, sustains a more far-reaching critique of the system as a whole.

Aboriginal leaders may be able to push a transitional justice framework even further, to demonstrate that the residential school system was itself part of a larger web of racist and oppressive government policies that have structured and limited Indigenous life and life chances. The residential school system was not an aberration in Canadian government policy towards First Nations. The system was of a piece with other racist and discriminatory practices that have structured Aboriginal life and life chances for the past three hundred years, mostly under the sheltering umbrella of the *Indian Act*. The government's acknowledgment of the injustice and cruelty of the residential school system offers an opening that Aboriginal people could use to highlight the injustices of other government policies, and the almost ludicrous effrontery of offering an apology for the residential school system alone, in light of the apocalyptic damage and harm the colonial and Canadian governments have perpetrated against Aboriginal peoples. To the extent a transitional justice paradigm supposes the existence of historic injustice, and implies that states have an obligation to redress such injustice, it may open space for a much broader conceptualization of the actual injustices post-colonial governments may be held responsible for.

II. The Temporal Implications of "Transitional" Justice

The first sentence of the "Mandate for the Truth and Reconciliation Commission" states, "There is an emerging and compelling desire to put the events of the past behind us so that we can work towards a stronger and healthier future." The scope of transitional justice is not only limited spatially, to a particular segment or type of injustice, it is also contested temporally. For the government, one goal of transitional justice is to draw a line through history, emphasizing that it takes responsibility for government abuses that are nevertheless firmly in the past. It thereby underlines the difference between the past and the present, and the distinction between present and past policy. It hopes also to bring an end to recriminations that keep it morally on the defensive. Such government initiatives as apologies, truth commissions, and reparations are designed in part to allow the government and the dominant (settler) society to say finally to Aboriginal peoples "OK, now we're even." The "transition" is to an even playing field in which the government can no longer be held accountable for past wrongs.

For Indigenous leaders, transitional justice is not a wall, but a bridge. Aboriginal peoples will have an interest in using apologies, compensation, and truth commissions to draw history into the present, and to draw connections between past policy, present policy, and present injustices. Indigenous peoples may wish to extend new conceptions of historical wrongs to demonstrate that certain present policies reinscribe historical injustices and relations of oppression. It has taken many years for non-Aboriginal Canadians to recognize and acknowledge that the residential school system was racist, abusive, and fundamentally wrong, not only in its practice but in its intent. Indigenous leaders may hope to use the moment of transitional justice to push this cognitive transformation, to question the legitimacy of present policies, and to draw conceptual links between present and past policies. Whereas the government may try to use transitional justice to signal a break with the past, Indigenous activists may try to use the past as a way to critique the present. For them, transitional justice is effective to the extent it links the past with the present. The "transition" is to a relationship in which connections between past and present are firmly acknowledged, and in which the past guides present conceptions of obligation.

The tension between government and Indigenous conceptions of how transitional justice affects the relationship between past and present is evident in reparations, the TRC, and the apology. The IRSSA provides "at least $1.9 billion" for "common experience" payments to former students who lived at one of the residential schools. Each student is entitled to $10,000 for the first year, or part of a year, that she or he spent at school, and $3,000 for each additional year. Common experience payments are not taxable. Family members of students are not eligible for compensation. Students who suffered sexual or serious physical abuse may additionally go through an "independent assessment process" to determine the extent of their abuse and, therefore, the extent of their compensation. As the public notice explaining the residential school settlement states, "Awards are based on a point system for different abuses and resulting harms. The more points the greater the payment."[40] The "independent assessment process" replaces the alternative dispute resolution process previously in place. Before the submission deadline in 2012, the government received 105,542 applications for the Common Experience Payment, and it had issued payments to 79,179 survivors.[41]

Once the settlement agreement was reached, former students of residential schools faced a stark choice. By filling out a claim form and accepting compensation, former students gave up the right to go through the courts in the future. The public notice of the settlement states, "Former students – and family members – who stay in the settlement will never again be able to sue the Government of Canada, the Churches who joined in the settlement, or any other defendant in the class actions, over residential schools."[42] Former students who wished to retain the right to sue had to submit a form to "opt out" of the class action by 20 August 2007. The government included a clause in the agreement that stipulated that if 5,000 people opted out of the common experience payment, the government could back out of the agreement altogether.

From the perspective of the government, the clear intent of the settlement agreement was to shut down the wave of litigation that propelled the issue of residential schools onto the political stage and kept the Canadian government on the defensive for more than fifteen years. If the settlement agreement did not accomplish that goal, the government

40 "Official Court Notice," Residential Schools Settlement, online: <www.residentialschoolsettlement.com/summary_notice.pdf>.
41 ICTJ Website "Where We Work: Canada," online: <https://www.ictj.org/our-work/regions-and-countries/canada>.
42 "Official Court Notice," Residential Schools Settlement.

explicitly and legally secured the right to back out of the agreement. Nevertheless, the agreement did accomplish that goal. "With only 340 people opting out by the 2007 deadline, the Settlement Agreement has effectively corralled residential schools claims into a standardized compensation process."[43] In 2006, there were roughly 12,000 claims lodged against the churches and the government, which were largely resolved by the settlement agreement.[44]

In a context of transitional justice, there are benefits to such a move. A compensation package limits the amount of compensation an individual can receive but offers reparation more broadly to all those affected. From the perspective of compensation alone, a widely disbursed "common experience payment," supplemented by additional payments for abuse, can be seen as fulfilling a commitment to justice. Pablo de Grieff makes the case that a disparity in the amount of an award does not necessarily produce an injustice to the extent that reparations programs obviate other costs associated with litigation: long delays, high costs, cross-examination, gathering evidence, and the possibility of an adverse decision.[45] AFN and other residential school survivor groups have pointed explicitly to these costs when they endorse the compensation package included in the settlement agreement.

Transitional justice nevertheless normally conceives such initiatives as criminal prosecutions, truth commissions, reparations, and memorialization as complementary:

[T]o be effective transitional justice should include several measures that complement one another. Truth-telling, in isolation from efforts to punish abusers and to make institutional reforms, can be viewed as nothing more than words. Reparations that are not linked to prosecutions or truth-telling may be perceived as "blood money" – an attempt to buy the silence or acquiescence of victims.[46]

43 Linda Popic, "Compensating Canada's Stolen Generations" (2008) 7:2 Indigenous Law Bulletin 15.
44 Ibid.
45 Pablo de Grieff, The Handbook of Reparations (New York: Oxford University Press, 2006) at 439.
46 Some survivors do in fact appear to view compensation through this lens, suggesting that the offer of money further compromised their integrity. The fact that so few survivors opted out of the compensation package should not be taken as evidence that most people are satisfied with it, or that compensation has put an end to grievance.

The settlement agreement had the potential to be perceived in this way precisely because it offered compensation only in exchange for an end to court battles.

Indeed, if reparations and truth commissions are offered as an alternative to law, they may even be the source of renewed grievance.[47] To the extent that transitional justice is perceived as a way of closing off legal avenues of redress, and of insulating the government (and churches) from the law, some of its reconciliatory potential may be squandered.

The mandate of the TRC reinforced this trade-off between law and transitional justice, making clear that the truth commission was not empowered to "hold formal hearings, act as a public inquiry, or conduct a formal legal process." The truth commission did not possess subpoena powers, nor was it allowed to make any findings or express any conclusion or recommendation regarding the misconduct of any person. Nor did the commission "name names in their events, activities, public statements, report, or recommendations, or make use of personal information or statements made which identify a person," neither did it "record the names of persons so identified" when they were named in testimony. These limitations make the Canadian TRC significantly weaker than many other truth commissions, such as in South Africa. The TRC was tasked solely with eliciting and documenting survivors' accounts of their residential school experience. That record may inscribe a "survivor narrative" into Canadian history and act as a bridge to the present, but it should also be clear that the TRC was also part of the process of putting an end to the government's legal liability.

The apology has also been used to draw a line through history. On 11 June 2008 Canadian Prime Minister Stephen Harper stood in the House of Commons and issued a statement of apology to victims of the residential school system. Against the backdrop of other Conservative government policies towards First Nations, the Harper apology is somewhat anomalous. The Conservative government firmly resisted demands for an apology until at least August 2007. In March 2007, Minister of Indian Affairs Jim Prentice insisted that an apology would not accompany the

---

47 A "lump sum" payment can also be challenging for receiving communities, creating divisions among beneficiaries and non-beneficiaries, including within families and extended families. In Canada, the lump sum payments have already been linked to suicides, a rise in substance abuse, and predatory marketing practices. Jack Branswell and Ken Meaney, "Aboriginal Settlements Bring Woes of Their Own: Abuse Payments Trigger Trauma, Linked to Deaths," *Ottawa Citizen* (26 January 2009).

TRC and the victims' reparations package ordered by the court in the Indian Residential Schools Settlement Agreement because it was not required by the agreement. He also suggested that no apology was necessary, since "fundamentally, the underlying objective had been to try and provide an education to Aboriginal children" – a benign motive, in his mind, that differentiated this case from that of Maher Arar's torture in Syria and the head tax paid by Chinese immigrants in the first half of the twentieth century – two other policies for which Harper had apologized in his first two years in office.[48] Prentice and Harper reportedly believed that if there was to be an apology, it should come after the TRC issued its final report – after the evidence was in, in other words.[49]

Nevertheless, after the House of Commons issued its own apology in May 2007, various MPs convinced Harper that an apology would help build trust and secure support for the First Nations initiatives the Conservatives hoped to advance. Bill C-44 was in front of the Aboriginal and Northern Affairs Committee in March through June of that year, and opposition committee members reported that they were under "considerable pressure" to pass the bill.[50] Residential school survivors were also dying at the rate of four per day, which would mean that most would not live to hear an apology at the end of the TRC mandate in five years. In his Speech from the Throne, given at the opening session of parliament in October 2007, Harper promised an apology.[51]

According to Indian Affairs Minister Chuck Strahl, the wording of the apology was shaped in part by "ongoing consultations" between Strahl, the prime minister, and residential school survivors. Nevertheless, Harper faced criticism that Indigenous leaders had not been sufficiently involved in drafting the apology. The government refused to circulate a draft of the apology, despite requests from the Assembly of First Nations and the National Residential Schools Survivors Society. NDP leader Jack Layton warned that the Conservative government "run[s] the risk of that kind of paternalistic attitude of 'we know best and First Nations will just have to accept what we dish out.'"[52]

---

48 "Why to Apologize for the Residential Schools," *Globe and Mail* (28 March 2007); "Mounting Sense of Urgency Was Apology's Catalyst," *Globe and Mail* (13 June 2008).
49 16 May 2007.
50 "AFN, Opposition Stiffen Resistance to Bill C-44."
51 "Mounting Sense of Urgency," *supra* note 48.
52 "Plan for Residential-School Apology Criticized," *Globe and Mail* (6 June 2008); "Native Groups Shut Out of Residential Schools Apology," *Canadian Press* (6 June 2008).

In fact, in the weeks leading up to the apology, the AFN ran itself ragged trying to ensure that Harper would deliver an appropriate apology in the appropriate way. On one level, AFN leaders were probably concerned that the apology could be offered in such a way that it failed to satisfy the needs of survivors to hear the government accept responsibility and express regret, and yet satisfied the government's obligation to issue an apology. Even if the apology was a poor one, it would probably be the last one residential school survivors would get. The AFN hoped to make sure the moment was not squandered.[53]

The spirit of the apology was belied somewhat when MP Pierre Poilievre, from the prime minister's own Conservative Party, said on the radio, just a few hours before the apology, "Now, along with this apology comes another $4 billion in compensation for those who partook in the residential schools over those years. My view is that we need to engender the values of hard work and independence and self-reliance." His outburst generated a torrent of email responses, much of it accusing him of undermining the apology. Although Poilievre issued his own apology in the House of Commons the next day, fully retracting his remarks, for many, his comments revealed the cynicism of the Harper apology against the backdrop of the Conservative government's otherwise regressive policies towards First Nations.[54]

Most residential school survivors and First Nations leaders nevertheless endorsed the apology and approved of its wording. Many were pleased that Harper had used the term "survivor" to refer to former students, because Ottawa has long resisted the terminology employed by most groups of former residential school students. Harper also acknowledged the damage that schools had caused to Indigenous communities and cultures, and not only to individual students, and to the capacity of First Nations to reproduce and pass down their languages

---

53 "AFN Chief Visits Trent" (24 November 2008), on file with the author.
   The AFN's concern over the wording, timing, and delivery of the apology can also be attributed to an interest in using the apology to create a legacy for Fontaine. As the elected leader of the Assembly of First Nations at the time, Fontaine hoped to take credit for government initiatives that took place while he was in office. When such initiatives fail, as they did, for example, in the case of the Kelowna Accord, his legacy suffers a setback. In particular because of his role in negotiating the Settlement Agreement, Fontaine's reputation is now tied to the success of the apology, compensation, and the TRC.
54 "MP Retracts Radio Remarks," *Globe and Mail* (13 June 2008); "Next Step: More Accountable and Transparent Native Governments," *Globe and Mail* (28 July 2008).

and traditions. Harper said explicitly, "We are sorry," and he was clear about what the government was sorry for.

He also, at least metaphorically, transferred responsibility for the residential schools experience from Indigenous communities to the government. Specifically, Harper said, "The burden of this experience has been on your shoulders for far too long. The burden is properly ours as a government, and as a country." He concluded by endorsing the truth and reconciliation commission and expressed hope in its ability to "educate all Canadians" about the residential school system and to forge a new relationship between Aboriginal and other Canadians. Most Indigenous commentators agreed that the text and tone of the apology was sincere.

The apology included both of the dimensions that have been identified as important components of reconciliation: the acceptance of responsibility and the expression of regret. The apology acknowledged that a norm was violated, and the acknowledgment re-established a common moral ground. In this case, Harper acknowledged that Indigenous judgments about the wrongness of residential schools were right after all, and the judgment of the government, the churches, and the dominant society was wrong. Many residential school survivors focused on this dimension of the apology. They insisted that the prime minister had to go beyond saying "We are sorry," and admit that they were *wrong*.[55] In his speech, Harper said three times that the government's residential school policy was wrong, and many Indigenous people claimed to draw strength from that admission. AFN leader Phil Fontaine explained, "For first nations, it will restore our dignity because it will say we were unjustly wronged as a people over generations simply because of who we were. The apology will affirm that we are as good as anyone."[56]

A surprising number of non-Indigenous Canadians were also aware of and supported the apology. In a survey conducted between 11 and 13 June 2008, 83 per cent of respondents were aware of the apology to residential school students. Among those who were aware, 71 per cent agreed or agreed strongly that the government should apologize,

---

55 Elise Stolte, "PM's Apology Must Go beyond Sorry, Aboriginals Say: Healing for Community Rests on Ottawa Taking Responsibility for Its Past," *Edmonton Journal* (9 June 2008).

56 Anne McIlroy and Bill Curry, "97 Years Later, Apology at Last," *Globe and Mail* (9 June 2008).

and only 18 per cent disagreed or strongly disagreed. Political affiliation nevertheless distinguished respondents, with only 66 per cent of
Conservatives expressing support for the (Conservative government's)
apology, compared with 75 per cent of Liberal voters and 82 per cent of
NDP voters. One-third of respondents said they were left with a more
favourable view of government, and the apology had the greatest positive impact among young people.[57]

Expectations about what will come of the apology nevertheless
diverge significantly. For many non-Indigenous Canadians, the apology was meant to close a chapter of Canadian history. By accepting
guilt, many expect to be able to move on, to draw a line that separates
the present from a shameful and unfortunate past. The point of an apology, many believe, is to put the past behind us. As one columnist wrote,
"It is much to be hoped that native Canadians accept the apology in the
spirit in which it was offered and now move on, lest a grievance culture
becomes so deep-rooted that they are unable to transcend it and self-
identify with victim status forevermore."[58]

Former Conservative party campaign manager Tom Flanagan
expressed a similar sentiment when he noted, with indignation, that
Indigenous leaders expected the apology to lead to something more.
"The Conservative government," he said, "is now being reminded of
the truism that one thing leads to another. The Aboriginal industry sees
the government's re-apology for Indian residential schools as a sign of
weakness, leading to a wave of demands to resuscitate the Kelowna
Accord." Instead, he insisted, the apology should have no effect on the
government's First Nations policy. "At this juncture, it is critical for the
government not to get knocked off its own agenda." Indeed, what Flanagan proposed as a next step is that First Nations reform their own
governments to demonstrate more transparency and accountability.
Apparently, the government's apology should lead to a quid pro quo –
some kind of acknowledgment that First Nations have been complicit
in their own misfortune, and also bear responsibility.[59]

For most Indigenous leaders and residential school survivors, however, this is not the obvious next step, although the presumption that

---

57 "School-Abuse Apology Widely Backed," *Globe and Mail* (14 June 2008).
58 John Ivison, "A Good Day for Canada, and for Stephen Harper," *Victoria Times
    Colonist* (12 June 2008).
59 "Next Step," *supra* note 54.

the apology implies further action is practically universal. As Grand Chief Edward John wrote on the eve of the apology, "An apology alone is not reconciliation. An apology cannot undo history."[60] Mary Simon, president of the Inuit Tapiriit Kanatami, reiterated that sentiment, insisting "that real and lasting forgiveness must be earned. It will be forthcoming only when it becomes clear that the government is willing to act."[61] AFN leader Phil Fontaine consistently invoked the apology as a source of legitimacy and momentum, implying not only that something must follow from the apology but that something must follow quickly. When Justice Harry La Forme resigned as chair of the TRC commission in October 2008, Fontaine issued a statement that said, among other things, "We are prepared to act quickly with due regard to Survivors, but we must not lose the momentum that was created by the Apology of June 11th. We cannot afford to be distracted from the purpose and intent of the TRC and its work that is vital to the future First Nations–Canadian relations in this country."[62]

In the months after the apology, Fontaine and others pointed repeatedly to the large gap between the rhetoric and intent of the apology and the TRC and the Conservative government's continued recalcitrance on social welfare policies towards First Nations. At a July 2008 meeting of premiers, Fontaine said the apology and the work of the commission were very important for the survivors and for the country. He added, however, that concrete actions were needed to back the rhetoric. In his statement, he pointedly recalled that the Conservatives had scuttled the Kelowna Accord, adding that "First Nations want more funding for education, training, and skills development for native children. What we want to see from the Council of the Federation is continuous support to fill the gap of quality of life between Canadians and us."

The sincerity of apologies cannot be judged by tone alone and will inevitably be seen in the context of "what comes next." Although

---

60 "Break from the Past: What's Expected from the Residential Schools Apology," *Vancouver Sun* (11 June 2008).
61 "Leaders Hope Apology Will Curb Prejudice: Truth and Reconciliation. 'Real and Lasting Forgiveness Must Be Earned,'" *[Montreal] Gazette* (14 June 2008).
62 "National Chief Issues Statement on Resignation of Justice Harry LaForme as the Chair of the Truth and Reconciliation Commission" (21 October 2008), online: <www.newswire.ca/en/story/277525/national-chief-issues-statement-on-resignation-of-justice-harry-laforme-as-the-chair-of-the-truth-and-reconciliation-commission>.

Indigenous reactions to the apology were very positive in the immediate aftermath, the sense of vindication, and of the beginning of a new era, dissipated within months as Indigenous people began to note that the apology was not followed by any tangible commitment. For many, a commitment to reconciliation signals a commitment to more concerted efforts, and greater funding, for Indigenous initiatives. Reconciliation, many Aboriginal leaders believe, should be signalled by government responsiveness to Aboriginal needs and demands. But there is no evidence of a "new dawn" in the relationship between Indigenous and non-Indigenous Canadians, and the more the evidence is missing, the more isolated and irrelevant the apology appears. One way to interpret the disappointment that followed so quickly on the heels of the apology is that First Nations saw it as a beginning, whereas the government viewed it as an end.

One of the most conspicuous connections between the residential school system and present government policy towards First Nations is child welfare. By some estimates, the Canadian child welfare system is responsible for roughly 27,000 Aboriginal children who have been removed from their homes into protective custody. According to a report issued by the AFN, there are more than three times as many Aboriginal children in the care of child welfare agencies as there were in residential schools at the height of the system. Whereas 1 out of every 200 children in the general population is placed in the care of child welfare, 1 out of every 10 Aboriginal children has been removed from his or her home by child welfare agencies.[63] Most children are removed from their families because they suffer from "neglect" associated with substance abuse. Many of those substance-abusing parents are residential school survivors.

Once removed, the relationship between parents and children is remanded to the courts. With inadequate understanding of the legal system, inadequate legal counsel, and limited or no translation services, court proceedings often terminate parental rights. Responsibility and accountability rest with the mandated child welfare and legal systems and away from First Nations families and communities.

Aboriginal peoples often draw connections between the residential school system and present child welfare policies that remove Aboriginal

---

63 Assembly of First Nations, "Leadership Action Plan on First Nations Child Welfare" (2006) at 1, online: <www.turtleisland.org/healing/afncf.pdf>.

children from their homes and communities. In November 2008, sixty First Nations residents of Regina protested outside a court hearing in which grandparents were attempting to regain custody of a five-year-old girl who had been removed from her home by child welfare services. The protestors compared this custody battle to the battle First Nations people faced in the past with the residential school system. As the organizer explained,

> It's been done in history ... where they took the kids out of the home and put them in the school. That caused a lot of problems with addictions and all the social ills because they couldn't take care of their families. The government apologized for that. They said they were sorry and they compensated, and now it's starting over again, but this time ... in a courtroom.[64]

First Nations seek jurisdiction over Aboriginal child welfare. Child welfare theorists have identified a set of best practices for Aboriginal children, including community-based intervention that empowers the community – family, friends, and neighbours – to be involved in decisions about the well-being of children in their community. In Northern Manitoba, one First Nations Child and Family Service Agency has implemented a family welfare program that operates outside of the regular child welfare and court systems, using traditional peacemaking methods and family mediation. The program brings together family, extended family, community members, elders, social workers, and community service providers in the resolution of child protection concerns through the use of properly trained *okweskimowewak* (family mediators).[65] The program explicitly operates outside of the provincial legal system and attempts to resolve child welfare issues using Cree norms and laws.

III. Sovereignty and Legal Pluralism

The issue of sovereignty may importantly distinguish attempts to use transitional justice measures in post-authoritarian and post-conflict societies from the use of transitional justice to address historic injustices

---

64 Derek Putz, "Case a Flashback to Residential School System: Protestor," *[Regina] Leader Post* (20 November 2008).

65 Joe Pintarics and Karen Sveinunggaard, "Meenoostahtan Menisiwin: First Nations Family Justice, Pathways to Peace" (2005) 2:1 First Peoples Family and Child Review 67.

against Indigenous peoples in societies that are not undergoing transition. States use transitional justice measures to make amends for human rights violations that they commit against their own citizens. The transitional justice framework is distinct from a human rights framework to the extent it balances demands for criminal prosecutions against a perceived need to sustain democratic institutions in a transitional setting where such institutions may be fragile.[66] Against this conceptual backdrop, it should be clear that using transitional justice measures in the absence of transition or regime change is of more than semantic concern. Transitional justice measures are designed in large part to reinscribe a common national identity, legitimate the government, and reestablish the moral authority of state sovereignty – all of this, without any transition.

Even governments that have not undergone transition may be able to employ the conceptual architecture of transitional justice to reinforce the sovereign authority of the state over its Indigenous population. Apologies highlight the ways in which the state failed a segment of *its own* population by failing to treat its citizens equally. Truth commissions aim in part to rewrite the history of a nation and to weave the Indigenous historical experience into a new common national narrative. Truth commissions also aim to achieve reconciliation, to restore trust in government, and to include Indigenous people in the creation of collective memory and history. Transitional justice measures aim to "promote confidence in the political arrangements and restore to citizens full membership in society."[67] They are about integration and the assertion of a common national identity.

Yet one historic injustice that lies at the heart of Indigenous identity is loss of sovereignty. Indigenous peoples are defined in part by the fact that their sovereignty was not recognized by colonial powers that appropriated territory and sovereignty under the doctrine of *terra nullius*. Indigenous identity is premised on a common experience of dispossession, and Indigenous politics draws its own legitimacy from the illegality of that usurpation of sovereignty. The demand for territorial self-government, which challenges the sovereign authority of the

---

66 Paige Arthur, "How 'Transitions' Re-shaped Human Rights: A Conceptual History of Transitional Justice" Hum Rts Q 31 (2009), 321–67.
67 Jaime Malamud-Goti, "Trying Violators of Human Rights: The Dilemma of Transitional Governments," in *State Crimes: Punishment or Pardon* (Queenstown, MD: Aspen Institute, 1989) at 26.

state, has emerged as the defining claim of the international Indigenous rights movement.[68]

The use of a transitional justice framework could undercut the conceptual and legal connection the Indigenous rights movement has drawn between the historical loss of sovereignty and the contemporary political presence of Aboriginal peoples. It could, as a result, practically limit their capacity to make some of the claims – to self-government and territorial autonomy – that define the Indigenous rights movement.

Indigenous leaders have sought to resist the legitimating function that transitional justice performs on behalf of the state. But they do so in a careful balancing act. Indigenous peoples also make other demands – demands that do rely on a presumption of state sovereignty and that rest on the fact that Aboriginal populations have been excluded from many of the social, economic, and political benefits of citizenship. Indigenous political claims derive not only from a history of forced inclusion, which has engendered demands for self-government, but also from exclusion, which has led to demands for full – social, economic, and political – rights in citizenship. To the extent they hope that transitional justice measures and rhetoric can animate these other claims, Indigenous leaders may welcome government willingness to acknowledge a historical debt that also implies present obligations.

Indigenous demands for such transitional justice measures as apologies and truth commissions highlight the emotional and psychological complexities of the history and relationship between Indigenous peoples, non-Indigenous citizens of the same state, and the government. Indigenous demands for recognition and acknowledgment are tempered by simultaneous claims to sovereignty. Indigenous demands for truth-telling stem in part from a desire to inscribe their own historical experience in the history of the nation, while nevertheless maintaining a separate identity. For Indigenous peoples, one aim of truth-telling, apologies, and reparations is to strengthen communities and self-governing capacities that were undermined by residential schools and other racist government practices.

---

68 While it is true that not all Indigenous peoples demand self-government, the demand is nevertheless the distinguishing feature and binding thread of the international Indigenous rights movement. As an organizing principle of Indigenous politics, it is an important condition of the political voice of the movement.

The potential contradictions generated by addressing Indigenous claims for justice through a transitional justice framework, and by the concept of reconciliation that sits at the heart of that framework, might be addressed by importing into transitional justice the conception of "reconciliation" already implicit in Canadian law. This concept is premised on recognition that First Nations were sovereign at all relevant moments in the formation of the Canadian state. Reconciliation entails balancing Aboriginal sovereignty with the sovereignty of Canada. More specifically, the Supreme Court has interpreted reconciliation as an obligation to reconcile Canadian and Aboriginal legal systems.[69] Since 1977 and the entrenchment of section 35 in the Constitution, Canadian jurisprudence has "moved away from governance under the Indian Act towards the general principle of reconciliation which the Supreme Court of Canada has said is at the heart of Aboriginal-Crown relations ... what is being reconciled is the pre-existence of Aboriginal societies, including their legal systems and their laws, with the assertion of Crown sovereignty."[70]

Transitional justice measures in Canada have taken this concept of reconciliation into account, extending the institutional and rhetorical spaces where Indigenous law may be applied and acknowledged. Truth and reconciliation commissions in particular can act as sites in which Indigenous conceptions of truth and reconciliation, along with Indigenous structures and procedures for achieving truth and reconciliation, can be employed. Such a precedent could have legal – juridical and jurisdictional – implications that extend beyond the moment of transitional justice. The legal principle of reconciliation might be used to mitigate some of the ways that transitional justice could threaten Aboriginal claims to autonomy in four ways.

One implication of reconciliation is negotiation among equals. In Canada, this model was approximated when AFN leader Fontaine short-circuited the political agreement offered by the government by bringing a class action suit against the churches and the Canadian government. The Indian Residential Schools Settlement Agreement

---

69 *Delgamuukw v British Columbia* [1997] 3 SCR 1010; *R v Van der Peet* [1996] 2 SCR 507.
70 Louise Mandell, in oral testimony before the Standing House Committee on Aboriginal Affairs, 5 June 2007, "AFN, Opposition Stiffen Resistance to Bill C-44, Legal Experts Cite Grave Problems with Bill." See also Jeremie Gilbert, "Historical Indigenous Peoples Land Claims: A Comparative and International Approach to the Common Law Doctrine on Indigenous Title" (2007) 56 ICLQ 583, esp. 591–92.

was the result of negotiations among the three parties, leading to an out-of-court settlement that was approved, and is enforceable, by the court. Once the opt-out option was closed, the Canadian government was legally bound to the agreement.

Transitional justice may also be especially well-equipped to deal with demands for legal pluralism. Truth commissions are already set up, in part, to do some of the work that court cases would do, most importantly to provide testimony, without the more onerous and adversarial characteristics of Western court proceedings such as rules of evidence, burden of proof, cross-examination, and expensive legal counsel. Truth and reconciliation commissions, in short, have already recognized the ways in which Western courts and legal norms are inadequate to the tasks of truth-telling and reconciliation. The TRC mandate empowered commissioners to recognize "the significance of Aboriginal oral and legal traditions in its activities."[71] The TRC also engaged tribal elders and others familiar with Indigenous law, in an attempt to install their knowledge and frameworks at the centre of the process.

A transitional justice framework also opens space for Aboriginal people to draw on international laws, conventions, and declarations that specifically address the rights of Indigenous peoples, including ILO Convention 169 and the United Nations Declaration on the Rights of Indigenous Peoples. Even though the declaration is non-binding and has no legal force, as a declaration it is a statement of principles that could be drawn down into Canadian jurisprudence in the future. How judges would respond is an open question, but transitional justice actors, including TRC commissioners, could be proactive in clarifying the status of the declaration in Canada and in creating opportunities to use and develop the principles of the declaration in the process of truth and reconciliation.

Finally, the Truth and Reconciliation Commission has offered a significant opportunity to develop and extend the concept of reconciliation beyond the law, into the domains of history, politics, human capacity building, and cultural revaluation. Meaningful reconciliation will have to go beyond law alone. Reconciliation should involve rewriting Canadian history to include Aboriginal narratives, not only about the residential school system but about the history of the nation more generally. Reconciliation will involve opening space and forging

---

71 Mandate for the Truth and Reconciliation Commission, Schedule N, 5.

mechanisms that will promote Aboriginal political voice and leverage. Reconciliation requires investing in Aboriginal well-being and capacity building. Reconciliation will entail revaluing Indigenous languages and cultures, lost and degraded in part through the residential school system. Reconciliation also demands that Canadian non-Aboriginals recognize the injustices committed in the past and demand that they implement the recommendations that will be outlined in the TRC's final report.

IV. Conclusion

Context matters. Whether transitional justice measures will primarily legitimate the status quo between post-colonial states, settler societies, and Aboriginal peoples, or will have transformational capacity will depend in part on the political context in which they take place. In Canada, the apology and the settlement agreement have been used in part to limit Aboriginal demands for social justice and constitutional transformation and to reinforce the individual rights framework of the Conservative Party's Aboriginal policy. Aboriginal activists have tried instead to leverage the moral obligation implied by the apology and the settlement agreement to extend the scope of state responsibility.

Yet by December 2012, the Harper government's persistent failure to assume that responsibility had precipitated the nationwide Idle No More protest. When transitional justice is applied to Indigenous peoples in cases where there has been no regime transition, its success must be measured by its capacity to transform the playing field. It is not enough for it to perform the standard functions of legitimation and national conciliation that it has been designed for in post-authoritarian and post-conflict situations. Idle No More, and the government's general stance of non-response to the protest, was not directly related to the limits of the TRC and the apology. But it was more deeply emblematic of the current relationship between the Canadian government and the Aboriginal peoples of Canada, belying any possible expectation that the government intended anything transformative or far-reaching when it agreed to implement the settlement agreement.

15 From Recognition to Reconciliation: Nunavut and Self-Reliance – An Arctic Entity in Transition

NATALIA LOUKACHEVA

The territory of Nunavut is located in Canada's Eastern and Central Arctic where the majority of the population is Inuit. The Inuit of Nunavut have secured constitutional protection of their Aboriginal and Treaty rights through section 35 of the *Constitution Act, 1982*, but in the current context the promise of reconciliation under this section is still a work in progress. Moreover, the process of reconciliation is often hampered by persistent socio-economic problems. Despite the existence of a growing body of knowledge relating to Nunavut's legal, political and socio-economic status, and increasing recognition of the challenges it faces,[1] a definitive answer about the strength of a future self-reliant Nunavut remains elusive. The tackling of the many challenges that the Nunavummiut (citizens of Nunavut) face can be regarded as a pre-condition for this reconciliation. Furthermore, the continuing constitutional development of the territory is linked to the devolution process, which is the next stage of recognition in the path towards reconciliation. However, the success of reconciliation and devolution in Nunavut is connected ultimately to the capacity of local actors to promote self-sufficiency in practice. After evaluating Nunavut's constitutional status, the socio-economic challenges it faces, and the promise of devolution,

---

1 See, for example, "Nunavut at 10" (2009) 43:2 Journal of Canadian Studies; relevant chapters in Frances Abele et al, eds, *Northern Exposure: People, Powers, and Prospects in Canada's North* (Montreal: Institute for Research on Public Policy, 2009); Jackie Price, "*Tukisivallialiqtakka*: The Things I Have Now Begun to Understand: Inuit Governance, Nunavut and the Kitchen Consultation Model (MA Thesis, University of Victoria, 2007); also see studies by Graham White, Peter Jull, Annis May Timpson, Jack Hicks, Ailsa Henderson, etc., and further footnotes.

it is argued that such legal and political settings, including a possible devolution deal, may not be a solution for the problems associated with Nunavut's desire for self-reliance. Sustainability and greater autonomy (self-governance) and, ultimately, reconciliation also depend upon people and their ability to make a difference.

The concept of reconciliation that is shaped in various ways (e.g., political, communal, personal, etc.), and often underpins contemporary political discourse on Indigenous peoples' rights, has been important to the Inuit and other Aboriginal peoples across Canada.[2] One substantive manifestation of reconciliation has been the response to the legacy of the residential schools (e.g., the 2006 Indian Residential Schools Settlement Agreement) and the subsequent establishment and work of a Truth and Reconciliation Commission (see chapter 14).

There is also an aspirational goal of Aboriginal self-governance that is often perceived as a measure of "achieving political and national reconciliation in which a sense of multinational citizenship is forged through recognizing diversity and self-determination."[3] Thus, internal self-determination has often been equated with reconciliation and the definition of the reconciliatory pre-conditions for Indigenous peoples (e.g., the overcoming of the colonial legacy; full Indigenous involvement in economic and political life; development of international standards).[4] Furthermore, the renewal of treaty relations and the implementation of Aboriginal rights, including the right to self-government, have been recognized by the government of Canada as a part of the reconciliation process.[5] The Canadian judiciary has also embraced the idea of reconciliation in their interpretation of section 35 of the *Constitution Act, 1982* (e.g., *R v Van der Peet*, para 31 – reconciliation is the key in Aboriginal rights law) and in some cases has also connected the idea of reconciliation with Aboriginal legal practices (e.g., *Ammaq et al v Canada (AG)*, paras 61–62).[6]

---

2 About this concept, see, for example, W Kymlicka & B Bashir, eds, *The Politics of Reconciliation in Multicultural Societies* (Oxford: Oxford University Press: 2008).

3 Mark D Walters, "The Jurisprudence of Reconciliation: Aboriginal Rights in Canada," in Kymlicka & Bashir, *ibid*, part III.

4 See, for example, Ian S McIntosh, "Visions of the Future: The Prospect for Reconciliation" (1999) 23:4 Cultural Survival Quarterly, online: <http://www.culturalsurvival.org/ourpublications/csq/article/visions-future-prospect-reconciliation>.

5 Indian and Northern Affairs Canada, *Gathering Strength: Canada's Aboriginal Action Plan* (Ottawa: Minister of Public Works and Government Services Canada, 1998), including "Statement of Reconciliation."

6 *R v Van der Peet* [1996] 2 SCR 507; *Ammaq et al v Canada (AG)* [2006] NuCJ 24 (CanLII).

The Inuit representatives have also expressed their own views on the ongoing process of reconciliation. These views do not generally perceive reconciliation as a legal term; instead they reflect on the value of culture and the need to improve understanding and trust between Inuit and non-Aboriginal (Qallunaat or non-Inuit) cultures: "[B]oth Aboriginal and non-Aboriginal cultures alike must respect one another in light of their historical experiences – they have to see eye to eye on healing, so to speak."[7] They also link reconciliation to Canada's fulfilment of its obligations "under historical and modern treaties" with Aboriginal peoples and to the need for socio-economic wellness and sustainability. In the words of Amagoalik, the "father of Nunavut," "Canada must put in place a long-term program to improve the socio-economic status of our people, to improve health and education, and to effectively deal with the housing crisis that faces our Aboriginal communities."[8]

Another Inuk leader, Nungak, has emphasized the need for a correction in the power relations between Aboriginal peoples and governmental jurisdictions, "from a lopsided Benefactor/Beneficiary set-up, to more of a Nation to Nation, equal-to-equal level jurisdictional field."[9] Indeed, the process of reconciliation does not stop once treaties are signed; its "normative" significance remains and implies that the government should stand by its obligations to implement those treaties that are also perceived as "living" agreements.

The settlement with the Inuit of the Nunavut Land Claims Agreement (NLCA) in 1993 and the establishment, in 1999, of a new territory of Nunavut (*Nunavut Act*, 1993) with an Inuit majority, was a significant part of this recognition, but further constitutional and political developments show that, even today, reconciliation in Nunavut is not complete. The NLCA is a land claim agreement within the meaning of section 35 of the *Constitution Act, 1982*. However, the negotiation of this agreement did not fulfil the promise of reconciliation entailed by this section. Furthermore, since 2006, the Nunavut Tunngavik Inc. (NTI) – an organization representing the beneficiaries of the NLCA, has been in the process of suing the government of Canada for breach of contract

---

7 David Joanasie, "Perspective on Reconciliation from an Inuk Youth," in Shelagh Rogers, Mike Degagné, & Jonathan Dewar, eds, *Speaking My Truth: Reflections on Reconciliation and Residential School* (Ottawa: Aboriginal Healing Foundation, 2012) at 104.
8 John Amagoalik, "Reconciliation or Conciliation: An Inuit Perspective," in Shelagh Rogers et al, *Speaking My Truth* at 41.
9 Nungak, cited in *ibid* at 41.

and for not carrying out the Crown's obligations under the NLCA. It has been argued that the NLCA is constitutionally protected under section 35 and thus Canada is under an obligation in its application of the NLCA "to act in good faith and in honour and integrity in a process of fair dealing and reconciliation."[10]

Further constitutional development of the territory is currently linked to the process of devolution, which can be seen as the next stage of recognition in the path to full reconciliation. De facto, the success of reconciliation and devolution in Nunavut is connected to the capacity of the Inuit and all Nunavummiut, in practice, to achieve sustainability. As Peter Jull notes, the Canadian "reconciliation" process, including Nunavut, was marked initially by misunderstandings and the complexity of disputes, which

> led gradually to greater openness, and then to discussions of citizenship entitlements, indigenous rights, use and benefit of territories and resources and devolution of central administrative power to local and regional indigenous or indigenous-dominated political entities … The decisive factor on the Inuit side was a determination to recover control of their lands and lives, with a flexibility about means.[11]

A primary element of "control" is self-reliance and fiscal autonomy. As such, we can usefully ask, Has this already been realized as part of the reconciliation process in Nunavut?

Self-Reliant Development and Nunavut

As has been noted above, reconciliation takes different forms. One is manifested in self-governance / internal self-determination, in which socio-economic development and self-reliance play a crucial role. As such, can the drive for self-reliance in Nunavut serve as a motor for wider reconciliation?

---

10 See further; quoted from the Nunavut Court of Justice, Amended Statement of Defence of the Third Parties to the Further Amended Third Party Notice, Court File 08-06-713-CVC, point 13.

11 See Peter Jull, "Reconciliation and Northern Territories, Canadian-Style: The Nunavut Process and Product" (1999) 30 Indigenous Law Bulletin, online: <http://www.austlii.edu.au/au/journals/ILB/1999/30.htm>.

The sustainability of Nunavut is conditioned by a variety of factors. However, the developments and outcomes involved have the potential to provide greater self-reliance for the Nunavummiut or, rather more problematically, to impede the self-sustainability of local communities. Furthermore, self-reliance and the economic viability of Nunavut depend not only on the legal and political settings in place, but also on the ability of local actors to respond to change.

In 1999, when Nunavut was carved out of the Northwest Territories (NWT), expectations of its potential for prosperous development were high. However, those expectations have been dampened by the realization that Nunavut continues to face harsh social, economic, environmental, and political problems, all of which challenge any self-reliant future for the territory while also render the prospects for sustainable governance uncertain.[12]

For the purposes of this chapter, the notion of Nunavut's self-reliance is deemed to be synonymous with that of sustainability, self-sufficiency, or self-sufficient development. Many of the challenges that Nunavut faces and the issues that they raise are not particular to Nunavut alone. Indeed, many of them are recognizable across the North. In the Canadian Arctic, sustainable development is focused on economic and social development, and environmental stewardship. The challenges to self-reliant development of Arctic jurisdictions such as Nunavut are manifold and inter-related:

1 Fiscal pitfalls (e.g., the shortage of financial institutions and the lack of fiscal resources for proper operational capacity; inadequate climate for investors; widening disparities in incomes, continuing high dependency on national transfers, despite the pragmatic expectations of self-sufficiency, and an inability to raise its own revenues due to the nature of fiscal federalism in Canada and the legal status of the territory, etc.).
2 Socio-economic factors (e.g., social wellness, fundamental social ills; educational and health problems; the importance of maintaining Inuit culture and values; underdeveloped infrastructure; high costs

---

12 See, for example, John Amagoalik, "There's Little to Celebrate on Nunavut's 10th Birthday: Inuit Territory Suffers from Unemployment, Chronic Social Problems, and High Dropout Rate," *Toronto Star* (1 April 2009); Jim Bell, "A Low-Key 10th Birthday," *Nunatsiaq News* (3 April 2009); Dru Oja Jay, "Nunavut Neglect Could Damage Canada's Arctic Claims," *Postmedia News* (10 July 2013).

of communications, living, and doing any kind of business; high structural unemployment; fluctuations in global market prices for renewable and non-renewable resources, dependence on increasingly expensive conventional sources of energy; underdevelopment of the private sector; reliance on the public sector as the primary employer and the major player in most development initiatives; balancing the desire to promote short-term strategies for resource extraction and benefiting from the royalties that accrue versus long-term economic planning for self-reliance, etc.).

3 Environmental issues (e.g., the impact of globalization and global warming on the development of trade in relation to traditional arts; bans on certain wildlife products; the impact of climate change on traditional economies, diets, and the general livelihood of the Inuit as well as on the preservation of Arctic ecology and fauna; the clash of Indigenous traditional subsistence economic activities and environmental interests with the pressure for industrial development, etc.).

4 Juridical-political challenges (e.g., international legal limitations or bans on the global trade of traditional arts, seal skins, or other wildlife products; inefficiency or non-implementation of the land claim agreement; overly complex structure of governmental and land claim bodies, which are based on Western law and modes of governance; nepotism, corruption, and lack of transparency; clash between Inuit and modern values; declining faith in democracy or communal involvement; lack of long-term strategic planning and high costs associated with maintaining the governmental bureaucracy; shortage of qualified manpower and of bureaucratic capacity to deal with the many problems associated with governing).

Understanding these factors that face Nunavut is thus of fundamental importance to appreciate the broader picture surrounding self-reliance. As such, its self-reliance is linked to the nature of legal and governance arrangements in place and to its de jure autonomy.

Furthermore, the capacity of Nunavut's system of governance to cope with change is crucial for its self-reliance. The sustainability of Nunavut depends not only on the efficiency of governmental policies or the comprehensiveness of its legal arrangements but also on the capacity of local communities to adapt and respond to changes, and to take the initiative. Thus, healthy and socially stable communities with well-educated human resources, youth who do not immediately relocate south for work and educational opportunities, and a holistic approach to tackling social ills and environmental problems are of the utmost importance for a self-reliable Nunavut. Finally, the efficiency of Nunavut's legal and governance arrangements cannot be divorced from its fiscal autonomy and jurisdictional capability to exert economic sustainability. As such, it is clear that Nunavut's process of reconciliation with the Canadian state is being hampered by persistent and deeply embedded socio-economic problems. What then are the challenges for the sustainable governance of Nunavut from a legal and governmental settings perspective?

Settings

Nunavut is struggling to gain greater political and economic autonomy within Canada, which could facilitate self-reliance of current and future generations. Negotiation of the territorial status of Nunavut was presented by the Inuit as an integral part of the Political Accord and the NLCA, 1993 (article 4). Thus, in 1999 a public government with "an Inuit face" was created alongside the existing land claims agreement. The NLCA in section 2.2.1 states, "The Agreement shall be a land claims agreement within the meaning of Section 35 of the *Constitution Act, 1982.*" Thus, on the one hand, the Inuit rights and structures endorsed by the NLCA are constitutionally protected under section 35 of the *Constitution Act, 1982.* On the other hand, they were given a territory with a public government with an Indigenous majority. In that sense, the promise of reconciliation in section 35 is not fully realized, as the Inuit of Nunavut still have the right to negotiate a separate self-government agreement in the future (e.g., if the Inuit of Nunavut became a minority within the territory).

With the settlement by the Inuit of the NLCA and the creation of the public government, representing the Inuit majority, the Nunavummiut should have become more self-reliant. Yet, in practice, it was not achieved, despite substantial financial assistance from federal authorities. Thus, the major legal and economic challenge is how to reconcile the idea of autonomy, self-reliance, and responsibility for Nunavut with external financial dependency.[13] In all its priority policy documents – plans for

---

13 Ninety per cent of GN's revenue comes from the federal government. Nunavut, Legislative Assembly, "2014–15 Main Estimates," 4th Leg 2nd Sess (May 2014) V; and see Impact Economics, "2013 Nunavut Economic Outlook, Nunavut's Next Challenge: Turning Growth into Prosperity" (Nunavut Economic Forum, December 2013) <neds2.ca/wp-content/uploads/2014/10/2013_Nunavut_Economic_FINAL_Jan_28_2014.pdf>.

development of Nunavut (1999–2004, 2004–9, 2009–13; 2013–18) – the government of Nunavut (GN) emphasized the need for self-reliance and reduced dependence as preconditions for future prosperity. The current GN in its Sivumut Abluqta vision stresses, "Our top priority is the development of self-reliance and optimism through quality education and training to prepare Nunavummiut for employment." In the Tamapta 2009–13 vision, the GN noted that by 2030 "[c]ommunities will be self-reliant, based on Inuit societal values, with reduced dependence on government."[14] Furthermore, in Aajiiqatigiinniq – a joint working strategy between the GN and the NTI – both authorities have chosen encouragement of self-reliance as a key priority. This document states, "For our Territory to be successful, Inuit must participate fully in its operation. We recognize that in order to increase self-reliance, we must first work towards providing communities with the tools necessary to achieve community wellness."[15] Thus, the development and implementation of anti-poverty and suicide prevention strategies and the raising of Inuit employment capacity are seen as crucial steps.

The social, economic, environmental, and political problems that dominate Canada's Arctic region question both the adequacy of current land claims and the governance systems in place. Do the provisions of the NLCA, the *Nunavut Act*, the Nunavut Political Accord, and other legal arrangements provide a sufficient framework for the Inuit and all Nunavummiut to become sustainable? Expectations of self-sufficiency and responsibility have become central to the generation of a self-governing capacity at the local government and communities level. The question remains whether the institutional governance and land claim structures are adequate to bring about self-reliance for the residents of Nunavut?

An analysis of the legal status of Nunavut[16] reveals that the Nunavummiut aspire to greater autonomy and self-reliance, despite limitations imposed by legal and governance structures. The negotiation of the

---

14 See *Sivumut Abluqta: 2013–18* (Iqaluit: GN, 2013); *Tamapta,* "Building Our Future Together: Government of Nunavut Priorities 2009–2013" (Iqaluit: GN, 2009).

15 *Aajiiqatigiinniq,* "Government of Nunavut and Nunavut Tunngavik Incorporated Working Together" (Iqaluit: GN and NTI, 20 April 2011) online: <www.gov.nu.ca>.

16 See Natalia Loukacheva, *The Arctic Promise: Legal and Political Autonomy of Greenland and Nunavut* (Toronto: University of Toronto Press, 2007); Alastair Campbell, Terry Fenge, & Udloriak Hanson, "Implementing the 1993 Nunavut Land Claims Agreement" (2011) 1:2 Arctic Review on Law and Politics 25.

NLCA was intended to enhance the sustainable development and self-reliance of the Inuit. The original goal of the land claim – to boost economic development and the self-sufficiency of the Inuit communities – has yet to materialize. Problems remain, particularly in limitations related to the land claim. It took many years to negotiate the NLCA. Thus, the original negotiators had a 1970s vision of industrial development and could not foresee future needs and challenges, such as impacts of climate change on wildlife use and natural resources, globalization, increased shipping, or the need for greater socio-economic development. As a result, the NLCA leaves much to be desired in terms of the Inuit socio-economic rights.

Furthermore, there are also problems with implementation of the land claim. For example, the auditor general of Canada noted that the government of Canada has failed to implement the spirit, goals, and intent of the NLCA. This undoubtedly undercut the potential for the NLCA to make a successful contribution to the economic growth and self-reliability of the Inuit beneficiaries.[17] As noted previously, in 2006 the NTI[18] sued the federal government for $1 billion for breach of contract and non-implementation of the NLCA. In 2012 the decision on the merits on part of the NTI claim was made by Mr Justice Johnson of the Nunavut Court of Justice, who issued a ruling in favour of the NTI on the failure of the government of Canada to establish a Nunavut General Monitoring Plan as required by the NLCA. The NTI was granted $14.8 million in damages. Other parts of the NTI's lawsuit (e.g., article 23 dealing with Inuit employment and article 24 dealing with government contracting) remain unresolved.[19]

Despite the many positive developments brought about by the NLCA, major challenges remain to its implementation.[20] Arguably, problems with the non-implementation of land claims are rooted in the Aboriginal land claims policy in Canada and in the lack of consensus on shared responsibilities by all the parties involved or sufficient

---

17 See, for example, Sheila Fraser, *Report of the Auditor General of Canada to the House of Commons*, November 2003, ch 8.

18 About NTI and its special role in Nunavut, see online: <www.nunavut.tunngavik.com>.

19 *The Inuit of Nunavut as Represented by NTI v R*. Claim by the NTI filed in the Nunavut Court of Justice, 5 December 2006, para 12. *NTI v Canada (AG)* 2012 NUCJ 11, para 354; the Government of Canada has appealed this decision but the appeal was dismissed. See "NTI Disappointed That Crown Appeals Historic Ruling," NTI news release, 21 August 2012. *Nunavut Tunngavik Incorporated vs Canada (AG)*, 2014 NUCA 02.

20 About those challenges, see Campbell, Fenge, & Hanson, *supra* note 16.

mechanisms implement existing land claims to fruition for Indigenous beneficiaries and the rest of Canada.

Another problem is the complexity of the regulatory system, which is entrenched in the prevailing co-management and resource management structures, and in the dysfunction of, and the fiscal burden carried by, many of the structures created under the NLCA. To deal with this, several measures have been taken to avoid overlaps and duplication in the functioning of several co-management boards while also reducing costs and providing better conditions for environmental monitoring, land use planning, and assessment.[21]

By itself the settlement of the NLCA did not bring about economic independence or substantial Inuit influence over the industrial development of their lands. With the settlement of the NLCA the Inuit could participate in the economic development of their land and improve socio-economic and wildlife matters affecting their people. At the same time the economic impacts of the land claim on the well-being and business development of Inuit communities depend on the variables chosen, and thus the results can be seen as questionable. One can argue that the land claim provided the Inuit with economic opportunities and benefits that are sufficient for their sustainability. For example, it opened the way for economic cooperation and business partnerships; allowed for the creation of economic institutions; included the possibility to negotiate the Impact and Benefits Agreements with companies willing to do business on the Inuit lands,[22] and guaranteed special measures to ensure the priority of the Inuit employment and training; brought monetary compensation and sub-soil title to some lands, etc. Overall, however, it can be argued that, despite these positive examples, the NLCA does not guarantee the sustainable future aspired to by the Inuit, nor has it succeeded in promotion of Indigenous self-sufficiency.

---

21 See, for example, Neil McCrank, "The Review of the Regulatory Systems across the North," report to Minister of Indian Affairs and Northern Development (Ottawa: Minister of Public Works and Government Services, May 2008). Also, in 2012 the Nunavut Marine Council was created to improve the implementation of the NLCA. See Natalia Loukacheva, "Inuit Perspectives on Arctic Ocean Governance: The Case of Nunavut" (2014) 28 Ocean Yearbook 348; and Nunavut Marine Council Business Case, 15 February 2012.

22 About problems with IBAs and Nunavut, see, for example, Dustin Fredlund, *Nunavummi Sivumuuqpallianiq [Nunavut Moving Forward]: Sustaining Northern Cultures in the Face of Progress* (Toronto: Walter & Duncan Gordon Foundation, 2012) at 22.

Historically, the development of the Eastern and Central Arctic (Nunavut) was rooted in substantial government activities and projects. Economic development occurred slowly and was induced in part as a result of government programs. Thus, when Nunavut was created, it had an underdeveloped economy, which, from the outset, set significant limitations on the territory's capacity to generate or expand its own revenue sources. However, since its inception the negotiation of the NLCA has been viewed by the Inuit as a part of their political development that would lead to the creation of the new territory. Thus, the land claim and the creation of the territory with a public government were considered crucial pre-conditions for Inuit economic progress and development.

Legal and governmental frameworks and provisions are not always sufficient or adequate to produce self-reliance for the Nunavummiut, and after fifteen years Nunavut is still a project in transition. The efficacy of Nunavut's governance machinery is subject to growing criticism and scrutiny by those who negotiated the creation of the new territory and those who daily witness mounting problems.[23] Over the years, the GN has faced significant criticism for its policy of decentralization, shortage of qualified staff, scandals involving senior government officials, and poor financial practices.[24] Furthermore, it is no secret that Nunavut's overstretched bureaucracy has been under scrutiny, particularly in the promotion of meetings, action plans, and strategies that lack a clear implementation vision, commitment to public debate, and transparency.[25] Although the GN has adopted strong fiscal management principles of being "forward-looking in our planning," "prudent in our budgeting," "responsible in our choices," "transparent in our reporting," and "accountable in our actions" as a core of their good governance operation,[26] it still remains to be seen how these principles will be operationalized. On several occasions many Nunavummiut remain confused and alienated by the number of bureaucratic structures created by the NLCA, the Political Accord, and the *Nunavut Act*.[27]

23 See *Nunatsiaq Online*: <www.nunatsiaqonline.ca>.
24 For example, "Financial Controls in Nunavut Still Lacking, Auditor General Says," CBC News (3 April 2009). Over the past decade, these issues have also been discussed in various publications, including the *Nunatsiaq News*.
25 See, for example, Nunavut, Legislative Assembly, *Hansard*, 2nd Leg (March 2008) Member's Statements, 363–2(4) (Tagak Curley).
26 2013–2014 Budget Highlights, GN, February 2013 at 1.
27 See, for example, Bell, *supra* note 12.

Socio-Economic Matters

In 1999 the creation of Nunavut was seen by the Inuit and others as the solution to their social malaise. It was expected to promote the revival of Inuit values and culture and provide the best way to build healthy and self-sufficient communities. Today, the array of social ills (e.g., high dropout rates from schools, violence, suicide, abuse, addictions, mental health problems, tuberculosis and sexually transmitted diseases, shortage of housing and hidden homelessness, growing poverty, welfare dependence, lower standards of living compared to that of other Canadians, etc.) compromise opportunities for economic development, self-sufficiency, adequacy and legitimacy of the land claim and the created governance structures, and, ultimately, the process of reconciliation itself. In the words of former premier Aariak, "We need healthy communities in order to start looking outwards, developing our sense of reliance and looking all the way out to the globe. If we have healthy individuals in healthy communities, then it is that much easier to work toward dealing with the situations that we are immersed in."[28]

The lack of a stable social environment is a serious impediment for the self-reliance of Nunavut and the movement towards reconciliation. Despite the positive prospects for future industrial development in the territory, especially in the mining sector, the economic sustainability of Nunavut is inescapably also interconnected with the issues of housing, education, environment, and social wellness. Nunavut is poised for economic growth due to increased private sector–led investment in recent years, primarily in the development of non-renewable resources, especially the mining sector, which is expected to become the major economic driver in Nunavut.[29] However, this development is not yet secure, as a clear need remains to promote more "favourable socio-economic and regulatory conditions" to boost investor interest in the mining

---

28 Quoted from "New Nunavut Premier Says Responding to Credit Crunch Impact on Mining Top Priority," Canadian Press (25 November 2008).
29 NEF and Impact Economics, "The 2010 Economic Outlook," Nunavut Economic Forum and Impact Economics, 2010, 59. High economic benefits and prospects for Nunavut are anticipated with the construction of the Mary Rive iron mine in 2013–2014. Canadian Chamber of Commerce, "Economic Outlook 2013–14," policy brief, December 2012 at 12. On mining prospects in Nunavut, see Justin Cooke, "Nunavut" in *The Territorial Outlook, Economic Forecast (Winter 2013)* (Ottawa: Conference Board of Canada 2013); and 2013 Nunavut Economic Outlook, *supra* note 13.

industry of Nunavut.[30] Hopes for further promotion of self-reliance, based on such resource developments remain uncertain and are linked to the constitutional matter of devolution. Furthermore, the expectations of substantial economic and employment opportunities from resource development clash with the necessity to preserve ecological balance, Inuit wildlife harvesting, and Arctic fauna. For example, the 2008 decision by the NTI to lift a moratorium on uranium exploration and mining on the Inuit-owned lands was not supported by all beneficiaries of the NLCA and environmental groups concerned with the impact of radioactive contaminants on the future generations of the Nunavummiut and the caribou calving grounds. In 2012 the GN released its Uranium Policy Statement, in which it emphasized that all its decisions will "support safe and responsible development that provides substantive and sustainable benefits to Nunavut without harming our environment."[31] Nevertheless, the issue of uranium mining in Nunavut has been controversial and has led to several actions by an independent NGO Nunavummiut Makitagunarningit calling for a comprehensive public inquiry on uranium mining and questioning why the Nunavummiut were deprived of the free, prior, and informed consent in this matter, as well as calls by the hunters and trappers organizations for a referendum on the uranium question.[32] There is clearly also rising tension between the necessity for mining and the maintenance of traditional hunting and harvesting.[33]

There are number of detailed studies on the economic outlook for Nunavut[34] that analyse the prospects and challenges for socio-economic prosperity. As such, it is well documented that the shortage of educational,

30 For example, in February 2012 Newmont Mining Corp (Hope Bay Project) put mineral activities on hold.

31 Minister Taptuna quoted in GN, "GN Announces Uranium Policy Statement," news release (6 June 2012).

32 This NGO was established in 2009. It has been active in lobbying and petitioning the NLCAs bodies and the GN on uranium mining problems. See Nunavummiut Makitagunarningit, "Submission to the United Nations' Special Rapporteur on the Rights of Indigenous Peoples on Extractive and Energy Industries in and near Indigenous Territories" (1 April 2013); "Nunavut Hunters' Organization Calls for Uranium Referendum," CBC News (15 July 2013).

33 About mining and environmental governance in Nunavut, see Laura Bowman, "Sealing the Deal: Environmental and Indigenous Justice and Mining in Nunavut" 2011 20:1 Review of European Community & International Environmental Law 19.

34 See, for example, 2013 Nunavut Economic Outlook, *supra* note 13; also see all previous reports and Nunavut Economic Strategy online: <www.nunavuteconomicforum.ca>.

organizational, regulatory, social, and human capital hampers the development of the private sector and the economy as a whole in Nunavut. It is also well known that Nunavut's underdeveloped infrastructure (e.g., clear need to develop roads, marine facilities, and upgrades for airports) impedes promotion of economic prosperity. However, one promising initiative – the upgrade of Iqaluit international airport as a result of a public-private partnership – is expected to bring substantial socio-economic benefits.[35] The possibility that a 1,300 km road will be built to connect the Southern Kivalliq region in Nunavut with Northern Manitoba is also seen as vital to successfully addressing many of the socio-economic issues faced by the territory.[36] There are also positive economic developments in Nunavut's arts and crafts sector and in its fledgling film industry, as well as emerging possibilities within community-based inshore fishing and different types of tourism (e.g., Arctic cruise tourism), but overall, the fishing and tourism industries are still in development.[37]

Because of climate change and future maritime developments, Nunavut is poised to gain from the economic opportunities that may emerge in the wake of the melting Arctic sea ice. However, Nunavut's lack of a basic maritime transport infrastructure, the need of harbour facilities, better navigational aids and supply chains, prevent the territory "from serving basic community needs, including safe transportation, and facilitating responsible economic resource, tourism, fishing and polar shipping development."[38]

Moreover, continuing high dependence on the public sector and over-reliance on government employment do not augur well for the promotion of a sustainable economy. Therefore massive fiscal transfers from Ottawa will continue to have an impact on the lives of the Nunavummiut and their attempt to generate economic progress in the near future. As such, the question of the struggle for self-reliance by Indigenous peoples, or of continuing "internal colonialism," as it is still often framed,

---

35 The federal government is planning to commit $77.3 million to this upgrade; a private partner will be chosen by GN. GN, news release, "Governments of Canada and Nunavut Demonstrate How Commitment to Public-Private Partnerships Benefits the Territory (20 September 2012).

36 Patrick White, "Have Road Will Travel: Rural Nunavut Hopes for a Way Out," *Globe & Mail* (23 August 2012).

37 2013 Nunavut Economic Outlook, *supra* note 13.

38 See John Higginbotham, "Nunavut and the New Arctic," CIGI Policy Brief No 27 (July 2013) at 1.

remains the focus of ongoing discourse.[39] Nunavut is the subject of much criticism as the model of economic reliance on a dominant public sector; federal funding and expectations of greater transfers from Ottawa simply cannot solve the long-term problem. As Exner-Pirot notes, the problem in all northern territories and especially in Nunavut "is not that the federal government is 'wasting' billions of dollars in transfers to the North. The problem is that the money it sends does not and cannot provide reasonable rates of literacy, employment, health outcomes and educational achievement, because the high level of federal transfers and the culture of dependency it breeds *is* the problem."[40] According to some evaluations,[41] the major solution to Nunavut's dependency is to deal with the devolution of natural resources and the constitutional status of the territory. According to the northern premiers, "The territories' lands and resources belong to northerners and must be managed, developed and protected according to northerners' needs and priorities. Devolution is essential to building prosperous, resilient and self-reliant communities throughout Canada's North."[42] Is devolution an answer to Nunavut's sustainability? Can the process of devolution be viewed as the next stage of recognition in Nunavut's path to reconciliation?

Devolution

Fiscally, the territory is 90 per cent dependent on transfers from the federal government. At the same time, the devolution of certain powers from

39 Charles Pinderhughes, "Toward a New Theory of Internal Colonialism" (2011) 25:1 Socialism and Democracy 235.
40 Heather Exner-Pirot, "Dead in the Arctic," Eye on the Arctic (16 August 2012), online: <www.rcinet.ca/eye-on-the-arctic/>.
41 See, for example, Kirk Cameron & Alastair Campbell, "The Devolution of Natural Resources and Nunavut's Constitutional Status" (2009) 43:2 Journal of Canadian Studies 198; on aspects of devolution in Nunavut, see Beth Elder, "Aboriginal Self-Government in Nunavut" (2012) 3:2 Sovereignty and Intervention Public Policy and Governance Review 21; Tony Penikett, "Destiny or Dream: Sharing Resources, Revenues and Political Power in Nunavut Devolution," in Natalia Loukacheva, ed, *Polar Law Textbook II* (Copenhagen: Nordic Council of Ministers, TemaNord 535, 2013) 199; Tony Penikett & Adam Goldenberg, "Closing the Citizenship Gap in Canada's North: Indigenous Rights, Arctic Sovereignty, and Devolution in Nunavut" (2013) 22:1 Michigan State University Journal of Int'l Law, 23; about financial considerations and benefits of devolution, see Anthony Speca, "Nunavut, Greenland and the Politics of Resource Revenue," *Policy Options* (May 2012) 62.
42 Northern Premiers, communiqué, "Premiers Continue to Build a Stronger North and Better Canada" (27 June 2012).

Ottawa to Nunavut is perceived by many Nunavummiut as the "magic measure" for the territory's self-reliance. The Nunavummiut are eager to obtain greater 'province-like' jurisdiction on lands and resources (e.g., inshore on Crown lands and offshore within Canada's internal waters). According to the Department of Executive and Intergovernmental Affairs of Nunavut, which is responsible for devolution negotiations and the implementation of a possible final agreement,

> Devolution is the transfer of federal jurisdiction over Nunavut's lands, resources and inland waters to the Government of Nunavut (GN). A devolution agreement will transfer this federal jurisdiction to the GN and will outline the transfer of federal programs and services, including the positions required to deliver them.[43]

Over the years the question of Nunavut's devolution has developed along several important key issues and expectations, which can be summarized as follows:

The legal-constitutional status of Nunavut (e.g., provincial status vs territorial), further constitutional evolution (e.g., devolving of jurisdiction as the culmination of nation-building and partnership with the North, a part of the constitutional process in Canada).

Implementation of the spirit and letter of certain provisions of the NLCA (e.g., article 15.4.2, the establishment of the Nunavut Marine Council[44]) which is expected to boost Nunavut's ability to deal with current issues and, it is perceived, would also help to generate the capacity to assume responsibility for and control over the devolved areas of jurisdiction.

Inuit offshore rights (including the waters of the Canadian Arctic Archipelago and sub-soil).[45] One unique feature of Nunavut is its large marine areas, which are vital to Inuit coastal communities and their marine culture. Thus, for example, the NTI presented a case that those areas are integral to Nunavut's devolution, and the NLCA provides substantial justification based on both law and policy that marine areas should be the subject of devolution and resource-revenue-sharing negotiations.[46]

---

43 See "Devolution," Department of Executive and Intergovernmental Affairs, online: <www.gov.nu.ca/eia/information/devolution>.
44 About the NMC and its mandate, see Loukacheva, *supra* note 21.
45 About Inuit offshore rights, see, for example, *ibid.*
46 NTI, "Devolution and Marine Areas," Discussion Paper, presented to Indian Affairs and Northern Development, Vancouver (2 February 2007) at 6.

Equality and non-discrimination (e.g., devolution is associated with hopes that devolved authority will guarantee equal opportunities and a quality of life for the Nunavummiut similar to that of southern Canadians).

Political development (e.g., a new relationship and partnership with national authorities; a new role for Nunavut in the Confederation; greater decision-making powers and political autonomy).

International significance (e.g., increased credibility for Nunavut as a viable destination for inward investment and as a place to do business; an example for the broader circumpolar community and beyond).

Arctic sovereignty (e.g., discourse on the contribution of the Inuit to the assertion of Canadian sovereignty in the North and the scope of devolved jurisdiction).

Fiscal autonomy (e.g., expectations that devolution will reduce territorial dependency and generate substantial revenues via royalties from resource extraction and other avenues).

Self-determination (e.g., with the settlement of the NLCA and the creation of the territory, the Inuit of Nunavut did not achieve a measure of self-determination that would allow them to have a self-sustainable existence and more control over the land and their lives).

Self-reliance (e.g., devolution can change the structure of Nunavut's economy and remedy many of the socio-economic ills and struggles that the territory currently encounters).

Devolution as the next stage along the path to reconciliation (e.g., several of the above-mentioned dimensions fit the ultimate goal of self-determination, autonomy, and socio-economic sustainability).

Arguably, all of these issues are interconnected. They also indicate that the question of Nunavut's devolution is rather complex. Nunavut's devolution process clearly remains a work in progress, in which determining the balance between various interests is often quite challenging. The conclusion of the devolution deal remains the top priority for the current GN as indeed it has been for previous GNs.

Despite the challenges to self-reliable development, one key to the creation of a prosperous future for Nunavut is clearly related to the estimated wealth of renewable (e.g., fish) and non-renewable (e.g., fossil fuels, precious metals, minerals) resources.[47] There are also, possibly substantial, offshore resources. This factor serves as major impetus for the Inuit leadership to get a devolution deal.

---

47 See, for example, 2013 Nunavut Economic Outlook report.

In the words of former premier Aariak, devolution is needed because, despite the settlement of the NCLA, the GN

> does not have direct control over the Crown Lands and waters of our territory ... Devolution is about equality. Canada's constitution guarantees that the lands, internal waters and resources within a province belong to the people who live there. Devolution is about ensuring Nunavummiut have the same economic opportunities as other Canadians. It is the next step in integrating the north as equal partners into the Canadian federation.[48]

With the settlement of the NLCA the Inuit gained ownership of 18 per cent of the land; about 80 per cent of the territory is Crown land. However, Nunavut's current territorial status does not imply the same constitutional rights to resources and offshore waters as provinces enjoy. Thus the question arises whether it would be better for Nunavut simply to become a province,

The feasibility of granting provincial status to Nunavut has been a question on the political agenda for some time and has been regularly featured in academic discourse.[49] However, it did not materialize in practice for various reasons including particularities and realities in the North (e.g., low population density, high costs, harsh climactic conditions, inadequate socio-economic base). As some authorities note, "[P]rovincial status as it is understood in today's context cannot do justice to the unique socio-political and cultural characteristics found in present-day Nunavut," and it is arguable "that there is an implicit constitutional presence for the Nunavut [Province] Territory in Canada."[50] For now, all three northern territories have been following the devolution path. The fact that the two other northern territories signed their final devolution agreements (the Yukon in 2003; the NWT in 2013)[51]

---

48 Eva Aariak, "Reflecting on Our Past, Looking to Our Future," in *Impacts on Decision-Making in Nunavut: Our Future Is Not Yet Set Nor Is Our Journey Complete* (2012). Devolution Division, Department of Executive and Intergovernmental Affairs, Government of Nunavut, online: <www.gov.nu.ca/eia/information/devolution>.

49 This issue has been raised in *Nunatsiaq News*. See also Gordon Robertson, *Northern Provinces: A Mistaken Goal?* (Montreal: Institute for Research and Public Policy, 1985). Cameron and Campbell, *supra* note 41 at 210–12.

50 Cameron and Campbell, *supra* note 41 at 210.

51 About NWT's devolution, see "Devolution of Lands and Resources of the Northwest Territories," online: <devolution.gov.nt.ca>.

has served as something of an inspiration and prompted the Nunavut leadership to pursue devolution talks with greater urgency. As noted previously, as an element of this devolution path, Nunavut wishes to gain powers similar to those of the Canadian provinces, including, for instance, territorial jurisdiction over natural resources on Crown lands and a resource-sharing benefit agreement. However, the possibility of gaining provincial status is not on the current agenda; rather, the aspiration is to gain "province-like" powers on those matters.

Challenges associated with devolution in Nunavut remain. Some are fiscal and deal with the system of territorial formula financing (TFF) and possible resource-revenue sharing.[52] Others deal with the capacity of the GN to operate and take on devolved responsibility.[53] There are also questions about "the adequacy of the resource base to be transferred" and "the resistance of the federal government to devolution in Nunavut's adjacent marine areas."[54]

The Inuit leadership has been very vocal about Nunavut's aspirations to devolution and have tried various tactics to prompt negotiations with the federal government on it. For example, different faces of the "Arctic sovereignty card" were played on different occasions in an effort to move the devolution talks further forward. Thus,

> on the one hand, Nunavut officials such as the former premier Okalik and representatives of the NTI made an argument that the Inuit will strengthen Canada's Arctic sovereignty claim, as they are proud to be Canadian,

---

52 About TFF and Nunavut's devolution, see Speca, *supra* note 41.
53 Paul Mayer, *Mayer Report on Nunavut Devolution* (Ottawa: Fasken Martineau Du-Moulin LLP, June 2007). In 2010, mismanagement of the Nunavut Housing Corporation ran up $110 million in cost overruns on its two social housing construction programs. See, for example, Deloitte & Touche LLP, *Nunavut Housing Corp Review of Nunavut Housing Trust* (22 September 2010). Weak financial operational capacity of the GN, human resources, and numerous other problems are well described in reports of the auditor general of Canada. See, for example, Sheila Fraser, *Report of the Auditor General of Canada to the Legislative Assembly of Nunavut – 2009, Report No. 2 Financial Management Practices – Follow-up on the 2005 Report to the Legislative Assembly of Nunavut* (Ottawa: Office of the Auditor General of Canada, 31 March 2009); Fraser, *Report of the Auditor General of Canada to the Legislative Assembly of Nunavut – 2010, Human Resource Capacity – Government of Nunavut* (Ottawa: Office of the Auditor General of Canada, 8 March 2010); Michael Ferguson, *Report of the Auditor General of Canada to the Legislative Assembly of Nunavut – 2012, Procurement of Goods and Services* (Ottawa: Office of the Auditor General of Canada, 28 February 2012).
54 Cameron and Campbell, *supra* note 41 at 217.

but in exchange they want to gain access to resources that are currently under the jurisdiction of the federal government. On the other hand, Nunavut was making a claim that the waters of the Arctic Archipelago are also Nunavut's internal waters. The territory, as a result of the devolution deal, should be granted sub-soil rights to the offshore region. The territory has asked the federal government for an equal partnership with regards to jurisdiction over sub-soil rights and royalties on resources located beneath the waters of the Arctic Archipelago.[55]

On numerous occasions and in speeches, former premier Okalik defended this position and further emphasized that "just like provinces have jurisdiction over Canadian internal waters within their borders Nunavut is seeking equal responsibility."[56] However, it is questionable whether this strategy of seeking to connect the devolution debate over resources, including those offshore, with the assertion of Arctic sovereignty has helped Nunavut to advance its claims. Indeed, this position was clearly not supported by Ottawa and clashed with its views on the scope of powers that can be devolved to Nunavut. The 2007 report of Special Representative Mayer on devolution in Nunavut concluded that the territory is not ready to assume new responsibilities as a result of its mounting problems and challenges with administration of its current affairs. In 2008 the federal government confirmed that it will follow a phased approach to devolution, and the question of Nunavut's jurisdiction over seabed resources beneath internal waters was not therefore going to be on the initial agenda.[57] Okalik's position subsequently softened and came to focus instead on the necessity of building healthy communities as a requirement for the exercise of sovereignty.

Despite tensions over the possible scope of devolution and the need to resolve the clashes among stakeholders involved (e.g., local interests, the territorial government, and national ambitions), the process of devolution culminated in the signing of the Lands and Resources Devolution Negotiation Protocol on 5 September 2008.[58] The protocol

---

55 Natalia Loukacheva, "Nunavut and Canadian Arctic Sovereignty" (2009) 43:2 Journal of Canadian Studies 99.
56 Paul Okalik, "Devolution and Nation Building in Canada's North (speech at the Northern Transportation Conference, Yellowknife, NWT, 13 December 2006) 4.
57 Mayer *supra* note 53; Stephen Harper, Letter from Prime Minister Harper regarding devolution (25 February 2008). Doc. 195–2(4). Available from the author.
58 The Lands and Resources Devolution Negotiation Protocol, Ottawa (5 September 2008).

excluded seabed resource management (i.e., offshore oil and gas) from the first stage of devolution negotiations and suggested that it would be discussed together with the onshore management of such resources during a future stage of devolution (paras 3.2 (b)(c)). The signing of the protocol was seen by all signatories (the GN, the NTI, and the government of Canada) as an important step towards a possible devolution agreement for the territory. However, despite these expectations, the process stalled and very little progress has subsequently been made. Former premier Aariak, like her predecessor, had been very vocal about the importance of the final devolution agreement for Nunavut. In 2011 the signing by the NWT of its agreement-in-principle on devolution was seen by the Nunavut leadership as providing an important impetus to re-starting its own devolution negotiations with Ottawa. Furthermore, in 2011 the NTI supported the GN's position and issued a special resolution on devolution urging all parties to re-commit to negotiations and conclude the final agreement. In this resolution the NTI emphasized the importance of "a mutually respectful and beneficial partnership" with Ottawa that would give the Inuit "both adequate control over resource development decisions and primary access to public sector revenues and other benefits."[59] In May 2012 the federal government appointed a chief federal negotiator for Nunavut's devolution process;[60] Nunavut also appointed its chief negotiator, but little progress has been made. Nunavut Premier Taptuna, talking about the future of smaller communities and their sustainability, has noted, "At this time there are no long-term viability plans from this government ... Nunavut does not have any means of generating its own revenues. We do not have devolution and all of our transfer money comes from Ottawa."[61] Thus, devolution is seen as a solution to many issues. In October 2014 the governments of Canada, Nunavut, and the NTI named negotiators who will go ahead with talks on the negotiation of the devolution agreement-in-principle. In the words of Taptuna, "It is an important day for Nunavummiut. It moves us closer to self-reliance and more control over our own resources ... What happens

---

59 NTI, Resolution RSA 11-11-14 Devolution, Annual General Meeting, Cambridge Bay (22–24 November 2011).
60 "Ottawa Names Nunavut Devolution Negotiator," *Nunatsiaq News* (22 May 2012).
61 Nunavut, Legislative Assembly, *Hansard* (12 June 2014) Question 171-4(2): Long-term Viability of Smaller Communities (Peter Taptuna).

in negotiations for devolution affects all Nunavummiut."[62] Thus, it is hoped that in the near future there will be progress on this matter.[63]

The complexity of devolution in Nunavut and the need to balance various interests present a number of challenges. Moreover, it is unclear whether the final outcome would really meet all, or indeed any, of these expectations in respect of the various challenges associated with the quest for self-reliance. It remains to be seen how the situation will unfold and whether devolution will constitute a meaningful stage in the path to reconciliation.

Conclusion

The jurisprudence of the Supreme Court of Canada notes, "Reconciliation is not a final legal remedy in the usual sense. Rather, it is a process flowing from rights guaranteed by s. 35(1) of the *Constitution Act, 1982*."[64] The NLCA is constitutionally protected under section 35, but settlement of the NLCA did not fulfil the promise of reconciliation under this section. Further, the NLCA or the creation of the territory with the system of public government represented by the Inuit majority is not a pre-condition of self-reliance. Per se, greater political autonomy is not a guarantee of sustainability, but it can assist in the achievement if this goal. Political empowerment through increased autonomy and improved economic possibilities is crucial for the sustainable development of Nunavut. However, the NLCA and Nunavut's governance structures still need to gain legitimacy among the Nunavummiut in order to be seen more generally as an efficient venue to achieve the pragmatic goal of sustainability.

Self-reliance in Nunavut is important, not just for the viability of legal arrangements, economic prosperity, and resolution of social ills. Moreover, it is crucial for the Inuit in their quest to overturn voluntary colonialism and to regain power by strengthening Indigenous identity, values,

---

62 Jim Bell, "Ottawa Accelerates Nunavut Devolution Talks," *NunatsiaqOnline* (3 October 2014), <www.nunatsiaqonline.ca/stories/article/65674ottawa_accelerates_nunavut_devolution_talks/>.

63 Steve Rennie, "Nunavut Premier Seeks Devolution Pact, Eyes Control over Land, Resources," *Globe and Mail* (3 February 2015), online: <www.theglobeandmail.com/news/national/nunavut-premier-seeks-devolution-pact-eyes-control-over-land-resources/article22777248/>.

64 *Haida Nation v British Columbia (Minister of Forests)*, 2004 SCC 73, [2004] 3 SCR 511 at para 32.

and culture. The transformation from a traditional nomadic subsistence culture to industrial modernity and the imposition of Western values, laws, and institutions on the Inuit is one of the most challenging impediments to Nunavut's self-reliance. For example, as noted by Anawak, in an attempt to reduce poverty there is a "need to reconcile Inuit forms of governance with the governance model we use in Nunavut today."[65] Bridging the culture clash and the gap in values often caused by the painful experience of colonization thus continues. One potential solution is in revival of traditional knowledge and values. Thus, maintenance of the *Inuit Quajimajatuqangit* ("IQ" – Inuit societal values and knowledge) has become the focal point of the Inuit land claim organizations, GN's policies, and public service. As such, Nunavut's drive for self-reliance is perhaps best expressed in the promotion of social wellness, human capacity-building, education, and the availability of a skilled manpower base able to accommodate local needs and Indigenous values.

However, self-reliance for Nunavut cannot be achieved through economic benefits from resources development, or prosperity as the outcome of the devolution deal with Ottawa alone. The path to self-reliance, internal self-determination (self-governance), and, ultimately, reconciliation, should nevertheless be considered in the context of the dimensions described above.

Despite much criticism of the "Nunavut project" and of limitations to its fulfilment, it is clear that a growing role of communities, promotion of the public initiative, investment in youth and in the wellness of future generations, and community-based strategic planning and economic activities are key for self-reliance. Improved partnership with the federal government, the engagement of private partners, and direct Inuit involvement in economic development are also important. Nunavut is an Arctic entity in transition where, despite the constitutional protection of Inuit rights under section 35 of the *Constitution Act, 1982*, the NLCA, and the creation of territory, the ultimate goals of reconciliation and self-reliance have not yet been attained. However, successfully addressing the many remaining challenges associated with socio-economic development and a greater realization of the possibilities associated with devolution could play a significant role in the attainment of these broader political goals.

---

65 Jack Anawak, quoted from GN, "Poverty Reduction Action Plan Focuses on Community Self-Reliance, Collaboration and Healing: The Makimaniq Plan – A Shared Approach to Poverty Reduction," news release (24 February 2012).

PART FIVE

Comparative Reflections

16 Constitutional Indigenous Treaty Jurisprudence in Aotearoa, New Zealand

Introduction

In the 1980s, both Canada and Aotearoa New Zealand sought to more formally recognize their Indigenous peoples in the law. In Canada, in 1982, the new *Constitution Act 1982* was enacted with section 35(1), in Part II, reading, "The existing aboriginal and treaty rights of the aboriginal peoples of Canada are hereby recognized and affirmed." In Aotearoa New Zealand, in 1986, the first statute was enacted that gave some legal standing to the *Treaty of Waitangi*. Section 9 of the *State Owned Enterprises Act* 1986 states, "Nothing in this Act shall permit the Crown to act in a manner that is inconsistent with the principles of the Treaty of Waitangi." More than 100 statutes now reference the *Treaty of Waitangi*. The judiciary in both countries have since contributed enormously to defining the Indigenous reconciliation discourse. The courts have often gazed at the other with approval.[1] But the legislative mechanism to

* My thanks to the Sandra Day O'Conner Law School, Arizona State University (particularly Professor Rebecca Tsosie), for hosting me for part of 2012 during my tenure as the Fulbright Nga Pae o te Maramatanga Māori Senior Scholar Award recipient, during which much of the draft of this chapter was written. I also thank Dr Abby Suszko for research assistance in preparing this work.

1 For a Canadian example, see McLachlin CJ judgment in *Haida Nation v British Columbia (Minister of Forests)*, 2004 SCC 73, [2004] 3 SCR 511 at para 46, where she references New Zealand Ministry of Justice *A Guide for Consultation with Māori* (Wellington: The Ministry, 1997). Aotearoa New Zealand courts have since referenced this Canadian decision: see *Proprietors of Wakatū Inc v AG* [2012] NZHC 1461; and *Paki v AG* [2009] 1 NZLR 72. Moreover, several New Zealand cases have cited *Delgamuukw v British Columbia* [1997] 3 SCR 1010 including *Takamore v Clarke*, 2011 NZCA 587, [2012] 1 NZLR 573; *Ngati Apa v AG* [2003] 3 NZLR 643; *McRitchie v Taranaki Fish and Game Council* [1999] 2 NZLR 139; and *Te Runanganui O Te Ika Whenua Inc Society v AG* [1994] 2 NZLR 20.

recognize reconciliation with Indigenous peoples is obviously different: in Canada it has been via formal constitutional recognition, whereas in Aotearoa New Zealand it has been via ad hoc statutory incorporation. The New Zealand judges are alive to this difference, although there is conflict as to whether the difference is significant or not. One thread of the general sentiment is that there is similarity,[2] even though Canada has the *Constitution Act 1982* and New Zealand has the *Treaty of Waitangi*,[3] and there should be no inference that "the rights of the Māori people are less respected than the rights of aboriginal peoples are in North America."[4] In contrast is the sentiment that the Canadian cases are irrelevant because they "reflect the different statutory and constitutional context in Canada."[5] This chapter thus focuses on the developing legislative and judicial considerations of the *Treaty of Waitangi* and whether it provides as section 35 in Canada does for its Indigenous peoples, or not. This chapter focuses on exploring some of the judgments of the courts compared to the reports of the Waitangi Tribunal. The core questions explored here are of constitutional role that the contemporary judiciary attributed to the *Treaty of Waitangi* and whether these judgments move beyond mere recognition of Māori and the treaty towards reconciliation with Māori.

Māori and the Law Generally

It is important to take a moment to provide a snapshot of who Māori are and what the law generally does for Māori, because this is the context in which the contemporary constitutional operation of the *Treaty of Waitangi* must be understood.

Māori first discovered and settled the lands and waters of Aotearoa New Zealand sometime after 800 CE.[6] Grouped into distinct peoples, the Māori tribes became, literally, the people of the land (*tangata whenua*),

---

2 *Proprietors of Wakatū Inc v AG, ibid* at para 309, Clifford J states, "is a clear point of similarity with the context in Canada."
3 *New Zealand Māori Council v AG* HC Wellington CIV-2007-485-000095, 4 May 2007 at para 61.
4 *Te Runanga o Muriwhenua Inc v AG* [1990] 2 NZLR 641 (CA) at p 655 per Cooke P.
5 *New Zealand Māori Council v AG*, 2007 NZCA 269, [2008] 1 NZLR 318 at para 81.
6 See Jacinta Ruru, "Asserting the Doctrine of Discovery in Aotearoa New Zealand: 1840–1960s" in Robert J Miller, Jacinta Ruru, Larissa Behrendt, and Tracey Lindberg, eds, *Discovering Indigenous Lands: The Doctrine of Discovery in the English Colonies* (Oxford: Oxford University Press, 2010). Note that Ranginui Walker, *Ka Whawhai Tonu*

living upon Papatuanuku, the earth mother, with Ranginui, the sky father, above. The common language (with regional dialectal differences) captured this world view. For instance, *hapū* means "sub-tribe" and "to be pregnant"; *whanau* means "family" and "to give birth"; and *whenua* means "land" and "afterbirth."[7] Of some forty distinct *iwi* (tribes), and hundreds of *hapū*, each derived its identity from the mountains, rivers, and lakes.[8] Today, Māori are visibly present throughout the country (currently constituting over 15 per cent of the population),[9] integrated into all parts of society and share a long history of intermarriage with *Pakeha* (the Māori word for Europeans) and others.[10] Since 1950s, Māori began a noticeable drift from rural to urban living, to the point that now more than 80 per cent of Māori live in cities, notably Auckland and Hamilton. Many Māori have retained strong cultural links to their tribal areas, in particular visiting *marae* (traditional meeting houses) for family celebrations and funerals. There is nonetheless a small but significant group of Māori who no longer know their tribal backgrounds and instead identify and participate as "urban Māori."[11]

In 1840, many Māori chiefs officially consented to Europeans living in Aotearoa New Zealand with the signing of the bilingual *Treaty of Waitangi*. The Māori language version, which contains the most signatures, records that Māori would retain *tino rangatiratanga* (sovereignty) over their lands and treasures but otherwise gave *kawanatanga* (governance) rights to the British Crown. The English version has some significant translational differences, where it states that Māori ceded sovereignty to the British Crown but Māori retained full exclusive and undisturbed possession of their lands, estates, forests, fisheries, and other properties.

Matou: Struggle without End, 2nd ed (Auckland: Penguin Books, 2004) 24 provides the 800 CE date, but others sometimes put it at about 1200 CE: *see* Michael King, *The Penguin History of New Zealand* (Auckland: Penguin Books, 2003) 48.

7 For an introduction to the Māori language, see HW Williams, *Dictionary of the Māori Language* (Wellington: GP Publications, 1992); and HM Ngata, *English-Māori Dictionary* (Wellington: Learning Media, 1993).

8 For an introduction to Māori mythology, see Ross Calman & AW Reed, *Reed Book of Māori Mythology*, 2nd ed (Wellington: Reed Books, 2004).

9 "People and Communities" online: Statistics New Zealand <www.stats.govt.nz/people> (showing New Zealand's current population).

10 Paul Callister, Robert Didham, & Anna Kivi, "Who Are We? The Conceptualisation and Expression of Ethnicity" (2009) 4 Official Statistics Research Series 1.

11 As an example, see the Te Whanau o Waipareira Māori Urban Authority in Auckland: "Home" online: Te Whānau o Waipareira <www.waipareira.com/>.

However, the future did not eventuate as Māori had expected. In 1840, the British assumed formal sovereignty of the country. In 1852, the *New Zealand Constitution Act* was enacted that created provincial councils throughout the country and a central General Assembly, that constituted the Governor-in-Chief of New Zealand, a Legislative Council, and a House of Representatives.[12] Many Māori tribes were unhappy with the colonial government regime. Some protest action was peaceful (travelling to England to petition Queen Victoria) and some was violent. By the 1860s, the violence had escalated into the New Zealand land wars.[13] By the 1870s, European settlers outnumbered Māori.

Today, Māori own an unknown quantity of general freehold land and own in fee simple about 6 per cent of the country's landmass in Māori freehold land title. There are no reserves, as in Canada. The colonial beginning point was that Māori owned the land. Following the signing of the *Treaty of Waitangi*, the British Crown set about acquiring land and by the early 1860s had become the owner of most of the land in the South Island and the lower part of the North Island (constituting about 60 per cent of New Zealand's land mass and where about 10 per cent of Māori lived).[14] The Crown then sold this land as general freehold land to the new European settlers. In the 1860s, legislation enabled the Crown acquisition of most remaining lands in the North Island through outright confiscation and the more subtle but equally successful waiver of the British Crown's right of pre-emption in favour of the creation of Māori freehold land titles.[15] The Native Land Court was established with the primary purpose to encourage Māori landowners to transfer

---

12 This historical Act can be viewed at "The New Zealand Constitution Act" (2012) online: Victoria University of Wellington Library <nzetc.victoria.ac.nz/tm/scholarly/tei-GovCons.html>.

13 See James Belich, *The New Zealand Wars and the Victorian Interpretation of Racial Conflict* (Auckland: Penguin, 1998); and Belich, *Making Peoples: A History of the New Zealanders from Polynesian Settlement to the End of the Nineteenth Century* (Auckland: Penguin, 1996).

14 Note that many of these early sales included clauses that promised to set aside some land for reserves, but it was rarely done, and even where it was done, Māori were not forced to reside on the reserved lands. See Waitangi Tribunal, *Te Whanganui A Tara Me Ona Takiwa: Report on the Wellington District*, Wai 145 (Wellington: Legislation Direct, 2003). Note tribunal reports can be viewed at the Waitangi Tribunal website: "Home" (2012) online: The Waitangi Tribunal <www.justice.govt.nz/tribunals/waitangi-tribunal>.

15 *Native Lands Act* 1865.

their customary holdings into a freehold title that would then enable them to alienate their lands as they wished.[16] In reality, many owners were forced to sell their lands to pay for financial debt incurred in the transaction process. Today, there is said to be virtually no Māori customary land remaining. The 6 per cent that is held in Māori freehold titles is mostly held in multiple in common titles, not inhabited, and in rural areas but with little arable value. Māori freehold land can be alienated, but legislation enacted in 1993 – *Te Ture Whenua Māori Act* / the *Māori Land Act* – has emphasized new twin principles to ensure that it is retained in Māori ownership and that it is used and developed. There are some remarkable financial success stories, mostly concerning forestry on Māori freehold land where the Māori trusts or Māori incorporations are returning profits of a million dollars and more.

Māori have a strong political presence. Since the 1860s Māori have had guaranteed representation in the House of Representatives,[17] with four electoral seats set aside for Māori voters.[18] It was not until 1975 that Māori had the choice to enrol in either the Māori or the General roll.[19] Since the 1990s, when the country moved from a first past the post to a mixed member proportional voting system, the Māori seats have been adjusted to reflect the number of the persons enrolled in the Māori seats. There are now seven Māori seats, and an increasing number of Māori being elected to Parliament on party lists, representing the spectrum of political ideologies. The Māori Party (first established in 2004) has a confidence and supply agreement with the National Party that currently leads government. One benefit of this arrangement is that the co-leader of the Māori Party is the minister of Māori affairs.[20]

Māori are regaining control of their affairs boosted by *Treaty of Waitangi* claim settlements. Since the mid-1980s, the Crown has sought to engage in a "fair and final" settlement process of claimed historical

---

16 *Native Lands Act* 1865.
17 The Parliament of New Zealand has two parts. One is the head of state, Queen Elizabeth II, who is represented by the governor-general. The other part is the House of Representatives, which comprises members of Parliament, who are elected every third year.
18 *Māori Representation Act*, No 47 1867, (NZ). See Andrew Geddis, "A Dual Track Democracy? The Symbolic Role of the Māori Seats in New Zealand's Electoral System" (2006) 5 ELJ 347.
19 *Electoral Amendment Act*, No 28 1975 (NZ).
20 See the Māori Party website for information about this party including this agreement: "Home" (2010) online: Māori Party <www.Māoriparty.org>.

breaches of the principles of the *Treaty of Waitangi.*[21] The settlements
aim to provide the foundation for a new and continuing relationship
between the Crown and the claimant group based on the *Treaty of Waitangi* principles. Settlements thus contain Crown apologies of wrongs
done, financial and commercial redress, and redress recognizing the
claimant group's spiritual, cultural, historical, or traditional associations with the natural environment. Some significant cultural redress
examples include the return of *pounamu* (nephrite jade/greenstone)
ownership to Ngai Tahu[22] and the new co-management of the Waikato
River.[23] More than twenty tribal groups have now received redress.[24]
In addition, there have been financially notable pan-tribal settlements
regarding commercial fisheries, commercial aquaculture, and forestry.[25]
The increased wealth of the tribes has enabled Māori to have more
national political clout[26] and the means to work with their tribal members to grow their tribal assets and provide many social benefits.

Since 1975, Māori have had the opportunity to present arguments to
the specially created permanent commission of inquiry – the Waitangi
Tribunal – on alleged Crown contemporary breaches of the principles
of the *Treaty of Waitangi.*[27] From 1985 to 2010, Māori were able to lodge
arguments that the Crown actions, policies, or laws between 1840 and
1992 breached the treaty principles.[28] The Waitangi Tribunal consists of
both Māori and non-Māori Māori Land Court judges and other notable appointed persons. It is a powerful bicultural place where hearings
are often heard in *marae* (Māori meeting houses), with Māori protocols

21 See Office of Treaty Settlements, *Ka tika a muri, ka tika a mua / Healing the Past, Building a Future,* 2nd ed (Wellington: Office of Treaty Settlements, 2002); and R Joseph,
"Contemporary Māori Governance: New Era or New Error?" (2007) 22 NZULR 628.
22 *Ngai Tahu (Pounamu Vesting) Act,* No 81 1997 (NZ).
23 *Waikato-Tainui Raupatu Claims (Waikato River) Settlement Act,* No 24 2010 (NZ).
24 See the Office of Treaty Settlements website, "Progress of Claims" for a current list
of negotiated settlements, online: Office of Treaty Settlements <nz01.terabyte.co.nz/
ots/fb.asp?url=livearticle.asp?ArtID=-1243035403>.
25 *Treaty of Waitangi (Fisheries Claims) Settlement Act,* No 121 1992 (NZ); *Māori Fisheries
Act,* No 78 2004 (NZ); *Māori Commercial Aquaculture Claims Settlement Act,* No 107
2004 (NZ); *Central North Island Forests Land Collective Settlement Act,* No 99 2008 (NZ).
26 For example, in 2005 the Iwi Chairs Forum was established; see "Kaupapa" (2008)
online: Iwi Chairs Forum <www.iwichairs.Māori.nz/Kaupapa/>.
27 Paul Hamer, "A Quarter-Century of the Waitangi Tribunal: Responding to the Challenge" in Janine Hayward & Nicola Wheen, eds, *The Waitangi Tribunal: Te Roopu
Whakamana i te Tiriti Waitangi* (Wellington: Bridget Williams Books, 2004).
28 *Treaty of Waitangi Amendment Act,* No 148 1985 (NZ), s 3(1).

and Māori language often utilized. The tribunal has released numerous reports on tribe-region-specific claims alleging historical breaches throughout the country and has reported on an array of generic issues ranging from the use of the Māori language, customary fishing, to the allocation of radio frequencies, petroleum, aquaculture, and water. In some instances the government has accepted the tribunal's recommendations for redress and enacted appropriate legislation (e.g., the *Māori Language Act 1987* and the *Māori Commercial Aquaculture Claims Settlement Act 2004*), but denied several others (e.g., the reports on petroleum, and the foreshore and seabed).[29]

In regard to who are Māori, legislation simply affirmed that "Māori means a person of the Māori race of New Zealand; and includes a descendant of any such person."[30] This is perceptibly different from the detailed legal definitions used to define the Aboriginal peoples in Canada. The contemporary descent definition, rather than the historically used legal blood quantum classification, is much more aligned to a Māori perspective of identification – "When children are born with whakapapa they are grandchildren or 'mokopuna of the iwi.' They are Māori."[31] However, for Māori people, while descent from a Māori ancestor is a minimum requirement, being Māori is primarily a matter of subjective, social identification with other Māori and within that wider group with particular *iwi* and *hapū*.[32]

The law today recognizes the Māori language as an official language of the country.[33] Many statutes recognize Māori cultural values, including *kaitiakitanga*,[34] and *taonga*.[35] Numerous statutes across a wide spectrum, from environmental management, to family property division, to land transport require decision-makers to have some level of regard for the principles of the *Treaty of Waitangi* as discussed below.

---

29 Waitangi Tribunal, *The Petroleum Report*, Wai 796 (Wellington: Legislation Direct, 2003); Waitangi Tribunal, *Report on the Crown's Foreshore and Seabed Policy*, Wai 1071 (Wellington: Legislation Direct, 2004).

30 Section 4 of *Te Ture Whenua Māori Act 1993 / Māori Land Act*, No 4 1993 (NZ).

31 Moana Jackson, "The Part-Māori Syndrome," *Mana Magazine* (June–July 2003) at 62. For a past example of how Māori were historically defined in legislation, see s 2 of the *Native Land Court Act*, 1894.

32 See Natalie Coates, *Kia tū ko taikakā: Let the Heartwood of Māori Identity Stand – An Investigation into the Appropriateness of the Legal Definition of "Māori" for Māori* (BA [Hons] diss., Te Tumu: School of Māori, Pacific and Indigenous Studies, 2008) online: <https://ourarchive.otago.ac.nz/handle/10523/5171>.

33 *Māori Language Act*, No 176 1987.

34 For example, *Resource Management Act*, No 69 1991 (NZ), s 7(a) [RMA].

35 For example, *Property (Relationships) Act*, No 166 1976 (NZ), s 2.

Nonetheless, Māori still constitute all the wrong side of the statistics for health, education, imprisonment, and unemployment.[36] Past legislation legitimated horrendous actions against Māori, including taking their lands and treasures, and encouraging the demise of the Māori language and Māori culture. While the country is reconfiguring towards reconciliation, the relationship between Māori and government and society generally is still tense at times. In 2003 and 2004 the country's race relations erupted concerning the issue of possible Māori ownership of the foreshore and seabed.[37] In 2012, disquiet emerged about possible Māori ownership of freshwater.[38]

This overall account of Māori and the law is similar in some ways to the general experiences of Aboriginal peoples in Canada. Aboriginal peoples have similarly been disposed of much of their lands and treasures, lost many of their languages and much of their cultural knowledges, but have retained collective strength in who they are and what they desire. There are, of course, differences arising in part from the different colonial tools used. For instance, in Canada there is the *Indian Act* and reserves, a history of residential native schooling, and no single treaty or judicial institutions similar to the Māori Land Court or the Waitangi Tribunal. This chapter now turns to consider the specific legal role of the *Treaty of Waitangi*.

Parliament's Treatment of the *Treaty of Waitangi* Specifically

Aotearoa New Zealand has a unicameral legislature. Under its constitutional system, Parliament is supreme and has no formal limits to its law-making power.[39] The *Treaty of Waitangi* is not part of the domestic

---

36 See "Browse for Statistics" online: Statistics New Zealand <www.stats.govt.nz/browse_for_stats.aspx>.

37 See Abby Suszko, "The Marine and Coastal Area (Takutai Moana) Act 2011: A Just and Durable Resolution to the Foreshore and Seabed Debate?" (2012) 25 NZULR 148.

38 For example, see "Māori Council Readies for Court Action" 3 *News* (17 September 2012) online: 3 News <www.3news.co.nz/politics/Māori-council-readies-for-court-action-2012091706#axzz3O4xxyFW0>. See Jacinta Ruru, "Indigenous Restitution in Settling Water Claims: The Developing Cultural and Commercial Redress Opportunities in Aotearoa New Zealand" (2013) 22:2 Pacific Rim Law & Policy Journal 311.

39 To better understand New Zealand's constitutional system, see Phillip Joseph, *Constitutional and Administrative Law in New Zealand*, 2nd ed (Wellington: Thompson Brookers, 2007); Matthew Palmer, "Constitutional Realism about Constitutional Protection: Indigenous Rights under a Judicialized and a Politicized Constitution" (2007) 29 Dalhousie LJ 1.

law. Since the 1980s, the treaty is commonly said to form part of the country's informal constitution, along with the *New Zealand Bill of Rights Act 1990*, the *Electoral Act 1993*, and the *Constitution Act 1986*.[40] But for the judiciary or those acting under the law, the treaty itself usually becomes relevant only if it has been expressly incorporated into statute.[41] Even so, statutory incorporation of the treaty has been a relatively recent phenomenon. It was once endorsed in the courts "as a simple nullity."[42] It was not until the 1970s, when Māori visibly took action to highlight treaty breaches, that the treaty began to gain mainstream recognition and, in turn, the attention of those in Parliament and the judiciary.[43]

The *Treaty of Waitangi Act 1975* was the first statute to use the term "the principles of the Treaty of Waitangi" and the first statute to permit interpretation of the *Treaty of Waitangi*. Hence the treaty jurisprudence was initially developed in the Waitangi Tribunal.[44] The courts entered this terrain post-1986, via the opening provided in the *State Owned Enterprises Act 1986*.[45] Section 9 states, "Nothing in this Act shall permit the Crown to act in a manner that is inconsistent with the principles of the Treaty of Waitangi." This wording was unique – no other statute had ever confined those with statutory power to have some level of regard for the *Treaty of Waitangi*.

Today, more than one hundred statutes reference the *Treaty of Waitangi*, but there are various reasons and methods for the incorporations.

---

40 The *Constitution Act*, No 114 1986 (NZ) sets out New Zealand's system of government, in particular the executive, legislature, and judiciary, and it holds that the sovereign in right of New Zealand is the head of state, and the governor-general is the sovereign's representative. See generally Geoffrey WR Palmer & Matthew Palmer, *Bridled Power: New Zealand's Constitution and Government*, 4th ed (Auckland: Oxford University Press, 2004).

41 *Te Heuheu Tukino v Aotea District Māori Land Board* [1941] NZLR 590, [1941] AC 308 (PC).

42 *Wi Parata v Bishop of Wellington* [1877] 3 NZ Jur 72, 78 (NS) (SC).

43 See Walker, *supra* note 6.

44 For commentary on treaty principles, see Te Puni Kokiri, Ministry of Māori Development, *He Tirohanga o Kawa ki te Tiriti o Waitangi / A Guide to the Principles of the Treaty of Waitangi as Expressed by the Courts and the Waitangi Tribunal* (Wellington: Te Puni Kokiri, 2001).

45 The courts have defined the relationship by stating that the tribunal's opinions "are of great value to the Court" (*New Zealand Māori Council v AG* [1987] 1 NZLR 641 at p 662 (CA) [Lands Case]) and "are entitled to considerable weight" (*Moana Te Aira Te Uri Karaka Te Waero v The Minister of Conservation and Auckland City Council* HC Auckland M360-SW01, 19 February 2002 at para 59) but can be freely dismissed.

For example, the *Treaty of Waitangi* settlement statutes reference the historical signing of the treaty and record Crown apologies for breaching the principles of the *Treaty of Waitangi*. Those statutes that actually direct decision-makers acting under a statute to have some level of regard to the Treaty principles do not use uniform orders. Section 9 of the *State Owned Enterprise Act* cited above is obviously one example of a directive. However, it is more common for the treaty principles directive to be positioned as a positive, rather than a negative, duty. The directives usually take one of the following forms:[46]

- *Give effect to* the treaty principles,[47]
- *Give particular recognition to* the treaty principles,[48]
- *Take into account* the treaty principles,[49]
- *Ensure full and balanced account of* the treaty principles,[50]
- *Have regard for* the treaty principles,[51]
- *Acknowledge* the treaty principles,[52] and
- *Recognize and respect* the treaty principles.[53]

---

46 Note that this summary is taken from the Constitutional Advisory Panel, *New Zealand's Constitution: The Conversation So Far* (Sept 2012) at 56, online: Constitutional Advisory Panel <www2.justice.govt.nz/cap-interim/Resources.html>.

47 For example, *Conservation Act*, No 65 1987 (NZ), s 4, states, "This Act shall so be interpreted and administered as to give effect to the principles of the Treaty of Waitangi."

48 For example, *Royal Foundation for the Blind Act*, No 3 2002 (NZ), s 10, states that one object of the foundation is to "give particular recognition to the principles of the Treaty of Waitangi and their application to the governance and services of the Foundation."

49 For example, RMA, *supra* note 34, s 8, requiring that the exercise of functions and powers under the Act "take into account the principles of the Treaty of Waitangi."

50 The Preamble of the *Environment Act*, No 127 1986 (NZ), states that one purpose of the Act is to "[e]nsure that, in the management of natural and physical resources, full and balanced account is taken of … (iii) The principles of the Treaty of Waitangi."

51 For example, *Crown Minerals Act*, No 70 1991 (NZ), s 4, requires that the exercise of functions and powers under the Act "shall have regard to the principles of the Treaty of Waitangi."

52 For example, *Education Act*, No 80 1989 (NZ), s 181, states that one duty of a council of an institution in exercising its functions and powers under the Act will be to acknowledge the treaty principles.

53 For example, *Exclusive Economic Zone and Continental Shelf (Environmental Effects) Act*, No 72 2012 (NZ), s 12, outlines what is required "in order to recognise and respect the Crown's responsibility to give effect to the principles of the Treaty of Waitangi for the purposes of this Act."

The latest trend for statutory incorporation of the treaty principles is to be more prescriptive. For example, a recent statutory inclusion is found in section 12 of the *Exclusive Economic Zone and Continental Shelf (Environment Effects) Act 2012*. This section reads:[54]

Section 12 – Treaty of Waitangi
In order to recognise and respect the Crown's responsibility to give effect to the principles of the Treaty of Waitangi for the purposes of this Act, –
(a)
section 18 (which relates to the function of the Māori Advisory Committee) provides for the Māori Advisory Committee to advise the Environmental Protection Authority so that decisions made under this Act may be informed by a Māori perspective; and
(b)
section 32 requires the Minister to establish and use a process that gives iwi adequate time and opportunity to comment on the subject matter of proposed regulations; and
(c)
sections 33 and 59, respectively, require the Minister and the EPA to take into account the effects of activities on existing interests; and
(d)
section 45 requires the Environmental Protection Authority to notify iwi authorities, customary marine title groups, and protected customary rights groups directly of consent applications that may affect them.

The next part of this chapter considers how the courts have interpreted these legislative phrases.

The Courts' Interpretations of the *Treaty of Waitangi*

Aotearoa New Zealand's present appeal courts constitute, in order, the High Court, Court of Appeal, and the Supreme Court.[55] Prior to the

---

54 Note Bill 327-1, *Heritage New Zealand Pouhere Taonga Bill*, 49th–50th Parl, 2011, cl 7 proposes to adopt this format. But section 4 of the *Environmental Protection Authority Act*, No 14 2011 (NZ) did not as it uses the phrase "to take appropriate account of the Treaty of Waitangi."
55 See *Supreme Court Act*, No 53 2003 (NZ). The lower courts include the Environment Court, the District Court, the Family Court, and the Māori Land Court. Note that Māori Land Court decisions are appealed first to the Māori Appellate Court and then onto the High Court and above.

2002, the Privy Council was Aotearoa New Zealand's top appeal court. All of these appeal courts have considered and developed the principles of the *Treaty of Waitangi* jurisprudence. This part explains, first, how the courts describe the standing of the treaty, then how the courts have interpreted the general phrase "the principles of the *Treaty of Waitangi*." This part then considers how the courts have specifically interpreted the strongest legislative treaty principles directive that exists in section 4 of the *Conservation Act 1987*.

In 1987, Māori took the first opportunity afforded to utilize the treaty in a legal argument before the courts. The New Zealand Māori Council relied on section 9 of the *State Owned Enterprises Act 1986* to argue in the courts that the Crown had to act consistently with the treaty in transferring Crown assets into state-owned business-focused enterprises. They were successful. This case, *New Zealand Māori Council v AG,*[56] commonly referred to as the *Lands* case, has become the landmark decision for reconciliation treaty jurisprudence.

In this *Lands* case, the Court of Appeal justices discussed the status of the *Treaty of Waitangi*. They all accepted the orthodox position established by the Privy Council in 1941 that the "Treaty cannot be enforced in the Courts except in so far as a statutory recognition of the rights can be found."[57] But even so the justices were comfortable in discussing the treaty as having a like constitutional status (but not constitutional in the sense that it could override over statutes or bind Parliament in any manner).[58] For example, President Cooke said that he accepted the submissions that argued that "the Treaty is a document relating to fundamental rights; that it should be interpreted widely and effectively and as a living instrument taking account of the subsequent developments of international human rights norms; and that the Court will not ascribe to Parliament an intention to permit conduct inconsistent with the principles of the Treaty."[59] Justice Richardson, in this case, said that "the Treaty is a positive force in the life of the nation and so in the government of the country."[60] In a later case, Cooke P stated that

---

56 Lands Case, *supra* note 45. To appreciate the importance of this case, see Jacinta Ruru, ed, *"In Good Faith" Symposium Proceedings Marking the 20th Anniversary of the Lands Case* (Wellington: New Zealand Law Foundation, 2008).

57 *Ibid* at 655 per Cooke P citing *Te Heuheu Tukino v Aotea District Māori Land Board, supra* note 41.

58 Lands case, *ibid* at 655 per Cooke P.

59 *Ibid.*

60 *Ibid* at 682 per Richardson J.

"the Treaty is a living instrument and has to be applied in the light of developing national circumstances,"[61] and, "The Treaty obligations are ongoing. They will evolve from generation to generation as conditions change."[62] But the courts have mostly also stressed that the treaty does not give rise to legal rights on its own. This stance is particularly repeated in criminal cases where the treaty has not been incorporated into any relevant criminal legislation.[63] However, at times a contrasting approach has been pronounced in family cases. Despite no family legislation citing the treaty principles, the High Court hearing an appeal from the Family Court said in dictum that "all Acts dealing with the status, future and control of children, are to be interpreted as *coloured by* the principles of the Treaty of Waitangi."[64] The Court justified this approach because:[65]

> We are of the view that since the Treaty of Waitangi was designed to have general application, that general application must colour all matters to which it has relevance, whether public or private and that for the purposes of interpretation of statutes, it will have a direct bearing *whether or not there is a reference to the Treaty in the statute*. We also take the view that the familial organisation of one of the peoples a party to the Treaty, must be seen as one of the taonga, the preservation of which is contemplated. (Emphasis added.)

The appeal courts have since referenced this observation several times.[66] The different judicial approaches remain unresolved. In the *Lands* case, Richardson J made a remark that is now twenty-five years old but just as relevant today: "Much still remains in order to develop a full understanding of the constitutional, political and social significance

---

61 *Te Runanga o Muriwhenua Inc v AG, supra* note 4 at 655.
62 *Ibid* at 656.
63 For example, see *Grubmayr v Bloxham* [2010] NZAR 256 (HC); *R v Ransfield* HC Rotorua T030059, 20 February 2004; and *Nga Uri O Te Ngahue v Wellington City Council* CA CA407/03, 18 February 2004.
64 *Barton-Prescott v Director-General of Social Welfare* [1997] 3 NZLR 179 (HC) at p 184 [emphasis added].
65 *Ibid.*
66 See *Takamore v Clarke, supra* note 1 at para 248; *New Zealand Māori Council v AG, supra* note 5 at para 74; *Paki v AG, supra* note 1 at para 84. Note also the Family Court decision *DBH v JCK* FAMC North Shore FAM-2007-044-773, 29 August 2011 at para 189.

of the Treaty in contemporary terms and our responsibilities as New Zealanders under it."[67]

But what of the actual phrase "the principles of the *Treaty of Waitangi*"? How have the courts interpreted it? According to the *Lands* case, the hallmarks of this expression are partnership, reasonableness, and good faith. Cooke P, in this case, concluded, "[Treaty] principles require the Pakeha and Māori Treaty partners to act towards each other reasonably and with the utmost good faith. That duty is no light one. It is infinitely more than a formality."[68] He stressed the importance of not freezing treaty principles in time: "What matters is the spirit ... The Treaty has to be seen as an embryo rather than a fully developed and integrated set of ideas."[69] Richardson J observed that "the obligation of good faith is necessarily inherent in such a basic compact as the Treaty of Waitangi,"[70] and Somers J likewise stated, "Each party in my view owed to the other a duty of good faith."[71] Casey J emphasized the importance of an "on-going partnership,"[72] and Bisson J described the treaty principles as "the foundation for the future relationship between the Crown and the Māori race."[73]

In 1994, the Privy Council choose three different principles as the hallmarks of the treaty principles: reasonableness, mutual cooperation, and trust.[74] Here the Privy Council stressed that the principles do not impose on the Crown any obligations that are "absolute and unqualified," because this "would be inconsistent with the Crown's other responsibilities as the government of New Zealand and the relationship between Māori and the Crown."[75] The domestic courts have also

---

67 Lands case, *supra* note 45, at 672 per Richardson J.
68 *Ibid* at 667 per Cooke P.
69 *Ibid* at 663.
70 *Ibid* at 682 per Richardson J.
71 *Ibid* at 693 per Somers J.
72 *Ibid* at 703 per Casey J.
73 *Ibid* at 714 per Bisson J. Subsequent judicial decisions, including decisions from the Privy Council, have confirmed the underlying tenor of this landmark *Lands* decision, including respectfully not construing a finite list of treaty principles. For example, see *AG v New Zealand Māori Council (No 2)* [1991] 2 NZLR 147 (CA); *New Zealand Māori Council v AG* [1992] 2 NZLR 576 (CA); *New Zealand Māori Council v AG* [1994] 1 NZLR 513 (PC); *New Zealand Māori Council v AG* [1996] 3 NZLR 140 (CA); *Takamore Trustees v Kapiti Coast District Council* [2003] 3 NZLR 496 (HC); and *Carter Holt Harvey Ltd v Te Runanga o Tuwharetoa ki Kawerau* [2003] 2 NZLR 349 (HC).
74 *New Zealand Māori Council v AG* [1994] 1 NZLR 513; *ibid*, Lord Woolf at 517.
75 *Ibid*.

highlighted this point that the treaty principles do not "lay down what should be done"[76] but rather are a process to be considered in determining an appropriate option to proceed with. Cooke P said this in 1991: "If the Government, giving due weight to the Treaty principles, elects between the available options reasonably and in good faith, it seems to me that the Treaty is complied with. That would be so no matter what may be the precise legal status of the Treaty."[77]

How have the courts interpreted the strongest legislative directive concerning the principles of the *Treaty of Waitangi*? This directive is found in section 4 of the *Conservation Act 1987*, which states, "This Act shall so be interpreted and administered as to give effect to the principles of the Treaty of Waitangi."[78]

In 1988, the Māori Land Court was the first to consider this section.[79] This case concerned a dispute between a Māori land-owning trust and the Department of Conservation over land block boundaries bordering a forest park. Hingston J concluded that section 4 requires the Crown to[80]

act fairly, to ensure that the Māori people to be effected [*sic*] by any negotiations are properly represented. This at the very least, would require the Crown undertaking to meet the applicants [*sic*] legal and other costs irrespective of the outcome of negotiations. As well "partnership" means both parties *together* strive for an equitable solution and not approach the discussions as opponents. It may be difficult for those of us born to, and trained in the adversary method of solving problems to accept that there is another way – be that as it may – it has to be tried.

The most noteworthy case specific to section 4 is the Court of Appeal's *Ngai Tahu Māori Trust Board v Director-General of Conservation*[81] decision. Commonly referred to as the "whale-watch case," this 1995 decision clarified a significant point: the section 4 directive has relevance not solely to the *Conservation Act*, but also to those statutes listed in its

---

76 *AG v NZ Māori Council* [1991] 2 NZLR 129 (CA) at 135 per Cooke P.
77 *Ibid.*
78 Although note that the most recent legislative incorporations use this phrase but in a directed manner, see *supra* note 54.
79 *Re Pouakani Block Application* (1988) 65 Taupo MB 1 (MLC).
80 *Ibid* at para 11 [original emphasis].
81 *Ngai Tahu Māori Trust Board v Director-General of Conservation* [1995] 3 NZLR 553 (CA) [*Ngai Tahu*].

First Schedule. More than twenty statutes appear in the First Schedule, including the statute relevant to this case, the *Marine Mammals Protection Act 1978*. Other statutes listed include the *National Parks Act 1980*, *Reserves Act 1977*, and the *Wildlife Act 1953*. Yet the Court confined the ramifications of its section 4 findings on two fronts. While it accepted that a statute listed in the First Schedule should be interpreted and administered so as to give effect to the treaty principles, this should occur only where the statute does not contain an internal reference to the treaty, and then only to the extent that the provisions in the statute are not clearly inconsistent with the treaty principles. In other words, confronted with any clear conflict between a provision in a statute like the *Marine Mammals Protection Act 1978* and a treaty principle, the provision in the statute trumps the treaty principle, causing the treaty principle to lose. This interpretation has not been challenged in the higher courts as to whether it is correct or not. Undoubtedly, the interpretation as it stands dilutes in real terms the impression first gained from the strongly worded "to give effect to" section 4 direction.

The whale-watch case extracted several treaty principles relevant to the conservation estate. The Crown's right and duty to govern was emphasized – the rights and interests of everyone in New Zealand, Māori and Pakeha and all others alike, must be subject to the overriding authority in Parliament to enact comprehensive legislation for the protection and conservation of the environment and natural resources.[82] The Crown's fiduciary duties owing to Māori and Māori rights to exercise *tino rangatiratanga* (Māori sovereignty or unqualified exercise of chieftainship over their lands) were restated in reference to previous judicial decisions.[83] Emphasized was the point that the treaty principles "require active protection of Māori interests" and "to restrict this to consultation would be hollow."[84] Moreover, the Crown and Māori must act as reasonable treaty partners, and Māori have a right of development. The stated principles were entirely consistent with the treaty jurisprudence being developed at that time in the courts in cases like the Court of Appeal *Lands* case but not in the Waitangi Tribunal, as will be discussed later in this chapter.

---

82 *Ibid* at 558.
83 *Ibid* at 558–59.
84 *Ibid* at 560. For a more recent and comprehensive consultation case, see *Waikato Tainui Te Kauhanganui Inc v Hamilton City Council* [2010] NZRMA 285 (HC).

In 2002, the High Court, *Te Waero v Minister of Conservation and Auckland City Council*,[85] considered whether the minister of conservation was required by section 4 to consult with a specific *iwi* when classifying public land as recreation reserves under the *Reserves Act 1977* (an Act listed in the First Schedule of the *Conservation Act* like the *Marine Mammals Protection Act 1978*). Harrison J stated that "consultation is not of itself a discrete, substantive Treaty principle."[86] Rather, the need to consult arises only when a treaty interest has been identified. Harrison J held that there were no specific treaty principles relevant to the classification decision in this case.[87] Thus, there was no need to consult.[88] However, Harrison J observed in obiter, "The Department should have had a mechanism in place for specifically identifying any Treaty interests which may be relevant and thus should be taken into account by the Minister when considering classification."[89] Although this was an important rap on the knuckles for the department, the justice's choice of words is interesting. "Take into account" is the threshold test for decision-makers acting, for example, under the *Resource Management Act*,[90] but it is not the test for those operating under the *Conservation Act*, where to "give effect to" is the threshold test.

Another case that discussed section 4 is *McRitchie v Taranaki Fish and Game Council*.[91] In 1998, the majority of the Court of Appeal in deciding the *McRitchie* case held that Māori have no customary fishing rights to take trout. In reaching this conclusion several statutes were examined, including the *Conservation Act*. While the president of the Court, Richardson P, cited section 4 in his opening statement of the majority judgment, the section was not thereafter discussed. However, Thomas J, in his dissenting judgment, examined section 4 at length, along with

85 *Moana Te Aira Te Uri Karaka Te Waero v The Minister of Conservation and Auckland City Council, supra* note 45.

86 *Ibid* at para 61.

87 *Ibid* at para 70.

88 This case aligns with other judicial discussions; for example, see *Carter Holt Harvey Ltd v Te Runanga o Tuwharetoa ki Kawerau, supra* note 74 at paras 27–31. While Justice Heath in this case summarized treaty principles, consultation is not included. Instead, he states that the duty to consult arises out of the relationship of treaty partners; see paras 27–31.

89 *Moana Te Aira Te Uri Karaka Te Waero v The Minister of Conservation and Auckland City Council, supra* note 45 at para 67.

90 RMA, *supra* note 34, s 8.

91 *McRitchie v Taranaki Fish and Game Council, supra* note 1.

another provision in the Act, section 26ZH. This section states, "Nothing in this Part of this Act shall affect any Māori fishing rights." Thomas J stated,[92]

> Section 4 recognises the fundamental constitutional status of the treaty, and it and s 26ZH are not to be demeaned. Parliament should not be thought to have enacted these provisions as mere window-dressing. If, therefore, it is found that the guarantee of "their ... Fisheries" to Māori under the treaty includes the right to fish for food, irrespective of the species inhabiting the particular fishery, s 4 requires effect to be given to that guarantee. It requires the Act to be "interpreted" as well as administered to give effect to the principles of the treaty.

However strong, this statement still comprises only part of the dissenting judgment and has not yet been picked up on in later cases.

In summary, in many ways the judiciary is still in its infancy in interpreting the ambit of the principles of the *Treaty of Waitangi* and thus reconciliation. The most comprehensive decision on the phrase remains the *Lands* case. In 2005, Justice Baragwanath provided a pivotal summary of the *Lands* case in an attempt to clarify the "partnership" commitment:[93]

> When Cooke P in [the *Lands* case] said that the Treaty "signified a partnership between races," his focus was on the treaty between two high authorities – the Māori Chiefs who were signatories on behalf of their tribes and Captain Hobson who signed as representative of Queen Victoria on behalf of "the Crown," who were together creating a new society. He did not suggest that the new society of New Zealanders created by the Treaty would be a divided one with Māori on one side and non-Māori on the other side of a gap. Read fairly in context Lord Cooke's concept has precisely the opposite sense. So does the language of the Treaty.
>
> It contemplated that the British Crown and the Māori signatories would create a new community of both Māori and immigrants. Both Māori and non-Māori citizens were to have the rights as British subjects in the new community. The need for its "Laws and Institutions [was] alike to the native population and to Her subjects." Both Hobson and the signatory

---

92 *Ibid* at 162.
93 *Ngati Maru Ki Hauraki Inc v Kruithof* [2005] NZRMA 1 (HC) at paras 49 and 50.

Chiefs agreed to what Sir Hugh translated as "the Queen's Government being established over all parts of this land ..." That Government, of an age before universal franchise, has evolved into the present democratic New Zealand Government that represents and is answerable to all New Zealanders. Hence Cooke P's description ... of the New Zealand Government as "in effect one of the Treaty partners." Its obligation to give due effect to the Treaty is a continuing one.

In comparison to the courts, the Waitangi Tribunal has explored in much more depth the treaty principles – unsurprising because the jurisdiction of the tribunal is centred on the treaty principles. The tribunal's jurisprudence is now discussed.

In Contrast: The Waitangi Tribunal's Interpretation of the *Treaty of Waitangi*

The Waitangi Tribunal has a remarkably different interpretation of the appropriate constitutional role of the *Treaty of Waitangi* to the courts. Early on, the tribunal asserted a strong constitutional place for the treaty in New Zealand.[94] For example, in 1984 the Kaituna River Tribunal observed,[95]

From being "a simple nullity" the Treaty of Waitangi has become a document of importance approaching the status of a constitutional instrument so far as Māoris are concerned. It is not truly a constitutional instrument because conflict between an Act of Parliament of Regulation and the Treaty does not render the statute null and void. But it does expose the Crown to the risk of a claim that the statute in question is in conflict with the Treaty and to that extent it would seem prudent for those responsible for legislation to recognise the danger inherent in drafting statutes or regulations without measuring such instruments against the principles in the Treaty.

By 1988, the tribunal had coined its most powerful and enduring classification of the treaty as Aotearoa New Zealand's "basic constitutional

---

94 Note, for further discussion on this material, see Jacinta Ruru, "The Waitangi Tribunal" in Malcolm Mulholland and Veronica Tawhai, eds, *Weeping Waters: The Treaty of Waitangi and Constitutional Change* (Wellington: Huia, 2010) 127.
95 Waitangi Tribunal, *Report of the Waitangi Tribunal on the Kaituna River Claim*, Wai 4 (Wellington: Waitangi Tribunal, 1984) at 26.

document."⁹⁶ In 1991, the Ngai Tahu Tribunal agreed with this state-ment,⁹⁷ but not that "the power of Parliament will be curbed by its obli-gations to respect the terms of the Treaty."⁹⁸ The tribunal here observed that there would "appear to be formidable difficulties" in reaching that conclusion "in the absence of further legislative action."⁹⁹ In 1994, the Māori Electoral Option Tribunal recognized the Privy Council's articu-lation that the "Treaty records an agreement executed by the Crown and Māori, which over 150 years later is of the greatest constitutional impor-tance to New Zealand."¹⁰⁰ In 2001, the Napier Hospital Tribunal stated that "the Treaty of Waitangi is the foundation document for modern constitutional government in New Zealand."¹⁰¹ In 2009, the Te Urew-era Tribunal declared the treaty "a fundamental document in New Zea-land's constitutional arrangements."¹⁰² In 2011, the tribunal declared the treaty to be "this country's pre-eminent constitutional document"¹⁰³ and "a constitutional instrument of overriding significance."¹⁰⁴

In regard to the treaty principles phrase, the tribunal, in comparison to the courts, has focused on the relationship between the Crown's right to govern and the Māori right to retain sovereignty. The tribu-nal has been consistent in its interpretation that the treaty principle that gives the Crown the right to govern – *kawanatanga* (acquired via article 1 of the Māori version of the treaty) is qualified by Māori

96 Waitangi Tribunal, *Report of the Waitangi Tribunal on the Muriwhenua Fishing Claim*, Wai 22 (Wellington: Waitangi Tribunal, 1988) at 188.
97 Waitangi Tribunal, *The Ngai Tahu Report*, Wai 27 (Wellington: Brooker & Friend, 1991) at 224. Also expressed as such in the Waitangi Tribunal, *Report of the Waitangi Tribunal on Claims Concerning the Allocation of Radio Frequencies*, Wai 26 (Wellington: Brooker & Friend, 1990); and Waitangi Tribunal, *The Ngai Tahu Sea Fisheries Report*, Wai 27 (Wellington: Legislation Direct, 1992).
98 *Ngai Tahu Report, supra* note 98 at 224.
99 *Ibid.*
100 Waitangi Tribunal, *Māori Electoral Option Report*, Wai 413 (Wellington: Brookers, 1994) at para 3.2. The tribunal is citing *New Zealand Māori Council v AG* [1994] 1 NZLR 513, *supra* note 74 at 3.
101 Waitangi Tribunal, *The Napier Hospital and Health Services Report*, Wai 692 (Welling-ton: Legislation Direct, 2001) at 44.
102 Waitangi Tribunal, *Te Urewera: Pre Publication*, Part 1 (Wellington: Legislation Direct, 2009) at 125.
103 Waitangi Tribunal, *Ko Aotearoa Tēnei: A Report into Claims Concerning New Zealand Law and Policy Affecting Māori Culture and Identity*, Taumata Tuatahi, Wai 262 (Wel-lington: Legislation Direct, 2011) at 24.
104 *Ibid* at 166–67.

sovereignty – *tino rangatiratanga* (retained by Māori via article 2 of the Māori version of the treaty). For example, the Orakei Claim Tribunal, in its 1987 report, stated that *kawanatanga* "is less than the supreme sovereignty of the English text and does not carry the English cultural assumptions that go with it, the unfettered authority of Parliament or the principles of common law administered by the Queen's Judges in the Queen's name."[105] Moreover, the Ngai Tahu Tribunal, in its 1991 report, stated that *tino rangatiratanga* "necessarily qualifies or limits the authority of the Crown to govern. In exercising its sovereignty it must respect, indeed guarantee, Māori rangatiratanga – mana Māori – in terms of article 2."[106] Or as the Mohaka River Tribunal put it, the Crown is required to "exercise its kawanatanga with due respect for tino rangatiratanga."[107] These reflections have been endorsed in subsequent tribunal reports.[108] Throughout these reports, the tribunal has referred to this qualification as the principle of reciprocity.

While the tribunal has emphasized that there is "unity" and "considerable overlap" among the treaty principles and thus they must be read together,[109] this principle of reciprocity stands out as the "'overarching principle' that guides the interpretation and application of other principles, such as partnership."[110] The tribunal accepts that it is a legitimate exercise of the Crown's governance role to make national laws, and make national laws that constrain the actions of members of society, because article 1 endorsed the Crown as the "only centralised body with the overview and capability necessary"[111] to enact laws for

---

105 Waitangi Tribunal, *Report of the Waitangi Tribunal on the Orakei Claim*, Wai 9 (Wellington: Waitangi Tribunal, 1987) at 180, as cited in *Te Raupatu o Tauranga Moana: Report on the Tauranga Confiscation Claims*, Wai 215 (Wellington: Waitangi Tribunal, 2004) at 20.

106 *Ngai Tahu Report, supra* note 98, vol 3, 236–37 as cited in *Te Raupatu o Tauranga Moana, ibid* at 20.

107 Waitangi Tribunal, *The Mohaka ki Ahuriri Report*, Wai 201 (Wellington: Legislation Direct, 2004) at 28.

108 For example, see *Te Raupatu o Tauranga Moana, supra* note 106; and *Ko Aotearoa Tenei*, note 104 at 24.

109 For example, see Waitangi Tribunal, *The Tarawera Forest Report*, Wai 411 (Wellington: Legislation Direct, 2003) at 22.

110 Waitangi Tribunal, *Report on the Crown's Foreshore and Seabed Policy, supra* note 29 at 130, and see note 6 at 130 of the report for a reference to other tribunal reports that have endorsed this sentiment.

111 Waitangi Tribunal, *He Maunga Rongo: Report on Central North Island Claims*, amended ed, Wai 1200 (Wellington: Legislation Direct, 2008) at 1238.

the benefit of all in society. But the tribunal adds that the Crown must exercise its legitimate governance capabilities by exercising a "careful balancing"[112] act that is consistent with its treaty obligations. According to the tribunal, the "'test' is reasonableness, not perfection."[113]

Thus, when would it be reasonable for the Crown to override Māori *tino rangatiratanga*? The Turangi Township Tribunal set the standard test: the Crown will be justified in doing so only "in exceptional circumstances and as a last resort in the national interest."[114] Other reports have developed this sentiment. For example, in the context of natural resources, the Central North Island Tribunal claimed that it might be reasonable for the Crown, having first conducted a careful balancing act, for the needs of other sectors of the community to trump its treaty obligations to Māori. This might occur in five instances: (1) in exceptional circumstances such as war; (2) for peace and good order; (3) in matters involving the national interest; (4) in situations where the environment or certain natural resources are so endangered or depleted that they should be conserved or protected; and (5) where Māori interests in natural resources have been fully ascertained by the Crown and freely alienated.[115] The tribunal does not perceive that the Crown's qualified right to govern creates "a constitutional problem," because few "western governments enjoy unqualified sovereign power" as a result of entrenched constitutions or international agreements.[116]

Finally, what has the tribunal specifically said about section 4 of the *Conservation Act*? In summary, the tribunal's position is manifest in two ideas. First, the section 4 expression means that while the Crown has a right to govern, this right is qualified by the Māori right to exercise *rangatiratanga*. Although in exceptional circumstances the Crown may override this fundamental right of *rangatiratanga*, it may do so only as a last resort and if this is in the national interest. However, the "national interest in conservation is not a reason for negating Māori rights of property."[117] Second, if the resource in question is highly valued and of great spiritual and physical importance, then it is to be considered a

---

112 *Ibid.*
113 *Ibid.*
114 Waitangi Tribunal, *The Turangi Township Report*, Wai 84 (Wellington: Brookers, 1995).
115 Waitangi Tribunal, *supra* note 111 at 1239.
116 Waitangi Tribunal, *supra* note 115 at 285.
117 Waitangi Tribunal, *The Whanganui River Report*, Wai 167 (Wellington: GP Publications, 1999) at 330.

taonga, and the Crown is under an affirmative obligation to ensure its protection to the fullest extent reasonably practicable.[118]

The tribunal has developed its first idea (that is that *kawanatanga* [governorship] is generally subject to *rangatiratanga*) to a level where the courts, including the Court of Appeal, have not gone. The tribunal has emphasized that cession of sovereignty to the Crown by Māori was qualified by the retention of *tino rangatiratanga*. While the Court of Appeal in the whale-watch case recognized the Crown's right to govern and the Māori right to exercise *tino rangatiratanga*, it did not consider how the two should operate together. Instead it focused on the first right, the Crown's governance right: "The rights and interests of everyone in New Zealand, Māori and Pakeha and all others alike, must be subject to that overriding authority."[119] Even though it emphasized *kawanatanga*, it skipped how *kawanatanga*, as an overriding authority, might relate to the Māori right to exercise *tino rangatiratanga*. The Court of Appeal simply focused on fiduciary duties, active protection, good faith, and so on – in other words, how the treaty parties should operate towards one another. It did not turn on what a right of *tino rangatiratanga* encompassed or how it could operate alongside a Crown right to govern.

The tribunal's and the Court of Appeal's understandings of the treaty fail to mirror each other essentially because the tribunal says *kawanatanga* is subject to *rangatiratanga*, whereas the Court of Appeal says *rangatiratanga* is subject to *kawanatanga*. A future re-examination of the Court of Appeal's decision may disrupt the Court's interpretation that other legislative provisions override treaty principles. However, this would succeed only if the courts developed the tribunal reasoning and accepted that the national interest in conservation is not a reason for negating Māori rights of property. For example, the court would have to hold that any inconsistency between a policy directive, such as conservation or preservation, should give way to a treaty principle. It is certainly arguable that this should be the true interpretation of the strongly worded section 4 directive to give effect to the principles of the treaty. However, the majority judgment in the *McRitchie* case does not suggest movement in this direction to any extent – in fact, it is

---

118 See Waitangi Tribunal, *Preliminary Report on the Te Arawa Representative Geothermal Resource Claims*, Wai 153 (Wellington: Brooker & Friend, 1993); and Waitangi Tribunal, *Mohaka River Report*, Wai 119 (Wellington: Brooker & Friend, 1992).

119 *Ngai Tahu, supra* note 81 at 558.

silent on the implication of section 4. Moreover, the Waitangi Tribunal jurisprudence is, of course, not binding on the courts. Even though the courts have stated that the tribunal's opinions "are of great value to the Court"[120] and "are entitled to considerable weight,"[121] the courts are free to dismiss these tribunal statements.

Nonetheless, in regard to the second part of the tribunal's position, there appears to be more alignment between the Court of Appeal and the tribunal. Both seem to accept that the requirement for a natural resource or activity must fall within the category of a *taonga* before the Crown should be subjected to certain duties to protect it. The Court of Appeal appears prepared to read *taonga* broadly: "Although a commercial t-watching business is not taonga or the enjoyment of a fishery within the contemplation of the treaty, certainly it is so linked to taonga and fisheries that a reasonable treaty partner would recognise that treaty principles are relevant."[122]

Moreover, in 2011, the Waitangi Tribunal made a powerful critique of the Department of Conservation – the department that gains its powers from the *Conservation Act*. In this *Ko Aotearoa Tenei* report, the Tribunal positions that partnership is the intellectual framework for understanding the principles of the Treaty of Waitangi and thus[123]

> the department must be looking for partnership opportunities in everything that it does ... opportunities to share power with tangata whenua should be a core performance indicator for the department rather than ... the exceptional outcome driven by the wider pressures of Treaty settlements it now is.

The tribunal stated that the department "must take a broad and unquibbling approach, one that is based on forward-looking partnership, not on damage control."[124] One conclusion reached by the tribunal reads that the General Conservation Policy and General Policy for National Parks[125]

---

120 *New Zealand Māori Council v AG, supra* note 45 at 662 per Cooke P.
121 *Moana Te Aira Te Uri Karaka Te Waero v The Minister of Conservation and Auckland City Council, supra* note 45 at para 59.
122 *Ngai Tahu, supra* note 82 at 560.
123 *Ko Aotearoa Tenei, supra* note 104 at 324.
124 *Ibid.*
125 *Ibid.*

[m]ust be amended to reflect the full range of relevant Treaty principles as articulated by the courts. The terms of section 4 plainly make that mandatory. Indeed DOC's failure to include these in its lead general policy documents probably renders those documents in breach of that section. While Treaty principles as articulated by the Tribunal do not bind the department as a matter of law, it would be unduly restrictive for the department to treat them as irrelevant to its work.

Hence, this discussion – especially that concerning section 4 of the *Conservation Act* – highlights the fact that even with a strongly worded treaty directive and the existence of this directive for twenty-five years, the courts have not facilitated a radical rethink of the conservation estate – an estate that encompasses one-third of Aotearoa New Zealand's landmass. Change has certainly occurred in the past two decades, but the government has led this through the *Treaty of Waitangi* negotiated settlements.[126] The courts have not been at the forefront of supporting Māori in reconnecting to their lands and waters that lie within the conservation estate. While the courts are recognizing Māori, the courts appear not to be committed as such to any radical new reconciliation. The question that remains is whether the courts would become more proactive if the treaty was given a more formal role in our constitution.

Should the Treaty Be Constitutionalized?

Would Māori benefit from the *Treaty of Waitangi* having a more formal role in our constitution?[127] Even if the treaty does acquire more formal constitutional recognition, remember Parliament will still remain supreme. Are there lessons from Canada for New Zealand to consider?

In developing the *Treaty of Waitangi* principles, on occasion the New Zealand courts have discussed some of the Canadian judicial decisions,

---

126 Importantly, see Te Urewera-Tuhoe Bill (introduced into the House of Representatives on 7 August 2013) online: <www.parliament.nz/en-nz/pb/legislation/bills/00DBHOH_BILL12374_1/te-urewera-tuhoe-bill>.

127 Note that much impressive work has been written on the constitutional status of the treaty. In particular, see PG McHugh, "'Treaty Principles': Constitutional Relations inside a Conservative Jurisprudence" (2008) 39 VUWLR 39; BV Harris, "The Treaty of Waitangi and the Constitutional Future of New Zealand" (2005) NZLR 189; DV Williams, "The Treaty of Waitangi: A 'Bridle' on Parliamentary Sovereignty?" (2007) 22 NZULR 596; Matthew SR Palmer, *The Treaty of Waitangi in New Zealand's Law and Constitution* (Wellington: Victoria University Press, 2008).

particularly within the context of considering whether the Crown owes fiduciary duties to Māori. In 1987, in the *Lands* case, Cooke P defined the relationship between the Crown and Māori as creating "responsibilities analogous to fiduciary duties."[128] He did so without reference to the like precedents developing in Canada. However, in subsequent cases some mention has been made of some cases Canadian cases, namely *Guerin v R and National Indian Brotherhood* that described the Crown's obligations to Aboriginal peoples as not a public law duty or private law duty in a strict sense but "in the nature of a private law duty" and "therefore, in this *sui generis* relationship, it is not improper to regard the Crown as a fiduciary."[129] In 1990, Cooke P reflected on the *Guerin* case by stating,[130]

> More recently in Canada Indian rights have been identified as pre-existing legal rights not created by Royal Proclamation, statute or executive order. It has been recognised that, in some circumstances at least, the Crown is under a fiduciary duty to holders of such rights in dealings relating to their extinction. The judgments in *Guerin* ... seem likely to be found of major guidance when such matters come finally to be decided in New Zealand. The approach of this Court in the *Māori Council* case to the principles of the Treaty of Waitangi and the partnership and fiduciary analogies there drawn are consistent with them ... There are constitutional differences between Canada and New Zealand, but the *Guerin* judgments do not appear to turn on these. Moreover, in interpreting New Zealand parliamentary and common law it must be right for New Zealand Courts to lean against any inference that in this democracy the rights of the Māori people are less respected than the rights of aboriginal peoples are in North America.

Two years later, in *Te Runanga o Wharekauri Rekohu Inc v AG*,[131] Cooke P reflected on a subsequent Supreme Court of Canada decision, *R v Sparrow*,[132] and the Australian High Court decision, *Mabo v Queensland (No 2)*.[133] He cited these cases as evidence that "continuance after British sovereignty and treaties of unextinguished aboriginal title gives rise to

---

128   *New Zealand Māori Council v AG* [1987] 1 NZLR 641 (at 664) (per Cooke P).

129   *Guerin v R and National Indian Brotherhood* (1984) 13 DLR (4th) 321; [1984] 2 SCC 335 (SCC), at para 100.

130   *Te Runanga o Muriwhenua Inc v AG* [1990] 2 NZLR 641 (CA) (at 655).

131   *Te Runanga o Wharekauri Rekohu Inc v AG* [1993] 2 NZLR 301 (CA).

132   *R v Sparrow* (1990) 70 DLR (4th) 385 (SCC).

133   *Mabo v Queensland (No 2)* (1992) 175 CLR 1 (HCA).

a fiduciary duty and a constructive trust on the part of the Crown."[134] Cooke P specifically cited the passage from *Sparrow* that reads, "The *sui generis* nature of Indian title, and the historic powers and responsibility assumed by the Crown constituted the source of such a fiduciary obligation."[135] Cooke P observed that "clearly there is now a substantial body of Commonwealth case law pointing to a fiduciary duty."[136] He added,[137]

> In New Zealand the Treaty of Waitangi is major support for such a duty. The New Zealand judgments are part of widespread international recognition that the rights of indigenous peoples are entitled to some effective protection and advancement. The only real difference is that, whereas the Canadian Supreme Court required more than 18 months before delivery of its decision in *Sparrow* and the High Court of Australia slightly more than a year before delivery of their decision in *Mabo*, in New Zealand circumstances this Court has had to move more quickly – possibly at the cost of some public and other understanding of the complexity of the task.

The observations have not been limited to Cooke P. In 2000, Anderson and Paterson JJ, in the High Court, strongly articulated that in a case of public significance such as the Māori fisheries litigation "a Court might have recourse to a full armoury of jurisprudential principles to do justice."[138] In contrast, McGechan J, in 2003, did not accept the basis of an argument that the Crown had obligations, including those of a fiduciary character, under the *Treaty of Waitangi*. This was a High Court case where Te Runanga o Ngai Tahu sought judicial review against the attorney general, the minister of fisheries, and the Treaty of Waitangi Fisheries Commission.[139]

---

134 *Te Runanga o Wharekauri Rekohu Inc v AG* [1993] 2 NZLR 301 (CA) (at 306).

135 *R v Sparrow* (1990) 70 DLR (4th) 385 (SCC) (at 406, 406–09 per Dickson CJC and La Forest J).

136 *Te Runanga o Wharekauri Rekohu Inc v AG* [1993] 2 NZLR 301 (CA) (at 306).

137 *Ibid* at 306. Cooke P proceeded to make further supportive obiter comments about the existence of a fiduciary duty. See *Te Runanganui o Te Ika Whenua Inc Society v AG* [1994] 2 NZLR 20 (CA) (at 26); and *Ngai Tahu Māori Trust Board v Director-General of Conservation* [1995] 3 NZLR 553 (CA) (at 559).

138 *Te Waka Hi Ika o Te Arawa v Treaty of Waitangi Fisheries Commission* 7/3/00, Anderson and Paterson JJ, HC Auckland CP395/93 (at para 11).

139 *Te Runanga o Ngai Tahu v AG* 6/11/03, McGechan J, HC Auckland CIV-2003-404-1113 (see in particular paras 8 and 9).

In 2007, the High Court and Court of Appeal explicitly disagreed on the extent of fiduciary obligations. In *New Zealand Māori Council v AG*, Gendall J in the High Court held that "the fiduciary duties exist because of the partnership relationship, a well as the vulnerability of Māori in the sense that they are subject to the Crown's ultimate power to legislate."[140] Gendall J then traversed some of the Supreme Court of Canada's case law including *Guerin* and stated,[141]

> The Canadian cases involved the Constitution Act 1982. The Courts said this Act casts upon the Canadian Government the duty to act in a fiduciary capacity which, whilst not guaranteeing immunity from Government regulation, required the Government to justify legislation having a negative effect on any Aboriginal right protected under that Act. In New Zealand there is no similar constitution act, but there is the Treaty of Waitangi.
>
> The New Zealand Court of Appeal has followed the lead of the Canadian Courts and imposed upon the New Zealand Government duties of a fiduciary nature in respect of the Māori people. The Lands case recognises that the Treaty created a continuing relationship of a fiduciary nature, akin to a partnership, and that there is a positive duty to each party to act in good faith, fairly, reasonably and honourably towards the other.

On appeal, in the Court of Appeal, William Young P, O'Regan and Robertson JJ took a different stance to Gendall J.[142] In a joint judgment delivered by O'Regan J, the Court of Appeal focused on one of the cases cited by Gendall J and declared Gendall's J reliance on it incorrect. According to the Court of Appeal, Gendall J had incorrectly relied on *AG v New Zealand Māori Council*[143] (the *Radio Frequencies* case) because it is a case that does not stand "for the proposition that fiduciary duties, sourced from the Treaty itself, can form the basis of an action in New Zealand."[144] O'Regan J stated,[145]

---

140 *New Zealand Māori Council v AG* 4/5/07, Gendall J, HC Wellington CIV-2007-485-95 (at para 54). See also discussion at para 58.
141 *Ibid* at para 61.
142 *New Zealand Māori Council v AG* [2008] 1 NZLR 318 (CA).
143 *AG v New Zealand Māori Council* [1991] 2 NZLR 129 (CA).
144 *New Zealand Māori Council v AG* [2008], *supra* note 142 at 336.
145 *Ibid* at 337. Note that the Supreme Court recorded a statement in its minute to the court in relation to this decision, stating, "The parties acknowledge that the comments of the High Court and Court of Appeal in their judgments, of 4 May 2007 and 2 July 2007 respectively, concerning the Crown's fiduciary obligations to Māori under

We do not intend to traverse the arguments made to us on the basis of the recent Canadian authorities as to the nature of the duty owed by the Crown to aboriginal peoples in that country. Those decisions reflect the different statutory and constitutional context in Canada. The decisions of this Court contain clear statements to the effect that the Crown's duty to Māori is analogous with a fiduciary duty and we see no proper basis for us to revisit them. The law of fiduciaries informs the analysis of the key characteristics of the duty arising from the relationship between Māori and the Crown under the Treaty: good faith, reasonableness, trust, openness and consultation. But it does so by analogy, not by direct application. In particular, we see difficulties in applying the duty of a fiduciary not to place itself in a position of conflict of interest to the Crown, which, in addition to its duty to Māori under the Treaty, has a duty to the population as a whole. The present case illustrates another aspect of this problem: the Crown may find itself in a position where its duty to one Māori claimant group conflicts with its duty to another. If Gendall J was saying that the Crown has a fiduciary duty in a private law sense that is enforceable against the Crown in equity, we respectfully disagree.

The most recent series of cases on point is *Paki & Ors v AG*.[146] In the High Court, the representatives of the Pouakani people pled that the Crown owed the original owners of land adjoining the Waikato River a fiduciary duty based on four arguments that were collapsed into two streams of authority by Harrison J: the *Treaty of Waitangi* jurisprudence and related authority on the Crown's duty on extinguishment of customary rights.[147] Harrison J held against the Pouakani people on an earlier point of law but still progressed to consider the claim of alleged breach of fiduciary duty. He prefaced his discussion as "strictly obiter."[148] Harrison J rejected all arguments. At one point he stated,

> The Canadian authorities are settled. The Crown does not owe a fiduciary duty at large to its indigenous people or a group of them. An express undertaking assumed or implied from a particular instrument to represent or protect a specific interest is required.

---

the Treaty of Waitangi are obiter dicta (paragraphs 61–82 in the Court of Appeal judgment, and paragraphs 52–53, 57–70, and 94 of the High Court judgment)" *see New Zealand Māori Council v AG* November 2008 SC 49/2007, SC 50/2007 (para 2(b)).

146 *Paki & Ors v AG* 30/7/08, Harrison J, HC Hamilton CIV-2004-419-17.

147 *Ibid* at paras 25 and 108.

148 *Ibid* at para 107.

The Court of Appeal dismissed the appeal and focused only on the fiduciary duty point in obiter without precise reference to Canadian cases. The Court instead emphasized "our jurisprudence in this area must be that of New Zealand: the solution lies within this country."[149] The Supreme Court has yet to release its judgment on this part of the case.[150]

Returning to the question whether the courts would become more proactive if the treaty was given a more formal role in our constitution, it is interesting to consider the comparative experience of Canada's Aboriginal peoples within the similar context of conservation lands. Section 2(2) of the *Canada National Parks Act 2000* states, "For greater certainty, nothing in this Act shall be construed so as to abrogate from the protection provided for existing aboriginal or treaty rights of the aboriginal peoples of Canada by the recognition and affirmation of those rights in s. 35 of the Constitution Act 1982." Has this recognition provided a means for the Aboriginal peoples of Canada to reconnect with their lands and waters that lie within national parks? Moreover, has this recognition sparked new reconciliation between Aboriginal peoples and Canada?

The most relevant case concerning Aboriginal peoples and national parks is the *Mikisew Cree First Nation v Canada (Minister of Canadian Heritage)*[151] Supreme Court of Canada case. This case, decided 24 November 2005, concerned the process for the proposed placement of a winter road and its 200-metre no-firearm corridor to track the boundary of the Peace Point First Nations reserve that lies within the boundaries of the Wood Buffalo National Park. At issue were what rights Mikisew had under Treaty 8 to be consulted in the placement of this road. Mikisew argued that the construction of the road and the corridor would adversely affect their rights to hunt, fish, and trap, and that therefore the duty to consult was triggered. The Supreme Court agreed. Justice Binnie, for the Court, held that the "Crown has a treaty right to 'take up' surrendered lands for regional transportation purposes, but the Crown is nevertheless under an obligation to inform itself of the impact its project will have on the exercise by the Mikisew

149 *Paki v AG* [2009] NZCA 584; [2011] 1 NZLR; at para 116.
150 See *Paki v AG* [2012] NZSC 50; [2012] 3 NZLR 277. Postscript: this case has now been decided; see *Paki v Attorney-General (No 2)* [2014] NZSC 118.
151 *Mikisew Cree First Nation v Canada (Minister of Canadian Heritage)* 2005 SCC 69, [2005] 3 SCR 388, 259 DLR (4th) 610. For discussion of the lower court decisions on this case, see Dayna Nadine Scott, "Standing in the Road: The Battle for Wood Buffalo National Park" (2004) 13 J Environ Law Pract 145.

of their hunting and trapping rights, and to communicate its findings to the Mikisew."[152] The Court grounded this finding in the honour of the Crown and its associated duty-to-consult principle.

The *Mikisew* decision clearly recognizes the continuing Indigenous place of the lands encased within Wood Buffalo National Park: it has been "inhabited by First Nation peoples for more than over 8,000 years, some of whom still earn a subsistence living hunting, fishing and commercial trapping within the Park boundaries."[153] The Court explicitly recognized the impact of signing Treaty 8 in 1899: "It is not as though the Treaty 8 First Nations did not pay dearly for their entitlement to honourable conduct on the part of the Crown; surrender of the aboriginal interest in an area larger than France is a hefty purchase price."[154] Moreover, the Court set its judgment firmly within the context of reconciliation and recognized this as an evolving aspiration that began in this instance in 1899 with the signing of the treaty but that was the "first step in a long journey that is unlikely to end any time soon."[155]

Another instrumental case is the Federal Court of Canada decision, *Moresby Explorers Ltd v Canada (AG)*, where this court held in 2007 that the Archipelago Management Board for the Gwaii Haanas National Park Reserve and Haida Heritage Site was capable of limiting non-Haida tour operators access to the park.[156] As the Court put it, "In the end the question is whether the allocation of access to the Park between Haida and non-Haida tour operators is contrary to public policy."[157] The Court held no, because[158]

> [d]iscrimination on the basis of race is contrary to public policy when the discrimination simply reinforces stereotypical conceptions of the target group. However, there is legislative support for the proposition that discrimination designed to ameliorate the condition of a historically disadvantaged group is acceptable.

---

152 *Ibid* at para 55.
153 *Ibid* at para 6.
154 *Ibid* at para 52.
155 *Ibid* at para 56. For discussion of this case within the context of consultation, *see* Heather L Treacy, Tara L Campbell, & Jamie D Dickson, "The Current State of the Law in Canada on Crown Obligations to Consult and Accommodate Aboriginal Interests in Resource Development" (2007) 44 ALR 571.
156 *Moresby Explorers Ltd v Canada (AG)*, 2007 FCA 273, [2008] 2 FCR 341.
157 *Ibid* at para 30.
158 *Ibid* at para 31.

In a judgment dated 17 December 2010, the New Brunswick Provincial Court heard a case where a father and son had been charged with offences relating to unauthorized harvesting of soft-shelled clams within the Kouchibouguac National Park.[159] The father and son admitted to the facts but claimed a constitutionally protected right under section 35 of the *Constitution Act 1982* as Metis to fish for food within the park. The case turned on whether a distinctive Metis community ever emerged in the relevant area, and if so, whether such a community continued over time with rights that might be exercised within the park.[160] The Court answered no and held that "a constitutionally protected aboriginal right cannot be rooted in a community that never had any visibility."[161] And so the claimed constitutional right to take clams was not explored.

There are several cases that concern national parks generally (not issues arising under section 2(2)). For example, there is a 2008 Canadian Public Service Labour Relations Board case that concerned what matters can be included in an essential services agreement for Parks Canada staff.[162] The employer, Parks Canada, argued that it could not impede public access to the Pukaskwa National Park of Canada, and as custodians of the park, it must ensure that people are safe within the park. As part of this discussion and as evidence of a right of access, the board recognized that "members of two nearby First Nations have a right of access to the park, including the right to exercise treaty rights (hunting, fishing and trapping) within the park."[163] Of interest, in obiter dicta, the board later observed that the "the issue of a right of access to the park by virtue of aboriginal treaty is also salient. At the very least, no evidence was placed before the Board that the employer could lawfully interfere with the presence in the park of those First Nations' members to whom treaty rights apply, even if the park is formally closed to the rest of the public."[164]

These legislative provisions have provided some relief for the Aboriginal peoples of Canada, namely for Mikisew, for stopping the building of a road within a park. Overall, though, it seems that while

---

159 *Canada v Vautour* 2010 NBPC 39, [2011] 1 CNLR 283.
160 *Ibid* at para 4.
161 *Ibid* at para 79.
162 *Public Service Alliance of Canada v Parks Canada Agency* 2008 PALRB 97.
163 *Ibid* at para 39.
164 *Ibid* at para 199.

constitutional recognition of Indigenous peoples is undoubtedly a good and nice thing to do, it of itself may do little to dramatically rectify more than a hundred years of colonial law that has displaced Indigenous peoples from their lands and waters.

Conclusion

The *Treaty of Waitangi* is a unique contractual document entered into by our ancestors more than 170 years ago. It is the founding document for our contemporary society and provides a blueprint for respectful relations between Māori and the Crown. The treaty ought to have a central formal part in our constitutional framework, and the government is considering this proposition.[165] With formal recognition, the treaty would become relevant across the entire legal and political spectrum of the country. But constitutional protection is unlikely to give Māori much more legally than Māori already have if the current judicial interpretation of the treaty remains a guide. The courts, for the most part, have not yet moved beyond simply recognizing Māori and the treaty as important considerations. Precedents such as treaty principles can be trumped if they are inconsistent with core principles of the relevant statute, and emphasis on the Crown's right to govern illustrate this point. While the Waitangi Tribunal provides an alternative view to how the treaty principles ought to be interpreted and applied, and in fact reflect a true aspiration for reconciliation, there is no developing judicial trend in the courts to adopt the tribunal's reasoning.

Māori often lose in the courts, but so do Aboriginal peoples in Canada. What then is the solution if it does not lie entirely within constitutionalising rights? For Māori, there are opportunities in influencing legal and policy formation at the national level, because Māori have representation in Parliament, and Māori tribes have some political strength in negotiating with government. There are also increasing opportunities for Māori to influence decision-making at the local regional level

---

165 See "Home," *Constitutional Advisory Panel*, online: Constitutional Advisory Panel <www.ourconstitution.org.nz/>. See Constitutional Advisory Panel, *New Zealand's Constitution: A Report on a Conversation* (Wellington: Ministry of Justice, 2013). Note that many Māori want constitutional recognition of the treaty: see Malcolm Mulholland & Veronica Tawhai, eds, *supra* note 95. See *Māori Law Review* special issue "The Treaty of Waitangi and the Constitution" (July 2013) online: <http://maorilawreview.co.nz/2013/07/>.

because of *Treaty of Waitangi* claim settlements that sometimes go as far as implementing co- or joint management of specific natural resources. It is important to recognize these factors, but even so, Māori rights remain vulnerable, because, in the end, Parliament is and will remain supreme. Māori rights are most vulnerable if the majority public opinion is hostile or unsympathetic to Māori rights. While the treaty ought to form the central part of our constitution, we should not be fooled to think that overnight this would reinstate Māori as partners in creating a new reconciled bicultural society. The experiences of the Aboriginal peoples in Canada with section 35 show us this.

17 Constitutional Reform in Australia: Recognizing Indigenous Australians in the Absence of a Reconciliation Process

MEGAN DAVIS AND MARCIA LANGTON

I. Introduction

The modern Australian nation constituted at Federation in 1901 excluded Aboriginal people from the state. Aborigines inhabited a political no-man's land until a referendum proposing to include Aboriginal people within the jurisdiction of the Commonwealth Parliament in 1967 succeeded at the ballot.[1] Throughout Australian history, entrepreneurial, evangelical, and other humanitarian figures have attempted by various means, including treaties, to resolve the hostile relationship between the Indigenous and settler Australians. However, unlike in other settler societies, no treaty documents or treaty proposals were officially recognized by the state. Judicial decisions declared Australia uninhabited wasteland.[2] Consequently, the large body of law centred upon treaty rights in the United States and in Canada has not developed in Australia.

To many Indigenous Australians, Canada is regarded as a model of best practice for Aboriginal rights among liberal democracies – a kind of constitutional utopia. This is because of the existence of treaties and section 35 of the Canadian Constitution,[3] in addition to the *Canadian*

---

1 See John Chesterman and Brian Galligan, *Citizens without Rights: Aborigines and Australian Citizenship* (Cambridge: Cambridge University Press, 1997).
2 *Cooper v Stuart* (1889) 14 App Cas 286.
3 *Constitution Act 1982*, being Schedule B to the *Canada Act 1982* (UK), 1982, c 11.

Megan Davis and Marcia

Langton

Charter of Rights and Freedoms.[4]Also, Canada has taken seriously the notion of reconciliation in a way that Australia has been unable to. The concept of a judicially endorsed notion of reconciliation is incomprehensible to Aboriginal people who have experienced the acute injustice of High Court originalism.Furthermore, the attempt at a "reconciliation" process in the 1990s has since faltered. Reconciliation was a political conveniencethat emerged from a failed executive promise to enter into negotiations for a national land rights framework and a treaty with Aboriginal people in the 1980s.Today, the contemporary version of reconciliation is focused on employment covenants that, while meritorious, avoid engaging with the substantive questions of all reconciliation movements globally: truth and justice. It is unsurprising, scholars note, that Australia's reconciliation process rarely features in the literature on Indigenous peoples and reconciliation globally.[5]

Aboriginal advocacy for constitutional "recognition" over the past fifty years has not always been accompanied by or traversed a reconciliation process. The historical trajectory of Aboriginal political advocacy reveals that Aboriginalnotions of "recognition" are diverse and have included but are not limited to a constitutionally entrenched agreement-making "treaty" power, designated parliamentary seats, recognition of Aboriginal land and law, and a racial non-discrimination clause.The trajectory of the state, on the other hand, has been the converse: it has shifted from once entertaining strong forms of "recognition," such as a constitutional treaty-making power or a non-discrimination clause, to the past two decades of weak"recognition" – recognition as a passing preambular nod (accompanied by a non-justiciability clause; dare the High Court of Australia read anysubstance into such symbolism). The declining trajectory of substance in state-endorsed notions of constitutional recognition also runs parallel to the declining interest of the state in a formal reconciliation process diluted now to focus on those things all citizensshould be entitled to.

This chapter tracks competing notions of "recognition" and "reconciliation" preceding the current round of constitutional recognition. We say "competing" because these concepts are often confused,

---

4 See *Canadian Charter of Rights and Freedoms*, s 2(b), Part I of the *Constitution Act, 1982*, being Schedule B to the *Canada Act 1982*(UK), 1982, c 11, pt 1.
5 Damien Short, *Reconciliation and Colonial Power: Indigenous Rights in Australia* (Farnham, UK: Ashgate, 2008) 17.

conflated, and highly contested in Australia. They lack the distinctiveness of the Canadian approach. Part II provides a background to Aboriginal peoples and the Australian Constitution, explaining the status of Aboriginal people during the Federation period and their exclusion from the Constitution. It goes on to track Aboriginal political advocacy through to the current iteration of constitutional recognition overlaid by the state's ever-declining notion of recognition and reconciliation. Part III explains the current process of reform spearheaded by a Prime Minister's Expert Panel on the Recognition of Aboriginal and Torres Strait Islander peoples in the Constitution. This section includes an explanation as to why the expert panel – which included Indigenous and non-Indigenous leaders – resolved not to recommend a treaty-making power and why recognition of sovereignty was eschewed. Part IV concludes this chapter by explaining why recommendations similar to those contained in the Canadian Constitution or recommendations contemplating the negotiation of treaties or an acknowledgment of Indigenous sovereignty will never progress in Australia.

II. Citizenship

The Text of the New Constitution

Aboriginal people played no role in the drafting of the Constitution. Technically, male Aboriginal persons had the right to vote in South Australia from 1856, in Victoria from 1857, in New South Wales from 1858, and in Tasmania from 1896. However, they were not encouraged to vote, and polling booths were not erected in Aboriginal areas. And when the popularly elected constitutional conventions took place, Aboriginal people were not able to vote for delegates. As a result, there was no Aboriginal input into the discussions of the new Constitution.

While the Constitution as drafted did not formally exclude Aborigines from Australian citizenship or the vote, two sections did discriminate against Aborigines: section 51 (xxvi) and section 127. Section 51 (xxvi) is known as the "races power" and is contained within section 51 of the Constitution, which enumerates the heads of power for the Commonwealth. It reads,

> The Parliament shall, subject to this Constitution, have power to make laws for the peace, order, and good government of the Commonwealth

with respect to ... (xxvi) The people of any race, other than the aboriginal people in any State, for whom it is necessary to make special laws.

Section 127 disallowed Aborigines from being counted in the population of Australia: "In reckoning the numbers of the people of the Commonwealth, or of a State or other part of the Commonwealth, aboriginal natives should not be counted."

The lack of interest in Aborigines during the drafting of the Constitution was informed by notions of racial superiority and the "dying race" theory.[6] It is incontrovertible that the Constitution is imbued with racism. Section 51(xxvi) was clearly intended to authorize racially discriminatory laws. During the Constitutional Convention debates of the 1890s, the future premier of Western Australia, Sir John Forrest, contended, "It is of no use for us to shut our eyes to the fact that there is a great feeling all over Australia against the introduction of coloured persons. It goes without saying that we do not like to talk about it but still it is so."[7] The discriminatory tenor of these debates would further diminish Aboriginal rights, as the High Court in future cases uses the convention debates to interpret the "original" intent of the drafters.

To properly understand the exclusion of Aboriginal people from the Constitution, it is important to understand Aboriginal citizenship rights leading into and following Federation. Indeed, since the nineteenth century, confusion about the Aboriginal right to vote and the details of Aboriginal rights of citizenship have been poorly understood in the Australian polity. Discussions of Aboriginal citizenship rights – or lack of such rights – have been confused by the effect of the 1901 Constitution on the franchise statutes of each of the states.

Grimshaw suggests that the confusion about Aboriginal voting rights arose because, in the early colony, the British government created administrative barriers for gender and property on voting but not colour.[8] When the southeast Australian colonies became fully self-governing, they moved swiftly to extend the franchise to all men. This meant that a few Aboriginal men did enrol and cast votes over the next decades, but this was not the universal approach:

---

6 Andrew Markus, *Australian Race Relations 1788–1993* (Sydney: Allen and Unwin, 1994).
7 Official Record of the Debates of the Australasian Federal Convention (1891–1898) (1986 ed) vol 4, Melbourne 1898, 666.
8 Patricia Grimshaw & Katherine Ellinghaus, "White Women, Aboriginal Women and the Vote in Western Australia" (1999) 19 Studies in Western Australian History 39.

By contrast, however, Queensland's and Western Australia's settler governments, presiding over the colonies where most surviving Aborigines lived, did move explicitly to exclude Aborigines from the franchise. By the time women received the vote in Western Australia, Aboriginal men had been debarred from voting (unless by remote chance [they were] property holders) and hence Aboriginal women were similarly excluded from the vote. These states' interests would affect the rest in the federation settlement.[9]

The idea of citizenship, and whether it extended to Aborigines, was further confused by the effect of section 41 of the Constitution on state franchise acts. Section 41 provided that

[n]o adult person who has or acquires a right to vote at elections for the more numerous Houses of the Parliament of a State shall, while the right continues, be prevented by any law of the Commonwealth from voting at elections for either House of Parliament of the Commonwealth.

Section 41 was a compromise sought by South Australia, which had extended women the vote at state elections. It guaranteed that if one could vote at a state election in 1901 then that person automatically had the right to vote in Commonwealth elections. While section 41 "appeared to deal a blow to their citizenship," this one clause held out some possibilities for the Aborigines of the southeast.[10]

Federation

The establishment of the Australian Federation was contemporaneous with the removal of Aboriginal people from their traditional lands to reserves.[11] Each state and territory passed "protection" legislation. Notably, one of the first acts of the newly federated nation was to pass the White Australia Policy: legislation that favoured immigration to Australia from white European countries and institutionalized racist attitudes towards other cultures in Australian society.

The protection legislation was consistent with the dying race, Social Darwinist theory, influencing the constitutional drafters. There was a

---

9 Grimshaw & Ellinghaus, *supra* note 8.
10 *Ibid.*
11 Bain Attwood, "The Paradox of Australian Aboriginal History" (1994) 38:1 Thesis Eleven 118.

growing awareness of the need to protect Aboriginal people from frontier violence known as the Killing Times, and the spread of diseases was decimating Aboriginal populations. The legal rights of Aboriginal people were severely limited by Commonwealth and state protection legislation, such that, even given the variation between the jurisdictions, the majority of Aboriginal people could not vote, receive social welfare such as the old-age pension and unemployment benefits, move freely from place to place, choose their place of residence, make basic decisions concerning their own lives such as where to work, what to do with their earnings, and any property they acquired, and whom they might marry[12] (see table 1). Their children could be – and were in the thousands – removed and placed in institutions, in employment, or in the custody of strangers.[13]

It was not until 1949 that the *Commonwealth Electoral Act* was amended to give the vote to "an aboriginal native of Australia ... [who] is entitled under the law of the State in which he resides to be enrolled as an elector of that State and, upon enrolment, to vote at elections for the more numerous Houses of Parliament of that State." In 1962, the national Aboriginal association that spearheaded the fight for Aboriginal citizenship rights distributed a pamphlet that set out the rights of Aborigines in five states and the Northern Territory. In Western Australia and Queensland, Aborigines did not have voting rights. Aborigines were denied the vote, not by the letter of federal law, but by the administrative practices of the Aboriginal "protection and welfare" regimes in most state jurisdictions, and in the two most numerous states, by statutes.

The 1967 Referendum

In the decades leading up to the 1967 referendum, attitudes changed in the Australian polity. The shift was informed by external geopolitical

12 See, e.g., *Aboriginal Protection and Restriction of the Sale of Opium Act* 1897 (Qld); *Aboriginal Protections Act* 1909 (NSW); *Northern Territory Aboriginals Act* 1910 (SA); *Aboriginals Ordinance* 1911 (Cth); *Aboriginals Ordinance* 1918 (Cth); *Welfare Ordinance* 1953 (Cth); *Aboriginal and Torres Strait Islanders Affairs Act* 1965 (Qd); *Aborigines Act* 1911 (SA); *Aborigines Act* 1934 (SA); *Aboriginal Affairs Act* 1962 (SA); *Aborigines Protection Act* 1886 (WA); *Aborigines Act* 1905 (WA); *Native Welfare Act* 1963 (WA); *Natives Administration Act* 1905–36 (Vic); *Aborigines Act* 1890 (Vic); *Cape Barren Island Reserve Act* 1912 (Tas).
13 Bain Attwood and Andrew Markus, in collaboration with Dale Edwards and Kath Schilling, *The 1967 Referendum, or, When Aborigines Didn't Get the Vote* (Canberra: Australian Institute of Aboriginal and Torres Strait Islander Studies, 1997) at 14.

Table 1. Rights Enjoyed by Aborigines on Settlements and Reserves in Five States and the Northern Territory

	NSW	VIC	SA	WA	NT	QLD
Voting rights (state)	Y	Y	Y	N	Y	N
Marry freely	Y	Y	Y	N	N	N
Control own children	Y	Y	N	N	N	N
Move freely	Y	N	N	N	N	N
Own property freely	Y	N	Y	N	N	N
Receive award wages	Y	N	N	N	N	N
Alcohol allowed	N	N	N	N	N	M

Source: Bain Attwood and Andrew Markus, in collaboration with Dale Edwards and Kath Schilling, *The 1967 Referendum, or, When Aborigines Didn't Get the Vote* (Canberra: Australian Institute of Aboriginal and Torres Strait Islander Studies, 1997) at 14.

developments, including the creation of the United Nations after the Second World War and a growing international commitment to equality and non-discrimination. Two world wars and the controversy of apartheid in South Africa also contributed to this shift.[14] In 1962, the prohibition on Aboriginal people voting in federal elections ended. In addition there was a gradual realization that section 127, for example, that excluded Indigenous populations from the calculation of the census, was discriminatory. Equally problematic was the lack of Commonwealth head of power to makes laws for Aboriginal people.

A 1967 referendum amended two sections of the Constitution relating to Aboriginal people. The first was the "races power," section 51(xxvi), that empowered the federal Parliament to make laws with respect to "[t]he people of any race, other than the aboriginal race in any State, for whom it is deemed necessary to make special laws." This meant the states had responsibility for Aboriginal peoples and not the federal Parliament. The 1967 referendum had the effect of deleting the words "other than the aboriginal race in any State." In addition, the 1967 referendum repealed the aforementioned section 127, which stipulated that "[i]n reckoning the numbers of the people of the Commonwealth, or of

14 Jennifer Clark, *Race, Aborigines and the Coming of the Sixties to Australia* (Perth: University of Western Australia Press, 2008) 195; John Maynard, *Fight for Liberty and Freedom: The Origins of Australian Aboriginal Activism* (Canberra: Australian Institute of Aboriginal and Torres Strait Islander Studies, 2007).

a State or other part of the Commonwealth, aboriginal natives shall not be counted."

The outcome of the 1967 referendum, enabled the Commonwealth to legislate for Aborigines for the first time. While one racist provision was repealed and one amended in 1967 – with the overwhelming support of Australian voters – the Constitution still contains two provisions that permit racist acts or legislation: section 25 and section 51 (xxvi). While section 25 is a provision that contemplates that a state can discriminate against a race in voting,[15] section 51(xxvi) – despite 1967 – remains a concern, because it contains no restriction on the Commonwealth power to exercise it in a beneficial or detrimental way.[16]

Over the course of the next four decades there was a gradual realization that the 1967 referendum barely warrants the amount of celebration it attracts.[17] This is because, first, the Constitution remains discriminatory, and second, section 51 (xxvi) never delivered the political program that Aboriginal people had hope for.[18] Another important explanation for the caution in overstating the success of 1967 is that it shared the ballot box with another proposal that was listed first and was far more controversial. This was a proposal – known as "the nexus question" – to alter section 24 of the Constitution so that the number of members of the House of Representatives may be increased without increasing the number of senators. It attracted intense public and political scrutiny. The Aboriginal question barely rated a mention in the Cabinet notes leading up to the referendum. In the day after the referendum, the front pages of newspapers carried the story of the failed nexus question; the Aboriginal question barely rated a mention.[19]

15 Dylan Lino & Megan Davis, "Speaking Ill of the Dead: A Comment on s 25 of the Constitution" (2012) 23:4 Public Law Review 231.
16 George Williams, "Race and the Australian Constitution: From Federation to Reconciliation" (2000) 38:4 Osgoode Hall LJ (Winter 2000) 643.
17 Bain Attwood and Andrew Markus, The 1967 Referendum: Race, Power and the Australian Constitution (Canberra: Aboriginal Studies Press, 2007); John Chesterman, Civil Rights: How Indigenous Australians Won Formal Equality (Brisbane: University of Queensland Press, 2005); Tim Rowse, "The Practice and Symbolism of the 'Race Power': Rethinking the 1967 Referendum" (2008) 19 Australian Journal of Anthropology 89.
18 Attwood and Markus, 1967 Referendum, supra note 18.
19 George Williams and David Hume, People Power: The History and Future of the Referendum in Australia (Sydney: UNSW Press, 2010) 140–54.

The Failed Promises

Following the 1967 referendum, the federal Parliament was slow to utilize the races power – the constitutional authority it had been granted to make laws for Aboriginal people by the Australian people.[20] It was not until the Whitlam government in 1972 that the promised new era of Indigenous law and policy, as a consequence of section 51 (xxvi), arrived. This era was defined by the formal state policy of Aboriginal self-determination.[21] The Whitlam government legislated for the establishment of Aboriginal legal and medical services and ratified the International Convention on the Elimination of All Forms of Racial Discrimination;[22] enacting the *Racial Discrimination Act 1975*, which was to become a significant law for Indigenous peoples in the absence of a statutory or constitutional bill of rights.

Land rights were also a prominent feature of this government's agenda. Prior to the 1971 election, the Yolgnu sought an injunction in the Supreme Court of the Northern Territory against mining company Nabalco and the Commonwealth, to cease mining at Gove. Justice Blackburn set aside Yolgnu claims to Aboriginal land rights, finding that the property law system did not support Aboriginal title.[23] The Whitlam government established a land commission to examine how land rights could be protected in the Northern Territory. It was at this time that the National Aboriginal Conference (NAC) – a national Indigenous representative body – commenced its campaign for a treaty.[24] By 1979 the NAC were consulting communities on the concept of a *makarrata* – a Yolgnu word that has been interpreted as meaning a peaceful settlement to a dispute or "things are all right again after a conflict" or "coming together after a struggle."[25] At this time, Aboriginal political advocacy was further animated by the High Court's rejection of Aboriginal sovereignty in *Coe v Commonwealth*.[26] After consultations with communities, the NAC

---

20 Chesterman, *Civil Rights, supra* note 18.
21 Gough Whitlam, "It's Time for Leadership: 1972 Campaign Launch for the Australian Labor Party" (speech delivered at the Blacktown Civic Centre, 13 November 1972).
22 *International Convention on the Elimination on All Forms of Racial Discrimination*, opened for signature 7 March 1966, 660 UNTS 195 (entered into force 4 January 1969).
23 *Milirrpum v Nabalco Pty Ltd* (1971) 17 FLR 141.
24 Tim Rowse, *Obliged to Be Difficult* (Melbourne: Cambridge University Press, 2000) 179.
25 LR Hiatt, "Treaty, Compact, Makarrata …?" (1987) 58 Oceania 140.
26 *Coe v Commonwealth* [1979] HCA 68.

subcommittee developed a framework for an agreement and included designated parliamentary seats at federal, state, and local government. The Fraser government did entertain the proposal of a treaty, including exchanging letters, but when they lost power, the NAC wound to a halt as the incoming government abolished it in 1985.

The new government, led by Prime Minister Hawke, was elected on a platform that included a commitment to a national land rights framework. However, not long into its term, it abandoned the promise of national land rights, because of resistance from conservative state governments and concern for re-election. This decision to abandon land rights after being elected with such a policy "intensified the divisions ... deepened the historic Aboriginal conviction that the white man is devious, two-tongued and not to be trusted."[27] Meanwhile the government prepared for Australia's bicentenary in 1988, by constituting a commission to review the Australian Constitution. The final report contained a number of recommendations on Aboriginal and Torres Strait Islander peoples,[28] including deletion of section 25 of the Constitution, arguing that it was "no longer appropriate to include in the Constitution a provision which contemplates the disqualification of members of a race from voting." The commission also raised section 51 (xxvi), noting that Parliament could pass both "special and discriminating laws" that could be beneficial or adverse and so recommended the insertion of a racial non-discrimination clause. It also recommended the insertion of a new power of the Commonwealth to enter into an agreement with representatives of the Aboriginal people, although the power could not be used until the agreement is negotiated.

During the year of Australia's bicentenary, the prime minister was presented with the Barunga statement, a petition of political demands that called upon the Commonwealth to use the race power conferred upon it by the Australian people to recognize Aboriginal and Torres Strait Islander peoples' right to self-determination. The statement called for a national elected organization to oversee Aboriginal and Islander affairs, a national system of land rights, a police and justice system, a treaty recognizing prior ownership, continued occupation, and recognition of sovereignty. In reply the prime minister declared there would be a treaty within the life of his Parliament.

---

27 Rowse, *Obliged To Be Difficult, supra* note 25 at 195.
28 Constitutional Commission, Final Report of the Constitutional Commission (1998).

As with the election promise of a national land rights framework, the prime minister did not deliver on a treaty. Aboriginal leaders were disappointed and the government was heavily criticized. Instead the government contrived a reconciliation process, a political compromise designed to ameliorate the disappointment of Aboriginal and Torres Strait Islander people.

Setbacks for Aboriginal Reconciliation

"Reconciliation" commenced in 1991. Empowered by the *Council for Aboriginal Reconciliation Act 1991*, the Council for Aboriginal Reconciliation (CAR) was established to lead a reconciliation process.[29] CAR ably led this movement for over a decade, often in very difficult conditions inimical to meaningful reconciliation. Some of these conditions are important to recall, because they raise questions about the sincerity of the state in the midst of a reconciliation process.

One setback was in the aftermath of the High Court's 1988 decision in *Mabo* overturning the doctrine of *terra nullius*.[30] Following *Mabo*, the High Court handed down its decision in *Wik* on 23 December 1996, finding that pastoral leases could coexist with native title to the extent of inconsistency.[31] The amendments to the *Native Title Act* provided the "bucket loads of extinguishment" that the government promised farmers and pastoralists, and downgraded native title as a property right while simultaneously manufacturing fear of an imminent race election to justify its action. The amendment bill also suspended the operation of the *Racial Discrimination Act*. This episode illustrates the ease with which the federal government can discriminate against Aboriginal people in the absence of a bill of rights or any entrenched freedom from racial discrimination.[32]

All of this occurred during the so-called reconciliation era that Prime Minister Howard had reluctantly inherited from the previous

---

29 See Short, *Reconciliation and Colonial Power, supra* note 5; Elizabeth Moran, "Is Reconciliation in Australia a Dead End?" (2006) 12:1 Australian Journal of Human Rights 109.

30 *Mabo v Queensland* (No 1) (1988) 166 CLR 186.

31 *Wik Peoples v Queensland* [1996] 187 CLR 1.

32 Gillian Triggs, "Australia's Indigenous Peoples and International Law: Validity of the Native Title Amendment Act 1998 (Cth)" (1999) 23 Melbourne University Law Review 372.

government. Aside from Howard's notorious refusal to apologize for the Stolen Generations (the Aboriginal and Torres Strait Islander children removed from their families) because he did not believe the current generation of Australians should have to apologize for the previous generation's actions, the other setback was the High Court decision in *Kartinyeri* in 1998.

When Prime Minister Howard came to power in 1996, his government enacted legislation to deprive the Ngarrindjeri Aboriginal women from using the Aboriginal and Torres Strait Islander *Heritage Protection Act 1984* (Cth) to prevent the construction of a bridge over an area that encompassed secret women's business. The *Hindmarsh Island Bridge Act 1997* (Cth) suspended the *Heritage Act* so it applied everywhere in the country except for Hindmarsh Island. This legislation was challenged by the Ngarrindjeri women in the High Court on the basis that the races power – as amended in 1967 – cannot be used in an adverse or detrimental manner by the Commonwealth. The Commonwealth argued that there were no limits on the power so long as the law has a consequence based on race. In *Kartinyeri v Commonwealth*, the High Court upheld the legislation undermining the Ngarrindjeri women's argument.[33] The Court split on whether the races power can be used to discriminate against Indigenous peoples. The 1988 Constitutional Commission's prescience about the races power came to the fore. The judgment – unsatisfactorily – left open the possibility that the Commonwealth still possesses the power to enact racially discriminatory laws.

The Failed Republic

In Howard's second term a referendum was held on a republic. As a part of that, Aboriginal and Torres Strait Islander peoples were proposed by a peoples convention to be "recognized," alongside many other people and values in a preamble to the Constitution.[34] This was a dramatic departure from the substantive change Aboriginal people had been pursuing contemporaneously. Their political agenda was cherry-picked in favour of a symbolic gesture guaranteed to achieve political bipartisanship. The peoples convention drafted a preamble.

---

33 (1998) 195 CLR 337.
34 Mark McKenna, Amelia Simpson, & George Williams, "First Words: The Preamble to the Australian Constitution" (2001) 24 University of New South Wales Law Journal 382.

However, Prime Minister Howard eschewed that version and took it upon himself to draft a preamble with Aboriginal Democrats Senator Aden Ridgeway.[35] The final proposed preamble was widely publicly criticized for many reasons, including its recognition of "mateship" as an Australian value. Aboriginal leaders criticized it because it used the word "kinship" instead of "custodianship," failed to capture the nature of the Aboriginal connection to land, and lacked legitimacy because Aboriginal leaders were not consulted.[36] Even more insulting was the fact that the preamble was accompanied by a no-legal effect clause: the "preamble [should] not be used to interpret other provisions of the Constitution."[37] The preamble was rejected by Australians in 1999 in every state and territory and nationally by 60.7 per cent.[38] The rejection was acute in Aboriginal and Torres Strait Islander electorates.

The End of Reconciliation

Following the failed republic referendum, after a decade, the reconciliation process was winding up. The reconciliation documents were handed to the prime minister at a formal ceremony at the Sydney Opera House in 2000. Recommendations included the Commonwealth Parliament preparing legislation for a referendum to recognize Aboriginal and Torres Strait Islander peoples as the first peoples of Australia in a new preamble to the Constitution, and remove section 25 of the Constitution and introduce a new section making it unlawful to adversely discriminate against any people on the grounds of race.[39] The event was overshadowed by the animosity displayed towards the prime minister when attendees stood up and turned their backs to him.

---

35 See Mark McKenna, Amelia Simpson, & George Williams, "With Hope in God, the Prime Minister and the Poet: Lessons from the 1999 Referendum on the Preamble" (2001) 24 University of New South Wales Law Journal 401.
36 "New Constitution Preamble," ABC Television, 7.30 Report, 11 August 1999; Damien Murphy, "Aborigines and Hanson Attack the Latest Wording," *Sydney Morning Herald*, 12 August 1999; Lauren Martin, "Ridgeway Criticised …," *Sydney Morning Herald*, 13 August 1999; McKenna, Simpson, & Williams, *supra* note 35 at 382.
37 Bills Digest No 32 Constitutional Alteration (Preamble) 1999, online: <www.aph.gov.au/Parliamentary_Business/Bills_Legislation/bd/Bd9900/2000bd032>.
38 Anne Winckel, "A 21st Century Constitutional Preamble" (2001) 24 University of New South Wales Law Journal 636.
39 Council for Aboriginal Reconciliation, *Final Report of the Council for Aboriginal Reconciliation to the Prime Minister and Commonwealth Parliament* (2000) ch 10 (Recommendations).

The reconciliation documents – the final submitted at the end of 2000 – provoked the prime minister into rejecting a treaty, declaring there would never be a treaty in Australia, because a nation cannot have a treaty with itself.[40]

The Aboriginal and Torres Strait Islander Commission (ATSIC) attempted to continue the work of CAR in facilitating a community conversation on a treaty, but it was criticized by government for focusing on "symbolic reconciliation" rather than "practical reconciliation," which makes central economic development, employment, and education. In any event, ATSIC was abolished by the government.[41] And with ATSIC went bipartisan support for the right to self-determination as a policy; it was "eviscerated from the lexicon of Australian politicians, policymakers and Australian journalists and political commentators and inelegantly dismissed as a 'failed experiment' and antithetical to Aboriginal economic development."[42] In Australia the concept of "self-determination" is conflated with ATSIC and the "rights agenda" – and disparaged as being irrelevant to health and well-being of Aboriginal and Torres Strait Islander peoples.

Recognition

Indigenous political advocacy for a treaty or any other constitutional reform went into hiatus. Three days prior to the federal election in 2007, Prime Minister Howard declared renewed support for recognition of

---

40 See generally John Howard, "Politics and Patriotism: A Reflection on the National Identity Debate" (Speech, Melbourne, 13 December 1995); John Howard, "The Liberal Tradition: The Beliefs and Values Which Guide the Federal Government" (Sir Robert Menzies Lecture, Melbourne, 18 November 1996); Sean Brennan, "Reconciliation in Australia: The Relationship between Indigenous Peoples and the Wider Community" (2004) 11 Brown Journal of World Affairs 149.

41 John Howard, "Practical Reconciliation" in Michelle Grattan, ed, *Reconciliation: Essays on Australian Reconciliation* (Melbourne: Bookman, 2000) 89; see generally Jon Altman & Boyd Hunter, "Monitoring 'Practical' Reconciliation: Evidence from the Reconciliation Decade, 1991–2001' (Discussion paper no 254, Centre for Aboriginal Economic Policy Research, 2003) v; William Sanders, "Journey without End: Reconciliation between Australia's Indigenous and Settler Peoples" (Discussion paper no 237, Centre for Aboriginal Economic Policy Research, 2002); Boyd Hunter and Robert Schwab, "Practical Reconciliation and Continuing Disadvantage in Indigenous Education" (2003) 4:2 *Drawing Board* 83.

42 Megan Davis, "NARRM Oration 2012 – Aboriginal Women: The Right to Self-Determination" (2012) 16:1 Australian Indigenous Law Review 78.

Aboriginal and Torres Strait Islander people in a new preamble to the Constitution.[43] This provided continuity to his advocacy for recognition of Indigenous peoples in a preamble in the 1999 referendum, which was so resoundingly rejected by the people.

Howard was defeated and the new Rudd government distinguished itself from the previous government by making its first act as a new government an Apology to the Stolen Generations on behalf of the Parliament and the Australian people.[44] And soon after, constitutional "recognition" was back on the agenda. In 2008, Rudd was handed a Yolngu and Bininj Leaders Statement of Intent by members of those communities who expressed their desire for constitutional protection for traditional land and cultural rights.[45] The communiqué was written on behalf of Yolgnu and Bininj clans living in Yirrkala, Gunyangara, Gapuwiyak, Maningrida, Galiwin'ku, Milingimbi, Ramingining, and Laynhapuy homelands, constituting approximately 8000 Indigenous people in Arnhem land. The document was developed following meetings at Maningrida in West Arnhem Land on 1 July 2007 and other related meetings over the previous eighteen months. The prime minister responded to the demand for constitutional recognition of our prior ownership and rights by pledging his support for recognition in preamble to the Constitution.[46]

The assumption, without serious contemplation of the contents of the communiqué – much in the same manner as Howard and treaty – highlights the manner in which the state cherry-picks Aboriginal aspirations to suit their own agenda – one that seeks minimal disruption to their own public institutions. While in the 1980s, Hawke and the Constitutional Commission had given serious thought to recognition

---

43 John Howard, "A New Reconciliation" (2007) 19:4 Sydney Papers at 108–9; "The Prime Minister on the New Preamble," ABC Television, 7.30 Report, 11 August 2007; Noel Pearson, "Reconciliation U-Turn Shows Leader's True Colours," *[Sydney] Weekend Australian*, 24 November 2007.

44 Commonwealth, *Parliamentary Debates*, House of Representatives, 13 February 2008, 172 (Kevin Rudd, Prime Minister) ("Apology to Australia's Indigenous Peoples").

45 "Yolngu and Bininj Leaders' Statement of Intent," Yirrikala, 23 July 2008 (Copy on file with author).

46 "Rudd Pledges Indigenous Recognition in the Constitution," ABC PM, 23 July 2008; Kevin Rudd, "Joint Press Conference with the Chief Minister of the Northern Territory, Paul Henderson" (transcript of media conference, 24 July 2008); "Indigenous Leaders Call for Constitutional Recognition," ABC News, 8 June 2008, online: <www.abc.net.au/news/2008-06-08/indigenous-leaders-call-for-constitutional/2464522>.

of Aboriginal land rights, treaty and Indigenous rights in the operative text of the Constitution, twenty years later the preference is for recognition in the Preamble.

III. The Expert Panel on Recognition in the Constitution

The next significant event occurred in 2010 when Prime Minister Julia Gillard constituted an expert panel to report to government on possible options for constitutional change to give effect to Indigenous constitutional recognition. Gillard constituted the panel only because she was forced to by the Green Party and an Independent MP Rob Oakeshott during negotiations for power after the 2010 election led to a hung Parliament. It is important to keep this in mind, because, again, it was not a process borne out of an organic or sincere desire to achieve recognition. It was a political contrivance.

It is significant that the Prime Minister's Office selected the word "recognition." Prior to 2010, "recognition" was not a prominent word in discussion or debate about Indigenous constitutional matters.[47] We suggest that "recognition" was chosen partly because, despite the quite broad terms of reference, the government was thinking primarily about symbolic recognition. By this point in Australian history, it was accepted wisdom that in order to achieve constitutional change, bipartisan support was critical. For that reason, amendment proposals are, by necessity, minimalist. Also, "recognition" may be have been chosen because of Howard's announcement in 2007 of recognition in a preamble to the Constitution. In addition, Queensland, New South Wales, Victoria, and South Australia had all enacted "recognition" clauses in their state constitutions (even though the accompanying non-justiciability clause in each of these recognition gestures provoked some Aboriginal leaders to label it as "non-recognition"). In any event, the introduction of the word "recognition" proved problematic for the expert panel because of the non-specific nature of the commitment it implies, juxtaposed against the very specific and concrete recommendations the panel made.

The panel consulted the Australian community and the Aboriginal community over the course of a year. It adopted a number of approaches to facilitate consultation: it published a discussion paper, developed a

---

47   Barbara A Hocking, ed, *Unfinished Constitutional Business?: Rethinking Indigenous Self-Determination* (Canberra: Aboriginal Studies Press, 2005).

website and digital communications strategy, and held public meetings and events. Also, a short film summarizing the discussion paper was translated into fifteen Aboriginal and Torres Strait Islander languages, and interpreters of Aboriginal and Torres Strait Islander languages were at consultations, as needed and where possible. In terms of methodology, the panel adopted four principles to guide its assessment of proposals for constitutional recognition of Aboriginal and Torres Strait Islander peoples, that each proposal must (1) contribute to a more unified and reconciled nation; (2) be of benefit to and accord with the wishes of Aboriginal and Torres Strait Islander peoples; (3) be capable of being supported by an overwhelming majority of Australians from across the political and social spectrums; and (4) be technically and legally sound. In January 2011 the panel handed its *Final Report of the Expert Panel*[48] to the prime minister containing five recommendations:

1. Section 25: disqualification of voters on basis of race
   Recommendation 1 was that s 25 be repealed. Section 25 is a provision which contemplates the possibility of state laws disqualifying people of a particular race from voting at State elections. There was multi party support for the deletion of s 25.
2. Deletion of s 51(xxvi)
   Recommendation 2 was that s 51(xxvi) be repealed. It was then recommended that a new s 51 A be inserted into the Constitution; a proposal that is designed to include a statement of recognition as introductory words to a new head of legislative power replacing s 51 (xxvi). The Panel decided to place a statement of recognition in a preamble to the substantive power replacing the race power because of the unanimous legal view that one cannot have a preamble to the UK Act as a whole. Furthermore Aboriginal and Torres Strait Islander peoples almost universally did not want a preamble at the beginning of the Constitution and were especially opposed if any such preamble contained a non-justiciability clause. The new "section 51A" to be inserted reads:
3. Section 51A Recognition of Aboriginal and Torres Strait Islander peoples

---

48 Expert Panel on Constitutional Recognition of Indigenous Australians, *Recognising Aboriginal and Torres Strait Islander People in the Constitution: Report of the Expert Panel* (Canberra: Expert Panel, 2012) 211, online: <www.youmeunity.org.au/finalreport> [*Expert Panel Report*].

Recognising that the continent and its islands now known as Australia were first occupied by Aboriginal and Torres Strait Islander peoples;

Acknowledging the continuing relationship of Aboriginal and Torres Strait Islander peoples with their traditional lands and waters;

Respecting the continuing cultures, languages and heritage of Aboriginal and Torres Strait Islander peoples;

Acknowledging the need to secure the advancement of Aboriginal and Torres Strait Islander peoples;

the Parliament shall, subject to this Constitution, have power to make laws for the peace, order and good government of the Commonwealth with respect to Aboriginal and Torres Strait Islander peoples.

4. Racial non-discrimination clause

The Panel recommended a new racial non-discrimination clause to be inserted a new "section 116A" based on the *Canadian Charter of Rights of Freedoms*.

5. Aboriginal languages

Finally the Panel recommended that a new "section 127A" Recognising Aboriginal languages be inserted, along the following lines:

5. Section 127A Recognition of languages

(1) The national language of the Commonwealth of Australia is English.

(2) The Aboriginal and Torres Strait Islander languages are the original Australian languages, a part of our national heritage.

Why No Recognition of Sovereignty or a Treaty?

Given that the panel had established a methodology by which proposals were assessed for reform, it was important for the panel to accurately record the views of Aboriginal and Torres Strait Islander peoples, as one criterion to assess proposals was that they "be of benefit to and accord with the wishes of Aboriginal and Torres Strait Islander peoples."[49] Many submissions to the panel and consultations revealed that they were concerned with treaty,[50] sovereignty, and free, prior, and informed consent. Surprisingly, the panel also found that there was strong support among the non-Indigenous community for forms of binding agreements between Aboriginal and Torres Strait Islander communities and

---

49 *Ibid* at 4.
50 *Ibid* at 201.

governmental and non-governmental parties. The panel also found that the experience of Aboriginal people in Canada, particularly in relation to treaties and post-colonial treaty-making, was referenced in many submissions and in consultations. The panel devoted two separate chapters to treaty and sovereignty. Each is addressed in turn.

Why No Recommendation for a Treaty?

There is growing confidence in the process of agreement-making with Indigenous people, and, at the same time, there is increasing understanding of the flaws in the process that arise from the intransigence of state and federal governments in recognizing these agreements.[51] This intransigence prevents the formalization of critically important aspects of these agreements, such as their ability to run the land. Such uncertainty is precisely the outcome desired by federal and state governments in order to discourage agreement-making with Aboriginal people.

Since the first agreements signed under the provisions of the *Aboriginal Land Rights Act* in the Northern Territory more than twenty years ago, there has been an astonishing proliferation of agreements between Australian Indigenous people and resource extraction companies, railway, pipeline, and other major infrastructure project proponents, local governments, state governments, farming and grazing representative bodies, universities, and many other institutions and agencies.[52] Some are registered under the terms of the *Native Title Act*. Others are simple contractual agreements that set out the framework for future developments.

These developments in relations between Indigenous and non-Indigenous Australians are evidence of creative thinking by those involved in grappling with the legacy of the Australian frontier. While the many attempts at treating with Aborigines in colonial times and in the early twentieth century were not translated into enduring outcomes, it is clear that the need for agreements is both desirable and appropriate for several reasons, although there is formidable resistance

---

51 Marcia Langton, "A Treaty between Our Nations? (2000) 84 Arena Magazine 8–9.
52 Marcia Langton, Maureen Tehan, Lisa Palmer, Kathryn Shain, & Odette Mazel, "Sharing Land and Resources: Modern Agreements and Treaties with Indigenous People in Settler States," in Langton, Tehan, Palmer, Shain, and Mazel, eds, *Settling with Indigenous People: Modern Treaty and Agreement-Making* (Annandale, NSW: Federation, 2006) 1.

to agreement-making with Aboriginal people. The agreements negotiated since the 1970s are evidence of a willingness to do what the colonial settlers were unable to countenance: that is, to acknowledge that another group of people were the owners and custodians of the lands and waters of Australia; that their descendants have a right to possess, use, and enjoy those lands and waters; to govern, within the limits of Australian law, their use and access by others, and to reap any benefits arising from that use and access by others, as would any other group of people in rightful possession of a place.

There were 164 submissions that recommended agreement-making,[53] and the majority supported the inclusion of an agreement-making power in the Constitution. The Law Council of Australia supported the recommendation by the Constitutional Commission in 1988 to vest in the Commonwealth power to make agreements with Aboriginal and Torres Strait Islander peoples on a range of subjects, and that it might provide, like section 105A, for the agreement to override other laws. The Law Council argued,

> This approach would obviate the need to put to referendum an extensive catalogue of rights or detailed arrangements and provide, at the same time, a source of Constitutional authority for such agreement/agreements. It would also provide opportunities for properly resourced consultations with Aboriginal and Torres Strait Islander communities and organisations, and wider community education, in relation to appropriate arrangements for addressing much of the unfinished business, including in relation to sovereignty, self-determination, political representation (including through guaranteed seats in Parliament), recognition of customary law and land rights.[54]

This was consistent with other submissions that also concurred that agreement-making would "help redress past wrongs and heal the relationship between indigenous and non-indigenous Australians, facilitate the making of a treaty or agreements at national, State and Territory, and regional levels, and go some way towards recognising the sovereignty and self-determination rights of Aboriginal and Torres

---

53 *Expert Panel Report, supra* note 49 at 201.
54 *Ibid* at 200.

Strait Islander peoples."[55] Also it was suggested that agreements might improve health and education outcomes.

However, the panel concluded that, on the basis of its methodology, proposals must "be capable of being supported by an overwhelming majority of Australians from across the political and social spectrums," and that a recommendation for treaty or agreements would not receive sufficient support. It argued that "at the present time, any proposal for a form of constitutional backing for a treaty or other negotiated agreements with Aboriginal and Torres Strait Islander peoples would be likely to confuse many Australians, and hence could jeopardise broad public support for the Panel's other recommendations."[56] Importantly, however, it did note that the Commonwealth already has the power to conclude agreements under sections 51(xxvi) and 61 of the Constitution.

Sovereignty

Sovereignty dominated the consultations and submissions of Aboriginal and Torres Strait Islander peoples to the panel.[57] Indeed, when the National Congress of Australia's First Peoples polled its membership on the three most important policy areas for members, they were health, education, and sovereignty, and "88 per cent of Congress members identified constitutional recognition and sovereignty as a top priority."[58] The panel found that sovereignty had different meanings for Aboriginal people. Tom Trevorrow, chair of the Ngarrindjeri Regional Authority in South Australia, argued, "Ngarrindjeri will continue to assert to Government its own sovereignty over its own people, place and knowledge."[59] A major legal concern raised by Aboriginal and Torres Strait Islander peoples was that symbolic "recognition" in the Constitution would compromise sovereignty. According to legal advice that the panel sought,

[T]he sovereignty of the Commonwealth of Australia and its constituent and subordinate polities, the States and Territories, like that of their

---

55 *Ibid* at 193.
56 *Ibid* at 212.
57 *Ibid* at 205.
58 *Ibid* at 210.
59 *Ibid* at 211.

predecessors, the Imperial British Crown and its Australian colonies, does not depend on any act of original or confirmatory acquiescence by or on behalf of Aboriginal and Torres Strait Islander peoples. It derives from the majority view of the High Court in Mabo v Queensland (No 2) that the basis of settlement of Australia is and always has been, ultimately, the exertion of force by and on behalf of the British arrivals. Advice to the Panel is that recognition of Aboriginal and Torres Strait Islander peoples in the Constitution as equal citizens could not foreclose on the question of how Australia was settled. Nor should Constitutional recognition in general have any detrimental effect, beyond what may already have been suffered, on future projects aimed at a greater place for customary law in the governance of Australia.[60]

For the same reasons as the panel rejected treaty, it found recognition of the sovereign status would not attract broad public support.[61]

Finally, one consequence of use of the word "recognition" was that people fixated on what "recognition" meant. On the one hand Conservatives posited that "recognition" was – by its textual meaning – minimal, whereas Aboriginal and Torres Strait Islander peoples argued that it meant "recognition" of racial discrimination, marginalization, and exclusion. On the other hand, in regard to symbolic "recognition," there is an Indigenous perspective that they do not need to be "recognized" by the state.[62] The spectre of "recognition" politics of this iteration of constitutional reform has meant that soft recognition dominates the public discourse because it is inoffensive and presented at a high level of generality. In the same way that the 1967 referendum asked for, and the Reconciliation era required, a "non-specific commitment," this iteration of constitutional reform is demanding not more than a non-specific commitment of the Australian people. The consequences will be the same as those of 1967: disappointment and unrealistic expectations of what can be achieved through the law.

---

60 *Ibid* at 212.
61 *Ibid* at 213.
62 For more in-depth discussion of "recognition" of marginalized groups in written constitutions, see Charles Taylor, "The Politics of Recognition," in Amy Gutmann, ed, *Multiculturalism and "The Politics of Recognition"* (Princeton: Princeton University Press, 1992) 25.

IV. Conclusion

The chapter has traversed the period of Federation and the exclusion of Aboriginal people in the drafting of the Constitution to the 1967 referendum, the so-called reconciliation phase to the contemporary period of "recognition" – a concept embraced by the state only as long as it means symbolism and non-justiciability. The preference for symbolism and non-substance reflects the resignation of the state to the conservative nature of the polity evidenced by the few times the Constitution has been amended. Eight out of forty-four referendums have succeeded since 1901, and the distinguishing feature of success was support from both political parties.[63] In addition these changes have occurred under conservative government that has heightened the hysteria around who can and cannot drive constitutional reform. The starting point for the state on constitutional reform has shifted from what is best for the Australian people and what legally and technically robust to what minimal, inoffensive gesture will get support.

The other difficulty is Australia's "rights reluctance"[64] – not only Aboriginal rights but any rights. Unlike most common law countries, Australia has retained a very strong faith in Westminster parliamentary sovereignty. The prevailing sentiment in Australian Parliaments is that their power should not be impinged upon by constraints like "rights," especially a racial non-discrimination clause or any Aboriginal rights. This is reflected in the timidity of the Australian Bill of Rights / Charter of Rights movement that is at great pains to insist to its detractors that any future statutory Charter will have very little impact upon Parliaments' capacity to make laws. For example, Parliaments would still be empowered to pass discriminatory laws against Aboriginal people, so long as they acknowledged what they are doing. This provides little comfort to Aboriginal people.

However, the third difficulty is the paucity of a reconciliation process. Unlike Canada, Australia has no formal or continuous reconciliation process – not in the true sense of the word. There have been moments of significant, historical retelling, as exercised during the National Inquiry into the Separation of Aboriginal and Torres Strait Islander Children

---

63 Tony Blackshield & George Williams, *Australian Constitutional Law and Theory: Commentary and Materials*, 5th ed (Sydney: Federation, 2010) 1340.
64 Hilary Charlesworth, *Writing in Rights* (Sydney: UNSW Press, 2002).

from Their Families,[65] the Royal Commission into Aboriginal Deaths in Custody,[66] and the Apology to the Stolen Generations.[67] Yet for other historical wrongs such as the Killing Times[68] (Frontier Wars) or the mass fraud perpetrated by the state during the Protection era (Stolen Wages),[69] acknowledgment by the polity is virtually non-existent. Australian reconciliation is characterized by an "intense resistance to any change in the colonial structures that continue to dominate and subordinate indigenous peoples."[70]

Reconciliation in Australia has failed. It was a statutory process set up after the state reneged on a national framework for land rights and a treaty process. Once the Act lapsed, so did the process. Indeed at the end of the reconciliation phase, the recommendations were colloquially labelled "unfinished business," demonstrating that reconciliation was not about truth and justice or addressing aspirations of Aboriginal and Torres Strait Islander peoples. Reconciliation in Australia has always been state-driven. Despite the contemporary fashion for symbolic recognition, there is a growing sentiment that the political conditions in

65 Human Rights and Equal Opportunity Commission, Bringing Them Home Inquiry, *Bringing Them Home: Report of the National Inquiry into the Separation of Aboriginal and Torres Strait Islander Children from Their Families* (Sydney: Human Rights and Equal Opportunity Commission, 1997).

66 Commonwealth, Royal Commission into Aboriginal Deaths in Custody (RCIADIC), National Report (Canberra: Australian Government Publishing Service, 1991).

67 Commonwealth, *Parliamentary Debates*, House of Representatives, 13 February 2008, 172 (Kevin Rudd, Prime Minister) ("Apology to Australia's Indigenous Peoples").

68 John Connor, *Australian Frontier Wars 1788–1838* (Sydney: UNSW Press); Henry Reynolds, *Forgotten War* (Kensington, NSW: NewSouth, 2013); Robert Foster & Amanda Nettelbeck, *Out of Silence: The History and Memory of South Australia's Frontier Wars* (Cambridge, MA: Wakefield, 2012); Timothy Bottoms, *Conspiracy of Silence* (Sydney: Allen and Unwin, 2013).

69 See, e.g., Rosalind Kidd, *Trustees on Trial* (Canberra: Aboriginal Studies Press, 2006); Rosalind Kidd, *The Way We Civilise* (St Lucia, Qld: University of Queensland Press, 1999).

70 Damien Short, *Reconciliation and Colonial Power: Indigenous Rights in Australia* (Farnham, UK: Ashgate, 2008); Mick Dodson & Lisa Strelein, "Australia's Nation-Building: Renegotiating the Relationship between Indigenous Peoples and the State" (2001) 24 University of New South Wales Law Journal 826; Megan Davis, "Chained to the Past: The Psychological Terra Nullius of Australia's Public Institutions," in Tom Campbell, Jeffrey Goldsworthy, & Adrienne Stone, eds, *Protecting Rights without a Bill of Rights: Institutional Performance and Reform in Australia* (Farnham, UK: Ashgate, 2006) 175; Barbara Hocking, ed, *Unfinished Constitutional Business: Rethinking Indigenous Self-Determination* (Canberra: Aboriginal Studies Press, 2005).

Australia are ill-suited to permit public institutions to evolve in a way that is inclusive, pluralist, and accommodating of first peoples. To achieve that would require extraordinary, once-in-a-lifetime leadership – moving a nation to do in the twenty-first century what should have been done a century ago. While Aboriginal and Torres Strait Islander peoples in Australia do look to Canada as the gold standard of a post-colonial state dealing with first peoples – section 116A of the panel's recommendations is based on the *Charter* – comparative analysis is limited. Fashioned by Canada's unique history – treaties at first contact, post-colonial agreement-making, statutory and constitutionally entrenched human rights, and measures such as a truth and reconciliation commission or a royal commission into Aboriginal Peoples – these are simply out of reach for Aboriginal peoples in Australia.

18   Legislation and Indigenous Self-Determination in Canada and the United States

JOHN BORROWS

Canada and Indigenous peoples should work together to produce legislation that enhances Indigenous self-determination.[1] This should occur even though such engagement presents significant risks and challenges for Indigenous peoples and governments.[2] While legislation involving Indigenous peoples raises distinctive issues,[3] drafting effective law is

1 This chapter builds on legislative proposals made in John Borrows, *Canada's Indigenous Constitution* (Toronto: University of Toronto Press, 2010) at 177–206. The *Declaration on the Rights of Indigenous Peoples* proclaims that "Indigenous peoples have a right to self-determination." A discussion of the development and implications of this fact is found in Erica IA Diaz, "Equality of Indigenous Peoples under the Auspices of the United Nations: Draft Declaration on the Rights of Indigenous Peoples" (1995) 7 St Thomas L Rev 493; James Anaya, *Indigenous Peoples in International Law* (New York: Oxford University Press, 1996) at 151–82; Sharon Venne, *Our Elders Understand Our Rights: Evolving International Law Regarding Indigenous Rights* (Princeton: Theytus Books, 1998) at 107–71.
2 For excellent critiques of the perils of working with Canadian governments for Indigenous peoples, see Taiaiake Alfred, *Peace, Power, Righteousness: An Indigenous Manifesto* (Toronto: Oxford University Press, 1999); Alfred, *Wasase: Indigenous Pathways to Action* (Peterborough, ON: Broadview, 2005); Glen Coulthard, "Resisting Culture: Seyla Benhabib's Deliberative Approach to the Politics of Recognition in Colonial Contexts" in David Kahane, Dominique Leydet, Daniel Weinstock, & Melissa Williams, eds, *Realizing Deliberative Democracy* (Vancouver: University of British Columbia Press, 2009): Glen Coulthard, "Beyond Recognition: Indigenous Self-Determination as Prefigurative Practice" in Leanne Simpson, ed, *Lighting the Eighth Fire: The Liberation, Resurgence, and Protection of Indigenous Nations* (Winnipeg: Arbeiter Ring, 2008) at 187.
3 This issue is explored in greater detail in John Borrows, "Stewardship and the First Nations Governance Act" (2003) 29 Queen's LJ 103; Robert Williams Jr, "Taking Rights Aggressively: The Perils and Promise of Critical Legal Theory for Peoples of Color" (1987–88) 5 Law & Ineq 103 at 121–27.

challenging in any policy field.[4] The political world in which we live is chaotic, hostile, and full of contradictions and cross-cutting interests.[5] It is also generally averse to Indigenous political aspirations.[6] Thus, one could effectively critique any action designed to support Indigenous peoples within the nation state.[7] Yet, as this chapter argues, communities could be strengthened and lives could be improved through legislation aimed at implementing international and domestic commitments and obligations regarding Aboriginal peoples.[8] There are reasons to act, even though our interventions will never produce certainty, determinacy, and truth.[9] There is no escape from our always less-than-perfect circumstances, and though one must ever be appropriately cautious and critical, there is room for improvement, even within the nation state. As long as broader implications are considered and addressed, and longer-term aspirations are not fatally compromised, working to recognize and affirm Indigenous self-determination in conjunction with Canada can produce real-world benefits.

This chapter compares federal legislation concerning Indigenous peoples in Canada and the United States with the goal of prompting

---

4 For a discussion critically questioning the value of legislation, see John Griffiths, "Is Law Important?" (1979) 54 NYUL Rev 339. For a discussion of the positive possibilities of statutory interpretation more generally, see William Eskridge, *Dynamic Statutory Interpretation* (Cambridge, MA: Harvard University Press, 1994).

5 Jim Tully, *Public Philosophy in a New Key: Vol 1, Democracy and Civic Freedom* (Cambridge: Cambridge University Press, 2008) at 240: Our political lives are "shot through with relations of inequality, force and fraud, broken promises, failed accords, degrading stereotypes, misrecognition, paternalism, enmity and distrust."

6 Johnny Mack, *Thickening Totems and Thinning Imperialism* (LLM Thesis, University of Victoria, Victoria, British Columbia, 2009) [unpublished].

7 See Frantz Fanon, *The Wretched of the Earth* (New York: Grove, 2004).

8 For a general discussion of where improvement is needed in the lives of Indigenous peoples in Canada as well as the United States, see Angela Mashford-Pringle, "How'd We Get Here from There? American Indians and Aboriginal Peoples of Canada Health Policy" (2011) 9(1) Pimatisiwin 153. For a general discussion of improving Aboriginal socio-demographic circumstances for Aboriginal peoples in Canada, see JB Waldram, DA Herring, & TK Young, *Aboriginal Health in Canada: Historical, Cultural, and Epidemiological Perspectives*, 2nd ed (Toronto: University of Toronto Press, 2006).

9 For a philosophical discussion related to pursuing legal action, despite indeterminacy and power imbalances, see Williams Jr, supra note 3 at 121–27. For arguments that law is never built on rational certainties and absolutes, see Joseph Singer, "The Player and the Cards: Nihilism and Legal Theory" (1984–85) 94 Yale LJ 1; Drucilla Cornell, "Toward a Modern/Post-Modern Reconstruction of Ethics" (1985) 133 U Pa L Rev 291; David Kennedy, "The Turn to Interpretation" (1985) 58 S Cal L Rev 251.

legislative innovation in Canada.[10] While there are significant problems between indigenous peoples and governments in both counties, this chapter demonstrates that Canada is much less supportive of Indigenous people in the legislative field.[11] This is true, despite the fact that Aboriginal and treaty rights are constitutionally recognized and affirmed in section 35(1) of Canada's *Constitution Act, 1982*, which proclaims, "The existing aboriginal and treaty rights of the aboriginal peoples of Canada are hereby recognized and affirmed."[12] The recognition and affirmation of Native American rights does not exist in the US Constitution.[13] Nevertheless, the constitutions of Canada and the United States are similar in one important respect: both allocate authority for legislation in relation to Indians to the federal government.[14] This power could be used more effectively in both countries, but, in spite of the seeming advantage of Canadian constitutional recognition, Native American people in the United States enjoy greater practical legal

---

10 For a comparison of Canadian and US Indian policy, see Roger L Nichols, *Indians in the United States and Canada: A Comparative History* (Lincoln: University of Nebraska Press, 1999); Jill St Germain, *Indian Treaty-Making Policy in the United States and Canada, 1867–1877* (Lincoln: University of Nebraska Press, 2001).

11 A similar conclusion can be found in Dan Russell, *A People's Dream: Aboriginal Self-Government in Canada* (Vancouver: UBC Press, 2000) at 14–40.

12 *Constitution Act, 1982*, being Schedule B to the *Canada Act 1982* (UK), 1982, c 11.

13 For an argument that the United States constitution should formally recognize Native American rights, see Frank Pommersheim, *Broken Landscape: Indians, Indian Tribes, and the Constitution* (New York: Oxford University Press, 2009) at 309–11. Arguments have also been offered that would allow tribes to consensually incorporate themselves with the United States through compact; see Alex Tallchief Skibine, "Redefining the State of Indian Tribes within 'Our Federalism': Beyond the Dependency Paradigm" (2006) 38 Conn L Rev 667.

14 Section 91(24) of the *Constitution Act, 1867* declares that exclusive legislative authority of the Parliament of Canada extends to "Indians, and Lands reserved for the Indians," *British North America Act, 1867*, 30–31 Vict, c 3 (UK). The "Indian trade and commerce clause," located in art 1, s 8, cl 3 of the United States constitution, states that the federal Congress shall have power "[t]o regulate commerce with foreign Nations, and among the several States, and with the Indian Tribes." For a critique of the United States Supreme Court's treatment of the Indian commerce clause power see Nell Jessup Newton, "Plenary Power over Indians: Its Scope, Sources and Limitations" (1984) 132 U Pa L Rev 195; Philip Frickey, "Domesticating Federal Indian Law" (1996) 81 Minn L Rev 31; Robert Clinton, "There Is No Federal Supremacy Clause for Indian Tribes" (2002) 34 Ariz St LJ 113.

recognition in relation to governance, culture, and the environmental conservation and development.[15]

What explains the relative success of legislative initiatives in the United States? The answer is, quite simply, that Indigenous peoples in the United States have created receptive policy frameworks with Congressional allies that build law on principles of self-determination.[16] Indigenous peoples and parliamentarians in Canada have not been very successful in this regard.[17] The US federal government is more willing to use its power to pre-empt state law's application to Indian reservations, thus carving out a space for Indigenous governance.[18] Canadian governments have been extraordinarily reluctant to displace

---

15 The words of Roger Gibbons, written in 1984. are prophetic:

> [W]hile the search for a new constitution appeared at first to be an important opportunity for Indians, it has turned out to be a policy trap. The constitutional debate has brought a new set of environmental factors to bear on Indian affairs which are largely beyond the control of Indian political organizations, and which threaten to constrain severely Indian policy options in the years ahead. Because Indian affairs have become entangled in broader constitutional issues, Indian control over those public policies which shape their very lives and futures may be further weakened.

Roger Gibbons, "Canadian Indian Policy: The Constitutional Trap" (1984) 4 Canadian Journal of Native Studies 1 at 2.

16 "The social, political and legal activism of Indian leaders and their advocates in the 1950's, 60's and 70's resulted in an unprecedented volume of Indian legislation, most of it favorable to Indian interests, and all of it enacted at the behest of the tribes or at least with their participation." David Getches, Charles Wilkinson, Robert Williams, Jr, & LM Fletcher, eds, *Cases and Materials on Federal Indian Law* (St Paul, MN: West, 2011) at 220.

17 For an insightful film chronicling the challenge of constitutional negotiations among Canadian federal, provincial, and Aboriginal leaders, see Maurice Bulbulian, *Dancing around the Table, Part One and Part Two* (Montreal: National Film Board of Canada, 1987). For a general discussion of these conferences, see Michael Asch, *Home and Native Land: Aboriginal Rights and the Canadian Constitution* (Vancouver: University of British Columbia Press, 1993). For a view that these conferences did produce benefits, see Kathy Brock, "The Politics of Aboriginal Self-Government: A Canadian Paradox (2001) 34 Canadian Public Administration 272.

18 For a discussion of the pre-emption power in federal Indian law, see *Williams v Lee* (1959) 358 US 277, 79 S Ct 269 (USSC); *Warren Trading Post v Arizona Tax Commission*, (1965) 380 US 685 (USSC); *McClanahan v Arizona State Tax Commission*, (1973) 411 US 164 (USSC); Robert Clinton, "Isolated in Their Own Country: A Defense of Federal Protection of Indian Autonomy and Self-Governance" (1981) 33 Stan L Rev 979; Jackie Gardina, "Federal Preemption: A Roadmap for the Application of Tribal Law in State Courts" (2010–11) 25 Am Indian L Rev 1.

provincial power in favour of Indigenous governmental authority.[19] As a result, Indigenous self-determination does not animate Canadian legislation in any significant way.[20] By way of contrast, in the United States it has been observed that "[t]ribal sovereignty forms the bedrock of the modern courts decisions and statutes."[21] With this starting point, tribes in the United States are more willing to creatively work with the federal government because it has generally proceeded "on the principle that Indian tribes are, in the final analysis, the primary or basic governmental unit of Indian policy."[22] While it is important to emphasize that there are exceedingly difficult policy challenges for Indigenous peoples in the United States too,[23] particularly related to the Supreme Court,[24] the modern statutory acceptance of self-determination has made a notable difference.[25] It has meant that "no Indian legislation has been passed over Indian opposition since ... 1968."[26]

---

19 See, generally, J Anthony Long and Menno Boldt, eds, *Governments in Conflict?: Provinces and Indian Nations in Canada* (Toronto: University of Toronto Press, 1988).
20 The paradigmatic legislation in Canada is the *Indian Act*, which was designed to undermine Indigenous self-determination; see John Tobias, "Protection, Civilization, Assimilation: An Outline History of Canada's Indian Policy" in Ian Getty & Antoine Lussier, eds, *As Long as the Sun Shines and Water Flows: A Reader in Canadian Native Studies* (Vancouver: University of British Columbia Press, 1990) at 29.
21 Charles Wilkinson, *Blood Struggle: The Rise of Modern Indian Nations* (New York: WW Norton, 2005) at 248.
22 Nell Jessup Newton, Robert Anderson, et al, eds., *Cohen's Handbook of Federal Indian Law* (Newark, NJ: LexisNexis, 2005) at 99.
23 For an excellent critique of federal legislative initiatives over the last forty years, see Jeff Corntassel & Richard Witmer II, *Forced Federalism: Contemporary Challenges to Indigenous Nationhood* (Norman: University of Oklahoma Press, 2008). The authors argue that tribes are compelled to negotiate with states under many of the federal laws outlined in this chapter, and that this results in a dilution of the tribe's nationhood and self-determination.
24 For a critique of the US Supreme Court's approach, see Walter Echo-Hawk, *In the Courts of the Conqueror: The 10 Worst Indian Law Cases Ever Decided* (Golden, CO: Fulcrum, 2010); Robert Williams Jr, *Like a Loaded Weapon: The Rehnquist Court, Indian Rights, and the Legal History of Racism in America* (Minneapolis: University of Minnesota Press, 2005); David Wilkins, *American Indian Sovereignty and the U.S. Supreme Court: The Masking of Justice* (Austin: University of Texas Press, 1997).
25 See, generally, John Wunder, ed, *Native American Sovereignty* (New York: Taylor & Francis, 1999).
26 Charles Wilkinson, *American Indians, Time and the Law* (New Haven, CT: Yale University Press, 1987) at 83. The issue of Indian "consent" in other areas of US law is much more troubling; see Matthew Fletcher, "Tribal Consent" (2012) 8 Stan J Civil Rights & Civil Liberties 45.

Legislation furthering Indigenous self-determination in the United States has generally focused on three areas: (1) Indigenous control over federal services for Indigenous people, (2) the protection of Indigenous cultures and communities, and (3) Indigenous control in relation to natural resources and economic development.[27] Each of three areas will be briefly examined in the body of this chapter to highlight potential fields for Canadian legislative action. This short review reveals the impressive scope of US law dealing with Indigenous issues, which, as noted, dramatically contrasts with the dearth of statutory activity in Canada.[28]

Indigenous Control of Federal Services

Like Canada, the United States has experienced a deeply troubling colonial history in its relation with Indigenous peoples.[29] Change has been slow to develop. Over forty years ago, President Nixon began a new chapter in the relationship between Native American tribes and the federal legislative and executive branches of government.[30]

---

27 Robert Anderson, Bethany Berger, Philip Frickey, & Sarah Krakoff, eds, *American Indian Law, Cases and Commentary* (St Paul, MN: West, 2010) at 155.

28 There are well over forty significant pieces of legislation addressing Indigenous self-determination in the United States; see United States Code (USC) Title 25 – Indians. The words of Roger Gibbons, written in 1984 still ring true: "Unlike the situation in the United States where over 4000 separate unsystematized statutory enactments relating to Indian policy exist …, Canadian public policy in the field of Indian Affairs is concentrated within a … single piece of legislation, last subjected to any comprehensive revision in 1951." Roger Gibbons, "Canadian Indian Policy: The Constitutional Trap" (1984) 4 Can J Native Studies 1 at 2.

29 Robert J Miller, Jacinta Ruru, Larissa Behrendt, & Tracey Lindberg, *Discovering Indigenous Lands: The Doctrine of Discovery in the English Colonies* (Oxford: Oxford University Press, 2010); Lindsay G Robertson, *Conquest by Law: How the Discovery of America Dispossessed Indigenous Peoples of Their Lands* (New York: Oxford University Press, 2007); Stuart Banner, *How the Indians Lost Their Land: Law and Power on the Frontier* (Cambridge, MA: Harvard University Press, 2007); Robert Williams Jr, *The American Indian in Western Legal Thought: The Discourses of Conquest* (New York: Oxford University Press, 1990).

30 Unfortunately, the United States Supreme Court, which had been somewhat supportive of Native claims in previous decades, became increasingly unreceptive to Indigenous arguments from the late 1970s through to the present day; see Sarah Krakoff, "Undoing Indian Law One Case at a Time: Judicial Minimalism and Tribal Sovereignty" (2001) 50 Am U L Rev 1178; Philip P Frickey, "A Common Law for Our Age of Colonialism: The Judicial Divestiture of Indian Tribal Authority over Nonmembers" (1999) 109 Yale LJ 1.

He officially renounced past practices that attempted to "terminate" tribes.[31] At the same time he formally announced a national policy goal of "strengthening the Indian's sense of autonomy without threatening his sense of community."[32] Congress soon followed President Nixon's lead.[33] In 1975 it passed the *Indian Self-Determination and Educational Assistance Act* to facilitate Indian control of federal services.[34] Among the congressional findings, which are embedded in the Act and outline its purpose, is the recognition that "the Indian people will never surrender their desire to control their relationships both among themselves and with non-Indian governments, organizations and persons."[35] The Act enhances Indian control by allowing tribes to enter into contracts and receive grants to administer federally funded services. In 1994 this Act was supplemented by the *Tribal Self-Governance Act*, which allows for the transfer of federal programs to tribes and facilitates congressional support of projects designed to enhance self-determination.[36] These Acts compel the federal government to fund tribal programs that are planned and administered by Indian nations themselves.

31 Unfortunately, termination can still occur through judicial disestablishment; see Judith V Royster, "The Legacy of Allotment" (1995) 27 Ariz St LJ 1; Charlene Koski, "The Legacy of Solemn v Bartlett: How Courts Have Used Demographics to Buy Congress and Erode the Basic Principles of Indian Law" (2009) 84 Washington L Rev 723.
32 Richard Nixon, "Message from the President of the United States Transmitting Recommendations for Indian Policy" (8 July 1970) *H.R. Doc. No. 91-363*, 91st Congress, 2nd Sess.
33 In Canada, during this period, Prime Minister Trudeau proposed the assimilation of First Nations in Canada; for an influential critique of this policy, see Harold Cardinal, *The Unjust Society* (Vancouver: Douglas & McIntyre, 1969).
34 *Indian Self-Determination and Educational Assistance Act* 25 USC 450; David H Getches, "Conquering the Cultural Frontier: The New Subjectivism of the Supreme Court in Indian Law" (1996) 84 Cal L Rev 1573.
35 *Indian Self-Determination and Educational Assistance Act* 25 USC 450.
36 *Tribal Self-Governance Act*, 25 USC 450n, 458aa to 458gg. This *Act* also builds on the same base as the *Indian Self-Determination and Assistance Act* by proclaiming, "The Tribal right of self-governance flows from the inherent sovereignty of Indian Tribes and nations." The Office of Self-Governance, which administers the *Tribal Governance Act*, oversees a budget of close to $500 million to ensure that tribes continue to develop their governance capacity. For general commentary, see Tadd Johnson & James Hamilton, "Self-Governance for Indian Tribes: From Paternalism to Empowerment" (1994–95) 27 Conn L Rev 1251. For an examination of the Act's operation in one field, see Mary Ann King, "Co-Management or Contracting: Agreements between Native American Tribes and the U.S. National Park Service Pursuant to the 1994 Tribal Self-Governance Act" (2007) 31 Harv Envtl L Rev 475.

Legislation facilitating Indian control of government services also extends to tribally controlled colleges and universities,[37] primary and secondary schools,[38] housing,[39] social assistance,[40] policing,[41] and health care.[42] These Acts mark a legislative revolution.[43] They are slowly peeling away layers of federal domination in Indian affairs.[44] When these initiatives began in the early 1970s, tribes controlled only 1.5 per cent of the delivery and administration of federal services to Indian people, whereas today they control over 50 per cent of this sector.[45] While there is much work ahead, Indian control of Indian services has made a significant difference in the United States because it has strengthened the economic, social, and cultural health of Indian tribes.[46]

Indigenous peoples in Canada do not generally plan and deliver services to the same degree as in the United States.[47] In fact, First Nations policy development and delivery in Canada is almost exclusively under federal control. The main piece of legislation dealing with First Nations governance in Canada is the *Indian Act*.[48] It is designed

37 *Tribally Controlled Colleges and Universities Assistance Act*, 25 USC 1801.
38 *Indian Education Act*, 25 USC 2601–51.
39 *Native American Housing Assistance Self-Determination Act*, 25 USC 4101.
40 Programs administered by the tribes include Temporary Assistance for Needy Families, Food Stamps, Child Support Enforcement, etc.; see Nell Jessup Newton, Robert Anderson et al, eds, *Cohen's Handbook of Federal Indian Law* (Newark, NJ: LexisNexis, 2005) at 1400–02.
41 *Indian Law Enforcement Reform Act*, 25 USC 2801–09.
42 *Indian Health Care Act*, USC 1613–82; *Indian Alcoholism and Substance Abuse Prevention and Treatment Act*, 25 USC 2401–78.
43 For a discussion of the transformation of federal Indian law and policy in the years after Nixon, see George Pierre Castile, *To Show Heart: Native American Self-Determination and Federal Indian Policy, 1960–1975* (Tucson: University of Arizona Press, 1998).
44 George Pierre Castile, *Taking Charge: Native American Self-Determination and Federal Indian Policy, 1975–1993* (Tucson: University of Arizona Press, 2006).
45 Robert Anderson, Bethany Berger, Philip Frickey, & Sarah Krakoff, eds, *American Indian Law, Cases and Commentary* (St Paul, MN: West, 2010) at 155.
46 Miriam Jorgensen, ed, *Rebuilding Native Nations: Strategies for Governance and Development* (Tucson: University of Arizona Press, 2007) at 146–74, 223–45.
47 Emmanuel Brunet-Jailly, "The Governance and Fiscal Environment of First Nations' Fiscal Intergovernmental Relations in Comparative Perspectives" (Prepared for National Centre for First Nation Governance, March 2008) at 9–15, online: <fngovernance.org/ncfng_research/emmanual_brunet-jailley.pdf>.
48 One small step away from the *Indian Act* is the *First Nations Land Management Act*, SC 1999, c 24, which allows First Nations to opt out of certain sections of the *Indian Act* "to create their own system for making reserve land allotments to individual First

explicitly to break down First Nations socio-political relations and forcibly absorb individual nation members within broader Canadian society.[49] Its provisions narrowly define and heavily regulate Indigenous peoples' citizenship,[50] land rights,[51] succession rules,[52] political organization,[53] economic opportunities,[54] fiscal management,[55] and educational patterns and attainment.[56] Particularly troubling is the fact that the *Indian Act* makes First Nations largely subject to provincial legislation and regulation without their consent.[57] Such an idea usurps First Nations' authority.[58] In particular, section 88 of the *Indian Act* drastically constrains jurisdictional spaces that should be filled by

---

Nation members. They also have authority to deal with matrimonial real property interests or rights." For commentary, see Tom Flanagan, Christopher Alcantara, & André Le Dressay, *Beyond the Indian Act: Restoring Aboriginal Property Rights* (Montreal & Kingston: McGill-Queen's University Press, 2010).

49 John Tobias, "Protection, Civilization and Assimilation: An Outline History of Canada's Indian Policy" in James Miller, ed, *Sweet Promises: A Reader on Indian-White Relations in Canada* (Toronto: University of Toronto Press, 1991) at 127; Brian E Titley, *A Narrow Vision: Duncan Campbell Scott and the Administration of Indian Affairs in Canada* (Vancouver: University of British Columbia Press, 1986), particularly the chapter entitled "General Aspects of Policy and Administration" at 37–59.

50 Larry Gilbert, *Entitlement to Indian Status and Membership Codes in Canada* (Toronto: Carswell, 1996); Bonita Lawrence, *"Real" Indians and Others: Mixed Blood Urban Native Peoples and Indigenous Nationhood* (Vancouver: UBC Press, 2004).

51 The reserve system is described in Richard Bartlett, *Indian Reserves and Aboriginal Lands in Canada: A Homeland* (Saskatoon: University of Saskatchewan Native Law Centre, 1990); broader land issues are discussed in Kerry Wilkin, ed, *Advancing Aboriginal Claims: Visions / Strategies / Directions* (Saskatoon: Purich, 2004).

52 Shin Imai, *Aboriginal Law Handbook*, 2nd ed (Toronto: Carswell, 1999) at 240–44.

53 Brian Crane, Robert Mainville, & Martin Mason, *First Nations Governance Law* (Toronto: LexisNexis, Butterworths, 2006) at 101–29; Robert A Reiter, *The Law of First Nations* (Edmonton: Juris Analytica, 1996).

54 Royal Commission on Aboriginal Peoples, *The Report of the Royal Commission on Aboriginal Peoples*. 5 vols (Ottawa: Minister of Supply and Services, 1996).

55 Skeena Native Development Society, *Masters in Our Own House: The Path to Prosperity* (Terrace, BC: Skeena Development Society, 2003) at 59–74.

56 For an annotated description of the *Indian Act*, see Shin Imai, *Indian Act and Constitutional Provisions* (Toronto: Thomson Carswell, 2006).

57 Darlene Johnston, *The Taking of Indian Lands in Canada: Consent or Coercion* (Saskatoon: University of Saskatchewan Native Law Centre, 1989).

58 An innovative argument that develops First Nations autonomy in Canada along familiar constitutional lines is Bruce Ryder, "The Demise and Rise of the Classical Paradigm in Canadian Federalism: Promoting Autonomy for the Provinces and the First Nations" (1991) 36 McGill LJ 308.

Indigenous sovereignty.[59] It does so by delegating vast fields of political activity to provincial governments by referentially incorporating, as federal law, provincial laws of general application.[60] This severely limits First Nations' political power in Canada.[61] It also creates very few incentives for the federal government to work with First Nations and pass legislation recognizing and affirming Aboriginal and treaty rights throughout the country. The federal government's "transfer" of legislative responsibility from itself and First Nations to provincial governments is a significant reason why Canada lags behind the United States in developing politically healthier Indigenous communities.

As a result of this approach, unlike in the United States, First Nations in Canada remain largely subject to federal control when federal services are delivered to their members. The auditor general of Canada (AGC) identified three problems with this arrangement as it relates to First Nations.[62] First, the federal government has not created clarity about the service levels that First Nations receive relative to the general population. This has resulted in First Nations receiving substantially fewer dollars per capita than others when it comes to basic government service. Such glaring disparities raise concerns related to unfairness and discrimination. First Nations and First Nations organizations have challenged this funding gap in court.[63] These discrepancies create the impression that governments are working towards the assimilation

59 For a history and legal analysis of section 88 of the *Indian Act*, see Kerry Wilkins, "Still Crazy after All These Years: Section 88 at Fifty" (2000) 38 Alta L Rev 458.
60 See *R v Dick*, [1985] 2 SCR 309; *Kitkatla Band v British Columbia (Minister of Small Business, Tourism and Culture)* [2002] 2 SCR 146.
61 For arguments questioning the constitutionality of section 88 of the *Indian Act*, see Leroy Little Bear, "Section 88 of the Indian Act and the Application of Provincial Laws to Indians" in J Anthony Long and Menno Boldt, eds, *Governments in Conflict? Provinces and Indian Nations in Canada* (Toronto: University of Toronto Press, 1988) at 175; Kent McNeil, "Aboriginal Title and Section 88 of the Indian Act" (2000) 34 UBC L Rev 157.
62 Office of the Auditor General of Canada, *2011 June Status Report of the Auditor General of Canada*, at chapter 4. Metis people are even further disenfranchised because governments in Canada do not recognize Metis governance, even in limited ways found in the *Indian Act*.
63 For challenges in the area of child welfare, see *Canada (AG) v First Nations Child and Family Caring Society of Canada*, 2010 FC 343 (CanLII). For challenges in the area of education, see First Nations Child and Family Caring Society, *Information Sheet #2: First Nations Education* (July 2013), online: <www.fncaringsociety.com/sites/default/files/Information%20Sheet%202_First%20Nations%20Education_1.pdf>.

of First Nations by creating negative incentives that impel people to leave the reserves and seek services elsewhere.[64] As the AGC wrote, "It is not always evident whether the federal government is committed to providing services on reserves of the same range and quality as those provided to other communities across Canada."[65]

Second, First Nations in Canada do not effectively plan and control the delivery of services because the federal government has not created a legislative base to hold themselves accountable in this field. In this respect, the AGC observed,

First Nation children on reserve are underfunded $2,000–$3,000 per child (First Nations Child and Family Caring Society [FNCFCS], 2013; Assembly of First Nations [AFN], 2010). Unlike provincial schools, the federal government provides $0 for libraries; $0 for computers, software, and teacher training; $0 for extracurricular activities; $0 for First Nation data-management systems; $0 for second- and third-level services (including core funding for special education, school boards, governance and education research); $0 for endangered languages; and $0 for principals, directors, pedagogical support, and the development of culturally appropriate curricula (AFN, 2010; FNCFCS, 2013). In 2010/11, AANDC provided $1.5 billion for First Nation education on reserve and $304 million for building construction and maintenance. The parliamentary budget officer released a report in 2009 with an analysis of actual costs for the delivery of education, finding that schools on reserve are systematically underfunded by less than half (58 per cent) of the actual costs needed to provide equal and equitable access to safe schools and education. See Ashutosh Rajekar and Mathilatath Ramnarayanan, *The Funding Requirement for First Nations Schools in Canada* (Ottawa: Office of the Parliamentary Budget Officer, 2009) <www2.parl.gc.ca/sites/pbo-dpb/documents/INAC_Final_EN.pdf>.

64 The *Indian Act* is designed to assimilate First Nations; see "The Indian Act" in *Report of the Royal Commission on Aboriginal People, Volume 1, Looking Forward, Looking Back* (Ottawa: Minister of Supply and Services Canada, 1996) at 255–332; John Tobias, "Protection, Civilization and Assimilation: An Outline History of Canada's Indian Policy" in James Miller, ed, *Sweet Promises: A Reader on Indian-White Relations in Canada* (Toronto: University of Toronto Press, 1991) at 127; Brian E Titley, *A Narrow Vision: Duncan Campbell Scott and the Administration of Indian Affairs in Canada* (Vancouver: University of British Columbia Press, 1986). In the late 1960s the Trudeau government proposed completing the process of assimilation through the White Paper; see Sally Weaver, *Making Canadian Indian Policy: The Hidden Agenda 1968–1970* (Toronto: University of Toronto Press, 1981). After the constitution was patriated, First Nations suspected the White Paper was still government policy that was being pursued by devolution of federal services to the provinces; see J Anthony Long and Menno Boldt, *Governments in Conflict? Provinces and Indian Nations In Canada* (Toronto: University of Toronto Press, 1988).

65 Office of the Auditor General of Canada, *2011 June Status Report of the Auditor General of Canada* at chapter 4.

[F]or First Nations members living on reserves, there is no legislation supporting programs in important areas such as education, health, and drinking water. Instead, the federal government has developed programs and services for First Nations on the basis of policy. As a result, the services delivered under these programs are not always well defined and there is confusion about federal responsibility for funding them adequately.[66]

When governments act through policy, as opposed to legislation, they retain greater discretion in carrying out their plans. This allows them to exercise broader control over those whom their policies affect. In contrast, when governments act through legislation and regulation, they signal a higher level of commitment. This is because legal consequences follow when there is a departure from prescribed legislative standards. Acts done contrary to legislation can be challenged in court, and remedies can be secured to compel or constrain government or private actors. There are no such consequences when a government acts contrary to its policies. Since the federal government in Canada, unlike the United States, has not committed itself to measurable standards in the provision of services, it is difficult to maintain legal challenges to unequal service delivery. The federal government has not cultivated its own accountability and transparency in relation to First Nations service delivery. This is ironic, given the decade-long federal fetish focusing on First Nations accountability-related service delivery.[67] By way of contrast, the United States federal government has held itself to an appreciably higher level of accountability in its relations with Indigenous peoples.[68]

Third, as a result of problems in federal funding mechanisms, First Nations in Canada do not effectively "control their relationships both among themselves and with non-Indian governments, organizations and persons," as is the legislative goal in the United States. The failure to provide such mechanisms in Canada has led to great uncertainty about funding levels within First Nations. This makes it nearly

66 *Ibid.*
67 John Borrows, "Stewardship and the First Nations Governance Act" (2003–04) 29 Queen's LJ 103.
68 More generally, the United States Supreme Court has recognized general congressional trust responsibilities in *United States v Sioux Nation* (1980) 448 US 371 (USSC). For executive trust responsibilities to tribes, see *Seminole Nation v United States*, (1942) 316 US 286 (USSC); *Morton v Ruiz* (1974) 415 US 199 (USCC); however, the Supreme Court has loosened these standards in recent years; see *Lincoln v Vigil* (1993) 508 US 182 (USSC); *United States v Navajo Nation* (2003) 537 US 488 (USSC).

impossible for these communities to engage in stable long-term planning. The AGC has noted that the Canadian government's ambiguous funding mechanism also creates problems related to the day-to-day management of reserves. Money to operate First Nations' governments is often received months after approved programs have already begun, placing great strain on community resources. Moreover, most funding agreements have only a one-year lifespan and thus create high transaction costs, which include duplicative and burdensome negotiation and reporting mechanisms. This places further stress on scarce community administrative resources. Finally, in the area of First Nations control of services, the auditor general reported that there is a lack of organizational assistance to support local service delivery. As a result, First Nations have not been able to develop a stable and efficient bureaucracy to ensure certainty, transparency, and accountability in the administration of their resources.[69] These three problems alone reveal the stark differences between Canada and the United States when it comes to Indigenous control of Indigenous services. Canada is severely behind the United States in this respect and this has negative consequences for First Nations administration and governance.

Protection of Indigenous Cultures and Communities

Canada also falls drastically behind the United States in the second area of legislative focus, the protection of Indigenous cultures and communities. Legislation dealing with these issues in the United States is detailed, supportive of self-determination, and calibrated to recognize important differences among tribes. One of the most significant pieces of legislation in this regard is the *Indian Child Welfare Act of 1978* (*ICWA*).[70] The Act was designed to prevent high rates of removal of

---

69 For a discussion of the importance of effective bureaucracies in First Nations, see Stephen Cornell & Joseph Kalt, *What Can Tribes Do?: Strategies and Institutions in American Indian Economic Development* (Los Angeles: UCLA American Indian Studies Center, 1994).

70 *Indian Child Welfare Act*, 25 USC 1901–1931. *ICWA* states, "The Congress hereby declares that it is the policy of this Nation to protect the best interests of Indian children and to promote the stability and security of Indian tribes and families by the establishment of minimum Federal standards for the removal of Indian children from their families and the placement of such children in foster or adoptive homes which will reflect the unique values of Indian culture, and by providing for assistance to Indian tribes in the operation of child and family service programs."

Indian children from their families and communities[71] and has been very successful in this regard.[72] Congress has also passed legislation related to religious freedoms,[73] cultural heritage,[74] the protection and enhancement of Indigenous languages,[75] the encouragement, development, and

---

71 Prior to the enactment of *ICWA*, state government agencies removed 25–35 per cent of all Indian children from their families, nationwide; see Matthew Fletcher, "The Origins of the Indian Child Welfare Act: A Survey of the Legislative History," Indigenous Law & Policy Center Occasional Paper 2009-04 (10 April 2009) online: <www. law.msu.edu/indigenous/papers/2009-04.pdf>; for further context, see Matthew Fletcher, Wenona T Singel, and Kathryn E Fort eds, *Facing the Future: The Indian Child Welfare Act at 30* (Lansing: Michigan State University Press, 2009).

72 After *ICWA*, Indian children now represent only approximately 3 per cent of children in care; see General Accounting Office, GAO-05–290, *Indian Child Welfare Act, Existing Information on Implementation Issues Could Be Used to Target Guidance and Assistance to States* 4 (2005) at 1. The leading case concerning *ICWA* is *Mississippi Band of Choctaw Indians v Holyfield*, (1989) 490 US 30, 109 SCt 1597, 104 LEd 2nd 29 (USSC). However, see *Adoptive Couple v Baby Girl* (2013) 398 SC 625, 731 SE 2d 550, where the Supreme Court reads *ICWA* to apply only to "intact" Indian families, which opens room for undermining the statute when Indian families are in disarray.

73 *American Indian Religious Freedom Act*, 42 USCA 1996. Section 1 of the Act states that "it shall be the policy of the United States to protect and preserve for American Indians their inherent right of freedom to believe, express, and exercise the traditional religions of the American Indian, Eskimo, Aleut, and Native Hawaiians, including but not limited to access to sites, use and possession of sacred objects, and the freedom to worship through ceremonials and traditional rites." The Act accomplishes its purposes by creating policy space for tribes to work with federal agencies to identify and protect sacred places. For leading cases related to this Act, see *Employment Division v Smith*, 494 US 872 (1990); *Lyng v Northwest Indian Cemetery Protective Assn*, 485 US 439 (1988). For commentary, see John Celichowski, "A Rough and Narrow Path: Preserving Native American Religious Freedom" (2000) 25 Am Indian L Rev 1.

74 *Native American Graves Protection and Repatriation Act* (NAGPRA), Pub L 101–601, 25 USC 3001 et seq, 104 Stat 3048.

75 *Native American Languages Act*, 1990, 25 USC 2901–06. The Act begins by reciting the following provisions:

The Congress finds that –
(1) the status of the cultures and languages of Native Americans is unique and the United States has the responsibility to act together with Native Americans to ensure the survival of these unique cultures and languages;
(2) special status is accorded Native Americans in the United States, a status that recognizes distinct cultural and political rights, including the right to continue separate identities;
(3) the traditional languages of Native Americans are an integral part of their cultures and identities and form the basic medium for the transmission, and thus

protection of Indigenous arts and crafts,[76] and the development of a national museum.[77]

In comparison to these robust legislative protections, Canadian legislation is exceedingly thin when recognizing, protecting, and enhancing First Nations cultures.[78] For example, while the provinces have acted in the field of Indigenous child welfare,[79] there is no national legislation dealing with issue, despite the inordinate number of children in care.[80] Thus, unlike in the United States, where the proportion of Native

---

survival, of Native American cultures, literatures, histories, religions, political institutions, and values ...

(8) acts of suppression and extermination directed against Native American languages and cultures are in conflict with the United States policy of self-determination for Native Americans.

76 *Indian Arts and Crafts Enforcement Act*, 2000, Pub L No 105-497, 25 USCA 305–05(e). The Act prohibits misrepresentation in marketing of Indian arts and crafts and authorizes the recovery of damages for all gross profits accrued by the seller or fake Indians arts and crafts.

77 *National Museum of the Indian Act Amendments* of 1996, PubL No 104-278, 20 USCA 80q.

78 Sonia Harris Short, *Aboriginal Child Welfare, Self-Government and the Rights of Indigenous Children: Protecting the Vulnerable under International Law* (Burlington, VT: Ashgate, 2012).

79 *Child, Family and Community Service Act* [RSBC 1996] c 46; see ss 2 (*e*) & (*f*), 4(1), 35(1) (*b*), 70 (1)(*j*), 71(3); *Child and Family Services Act*, 1990 C-11 ss 1(2)4, 1(2)5, 13(3), 34(2) (*d*), 34(10)(*f*), 35(1)(*e*), 36(4)(*c*), 37(3)3, 37(4), 39(1)4, 47(2)(*c*), 54(3)(*f*), 57(5), 58(2)(*b*), 58(4), 61(2)(*d*), 64(4)(*d*), 64(6)(*e*), 69(1)(*e*), 80(4)(*f*), Part X, 223 (Ontario); *Youth Protection Act*, 2002, P-34.1, ss 2.4(5)(*c*), 37.5 (Quebec); *Child and Family Services Act*, C-7.2 1989–90, ss 4(*c*), 23, 37(4)(*c*), 37(10), 37(11), 53, 61 (Saskatchewan); *Child, Youth and Family Enhancement Act*, RSA 2000, c C-12 (Alberta); *Children and Family Services Act* c 5, 1990, Preamble, ss 2(*g*), 7(2), 6(1), 9(*i*), 20(*d*), 36(3), 39(8)(*c*), 42(3), 44(3)(*c*), 47(5), 88(1)(*e*) (Nova Scotia); *Children's Act* c 22, ss 107, 109, 131(*k*) (Yukon); *Family Services Act* c F-2.2 1980 ss 1(*g*), 3(1), 45(1)(*a*), 45(3)(*a*) (New Brunswick); *Child, Youth and Family Services Act*, c-12.1 1998, ss 7(*f*), 7(*g*), 9(*c*), 75(2)(*e*) (Newfoundland); *Child and Family Services Act*, SNWT 1997, c 13, Preamble, ss 2(*f*), 2(*i*), 2(*l*), 3, 7(*l*), 7(*m*), 7(*n*), 15, 25 (*b*.1), 25 (*c*), 54 (3), 56, 57, 58, 58.1, 58.2, 59, 91(*i*) (Northwest Territories); *Consolidated Child and Family Services Act (Nunavut)* SNWT 1997, c 13, Preamble, ss 2(*f*), 2(*i*), 2(*l*), 3, 7(*l*), 7(*m*), 7(*n*), 15, 25 (*b*.1), 25 (*c*), 54 (3), 56, 57, 58, 58.1, 58.2, 59, 91(i) (Nunavut).

80 In February 2007 the Assembly of First Nations estimated that there were 27,000 First Nation children in care in First Nations and provincial agencies, off reserve. They made the point that this number is three times the number of children that were in residential schools at the height of their operation; see Assembly of First Nations, First Nations Child and Family Services, Questions and Answers, online: <nationtalk.ca/story/speaking-notes-for-assembly-of-first-nations-national-chief-phil-fontaine-international-conference-on-ethics/>.

American children in care is now very low, in Canada an Aboriginal child is 9.5 times more likely than a non-Aboriginal child to be in government-supervised care. The situation is particularly troublesome in the west. In British Columbia, Aboriginal children comprise over 50 per cent of the children in care, though Aboriginal children make up only 9 per cent of the general population. In Manitoba, over 13 per cent of Aboriginal children are not living with their parents but are in government care. In fact, Aboriginal children comprise about 20 per cent of the child population but represent over 70 per cent of the children in care in Manitoba. In Saskatchewan, approximately 2 per cent of children in the province are Aboriginal, yet they also represent over 67 per cent of the children in care.[81] Lamentably, these numbers are much higher than was the case when the US government passed *ICWA* decades ago, in 1978. Furthermore, Canadian numbers are shockingly higher than contemporary US rates where Indian children now represent only approximately 3 per cent of children in care. Federal law recognizing self-determination seems to have stemmed the flood of Indigenous children leaving their communities and families, while generally supportive provincial legislation has made little difference in Canada. The crisis in Canada is compounded by the severe underfunding of federal First Nations child welfare services, particularly when compared to the broader population.[82] Litigation is being pursued by First Nations advocates to address these deficiencies.[83] In light of these facts, it is plain to see that, despite the strong provincial presence in

81 Justice Ted Hughes, *BC Children and Youth Review: An Independent Review of BC's Child Protection System* (7 April 2006) at 48; Manitoba Aboriginal Affairs Secretariat, *Aboriginal People in Manitoba* (Winnipeg: Aboriginal Affairs Secretariat, 2006) at 42; Saskatchewan Institute of Public Policy, "A Profile of Aboriginal Children in Regina" in *Commission on First Nations and Metis Peoples and Justice Reform* (Saskatoon: np, 2004) at 10–7.
82 Auditor General, *2011 June Status Report of the Auditor General of Canada*, ch 4, at 23–25, online: <www.oag-bvg.gc.ca/internet/docs/parl_oag_201106_04_e.pdf>.
83 The First Nations Child and Family Caring Society and the Assembly of First Nations filed a human rights complaint alleging that the inequitable funding of child welfare services on First Nations reserves amounts to discrimination on the basis of race and national ethnic origin, contrary to section 5 of the *Canadian Human Rights Act*, RCS 1985, c H-6 [the Act]. They have also filed a claim of retaliation alleging that the Canadian government, NAC, and Department of Justice officials monitored Cindy Blackstock's personal and private Facebook page. See *First Nations Child and Family Caring Society of Canada et al v AG (for the Minister of Indian Affairs and Northern Development Canada)*, 2013 CHRT 16 (CanLII); *First Nations Child and Family Caring Society of Canada et al v AG (for the Minister of Indian and Northern Affairs Canada)*, 2012 CHRT 24 (CanLII).

the field of Native child welfare, US federal legislative initiatives recognizing tribal jurisdiction are dramatically more effective in keeping families together.[84]

Indigenous peoples in Canada also do not enjoy targeted legislative protection in relation to religious freedom. It is true that Human Rights Acts exist in federal and provincial law and have provisions that provide for "a right to equal treatment with respect to services, goods and facilities, without discrimination because of ... creed."[85] Furthermore, as a result of section 67 of the *Canadian Human Rights Act*, similar protections apply on First Nations reserves.[86] These provisions make it possible for First Nations to challenge actions that limit their religious freedoms related to non-government action.[87] However, scanning the

---

84 In fact, *ICWA* recognized that state jurisdiction was a significant problem for Native families. *ICWA*'s congressional finding 5 reads that "the States, exercising their recognized jurisdiction over Indian child custody proceedings through administrative and judicial bodies, have often failed to recognize the essential tribal relations of Indian people and the cultural and social standards prevailing in Indian communities and families." *Indian Child Welfare Act*, 25 USC 1901–1931.

85 For example, Ontario's *Human Rights Code* provides for "a right to equal treatment with respect to services, goods and facilities, without discrimination because of race, ancestry, place of origin, colour, ethnic origin, citizenship, creed, sex, sexual orientation, age, marital status, family status or disability." RSO 1990, c H19, s 1; 1999, c 6, s 28 (1); 2001, c 32, s 27 (1); 2005, c 5, s 32 (1).

86 *An Act to amend the Canadian Human Rights Act* SC 2008, c 30, s 67 the Act reads:

1. Section 67 of the *Canadian Human Rights Act* is repealed.

    1.1 For greater certainty, the repeal of section 67 of the *Canadian Human Rights Act* shall not be construed so as to abrogate or derogate from the protection provided for existing aboriginal or treaty rights of the aboriginal peoples of Canada by the recognition and affirmation of those rights in section 35 of the *Constitution Act, 1982*.

    1.2 In relation to a complaint made under the *Canadian Human Rights Act* against a First Nation government, including a band council, tribal council or governing authority operating or administering programs and services under the *Indian Act*, this Act shall be interpreted and applied in a manner that gives due regard to First Nations legal traditions and customary laws, particularly the balancing of individual rights and interests against collective rights and interests, to the extent that they are consistent with the principle of gender equality.

    As a result of this legislation, First Nations will be challenged by their own members to comply with human rights law in the coming years.

87 Moreover, though not legislatively based, First Nations have access to the Canadian Charter of Rights and Freedoms which, in section 2(a), reads, "Everyone has the following fundamental freedoms: (a) freedom of conscience and religion." First Nations could also make claims to religious freedoms under s 35(1) of the *Constitution Act,*

judgments of these tribunals makes it clear that human rights codes play next to no role in addressing Indigenous religious freedoms.[88] Furthermore, governments have frequently undermined Indigenous spirituality throughout the past through the operation of residential schools,[89] the outlawing of potlatches, giveaways, feasts, and dances,[90] and the planning, approval, and implementation of settlement and development on Indigenous sacred sites.[91] The government in Canada has not passed any stand-alone legislation limiting its own actions relative to such actions. Unlike in the United States, there are no broad-based legislative constraints addressing governmental responsibilities regarding Indigenous religious freedom in Canada. Furthermore, the government has not passed laws that prevent corporations, farmers, developers, provinces, and municipalities from undermining Indigenous religious freedoms, particularly in relation to land and resources.[92] Indigenous spirituality is often tied to lands, rivers, mountains, forests,

---

1982. For a discussion of the challenges in constitutional recognition of First Nations religious freedoms, see John Borrows, "Living Law on a Living Earth: Aboriginal Religion, Law and the Constitution" in *Constitutional Law, Religion and Citizenship in Canada*, edited by Richard Moon (Vancouver: UBC Press, 2008) 16.

88 Only a handful of Human Rights Board decisions deal with Aboriginal religion, and they have not found discrimination of the basis of religion; see *Blais v Canadian Union of Public Employees Local 3902*, 2011 HRTO 2113 (CanLII); *MacDonald v Anishnawbe Health Toronto*, 2010 HRTO 329 (CanLII); *Kelly v BC (Ministry of Public Safety and Solicitor General) (No. 2)*, 2009 BCHRT 363 (CanLII); *George v Jamin and others*, 2009 BCHRT 19 (CanLII); *Smith v BC (Ministry of Public Safety and Solicitor General) and another*, 2008 BCHRT 36 (CanLII).

89 JR Miller, *Shingwauk's Vision: A History of Native Residential Schools* (Toronto: University of Toronto Press, 1996); John S Milloy, *A National Crime: The Canadian Government and the Residential School System, 1879–1986* (Winnipeg: University of Manitoba Press, 1999).

90 Douglas Cole and Ira Chaikin, *An Iron Hand upon the People: The Law against the Potlatch on the Northwest Coast* (Vancouver: Douglas & McIntyre: 1990); Constance Backhouse, *Colour-Coded: A Legal History of Racism in Canada, 1900–1950* (Toronto: University of Toronto Press, 1999) at 56–102; Sidney L Harring, *White Man's Law: Native People in Nineteenth-Century Canadian Jurisprudence* (Toronto: University of Toronto Press, 1998) at 268–70.

91 Michael Lee Ross, *First Nations Sacred Sites in Canada's Courts* (Vancouver: UBC Press, 2005).

92 While environmental assessment legislation and planning laws might have some role to play in this regard, such legislation is generally ineffective in preventing negative impacts on First Nations spiritual practices; see Heather Dorries, "Rejecting the 'False Choice': Foregrounding Indigenous Sovereignty in Planning Theory and Practice" (PhD Thesis, University of Toronto, 2012) [unpublished].

and other physical sites and should thus be given legislation protection to limit government impact on such practices.

Indigenous peoples in Canada also lack rigorous national legislative protection of cultural heritage.[93] In contrast, the United States has a relatively strong regime of heritage protection in the *Native American Graves Protection and Repatriation Act* (*NAGPRA*).[94] *NAGPRA* directs federal agencies and museums to return Native American human remains and sacred objects to appropriate native groups and organizations. It also prevents the appropriation and disturbance of grave sites and provides for the return or proper care of such objects through consultation with the tribes. While there are clear limits to the Act's effectiveness (as is the case with any legislative action), *NAGPRA* has been very important in symbolically and practically enhancing respect for historic Native American material culture.[95] As noted, Canada lacks a comparable legislative framework recognizing and affirming broad-based Indigenous cultural and intellectual property protection.[96] Furthermore, provincial legislation in this area has also proven to be significantly deficient in recognizing and affirming Indigenous culture and heritage.[97]

93 Royal Commission on Aboriginal Peoples, *Report of the Royal Commission on Aboriginal Peoples, Vol 3: Gathering Strength* (Ottawa: Queen's Printer, 1996), ch 6, "Arts and Heritage" at 585–651. For a discussion of the limited ways in which Indigenous cultural heritage is protected in national legislation, see Catherine Bell & Robert Patterson, eds, *Protection of First Nations Cultural Heritage: Laws, Policy, and Reform* (Vancouver: UBC Press, 2009) at 35–37. Catherine Bell & Val Napoleon, eds, *First Nations Cultural Heritage and Law: Case Studies, Voices, and Perspectives* (Vancouver: UBC Press, 2009) at 367–414. However, it is important to note that the *Cultural Property Export and Import Act*, RSC, 1985, c C-51, does provide a way to secure the return of cultural items taken from First Nations.
94 *Native American Graves Protection and Repatriation Act* [*NAGPRA*], 25 USC 3001–13.
95 Julia A Cryne, "NAGPRA Revisited: A Twenty-Year Review of Repatriation Efforts" (2010) 34 Am Indian L Rev 99; Steven J Gunn, "The Native American Graves Protection and Repatriation Act at Twenty: Reaching the Limits of Our National Consensus" (2010) 36 Wm Mitchell L Rev 503.
96 For examples of impact of this failure, see Jennifer Kramer, *Switchbacks: Art, Ownership and Nuxalk National Identity* (Vancouver: UBC Press, 2006); Susan Roy, *These Mysterious People: Shaping History and Archaeology in a Northwest Coast Community* (Montreal & Kingston: McGill-Queen's University Press, 2010); Barry Steven Mandelker, "Indigenous People and Cultural Property Appropriation: Intellectual Property Problems and Solutions" (2000) 16 Can Intellectual Property Rev 367.
97 For example, British Columbia's *Heritage Conservation Act* has not protected First Nations burial sites or culturally modified trees; see *Heritage Conservation Act*, RSBC 1996, c 187, s 13(b); *Nanoose Indian Band v R*, 1994 CanLII 1806 (BC SC); *Kitkatla Band*

First Nations in Canada also lag appreciably behind the United States in formalized language protection.[98] Language nourishes culture, identity, and health.[99] It encodes unique world views, which enhance our understanding of the world around us.[100] Canada is officially bilingual (French and English) but there is no legislation recognizing and affirming the country's original languages. This is a problem because Indigenous peoples have lost ten of their fifty languages in the last hundred years as a result of modernization and colonization.[101] Furthermore, only a minority of Indigenous people within Canada speak or understand an Aboriginal language.[102] At current rates of support and transmission, it is estimated that only three Indigenous languages will survive until 2100.[103] Fortunately, there is evidence that endangered languages can be saved.[104] In fact, the strong desire to learn Aboriginal languages is apparent in Canada. There are more second-language Indigenous speakers in Canada than those who speak them as a mother tongue.[105]

---

v British Columbia (Minister of Small Business, Tourism and Culture), [2002] 2 SCR 146, 2002 SCC 31 (SCC). Ontario's *Cemeteries Act*, RSO 1990 c C.4 has also not provided significant protection for Aboriginal burial sites; see Peggy Blair, "The Non-Protection of Canadian Aboriginal Heritage (Burial Sites and Artifacts)" (October 2005) at 6–7, online: Scow Institute online: <scow-archive.libraries.coop/library/documents/RPHeritageSites.pdf>.

98 Royal Commission on Aboriginal Peoples, *supra* note 92 at 602–21.

99 Darcy Hallett, Michael J Chandler, & Christopher E Lalonde, "Aboriginal Language Knowledge and Youth Suicide" (2007) 22 Cognitive Development 392; UNESCO, *Why Language Matters for the Millennium Development Goals* (Bangkok: United Nations Education Social Cultural Organization, 2012).

100 James Fife, "The Legal Framework for Indigenous Language Rights in the United States" (2005) Willamette L Rev 325 at 328–29.

101 Mary Jane Morris, "Aboriginal Languages in Canada: Emerging Trends and Perspectives on Second Language Acquisition" (Ottawa: Statistics Canada, 2007) online: Statistics Canada <www.statcan.gc.ca/pub/11-008-x/2007001/9628-eng.htm>.

102 *Ibid.*

103 *Ibid.*

104 JA Fishman, ed, *Can Threatened Languages Be Saved? Reversing Language Shift, Revisited: A 21st-Century Perspective* (Clevedon, UK: Multilingual Matters, 2001); Summer Kupau, "Judicial Enforcement of 'Official' Indigenous Languages: A Comparative Analysis of Maori and Hawaiian Struggles for Cultural Language Rights" (2004) 26 U Haw L Rev 495–535.

105 In 2001, more people speak an Aboriginal language than had an Aboriginal mother tongue (239,600 versus 203,300). This suggests that some speakers must have learned their Aboriginal language as a second language. It appears that this is especially the case for young people. Learning an Aboriginal language as

Canada could build on these developments and officially act to reverse Indigenous language loss throughout the country. A necessary first step would be the development of legislation encouraging Indigenous language retention and uptake.[106] As noted, this has occurred in the United States through the *Native American Languages Act*.[107] Of course, language legislation must be reinforced by financial and

---

a second language cannot be considered a substitute for learning it as a first language. Nevertheless, increasing the number of second language speakers is part of the process of language revitalization, and may go some way towards preventing, or at least slowing, the rapid erosion and possible extinction of endangered languages.

Mary Jane Morris, "Aboriginal Languages in Canada: Emerging Trends and Perspectives on Second Language Acquisition" (Ottawa: Statistics Canada, 2007) online: <www.statcan.gc.ca/pub/11-008-x/2007001/9628-eng.htm>.

106 Joshua Fishman has discussed the strengths and limits of legislative intervention in revitalizing endangered languages. Fishman, *supra* note 103 at 1–23; Nancy H Hornberger & Martin Pütz, eds, *Language Loyalty, Language Planning, and Language Revitalization: Recent Writings and Reflections from Joshua A Fishman* (Clevedon: Multilingual Matters, 2006).

107 Section 104 of the US *Native American Languages Act* states,

It is the policy of the United States to – (1) preserve, protect, and promote the rights and freedom of Native Americans to use, practice, and develop Native American languages; (2) allow exceptions to teacher certification requirements for Federal programs, and programs funded in whole or in part by the Federal Government, for instruction in Native American languages when such teacher certification requirements hinder the employment of qualified teachers who teach in Native American languages, and to encourage State and territorial governments to make similar exceptions; (3) encourage and support the use of Native American languages as a medium of instruction in order to encourage and support – (A) Native American language survival, (B) educational opportunity, (C) increased student success and performance, (D) increased student awareness and knowledge of their culture and history, and (E) increased student and community pride; (4) encourage State and local education programs to work with Native American parents, educator, Indian tribes, and other Native American governing bodies in the implementation of programs to put this policy into effect; (5) recognize the right of Indian tribes and other Native American governing bodies to use the Native American languages as a medium of instruction in all schools funded by the Secretary of the Interior; (6) fully recognize the inherent right of Indian tribes and other Native American governing bodies, States, territories, and possessions of the United States to take action on, and give official status to, their Native American languages for the purpose of conducting their own business; (7) support the granting of comparable proficiency achieved through course work in a Native American language the same academic credit as comparable proficiency achieved through course work in a foreign language, with

administrative mandates, which has not occurred in the United States.[108] Nevertheless the Act creates an important framework and starting point for supporting Indigenous language revitalization. While legislation must always be supported by broader action, Canada has not even taken this initial step towards enhancing Indigenous self-determination in this respect.[109]

Another area that is vital to Indigenous self-determination is dispute resolution.[110] When Indigenous peoples practise their own laws, they identify and apply the principles they want to guide their lives.[111] This reinforces respect for community authorities, including ancient teachings and present-day norms.[112] The Canadian Parliament, unlike the federal Congress, has not recognized and affirmed inherent Indigenous

---

recognition of such Native American language proficiency by institutions of higher education as fulfilling foreign language entrance or degree requirements; and (8) encourage all institutions of elementary, secondary and higher education, where appropriate, to include Native American languages in the curriculum in the same manner as foreign languages and to grant proficiency in Native American languages the same full academic credit as proficiency in foreign languages.

Native American Languages Act, 1990, 25 USC 2901–06, s 104.

108 Allison Dussias, "Indigenous Languages under Siege: The Native American Experience" (2008) 3 Intercultural Hum Rts L Rev 5; Allison Dussias, "Waging War with Words: Native Americans' Continuing Struggle against the Suppression of Their Languages" (1999), 60 Ohio St LJ 901; James Fife, "The Legal Framework for Indigenous Language Rights in the United States" (2005) Willamette L Rev 325 at 355–57.

109 Brock Pitawanakwat, "Anishinaabemodaa Pane Oodenang / A Qualitative Study of Anishinaabe Language Revitalization as Self-Determination in Manitoba and Ontario" (PhD Dissertation, University of Victoria, 2009).

110 For two excellent detailed examples of Indigenous self-determination and the practice of tribal law, see Raymond Austin, *Navajo Courts and Navajo Common Law: A Tradition of Tribal Self-Governance* (Minneapolis: University of Minnesota Press, 2009); Justin Richland, *Arguing with Tradition: The Language of Law in Hopi Tribal Court* (Chicago: University of Chicago Press, 2008).

111 Tom Tso, "The Process of Decision Making in Tribal Courts" (1989) 31 Ariz L Rev 225; Frank Pommersheim, *Braid of Feathers: American Indian Law and Contemporary Tribal Life* (Berkeley: University of California Press, 1995); Gloria Valencia-Weber, "Tribal Courts: Custom and Innovative Law" (1994) 24 NML Rev 225; Elizabeth E Joh, "Custom, Tribal Court Practice, and Popular Justice" (2000/01) 25 Am Indian L Rev 117.

112 For discussion and examples, see Justin Richland and Sarah Deer, eds, *Introduction to Tribal Legal Studies*, 2nd ed (Lanham, MD: Altamira, 2010) at 312–26.

authority in this field.[113] Thus, Indigenous peoples in Canada have experienced greater difficulty emphasizing and strengthening their own values and aspirations, particularly when individuals and non-Native governments act contrary to their legal orders.[114] In the United States, while tribal courts were initially designed to assimilate Indigenous peoples,[115] tribes are slowly subverting these plans and are making courts vehicles for self-determination.[116] They are slowly transforming communities' conceptualization of their own powers.[117] Thus, while the US Supreme Court has not always supported these institutions,[118] Congress has recognized their importance for maintaining law and order for many years.[119] In fact, Congress recently passed the *Tribal Law and Order Act* to strengthen tribal courts and thereby more effectively confront public safety challenges facing reservation communities.[120] With

---

113 Parliament's failure to more formally recognize Indigenous legal orders is inconsistent with provisions in the *Declaration on the Rights of Indigenous Peoples*, UN General Assembly, *United Nations Declaration on the Rights of Indigenous Peoples*, GA Res (2 October 2007), A/RES/61/295, online: <http://www.refworld.org/cgi-bin/texis/vtx/rwmain?docid=471355a82>. Article 9 asserts, "Indigenous peoples have the right to belong to indigenous communities or nations *according to their own traditions and customs.*" Article 19 provides that "Indigenous peoples have the right ... to maintain and develop their own decision making institutions." Article 33 recognizes that Indigenous peoples have the "right to maintain a justice system in accordance with their legal traditions."

114 Limited exceptions to the Canadian resistance to tribal courts is found in the Metis Settlement Appeals Tribunal; see Cathy Bell, *Contemporary Métis Justice* (Saskatoon: Native Law Centre, 1999); and treaty settlements such as the Nisga'a Agreement, see RSC 2000, c 7; SBC 1999 c 2.

115 Vine Deloria & Clifford Lytle, *American Indians and American Justice* (Austin: University of Texas Press, 2003) at 111–16.

116 Christine Zuni, "Strengthening What Remains" (1997) 7 Kan JL & Pub Pol'y 18. For a discussion of how tribal court power can continue to grow, by pushing back jurisdictional intrusions by federal courts, see Matthew Fletcher, "Indian Courts and Fundamental Fairness: 'Indian Courts and the Future' Revisited" (2010) 81 U Colo L Rev 973.

117 Matthew LM Fletcher, "Rethinking Customary Law in Tribal Court Jurisprudence" (2007) 13 Mich J Race & L 57.

118 Joseph Singer, "Canons of Conquest: The Supreme Court's Attack on Tribal Sovereignty" (2002–03) 37 New Engl L Rev 641.

119 However, Congress has not usually provided sufficient resources for tribal courts to ensure their most effective operation; see Nell Jessup Newton, "Tribal Court Praxis: One Year in the Life of Twenty Indian Tribal Courts" (1997/98) 22 Am Indian L Rev 285.

120 *Tribal Law and Order Act*, 25 USC 1302 (3)(a)–(f). For commentary, see David Patton, "Tribal Law and Order Act of 2010: Breathing Life into the Miner's Canary" (2012) 47 Gon L Rev 767. See also *Indian Tribal Justice Technical and Legal Assistance Act*, 25 USC 3651–81; *Indian Child Protection and Family Violence Act*, 25 USC 3201–11.

such support alongside their continued internal development and sophistication, tribal courts will continue to play a vital role in facilitating self-determination for some time.[121] While much is distinctive in Canada, as Indigenous peoples continue to develop their legal traditions, they could greatly benefit from US examples if they sought to secure formal recognition of their dispute resolution structures through statutes and regulations.[122] Tribal courts are developing as significant cultural forces in the United States. Canada would do well to facilitate Indigenous dispute resolution in ways that enhance self-determination throughout the country.

Indigenous Control in Relation to Economic Development, Environment, and Natural Resources

A people's self-determination is strongest when their lands and people are physically healthy and self-sustaining.[123] This occurs when they have the capacities and resources to work and grow on their own terms in cooperation with others.[124] Indigenous peoples in Canada do not enjoy the same level of legislative support in these matters, when compared to the United Sates.[125] Canada has done much less to advance Indigenous

---

121 An excellent compilation of materials and cases from tribal courts in the United States is found in Matthew LM Fletcher, *American Indian Tribal Law* (New York: Aspen, 2011).

122 For further discussion, see John Borrows, *Canada's Indigenous Constitution* (Toronto: University of Toronto Press, 2010) at 206–18.

123 For a discussion of First Nations development in Canada, see Robert Anderson, *Aboriginal Entrepreneurship and Business Development* (North York, ON: Captus, 2002); Wanda Wuttenee, *Living Rhythms: Lessons in Aboriginal Economic Resilience and Vision* (Montreal & Kingston: McGill-Queen's University Press, 2004); Dwight Dorey & Joseph Magnet, *Legal Aspects of Business Development* (Toronto: LexisNexis Butterworth's, 2005); Harold Bherer, Sylive Gagnon, & Jancinte Roberge, *Wampum and Letters Patent: Exploratory Study of Native Entrepreneurship* (Montreal: Institute of Research on Public Policy, 1990); Rosalyn Kunin, *Prospering Together: The Economic Impact of Aboriginal Title Settlements in BC* (Vancouver: Laurier Institution, 2001); Skeena Native Development Society, *Masters in Our Own House: The Path to Prosperity* (np: Skeena Native Development Society, 2003).

124 For a discussion of development as it relates to capabilities, see Amartya Sen, *The Idea of Justice* (Cambridge, MA: Belnap, 2009).

125 It should be noted that success in the United States related to tribal economic development started only about forty years ago, during the Nixon administration. Before this time, as the Cohen Handbook observes, "For much of the past two

self-determination in the fields of economic development and natural resource protection. Among the legislative supports enjoyed by Indigenous peoples in the United States related to economic development are the *Indian Gaming Regulatory Act*,[126] *Indian Financing Act*,[127] *Indian Tribal Regulatory Reform and Business Development Act*,[128] *Indian Tribal Economic Development and Encouragement Act*,[129] *Native American Business Development, Trade Promotion, and Tourism Act*.[130] Legislation relating to Native American control over the environment and natural resources is found in the *Clean Air Act*,[131] *Clean Water Act*,[132] *National Indian Forest Resources Management Act*,[133] *American Indian Agricultural Resource Management Act*,[134] and the *Indian Mineral Development Act*.[135] While many challenges remain, these legislative initiatives have boosted living standards for Native peoples in the United States.[136] This has also helped them to make significant gains in protecting their lands and resources.[137]

---

centuries, federal Indian policies inhibited tribal economic development." Felix Cohen, *Cohen's Handbook of Federal Indian Law*, ed by Nell Jessup Newton (Newark, NJ: LexisNexis, 2005) at 21.01. Furthermore, Indian tribes in the United States still suffer from higher rates of socio-economic dislocation than other groups; see Jonathan B Taylor & Joseph P Kalt, *American Indians on Reservations: A Databook of Socioeconomic Change between the 1990 and 2000 Censuses* (Harvard Project on American Indian Economic Development, January 2005) online: <hpaied.org/images/resources/publibrary/AmericanIndiansonReservationsADatabookofSocioeconomicChange.pdf>. However, at times there have been significant exceptions to these patterns; see Alexander Harmon, *Rich Indians: Native People and the Problem of Wealth in American History* (Chapel Hill: University of North Carolina Press, 2010).

126 *Indian Gaming Regulatory Act*, 25 USC 2701–21.
127 *Indian Financing Act*, 25 USC 1451–1544.
128 *Indian Tribal Regulatory Reform and Business Development Act*, 1999, PubLNo 106–447.
129 *Indian Tribal Economic Development and Encouragement Act*, 25 USC 4301–07.
130 *Native American Business Development, Trade Promotion* and *Tourism Act*, 25 USC 4301–07.
131 *National Indian Forest Resources Management Act*, 25 USC. 3101–20.
132 *Clean Air Act*, 42 USC 7474(c).
133 *Clean Water Act*, 33 USC 1377(e).
134 *American Indian Agricultural Resource Management Act*, 25 USC 3701–13.
135 *Indian Mineral Development Act*, 25 USC 2101–08.
136 Taylor & Kalt, *supra* note 24; Lorie Graham, "An Interdisciplinary Approach to American Indian Economic Development" (2004) 80 NDL Rev 597; Steven Andrew Light, Alan P Meister, & Kathryn RL Rand, "Indian Gaming and Beyond: Tribal Economic Development and Diversification" (2009) 54 SDL Rev 375.
137 Douglas Brockman, "Congressional Delegation of Environmental Regulatory Jurisdiction: Native American Control of the Reservation Environment" (1992) 41 Wash UJ Urb & Contemp L 133; Dean Suagee, "Tribal Environmental Policy Acts and the Landscape of Environmental Law" (2009) 23 Natural Resources & Environment 56.

For example, US legislation in the field of gaming has created enormous revenue for Indigenous peoples, growing from $200 million in 1988 to exceed $25 billion in net revenue during the last few years.[138] Furthermore, substantial revenue has been generated as spin-offs from gaming facilities (hotels, restaurants, entertainment, and shopping) exceed $3 billion.[139] Moreover, "Indian gaming facilities, including non-gaming operations, directly support approximately 346,000 jobs and pay about $12 billion in wages to employees."[140] While these benefits are not evenly spread among tribal entities,[141] they do represent a significant gain for reservation economies. In fact, in some areas, tribal growth has significantly benefited entire regions far beyond reservation boundaries.[142] Non-native people benefit greatly from tribal development where this has occurred.[143] This has not generally happened in Canada. Indigenous peoples do not have solid federal support for gaming.[144] The federal *Criminal Code* simultaneously prohibits gambling and creates exceptions to allow provinces to regulate the field.[145] Since First Nations were not successful in establishing gaming as an Aboriginal right within section 35(1) of the Constitution,[146] Indigenous peoples

---

138 Thaddieus Conner & William A Taggart, "Indian Gaming and Tribal Revenue Allocation Plans: A Case of 'Play to Pay'" (2011) 15 Gaming L Rev & Economics 355.

139 Alan Meister, *Casino City's Indian Gaming Industry Report* (Newton, MA: Casino City 2008) at 10–11, 14.

140 *Ibid.*

141 Stephen Cornell, "The Political Economy of American Indian Gaming" (2008) 4 Annual Rev L & Social Science 63; Matthew Fletcher, "Bringing Balance to Indian Gaming" (2007) 44 Harv J Legislation 39.

142 For a discussion of backlash against this expansion, see Matthew Fletcher, "Indian Tribal Businesses and the Off-Reservation Market" (2008) 12 Lewis & Clark L Rev 1047.

143 For a Canadian discussion of the benefits to non-Aboriginal peoples, resulting from Indigenous economic development, see Andre LeDrassay, "A Brief Tax (On A Me) of First Nations Taxation and Economic Development" in Royal Commission on Aboriginal Peoples, *Sharing the Harvest: The Road to Self-Reliance* (Ottawa: Supply and Services, 1993) 215.

144 William V Ackerman and Rick L Bunch, "A Comparative Analysis of Indian Gaming in the United States" (2012) 36 Am Indian Q 36. For a discussion of the wider context of Aboriginal gaming in Canada, see Yale Belanger, *Gambling with the Future: The Evolution of Aboriginal Gaming in Canada* (Saskatoon: Purich, 2006).

145 *Criminal Code*, RSC 1985, c C-46 ss 206–07.

146 *R v Pamajewon*, [1996] 2 SCR 821. For commentary on this case, see Bradford W Morse, "Permafrost Rights: Aboriginal Self-Government and the Supreme Court in R. v. Pamajewon" (1997) 42 McGill LJ 1011; John Borrows, "Frozen Rights in Canada: Constitutional Interpretation and the Trickster" (1997) 22 Am Indian L Rev 37.

generally must work with the provinces to participate in this activity.[147] While there have been some limited successes in this regard,[148] provincial control has meant that Indigenous peoples in Canada do not enjoy the wider benefits gaming has created for tribes in the United States. The failure of the Canadian federal government to legislatively recognize and affirm First Nations in a manner similar to the US *Indian Gaming Regulatory Act* represents a significant loss of economic opportunity for Indigenous peoples in Canada.

First Nations in Canada also lack legislative support related to business development. There is an exceedingly weak policy framework for encouraging economic development among First Nations communities, which focuses merely on decision-making, assessment, and communications.[149] In contrast, as noted above, the United States has numerous legislative mechanisms to facilitate Native American economic self-determination.[150] The *Indian Reorganization Act* created tribal business committees that enabled communities to have the legal personality necessary to enter into contracts and other transactions.[151] The *Indian Financing Act* creates access to reimbursable private capital funds for economic activities by tribes or tribal members.[152] It also guarantees and insures commercial loans to individual Indians and organizations. The *Indian Tribal Regulatory Reform and Business Development Act* provides mechanisms for congressional review of law and regulations that effect

---

147 *R v Bear Claw Casino Ltd*, [1994] SJ No 485, [1994] 4 CNLR 81 (Sask Prov Ct); *Saskatchewan Indian Gaming Authority (SIGA) v National Automobile, Aerospace, Transportation and General Workers Union of Canada*, [2000] SJ No. 266 (Sask QB) (SIGA) at para 11.

148 David Potter, Brenda Pritchard, & Paul Seaman, "Betting on Reconciliation: Law, Self-Governance, and First Nations Economic Development in Canada" (2011) 15 Gaming L Rev & Economics 207 at 208; Yale Belanger, Robert Williams, & Jennifer Archer, "Casinos and Economic Well-Being: Evaluating the Alberta First Nations' Experience" (2011) 5 J Gambling Business & Economics 23.

149 See Aboriginal Affairs and Northern Development Canada, "Federal Framework for Aboriginal Economic Development (Ottawa: Minister of Indian Affairs and Northern Development and Federal Interlocutor for Métis and Non-Status Indians, 2009) online: <www.aadnc-aandc.gc.ca/eng/1100100033501>.

150 For a contextual treatment of these laws, see Robert Miller, *Reservation "Capitalism": Economic Development in Indian Country; Native America – Yesterday and Today* (Santa Barbara: AFL-CLIO, 2012).

151 *Indian Reorganization Act*, 25 USC 477.

152 *Financing Economic Development of Indians and Indian Organizations*, 25 USC 1451–544.

business on reservations.[153] The *Indian Tribal Economic Development and Encouragement Act* removes uncertainty when entering into contracts with tribes by ensuring that Congress and the courts do not "second-guess" tribal bargains.[154] At the same time, the statute mimics consumer protection and fair dealing statutes to facilitate fairness in tribal transactions.[155] In addition the *Native American Business Development, Trade Promotion and Tourism Act* enhances tribal sovereignty by providing for financial, technical, and administrative assistance in growing Indigenous economies.[156] The US Congress regards economic success as vital to tribes. In fact section 6 of the Act is premised on the congressional finding that "the United States has an obligation to guard and preserve the sovereignty of Indian tribes in order to foster strong tribal governments, Indian self-determination, and economic self-sufficiency among Indian tribes."[157] There are no similar statements regarding Indigenous economic development in Canadian law. While legislative action in any country usually fails to meet legislators' highest aspirations for their laws, these and other US economic development initiatives demonstrate substantial support for tribal businesses. When one examines the Canadian legislative record, it is clear that Canadian Indigenous peoples do not enjoy this same level of support.[158]

---

153 *Indian Tribal Regulatory Reform and Business Development Act*, 1999, PubLNo 106–447.

154 *Indian Tribal Economic Development and Encouragement Act*, 25 USC 4301–07. For commentary on this act, see Anna-Emily C Gaupp, "The Indian Tribal Economic Development and Contracts Encouragement Act of 2000: Smoke Signals of a New Era in Federal Indian Policy?" (2001) 33 Conn L Rev 667.

155 In particular, the statute insists that the tribes give notice of their sovereign immunity when making contracts. For a discussion of tribal sovereign immunity as it relates to contracts in Indian country, see Chloe Thompson, "Exercising and Protecting Tribal Sovereignty in Day-to-Day Business Operations: What the Key Players Need to Know" (2010) 49 Washburn LJ 661.

156 *Native American Business Development, Trade Promotion* and *Tourism Act*, 25 USC 4301–07.

157 Moreover, the Act creates the Office of Native American Business Development in the Department of Commerce to provide resources to tribes. Furthermore, as one avenue of development, it requires the secretary of the interior to establish projects to enhance tourism opportunities for tribal entities; see 25 USC s 4305.

158 Legislation facilitating economic development in Canada is limited largely to enhancing taxation powers under the *Indian Act*. For example, First Nations can also implement property taxation under the *First Nations Fiscal and Statistical Management Act*, SC 2005, c 9. The *FSMA* created four First Nation institutions to facilitate

The situation is unfortunately similar when one compares US to Canadian legislation in the field of environmental and resource rights and protections. In Canada there are a very few statutes that single out and recognize the ability of First Nations to develop and conserve environments and resources in accordance with their own aspirations. There is one exception to this pattern, where Canadian and US law is somewhat similar in oil and gas legislation. In Canada the *Indian Oil and Gas Act* enables First Nations to manage and develop these resources on reserve land with federal intervention and assistance.[159] In the United States the *Indian Mineral Development Act* authorizes tribes to enter into agreements for the extraction, processing, or other development of energy resources, including oil and gas.[160] Both jurisdictions seek to maximize energy resource exploitation, though the structures and institutions they employ are somewhat different.

---

development: First Nations Tax Commission, First Nations Financial Management Board, First Nations Finance Authority, and First Nations Statistical Institute. These institutions are still fragile and, except for the First Nations Tax Commission, are still being established. Unfortunately, in 2012 the federal government withdrew financial support for the First Nations Fiscal Institute, which will make it more difficult for the First Nations Financial Management Board and First Nations Finance authority to do their work; see (2012) 30 *Windspeaker* online: <www.ammsa.com/publications/windspeaker/ottawa-kicks-peg-out-foundational-organizations>. For a discussion of the operation of these boards, see Aboriginal Affairs and Northern Development Canada, *A Report to Parliament on the Legislative Review of the* First Nations Fiscal and Statistical Management Act (March 2012) online: <www.aadnc-aandc.gc.ca/eng/1334169647868/1334169697578>. Parliament also passed the *First Nations Commercial and Industrial Development Act*, SC 2005, c 53, to provide for the adoption of provincial regulations on reserve, compatible with those off reserve. Unlike U.S. models, which work from a self-determination framework, this Act seeks to assimilate reserve-based activities into provincial law. In 2010, *FNCIDA* was amended by Bill C-24, the *First Nations Certainty of Land Title Act*, SC 2010, c 6.

159 *Indian Oil and Gas Act*, RSC, 1985, c I-7. This Act is complemented by the *First Nations Oil and Gas and Moneys Management Act*, SC 2005, c 48, which allows First Nations to opt out of the *Indian Oil and Gas Act* and manage their own exploration activities revenues from oil and gas. Furthermore, the *Indian Oil and Gas Regulations*, SOR/94-753, provides for the manner in which oil resources on reserve are developed. For commentary on this Act and regulations, see Andrew Black, "Devolution of Oil and Gas Jurisdiction to First Nations in Canada" (2008) 45 Alta L Rev 537.

160 *Indian Mineral Development Act*, 25 USC 2101–08. For complementary legislation, see the *Indian Energy Act*, 25 USC 37 3501–06, which assists tribes in energy development through grants, loans, technical assistance, and streamlined approval procedures.

Unfortunately, when it comes to comparing legislation dealing with environmental and resource protection in the two countries, it is clear that Canadian law is also significantly behind that of the United States. For example, there is nothing in Canada remotely similar to the *National Indian Forest Resources Management Act, Clean Air Act, Clean Water Act,* and the *American Indian Agricultural Resource Management Act.*[161] In the United States each of these Acts recognizes significant inherent authority within tribes to exercise all the powers of states in protecting their environments. The *National Indian Forest Resources Management Act* allows tribes to protect, conserve, utilize, manage, and enhance their forest lands. It provides for civil actions against trespass, which can be enforced in tribal courts, and it mandates that such judgments are required to be given full faith and credit by tribal and state courts.[162] The *American Indian Agricultural Resource Management Act* creates a similar regime in relation to arable and range lands. The *Clean Air Act* and *Clean Water Act* are pinnacle pieces of legislation, and both provide that "tribes shall be treated as states under these laws and have the option of taking over federal responsibility for setting and enforcing environmental standards on reservations."[163] It is regrettable that similar initiatives have not been undertaken in Canada, despite the unique constitutional protections Indigenous peoples enjoy in Canada.

In fact, in the Canadian context, Parliament has even rolled backed the relatively weak environmental and resource protections that once existed relative to Indigenous lands. In 2012 two omnibus legislative initiatives made it easier for the Canadian government to develop lands over which Indigenous peoples may have Aboriginal title, rights,

---

161 *National Indian Forest Resources Management Act*, 25 USC 3101–20; *Clean Air Act*, 42 USC 7474 (c); *Clean Water Act*, 33 USC 1377(e); *American Indian Agricultural Resource Management Act*, 25 USC 3701–13.

162 For commentary on this Act, see Daria Mondon, "Our Land Is What Makes Us Who We Aare: Timber Harvesting on Tribal Reservations after NIFRMA" (1997) 21 Am Indian L Rev 259.

163 Robert Anderson, Bethany Berger, Philip Frickey, & Sarah Krakoff, eds, *American Indian Law, Cases and Commentary* (St Paul, MN: West, 2010) at 157. For commentary, see James Grivala, "The Origins of EPA's Indian Program" (2006) 15 Kan JL & Pub Pol'y 191; Regina Cutler, "To Clear the Muddy Waters: Tribal Regulatory Authority under Section 518 of the Clean Water Act" (1999) 29 Envtl L 721; Judith V Royster, "Practical Sovereignty, Political Sovereignty, and the Indian Tribal Energy Development and Self-Determination Act" (2008) 12 Lewis & Clark L Rev 1065.

or treaty protections.[164] While Parliament cannot avoid constitutional obligations by passing permissive legislation,[165] removing statutory protection makes it more difficult to use the legal system to uphold constitutional rights and interests.[166] In this case, in passing permissive omnibus legislation, Parliament removed specific protections in the *Navigable Waters Protection Act,* which previously triggered federal environmental assessments and Crown duties to consult and accommodate Indigenous peoples. Pipelines were also specifically exempted from review under the omnibus bills (although the National Energy Board must still consider navigations issues through its approval process). Furthermore, the *Canadian Environmental Assessment Act* was replaced with changes that completely eliminate environmental assessments for so-called minor projects. In addition, the *Fisheries Act* was modified to more directly protect fish, but not fish habitat, and a definition of Aboriginal fisheries was imposed, which requires "serious harm" to stop developments harmful to such fisheries. Changes that will have negative effects on Indigenous environments and resources were also made to the following acts: *Hazardous Materials Information Review Act, Canada Oil and Gas Operations Act, National Energy Board Act, Species at Risk Act, First Nations Fiscal and Statistical Management Act,* and *Indian Act.* These Acts are not attentive to Indigenous self-determination in structuring Canada's wider policy framework. In fact, this legislation is likely to harm Indigenous peoples' abilities to "control their relationships both among themselves and with non-Indian governments, organizations and persons," which is the goal of US legislation and policy.[167]

Conclusion

This chapter is based on the recognition that the constitutional rooting of Aboriginal and treaty rights in Canada's constitution has not led to

---

164 See *Jobs, Growth and Long-Term Prosperity Act,* SC, c 19, 29 June 2012 (Bill C-38); and *Jobs and Growth Act, 2012,* SC, c 31, 14 December 2012 (Bill C-45).

165 *R v Sparrow,* [1990] 1 SCR 1075, at 1112; *R v Marshall,* [1999] 3 SCR 456 at para 48; *Haida Nation v British Columbia (Minister of Forests),* [2004] 3 SCR 511 at para 53.

166 For a more general discussion of the necessity of legislative action in constitutional development, see Aharon Barak, *Proportionality: Constitutional Rights and Their Limitations* (Cambridge: Cambridge University Press, 2012).

167 *Indian Self-Determination and Educational Assistance Act* 25 USC 450.

significant legislative recognition and affirmation of those rights.[168] In contrast, as the foregoing review demonstrates, the US Congress has done much more to recognize and facilitate Indigenous peoples' self-determination in the areas of Indigenous control of federal services, culture, economic development, resources, and the environment. Ideas drawn from this experience, for potential application in Canada, must be applied with the knowledge that they will not necessarily address the deeper challenges between the parties. There will be significant challenges in the relationship between Indigenous peoples and others, just as occurs in the United States, despite supportive legislation. However, while legislation is never a panacea for some of the deepest conflicts we experience, it can be a necessary though not sufficient way to begin the process of decolonizing Canada. It can strengthen communities and improve lives, as this chapter has demonstrated. The modest ideas presented here, if applied with the goal of self-determination at their heart, could assist in hastening this process.

---

168 Prime Minister Stephen Harper recently recognized that legislative reform should occur in Canada, related to Indigenous peoples. However, self-determination was given as a justification for such change. He said,

Why would we wish to change the rules?
   Because "from the rules you set come the results you get," and the incentives buried in the *Indian Act* self-evidently lead to outcomes that we all deplore.
   To be sure, our government has no grand scheme to repeal or to unilaterally rewrite the *Indian Act*: After 136 years, that tree has deep roots. Blowing up the stump would just leave a big hole. However, there are ways, creative ways, collaborative ways, ways that involve consultation between our government, the provinces, and First Nations leadership and communities, ways that provide options within the Act, or outside of it, for practical, incremental, and real change.
   So that will be our approach, to replace elements of the *Indian Act* with more modern legislation and procedures, in partnership with provinces and First Nations. It is an approach that has already shown promise. With inspired leadership, energy, and enterprise, some bands have already shown that First Nations people are as quick to prosper, as capable of excellence, and as able to enjoy all that Canada's vibrant economy has to offer.

"PM Addresses the Crown–First Nations Gathering," 24 January 2012, Ottawa, online: <www.afn.ca/uploads/files/cfng/pm-cfng.pdf>.

Afterword: The Indigenous International and a Jurisprudence of Jurisdictions

MICHAEL IGNATIEFF*

In this commentary on the significance of section 35, I want to situate the discussion in what should be called the Indigenous "international." Estimates vary, but there are 350 million people around the world who self-identify as Indigenous people and who identify with similar peoples around the globe. Over the last twenty years, this sense of belonging to an Indigenous identity that is both local and global has been strengthened by the shared struggle to secure the United Nations Declaration on the Rights of Indigenous Peoples.[1] In the process, Indigenous peoples everywhere came to understand that they share common battles. For too long, official Canada opposed the declaration, and its reluctance has cost it a leadership role within this Indigenous international.

The opportunities for Canadian leadership became clear to me during a visit to New Zealand in 1999 when the only issue that anybody wanted to talk to me about was section 35. The lawyers and legal experts I talked to knew more about Aboriginal peoples in Canada and Canadian law than I did at the time. What I observed in New Zealand was a society being transformed by a collective rediscovery, shared by all New Zealanders, of the central salience of its Maori past to contemporary New Zealand identity.

Since the 1960s, all societies with a significant Indigenous presence have been rediscovering the place of Indigenous peoples in their collective identity and re-questioning the rules of sovereignty by which they are governed. We could include Peru, Bolivia, and many other

---

* I am indebted to Karen Blake and Patrick Healy for their assistance in the preparation of this chapter.
1 *United Nations Declaration on the Rights of Indigenous Peoples*, GA Res 61/295, UN Doc A/RES/61/295 (13 September 2007).

Latin American societies in this process. More than identity is at stake. Indigenous peoples have pressed for the right to benefit from economic development on their lands; they have sought protection for cultural and linguistic rights; and, above all, they have insisted on recognition of their historical place in the founding narratives of their countries.

These Indigenous demands are unsettling precisely because they are foundational. They force all citizens to ask, "What is the ground under our feet; what is the ground we share?" Often, in the past sixty years, both sides, Indigenous and non-Indigenous, have asked themselves, in bitter disputes and confrontations, whether there is any common ground at all. Yet the search for common ground does not end, because it cannot. There is no alternative but to live together, preferably in justice.

Finding a way to live together is not about tinkering with this or that Aboriginal policy or about expanding this or that feature of constitutional law. It's an opportunity to reimagine our common future as a people. The Indigenous issue, when seen in this light, becomes a question about what countries like Canada, Australia, New Zealand, Peru, and Bolivia might become if they sustained a commitment to put justice for Indigenous peoples at the centre of their political agenda. Moreover, if Canada saw itself as part of the Indigenous international, it could seize opportunities for learning and leadership. This would in turn require the Canadian government to draw chiefs and Aboriginal leaders across the country into the work of speaking both for their own peoples and for their country in the larger world.

This is the broader international context in which we need to think about the historical significance of section 35 in our constitution. The point is, the world of Indigenous peoples pays some attention to what we do in Canada, and we need to act with a sense that we can lead and inspire others. When seen in this light, section 35 is the constitutional recognition of the constitutive place of Aboriginal peoples in the political identity and legal order of our country. It recognizes their place in the founding narrative of Canada and acknowledges the state's obligations to fulfil specific treaty rights and Crown duties inherited from the past. That is the backward-facing element of section 35. Section 35 also has a generative, future-directed aspect, one that aims to create a practice of inter-societal law. It is designed to facilitate dialogue between two legal systems, on the basis of a primary recognition of existing rights and obligations.

In addition to recognizing the past and charting a shared future, section 35 also tacitly distinguishes between a jurisprudence focused on sovereignty and one attending to jurisdiction. It is a permanent feature of Canadian life, of course, that some of our citizens question the sovereignty of Canada. Québécois citizens who want an independent Canada contest the legitimacy of the political order in which they live, and notably, they question the legitimacy of the *Constitution Act, 1982* because it was not ratified by the Assemblée Nationale. Equally, there are Aboriginal leaders in Canada who question whether Canadian law is sovereign over their lands. Our country is not unique in having groups of citizens who contest their country's sovereignty, but Canada has proved especially successful in maintaining a democratic constitutional order without abridging the rights of those who no longer want to be part of it.

Constitutional orders, to be democratic, have to protect the rights of those who contest their legitimacy, but they cannot be equivocal about where ultimate sovereign legitimacy lies. In my reading, section 35, being a part of the Constitution of Canada, tacitly restates the ultimate supremacy of Canadian law. It then goes on to frame the possibility of a jurisprudence of jurisdictions. For section 35 jurisprudence, the question is not whose this country is. Sovereignty questions are tacitly resolved in favour of Canada. Instead, section 35 opens up a practical jurisprudence of jurisdictions whose ruling question is "who does what?"

Thirty years later, we still haven't solved the jurisdictional question. The *Indian Act* of 1876 remains in force, conferring on the federal government an imperial and colonial tutelary role that it lacks the will or the capacity to enforce, and which Aboriginal peoples deeply resent. Band councils don't have the authority, the revenue-raising powers, or the resource base they need to provide their people with accountable and responsible government. Disputes over jurisdiction between provincial and federal governments in the field of health and child protection, to name but two, leave many Aboriginal children abandoned by both jurisdictions. Uncertainty about jurisdictional issues holds back responsible resource development. Federal and provincial review panels may approve pipelines and mines, but companies know that lines can be cut and shaft-digging stopped if Aboriginal resistance is sufficiently determined. The companies have the watches but Aboriginal peoples have the time.

These jurisdictional stand-offs hurt Aboriginal peoples most, of course. Solutions are possible, and they are likely to come in the political arena, rather than the courts, if the leadership is there and chiefs, companies, provinces, and federal authorities are willing, problem by problem, to consult, negotiate, and deliver on promises in good faith. Until these political negotiations bear fruit, a question will hang over any historical estimate of the good or ill that section 35 has done. The ultimate test of section 35, of course, is whether, yesterday, today, and tomorrow it will make a positive difference to the lives of Aboriginal Canadians. Because the essential question – who does what? – has not been answered, the jury is out on section 35's historical significance.

We can observe, however, that section 35 has shifted the constitutional balance between the Supreme Court and Parliament in the handling of Aboriginal issues in Canada. Thanks to section 35, courts have taken an ever-increasing role in adjudicating conflicts over Aboriginal rights in Canada. We have "judicialized" the question of Aboriginal rights in our country, and the results have been ambiguous. As someone who was once a practising politician, I was struck, during my time in Parliament, by the way in which section 35 led to a kind of quiescence on the part of Canadian politicians vis-à-vis Aboriginal affairs. It allowed them to sit back and let the Supreme Court "sort it out." The coming of section 35 has been part of a primal rebalancing of our constitutional architecture in which the courts have gained at the expense of Parliament. In turn, a Parliament on the British model gives the legislative initiative to the prime minister and gives individual members of Parliament little real capacity to introduce legislation that has any possibility of becoming law. This is in sharp contrast to the US Congress where individual congressmen and senators can introduce legislation in relation to Indian nations, and where, as a result, the legislative contribution to their welfare is less restricted than it is in Canada.

A second consequence of the judicialization of Aboriginal issues, as a result of section 35, is that it has turned political questions into legal ones. Whenever band council leaders used to come to see me on Parliament Hill, during my time in politics, I was struck by the sheer amount of legal jargon their presentations were required to include. I never met a group with greater mastery of legal arcana. Section 35 has legalized a battle that ought instead to be a political battle for recognition and resources. Chiefs will tell you – and they are right – that in the absence of any political will on the part of the federal government to negotiate and settle outstanding treaty and land disputes, they have no recourse but to go to the courts and exercise their section 35 rights. But this has a tragic side. Aboriginal leaders are forced to spend money on lawyers, when they should be spending what little resources they have on housing or water treatment or health care. It would be grotesque indeed if the only real beneficiaries of Canada's constitutional revolution were the lawyers.

If jurisdictional disputes have been taken over by the lawyers, and if the federal government, as chiefs recurrently charge, will not negotiate closure and settlements in good faith, it becomes inevitable that some Aboriginal leaders start dreaming of opting out of the process altogether, of constituting a self-sufficient Aboriginal sovereignty that does not have to deal with Canada at all. While this is a natural reaction to a sense of futility and deadlock, the pursuit of exclusive Aboriginal sovereignty strikes me as a dead end. A more constructive discussion might address the ways in which we share jurisdiction in Canada. We've been doing it for a very long time. We do not have unitary jurisdiction in Canada because we have always had to accommodate the French civil law tradition in Quebec. From the very beginning, therefore, we had to allow for the jurisdictional accommodation of difference and that's why we're still together. If we're looking to go forward, we need to bring Canadian and Aboriginal jurisdictions into a more equal balance. Aboriginal communities need to have a resource and taxation base. No taxation without representation, no representation without taxation: this principle of democratic legitimacy should be our guide. In other words, if we believe, as we should, in Aboriginal self-government, then these governments need to be able to tax and raise revenue and be accountable to their people for their expenditure decisions. This means, in turn, allowing those Aboriginal communities that are ready, to break free of the *Indian Act* and begin to act as responsible municipal governments, providing services and being accountable as other municipal orders of government in Canada mostly are.

Section 35 does point us this way. Since it acknowledges treaty rights, it recognizes that Aboriginal bands constitute political communities. Once you acknowledge bands as political communities, and once you concede, as you should, that they must enjoy the revenue and resource base necessary to enjoy equality of citizenship with other Canadians, then you have embarked on a path that leads both to real self-government, under the supremacy of Canadian law.

In any new vision of Indigenous-Canadian relations, there must be a way to reconcile maintaining the integrity of the communal land base of a band with the freedom for individuals to own and sell property. No one-size solution, mandated by the federal government will work. The solutions will have to be locally generated and locally owned, but

I can't see how you can have equality of opportunity for Aboriginal Canadians without the capacity to own real property and hand it on to your heirs. I also can't see any solution to the endemic Aboriginal housing crisis unless Aboriginal Canadians can own and improve their own properties.

We shall also have to clarify what we both mean by the duty to consult, especially on resource development projects. The duty to consult should imply a duty to share the benefits of resource development, with more careful apportionment of the costs, shifting them from Aboriginal communities to those who stand to profit. We need a democratic process of consultation on resource development that gives Aboriginal peoples the standing to say yes or no to development on their land, while providing certainty that resource development needs if it is to secure finance. We don't have this now, and it is holding back development and embittering Aboriginal communities.

If we are to have genuinely shared benefits from resource development, we have to start moving towards political agreements that can stick. A crucial conclusion of many of the chapters in this collection has been that law can't substitute for politics; we're stuck with the politics of negotiation. Law can set up the constraints on that negotiation. We can't agree to just anything; there are some things that are off the table. We meet as equals. We treat each other as equals. There are bounded constraints in terms of treaty. There are bounded constraints in terms of the *Charter*. We sit down as equals face-to-face, and we negotiate. And we absolutely have to.

Any thoughtful observer must be struck by the inescapable fact that Aboriginal issues lie at the centre of our economic prospects as a country. We need to remedy the impasse; the status quo is simply unsustainable. People will not invest in this country, people will not create jobs, unless we can begin to attain jurisdictional clarity about who does what. Section 35, the *Constitution Acts 1867* and *1982*, and the treaties create a framework for action but, ultimately, the solution will be political and not constitutional.

The issues at stake in section 35 therefore go beyond any purely intellectual exercise. They challenge our definition of what it is to be Canadian; they are absolutely central to the economic and political future of our country. All political leaders in our country should have a very practical respect for the power of Aboriginal peoples, for the potential veto power that they exercise over resource and economic development in the northern and remote parts of our country where our future will be created. We are dealing with people who have power, and that power must be respected.

I want to conclude with a final point: recognition is a mutual process. I want a process of mutual recognition that is grounded on the conclusions of the Supreme Court in *Delgamuukw*: "We are all here to stay."[2] None of us are settlers anymore. None of us have anywhere else to go; we're stuck with each other; we're stuck with the plurality, the diversity, and with the pain of the past. There's nothing we can do to change the past. But we can acknowledge it in full, accept deep responsibility for it, and then move on into the future: equal in rights, equal in respect. Our shared question is, who does what to create a shared home?

---

2 *Delgamuukw v British Columbia*, [1997] 3 SCR 1010, at para 186.

Contributors

John Borrows is the Canada Research Chair in Indigenous Law at the University of Victoria Law School. His publications include *Recovering Canada*, as well as *The Resurgence of Indigenous Law* (Donald Smiley Award for the best book in Canadian Political Science, 2002), *Canada's Indigenous Constitution* (Canadian Law and Society Best Book Award, 2011), *Drawing Out Law: A Spirit's Guide*, all from the University of Toronto Press, and *Aboriginal Legal Issues: Cases, Materials, and Commentary*, 4th ed. (Butterworths 2012). Professor Borrows is a recipient of an Aboriginal Achievement Award in Law and Justice, a fellow of the Trudeau Foundation, and a fellow of the Academy of Arts, Humanities, and Sciences of Canada (RSC), Canada's highest academic honour. He is a recipient of the 2012 Indigenous Peoples Counsel designation from the Indigenous Bar Association. He is Anishinaabe/Ojibway and a member of the Chippewa of the Nawash First Nation in Ontario, Canada.

Michael J. Bryant has worked as a litigator, negotiator, scholar, teacher, and cabinet minister in Aboriginal affairs, over the past twenty-five years. He was Ontario's first Minister of Aboriginal Affairs, and previously served as Minister Responsible for the Aboriginal Affairs Secretariat during his tenure as Attorney General. In the 1990s, he worked on Aboriginal rights appeals for BC First Nations at Blakes LLP, and then under the Hon. Ian Binnie at McCarthy Tetrault LLP. In addition to publishing articles and chapters on Aboriginal rights, Mr Bryant taught Aboriginal politics at the University of Toronto, and served as lecturer in law, adjunct professor, and visiting professor at King's College London, University of Toronto, and Osgoode Hall Law School. Mr Bryant earned graduate degrees in Aboriginal affairs at Harvard University (LLM) and the University of British Columbia (MA) and a JD from Osgoode Hall Law School. He is a former Supreme Court of Canada law clerk who served as special advisor, at Norton Fulbright LLP in Toronto, specializing in natural resources, energy, and Aboriginal affairs. He currently works as a consultant and negotiator with Ishkonigan Consulting and Mediation and as chair of the Public Accountants Council for the province of Ontario.

Megan Davis is a professor of law and director, Indigenous Law Centre, Faculty of Law at the University of New South Wales. Professor Davis is a UN expert member of the United Nations Permanent Forum on Indigenous Peoples and holds the following portfolios: Administration of Justice, Gender and Women, and Intellectual Property and Indigenous Knowledge. In 2012, Professor Davis was the rapporteur of the UNPFII Expert Group Meeting on Violence against Indigenous Women in New York. She is a commissioner of the NSW Land and Environment Court and a fellow of the Australian Academy of Law. Professor Davis is also the Australian member of the International Law Association's Indigenous Rights Committee. In 2011, Professor Davis was appointed by the federal government to the Expert Panel on the Recognition of Aboriginal and Torres Strait Islander Peoples in the Constitution. She teaches, writes, and researches in the areas of public law and international law, especially violence against Indigenous women. In particular, Professor Davis is interested in constitutional law and constitutional reform and democratic theory and governance. Professor Davis has extensive experience as an international human rights lawyer and participated in the drafting of the UNDRIP from 1999 to 2004. She is a former UN fellow of the UN Office of the High Commissioner for Human Rights in Geneva and has participated as an international lawyer in Indigenous legal advocacy, UN working groups, and expert seminars at the United Nations for over a decade. Professor Davis was also the director of the Bill of Rights Project, Gilbert + Tobin Centre of Public Law. Professor Davis was the 2010 NAIDOC Scholar of the Year.

Kirsty Gover is associate professor at Melbourne Law School. Her research addresses the law, policy, and political theory of Indigenous rights, institutions, and jurisdiction. She is interested in the role played by Indigeneity in settler-state political theory and international law. Dr Gover is the author of *Tribal Constitutionalism: States, Tribes, and the Governance of Membership* (Oxford University Press, 2010) and is working on a book entitled *When Tribalism Meets Liberalism: Political Theory and International Law* (Oxford University Press), examining the ways in which Indigenous self-governance influences the development of international law and international legal theory by altering the behaviour of settler states. Dr Gover is a graduate of the New York University JSD Doctoral Program, where she was an Institute for International Law and Justice Graduate Scholar and New Zealand Top Achiever Doctoral Fellow. She is co-director of Melbourne Law School's Indigenous Peoples in International and Comparative Law Research Program.

Sari Graben is assistant professor in the Department of Law, Ryerson University. Professor Graben's primary theoretical interests are in the field of Indigenous law and development, with a special focus on regulatory institutions, emergent property systems, and governance. Her research analyses key challenges that arise from the regulation of Indigenous rights and engages with analytical methods that deepen comparative frameworks used for pragmatic experimentation. She publishes widely in the field and is currently co-editing a book (with Angela Cameron and Val Napoleon) entitled *Indigenous Peoples and Real Property: Beyond Privatization*. Professor Graben obtained her doctorate from Osgoode Hall Law School, held a SSHRC postdoctoral fellowship at University of California – Berkeley Law, and held the Canada-US Fulbright Visiting Research Chair at the University of Washington (Seattle). Her teaching areas are business law, Aboriginal law, natural resource law, and international law.

Sébastien Grammond is a professor at the University of Ottawa's Civil Law Section. Professor Grammond obtained his LLB (1992) and his LLM (1993) from the Université de Montréal, and he completed a doctorate in law at Oxford University in 2004. After his clerkship with Chief Justice of the Supreme Court of Canada Antonio Lamer, he began practising law in Montreal in 1994 with Fraser Milner Casgrain LLP, where he specialized in Aboriginal law, constitutional law, and administrative law. He became a professor in the Civil Law Section in 2004, and has since taught courses on contractual obligations, civil procedure, and Aboriginal law. He also occupied the position of vice-dean of research from 2005 to 2008 and that of dean from 2008 to 2014. His research focuses on the rights of minorities and Indigenous peoples, with a particular emphasis on the relationships between law and Indigenous identity. He has also published *Identity Captured by Law: Membership in*

Canada's Indigenous Peoples and Linguistic Minorities (McGill-Queen's University Press, 2009), as well as *Terms of Coexistence: Indigenous Peoples and Canadian Law* (Carswell, 2013). In matters of private law, his interests include the interpretation of contracts and contractual justice.

Michael Ignatieff is a former leader of the Liberal Party of Canada and is Edward R. Murrow Professor of the Practice of Politics, the Press, and Public Policy at the Harvard Kennedy School. He holds a doctorate in history from Harvard University and has held academic posts at Kings College, Cambridge, the University of Toronto, and the University of British Columbia. His books include *The Needs of Strangers* (Viking, 1984), *Scar Tissue* (Farrar, Straus and Giroux, 1992), *Blood and Belonging: Journeys into the New Nationalism* (Farrar Straus, 1993), *The Warrior's Honour: Ethnic War and the Modern Conscience* (Henry Holt, 1997), *Isaiah Berlin: A Life* (Henry Holt, 1998), *The Rights Revolution: The Massey Lectures* (Stoddart, 2000), *Human Rights as Politics and Idolatry* (Princeton University Press, 2001), *The Lesser Evil: Political Ethics in an Age of Terror* (Princeton University Press, 2004), and *Fire and Ashes: Success and Failure in Politics* (Random House Canada, 2013).

Courtney Jung is a professor of political science at the University of Toronto. She joined the department in 2008 from the New School for Social Research in New York, where she was an associate professor of political science. Professor Jung works on identity and identity formation at the intersection of comparative politics and contemporary political theory. Her books engage normative debates about liberalism, multiculturalism, and democratic participation through research into political identity formation, mainly in South Africa and Mexico. She has received awards from the Social Sciences and Humanities Research Council (2009–13), Fulbright New Century Scholars Program (2003), the Mellon Foundation (2002–4), and the National Endowment for the Humanities (2001–2). She was a member at the Institute for Advanced Study in 2001–2 and has held visiting positions at Yale University, Central European University, and University of Cape Town. Her publications include *The Moral Force of Indigenous Politics: Critical Liberalism and the Zapatistas* (Cambridge University Press, 2008), and *Then I Was Black: South African Political Identities in Transition* (Yale University Press, 2000). She has also written about the truth and reconciliation commission in Canada. Her current research tracks the constitutional entrenchment of economic and social rights. Her data set is available online at www.tiesr.org.

Marcia Langton is the chair of Australian Indigenous studies with the Centre for Health & Society at the Melbourne School of Population Health. Professor Langton has held the foundation chair of Australian Indigenous studies at the University of Melbourne since February 2000. An anthropologist and geographer, she has made a significant contribution to Indigenous studies at three universities, and to government and non-government policy and administration throughout her career. Her research has concerned Indigenous relationships with place, land tenure, and environmental management, agreement-making, and treaties in the Northern Territory and Cape York Peninsula. Her work in anthropology and the advocacy of Aboriginal rights was recognized in 1993 when she was made a member of the Order of Australia. She became a fellow of the Academy of Social Sciences in Australia in 2001 and was awarded the inaugural Neville Bonner Award for Indigenous Teacher of the Year in 2002.

Jean Leclair holds the position of professeur titulaire at the Université de Montréal. He obtained an LLM from the Université de Montréal, where he was the recipient of the Duff-Rinfret scholarship awarded by the Department of Justice, Government of Canada. He served as a judicial law clerk to Madam Justice Desjardins with the Federal Court of Appeal from 1986 to 1988. His teaching and research interests include legal theory, Canadian legal history, constitutional law (federalism and fundamental rights), and Aboriginal legal issues. He was one of the four Pierre Elliott Trudeau Foundation fellows for 2013. He was also a founding member of Les Veilleurs de Nuit theatre company. Some of his most recent publications relating to Aboriginal issues include "Le fédéralisme comme refus des monismes nationalistes," in Dimitrios Karmis & François Rocher, eds, *La dynamique confiance-méfiance dans les démocraties multinationales: Le Canada sous l'angle comparatif* (Presses de l'Université Laval, 2012); "Les droits ancestraux en droit constitutionnel canadien: quand l'identitaire chasse le politique," in Alain Beaulieu, Stéphan Gervais, & Martin Papillon, eds, *Les Autochtones et le Québec* (Les Presses de l'Université de Montréal, 2013); and "Le fédéralisme: un terreau fertile pour gérer un monde incertain," in Ghislain Otis & Martin Papillon, eds, *Le fédéralisme et les peuples autochtones: principes et enjeux de la gouvernance relationnelle / The Relational Dimension of Indigenous Governance and Federalism: Theories and Practices* (Les Presses de l'Université d'Ottawa, 2013).

Natalia Loukacheva is Canada Research Chair in Aboriginal Governance and Law and associate professor of political science at the University of Northern British Columbia. Prior to joining the faculty in 2014, she was a research associate at the Munk School of Global Affairs, University of Toronto (2004–13); the first visiting Nansen Professor of Arctic Studies in Iceland (Norway-Iceland initiative of the Ministries of Foreign Affairs, 2013). She is also an adjunct professor of law at Osgoode Hall Law School, York University; a fellow with the Canadian Defence and Foreign Affairs Institute (Ottawa); and associate scientist with the Stefansson Arctic Institute in Iceland. She was the founding director of the Graduate Polar Law Program and taught polar law at the University of Akureyri, Iceland (2008–10). She holds a doctor of juridical science from the Faculty of Law, University of Toronto, and a doctor of philosophy (law) from the Urals State Law Academy (Russian Federation). Dr Loukacheva specializes in international and comparative constitutional law, with research interest in the Arctic. She is the author of *The Arctic Promise: Legal and Political Autonomy of Greenland and Nunavut* (University of Toronto Press, 2007), the editor and project leader of the first ever *Polar Law Textbook* (Nordic Council of Ministers, Tema Nord 538, 2010), of the *Polar Law Textbook II* (2013), of *Polar Law and Resources* (2015) and special editor of the *Yearbook of Polar Law*, vol. 2 (2010) and of the *Arctic Review on Law and Politics* 2 (2012). Since 2012 she also has served as an associate editor of the *Arctic Review on Law and Politics*. Dr Loukacheva chairs an International Thematic Network group on Legal Issues in the Arctic of the Northern Research Forum, and from 2011 to 2015 she chaired an Arctic Governance group of the Arctic Law Thematic Network of the University of the Arctic. She is the author of numerous publications on legal and political issues in the Arctic, Indigenous peoples' rights, and governance in the North.

Patrick Macklem is the William C. Graham Professor of Law at the University of Toronto Faculty of Law. He holds law degrees from Harvard and Toronto, and an undergraduate degree in political science and philosophy from McGill. He served as law clerk for Chief Justice Brian Dickson of the Supreme Court of Canada and as a constitutional advisor to the Royal Commission on Aboriginal Peoples. He is a recurring visiting professor at Central European University. He has been a visiting scholar at Stanford Law School and UCLA School of Law. In 2003, he was selected as a Fulbright New Century Scholar, taught at the European University

Institute, and was a visiting scholar at Harvard Law School. In 2006–7 he was a senior global research fellow at the Center for Human Rights and Global Justice at NYU School of Law. In 2007–8 he was a member of the Institute for Advanced Study in Princeton, New Jersey. Professor Macklem's teaching interests include constitutional law, international human rights law, Indigenous peoples, ethnic and cultural minorities, and labour law and policy. He is the author of *Indigenous Difference and the Constitution of Canada* (University of Toronto Press, 2001), co-editor of *Canadian Constitutional Law* (Emond Montgomery, 2003), *The Security of Freedom: Essays on Canada's Anti-Terrorism Bill* (University of Toronto Press, 2001), and has published numerous articles on constitutional law, labour law, Indigenous peoples and the law, and international human rights law. He is a fellow of the Royal Society of Canada.

P.G. McHugh is a professor of law and legal history at the University of Cambridge and a fellow of Sidney Sussex College. He is the author of two major books, *Aboriginal Societies and the Common Law* (2006) and *Aboriginal Title* (2011), as well as numerous articles and essays. Professor McHugh is a leading authority on Aboriginal title throughout the common law world. The most pointed and controversial application of his scholarship was to Maori rights around the New Zealand coastline, leading to the country's foreshore and seabed controversy. He is also known as an imperial legal historian and has published widely on the historical aspects of Crown–tribe relations during the imperial and early national periods (especially in Canada and New Zealand).

Dwight Newman is professor of law and Canada Research Chair in Indigenous Rights in Constitutional and International Law at the University of Saskatchewan. He served a three-year term as associate dean of the University of Saskatchewan College of Law from 2006 to 2009, and he has been a visiting scholar at the McGill Faculty of Law and an honorary senior research fellow at the University of the Witwatersrand School of Law. He completed his doctoral work at Oxford University, where he was a Rhodes Scholar and, later, a SSHRC doctoral fellowship holder. While at Oxford, he also taught in the undergraduate jurisprudence and public international law courses. He served as a law clerk to Chief Justice Antonio Lamer and Justice Louis LeBel at the Supreme Court of Canada in 1999–2000, and he has worked for human rights organizations in Hong Kong and South Africa. He is a member of the Ontario and Saskatchewan bars. He has published widely, including books entitled *The Duty to Consult: New Relationships with Aboriginal Peoples* (Purich, 2009) and *Community and Collective Rights: A Theoretical Framework for Rights Held by Groups* (Hart Publishing, 2011), the co-authored *Law of the Canadian Constitution* (Toronto: LexisNexis, 2013), *Natural Resource Jurisdiction in Canada* (Toronto: LexisNexis, 2013), and *Revisiting the Duty to Consult Aboriginal Peoples* (Saskatoon: Purich, 2014).

Jacinta Ruru is an associate professor at the Faculty of Law, University of Otago, centre associate at the Indigenous Law Centre, University of New South Wales, and part of the research leadership team for Nga Pae o te Maramatanga (New Zealand's Maori Centre of Research Excellence). Her research focuses on exploring Indigenous peoples' legal rights and interests to own, manage, and govern land and water. She has led or co-led several national and international research projects, including on the common law doctrine of discovery, Indigenous rights to fresh water, and multidisciplinary understandings of landscapes. Her PhD is from the University of Victoria, Canada, and explored Maori and Aboriginal peoples' rights to national parks. Some of her work is interdisciplinary especially with the social sciences and comparative with Australia, Canada, the United States, and the Nordic countries. She has published widely including co-authoring *Discovering Indigenous Lands: The Doctrine of Discovery in the English Colonies* (Oxford University Press, 2010). Research awards include the University of Otago's Rowheath Trust and Carl Smith Medal for outstanding scholarly achievement across all disciplines (2010) and the Fulbright Nga Pae o te Maramatanga Senior Maori Scholar Award (2012).

Douglas Sanderson is an associate professor at the University of Toronto Faculty of Law. He was managing editor of the inaugural edition of the *Indigenous Law Journal* in 2002 while a student in the JD program. He went on to get his LLM from Columbia University. Professor Sanderson is a member of the Opaskwayak Cree Nation. From 2004 to 2007 he was a senior advisor to the government of Ontario, first in the Office of the Minister Responsible for Aboriginal Affairs, and later to the attorney general. Professor Sanderson's research areas include Aboriginal and legal theory, as well as private law (primarily property law) and public and private legal theory. Moving beyond the framework of common law property rights and constitutional land/treaty rights, his scholarship focuses on Aboriginal institutions, postcolonial reconciliation, and rebuilding community.

Abbey Sinclair is an associate lawyer at Rueter Scargall Bennett LLP. She articled with the Ontario Ministry of the Attorney General in the Legal Services Branch of the Ministry of Energy and Ministry of Infrastructure. She holds an undergraduate degree in international studies and political science from Glendon College, York University, and a master's degree in comparative politics from the London School of Economics. She obtained her juris doctor from Queen's University, where she was a member of the senior editorial board of the *Queen's Law Journal*. Prior to attending law school she worked for an international non-profit organization developing microfinance, health, and education initiatives in Indigenous communities in Latin America.

Brian Slattery is professor of law and Distinguished Research Professor at Osgoode Hall Law School, York University, having previously held positions at McGill University, the University of Dar es Salaam, and the University of Saskatchewan. He graduated from the Faculty of Law at McGill University and completed his doctorate at Oxford University. Professor Slattery has devoted much of his scholarship to overhauling the standard conception of the Canadian Constitution in a way that takes account of the distinctive rights and historical contributions of Aboriginal peoples. In other scholarly work, Professor Slattery has explored the philosophical foundations of human rights and the continuing vitality of the natural law tradition. In the 1990s, Professor Slattery served as a senior advisor to the Royal Commission on Aboriginal Peoples. He was named a fellow of the Royal Society of Canada in 1995. He continues to research and write on Aboriginal and treaty rights, constitutional law, and legal theory.

Dale Turner is an associate professor of government and of Native American studies at Dartmouth College. He was the research associate for the two co-directors of research for the Royal Commission on Aboriginal Peoples. He is the author of *This Is Not a Peace Pipe: Towards a Critical Indigenous Philosophy* (University of Toronto Press, 2006) and is co-editor (with Tony Lucero) of *The Oxford Handbook of Indigenous Peoples' Politics* (Oxford University Press, 2015). He is currently working on a project that focuses on the role that Indigenous knowledge plays in river restoration co-management agreements in three Indigenous communities. He is a citizen of the Temagami First Nation on Lake Temagami, Ontario.

Mark D. Walters is a professor at the Queen's University Faculty of Law. His research focuses on constitutional law, legal history, and legal theory. Professor Walters's focus is the status of Aboriginal customary laws and government in colonial Canada. In particular, he is interested in exploring what may be labelled the "covenant-chain constitution" that existed in pre-Confederation Canada – the covenant chain being the series of treaties that bound the Crown and Aboriginal nations in the Great Lakes region. He is also interested in general theoretical problems arising in constitutional law, and how approaches to them affect approaches to practical legal issues. An example that he has been considering is the notion of the "unwritten" constitution. Finally, he is exploring the evolution of jurisprudential and constitutional theory.

Jeremy Webber is dean of law at the University of Victoria. He held the Canada Research Chair in Law and Society at UVic from 2002 to 2014 and has been a Trudeau Fellow since 2009. He taught in the Faculty of Law at McGill University from 1987 to 1998 and was dean of law at the University of Sydney from 1998 to 2002. Dean Webber has published widely in the fields of legal and political theory, comparative constitutional law, and Indigenous rights (in both the Canadian and Australian contexts), including *Reimagining Canada: Language, Culture, Community, and the Canadian Constitution* (McGill-Queen's University Press, 1994) and *The Constitution of Canada: A Contextual Analysis* (Hart, 2015). He is co-editor of four collections of essays: *Let Right Be Done: Aboriginal Title, the* Calder *Case, and the Future of Indigenous Rights* (UBC Press, 2007); *Between Consenting Peoples: Political Community and the Meaning of Consent* (UBC Press, 2010); *Storied Communities: Narratives of Contact and Arrival in Constituting Political Community* (UBC Press, 2011); and *Recognition versus Self-Determination: Dilemmas of Emancipatory Politics* (UBC Press, 2014).